Fundamental Skills
and Concepts
in Patient Care

Fundamental Skills and Concepts in Patient Care

LuVerne Wolff Lewis, MA, RN and
Barbara Kuhn Timby, MA, BSN, RN

Adapted and edited for the UK from Lippincott's **Fundamental Skills and Concepts in Patient Care** *(Fourth edition) by Bernadette Frawley and Jan Cooper, with contributions from Alison Dines, Jennie Wilson, Ann Young, Bernie Gardiner*

CHAPMAN & HALL
London · Glasgow · New York · Tokyo · Melbourne · Madras

Published by Chapman & Hall, 2–6 Boundary Row, London SE1 8HN

Chapman & Hall, 2–6 Boundary Row, London SE1 8HN, UK

Blackie Academic & Professional, Wester Cleddens Road, Bishopbriggs, Glasgow G64 2NZ, UK

Chapman & Hall, 29 West 35th Street, New York NY10001, USA

Chapman & Hall Japan, Thomson Publishing Japan, Hirakawacho Nemoto Building, 6F, 1-7-11 Hirakawa-cho, Chiyoda-ku, Tokyo 102, Japan

Chapman & Hall Australia, Thomas Nelson Australia, 102 Dodds Street, South Melbourne, Victoria 3205, Australia

Chapman & Hall India, R. Seshadri, 32 Second Main Road, CTT East, Madras 600 035, India

First edition 1993

© 1993 Chapman & Hall

Adapted from *Fundamental Skills and Concepts in Patient Care*, Fourth edition. Copyright © 1988 by J.B. Lippincott Company. Copyright © 1984, 1980, 1976 by J.B. Lippincott Company.
Adapted by arrangement with J.B. Lippincott Company, 227 East Washington Square, Philadelphia, PA 19106-3780, USA.

Typeset in Palatino by Best-set Typesetter Ltd., Hong Kong
Printed in Hong Kong by Thomas Nelson

ISBN 0 412 43960 3

A catalogue record for this book is available from the British Library

Printed on permanent acid-free text paper, manufactured in accordance with the proposed ANSI/NISO Z 39.48-199X and ANSI Z 39.48-1984

Contents

Part 2   Nursing Skills for Health Promotion and Maintenance

Part 4   Nursing Skills Related to Health Restoration

Part 5 Nursing Skills Associated With the Dying Patient

Contributors

Bernadette Frawley
Harley Street Clinic
35 Weymouth Street
London
W1N 4BJ

Jan Cooper
72 St Andrew Terrace
Hamilton
New Zealand

WITH
Alison Dines
Department of Nursing Studies
King's College London
Cornwall House
Waterloo Road
London
SE1 8TX

Jennie Wilson
Infection Control Nurse Coordinator
Charing Cross Hospital
Fulham Palace Road
London

Ann P. Young
Deputy Registrar
Nightingale and Guy's
   College of Health
Guy's Hospital
London SE1

Bernie Gardiner
9 St Andrews Road
West Kensington
W14 9SX

Foreword

The delivery of care to the patient either in the home or hospital has changed drastically in the past decade. These changes have tended to occur as a quiet evolution rather than as an overnight process, but nevertheless have altered completely the traditional picture of the sick person as one who is confined to bed or who needs to lie in their bedroom behind closed curtains. Hospital in-patient stays are now much shorter; day care in all specialities is commonly provided, and the transfer of patients needing acute care in the home from hospital to the community nursing services occurs more frequently.

Technological advances in care have created new levels of knowledge and skills amongst health care workers both in the home and in the hospital. Nurses in the community now also commonly provide "high tech" care and support to patients and their families: examples would include those with Hickman lines in position, and children and young infants who are oxygen dependant. A decade or so ago, all these patients would have been in an intensive care situation in the hospital.

Other evolutionary influences on patient care recognized in this text include the concept of primary nursing. Fundamentally designed to enable each patient to relate to "my nurse" and for each nurse to develop their own special relationship with "my patient" primary nursing is thus aimed at enhancing care wherever it is provided.

To underpin understanding of these changes, the authors provide a knowledge base which is founded wherever possible on research data, with references from both sides of the Atlantic. Some may wish to ponder on why there is a need to adapt or anglicise an American text—when after all we all speak English? But the realist will appreciate that whilst there are many similarities in philosophies and approaches to care, there are also some fundamental differences, notably in terminology and organizational approaches. The adaptors have recognized this and have sought to make the appropriate changes and modifications where needed for the health care worker in the UK, thus enabling the easier transfer of knowledge and ideas for everyday practice in this country.

The text's broad aim is to provide the reader with a framework to use when providing care for patients in a variety of situations and settings. Practical, relevant information is presented within the context of the nursing process in a user friendly way. Learning objectives are defined for each chapter, thus encouraging the reader to self-evaluate progress through the complexities of providing informed, sensitive and appropriate care.

Barbara F Weller, MSc, RGN, RSCN, RNT

July 1992

Part 1

The Nurse
and the Patient

1

The concept of nursing

Learning objectives

When the content of this chapter has been mastered, the learner should be able to:

Define the terms appearing in the glossary.
Identify the changes that have occurred in definitions of nursing.
List three objectives of nursing.
Describe four basic skills required of nurses.
List three components that provide a basis for the skills used by nurses.
Describe the nursing competencies.

Glossary

Active listening Hearing the content of what the patient says as well as the unspoken message.

Activities of daily living Common acts that people carry out each day in the normal course of living.

Assessment skills Collecting information by interviewing, observing, and examining a patient.

Caring The concern and attachment that occur from the close relationship of one human being with another.

Caring skills Those skills that restore or maintain an individual's highest state of functioning.

Comforting skills Those skills that convey to the patient that his feelings are understood and accepted.

Continuing education Formal or informal education offered to nurses who have completed their basic training programme.

Counselling skills Communication skills that involve both talking and listening.

Empathy Detached awareness of what the patient is experiencing.

Health care Services provided to individuals who are sick or well for improving a state of well-being.

Health practitioner Any individual whose skills improve an individual's state of health.

Health promotion Care intended primarily to help people stay well. Synonym for *preventive nursing care*.

Medical care Care provided or directed by a doctor to assist a sick individual to get well.

Nursing process A method of problem solving in which the nurse assesses, plans, implements, and evaluates patient care.

Preventive nursing care Care intended primarily

to help people stay well. Synonym for *health promotion*.

Principle An undisputed fact on which certain outcomes can be predicted.

Rehabilitation The art and skill of helping handicapped persons regain function and use remaining abilities in the best way possible.

Rehabilitative nursing care Care commenced immediately upon a patient's admission to maintain or restore physical functions.

Self-image A personal view of oneself.

Sympathy Feeling so similarly to the patient that one's objectivity is lost.

Introduction

Nurses use specialized skills to care for people who are sick or well. All nurses, regardless of their choice of educational preparation, learn basic skills that are fundamental to the practice of nursing. Nursing practice involves the application of knowledge and the performance of skilled tasks that improve an individual's level of health.

Many individuals, besides nurses, can provide health care. *Health care* consists of services offered to people who are sick or well. Individuals such as nurses, dietitians, physiotherapists and occupational therapists are called *health practitioners*. Each health practitioner has been educated to provide unique skills that may improve an individual's state of health. Some of those skills may be provided independently of a doctor. The regulation of each health practitioner's skills is defined by their individual governing body.

Health practitioners also work interdependently with the doctor as a team. When a doctor requests that a health practitioner carry out a specific task, the term *medical care* is used. Medical care refers to care provided or directed by a doctor to help a sick individual get well.

Definitions of nursing

Nursing has probably been practised since the beginning of human existence. It has changed and continues to change as scientific knowledge increases and technological advances occur. Social circumstances have also influenced the development of nursing. Back in the 1800s standards of nursing were low; many of the sick were found in workhouses and much of the care was provided by the poor

themselves. Problems existed with diet, sanitation and general hygiene. At this time most of the nurses were drawn from the working class and drunkenness and immorality prevailed amongst them.

Charles Dickens' depictions of Sarah Gamp and Betsy Prig in Martin Chuzzlewit were considered to be fair representations of the typical hospital nurse of the early 19th Century. The time was therefore ripe for reform. (Jolley and Allen, 1982.)

It was during this time that two of the early pioneers of nursing emerged: Elizabeth Fry and Florence Nightingale. Fry gathered a small group of nurses together who attended Guy's Hospital one day a week to gain knowledge from the ward sisters.

They worked amongst the poor, and were respectable women, committed to what they did. Various branches of nursing groups were set up across England and other countries including those of the Sisters of Mercy and the Irish Sisters of Charity.

Following improvements to nursing outside hospitals, reforms in nursing within hospitals commenced. Training schemes were initiated lasting approximately two years which warranted the award of a certificate on completion. Despite these early changes in nursing there was still a void to be filled in the development of nursing practice alongside social and health reforms.

Florence Nightingale (1820–1910) is the individual credited with changing the direction and thus the definition of nursing in modern times. She felt nursing was a "calling", but one that should be based on more than just dedication and intuition. She demonstrated that the health of the sick and wounded could be improved through the classroom and clinical education of nurses. Nursing programmes continue to follow that model. Florence Nightingale proposed that "nursing is putting us in the best possible condition for nature to restore and preserve health".

The decline in death rates among those for whom she directed care was probably due to the use of physical skills in the areas of improved sanitation, hygiene, and nutrition. However, she equally demonstrated the value of emotional and spiritual nursing skills as she tended the wounded of the Crimea. The use of these nursing skills earned her the respect of a nation and the title "Lady with a Lamp".

Nursing history is rich in the definitions of nursing provided by those who have been recognized as authorities and therefore qualified spokespersons on the practice of nursing. The changing definitions reflect the transformations into which nursing continues to evolve.

The definition that broadened Nightingale's description of nursing to include health promotion was proposed by Virginia Henderson in 1955 and modified again in 1966.

> *The unique function of the nurse is to assist the individual, sick or well, in the performance of those activities contributing to health or its recovery (or to a peaceful death) that he could perform unaided if he had the necessary strength, will or knowledge. And to do this in such a way as to help him gain independence as rapidly as possible.*

In her writing and speaking, Henderson criticized definitions of nursing that limited the nurse to carrying out medical orders in the care of the sick. She identified fourteen skills that applied to all the health needs of individuals who require nursing assistance. These functions are listed in Table 1-1.

Table 1-1. Nursing skills provided to patients

Nursing skills help patients:
1. Breathe normally.
2. Eat and drink adequately.
3. Eliminate body wastes.
4. Move and maintain desirable postures.
5. Sleep and rest.
6. Select suitable clothing—dress and undress.
7. Maintain body temperature within normal range by adjusting clothing and modifying the environment.
8. Keep the body clean and well groomed and protect the integument.
9. Avoid dangers in the environment and avoid injuring others.
10. Communicate with others in expressing emotions, needs, fears, or opinions.
11. Worship according to one's faith.
12. Work in such a way that there is a sense of accomplishment.
13. Play or participate in various forms of recreation.
14. Learn, discover, or satisfy the curiosity that leads to normal development and health and use of the available health facilities.

From Henderson (1966).

No doubt as the role of the nurse changes and society's health needs change so will new definitions of nursing be developed to describe the functions of the nurse.

Men in nursing

For many years nursing was viewed as a career for women and indeed the majority of nurses today are still female, with only 10% being male. The reason for this may well stem from nursing in its early days when the "matron" was responsible for ensuring that all domestic standards were maintained, including patients looking neat and tidy prior to the consultant's round! Society's views on the sexes has also stereotyped women as the mothers and home makers, whilst men have traditionally been known as the "breadwinners". However, this attitude is changing and now many women are developing careers alongside men. Similarly, as nursing has changed more men are entering into it.

Resistance to men in nursing not only stemmed from public opinion but sometimes from within the profession. It was not until 1960 that men were allowed to join the Royal College of Nursing (RCN). At one time male nurses would only be seen in psychiatry. However, now there are men in all aspects of nursing, including midwifery.

Jane Salvage (1985) states: "The ratio of men to women in nursing averages 1 to 8.5, but the higher you go in the career ladder, the greater the concentration of men. There is one male auxiliary to every nineteen women, but the ratio in senior posts is 1:1". This viewpoint was supported by work undertaken by Nuttall (1983) who demonstrated that while male nurses numbered only 10% of the total nursing workforce at that time, in top posts in nursing such as District Nursing Officers, the ratio was one to one.

Hutt (1985) found that 80% of chief nursing posts were filled by men. Some explanations for this are given in *Nursing Today* (1989) as listed below:
1. In terms of female commitments men are better placed to remain in nursing full time and thus to go for promotion.
2. Possibly some men are anxious to move away from the clinical side of nursing. (This is in line with the view that nurses, be they male or female, realize that promotion to management positions means moving away from the bedside.)
3. Men may be under pressure to earn more, and

thus actively seek promotion, especially if they are the sole breadwinner of the family.

Despite the adverse opinions of some nurses towards men in nursing, many others both male and female welcome men in nursing. They support the view that if nursing practice is to be based on research and science, men can be influential in raising the status of nursing. Traditionally men have been associated with scientific discovery and are therefore more likely to be able to put forward a stronger argument for nursing and nursing research, not only to medical colleagues but also to politicians.

Objectives of nursing skills

Nursing involves skills that can be beneficial to sick or well individuals. Nurses now provide services in many diverse settings such as schools, industry, hospitals and home care. The following discussion elaborates and points out the major goals of nursing today.

Nursing works to promote health and prevent disease. Nurses today have an increasingly important responsibility to help people stay well. This is often called *preventive nursing care* or *health promotion*.

Promotion of physical health may be seen in the field of nutrition, in which the body's requirements are well known and the results of poor eating have been demonstrated. Nurses have knowledge of normal nutritional needs. Nurses use teaching skills related to nutrition to help people learn how to select, prepare, or modify their diets in order to meet their daily requirements. Eating a variety of foods in the proper amount promotes a healthy state.

Promoting the state of an individual's health will assist in the prevention or reduction in the occurrence of illness. Much work is being done to prevent illnesses that continue to strike humanity. Heart disease and cancer, for example, are being studied in many countries by people of varying professions. Nurses often assist in these studies. The purposes of such programmes are to find how these diseases are caused, how they can be treated when present, and how they can be prevented through health promotion measures.

Health practitioners have studied how stress affects health. Based on the findings of researchers, programmes that help us deal with stress are making it possible for more people to enjoy better health. Nurses are now assisting those individuals who demonstrate unhealthy physical responses to stress.

High blood pressure is a common stress response in the human body. By promoting stress management techniques, nurses can help individuals reduce their blood pressure to safer levels. Maintaining blood pressure at normal levels prevents many potential health problems.

Nursing is concerned with restoring health. Even with care that promotes health, disease attacks humans. The most basic component of nursing has been the use of skills that help sick people regain health. Nurses take care of the sick by giving aid, comfort, nourishment, protection, and support.

Assisting people to overcome handicaps by helping to return function to a part of the body or by making the best possible use of remaining abilities is often called *rehabilitation*. Until recently, rehabilitation was usually thought of as a specialized field of work done by people who helped severely handicapped patients. Today, nurses plan and utilize skills that prevent or restore physical functions immediately upon a patient's admission. Some refer to this kind of nursing care as *rehabilitative nursing care*. A nurse is giving rehabilitative care when she exercises a partially paralysed arm to help bring back its normal functioning.

Nursing is concerned with relieving suffering. Many individuals for whom nurses care may have life-threatening illnesses. Nurses recognize that there is an end to all human life. Health is not a state that can be sustained forever. The nurse who cares for a patient who is terminally ill also provides special skills to meet the individual's needs. The dying patient may present the greatest challenge to the nurse's skills. There is a sensitivity among nurses to the dying person's need for pain relief, physical care, and psychological care. The nurse's presence serves to relieve the burden of lonely suffering in the absence of close friends and/or family.

Skills basic to nursing

To provide comprehensive care, the nurse uses skills that are basic to any setting in which nursing is practised. These skills involve the application of sciences such as anatomy, physiology, sociology, and psychology, which form part of the knowledge base of nursing.

Assessment skills

Before the nurse can determine what type of care to provide, the needs and problems of the patient must be determined. This requires the use of assessment skills. *Assessment skills* are those acts of interviewing, observation, and examination for the purpose of collecting information. The nurse gathers information from various resources. The patient is the primary source, but the family, the medical record, and verbal information from other health practitioners are also helpful.

The nurse uses verbal skills to interview the patient or family. Certain questions about health and illness can provide facts about the individual's current and past health problems. It is also possible at this time to acquire the patient's view of his health state and expectations for care. Communication with the doctor or others involved with the patient may help the nurse gather information and avoid duplication.

The senses of vision, hearing, touch, and smell can aid in collecting facts about the person's health state through observation. Slurred speech may indicate that the patient has had a stroke; a fruity odour to the breath may indicate a complication of diabetes; bruises may indicate a recent fall; cold skin may mean poor circulation. The nurse uses knowledge of what is normal to interpret that which is abnormal.

Finally, the nurse uses examination skills as part of assessment. Various kinds of equipment such as a thermometer and a stethoscope are used by the nurse to provide information about the patient. The nurse follows a systematic pattern of assessing the patient from head to toe. Any deviation from normal provides the nurse with more clues for identifying the individual's actual or potential health problems. Various nursing skills may be useful in reducing, eliminating, or preventing those identified health problems. Assessment skills are dealt with in more detail in Chapter 4.

Caring skills

Nurses are and have always been care givers. This has been the most traditional role for nurses. *Caring skills* are those that restore or maintain an individual's highest state of functioning. For some patients this may involve something as minimal as assisting the patient with activities of daily living. *Activities of daily living* is a term used to describe acts that people do in the normal course of living. Such activities include eating, sleeping, elimination, working, moving about, socializing, and so on.

More and more nurses are being required to provide complex care skills such as the monitoring and use of highly technical equipment. This textbook is primarily written about the caring skills that nurses commonly provide in the practice of nursing.

No matter what level of care is provided, the nurse wants the patient eventually to be independent. The nurse who gives too much tender loving care may delay the patient from moving toward wellness and being able to resume normal activities of daily living.

Caring also involves the concern and attachment that occurs from the close relationship of one human being with another. Nurses maintain that their priority is the caring for the patient above all other tasks that may be involved.

Counselling skills

To promote active participation in decision making, nurses guard against giving advice to patients. Nurses believe that every individual or his family retains the right to make decisions and choices on matters affecting health and illness care. Therefore, nurses use many skills in communication that involve both talking and active listening.

The nurse provides information to the patient by responding to questions, by providing written information, and by using charts, models, or diagrams. Doing so promotes the patient's ability to analyse how his life is affected by his health problem or its treatment. The patient can then choose from several options that which is most appropriate for him, thus making an informed choice.

At times counselling involves teaching. While giving care, the nurse finds many opportunities to teach patients how to promote healing processes, how to stay well, how to prevent illness, and how to carry out activities of daily living in the best possible way. People know much more about health and health care today. They expect nurses to share accurate information with them.

Patients do not always ask questions or communicate their concerns. Another counselling skill is the use of empathy. *Empathy* is a detached awareness of what the patient is experiencing. The nurse uses empathy to anticipate the patient's emotional state and his desire or need for information. This skill involves being able to remain impartial in order to evaluate the situation. This quality differs from sympathy. *Sympathy* is feeling so similarly to the patient that the nurse loses objectivity and the ability to help the patient through his problem.

There are times when counselling skills involve active listening. *Active listening* is hearing the content of what the patient says as well as the unspoken message. Patients sometimes appreciate the opportunity to describe their feelings or concerns. Doing so helps the patient organize his thoughts and evaluate the situation more realistically. Often, the only requirements for the nurse are the provision for uninterrupted time with the patient and full attention to what is being said.

Comforting skills

All individuals possess a personal view of themselves. *Self-image* involves a mental attitude about who and what we are. A state of health is one of the usual characteristics of self-image, since it is the predominant experience for most individuals. When health is threatened, it will probably cause a person to reexamine his self-image. It may cause feelings of insecurity. What the patient assumed about himself, or even took for granted, may no longer be accurate. This change in mental attitude can threaten the foundation on which an individual is able to cope with current and future problems. The patient feels very vulnerable.

It is then that the nurse uses *comforting skills* to convey to the patient that his feelings are understood and accepted. Because the family or other supportive persons may not be continuously available for the patient, the nurse becomes the stabilizing figure during the patient's temporary state of illness.

Basis for nursing skills

Nursing began as an extension of nurturing. The early skills were often an accumulation of practices that were handed down from one generation to another. Those who were most successful and willing to assume the functions associated with nursing were entrusted with that responsibility. The present basis for nursing involves more than just apprenticed knowledge.

Scientific knowledge

The foundation for promoting health is based on information that has been discovered in the sciences. Nursing is said to make use of the applied sciences. Once anatomy and physiology are understood, assessment skills can be applied to identify the characteristics associated with health or disease. Once a knowledge of chemistry and physics is acquired, an understanding of therapeutic treatment such as pharmacology, fluid replacement, and

inhalation therapy can be applied. Understanding how organisms grow and multiply through the study of microbiology provides a basis for applying nursing skills that can protect individuals from infection.

Nurses also apply knowledge from the social sciences, such as sociology and psychology. By learning how individuals live and rely on social interaction, nurses can apply skills based on family and group structures. Human behaviour has been studied by psychologists. The information from this body of scientists provides information from which the nurse may use skills to help a patient change or modify his behaviour.

Research

Nurses have long participated in the research studies of other scientists. Now nurses are designing and conducting their own research. Many inquisitive nurses are not content to implement the skills and practices that have been perpetuated from tradition. Progress in any practice is often the result of challenging long-held beliefs. Many nurses are daring to ask why and why not. This has and will continue to promote the accumulation of scientific knowledge unique to the practice of nursing. It provides a basis for the change or addition of nursing skills that can be used to promote health and to prevent disease.

Nursing journals often publish the written contributions of nurses to promote current skills and knowledge.

Proven principles

Principles are undisputed facts on which one can predict certain outcomes. Principles usually develop from research. For the findings of research to be considered valid, they must have included a large or long-term test. In addition, the findings must be duplicated by other independent researchers. Once this occurs, the findings are considered proven principles. Nursing skills shoud be based on proven principles. Principles provide nurses with the reasons, or whys, that guide their actions. All skills for patient care should reflect a scientific rationale.

Consider the following example. Research has shown that the moist particles, called droplets, expelled during sneezing and coughing can carry live organisms from a person's nose and throat. These droplets are often carried considerable distances, and if someone else inhales them, he may become infected with the microorganisms. However, when the droplets are trapped with a tissue, these microorganisms do not reach others. The suggested nursing action, then, is to teach the patient to cover his nose and mouth when sneezing and coughing. The principle, or reason, for the action is that a tissue forms a physical barrier controlling the transmission of infectious microorganisms.

The nurse selects an appropriate skill based on knowledge of scientific research. The proven principle is the rationale for the nurse's action. Knowing the *why* of one's action and being able to predict its effect is important when implementing nursing skills. Good nursing care requires sound nursing judgment, which becomes possible only when the nurse has knowledge of principles and the results to expect when performing nursing actions.

Project 2000—the future nurse practitioner

In May 1988 the government gave its approval to a new report which was to change nurse education and training radically; it was known as Project 2000. However, work on the project had commenced long before 1988; back in 1986 the UKCC unanimously agreed to proposals of the project which were the culmination of work presented by a special working party looking at the future of the nurse education. Since then the project and its proposals have been widely publicized in the nursing press and they have generated much discussion amongst nurses at all levels (Table 1-2).

Table 1-2. *Project 2000: summary of major recommendations*

1. There should be a new registered practitioner competent to assess the need for care, provide care, monitor and evaluate and to do this in institutional and noninstitutional settings.
2. Preparation for the new registered practitioner should normally be completed within three years.
3. All preparation for registration should begin with a common foundation programme followed by branch programmes.
4. The common foundation programme should be a substantial part of preparation.
5. Branch programmes should be available, in mental illness, mental handicap, nursing of adults and nursing of children.
6. In the case of midwifery, there should also be an 18-month post registration preparation.
7. There should be a new, single list of competencies applicable to all registered practitioners at the level of registration and set out in Training Rules.
8. All future practitioners should register with Council. The area of practice should be indicated on the register.
9. Midwives should debate the new registered practitioner outcomes in the light of their special needs.
10. There should be a coherent, comprehensive, cost-effective framework of education beyond registrations.
11. There should be specialist practitioners, some of whom will also be team leaders, in all areas

of practice in hospital and community settings. The requisite specialist qualifications will be recordable on Council's register.
12. Health visiting, occupational health nursing and school nursing should be specialist qualifications in health promotion which are recordable on Council's register.
13. District nursing, community psychiatric nursing and community mental handicap nursing should be specialist qualifications which are recordable on Council's register.
14. Students should be supernumerary to NHS staffing establishments throughout the whole period of preparation.
15. There should be a new helper, directly supervised and monitored by a registered practitioner.
16. Students should receive training grants which are primarily NHS-controlled. These should be administered via National Boards and should derive from a separately identified education budget.
17. The position of teaching staff should be improved with a view to enhancing performance and allowing teachers opportunities for further training and for full participation in wider educational activities.
18. The full range of means to achieve the appropriate concentrations of educational resources should be considered, including re-establishments, partnerships consortia etc.
19. Educational costs should be clearly identified

Continued

Table 1-2. Continued

and heads of educational institutions should be given responsibility for management of a more comprehensive and clearly delineated education budget. 20. Practitioners should have formal preparation for teaching roles in practice settings. 21. Moves should be made to establish teaching qualifications at degree level for teachers of nursing, midwifery and health visiting. 22. Joint professional and academic validation should be pursued from the very outset of	change, in order to achieve academic recognition for professional qualifications. 23. Programmes of training for entry to the EN parts of the register should cease as soon as is practicable. 24. The enhancement of opportunities for ENs to enter RGN, RMN, RNMH and RSCN parts of the register should now be given priority. 25. Urgent consideration should be given to creating a new organization structure to implement the proposals of Project 2000.

Adapted from UKCC (1986) Project 2000—A New Preparation for Practice.

Funding was allocated by the government for one College of Nursing and Midwifery per district, to act as a demonstration area for Project 2000 nurse training. These demonstration areas commenced the Project 2000 programmes in the latter part of 1989.

The Project 2000 course (UKCC, 1986) consists of an 18-month common foundation programme followed by an 18-month branch programme in one of the following areas:

- Adult health
- Child health
- Mental illness
- Mental handicap

The Colleges of Nursing are linked to Higher Education establishments such as polytechnics. The courses consequently have conjoint validation from the appropriate National Board and the Council for National Academic Awards, (CNAA) or university body. Biological, sociological and behaviourial sciences provide a basis for Project 2000 training.

The course content also focuses on ethical, legal, environmental and political issues which affect health and nursing. Throughout the majority of the course the student has supernumerary status and takes up placements in both institutional and noninstitutional settings, developing the knowledge and skills to practise nursing according to the competencies for nurses on parts 12, 13, 14 or 15 of the register.

Most nurses welcome the reforms of Project 2000 but there are still some concerns about its introduction. One of these is the loss of the "student workforce". To combat this the role of the "health care assistant" is being developed, but Health Authorities also need to look at launching recruitment schemes, as did Australia, where nurse training

and education was moved into colleges of higher education. With the shortage of 18-year-olds these recruitment drives must look at back to nursing courses, creche facilities and flexible working hours.

The development of the health care assistant is also under discussion; some nurses feel that we may be creating another two-tier system: the registered nurse and the health care assistant. It is thought that the health care assistant's role will not only encompass assisting with patient care under the direction and supervision of the trained nurse; but also incorporate clerical duties.

Opportunities are also being developed for enrolled nurses who wish to undertake an EN to RGN conversion course. Flexible conversion courses are also being considered using a creditation system as well as distance learning programmes leading to conversion, such as the "Nursing Times Open Learning" Course, lasting approximately two years. For those enrolled nurses who do not want to convert to RGN their role will be protected and they will be able to continue to practise as enrolled nurses.

Nursing competencies

In April 1979 parliament passed the Nurses, Midwives and Health Visitors Act (UK Parliament, 1979). It decreed the establishment of the UKCC, whose function was to establish and improve standards of training and professional conduct, for nurses, midwives and health visitors. The act also brought about the establishment of the four national boards (English, Welsh, Scottish and Northern Irish). Their remit was to work alongside the UKCC to improve training methods, look at alleged cases of misconduct and arrange for examinations to be held.

The act also said there would be a single register of nurses, midwives and health visitors, prepared and maintained by the council. The final handover of control from the previous nine bodies was in 1983 when they were dissolved along with their rules and regulations.

The Nurses, Midwives and Health Visitors Rules Approval Order (UK Statutory Instruments, 1983) set down the competencies expected of each nurse, midwife or health visitor according to what level of the register they were on. It is sometimes referred to as "rule 18" or the nursing competencies. With the commencement of Project 2000 the above Rules Approval Order has been amended (UK Statutory Instruments, 1989) to include new competencies for nurses on completion of any of the branch programmes of Project 2000, i.e. those nurses who will be on either part 12, 13, 14 or 15 of the register. All 15 parts of the register are listed in Chapter 7, "Legal Implications for Nursing". The competencies for each part of the register are reprinted below:

Statutory Instruments 1983 No. 873

Nurses, Midwives and Health Visitors Rules Approval Order 1983
Ref. (H83/1175)

1. *Courses leading to a qualification the successful completion of which shall enable an application to be made for admission to Part 1, 3, 5 or 8 of the register shall provide opportunities to enable the student to accept responsibility for her personal professional development and to acquire the competencies required to:*
   (a) *advise on the promotion of health and the prevention of illness;*
   (b) *recognise situations that may be detrimental to the health and well-being of the individual;*
   (c) *carry out those activities involved when conducting the comprehensive assessment of a person's nursing requirements;*
   (d) *recognise the significance of the observations made and use these to develop an initial nursing assessment;*
   (e) *devise a plan of nursing care based on the assessment with the co-operation of the patient, to the extent that this is possible, taking into account the medical prescription;*
   (f) *implement the planned programme of nursing care and where appropriate teach and co-ordinate other members of the caring team*

who may be responsible for implementing specific aspects of the nursing care;*
   (g) *review the effectiveness of the nursing care provided, and where appropriate, initiate any action that may be required;*
   (h) *work in a team with other nurses, and with medical and para-medical staff and social workers;*
   (i) *undertake the management of the care of a group of patients over a period of time and organise the appropriate support services;*
   related to the care of the particular type of patient with whom she is likley to come in contact when registered in that Part of the register for which the student intends to qualify.

2. *Courses leading to a qualification the successful completion of which shall enable an application to be made for admission to Part 2, 4, 6 or 7 of the register shall be designed to prepare the student to undertake nursing care under the direction of a person registered in Part 1, 3, 5 or 8 of the register and provide opportunities for the student to develop the competencies required to:*
   (a) *assist in carrying out comprehensive observation of the patient and care under the direction of a person registered in Part 1, 3, 5 or 8 of the register;*
   (b) *develop skills to enable her to assist in the implementation of nursing care under the direction of a person registered in Part 1, 3, 5 or 8 of the register;*
   (c) *accept delegated nursing tasks;*
   (d) *assist in reviewing the effectiveness of the care provided;*
   (e) *work in a team with other nurses, and with medical and para-medical staff and social workers;*
   related to the care of the particular type of patient with whom she is likely to come into contact when registered in that Part of the register for which the student intends to qualify.

Amended competencies for entry to parts 12, 13, 14 or 15 of the Register:

The Common Foundation Programme and the Branch Programme, shall be designed to prepare the student to assume the responsibilities and accountability that registration confers, and to prepare the nursing student to apply knowledge and skills to meet the nursing needs of individuals and of groups in health and in sickness in the area of practice of the Branch Programme and shall include enabling the student to achieve the following outcomes:

   (a) the identification of the social and health implications of pregnancy and child bearing, physical and mental handicap, disease, disability, or ageing for the individual, her or his friends, family and community;

   (b) the recognition of common factors which contribute to, and those which adversely affect, physical, mental and social well-being of patients and clients and take appropriate action;

   (c) the use of relevant literature and research to inform the practice of nursing;

   (d) the appreciation of the influence of social, political and cultural factors in relation to health care;

   (e) an understanding of the requirements of legislation relevant to the practice of nursing;

   (f) the use of appropriate communication skills to enable the development of helpful caring relationships with patients and clients and their families and friends, and to initiate and conduct therapeutic relationships with patients and clients;

   (g) the identification of health related learning needs of patients and clients, families and friends and to participate in health promotion;

   (h) an understanding of the ethics of health care and of the nursing profession and the responsibilities which these impose on the nurse's professional practice;

   (i) the identification of the needs of patients and clients to enable them to progress from varying degrees of dependence to maximum independence, or to a peaceful death;

   (j) the identification of physical, psychological, social and spiritual needs of the patient or client; an awareness of values and concepts of individual care; the ability to devise a plan of care, contribute to its implementation and evaluation; and the demonstration of the application of the principles of a problem-solving approach to the practice of nursing;

   (k) the ability to function effectively in a team and participate in a multi-professional approach to the care of patients and clients;

   (l) the use of the appropriate channel of referral for matters not within her sphere of competence;

   (m) the assignment of appropriate duties to others and the supervision, teaching and monitoring of assigned duties.

Strategy for nursing

In April 1989 the Department of Health's Nursing Division published its unique blueprint for the nursing professions, *A Strategy for Nursing*. This was the culmination of three years' work by leaders of the profession aimed at preparing nursing to meet health care changes not only in the next decade but into the next century (Department of Health Nursing Division, 1989).

The strategy is made up of 44 targets for the nursing professions set out under following headings:

- Targets for Practice
- Targets for Manpower
- Targets for Education
- Targets for Leadership and Management

The strategy encompasses the Project 2000 reforms, as well as stating the need for greater flexibility in the practitioner's role within the community. The strategy also looks at the need to develop leaders within the profession and the development of innovative roles for nurses, midwives and health visitors.

Many of the strategy's concepts are already in operation somewhere in the country, but they need evaluation and development. Others present widespread national challenges and their implementation will occupy us for many years to come. If they are to be achieved they will bring major benefits not only to nurses, midwives and health visitors but, more significantly, to the people we serve, their families and the community at large. (Poole, 1989.)

The strategy was introduced to help nurses meet the changing health needs of the public, and provide them with a structure to move forward as a profession in order to achieve specific goals and objectives.

The strategy provides a framework which can be adapted to meet the needs of other countries within the UK; for example, Wales and Scotland have produced their own strategies. In England each region is assessing how to move the strategy forward. Printed below are the targets for action. It is up to nurses, midwives and health visitors at all levels to look at these targets, within their health settings and organizations, in order to devise a timetable for their implementation.

Targets for practice

   1. The full accountability of nursing, midwifery

and health visiting practitioners, with responsibility for individual patients or clients, should be recognized and applied in all health care settings.

2. The development of primary nursing should be encouraged.

3. New roles should be developed for practitioners to meet changing health care needs, improve care provision and realize the potential of clinical practice.

4. Health education and promotion should be a recognized part of health care; all practitioners should develop skills in, and use every opportunity for, health promotion.

5. The views and wishes of consumers should be taken into account in all decisions on the provision and delivery of health care.

6. There should be agreed policies and procedures for setting standards of care and monitoring their outcome; practitioners should develop a knowledge of quality assessment.

7. All clinical practice should be founded on up-to-date information and research findings; practitioners should be encouraged to identify the needs and opportunities for research presented by their work.

8. Academic faculties with departments of nursing should be encouraged to broaden their links with, and deepen their expertise in, research-based practice.

9. The nursing professions should be represented on, and contribute fully to the work of each ethical committee.

10. Practice-related and management information technology, of proven suitability, should be installed in all health care settings; all procedures—practice, organizational and managerial—should be examined and, where desirable, computerized.

11. All practitioners should be trained and experienced in the clinical use of information technology; they should be enabled to maintain and build on any computer literacy acquired at school or during professional training.

12. Health care facilities which could appropriately be led and managed by nurses, midwives or health visitors should be identified and developed.

13. Clinical practice and policies should take account of national and local strategies for health care.

14. The contribution of specialist practitioners should be explored and developed, in consultation with the medical profession where appropriate.

15. The special contribution of the enrolled nurse to nursing practice should be recognized; the position of the individual nurse and of standards of care should be safeguarded.

Targets for manpower

16. There should be strategic and operational plans for future manpower requirements which should be subject to regular review.

17. Systematic methods should be used to agree the number and deployment of staff in all health care settings.

18. The grading structure for nurses, midwives and health visitors should be fine tuned as appropriate to ensure that experience and responsibilities at all levels are recognized and acknowledged.

19. The skills and make up of each health care team, including the need for specialist skills, should be reviewed at intervals in the light of changing needs.

20. Sufficient ancillary, administrative and clerical staff should be provided in all health care settings to ensure that scarce professional skills are used to maximum effect.

21. Recruitment plans should be developed and implemented, paying particular attention to the needs of mature entrants and those re-entering the service.

22. Contact should be maintained with practitioners taking a career break, and flexible re-entry training programmes and conditions of service should be available to facilitate their return.

23. The particular needs of practitioners with family commitments and those from the ethnic minorities should be reflected in sympathetic and flexible personnel policies and practices.

24. Employment of practitioners re-entering the NHS should take account of skills and experience gained in other health care settings or outside the professions.

Targets for education

25. All staff delivering health care should be appropriately prepared for their practice.

26. There should be strategic and operational plans to meet the educational needs of the future professional workforce.

27. The proposals for educational reform detailed in the UKCC document Project 2000 should be implemented.

28. The education of nurses, midwives and health visitors should be regularly reviewed and adapted to ensure that it meets changing health care needs.

29. The number and organization of schools of nursing and midwifery should be rationalized, and linked with establishments of further and higher education.

30. All practitioners should have opportunities for continuing post-registration education appropriate to their work.

31. Opportunities for enrolled nurse conversion to the first level should be increased to recognize and enhance their contribution to care.

32. Practitioners should accept responsibility for ensuring their continued professional development and competence.

33. Periodic and continuing education within the area of post-registration education and practice should be examined.

34. The development of a comprehensive framework which allows the accumulation of credits towards graduate status should be pursued.

35. Future teachers must be able to demonstrate at an advanced level a knowledge of the theory and practice of nursing or midwifery. They must be qualified or clinically credible in the area of practice they teach and hold a recognized teaching qualification.

36. Support workers accountable to nurses should receive training, within the framework of the NCVQ, to an appropriate level.

37. Support workers with the qualifications, ability and desire to enter nursing education should be encouraged to do so.

38. Management should ensure that policies, practices and procedures meet the objectives of the organization.

39. Management should set performance targets to agreed standards and ensure that staff complements are appropriate to meet them.

40. Management should encourage and enable all practitioners to function at their highest level of ability.

41. Nurses, midwives and health visitors should have access to an experienced senior practitioner for advice on professional issues; procedures should be in place to resolve ethical issues arising from individual clinical practice.

42. Practitioners should be afforded personal appraisal of their performance and potential, advice on career options and appropriate training opportunities.

43. All staff should, throughout their careers, be given the opportunity to develop their professional skills and capabilities; those opting for careers in management should be given the appropriate training and opportunities.

44. Staff with special potential should be identified and given appropriate opportunities for development.

References

Continuing Nurse Education Open Learning for Nurses (1989) *Nursing Today*, Charlesworth, Huddersfield.

Department of Health Nursing Division (1989) *A Strategy for Nursing—A Report of the Steering Committee*, HMSO, London.

Henderson, V. (1966) *The Nature of Nursing—A Definition and Its Implications for Practice, Research and Education*, Macmillan, New York.

Hutt R. (1985) "Chief Officer Career Profiles", Study, Institute of Manpower Studies, Brighton.

Jolley, M. and Allen, P. (1982) *Nursing, Midwifery and Health Visiting Since 1900*, Faber and Faber, London.

Nuttall, P. (1983) Male takeover or female giveaway? *Nursing Times*, **79**(21), 10–11.

Poole A. (1989) Cited in Department of Health Nursing Division, *A Strategy for Nursing—A Report of the Steering Committee*, HMSO, London.

Salvage, J. (1985) *The Politics of Nursing*, Heinemann Nursing, London.

UKCC (1986) *Project 2000—A New Preparation for Practice*, United Kingdom Central Council for Nursing, Midwifery and Health Visiting, London.

UK Parliament (1979) The Nurses, Midwives and Health Visitors Act, HMSO, London.

UK Statutory Instruments (1983) Nurses, Midwives and Health Visitors Rules Approval Order, No. 873, HMSO, London.

UK Statutory Instruments (1989) Nurses, Midwives and Health Visitors (Registered Fever Nurses Amendment Rules and Training Amendment Rules) Approval Order, No. 1456, HMSO, London.

Further reading

Barry, J.T., Soothill K.L. and Francis B.J. (1989) Nursing the statistics: a demonstration study of nurse turnover and retention. *Journal of Advanced Nursing*, **14**, 528–35.

Bond, M. (1988) *Stress and Self Awareness: A Guide for Nurses*, Heinemann Nursing, London. (Reprint.)

Casey, N. (1990) A planned strategy. *Nursing Standard*, **4**(24), 20–1.

Chapman, C.M. (1983) The paradox of nursing. *Journal of Advanced Nursing*, **8**, 269–72.

Department of Health and Social Security (1986) *A Strategy for Nursing*, Report of a seminar organised by Nursing Division, HMSO, London.

Department of Health Nursing Division (1989) *"A Strategy for Nursing"—Seminar, 27 June*, HMSO, London.

Fisher, R. (1989) The role of men in nursing. *Nursing Standard*, **4**(12), 37–9.

Gallagher, P. (1990) Project 2000 in theory and practice. *Nursing Standard*, **4**(50), 30–1.

Henderson, V. (1978) The concept of nursing. *Journal of Advanced Nursing*, **3**, 113–30.

Hunt, M. (1991) Who flies highest. *Nursing Times*, **84**(7), 29–31.

Le Var, R. (1988) Quest—vital links. *Nursing Times*, **84**(45), 73–4.

Mason, P. (1991) Jobs for the boys. *Nursing Times*, **87**(7), 26–8.

McGrother, J. (1989) Project 2000—White Paper Education. *Nursing Standard*, **3**(32), 32.

Nightingale, F. (1946) *Notes of Nursing: What it is and What it is not*, J.B. Lippincott, Philadelphia.

Orlando, I.J. (1987) Nursing in the 21st century: alternate paths. *Journal of Advanced Nursing*, **12**, 405–12.

Orr, J. and Kratz, C. (1988) Widening the entry gate—the case for the case against. *Nursing Times*, **84**(31), 32–3.

Smith, L. (1982) Occasional papers—the influence of tradition in nursing. *Nursing Times*, **78**(12), 45–8.

Turner, C. (1989) Project 2000: learning from the American experience. *Senior Nurse*, **9**(4), 10–11.

Walsh, M. and Ford, P. (1990) *Nursing Rituals: Research and Rational Actions*, Heinemann Nursing, London. (Reprint.)

2

Nursing: the statutory bodies and patient services

Learning objectives

When the content of this chapter has been mastered, the learner should be able to:

Define the terms in the glossary.
Discuss the UKCC and its functions.
Describe what is meant by the "National Boards" and their major responsibilities.
Discuss the proposals of the PREPP report.
Discuss the structure and management of the NHS.
List the characteristics of "patient services".

Glossary

Advocacy Working indirectly or on behalf of someone.
Allege State or advance a fact.
Competence Having the necessary qualifications and/or ability as required by law.
Emotion A strong feeling such as love, hate or fear.
Holism The concept that all aspects of living—physical, emotional, social and spiritual—are interrelated and affect the individual as a whole.
Post basic Courses following registration as a nurse.
Psychology A science concerned with the way the mind functions and influences behaviour.
Register Official list.
Sociology A science concerned with relationships among people.
Standards Required degree of quality.
Statutory Of a legislative nature.

Introduction

In June 1970 the Committee on Nursing, chaired by Professor Briggs, was set up to look at the role of the nurse and the midwife in the hospital and community setting.

They were also asked to address the training and education required for those roles, in order to meet manpower needs and also those of an integrated health service.

In October 1972 the committee published their recommendations; these numbered 74 in all, of which one was to be of major importance to nursing:

There should be one single statutory organisation to supervise training and education and to safeguard and, when possible, to raise professional standards.

The committee suggested that the new statutory bodies should be set up in the following manner:

1. A single central council responsible for professional standards of education and discipline in nursing and midwifery in the UK.
2. National education boards responsible for the education organization and implementation of the council's policies.

These recommendations became a reality with the establishment of the UK Central Council (UKCC) and four National Boards by decree of the Nurses, Midwives and Health Visitors Act of 1979 (UKCC, 1979). They are independent bodies who work closely together. They replaced the nine previous statutory bodies which were dissolved in 1980 by the Secretary of State.

The UK Central Council

The UKCC is made up of 60 members who are elected every five years, and carries out the following main functions:

1. Maintaining a single professional register for nurses, midwives and health visitors.
2. Establishing and improving standards of education and training.
3. Improving standards of professional conduct and protecting the public from unsafe practitioners.

The professional register

The register is computer-based and was compiled by bringing together the registers and records of the nine bodies forming the previous statutory bodies. All nurses, midwives and health visitors on the register are allocated a Personal Identification Number (PIN).

Anyone entering nurse training in the UK is included in the index section of the Single Professional Register and Index of Training (SPRINT) by the relevant National Board. This means they will be told their PIN when entering into nurse training.

The PIN number is made up in the following manner;

'89'   B9988D
Year of commencement   Unique entrant number
of original training
(or year of first
registration in the
UK if trained abroad)

Registration after successful training will simply be a matter of changing the entry on "SPRINT".

Details of approved post basic courses and experience can be added to the register and changes in registration status of an individual can also be quickly entered and then disseminated where relevant.

Establishing standards of education and training

The Council and the four National Boards are required by the 1979 Act to establish and improve standards of training for nurses, midwives and health visitors (UK Parliament, 1979). The UKCC has a small team of professional officers who work with members through specialist committees. There is an Educational Policy Advisory Committee, a Midwifery Committee and a Committee on Research. The Health Visiting and District Nursing Committees are Joint Committees serving Council and Boards.

The Council have already agreed the educational preparation required for nurse training in the future in order to meet the health needs of the 1990s and beyond; i.e. Project 2000. In addition, they have also agreed that in the future all nurses and health visitors will be required to maintain their professional competence in order to practise. This has been a requirement for midwives since 1936! To look at the continuing education needs of the nurse practitioner, the UKCC set up an advisory committee who issued their report on Post Registration Education and Practice (PREPP) in August 1989.

> The project group was charged with developing a coherent and comprehensive framework for education and practice registration. In doing so, two key issues had to be incorporated: first meeting the needs of patients, clients and the health service, and second maintaining and enhancing standards of education and practice. (UKCC, 1990).

PREPP. The PREPP report views practice as a continuum for nurse practitioners to move along commencing with registration. With the changes in health care and the introduction of the NHS and Community Care Act there is a growing need for skilled up-to-date practitioners.

The recommendations of PREPP apply to *all* nurses on the register, i.e. enrolled nurses, midwives, registered nurses, etc. PREPP firstly considers the support which will be required by the newly qualified nurse practitioner. This will take the format of a preceptor system. The preceptors will act as role models providing effective support to build confidence and skills within the individual, for an agreed period of time. Once this is complete the "novice" will become a primary practitioner.

PREPP continues by looking at the continuing education of the practitioner—it recommends a minimum of five study days in three years. Nurses will be required to chart their progress and achievements in a personal professional profile. This portfolio will outline the individual's career progress, experience to date and achievements in practice. "The Council will need verification that profiles have been satisfactorily completed" (UKCC, 1990).

For nurse practitioners who have had a break from nursing practice for a period of five years or more, PREPP recommends they undertake a "Back to Nursing Programme" which has been validated by the appropriate National Board (ENB Course Number 902).

Further along the continuum of practice is the advanced practitioner. These will be nurses with proven advanced knowledge and skills. Advanced practitioners will need to have a Council approved qualification, the standard, kind and content of which is to be determined by the UKCC.

In order that continuing education and learning can be recognized, a credit and accumulation transfer system (CATS) will be introduced; this will also be used to recognize clinical experience.

A resumé of the PREPP recommendations is reprinted below.

1. There should be a period of support for all newly registered practitioners to consolidate the competencies or learning outcomes achieved at registration.
2. A preceptor should provide the support for each newly registered practitioner.

All the following recommendations will be statutory requirements:

3. All nurses, midwives and health visitors must demonstrate that they have maintained and developed their professional knowledge and competence.
4. All practitioners must record their professional development in a personal professional profile.
5. During the three years leading to periodic registration, all practitioners must complete a period of study or provide evidence of appropriate professional learning. A minimum of five days of study leave every three years must be undertaken by every registered practitioner.
6. When registered practitioners wish to return to practice after a break of five years or more, they will have to complete a return to practice programme.
7. The standard, kind and content of preparation for advanced practice will be specified by the Council. Advanced practitioners must have an appropriate Council-approved qualification recorded on the register.
8. To be eligible to practise, individuals must every three years:

   - submit a notification of practice;
   - EITHER provide verification that they have completed their personal professional profile satisfactorily; OR show evidence that they have completed a return to practice programme; and
   - pay their periodic fee.

9. Practitioners after a break of less than five years returning to practice using a specific registered qualification shall submit a notification of practice and, within the following calendar year, provide verification that they have completed their personal professional profile satisfactorily.

Improving standards of professional conduct

The Council is responsible for establishing and improving standards of professional conduct. It has formulated rules to determine the circumstances in which a person's name may be removed from or restored to the register. The Council has also produced a Code of Professional Conduct (UKCC, 1992) which sets out expected standards of conduct for nurses, midwives and health visitors. Each nurse, midwife and health visitor must read and understand it. A copy of the Code of Conduct is reprinted in Chapter 7, "Legal Implications of Nursing". The UKCC disciplinary procedure is also explained there.

In addition to the Code of Professional Conduct (UKCC, 1992), the UKCC has issued four supplementary documents:

1. Advertising by Registered Nurses, Midwives and Health Visitors (UKCC, 1985).
2. Administration of Medicines (UKCC, 1986).
3. Confidentiality (UKCC, 1987).
4. Exercising Accountability (UKCC, 1989).

These supplementary documents have been published to offer further advice to nurses, midwives and health visitors on specific areas related to the Code of Conduct and are available free of charge from the UKCC.

Who pays for the UKCC?

The bulk of the money required to run the Council comes from the periodic registration fees paid by nurses, midwives and health visitors. At the moment these fees are £30.00 every three years; there is no separate fee for each qualification held by an individual.

Major responsibilities of the National Boards

1. To arrange courses enabling people to qualify for registration and courses for post registration in accordance with the UKCC as to their content and standard.
2. To monitor and arrange nursing examinations.
3. To work with the UKCC to promote and improve nurse training.

The National Health Service

In order to understand the nature of patient services, it is necessary to take a brief look at the structure and function of the National Health Service (NHS), as the major health care promoter of this country.

The NHS was established by an act of parliament in 1946. The management of hospitals became entrusted to local committees or boards who acted as agents to the Minister of Health. The main aim of the National Health Service Act was "to promote the establishment in England and Wales of a comprehensive health service designed to secure improvement in the physical and mental health of the people of England and Wales and the prevention, diagnosis and treatment of illness" (National Association of Health Authorities, 1989). This meant the availability of a free health service to the population (various charges such as prescription fees were introduced later by amending acts).

The NHS was not an exclusive service—voluntary and commercially run hospitals were still allowed to be developed. However, the bulk of health care was provided by the NHS.

Family practitioner services were established under the 1911 National Insurance Act. All members of the population were eligible to register with a general practitioner. Executive Councils were established who administered contracts with members of the profession, made payments to them in line with national agreements and dealt with any complaints. (Pharmacists, dentists and opticians were paid per item of service.)

The Local Health Authorities took responsibility for the following:

1. Ambulance services.
2. Care of the mentally ill.
3. Home help services.
4. Provision of health centres.
5. Environmental health.

Fourteen Regional Health Boards (RHBs) were created to take over the organization and management of the hospitals. Members of the RHBs were appointed by the Minister of Health. "The boards in turn established hospital management committees (HMCs) in their region, to which they appointed the members and the chairman. The duty of HMCs was to control and manage their hospitals" (National Association of Health Authorities, 1989).

There was at least one teaching hospital per region—these were managed by Boards of Governors who were appointed and financed by the Minister.

Soon after the establishment of the NHS, Whitley Councils were organized to negotiate rates of pay. (Nurses' pay is now based on recommendations of a Pay Review Body.)

The NHS has always been funded by the government and this funding has been the subject of much criticism; unfortunately health care cannot be provided by a fixed cost for the whole nation. Many of the problems associated with financing and managing the NHS have led to its various re-organizations in order to provide a more cost effective system.

1974 Re-organization

The basic principle of the re-organization was the integration of services under two new types of health authorities:

1. Regional Health Authorities (RHAs) which replaced the RHBs.
2. Area Health Authorities (AHAs) (90 in total).

The RHAs were responsible for:

1. Allocation of funds.
2. Provision of some services.
3. Overall planning.

The AHAs were responsible for:
1. Planning and liaising with local authorities.
2. Management of personnel, supplies and ambulances.
3. Acting as employing authorities for consultants.

Districts became responsible to AHAs and Community Health Councils were established.

The main development from this organization meant that the service should be actively managed and planned. Management representation from every level up to the DHSS were responsible for devising strategic plans which would be periodically reviewed and also for issuing annual operational plans.

1982 Restructuring

This restructuring adopted the proposals of a consultative document entitled *Patients First* (Dept of Health, 1979), which was put together in response to criticism that the management of the NHS was becoming more expensive, whilst its efficiency was being reduced. This meant the abolition of the AHAs which were replaced by District Health Authorities (DHAs). Each district had to divide their services into units of management. The 90 Family Practitioners Committees became free standing (this happened three years later). Each year the Regional Chairman and his team met with the Minister to review health policies and plan and agree objectives for the following year. Regions held similar meetings with the Districts so that plans and objectives could be devised for their units.

The Griffiths Report (1983)

The Griffiths Report (UK Parliament Session 1983–84) chaired by Sir Roy Griffiths of Sainsbury's suggested that the NHS should be managed more like a business organization with a general management approach on all levels. The following proposals were implemented by 1986:
1. Health Services Supervisory Board, chaired by the Secretary of State based at the Department of Health.
2. Under the above the NHS Management Board comprising members from the Department, NHS and business.
3. Appointment of a General Manager for each Health Authority.
4. Management boards or groups.
5. Appointment of general managers at every level and unit managers. General managers were appointed on short term renewable contracts with pay increments related to performance.

The effects of these management changes were criticized by the public when hospitals and wards started to close. Many of the initial posts which were held by people outside of the service have subsequently been replaced by people from within the health service including nurses and medical officers.

The NHS and Community Care Act 1990

This is the latest act to introduce changes within the NHS based on the following points (UK Parliament, 1990):
1. *Self Governing Hospitals.* Those hospitals choosing to opt out will be run by NHS Trusts who will be responsible for financing their own resources and will be able to set up their own management structure. Self governing hospitals will be exempt from the NHS Management Executive.
2. *Funding and Contracts for Hospital Services.* Allocation of funds will be based on population, morbidity and costs of providing services. Contracts can be made between the private sector and within the NHS, as well as contracts between DHA managed hospitals and their parent authority. Training and research is to be funded by the RHA.
3. *Practice Budgets for General Medical Practitioners.* Costs of individual care over £5000 per annum will be charged to the DHA, not the GP practice. To qualify for a budget, practices must have a caseload of at least 11 000.
4. *Prescribing Budgets for General Medical Practitioners.* These will take account of:
   (a) Age and sex of patients.
   (b) Morbidity.
   (c) Temporary residents.
   (d) Cross boundary dispensing.
5. *Capital Charges.* This involves charges made for capital assets for which annual accounts will be kept, and "asset registers".
6. *Medical Audit.* This will include quality assurance programmes which will cover primary health care, hospital and community services.
7. *Consultant Appointments and Contracts.* This will include the appointment of more consultants and specific contract hours, stating how much time they must spend working within NHS hospitals.

8. *Changes in Family Practitioner Committees* (FPCs). FPCs will be reduced in size but will determine their own structure. They will be responsible for the overseeing of:
   (a) Prescribing budgets for GPs.
   (b) Medical audit.
   (c) Information technology to monitor GP prescribing and referral rates. FPCs will be directly accountable to the RHAs.

It is too early to say what the effects on health care will be following this latest act; but there are fears that the original concepts behind the NHS are being lost and replaced by health treatments and care based on the cheapest price rather than the individual needs of the patient.

Having reviewed the statutory bodies which govern nursing and the changes within the health care setting, i.e. the NHS, it is perhaps appropriate to consider what patients should expect from nurses when receiving care. Here follows a general overview of patient services and how they are interlinked to nursing.

Components of patient services

Although the study of man has often described his physical being separately from his emotional, social and spiritual being, each influences the other simultaneously. The concept that holds that every aspect of man is related one to the others is called *holism*. One way of defining holism is that it is concerned with the relationships between the person's mind and body and between his whole self and his environment.

Nurses recognize that patients have problems—physical, emotional, social, and spiritual—that all have an impact on health. Nurses therefore practise *holistic nursing* by providing services in one or all four of these general areas. As one problem is reduced, it generally has a similar effect on the other aspects of the patient's life.

To understand this concept more fully, consider a factory worker with heart disease who seeks care to overcome his physical disability. Assume that he is the family breadwinner with a wife and five children. He is presently unemployed because of his illness. To provide services that pertain only to his heart problem neglects consideration of the possible emotional, social, and spiritual influences of his illness. How will the family be supported until the patient is employable? Will he need to learn a new type of work when he recovers? How do he and his family feel about his becoming ill? Does the patient feel punished by a higher power? Does the community have services to help the patient? The answers to questions such as these show that physical health and mental health are closely related and that concern with both, as well as with the patient's environment, is important when providing holistic nursing services.

Physical services

Physical services involve the provision of nursing skills that assist the body in maintaining or returning to normal functioning. Physical services include skills such as providing nourishment and water, maintaining breathing, promoting urine and bowel elimination.

One of the most basic and most frequently provided services is that related to physical needs. Patients primarily associate the nurse with providing physical services. This text emphasizes methods that will prepare nursing students to perform the skills that relate to physical services.

Emotional services

An *emotion* is a strong feeling, such as love, hate or fear. The nurse often provides services related to the patient's emotional state. In doing so, the nurse applies principles of *psychology*, which is a science that studies the way the mind works and influences behaviour. There are common reasons for why people feel, act and think the way they do.

Terms frequently used to describe *emotional services* include caring, comforting, compassion and human kindness. These nursing skills encourage the expression of the patient's feelings and an understanding of their significance. Emotional care shows that the nurse has sincere respect, interest and concern for the patient as a person. Nursing is not really nursing unless it includes these patient services. It includes being there when the patient needs someone. Stated in another way, nursing includes giving a lot of one's heart. There may be times when the nurse does no more than offer the patient comfort with a firm handclasp or a smile. The nurse also shows compassion when allowing a patient the opportunity to express anger or frustration. Taking a few minutes to talk to a lonely patient shows kindness and understanding.

Social services

Humans live in groups. The most basic unit of society is the family. *Sociology* is a science about relationships among people. Nurses understand that if one member of a group experiences a health-related problem, it will affect all others with whom the patient has a significant relationship.

Illness may cause a temporary separation of family members. Providing a cot in a child's room so that parents may stay with a sick child is an example of a patient service that supports social aspects of care.

There may be financial hardships as a result of a health problem. For example, the individual may experience the loss of a job. The nurse can initiate referrals to various individuals, e.g. social workers, who may relieve the patient and his family of further worry.

In most instances, services that relate to emotional, social, and spiritual needs are provided after physical needs are met. Although there are differences in the way psychosocial needs are described, in general they are as follows, in order of priority:

1. The need for security and survival.
2. The need for affection and a feeling of belonging to a group.
3. The need for recognition for achievements.
4. The need for self-fulfilment.

Spiritual services

Religion helps humans understand their relationship with the universe around them. There are countless religious beliefs in the world. In this country, the most commonly practised religion is Christianity (Protestantism and Roman Catholicism). However, the nurse should expect to care for persons holding other beliefs as well such as Hinduism or Judaism. The nurse can provide *spiritual services* by understanding and providing opportunities for patients to practise rituals associated with their faith.

Some people do not accept any particular formal religious faith. Yet they may possess a personal belief about their relationship to a spiritual being and a code for moral behaviour. They, too, deserve respect for what they choose to believe.

The presence of religious items at the patient's bedside tells the nurse that he is practising a religious faith. He may wish to spend part of his day in prayer or other religious practices. Because some patients prefer privacy, it is a thoughtful gesture for the nurse to provide such privacy when desired.

Many hospitals have chapels in which patients may worship. Patients may be allowed to go to the chapel if their condition permits. Frequently, it is the nurse who can share information with a patient about the availability of a chaplain, a chapel, or scheduled religious services within the hospital. Patients have been known to improve physically and emotionally because of strong faith. Spiritual support is often the key to hope and determination when illness is present.

Although a person's religious faith often appears to help recovery, there are times when beliefs conflict with traditional care. For example, the doctrine of Jehovah's Witnesses does not permit blood transfusions. Certain vegetarians refuse meat, fish and poultry on religious grounds. If a particular religious practice presents a problem for the patient's care, the nurse may wish to consult with a clergyman, although the patient does have the right to refuse care. A clergyman, however, may very well be the person who can best help the patient accept necessary care. In many hospitals, clergymen of various faiths are available at all times.

The clergyman's visit is usually an important part of the patient's day. The thoughtful nurse will help the clergyman locate the patient and see whether he is able to receive the visit. Having the clergyman visit at an unsuitable or inconvenient time is embarrassing to both the patient and the clergyman. The nurse also will provide privacy as desired.

Characteristics of patient services

The services that are provided by nurses collectively set an example of the characteristics that make up the nurse–patient relationship.

Patient services preserve human dignity. Each patient is a human being and thus, in that respect, an equal of the nurse. When providing patient services, the nurse maintains an acceptance that others may be different but that they are no less or more deserving of nursing skills.

Patient services uphold the uniqueness of each person. Nurses accept differences in people and, therefore, treat each patient as a unique individual. Although in some ways we are all alike—we need food, water and oxygen to live, and we need to be able to get rid of wastes from our bodies—each of us is different from every other person. We react differently to events in our lives; we have different levels of intelligence; we play and work in different ways; we believe different things; we have different values; and so on. Understanding people and respecting their beliefs and rights come with experience.

Patient services are provided to all individuals throughout the life cycle. Care is provided regardless of the patient's age, sex, colour, creed, or socio-economic status. It includes the care of the sick and well throughout life.

Patient services include advocacy care. Working indirectly on behalf of someone is called *advocacy*, and the nurse becomes a *patient advocate* when working on behalf of a patient. Nurses usually offer direct services in face-to-face situations. However, there are times when nurses work indirectly on behalf of a patient. For example, a nurse helps a patient to receive the services of a social worker when required. A nurse makes a patient's needs known to the doctor or to other health workers. These examples illustrate patient advocacy.

Another view of advocacy is that the nurse shares information with the patient so that he can make the best possible decisions for himself. The nurse then supports his decision. This concept of advocacy takes health personnel out of the role of persons "who know best". It recognizes the right of rational adults to make their own decisions after having appropriate knowledge about courses of action open to them and the consequences of each course of action. However, the advocacy role still recognizes that making a decision for a patient may become necessary in certain emergency situations.

Patient services promote independence. Nurses are teachers. While giving care, the nurse finds many opportunities to teach patients how to promote healing processes, how to stay well, how to prevent illness, and how to carry out activities of daily living in the best possible way. Patients expect nurses to share accurate information with them. Nurses teach not only by telling and explaining things to patients, but also by displaying their own behaviour. Patients notice what nurses do. Many are heard to say that they do something in a particular manner because they saw a nurse do it that way. This being so, nurses should practise and teach good standards of health care. Many people learn more by example than from verbal teaching.

References

Department of Health (1979) *National Health Service Review Working Papers*, HMSO, London.

The National Association of Health Authorities (1989) *NHS Handbook* 4th edn, Macmillan Press, London.

UKCC (1985) *Advertising by Registered Nurses, Midwives and Health Visitors*, Advisory paper, United Kingdom Central Council, London.

UKCC (1986) *Administration of Medicines*, Advisory paper, United Kingdom Central Council, London.

UKCC (1987) *Confidentiality*, Advisory paper, United Kingdom Central Council, London.

UKCC (1989) *Exercising Accountability*, Advisory paper, United Kingdom Central Council, London.

UKCC (1990) *The Report of the Post Registration Education and Practice Project*, United Kingdom Central Council, London.

UKCC (1992) *The Code of Professional Conduct for Nurses, Midwives and Health Visitors*, 3rd edn, United Kingdom Central Council, London.

UK Parliament (1979) *The Nurses, Midwives and Health Visitors Act*, HMSO, London.

UK Parliament (1990) *The NHS and Community Care Act*, HMSO, London.

UK Parliament Session (1983–84) *NHS Management Enquiry* (published 1984), Macmillan Press, London.

Further reading

Carlisle, D. (1991) Take five. *Nursing Times*, **87**(6), 40–1.

Cole, A. (1991) Advance to go? *Nursing Times*, **87**(7), 48–9.

Cole, A. (1991) Outlook gloomy. *Nursing Times*, **87**(13), 24.

Davidson, L. (1991) Support for newly registered staff. *Nursing Times*, **87**(3), 51–2.

Davidson, L. (1991) Where there's a will . . . ? *Nursing Times*, **87**(13), 19–20.

Fardell, J. (1991) Maintaining a high profile. *Nursing Times*, **87**(5), 50–1.

Fatchett, A. and Hally, H. (1989) Community care up in the air. *Nursing Times*, **85**(31), 15–18.

Fielding, P. (1989) Opportunity knocks. *Nursing Times*, **85**(9), 47–8.

Friend, B. (1991) Brave new world. *Nursing Times*, **87**(13), 20–1.

Laurent, C. and Friend, B. (1991) Two sides of the coin. *Nursing Times*, **87**(13), 22.

Lee, S.J. (1989) Preparing personal profiles. *Nursing Standard*, **85**(14), 55–6.

McFarlane, J. (1989) Whitewashing the past. *Nursing Times*, **85**(14), 46–7.

McMillan, I. (1991) In the vanguard. *Nursing Times*, **87**(13), 23.

Morton-Cooper, A. (1991) Back on course. *Nursing Times*, **87**(4), 54–5.

Neuberger, J. (1989) Pawns in the game? *Nursing Times*, **85**(11), 50–1.

Nursing Times (1989) Focus on the NHS review. *Nursing Times*, **85**(6), 16–19.

Nursing Times (1989) Community care: the new mix. *Nursing Times*, **85**(29), 16–18.

Parrish, A. and Sines, D. (1989) Meeting the challenge. *Nursing Standard*, **3**(44), 20–2.

Roques, A. (1989) Up for grabs. *Nursing Times*, **85**(13), 44–5.

Rowden, R. (1989) What's in it for us? *Nursing Times*, **85**(8), 45–6.

Tingle, J. (1990) Accountability and the law: how it affects the nurse. *Senior Nurse*, **10**(2), 8–9.

3

Concepts of health

Learning objectives

When the content of this chapter has been mastered, the learner should be able to:

Define terms appearing in the glossary.

Discuss the components of health.

Describe various ways that the concept of health is interpreted.

Identify ways that nurses work towards the health of patients.

Differentiate the terms health and illness.

Discuss the relationship between health and illness.

Outline the various factors which influence health.

Discuss health as a resource.

Discuss the relationship between health and personal responsibility.

Outline one model of health promotion.

Discuss some key ideas in health promotion.

Describe the role of the nurse in health promotion.

Glossary

Acute illness An illness that comes on quickly and lasts a relatively short time.

Chronic illness An illness that comes on slowly and lasts a relatively long time.

Continuum A continuous line with extremes at either end.

Emotional health A state in which one feels good about life.

Empowerment Helping people to increase control over something.

Exacerbation A period during an illness when the symptoms become worse.

Figure and ground illusion A drawing which may be seen as two human faces or as a vase, depending upon what is viewed as the object and the surroundings.

Health A state of physical, emotional, social, and spiritual well-being.

Health education An activity which aims to increase well-being and reduce ill health, by influencing the knowledge, beliefs, attitudes and behaviour of individuals.

Health promotion The process of enabling people to increase control over, and improve their health.

Ill Having a disease. Synonym for *sick*.

Inequalities in health Different experier

wellness and illness between various groups of people.

Physical health A state in which the body organs are functioning normally.

Prevention An activity which reduces the likelihood of illness.

Remission An interval during an illness when the disease seems to have disappeared.

Resource A possession that is valuable because its supply is limited and for which there is no substitute.

Sick Having a disease. Synonym for *ill*.

Social stigma A mark of disapproval against an individual due to the violation of a group's value system.

Social health A state in which one feels safe, valued by others, and productive.

Spectrum The entire range of something, made of different segments which fit together.

Spiritual health A state in which an individual experiences an inner peacefulness in relation to himself and the meaning of life.

Well-being A state in which one is experiencing an acceptable quality of life.

Introduction

A predictable characteristic of being human is that there will be changes in health. It is impossible to be well and stay well, or get well and remain well forever. Health is a goal to which nursing is committed. All the patient services that nurses provide through the skills they perform are directed toward assisting individuals to improve their health.

How each person defines health is varied and personal. Some people have a very narrow definition where health is the absence of disease. Others have a much broader view; for example, the World Health Organization defined *health* as "a state of complete physical, mental, and social [most nurses would also add the word spiritual] well-being and not merely the absence of disease or infirmity". The term *well-being* means that a person is experiencing an acceptable quality of life as he defines it. The World Health Organization's definition of health has been criticized by many people, who state that it is too idealistic for a person to feel a "complete state of well-being" or to assume that life is static. Whatever we perceive health to be, it is clear that to each individual it is personal. It is therefore important that the nurse

ascertain from the individual what he regards health to be and not impose her own views.

Health

The fact that humans have physical, emotional, social and spiritual needs was discussed in Chapter 2. Nurses provide patient services to meet the individual's needs in each of those four areas. Health, the goal of nursing, may be assessed by considering these four components of physical, emotional, social, and spiritual health.

Physical health

Perhaps the most expected assistance from health personnel is an improvement in physical health. For most, *physical health* is a state in which the body organs are functioning normally. Remember that definitions of health are different among different people. For some, an ability to function without experiencing symptoms may fit the definition for physical health. For example, a diabetic whose disease is controlled with proper diet, exercise or medication may also consider himself physically well. For others, physical health may mean possessing the highest resistance against disease, which is perhaps the most desirable definition of all. It may include living a lifestyle that reduces a potential for illness. An individual with this concept of physical health may seek assistance from the nurse to stop smoking, maintain a desirable weight for his height, and start exercising regularly.

Emotional health

How one feels emotionally is also a part of health. Most would agree that a desirable life would include more than just normal physical functioning. A vegetative state is not usually associated with quality of life. Feelings add another dimension to life and are what distinguish being human.

There are common feelings that could be characterized as positive or desirable, such as happiness, contentment, joy and good humour. Negative or undesirable feelings would include anger, sadness, fear and loneliness. Life involves feeling both negative and positive kinds of emotions. One would not know the value of happiness without having experienced sadness. An emotionally healthy individual is often able to find something positive in even the worst feelings. An example of this is the old saying, "Better to have loved and lost than never to have loved at all".

Emotional health is a state in which one feels good about life. Again, keep in mind that there are variations in the interpretation of this definition. Some may view emotional health as simply an attitude that life involves a mixture of feelings while others may seek opportunities for experiencing them. The nurse may support or provide coping strategies and mechanisms, discussed in Chapter 2, that help to restore balance to the patient's emotional state.

Social health

Social health is a state in which one feels safe, valued by others and productive. Social health is concerned with the supportive interrelationships an individual enjoys with friends, relatives and the wider community.

Nurses treat each patient as someone of personal worth. There are some diseases that carry a *social stigma*; that is, there is some shame attached to an individual with a condition because it somehow violates a group's value system. A *value system* is a group of beliefs that form the framework for one's attitudes and behaviour. Examples of these conditions may include alcoholism, mental illness, AIDS, or obesity. The nurse promotes social health by conveying to the patient and other health workers that the patient deserves the same efforts and care for these diseases as for other illnesses.

Spiritual health

Spiritual health is a state in which an individual experiences an inner peacefulness in relation to himself and the meaning of life. This aspect of man's health provides a feeling that despite hardships there is a purpose for one's existence. Nurses promote health when they accept the patient's spiritual attitudes and beliefs. The definition of spiritual health is perhaps the most personal of all.

Illness

Being *sick* or *ill* means that the person has some disease. A sickness or illness may be physical, affecting primarily a physical process; or it may be due to an accident or injury. It may be a mental disease, affecting primarily a mental process. Although a person may be considered either mentally or physically ill, his body still functions holistically. Hence,

a person with a mental illness often has physical problems, and a physical illness influences most patients emotionally in some way.

Acute illness

An *acute illness* is one that comes on quickly and lasts a relatively short time. Since the discovery of antibiotic drugs, many acute illnesses, such as streptococcal sore throats, are treated with relative ease. Nevertheless, many acute illnesses, such as infectious hepatitis, an acute illness that affects the liver, and the common cold still remain difficult to treat, and medical research continues to look for their cure.

Chronic illness

A *chronic illness* is one that comes on slowly and lasts a relatively long time. Arthritis, a joint disease, is an example. The number of elderly people in our population is increasing, and these people especially tend to suffer with chronic diseases. The more we learn about chronic illnesses, the more we can do to prevent them. Also when they do appear, every effort is being made to start early treatment so that their effects on the body can be decreased.

Remission. Some patients with chronic diseases experience periods of remission. A *remission* is an interval during which the disease seems to have disappeared. This does not mean the disease has been cured. The disease is likely to be remanifested; when it reappears is unpredictable. Multiple sclerosis, a chronic disease of the nervous system, is an example of a condition in which periods of remission may occur.

Exacerbation. Patients with chronic diseases may also undergo exacerbation of their disease. An *exacerbation* is a period during which the symptoms of a disease become worse. A patient with emphysema, a chronic lung disease, may find his symptoms become worse when he catches a cold.

Health and illness

Although most people think of themselves as being well when they are not ill, health and illness usually fluctuate within a wide range. In other words, health may not necessarily be constant in nature. At times people who are considered healthy may not feel as well as they do at other times. For example, you may have a headache and not do as well as usual with

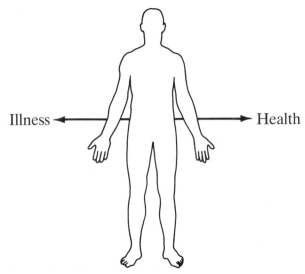

Illness ◄──────────► Health

Figure 3-1 The health-illness continuum, showing that there is no clear division between illness and health. Reproduced by permission of Oxford University Press from Catford, J.C., Positive Health Indicatiors —towards a new information base for health promotion, Community Medicine, vol. 5, pp 125–32, 1983.

and health at either end. As can be seen, there is no exact point at which health ends and illness begins. Health and illness are different for each person, and there may be a considerable range within which any one person may be considered ill or well. Other people have rejected the idea of the health-illness continuum (Downie, 1990) as some people may be healthy in some ways and not in others. For example, a terminally ill patient dying at home with the support of his general practitioner, community nurse and loving family and friends may be said to be physically ill but with good emotional health. In contrast, an anxious, lonely person with no interests and no job may be physically healthy but socially and emotionally ill. The relationship between health and illness may therefore be described as a *spectrum*, as illustrated in Figure 3-2. In this, the four components of physical, emotional, social and spiritual health are each composed of segments of health and illness. This demonstrates how some people may be *healthy in some ways and ill in others*.

your studying. Although you may not feel in peak form you probably do not think of yourself as being ill unless your headache continues or returns frequently. Likewise, people who are ill or diseased may find that they feel better at times and can do more for themselves than they can at other times. However, they still may be considered ill and unable to go to work or school.

Changes in health and illness have been described on a *health-illness continuum*, as illustrated in Figure 3-1. This is a continuous line with extremes of illness

An alternative to both these ideas is to see health and illness *as part of each other* as in the *"figure and ground" illusion* illustrated in Figure 3-3 (Brown, 1981). Health and illness are seen as too closely related to be separated. Thus all people have elements of illness and health within them over their life and one component of health affects another. For example, a depressed patient may be so inactive he develops a pressure sore. A patient with epilepsy may become socially isolated. In the illusion, whenever we talk about health, disease is in the background and whenever we talk about disease, health is present too.

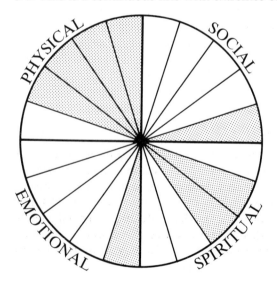

Health
Illness

Figure 3-2 The health-illness spectrum (copyright A. Dines).

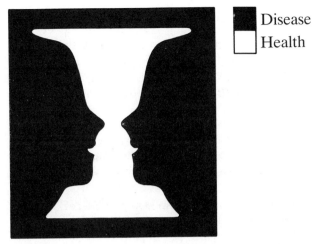

Figure 3-3 Health and illness as a figure and ground illusion. Reproduced with permission from Brown, V.A., Social Science and Medicine; published by Pergamon Press Ltd, 1981.

Influences on health

An individual's health is influenced by many factors. These include for example his work environment, exposure to contagious disease and whether he smokes or not. The main factors influencing health are illustrated in Figure 3-4. It has been shown that these influences affect different groups of people in various ways. These differences are sometimes referred to as inequalities in health (Townsend et al., 1988). For example, babies whose fathers have unskilled jobs run approximately twice the risk of stillbirth and death under one year than babies whose fathers work in the professions. In this example, social class is influencing health. Many studies have confirmed an association between suicide or attempted suicide and unemployment. Thus employment and unemployment may be influencing health. Women have higher levels of chronic and acute sickness than men. In this example gender is influencing health. The illness sickle-cell anaemia is far more common in people of Afro-Caribbean descent than other racial groups. Here, race is influencing health.

Health as a resource

Health is a valued resource. A *resource* is a possession that is valuable because its supply is limited and for which there is no substitute. Though health is an

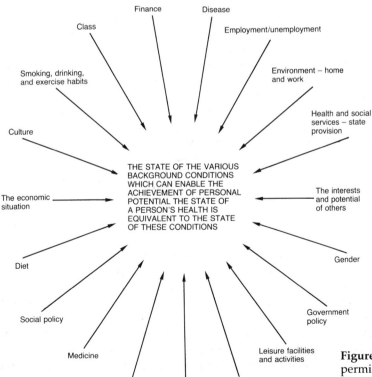

Figure 3-4 Factors influencing health. Reproduced by permission of John Wiley & Sons, Ltd. from Seedhouse, D., Health: The foundations for achievement; published by John Wiley, 1986.

intangible substance, it is nonetheless considered precious. People sometimes say, "as long as you have your health, you have everything". Nurses are committed to protecting, preserving and replenishing this personal resource through their work as health promoters.

One person who sees health as a resource is David Seedhouse. He sees health as the foundations for achievement. We need to have health in order to reach our potential (Seedhouse, 1986). The World Health Organization (WHO) also sees health as a resource: "health is . . . a resource for everyday life, not the objective of living" (WHO, 1986). The WHO encourages all people everywhere to work towards "Health for All by the year 2000 and beyond".

Health as a personal responsibility

Some people see health very much as a personal responsibility. The 1970s government publication *Prevention and Health: Everybody's Business* (DHSS, 1976) is such an example: "much of the responsibility for ensuring his own good health lies with the individual". Other people are wary of this emphasis on personal responsibility, for example, the World Health Organization: "It is often implied that people have the power to completely shape their own lives and those of their families so as to be free from the avoidable burden of disease. Thus when they are ill they are blamed for this and discriminated against" (WHO, 1984). More recently, the government, in its document *The Health of the Nation* (Dept of Health, 1991) has begun to emphasize *shared* responsibility for health: "Responsibilities for action to improve health are widely spread from individuals to government as a whole" (p. vii).

If the influences on health mentioned above are remembered, we can see that people may affect some influences more easily than others. Thus a person may improve his diet and be responsible for his health in this way. It is more difficult for someone to affect state provision of health services and the economic situation and thereby be responsible for these influences on his health. It is impossible for someone to alter their race or gender and influence their health in that way. Sometimes a person may not easily be able to alter his diet, for lack of money, or stop smoking because he is too stressed. This makes health as a personal responsibility a difficult area. This understanding will be important to the nurse as she works towards her goal of health promotion.

Health promotion

Health is a goal to which nursing is committed. Nurses work as health promoters to try and achieve this. The World Health Organization describes health promotion as "the process of enabling people to increase control over, and to improve their health "(WHO, 1984). People have different ideas about what health promotion involves (Downie et al., 1990; Research Unit in Health and Behavioural Change, 1989; Tones, 1986). One model is illustrated in Figure 3-5.

Health promotion is an umbrella term used to describe three overlapping areas, health education, prevention and health protection.

Health education aims to increase well-being and reduce illness by influencing the knowledge, beliefs, attitudes and behaviour of individuals and groups. For example a patient wishing to stop smoking asks for the nurse's help; by working with the patient, she acts as a health educator. A group of school governors are interested to see whether the school meals are as healthy as possible. They ask the school nurse to lead a session with them about the latest research on healthy eating. In so doing the school nurse works as a health educator.

Prevention aims to reduce the likelihood of illness. This may be thought of as primary, secondary and tertiary prevention. *Primary prevention* aims to stop particular diseases from occurring in the first place. For example, health visitors, practice nurses and general practitioners are involved in primary prevention when they immunise babies against diphtheria, tetanus, polio, whooping cough, measles, mumps and rubella. *Secondary prevention* aims to minimize the negative consequences of illness by detecting disease as early as possible and, by curing or limiting the disease, minimize the harm it causes to the person. Family-planning nurses, practice nurses and other health workers are involved with secondary prevention when they take a cervical smear test from a woman to screen for precancerous changes. *Tertiary prevention* aims to prevent complications or worsening of a disease that cannot be cured or eliminated. A nurse on a sugcial ward who sits a patient up in bed or in a chair as soon as possible after an operation to help prevent a chest infection is involved with tertiary prevention. Nurses working on a medical ward with confused and immobile patients, who make use of rating scales to help prevent pressure sores are also involved with tertiary prevention.

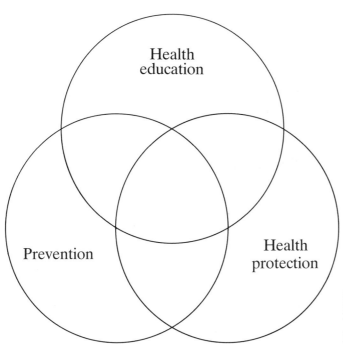

Figure 3-5 A model of health promotion. Reproduced by kind permission of the Health Education Authority from Tannahill, A., What is Health Promotion? Health Education Journal, 44(4), 1985.

Health protection concerns policies or laws at the local, national or international level which aim to prevent illness or increase well-being. Student nurses who press for a nonsmoking common room in their college are involved with health protection, as are people or pressure groups who lobby their MPs for changes in the law, for example to introduce the compulsory wearing of seat belts or provide better child-care provision.

Key ideas in health promotion

The World Health Organization, as has been mentioned, describes health promotion as "the process of enabling people to increase control over, and to improve their health" (WHO, 1984). There are a number of important ideas linked with this.

Health promotion aims to *enable* people; for this to occur, people need to *participate* in the health promotion activity. Health promotion is most likely to be successful where people start the activity themselves rather than have health professionals "impose" health upon them. This is sometimes called a "bottom-up" approach rather than a "top-down" approach. In the example of health education, the patient had decided to stop smoking himself, the nurse did not tell him he must do it.

A second important idea involves helping people to *increase control* over their health. This is sometimes called *empowerment*. In the case of the school nurse

sharing her knowledge of healthy eating with the school governors, the latter were then informed and in a position to decide what to do with the knowledge; they were empowered by it. In this example, the school governors already had some power. More difficult is the task of empowering people who have very little power. In one of the case studies below, Scottish council tenants were empowered to fight against poor housing which they saw as their main health problem.

A third important idea in health promotion is that of making *healthy choices easier choices*. This means that health promotion has a *political* dimension as policies and laws at the local, national and international level will affect the choices open to people. For example there is little point in people deciding to take regular exercise to promote their health if there are no leisure facilities in the area. Similarly, people will find it difficult to eat a high fibre diet if labelling on food does not display such information. For this reason, health promotion is sometimes described as *a multi-sectoral activity* affecting for example politicians, food manufacturers, the media, health professionals, local organizations and the public.

Case studies of health promotion

Case Study 1. Health protection. In Scotland council tenants have begun a fight against poor housing which they see as their main health problem

(Seymour, 1991). By forming residents associations or working alongside community health workers and health visitors in local projects, pressure has been put on local councils to improve their housing. In Glasgow, flats are beginning to be renovated and one widow, whose husband died from bronchial pneumonia, has been awarded damages against her local council because there was a clear link between damp and illness.

This case study illustrates a number of features of health promotion. It is mainly an example of health protection as local housing policies are changed in response to pressure from local people and professional workers. The health visitors and community workers used an enabling approach as local residents played a key role in the work. The example also illustrates empowerment as the local people identified and took control of their own health problem of poor housing. The work may also be seen as primary prevention of health problems related to damp housing.

Case Study 2. Prevention. Introducing a dog as a pet to elderly psychiatric patients in two wards has been found to be beneficial (Elliott and Milne, 1991). The patients were visited by Thistle, a Wheaten terrier. Although the patients were suffering from depression and senile dementia nurses reported an improvement in both the quality and quantity of patients' speech.

This is an example of tertiary prevention, as the patients' condition is improved, although not cured. If other nurses express an interest in this study and the results are shared with them, this sharing will be health educational. If these interested nurses later discuss this with their patients, who decide they would like to have dogs introduced as pets to the wards, then this becomes an example of health protection as ward policy is changed to prevent illness.

Case Study 3. Health education. Nurses can be highly effective in helping and supporting their patients to stop smoking (Clark et al., 1990). This is particularly true if the key ideas of participation and empowerment are followed. Where the patient identifies his smoking as a health problem for himself and is motivated to give up, rather than having this imposed upon him, the nurse is more likely to be sucessful in her role as health educator. Similarly when the patient is actively involved in the health education process and his real concerns about the negative aspects of giving up smoking, for example,

irritability and putting on weight, are dealt with, then the patient is more likely to be successful in his efforts.

This is an example of health education. If it is successful the nurse will have also been involved in primary prevention to prevent the occurrence of smoking-related disease.

References

Brown, V.A. (1981) From sickness to health: An altered focus for health care research. *Social Science And Medicine*, **15A**, 195–201.

Catford, J.C. (1983) Positive health indicators—towards a new information base for health promotion. *Community Medicine*, **5**, 125–32.

Clark, J., Haverty, S. and Kendall, S. (1990) Helping people to stop smoking: a study of the nurse's role. *Journal of Advanced Nursing*, **16**, 357–63.

Department of Health (1991) *The Health of the Nation*. HMSO, London.

DHSS (1976) *Prevention and Health: Everybody's Business*, HMSO, London.

Downie, R., Fyfe, C. and Tannahill, A. (1990) *Health Promotion Models and Values*, Oxford Medical Publications, Oxford.

Downie, R.S. (1990) Ethics in health education: an introduction, in Doxiadis, S. *Ethics in Health Education*, John Wiley, Chichester.

Elliott, V. and Milne, D. (1991) Patient's best friend. *Nursing Times*, **87**(6), 34–5.

Research Unit in Health and Behavioural Change (1989) *Changing the Public Health*, John Wiley, Chichester.

Seedhouse, D. (1986) *Health: the Foundations for Achievement*, John Wiley, Chichester.

Seymour, J. (1991) Whose health is it anyway? *Nursing Times*, **87** (April 10), 15.

Tannahill, A. (1985) What is health promotion? *Health Education Journal*, **44**(4), 167–8.

Tones, B.K. (1986) Health education and the ideology of health promotion: a review of alternative approaches. *Health Education Research*, **1**(1), 3–12.

Townsend, P., Davidson, N. and Whitehead, M. (1988) *Inequalities in Health*, Penguin, Harmondsworth.

WHO (1984) Health Promotion, Summary report of the Working Group on Concept and Principles of Health Promotion, Copenhagen, 9–13 July 1984.

WHO (1986) Ottawa charter for health promotion, International Conference on Health Promotion. 17–21 November 1986. Ottawa, Ontario, Canada.

Further reading

Ewles, L. and Simnett, I. (1985) *Promoting Health. A Practical Guide to Health Education*, John Wiley, Chichester.

Research Unit in Health and Behavioural Change (1989) *Changing the Public Health*. John Wiley, Chichester.

4

The nursing process: the model for nursing

Learning objectives

When the content of this chapter has been mastered, the learner should be able to:

Define terms appearing in the glossary.
List the four parts of the nursing process in the order in which they are carried out.
List seven characteristics of the nursing process.
Describe each of the steps in the four parts of the nursing process and give an example that illustrates each step.
Discuss the importance of effective communication.

Glossary

Actual problem A health problem that presently exists.

Assessment An action that involves collecting information.

Collaborative problem A potential health problem that would require the cooperative treatment efforts of the nurse and the doctor if it occurred.

Communication An exchange of information.

Contract An agreement among individuals about the responsibilities each has to the other.

Coping mechanisms Methods that reduce what an individual perceives to threaten his self-concept.

Coping strategies Activities one consciously uses to reduce stress.

Culture Everything a person learns from the groups of people of which he is a part.

Emotion A strong feeling, such as love, hate or fear.

Evaluation The process of measuring how well a goal or objective is reached.

Focus assessment A limited collection of a few specific, related facts.

Formal teaching The presentation of preplanned information at a scheduled time.

Goal An expected or desired outcome; the desired end result for which one works. Synonym for *objective*.

Holism The concept that all aspects of living— physical, emotional, social, and spiritual—are interrelated and affect the individual as a whole.

Holistic nursing The provision of patient services that integrate the concept that physical functions, emotions, group living, and spirituality all affect health.

Informal teaching The presentation of information

given in response to spontaneous questions whenever they occur.

Long-term goal A desired outcome that may take a few weeks or months to accomplish.

Need A necessity or a requirement.

Nonverbal communication The exchange of information without using words.

Nurse-patient relationship An association between a nurse and a patient in which the desired outcome is health. Synonym for *therapeutic relationship*.

Nursing diagnosis A statement describing a health problem that has the possibility of being resolved totally through nursing measures.

Nursing orders Specific, detailed directions for accomplishing goals.

Nursing process An organized sequence of steps that nurses use to solve the health problems of patients.

Objective An expected or desired outcome; the desired end result for which one works. Synonym for *goal*.

Objective information Information that can be measured.

Organization A process of grouping related information.

Pathophysiology The science that deals with the physical changes that occur when there is an altered state of health.

Patient One who actively participates with the nurse in identifying, planning and resolving health problems. Synonym for *client*.

Possible problem A situation in which some but not enough data have been collected to confirm the presence of a health problem.

Potential problem A health problem that may possibly occur in the future.

Problem Something that stands in the way of meeting a need; an unmet need.

Process A set of actions leading to a particular goal.

Regression Displaying a type of behaviour typical of an earlier age.

Relationship An association between people.

Short-term goal A desired outcome that may be accomplished within a few days or a week.

Subjective information Information that only the patient can experience and describe.

Validation A process of making sure information is factual.

Verbal communication The exchange of information through the use of words.

Introduction

In the past, nursing practice involved actions that were based mostly on common sense and the examples set by older, experienced nurses. The actual care of patients tended to be limited according to the medical orders given by a doctor. Nurses, today, continue to work interdependently with other health practitioners. However, now nurses are directing patient care more independently. In even stronger terms, nurses are being held responsible and accountable for providing appropriate patient care that reflects current accepted standards for nursing practice.

This change in attitude and practice occurred through the development of the nursing process. The nursing process is a problem-solving method. When nursing practice is based on the components of this method, the patient receives effective care which will meet his individual needs.

The nursing process is widely used in all areas of clinical nursing practice. All trained nurses are responsible for ensuring that care is given using an individualized approach. They are accountable for their patient's plan of care and also the nursing actions they perform. This accountability for care is clearly outlined in the nurses competencies which are reprinted in Chapter 1, ''The Concept of Nursing''. These competencies outline the responsibilities of the registered nurse and the enrolled nurse, whose role is to assist the registered nurse in the assessment, planning, implementation and evaluation of care. The contribution of the enrolled nurse when making decisions related to patient care must not be underestimated, as many through their experience will have a wealth of knowledge and skills to share with registered nurses. Similarly nurses in training can work alongside trained staff to develop their understanding of individual patient needs. Although they do not have accountability for planning patient care they can often make valuable contributions to the activities associated with the nursing process, whilst working within the ward team.

The nursing process

A *process* is a set of actions leading to a particular goal. The *nursing process* is an organized sequence of steps that nurses use to solve the health problems of patients. The goal of the nursing process is to provide care that will help a patient reach and maintain their optimum level of health.

The nursing process can be described as consisting of the following four steps:

1. Assessing the individual patient and his health care needs (identification of patient problems).
2. Planning the patient's care in order to resolve problems.
3. Implementing the required nursing care.
4. Evaluating the effectiveness and outcomes of the stated nursing actions.

If we accept that all patients are individuals, with different health needs as demonstrated in Henderson's (1966) definition of nursing, then it follows that if two patients from the same culture, who are the same age and sex, are admitted for the same operation they will have different health needs and problems. This individuality should be reflected in the patient's care plan and the nursing care which is implemented.

Characteristics of the nursing process

The nursing process is an effective method of problem solving. The actions necessary for solving problems are somewhat universal. A baker may seek to determine why a batch of bread does not rise; a scientist may seek a cure for HIV. Nurses help to solve the health problems of others. They deal with people, not objects or diseases. The nursing process, as a problem-solving method, contains some distinct characteristics. The nursing process is:

1. Within the legal scope of nursing. The definitions of nursing in nurse practice acts are expanding to describe nursing in terms of a more independent problem-solving role.
2. Based on knowledge. Nurses are increasing the depth and breadth of their knowledge. The ability to solve problems using the nursing process involves the application of the laws of science to patient care. Nurses now use their increased knowledge base to correlate a patient's health problem with the use of certain nursing skills to achieve a fairly predictable effect.
3. Planned. The steps of the nursing process are organized and systematic. One step leads to the next in an orderly fashion.
4. Patient centred. Each patient is unique with physical, psychological, social and spiritual needs. The nursing process involves a comprehensive appraisal of each patient. Nurses

encourage patients to become involved as active participants in various problem-solving steps.
5. Goal directed. It is important that the patient and the nurse understand the final expected outcome. The nursing process involves the cooperative efforts of the patient and nurse toward a target.
6. Prioritized. When the nursing process is used, some problems need to be solved before others. Those that are life threatening require immediate attention. First solving the problems that present the greatest potential for harm provides a strategy leading to improved health.
7. Dynamic. The health status of any patient is constantly changing. One problem is often related to another; as one problem changes, so may the other. The nursing process is like a continuous loop; when the last step has been completed, there is a need to begin all over again.

Nursing models

Before looking more closely at the stages involved in the nursing process, which provides a systematic approach for care, it is important to discuss nursing models. Models for care enable nurses to practise nursing with direction and continuity, reflecting their beliefs about nursing and its components.

Hunt and Marks Maran (1987) describe a nursing model as a "pictorial representation of a theory or an idea about nursing. The function of a model is to present a scaled-down picture or diagram about the relationship between beliefs, theories and concepts about nursing". Pearson and Vaugn (1986) simply explain a practice nursing model as "a descriptive picture of practice which adequately represents the real thing". They also state that approaches to nursing practice are based on an individual's belief about nursing, how nursing is classified and the subjects related to it, as well as theories which are believed to be true.

The above definitions can be more clearly understood by considering what the components which make up a nursing model are. Pearson and Vaugn (1986) explain the components in the following way:

1. Beliefs about man. The beliefs and values on which a model is based.
2. The goals of nursing practice. This is what the nurse aims to achieve.

3. The knowledge base. The knowledge and skills which the nurse needs to develop in order to achieve the goals of nursing.

The above three components within a model of nursing will constitute the direction of nursing practice.

Using the above components we can review how nursing care was practised when a medical model was followed:

1. Beliefs about man. Man was viewed as a biological being whose equilibrium became imbalanced due to disease.
2. Goals of care. To cure the disease through medical treatment.
3. The knowledge base. This was based on knowledge of the biophysical sciences such as microbiology, pathology and physiology (Pearson and Vaugn, 1985).

The aforementioned components of models can also be applied to nursing models, reflecting the underlying theory and philosophy of each model.

Nursing models fall into three types:

1. Developmental nursing models.
2. Systems nursing models.
3. Interactionist nursing models.

The classification of nursing models has been discussed by Fawcett (1984) and Aggleton and Chalmers (1987).

Developmental models

These models look specifically at what affects the developmental processes of an individual who is receiving nursing care, or about to receive care.

When using a developmental model of nursing, nursing intervention is required when through disease or illness the developmental processes of the individual are impaired. The aim of nursing care is to restore the individual's health in order to continue the developmental process in terms of maturing physically, psychologically and socially. An example of this type of model is Peplau's (1952) model. The components of Peplau's model are briefly outlined below:

Beliefs about man. Each person is an individual with physical and psychological needs. Individuals have the ability to continue to develop and learn throughout their lifespan. When stress occurs it creates tension which the individual will either channel positively and grow and learn from, or use poorly and regress. The individual's response is dependent on their ability to cope and their past experience. If an individual has a need which is not met, be it physical, psychological or social, then tension will occur. If the need continues to be unmet then the individual will regress. To resolve this the individual needs to learn positive behaviours to overcome the tension; this may include nursing intervention depending on the need deficit.

Goals of nursing. When using Peplau's model the goals of nursing can be defined as follows:

1. Establishment of a good rapport with the individual in order to overcome illness, and develop the individual's understanding of their health problems; thus preventing, where possible, future recurrences of illness.
2. The emphasis in today's world is based on the maintenance of health; therefore the nurse should develop her role as both a health educator and promoter.

"Peplau stresses that it is not only the patient or client who will develop but also the nurse through her increased understanding of the effects of universal stressors on different unique individuals" (Pearson and Vaugn, 1986).

Systems nursing models

These focus on the biological, psychological and social systems which make up the individual. When there is an imbalance in one or more of these systems then nursing intervention will be required. Systems nursing models suggest that there must be an equilibrium or stability between the biological, psychological and social systems of the individual. If there is a deficit in one or more of the systems then nursing intervention is aimed at restoring the balance or assisting the individual to adapt. An example of this type of nursing model is that of Roper et al. (1980), the components of which are briefly outlined below:

Beliefs about man. Throughout an individual's life span there are 12 activities of living which are common to all people. As individuals progress along the lifespan their ability to carry out these activities is influenced by psychological, social, physical, cultural and economic factors. The way in which the individual carries out these activities is therefore specific and individual to each person, for example, eating and drinking; a vegetarian will not eat meat whereas a non-vegetarian will.

When a need develops in one or more of these activities, then nursing intervention may be required.

Goals of nursing. These can be described as follows:

1. Assist the individual to regain or retain independence in the activities of living. Progress can be assessed by use of an independent-dependent continuum.
2. Assisting the individual to cope with dependence if independence is not possible or desirable.
3. Prevention of illness; when possible the nurse should act as a health educator and promoter.

Knowledge base. The knowledge base required for this model is an understanding of the body's structure and function in relation to the activities of living. This also encompasses understanding at what stage in the lifespan the individual will be independent or dependent. For example, babies of a few months of age will be dependent in the activity of elimination. The nurse needs to be able to decide how much nursing intervention is required and how much the individual can do to progress from dependence to the individual's optimum level of independence, in relation to each activity of living. Because all individuals carry out these activities of living differently, the nurse must also have a knowledge of the cultural, social and economic factors which affect individuals within her care.

Interactionist nursing models

These models focus on the individual's ability to communicate and interact in a meaningful way. Many of these models are based on work undertaken by a group of scientists known as the "symbolic interactionists".

Aggleton and Chalmers (1987) state the following:

According to interactionist models, nursing is needed on occasions when a person's self perceptions and/or those of others are such that role performances conducive to health cannot be easily adopted. In such circumstances, nurses may intervene to help individuals either acquire new roles or extend existing ones to cope with health related demands.

An example of an interactionist model is King's (1971), the components of which are briefly outlined below:

Beliefs about man. "Individuals react to other people, situations and objects within their lifespan, according to their personal perception and interpretation of them. An individual's behaviour is based on their past experience of the above, which will influence their behaviour in the future. Individuals react to their environment through social interaction in social relationships" (Pearson and Vaugn, 1986).

Goals of nursing. These can be described as follows:

1. Assist the individual to attain, maintain or restore health.
2. Establish good interpersonal skills with the individual and their family in order to meet the individual's health needs.
3. Provide appropriate health information for the individual.
4. Provide appropriate care for the individual when ill.
5. Employ preventative health measures and/or care.

Knowledge base. Nursing is viewed as a helping activity which provides care for individuals who are ill, whilst promoting health through education. To do this the nurse needs to have knowledge in relation to social systems, perception and interpersonal skills. The nurse also requires knowledge on how physiology, psychology and sociology relate to health and the individual. These skills are then employed to reflect the elements within King's model, i.e. action, reaction, interaction and transaction.

Selecting a model

When selecting a nursing model, nurses working together should be in agreement and choose a model which reflects their philosophy of care and will best meet the needs of their patients. Many nurses working together may decide to adapt a recognized model in order that it reflects more closely their philosophy and can thus be used to meet their patients' needs. Another alternative is that nurses may decide to evolve their own nursing model. Wright (1986) proposes three essential elements for evolving a nursing model:

1. Establish a shared philosophy.
2. Define and provide the knowledge and skills that nurses need.
3. Incorporate a problem-solving framework.

Wright also states that when evolving a nursing model, nurses must consider the circumstances in which it will be used and the people using it.

Whatever approach to choosing a nursing model is decided upon, the important point is that a nursing model is not imposed on nurses, as it will not be used effectively. Nurses must value and feel ownership for a nursing model so that it can reflect their nursing practice and needs of their patients.

For further information and details regarding nursing models, the reader is directed to the reference and further reading lists, at the end of the chapter.

Assessing the patient's health status

The nurse begins the nursing process by performing an assessment. *Assessment* is an action that involves collecting and organizing information. The purpose of assessment is to identify past, current, and possible future health problems. Assessment is ongoing and by comparing changes in information, the nurse may evaluate whether there is progress toward a goal.

Collecting information. The information may be gathered in different ways, such as by asking the patient or family questions, making observations while examining the patient, reading the patient's record, and asking other health workers about their observations of the patient. Information that is measurable, such as the patient's blood pressure, can be termed "objective". Information that only the patient can experience and describe, such as pain, can be termed "subjective". The opinions of others may also be called subjective because they are based on personal assumptions from within their own experience.

For the nursing process to be useful, the assessment must be thorough and accurate. It is important that the information reflects and relates to the individual's physiological, psychological, social, economic, cultural and spiritual aspects (Table 4-1). From this information the nurse will obtain a comprehensive base from which she can, in conjunction with the patient, plan the appropriate care. It is important that the nurse assesses the patient in accordance with an agreed nursing model, so that continuity of care and effective communication of patient's needs are maintained. The chosen model may be based, for example, on Roper's activities of living (Roper et al., 1980) or Orem's (1980) eight categories of needs.

It is essential that assessment information reflects the individuality of the patient; the nursing process loses its value if it is not patient centred.

Adding to the information collected. The process of assessment is continuous. Nurses gather information frequently throughout the nurse-patient relationship. The initial assessment information may be superficial and the nurse may need to explore some aspects of the information collected in more depth at a later time. At certain times a nurse will be assessing an individual for specific information, using observation, measurement and interpersonal skills, to determine if new problems are occurring which require nursing intervention. An example of this is when a patient returns from surgery; in the immediate postoperative period the nurse will assess the patient in the following areas:

1. Ability to maintain a clear airway.
2. Measurement of blood pressure and pulse to determine the presence of haemorrhage.
3. Observation of wound site and drains.
4. Patient's conscious level; recovery from anaesthesia.
5. Presence of and degree of pain.
6. Skin colour and temperature.

Ensuring accuracy. The nurse should have a good picture of the patient and his present state of health if the information has been gathered appropriately and accurately. To reduce the chance of interpreting the information incorrectly, the nurse should make sure it is factual. This is often called *validation*. In other words, the nurse should make sure that questionable information was not misinterpreted or collected with faulty equipment. The nurse may need to continue double-checking information in a variety of ways, making sure it is correct.

Organizing information. Interpretation of information is easier if the information is organized. *Organization* involves placing groups of related information into certain categories in much the same way that a cook files recipes. Some nurses use Maslow's or Kalish's hierarchy of needs to organize related information.

Recognizing needs or problems. While organizing information, the nurse may be thinking in terms of whether a need or problem exists. This requires the knowledge to recognize what is normal from what is abnormal. A *need* is a necessity or a requirement. Man has certain basic physical needs. For example, the needs for oxygen, food, water, and elimination are basic to life. Well-being requires that a person also meet his needs for security, love, self-esteem, and so on.

A *problem* is something that stands in the way of meeting a need. It is an unmet need. For example, to survive, a person must have oxygen. A person who is choking on food has a problem because his need for oxygen cannot be met. People have a need for self-

Table 4-1. *Functional health patterns*

Health Pattern	Type of Information
Health-perception/Health management pattern	Includes information about the patient's view of his health, the actions the patient has used in the past while healthy or ill, and his feelings about how his health care should be managed.
Nutritional-metabolic pattern	Includes information about the patient's habits of eating and drinking: amounts, types, times, use of supplements, physical characteristics that relate to the quantity and quality of food consumption, and cultural aspects.
Elimination pattern	Includes information about the patient's elimination of stool and urine. Some information would include the frequency, amounts, appearance, changes, and any use of medications or equipment that has been required.
Activity-exercise pattern	Includes information about the patient's daily routine, both work and recreation. Facts relating to what he is able to do, would like to do, and reasons for any differences between the two.
Cognitive-perceptual pattern	Includes information about the patient's use of language and his mental status. It also includes the patient's sensory abilities and the use of any artificial aids such as a hearing aid or glasses.
Sleep-rest pattern	Includes information about the patient's routine of sleep and inactivity. It would involve information related to the usual time for retiring and rising, and any customs or rituals the patient follows when preparing for sleep.
Self-perception/self-concept pattern	Includes information on the patient's attitudes about his personal strengths and weaknesses. Any behaviour that correlates with this, such as speaking with confidence, would also be included.
Role-relationship pattern	Includes information on how the patient interprets his functions and responsibilities within the group of people who are significant to him. This may include relatives, friends, and co-workers.
Sexuality-reproductive pattern	Involves information about the patient's analysis of the adequacy or inadequacy of his sexual behaviour. Also common reproductive information such as number of pregnancies, status of menstruation, and so on would be included.
Coping-stress-tolerance pattern	Involves information about the methods the patient uses when faced with problems and whether they assist him to a satisfactory outcome.
Value-belief pattern	Includes information about the patient's beliefs about the meaning and purpose of life. Any applications of these beliefs related to health and illness would be especially appropriate.

Reproduced with permission from Gordon, M., Manual of Nursing Diagnosis 1991–1992; published by Mosby-Year Book, 1991.

respect. A problem arises when a person dislikes himself. A problem in which a health need is not being satisfied ordinarily brings a person to seek help from health workers.

Learning to use the words *need* and *problem* correctly helps a nurse understand areas in which the patient has a strength, or a need that is being met. It also helps to identify a problem, or deficit, indicating that a need is not being met.

The assessment of a patient's health status may be summarized as having the following four steps:

1. Information about a patient is collected.
2. All information is checked for accuracy.
3. Information is organized under a list of categories.
4. The needs or problems of the patient are analysed by comparing the information about the patient with what is considered to be normal.

Nursing diagnosis

Most nurses are familiar with the term "diagnosis" in relation to doctors diagnosing medical conditions. The use of the term "nursing diagnosis" is still a relatively new concept to nursing within the UK, despite being well established in the USA.

If we accept that a "problem" arises when need is not met, then a nursing diagnosis can be described as

the reason why the problem occurs and why the nursing care needs to be given. According to Hunt and Marks Maran (1987) a nursing diagnosis statement should include the following:

1. Identification of the problem.
2. Identification of the cause of the problem if known.
3. Identification of how the patient is behaving in relation to the problem.

To illustrate the above, the following can be used as an example.

1. Difficulty in sleeping = problem.
2. Excessive intake of coffee = cause of problem.
3. Difficulty in falling asleep, feeling tired during the day and irritability with others = identification of patient's behaviour in relation to the problem.

When the nurse has completed her assessment of the patient (Table 4-2) she then identifies the problems. Having stated what the problem is, e.g. difficulty in sleeping, she can then incorporate the nursing diagnosis on the care plan following the problem statement, i.e. the cause of the problem and the behaviour exhibited by the patient in relation to the problem.

Identification of the cause of the problem is important as there may be many different causes; for example, difficulty in sleeping could be caused by:

Table 4-2. Summary of assessment findings

Mental and Physical State	Normal Findings	Abnormal Findings
Mental Status/Mood	Expresses feelings of contentment and satisfaction with life. Shows evidence of coping with everyday living. Appropriate grooming and personal hygiene.	Moody, depressed, anxious, worried, angry. Poor grooming and hygiene. Restless or motionless. Inappropriate responses to events.
Mental Status/Intellectual Ability	Has rational and coherent thought processes. Good attention span and memory.	Irrational, poor attention span and memory. Poor abstract thought. Unable to perform simple mental arithmetic.
Vision and the Eyes	Good visual ability with or without glasses or contact lenses. Appropriate colour perception. No visual field loss. Eyes are bright. Pink mucous membranes. Eyes move equally in all directions.	Poor visual ability or blindness. Colour blindness. Gaps in the field of vision. Dull or glossy eyes. Inflamed mucous membrane. Excessive tearing. Drainage from the eyes. Drooping eyelids.

Continued

Table 4-2. Continued

Mental and Physical State	Normal Findings	Abnormal Findings
Hearing and the Ears	Good hearing ability. Cerumen (wax) that is soft and easily removed. No drainage or discomfort. Skin that is intact, pink, warm and slightly moist.	Limited hearing or deafness. Drainage. Soreness when the ear is moved. Dry cerumen that plugs the ear canal.
Touch, Taste, Smell	Correct responses on both sides of the body to touch, texture, temperature, and vibration. Correct or very few incorrect responses to odours or flavours.	Absent, decreased, exaggerated, or unequal responses to the test substances.
Skin	Smooth, supple, and blemish free. Warm to the touch. No unusual colour.	Blisters, wounds, lesions, rashes, swelling. Cool, oedematous skin. Rough, dry, flaky skin.
Respiratory	Symmetric chest. Clear breath sounds. Normal respiratory rate and rhythm. No cough.	Abnormal chest contour. Noisy breath sounds. Laboured, slow, rapid or irregular respirations. Cough, with or without raising sputum. The presence of cyanosis.
Cardiovascular	Regular, strong heart beats. Blood pressure within normal range for age. Palpable peripheral pulses. Immediate return of colour to nailbeds.	Irregular heart beats. Rates slower or more rapid than normal. Weak or absent peripheral pulses. Low or high blood pressure. Poor capillary filling in nailbeds.
Neurological	Pupils are equal and react to light. Oriented to person, place and time. Alert and responds appropriately. Strong motor responses in all extremities.	Pupils sluggish or unequal. No response to light. Disoriented. Makes sounds that are not understandable. Weakness or paralysis in one or more extremities. No response to any stimuli.
Gastrointestinal	Pink, moist mucous membranes. Regularly spaced teeth or well-fitting dentures or bridges. Rough-surfaced tongue. Gag reflex present. Soft abdomen with active bowel sounds present. No impaction or haemorrhoids.	Pale or dry mucous membranes. Diseased or missing teeth. Smooth, dry tongue. Absent gag reflex. Rigid abdomen. Diminished or absent bowel sounds. Hard, dry stool within the rectum. Haemorrhoids present. Altered bowel habits, e.g. diarrhoea or constipation.
Genitourinary	Intact skin and normal distribution of pubic hair. Pink, moist, mucous membranes. No lesions, drainage, or odours. Bladder nonpalpable. Firm uterus postdelivery located at or below the midline of the umbilicus.	Discharge from the penis or vagina. Lesions on the penis or vaginal mucosa. Distended bladder with dribbling of urine. Boggy, postpartum uterus located above the midline of the umbilicus.
Musculoskeletal	Firm, strong muscles. Good muscle control and coordination. Good posture and balance. Normal range of motion in joints.	Muscle weakness, lack of control and coordination. Poor posture and balance. Limp or foot dragging during walking. Restricted range of motion.

1. Excessive intake of coffee.
2. Frequency of micturition.
3. Pain.
4. Anxiety.

If the cause of the problem is stated then the appropriate nursing actions can be planned.

Similarly, by stating the patient's behaviour in response to a problem, the nurse can evaluate the effectiveness of her nursing actions. This can be applied by using the same example of difficulty in sleeping due to excessive intake of coffee. If after implementing the appropriate plan of care the patient's sleep pattern improves and he becomes less irritable and tired during the day, the nurse can assume that the nursing actions are effective and continue with them until the problem is eliminated.

When using the nursing process, nurses are now being encouraged to incorporate nursing diagnosis so that individual patient problems can be more clearly stated. It is also useful for nurses in training to understand why deficits in needs occur, and the rationale behind nursing actions.

Differentiating actual, potential and possible health problems. An *actual health problem* is one that presently exists. Some human responses to illness or injury may not yet exist, but are likely to occur unless preventive nursing measures are taken. In this case the nurse would begin the problem statement with the word *potential*; for example, potential for impairment of skin integrity related to immobility. This would mean that the skin may break down and develop sores because the patient is not moving around enough to relieve the pressure from his body weight. The skin, however, is presently intact.

At times the nurse may suspect that a problem exists but may not have gathered enough information to be sure. In this case the nurse would use the term *possible* before the problem statement; for example, possible social isolation related to facial burn scars. In other words, the nurse thinks that perhaps the patient is avoiding going anywhere or being with anyone because he is self-conscious about his disfigurement. This may take more careful assessment; with more information the nurse may discover that this patient has felt satisfied with only a few close friends and has never cared to go to public places. The suspected diagnosis would thus not be appropriate in this case.

Note that any problem statement that indicates a potential or possible health problem only contains two parts: the problem and the cause. This is because the patient has not demonstrated any or enough signs that relate to it.

Identifying a collaborative problem. There are some problems that the nurse must look for, but whose treatment is outside the legal scope of nursing. The nurse must be aware that certain patients are at risk for developing disease or treatment complications. This requires the knowledge of pathophysiology. *Pathophysiology* is the science that deals with the physical changes that occur when there is an altered state of health.

The nurse must gather information that indicates the likelihood of these complications and notify the doctor if they occur. For all nursing personnel to be aware of the need to assess certain information, the nurse will write a statement that identifies the collaborative problem. This statement usually only contains two parts: the potential problem and its related cause. An example of a collaborative problem statement is: potential for bleeding related to anticoagulant medication. The nurse and other members of the nursing team would be aware and informed that this complication is possible. They would make certain observations, looking for signs of blood loss, and they would take precautions against any potential injury that would lead to bleeding. If signs of blood loss or haemorrhage occurred, nurses would be expected to use certain first-aid techniques to control bleeding. The doctor would need to be consulted about changing the dosage of the drug or replacing any blood that may have been excessively lost. Nurses may not legally prescribe medications, alter a dosage, or administer fluids such as blood without a written medical order.

The actions associated with the assessment aspect of the nursing process may be summarized as follows:

1. Analysing which problems can be solved by the nurse and which problems need cooperation with other members of the health care team.
2. Writing statements that clearly identify the problem, its cause, and, when applicable, the manifestations found in the patient.

Planning the patient's nursing care

To solve the patient's problems, a nurse must develop a plan of activities, and the patient should be included in the planning. The patient should be in agreement that the problems identified by the nurse do indeed exist, and he should agree to participate with the nurse in those activities that will lead to their solution. Unless there is agreement and cooperation, the worth of the plan decreases in value and effectiveness.

Setting priorities. The nurse needs to decide what problems are most important to work on in the length of time that the patient and nurse will be together. There are several ways to determine this. The first is to think in terms of the hierarchy of needs. Those problems that are interfering with the lower level needs should become a priority.

Another way to set priorities is to evaluate which problems can be solved or reduced in a short time and which ones will require more time. Finally, the nurse could examine which problems, if changed, will also result in a positive change in others. These criteria are used in the prioritized list of problems found in Table 4-3.

Establishing goals. A *goal* or *objective* is an expected or desired outcome, or the desired end result for which one works. The nurse may begin planning nursing care by stating one overall goal. However, there should be an additional goal for each problem identified. The goals may be short term, perhaps accomplished in a few days or certainly before the patient will be discharged from the hospital. Or the goal may be long term, taking weeks or months to complete. The written goals should indicate some specific, measurable fact showing that the patient's problem has been or is becoming resolved. It should also indicate an estimated target date for completion. The following are two examples of goal statements that show how a patient's improvement will be measured:

1. The patient will be able to walk 10 steps without assistance by July 30th.
2. The patient will be able to comb her own hair by August 3rd.

Having no goal for nursing care can be compared to buying an airline ticket without having a destination. Stating goals is an essential part of the process of planning nursing care with each patient.

Writing nursing actions. After the goals are clearly stated, measures that are most likely to help the patient reach those goals are selected. The plan is based on the knowledge that certain actions will produce a desired effect, which in turn will lead to accomplishing the goal. Any nurse who develops or contributes to the plan demonstrates accountability by signing each entry.

Table 4-3. Prioritized listing of problems

Problem Statement	Reason for Priority
Alteration in nutrition: less than body requirements related to fatigue associated with physical activity as manifested by eating only a few bites per meal, a weight loss of 5 pounds in three days, and a below normal haemoglobin level.	Eating is a basic human need. Without adequate nutrition cells die and death may occur. Until the nutrition is improved, the patient will not have the energy to move about.
Self-care deficit related to muscle weakness and fatigue as manifested by an inability to bathe, comb hair, or walk to the toilet without assistance.	Being unable to carry out these activities while in the hospital will not be a threat to survival. They may interfere with what the patient feels is the quality of life. They may affect his self-esteem, a higher level need. Improving nutrition may result in the patient's ability to care for himself.
Potential for impairment of skin integrity related to inactivity.	This problem has not yet occurred. It may be prevented with certain nursing measures. Certainly if the previous two problems are changed, they will also affect this problem.

The activities that are planned are written on the patient's plan of care. They are called nursing actions which are directions for the care that is to be carried out with the patient. Nursing actions are specific, detailed statements that direct who, what, when, where, and how much of an action should be done. They may also incorporate the activities that the doctor has indicated the nurse should perform. They must not be general or vague statements. The following is an example of a specific nursing action: "Position from side to side every two hours on the even hours. Place pillows between legs and upper arm for support. Place a small bath blanket under lower leg to keep the ankle from rubbing on the sheet". A vague statement would be one that states: "Turn frequently". This could be interpreted differently and carried out inconsistently.

Communicating the plan. Goal achievement depends on consistency and continuity of care. The nurse must share the plan with the patient, his family, and other members of the nursing team. The written plan becomes a permanent part of the record.

Planning nursing care for a patient may be summarized as having the following five steps.
1. Goals or objectives of nursing care are written.
2. The problems are ranked in order of their priority.
3. Actions that are most likely to help the patient reach goals of care are selected.
4. Nursing actions are written on the care plan.
5. The written plan is discussed with the patient and shared with other members of the nursing team.

Carrying out the plan of care

During the next part of the nursing process, the nursing care plan is put into effect by carrying out the nursing orders. Some nurses refer to this as nursing intervention or nursing implementation. Skills that the nurse uses during the implementation of the nursing actions are the subject of this book. These technical skills must be combined with the caring, comforting, and counselling skills so that the patient is treated holistically.

The term *nursing implementation* may be somewhat of a misnomer. Sometimes the nurse may carry out the activities alone, expecially when a patient is very ill. However, the nurse encourages patients to participate to whatever extent possible. Thus, some activities may be carried out by the patient independently, others may require that the nurse and the patient work together. For instance, the nurse may teach the patient how to do certain leg exercises; the patient would then do the exercises ten times every hour while awake. This is an example of the partnership that has been discussed between the nurse and patient.

Making pertinent observations. When giving nursing care, a nurse observes the patient to see how well or poorly he is responding to his care. There may be new information about the patient that has not been identified before. Assessment is a continuous process.

Charting the care. Charting is called documentation by some. The care plan and progress notes have the potential of being used as a legal documents, containing records of observations and activities related to the care of each patient. Everything written in the care plan and progress notes must be legible and accurate. If something is not recorded, it is assumed that it did not occur. To prove that the planned care was subsequently implemented, the nurse's recording of what took place should correlate with the plan. If there is a discrepancy between the plan of care and what is recorded, the nurse is responsible for determining its cause. This is another example of how nursing assumes accountability for patient care. This principle of accountability for carrying out nursing actions should not be any less than the accountability nurses demonstrate when carrying out the doctor's orders.

The patient's progress notes should also indicate the patient's level of participation. It should note any progress or regression that may have occurred as the plan was carried out. Quoting what the patient says at times during an interaction helps identify what is occurring from the patient's point of view. It safeguards individuals from making incorrect assumptions.

Carrying out the plan may be summarized as having the following three steps:
1. The nurse, along with the patient, puts the plan into action.
2. The patient is observed for his responses to nursing care.
3. The activities that are carried out and the patient's responses to them are recorded on the patient's progress notes.

Evaluating the results of nursing care

Evaluation is the process of measuring how well a goal or objective is reached. In terms of the nursing process, evaluation provides information on the degree to which a goal is being met through the use of specific nursing measures. Like assessment, it is an ongoing part of the nursing process.

Evaluation is more or less a scheduled event. Recall that the goal associated with each problem has an expected date for completion. As that date arrives, the nurse compares the patient's level of achievement with the measurable goal. Or, the nurses on a particular unit may establish a policy that all care plans will be reviewed on a certain routine. In other words, perhaps the care plans on all patients may be reviewed on Mondays and Fridays. Each nurse would write on the care plan that it had been reviewed for its current appropriateness.

There are three possible results from evaluation:

1. A goal of nursing care has been met; therefore, nursing actions to accomplish that goal are discontinued. *Example*: It is observed that a patient is using his crutches well and correctly; nursing orders about teaching and assisting him with crutch walking are discontinued.

2. A goal of nursing care has been unmet, but progress toward it has occurred; therefore, the nursing orders described in the plan should continue. *Example*: It is observed that a patient remains inactive but is free of bedsores; nursing actions to turn him at two-hourly intervals are continued.

3. A goal for nursing care is not being met; therefore, modifications and revisions in nursing care are necessary. *Example*: After a week of teaching a diabetic patient with reading and illustrated materials, it is observed that he is unable to select proper foods for his prescribed diet while using the exchange system. A modification in the nursing actions must be made.

Consulting with the patient and team members. It is important to discuss the progress toward goal achievement with the patient. In this way both the nurse and the patient can speculate on what activities need to be discontinued, added or changed. Other health team members who are familiar with a particular patient or problems similar to those of the patient may offer their expertise on those actions that have been previously successful for others. The evaluation of a patient's progress may be the subject of a nursing team conference.

Revising the plan. Unfortunately not all patient problems are solved with the nursing care that was originally planned. It is important to identify the factors that are interfering with goal achievement.

Some patients may have developed new problems. It may take some longer than expected. Some goals may be unrealistic. Some nursing actions may not be as effective as first hoped. Changing the goal, extending the date of expected accomplishment, or revising the nursing orders may result in improving the progress toward an improved state of health.

Evaluation can be summarized as having the following three steps:

1. The nurse determines how well the goals of nursing care are being met.
2. The nurse seeks the opinions of the patient and other health team members.
3. The results of evaluation are used to make changes.

The nursing process is generally accepted as an important method for planning and giving appropriate and competent nursing care. Principles of Care 4-1 describes the steps for using the nursing process. More detailed discussions of the nursing process can be found in speciality texts. A comprehensive list can be found in the reference and further reading lists at the end of this chapter.

Communication skills—introduction

In order to practise individual care effectively, using the four stages of the nursing process, it is important that the nurse employs good communication skills. This establishes a nurse-patient relationship based on mutual trust and respect.

Individual research studies carried out by Hayward (1975) and Boore (1984) demonstrate how effective communication can reduce the patient's anxiety and pain, hence aiding recovery from illness and surgery. Other studies undertaken in relation to communication look at the verbal interaction between patients and nurses; namely that of Macleod Clark (1983). From a study looking at conversations which took place between nurses and patients she concluded the following:

1. On the wards studied the nurse-patient interaction was limited both in time and quality.
2. Nurses employed strategies which blocked communication—nurses showed little evidence of using skills which promote communication.
3. There was a need to increase the amount of time allocated within nurse education programmes to developing nurses' understanding of the use of communication skills.

Principles of Care 4-1. *Utilizing the nursing process*

Nursing Action	Rationale
Collect information about the patient.	The nurse must determine what past, current, and potential health problems exist.
Validate all information.	Incorrect information may result in errors in the identification of problems.
Group information into categories.	Organizing related information simplifies the process of interpretation
Compare information about the patient to how he performs his activities of living normally.	Using standards for comparison helps identify any deviations that represent the patient's needs or problems.
Formulate the problem statements.	Clear identification of health problems directs the nurse to select skills that will improve the patient's health.
Determine how a successful outcome will be measured.	Meeting certain criteria will determine when nursing actions no longer need to be continued.
Rank problems in the order of their importance.	Working and solving some problems are more important than others for the patient's overall health to improve.
Select nursing measures that are most likely to meet the goals of nursing care.	Scientific knowledge based on research findings about the purpose of certain actions makes it possible for nurses to predict an expected effect.
Write nursing actions for the care of the patient.	Written information can provide consistency and continuity of care throughout each 24-hour period.
Discuss the plan with the patient, his family, and other nursing team members.	Communicating with everyone involved promotes cooperative efforts leading to success.
Put the plan into action.	Work produces results.
Observe the patient for his responses to the activities.	Any changes in the patient will affect each step of the nursing process.
Write down the activities that were carried out and the patient's responses.	Recording correlates the plan with the actions and verifies that it is being carried out.
Compare the patient's level of accomplishment with the identified criteria for a successful outcome.	There should be progress toward the goal if all the planning and care have been appropriate.
Discuss the progress or lack of it with the patient, his family, and health team members.	Pooling resources often results in better ideas for future plans.
Change the plan in areas that are no longer appropriate.	Alternative methods may be more successful in solving a problem.
Continue gathering information.	The nursing process is a continuous sequence of actions that are repeated until the patient and nurse are satisfied that the goals have been met.

Using communication skills

Communication is an exchange of information. Almost everything a person does communicates something. Communication is essential in the development of a nurse-patient relationship because no relationship can exist without it. Communication is a continuous process that occurs with every contact the nurse has with patients.

Verbal communication. *Verbal communication* is communication that uses words. It includes speaking, reading and writing. Messages of verbal communication may not be what we think they are. A patient may say that he is not eating because he has no appetite. When the nurse begins to feed him, however, he starts to eat. Does he want the attention of being fed or does he lack the strength to do so?

A word of caution is offered. It would be unwise to assume that everything the patient says must be viewed with suspicion and as a reason for probing and prying to find true meanings. Rather, the nurse will wish to accept what the patient says while being alert to the possibility that the patient may not always be able or willing to say what he really means. Therefore, the nurse will want to observe nonverbal communication carefully while still listening closely to what is said. Some communication techniques the nurse may want to utilize to achieve a specific purpose are given in Table 4-4.

Nonverbal communication. *Nonverbal communication* is the exchange of information without using words. It is what is *not* said. People communicate nonverbally through facial expressions, posture, gestures, general physical appearance, mode of dress, grooming, and voice inflections. Crying, laughing and moaning are also considered nonverbal communication because they do not use a language or words.

A person has less control over nonverbal than verbal communication. Words can be chosen with care, but a facial expression is harder to control. As a result, messages are often communicated more accurately through nonverbal communication. A patient may say he does not feel lonely, but the expression on his face, the way he moves, and the tone of his voice may all show signs of loneliness.

Table 4-4. Communication techniques

Technique	Purpose	Example
Informing	Provides facts.	"Your surgery is scheduled for 9:30 A.M."
Direct questioning	Obtains specific information.	"Are you having any pain?"
Open-ended questioning	Provides a means for the patient to be more descriptive.	"How does your pain feel?"
Reflecting	Provides a means of encouraging the patient to continue and explain more.	PATIENT: "I'm miserable." NURSE: "Miserable?"
Clarifying	Reduces the possibility of misinterpretation.	PATIENT: "Beyond every cloud there's a silver lining." NURSE: "Explain what that means to you."
Confronting	Calls attention to inconsistencies in behaviour or verbal statements.	"You say you want to go home but you haven't been doing your exercises."
Silence	Encourages the patient to initiate or continue the conversation.	PATIENT: "It is harder and harder to take care of myself at home." NURSE: (silence) PATIENT: "I get so short of breath climbing stairs."
Summarizing	Restates the areas covered in the conversation in brief form so that progress toward a goal can be identified.	"We've talked about your new diet and the difficulty you have in preparing food. Would you like to think about having a 'meals on wheels' service arranged for when you go home?"

The role of touch in communication. Touching someone carries nonverbal messages. Touch has different meanings to different people and therefore should be used with care. Some people do not like to be touched, and their feelings should be respected. One positive message touch often carries, when used appropriately, is that the person *cares* for the one he touches and is offering him support and comfort.

Touch is common in nursing because of the many times nurses and patients are in close physical contact. The nurse who holds a crying child in her arms gives the child a feeling of security and affection through the sense of touch. Healing has long been associated with the laying on of hands.

The role of silence in communication. Silence is often part of nonverbal communication. Periods of silence may have many different meanings. A patient may use silence as an escape; he may be afraid of an examination and remain silent in order to avoid talking about his fears. A husband and wife may often sit quietly without talking and still be communicating much about their love for one another. A comfortable and happy person may prefer silence to talking as an expression of his contentment. Silence may be used by someone who is exploring his feelings; to interrupt with conversation when someone is deep in thought disturbs his thinking process.

A common obstacle to effective communication is ignoring the importance of silence and talking excessively. Taking the role of silence into account when communicating with patients promotes the development of a nurse-patient relationship.

Communication barriers to a therapeutic relationship. It is important to treat each patient with dignity and respect. There are certain approaches that the nurse should avoid because they belittle the patient. The following approaches will undermine a mutually satisfying relationship:

    Giving orders to the patient
    Threatening the patient
    Shaming or criticizing the patient
    Lecturing the patient
    Giving advice to the patient
    Offering unrealistic reassurance

The role of listening in communication. Listening involves hearing and interpreting what is heard. A good listener pays close attention to what is said. It is difficult to overstress the importance of listening to patients when communicating with them. During the course of a busy day, it is easy to think about what must be done and to forget to listen to the patient. Many important signs of the patient's condition and how he feels are missed because a nurse fails to listen when a patient speaks.

Most people quickly learn when someone is pretending to listen. They usually can tell also when the listener is bored or impatient to get on with something else. For example, a nurse may look out a window, interrupt a patient, or have a faraway look while a patient speaks. It is easy to see that if the nurse becomes careless and does not listen, a productive nurse-patient relationship cannot be expected to develop.

A learned person once said that all wise men share one trait—the ability to listen. It is a comment worth every nurse's consideration.

Techniques to help promote communication. Various techniques may be used to promote effective communication between nurses and patients. They are described in Principles of Care 4-2.

Understanding the patient's responses to illness

All individuals are unique. Each patient brings to the relationship a different set of experiences and values that affect the significance he attaches to a certain situation. The more accurately the nurse interprets the patient's responses to his illness, the more appropriately the patient services can be adapted for the individual.

Culture and illness. Cultural factors often influence an experience with illness. *Culture* is everything that an individual learns from the groups of people of which he is a part.

Trying to understand a patient's cultural background helps the nurse understand that individual's behaviour. The nurse who feels a certain cultural background to be the best is biased and will tend to judge others with a certain amount of prejudice. Efforts to develop a helping nurse-patient relationship in such instances are almost certain to fail.

Common emotional responses. An actual or potential illness is a form of stress that presents a threat to an individual's survival. Because the mind and body are interrelated, the nurse can expect changes in the patient's usual emotional state. The nurse can anticipate certain common emotional reactions in those she is caring for. Some common responses are identified in Table 4-5.

Principles of Care 4-2. Promoting effective communication with a patient

Nursing Action	Rationale
Have a purpose for a conversation with the patient.	So-called idle talk may serve as an opener in a conversation, but having a purpose in mind for a conversation helps prevent drifting from important subjects into irrelevant chatter.
Identify the amount of time you can spend.	The patient will not misinterpret the reason for leaving.
Be knowledgeable about the subject being discussed with the patient.	The patient is very likely to realize when you are unfamiliar with the topic of conversation and to lose confidence in his care giver.
Admit not knowing about something and offer to obtain the information for the patient.	The patient soon recognizes when you do not have sufficient knowledge about a subject and will lose confidence and trust when he realizes you are speaking without having necessary information.
Focus a conversation on the patient and his needs and problems.	Communication has little value in terms of giving the patient needed care when attention is focused on you or on an activity you are performing for the patient.
Show interest in what the patient is saying.	Showing interest can be demonstrated by techniques such as using eye-to-eye contact (without staring) with the patient, thinking before talking, sitting down when convenient while conversing with the patient, relaxing while conversing, and listening to the patient. Most patients soon recognize when you pretend to be listening, and they then lose confidence in you.
Provide privacy while communicating with a patient.	Communication will usually be blocked if the patient thinks what he is saying will be overheard by others.
Assure the patient that a conversation with you will be held in confidence.	Although it is important to assure confidentiality, it is equally important to explain that you will have to share information with other health personnel if, in your judgment, what he tells you can influence his medical or nursing care. Serious problems may arise if you promise the patient you will tell no one about what he says. When the information is important for other health personnel to know, you will lose the patient's trust and confidence if you break your promise not to tell.
Keep your mind open and do not prejudge the patient.	Failing to keep your mind open obstructs communication because you may fail to receive correct messages.
Be as clear and concise as possible and use language the patient understands.	Most patients are unfamiliar with nursing and hospital jargon and there will be no communication if you describe things in a way that the patient does not understand.
Avoid giving the patient pat answers.	Pat answers such as "Everything will be all right," "Don't worry," "Everybody is afraid when sick," and "You patients are all alike" offer false assurance and are usually interpreted as a lack of interest in the patient.
Do not probe for information.	Probing for information puts the patient on the defensive and he is likely to stop a conversation with you.
Do not give advice unless the patient asks for advice.	The patient has a right to information so that he can make up his own mind. You are placing yourself in the position of "knowing best" if you give advice without being requested to do so. If the patient asks for advice, give it only if you have full and accurate information on the subject under discussion. If you do not, consult the nurse in charge.
Observe while you converse with a patient and use silence and touch appropriately.	The appropriate use of observation, silence, and touch are discussed in the text.

Table 4-5. Common emotional responses to illness

Emotional Response	Definition
Anxiety	An emotional state characterized by feelings of uneasiness about the unknown.
Worry	A mild form of anxiety characterized by preoccupation with a problem.
Fear	An emotional state characterized by expected harm or unpleasantness.
Depression	An emotional state characterized by unhappiness.
Anger	An emotional state characterized by feelings of resentment due to a real or supposed injury to oneself or others.
Overdependence	An emotional state characterized by feelings of helplessness beyond what is considered normal.
Self-pity	Feeling sorry for oneself.
Regression	Displaying a type of behaviour typical of an earlier age.
Apathy	An emotional state characterized by indifference to what is happening.

Table 4-6. Common coping mechanisms

Coping Mechanism	Definition	Example
Repression	Forgetting about situations that produced stress.	Being unable to remember the circumstances of a tragic traffic accident.
Denial	Refusing to believe information.	Not accepting a diagnosis despite medical evidence.
Rationalization	Minimizing a disappointment by finding something positive in the outcome.	Believing that it was better to have been passed over for a job promotion because the raise would have placed one in a higher tax bracket.
Compensation	Redirecting a desire for something unobtainable into efforts toward achieving or acquiring something similar.	Being unsuited to be a great athlete, but becoming a sports journalist instead.
Displacement	Redirecting anger toward one person onto an object or different person.	Kicking a wastebasket after being criticized by a supervisor at work.

Not all patients experience these emotions to the same degree. The extent to which some patients become distressed depends on the unique personality of the patient, past experiences related to illness, the severity of the health problem, and whether the patient is simultaneously experiencing other problems. Nurses may relieve some of the emotional discomfort of patients by following the suggested actions in Principles of Care 4-3.

Most individuals use methods to relieve their discomfort. The methods used are those that have been previously successful in relieving stress during an individual's life. These mechanisms are called coping strategies and coping mechanisms. *Coping strategies* are activities one consciously uses to reduce stress. Some commonly used strategies include the following.

1. Turning to a supportive person for reassurance.
2. Talking about problems with others.
3. Working at a physical activity such as squash.
4. Eating to restore a feeling of contentment associated with a full stomach.

Principles of Care 4-3. Providing emotional support

Nursing Action	Rationale
Watch for signs of stress such as rapid heart rate, crying, excessive cigarette smoking, excessive sleep or insomnia, loss of appetite or excessive eating.	Responses to stress are manifested through the sympathetic and parasympathetic nervous systems, which cause a speeding up or slowing down of body functions.
Sit in a relaxed position at eye level with the patient.	Power, authority, and control can be communicated in physical height and distance from the patient. The nurse can convey a nonjudgmental attitude by assuming a position similar to that of the patient.
Allow the patient to bring his emotions to the surface.	Identifying one's feelings and emotions is the first step in dealing with them. If the nurse chooses to ignore this aspect of care, holistic services are not provided.
Protect the patient from being overheard.	Most adults feel that admitting to feeling scared is a sign of weakness. Protecting the patient's public image reinforces a therapeutic relationship.
Share information with the patient.	The unknown can be fantasized beyond proportion and can escalate fear.
Indicate attention by gestures such as nodding the head at appropriate times.	Active listening involves concentration and participation in what is being said.
Don't dismiss or make light of what the patient is experiencing with statements like, "Don't worry, everything will be all right".	Each person attaches significance to a situation from his own experience. Being told by another that this is unnecessary overlooks that each patient is unique.
Allow time for discussing feelings.	Feelings are usually expressed with more difficulty than facts. Feeling pressed for time or being rushed may be interpreted as disinterest.
Allow the patient to express emotions such as anger and hostility without retaliation.	Patients usually do not mean to direct their feelings at the nurse personally. All behaviour has meaning, and the nurse may uncover it after the anger has been expressed.
Tolerate crying and protect the patient from being observed.	Crying is a result of feeling hurt and helpless. It is also associated with feeling out of control. The nurse who allows this reaction shows acceptance and a desire to stay and help the patient gain control.
Spend time with the patient at times other than when providing physical services.	Some patients may feel that the only reason a nurse spends time with them is because it is part of a job. Being with a patient at other times reinforces that he is important as an individual.

5. Sleeping to avoid dealing with a problem.
6. Using a symbolic object such as rabbit's foot or religious medal.

Coping mechanisms are methods, usually outside one's conscious awareness, that reduce what an individual perceives to threaten his self-concept. Some common coping mechanisms, their definitions, and examples can be found in Table 4-6.

Teaching the patient

One of the most important nursing skills while providing patient care is the promotion of independence of the patient. One way this can be achieved is through teaching. High-quality nursing care includes increasing the patient's knowledge of ways that will allow him to remain healthy. Limited hospitalization time has demanded that nurses identify learning needs of patients nearer the time of admission rather than discharge.

Formal and informal teaching. Teaching may be *formal* in that preplanned information is presented at a scheduled time. For example, students often attend specific classes with planned lessons. A classroom is set up for a lecture or demonstration. Nurses sometimes plan specific classes for groups of patients, such as pregnant women. But teaching may also be *informal*, occurring spontaneously at the patient's bedside with only the patient and a nurse present. As a health educator, the nurse often teaches in an informal manner, taking advantage of each opportunity to help the patient learn what he needs and wants to know.

Teaching, whether formal or informal, requires a plan. Without a plan, teaching becomes haphazard and the patient's need for information goes unattended. The student nurse may work with the team leader or the primary nurse in developing a teaching plan or carrying out certain specific parts that are identified on the patient's care plan. For a full explanation of primary nursing the reader is directed to the chapter in this book relating directly to methods of organizing patient care. Methods that the nurse should follow when formulating a teaching plan and implementing it are identified in Principles of Care 4-4.

Suggested measures for providing effective communication in selected situations

When the patient is an infant or child

Expect an infant to demonstrate emotional responses when his needs are not met with crying, kicking, thrashing about and irritability. An infant responds emotionally to cuddling, rocking, touching, and soothing sounds, including the sound of your voice.

Remember that youngsters need emotional support and display many of the same emotional responses to illness as do adults: fear, anger, worry

Principles of Care 4-4. Teaching patients

Nursing Action	Rationale
Find out what the patient wants to know.	Learning is facilitated when there is some personal interest.
Determine what the patient should know if he is to remain healthy.	Patients are not always aware that there is information that is vital to continued health and safety.
Teach when the patient appears ready and interested in learning.	Patients who are very ill or who are receiving visits from friends or relatives need to have teaching postponed.
Provide an environment that promotes learning.	Learning takes place best in a room that is well ventilated, well lighted, and of a comfortable temperature. Distractions and interruptions interfere with concentration.
Adjust teaching to a level the patient understands.	It is of little value to use terms that are not familiar to the patient, or to teach in such depth that he becomes confused.
Divide information into manageable amounts.	The patient may be overwhelmed by the amount of information and will not retain it.
Use different teaching aids, such as pamphlets, diagrams, models, and demonstrations.	People learn in a variety of ways. The more senses that can be stimulated, the more probable that the information will be learned.
Review previous information briefly.	Repetition increases retention of information.
Evaluate the patient's learning by asking the patient to make a list, draw a picture, or demonstrate a skill.	It is best to devise some method for assessing the patient's comprehension. The ability to recall with accuracy is proof that learning took place.
Document on the patient's record the information that has been taught and the patient's level of comprehension.	Following a teaching plan and reinforcing weak areas reduces duplication of efforts and facilitates goal achievement.

and so on. The nurse is a parent substitute during hospitalization of youngsters and must gain a child's confidence and trust.

Expect that many children regress when ill. *Regression* means that a person displays a type of behaviour typical of an earlier age. For example, a child that has been toilet trained regresses and soils himself or a child able to drink from a cup demands a bottle. Show respect for the child's need for extra dependence during illness and hospitalization, and help parents understand this temporary change in the child's behaviour.

Just as with adults, learn to accept a child's emotional outbursts, even when they are directed against you. Recognize that there is a cause for his behaviour. Patience and understanding help you to find reasons for behaviour; problems can then be better handled in a constructive manner.

Do not attack the behaviour, but attack its cause when behaviour becomes destructive.

Offer explanations of what you are going to do in ways a child can understand. Using dolls or puppets can be effective when explaining and gaining cooperation.

Keep in mind that from birth on, a person is developing his own unique behaviour throughout childhood. He has feelings and is learning to cope with problems through methods that will eventually prepare him for adulthood.

Take into account that among the strongest influences in the life of an adolescent is that of his peers. While he strives for individuality, he also wants to be like his peers. Failing to respect an adolescent's feelings in this regard does little to promote a therapeutic relationship.

Protect the parent-child relationship. Understand that parents are also under tension, and often suffer feelings of guilt, when a child is ill. Include the family in the child's care, to the greatest extent possible, and include family members in your teaching also.

When the patient is elderly

Take into account that a person's sensory system tends to fail with advanced age. Modified techniques that will subsequently be described may need to be adapted when providing pateint services.

Use touch but use it appropriately. Touch has been found to effectively help make up for other sensory losses in the elderly.

Show genuine respect and warmth with the elderly patient. Avoid using titles such as "granny", "gramps", "auntie", and the like, unless the patient wishes you to use them. You also show respect by talking to and treating the elderly as adults, not as children.

Give the patient opportunities to control whatever aspects of his life he can, such as the planning of his care and self-care. Dependence is often difficult for elderly patients to accept. Being allowed to maintain independence to the greatest extent possible is gratifying for them and promotes a helping relationship.

Allow the patient to self-pace his care when possible. This technique requires more time, but rushing the elderly often results in frustration, anger, and resentment.

Listen to the patient and allow him to reminisce. A conversation can be related to the present by gradually drawing attention to today's events.

Use family members as indicated for teaching purposes, for helping to strengthen family relationships, and for promoting a nursing relationship with people who are important to the patient.

When the patient is blind or has impaired vision

Identify yourself as you approach a blind patient and tell him when you are leaving. Explain to him what you are going to do while with him.

Explain your reason for touching a patient when you do. Avoid touching a blind patient suddenly because it is likely to frighten him.

Speak in a normal tone of voice. A blind person is not necessarily hard of hearing.

Be sure that the patient has his call bell handy and that he knows exactly where it is and how to use it.

Explain typical noises the patient can expect to hear that will be strange to him. Also familiarize the patient with the room's arrangement and furnishings.

Use the following techniques when the patient is not blind but has some impaired vision: have a bright light available for the patient; remove obstacles over which he could fall; and, when possible, provide him with a magnifying glass for reading.

When the patient is deaf or hard of hearing

Use devices such as a magic slate, chalkboard, flash cards, and writing pads to communicate.

Be thoughtful by keeping reading material handy for the patient.

Walk toward the patient slowly and allow him to see you as you approach. The patient will be easily frightened if someone suddenly appears in his line of vision.

If the patient reads lips, talk slowly, use simple language and speak in a natural tone of voice.

Use gestures as much as possible.

When the patient is hard of hearing, the following techniques are recommended: encourage the patient to wear his hearing aid if he has one, face the patient when you speak, enunciate clearly and speak loudly, use gestures as you speak, and question him to learn whether he has understood you.

When the patient cannot speak

Use special devices to communicate. Several examples follow:

1. A magnetic "talk board", which contains common phrases that the patient can select to communicate something. Phrases such as 'I am thirsty" and "I have pain" are common.

2. A "magic slate", which is a device on which one can write a message with a stylus. The message is removed by lifting specially treated paper, and the slate can then be used again.

3. Flash cards, which are cards about 3 by 5 inches, on which common phrases are written or symbols are drawn. The patient selects the appropriate phrase or symbol to convey a message. Extra cards or a writing pad on which the patient writes additional messages may also be used.

Use nonverbal communication to the greatest extent possible. For example, gestures and facial expressions carry a variety of messages. If the patient cannot move, use prearranged signals such as finger movements or eye blinking to convey a message.

Talk to a patient even though he cannot answer, and explain what you are going to do. It is a thoughtful gesture and also conveys caring and interest in the patient. Speak slowly, keep to one subject, use simple language, keep eye contact with the patient, use gestures, use consistent wording, and give the patient plenty of time to receive your message.

Be sure to keep a call bell handy for a patient who cannot talk and cannot call out for help.

Praise patients who are relearning how to talk as they make progress. Help the patient to relax and to speak slowly during reeducation.

When the patient is unconscious

Be careful about what is said in the presence of an unconscious patient. Hearing is believed to be the last sense lost; therefore, the patient may hear what is being said even though he cannot respond.

Assume that the patient can hear, and continue to talk with him as you normally would when giving care.

Speak to the patient before touching him; keep in mind that touch is an effective means of communication, even though the patient cannot respond.

Keep noises in the room at a low level so that the patient can focus on conversation, if it seems that he is receiving messages.

When the patient is from a different culture

Make a concerted effort to learn as much as possible about the beliefs and customs of the patient.

Make it as easy as possible for a hospitalized patient to carry out his cultural practices as long as they do not disturb others.

Modify care so that the patient's cultural practices and beliefs are not violated. To ignore them may result in his refusing care.

Use an interpreter whenever possible. Often a member of the patient's family can help. Also, a dictionary that translates one language into another is helpful.

Use gestures or pictures to demonstrate messages.

Be alert to nonverbal communication. Most nonverbal communication is universal and understood by everyone.

Prepare cards with a word in English on one side and its equivalent in the language the patient speaks on the other. The nurse and the patient can then select a particular card to convey a message to one another.

References

Aggleton, P. and Chalmers, M. (1987) Models of nursing, nursing practice and nurse education. *Journal of Advanced Nursing,* **12,** 573–81.

Boore, J. (1984) *A Prescription for Recovery,* Royal College of Nursing, London.

Fawcett, J. (1984) *Analysis and Evaluation of Conceptual Models of Nursing,* F.A. Davis, Philadelphia.

Hayward, J. (1975) *Information: A Prescription Against Pain,* Royal College of Nursing, London.

Henderson, V. (1966) *The Nature of Nursing—a Definition and Its Implications for Practice, Research and Education*, Macmillan, New York.

Hunt, J. and Marks Maran, D. (1987) *Nursing Care Plans—The Nursing Process at Work*, 2nd edn, John Wiley, Chichester.

King, I. (1971) *Toward a Theory for Nursing*, John Wiley, New York.

MacLeod Clark, J. (1983) An analysis of nurse-patient conversations on surgical wards, in *Nursing Research, Ten Studies in Patient Care* (ed. J.D. Wilson Barnett), John Wiley, Chichester.

Orem, D. (1980) *Nursing—Concepts of Practice*, 2nd edn, McGraw Hill, New York.

Pearson, A. and Vaugn, B. (1985) Nursing practice and the nursing process, in Open University Press, *A Systematic Approach to Nursing Care—An Introduction*, 2nd edn, The Open University Press, Milton Keynes.

Pearson, A. and Vaugn, B. (1986) *Nursing Models for Practice*, 2nd edn, Heinemann Nursing, London.

Peplau, H. (1952) *Interpersonal Relations in Nursing*, G.P. Putman, New York.

Roper, N., Logan, W. and Tierney, A. (1980) *The Elements of Nursing*, Churchill Livingstone, Edinburgh.

Wright, S. (1986) *Building and Using a Model of Nursing*, Edward Arnold, London.

Further reading

Barnett, D. (1985) Making your plans work. *Nursing Times*, **81**(24), 46–9.

Brooking, J. (1988) Occasional paper: "A scale to measure use of the nursing process". *Nursing Times*, **85**(15), 100–103.

Fitzpatrick, J. and Whall, A. (1989) *Conceptual Models of Nursing. Analysis and Application*, Appleton and Lange, New York.

Fraser, M. (1990) *Using Conceptual Nursing in Practice*, Harper and Row, London.

Great Britain: Statutory Instruments (1983) *Nurses, Midwives and Health Visitors Rules Approval Order*, HMSO, London.

McMahon, R. (1988) Who's afraid of nursing care plans? *Nursing Times*, **84**(29), 39–41.

Miller, A. (1985) Are you using the nursing process? *Nursing Times*, **81**(36), 100–103.

Richards, D. and Lambert, T. (1987) The nursing process: the effect on patients satisfaction with nursing care. *Journal of Advanced Nursing*, **12**, 559–62.

Teasdale, K. (1987) Partnership with patients? *The Professional Nurse*, September, 17–19.

Walsh, M. (1989) Model example. *Nursing Standard*, **3**(22), 22–3.

Webb, C. (1986) Nursing models—A personal view. *Nursing Practice*, **1**, 208–12.

Whitfield, S. (1989) Still struggling with the nursing process. *Nursing Standard*, **23**(3), 19–20.

Wilkinson, F. (1989) Care plan location—does it really matter? *Nursing Standard*, **3**(36), 35–7.

5

Research in nursing

Learning objectives

When the content of this chapter has been mastered, the learner should be able to:

Discuss the importance of research in nursing.
State the different types of research.
Describe the research process.
Consider the ethical implications of research.
Identify the factors to consider when reading a research report.

Glossary

Analysis Examination of the information and interpretation into an understandable format.

Control group The group of people or things who do not experience the variable introduced to the experimental group.

Data Information.

Ethics Science of morals.

Experimental group A group of subjects (people or things) who in the course of an experimental research project, are caused to experience the variable under consideration (Ogier, 1989).

Hypothesis A supposition which is made based on knowledge or information that has yet to be proved/disproved.

Independent variable The variable the researcher introduces or manipulates into the situation. This is used in experimental research.

Literature search A review of the research and associated studies previously undertaken, which are similar to the subject chosen to be researched. It provides the researcher with useful background information to the subject intended to be researched.

Methodology The way in which the researcher tries to fulfil the aim of the study; includes sample used, tools employed and analysis of data.

Null hypothesis A statement that predicts there will be no significant change or difference between the results of the control and experimental groups following introduction of a variable to the experimental group. For example a null hypothesis might state the following: "Adding 500 g of salt to a patient's daily bath water will have no effect on the incidence of wound infections in surgical patients" (Austin, 1988).

Pilot study A small preliminary study undertaken

prior to the main research study to help redefine the problem and test the proposed methodology.

Reliability The same test will give the same results when used in similar circumstances on different occasions.

Research A systematic inquiry to discover facts or test theories in order to obtain valid answers which have a scientific basis.

Validity The ability of the tools used in the study to obtain the required information or measure what they are supposed to measure.

Variable Any factor, characteristic, or attribute under study.

Introduction

Nursing research is a subject growing both in importance and quantity, whose findings will no doubt have profound effects on nursing practice, management and education in the future. This chapter is intended as an introduction to research in nursing, from its foundations through to the types of research and the terminology used in relation to research.

A good starting point is perhaps a definition of what is meant by research and how it relates to nursing. Many definitions have been offered in the past but one of the most succinct is that of Hockey (1984), who describes research as "an attempt to increase the sum of what is known, usually referred to as 'body of knowledge', by the discovery of new facts or relationships through a process of systematic scientific enquiry, the research process".

The importance of research in nursing

Many nurses, when considering research and nursing, view it as an academic exercise intended for nurse theorists. However, nurses working in the clinical situation have a responsibility for ensuring that they offer the best care for the individual. It is important that trained nurses question their nursing actions, and base them on proven scientific findings and not on established beliefs such as "this is the way we have always done it" or "Sister's policy is to do it this way". That is not to say that every nurse should undertake a research study but every nurse should possess an awareness of research and be able to critique various studies undertaken. By being able to do this, the nurse can objectively look at her care and see if she can apply research findings to her practice. One area of nursing practice which has been

researched by various people is communication with patients. Hayward (1975) undertook a research study to determine the effects of giving patients information preoperatively that was specifically related to their pre- and postoperative care. In particular he was interested to observe that if patients received specific information preoperatively, would their postoperative pain be reduced?

His findings showed that the group of patients who received specific information preoperatively required significantly less analgesic drugs than the control group of patients during the postoperative period.

Hayward's findings were supported by a similar study carried out by Boore (1978) who demonstrated, using physiological measures, that giving patients preoperative information reduced stress in the postoperative period. If we apply research findings such as the examples above to our practice we are in a position to set and maintain good standards of patient care.

Hockey (1984) stated that there were six main purposes of nursing research:

1. To establish scientific reasons for nursing activities.
2. To find ways of increasing the cost-effectiveness of nursing activities.
3. To satisfy the academic curiosity of nurses.
4. Identify strengths and weaknesses within nursing.
5. To establish evidence in support of required resources within nursing.
6. To help nursing attain professional status.

If there was not a need to increase our knowledge in relation to the study and practice of nursing, or this information could be obtained by different means, then there would not be a need for research. However, there are many unanswered questions in nursing and as it continues to grow so will the unanswered questions and the need for research.

The development of nursing research in the UK

Research in nursing did not really get underway until the 1950s; this may well be due to the fact that nurses did not possess the academic knowledge to attempt or undertake a research project. The need for nurses to have the opportunity to be able to gain qualifications in higher education became more apparent, especially following a survey by Carter (1954) who highlighted this point. It was Edinburgh University that first opened its doors to nurse tutor students in 1956. Undergraduate courses afforded nurses the knowledge and skills to be able to undertake research studies. Another problem which faced the early pioneers of nursing research was that apart from lacking the knowledge of the mechanics of the research process, technology was also not as advanced as it is today. These early researchers did not have computers which they could use to process their data or calculators to assist them with their statistics. In 1972 the Briggs Committee stated that "Nursing should become a research based profession, a sense of the need for research should become part of the mental equipment of every practising nurse and midwife" (Briggs, 1972).

Most nursing libraries now have an index to research studies in different areas and the Royal College of Nursing (RCN) in London houses the Steinberg collection which comprises many different research reports. The Index of Nursing Research (INR) which is based at the Department of Health library provides an information service to the nursing division of the department and the nursing profession. This was commenced in card form in 1975 but has since converted to an online computer data base in 1983, making searching and retrieval of information much easier. The main purpose of the INR is to promote the use of research in nursing information.

Additions to the INR can be purchased quarterly in the *Journal of Nursing Research Abstracts* from the Department of Social Services; backdated copies are also available.

Alongside the development of resource information related to nursing research, there has been an increase in the number of books available for nurses regarding various research studies which have already been undertaken. In addition, books are available offering advice on how to read research and the stages involved in a research study. Examples of these books can be found in the references and further reading lists at the end of the chapter.

Nursing journals such as the *Journal of Advanced Nursing* are solely concerned with research studies which nurses have undertaken. In the more general nursing magazines such as the *Nursing Times* and *Nursing Standard* the reader can frequently see abstracts from research studies which have been undertaken in various clinical specialities.

With the developing links of nursing with higher education has come the establishment of nursing research departments such as those at the University of London and the University of Surrey. Consequently, research fellowships have become pertinent areas of training for nurses. Dunn (1991) states that the objectives of these are "to give qualified practitioners the opportunity to acquire a thorough grounding in research methods and carry out a systematic study of an aspect of nursing care for a degree". These fellowships are flexible in that they allow for full or part time training at the polytechnic or university of the student's choice; they are also open to non-graduate nurses.

Recent years have also seen the creation of research posts at sister and senior nurse level, e.g. as liaison officers between the health service and higher education or as research officers within government health departments.

Funding for nurses to undertake research studies is available from three main sources; government research funds, funds at local level and private trusts and foundations (Hockey, 1986).

As research awareness has grown within nursing, so the curriculum for RGN training and post basic ENB courses have altered to accommodate research components such as an appreciation of research, and in some courses the students undertake a small research study of their own.

Similarly, alongside the introduction of the nursing process, nurses are being taught to meet the needs of individuals by basing their care on research related practice. An example of this is one of the earliest research studies undertaken by Doreen Norton where she developed a pressure sore risk calculator for geriatric patients (Norton et al., 1975). (Since then many other pressure sore risk calculators have been developed.) Throughout the chapters in this book, examples of research related to current nursing practice are cited.

There is also a post basic ENB course on research entitled "An Introduction to the Understanding and Application of Research" (ENB 871). This course is designed to develop the nurse's knowledge and appreciation of research; it is not intended to prepare nurses to carry out research.

Not all research which is undertaken is valid or reliable, but in order to be able to evaluate research reports or make sense of them, the nurse must understand the stages of the research process and the language involved.

The research process and associated "language"

Before looking at the main areas which compose a research report, it is important to examine the different types of research which the reader may come across.

Margaret Ogier (1989) in her most informative and interesting book *Reading Research* describes three main different types of research:

1. Descriptive research.
2. Experimental research.
3. Action research.

Descriptive research

This approach to research describes what it is, i.e., it sets out to establish what is happening in a particular situation by the use of both words and figures. Many of the research studies carried out by nurses use a descriptive approach and often conclude with questions being posed in which further research can be undertaken or based.

Experimental research

This approach to research differs from the above in that the researcher does not just make observations on a natural situation but also sets up a controlled situation in which certain factors or variables are introduced which are held constant. Both situations should be as similar as possible with the only difference being the variable introduced to the experimental group. The researcher can then observe and consider whether the variable introduced alters a given situation or causes change to occur.

An independent variable is the factor which is intentionally manipulated and given to the experimental group and withheld from the control group; for example providing patient education on discharge to patients following a heart attack. Both groups of patients can then be studied to see if by providing the education there was a change in the patient's behaviour and an improved recovery from illness. There are several types of experimental research the design of which is quite complex requiring considerable skills and statistical knowledge. As this chapter is intended as a simple introduction to research the reader is advised to refer to books listed in the further reading list to gain a greater understanding of the various types of experimental research study, and methods of setting them up.

Action research

In this type of research a particular problem or change in a situation is addressed, i.e. the researcher looks at how the problem was solved or observes certain changes being put into practice to see how effective they were. "The action researcher does not attempt to hold anything constant, but observes in a systematic manner how the people in a system cope with a local problem or how they adjust to an imposed change" (Macleod Clark and Hockey, 1989).

Fretwell (1982) studied factors affecting the ward learning environment and the role of the ward sister. Following this, she carried out an action research study which centred on a programme she had developed to assist sisters who experienced difficulties teaching in the ward learning environment (Fretwell, 1985). By implementing this programme she was able to introduce change and observe its effects.

The research process

Having chosen the area or subject to be researched, most researchers follow the stages outlined below for their study.

Introduction

This should include information on why the research has been undertaken and the significance of the problem addressed. The research proposal is stated identifying the reason for the research—be it to solve a problem or support a statement of belief with a scientific basis. The resources for the study are also clearly stated together with the proposed methodology.

Literature search

This gives information about previous research studies undertaken in respect of the chosen subject or problem being addressed. A literature search also enables the researcher to identify methodologies previously adopted. It helps the researcher to delineate the boundaries of the problem more clearly, illustrating its relation to previous research and also showing how the aspect being researched differs from similar studies previously undertaken. It is important that the researcher keeps an accurate record and complete references of papers and studies reviewed in the literature search, and it can be helpful to write a short resume on their strengths and limitations, methods used and relevance to planned research study.

Stating the hypothesis or null hypothesis

Ogier (1989) describes a hypothesis as "A statement based on knowledge or information that has yet to be proved or disproved". A null hypothesis is almost a negative statement or explanation; to suggest that by introducing a variable to a situation, there will be no significant change. Ogier, in her book, offers two good examples to illustrate both a hypothesis and a null hypothesis.

Hypothesis. "The preoperative giving of information about prospective treatment and care, and teaching exercises to be performed postoperatively, will minimise the rise in biochemical indicators of stress" (Boore, 1978).

Null hypothesis. In a study on women following episiotomies, "There would be no significant difference between the healing rates of women who had salt added to the bath water and those who did not" (Sleep, 1988). Not all research studies have a hypothesis or a null hypothesis; instead some pose questions, e.g. Closs et al.'s (1986) study "Factors Affecting Perioperative Body Temperature". The main questions posed in this study were:

1. "What factors influence fall in temperature during surgery?"
2. "Which patients are most at risk of developing a low body temperature?"
3. "Do nurses on the ward monitor the patient's body temperature postoperatively?"

Pilot study

This is a small study undertaken by the researcher prior to the main study. Its purpose is to test the research method and tools to be used so that the researcher can make the necessary alterations prior to starting the main study. The pilot study is usually written up in the methodology of the main study.

Research tools and methodology

These are the methods used to collect information. It also includes information on the population studied or more commonly known as the "sample" to be used. Within the study the researcher should state the reason why the chosen tool is preferred to another. Tools which are normally used include observation, interviews and questionnaires. When using observation of behaviour as a tool, the researcher may or may not be known to the group being studied. If known to the people being observed, the researcher must try not to be seen as a threat and must also try to make her observations objective. Similarly, if the observer is not known to the group, she may well be more objective but people may respond or act differently in her presence.

The researcher may use interviewing as a tool in order to obtain facts, ideas, impressions or opinions from the study subjects. Interviews can be structured or unstructured. When using the structured interview, each interview follows a set pattern whilst the unstructured interview uses more open ended questions. (The results from unstructured interviews are much more difficult to analyse.)

Questionnaires are another tool which the researcher may employ. The questions covered should be significant to the area being studied, and worded carefully to make sure that they are not misinterpreted. In order to test the questionnaire, it is a good idea to try it out on a similar group of people prior to using it in the main study. One of the problems with using questionnaires is that not everyone will return them; to help avoid this, the researcher should enclose a stamped addressed envelope. The number of questionnaires returned is termed the "response rate", i.e. the percentage of those approached who actually participated in the study. Questionnaires tend to be more useful to the researcher when those completing them are allowed to remain anonymous. This avoids people writing the answer they think the researcher wants to hear, rather than an honest response.

When looking at the research tools used, the validity and reliability should always be taken into account. The validity of a research tool refers to its ability to obtain the required information, i.e. that it measures what it is supposed to measure.

The reliability of a tool indicates its accuracy if used in similar circumstances, i.e. does the test produce the same results on a similar group on varying occasions?

Collating the results

It is from the results that the researcher draws her conclusions for further research. The results can be broken down and placed into groups such as percentages, rank order and mean scores. Statistics are used to help collate the results which can then be expressed in a graph or diagram format. Many nurses find this part of research either difficult to do or to interpret if reading a research report. In the further reading list there are recommended books which will give information on how to understand statistics as this text is too short to enter into the subject in greater detail. However, if it is not clear after further reading, help should be sought.

Drawing conclusions and communicating the findings

In this section of the report, the researcher discusses the results of the study in light of the original problem and hypothesis/null hypothesis. The conclusions are stated and the indications for further research discussed.

At this stage the author usually comments upon the findings of the research and discusses their implications for future nursing practice.

The researcher concludes with references and appropriate appendices. The study can then be submitted for publication either in its complete form or as a summarized version for one of the nursing journals.

Ethical aspects of research

When undertaking a research study there are certain factors which the researcher must consider; these offer protection to the subjects involved in the study. The most important factor that the researcher must ensure is that the people involved in the research study suffer no harm as a result of the study or the methods used.

The researcher must also ensure that the people involved in the study, be they patients, nurses or a certain population in the community, are informed of the purpose of the research and that their informed consent to participate in the study is obtained. (The term "informed consent" is clearly explained in Chapter 7.) The researcher also has to adhere to confidentiality, both of the individuals involved in the study, and the information which is collected.

Difficulties may arise for researchers when they are devising questionnaires; particularly if they are trying to obtain information in sensitive areas such as bereavement which may leave the person feeling upset or anxious; careful wording of questions is essential.

When observing care given to patients the researcher cannot stand by and allow unsafe practice to be carried out, for example, administering a nasogastric feed to a patient without first ensuring that the tube is correctly positioned. This could then affect the nurse-patient relationship as well as the research being undertaken.

To assist potential researchers, various ethical committees exist as well as guidelines to assist the researcher meet his/her responsibilities. The purpose of ethical committees is to ensure that the subjects involved in research studies are protected and also to vet the proposed study, to decide whether or not it is necessary. For example, if a particular group of people has been studied for the same purpose on previous occasions, the study may not be either required or acceptable, depending on the methods used. Although medical ethical committees have been established for some time, for the purpose of medical research, it is only in recent years that multidisciplinary committees have been formed, with some committees having a member who is a lay person, so that the views of the public can be represented. *Ethics Related to Research in Nursing* (RCN, 1977) provides the nurse with a summary of the ethical issues related to research.

It is suggested that anyone wishing to undertake a research study for the first time should seek the advice and support of someone who has proven expertise approaching and implementing research.

Application of research findings to practice

Although there are many research studies related to practice, management and education, it appears that nurses do not always use them. Hunt (1984) highlighted four main reasons why nurses do not use research findings:

1. Lack of knowledge.
2. Disbelief.
3. Lack of permission.
4. Lack of incentive.

Nurses often do not have access to professional libraries which house research studies; they tend to rely on what is available in their college library. Access to Nursing Unit libraries within universities or establishments like the Royal College of Nursing may not be possible due to travelling distance or the need for membership. Until recent years, research studies were normally only published in the academic nursing press. However, as previously mentioned, the more popular nursing journals do now publish extracts from research papers.

The ENB syllabus (1982) also contains a research section to be included in the RGN programme. Prior to this the inclusion of an introduction to research, its importance and methods was left to the discretion of Senior Nurse Teachers. Similarly one of the learning outcomes for Project 2000 is the "use of relevant literature and research to inform the practice of nursing" (ENB, 1989). With the inclusion of research studies within the syllabus, nurses should gain knowledge not only on how to read research reports, but also develop skills in relation to evaluating research and its application to practice.

Hunt (1984) suggests that although nurses may know of various research studies, they do not necessarily believe their findings. She also identifies that changing the established practice of years can be very difficult. However, this should not be a reason to ignore research; instead it is helpful to have more than one research report available on the area of practice which one intends to change. Equally important is ensuring that all staff involved in the

Table 5-1. Guidelines for reading research reports

Research Area	Questions to be Asked
Title	Is it understood, concise and informative?
Defining the problem	What is the problem to be investigated? Is the problem clearly defined? Is the hypothesis/null hypothesis clearly stated? Are the limitations of the study stated?
Reviewing the literature	Is the literature recent and is it relevant? Has similar research been previously undertaken? Does the literature suggest any ideas or implications which could be relevant to the proposed study? Does the review of the literature conclude with a brief summary?
Plan for the proposed research	What subjects were selected for the study— people? places? events? Is the sample large enough? Is the sample selected at random or selectively? Is the sample representative? What ethical considerations have been taken into account?
Pilot study	Was one carried out? Were any changes to the study made as a result of the pilot study?
Collection of the data (information)	How were the data collected? What research tools were used? How were the tools tested? Were the tools valid and reliable? Is the reason for using a specific tool stated? If a questionnaire is used was it designed by the researcher? Does the questionnaire miss important issues? Are the questions ambiguous? What was the response rate? Were interviews used in the study? What types of interview were used?
Analysis of the data	Are the results clearly presented? Are the statistics appropriate to the study? Are the tables/graphs understandable? Does the information answer the research questions?
Conclusions	Are the results discussed in terms of the hypothesis/null hypothesis? What conclusions does the researcher reach? Are the implications discussed? Are recommendations for further research suggested? Are the limitations of the study identified? Can the findings of the study be utilized in the readers area of clinical practice?

change process are consulted and involved at all stages. Staff should be encouraged to discuss problems and opinions so that the ward team can feel ownership of the proposed change, as opposed to something which is imposed on them, against their wishes.

Although nurses themselves may want to introduce research findings to their practice, they may not have the support of their senior managers. Nurse managers should be made aware of how research can improve standards of practice and can also be cost effective. It is important that educators provide the support and knowledge which is required at all levels.

The above leads on to Hunt's final point—lack of incentive. If nurses do not have adequate support when wanting to introduce research findings to change established practice, they will lose interest and become complacent, or move on to a more innovative area. If nurses are trying to introduce change in terms of research findings, nurse managers should provide positive feedback and encouragement, showing that they value what the individuals are trying to achieve whilst at the same time supplying recognition for their efforts.

Lelean (1982) states that "There is no easy way forward if we want nursing practice to be based upon firm scientific foundations. Each problem must be faced as a challenge for the future". She identifies that utilization of research findings should involve nurse practitioners, managers and educators examining the problems involved and then planning proposed changes together in order to move forward, thus assisting nursing to become a research based profession.

Guidelines for reading research reports

Although this chapter is intended as a brief introduction to research in nursing and the concepts involved, it is perhaps useful to conclude it with some guidelines to reading research reports in order for the reader to be able to evaluate them (Table 5-1). When reading research reports it is useful to have a series of questions in mind, related to the major areas of the report. This helps the reader to focus on the most important points in order to evaluate the study and its implications for practice. It is hoped that this chapter has given the reader an insight into research and highlighted its importance in relation to nursing and nursing practice.

For more in-depth information, it is suggested that the reader examines the books and articles quoted in the references and the further reading list.

References

Austin, L. (1988) The salt bath myth. *Nursing Times*, **84**(9), 79–83.

Boore, J.R.P. (1978) *Prescription for Recovery*, RCN Research Series, RCN, London.

Briggs, A. (1972) *Report of the Committee of Nursing*, HMSO, London.

Carter, G. (1954) University training for leadership and its relationship to the nursing profession. *Nursing Mirror*, **98**(21), 1391.

Closs, S.J., Macdonald, I.A. and Hawthorn, P.J. (1986) Factors affecting perioperative body temperature. *Journal of Advance Nursing*, **11**, 739–44.

Dunn, B. (1991) Who should be doing the research in nursing? *Professional Nurse*, **6**(4), 190–6.

ENB (1982) *Syllabus of Training, Professional Register*, (Part 3), ENB, London.

ENB (1989) *Project 2000—A New Preparation for Practice*, Working Document, ENB, London.

Fretwell, J.E. (1982) *Ward Teaching and Learning: Sister and the Learning Environment*, RCN Research Series, RCN, London.

Fretwell, J.E. (1985) *Freedom to Change, the Creation of a Ward Learning Environment*, RCN Research Series, RCN, London.

Hayward, J. (1975) *Information: A Prescription Against Pain*, RCN Research Series, RCN, London.

Hockey L. (1984) The nature and purpose of research, in *The Research Process in Nursing*, (ed. D.F.S. Cormack), Blackwell Scientific Publications, Oxford.

Hockey, L. (1986) Cited in Dunn, B. (1991) Who should be doing the research in nursing? *Professional Nurse*, **6**(4), 190–6.

Hunt, J. (1984) Why don't we use these findings? *Nursing Mirror*, **158**(8), 29.

Lelean, S.R. (1982) The implementations of research findings into nursing practice. *International Journal of Nursing Studies*, **19**(4), 223–30.

Macleod Clark, J. and Hockey, L. (1989) *Further Research for Nursing*, Education for Care Series, Scutari Press, London.

Norton, D., McLaren, R. and Exton-Smith, A.N. (1975) *An Investigation of Geriatric Nursing Problems in Hospital*, Churchill Livingstone, Edinburgh.

Ogier, M. (1989) *Reading Research*, Scutari Press, London.

RCN (1977) *Ethics Related to Research in Nursing*, RCN, London.

Sleep, J. (1988) Reported in Advances in midwifery research. *Senior Nurse*, **8**(1), 5.

Further reading

Behi, R. (1990) Types of research. *Nursing* **4**(3), 23–5.

Buckeldee, J. (1990) Carers concern. *Nursing Times* **6**(26), 58–9.

Clark, E. (1988) Research and common sense. *The Professional Nurse*, **3**(9), 344–7.

Hockey, L. (1986) *Nursing Research, Mistakes and Misconceptions*, Churchill Livingstone, Edinburgh.

Hunt, M. (1986) The process of translating research findings into nursing practice. *Journal of Advanced Nursing*, **12**, 101–10.

Kratz, C.R. (1982). Research, how can we challenge nursing practice? *Nursing Times*, **78**(32), 128.

Leach, M. (1990) Philosophical choices. *Nursing*, **4**(3), 16–18.

Macleod Clark, J. and Hockey, L. (1989) *Research for Nursing, A Guide for the Enquiring Nurse*, John Wiley, Chichester.

McSweeny, P. (1990) How to conduct a literature search. *Nursing*, **4**(3), 19–22.

Morle, K. (1990) We need more research. *Nursing*, **4**(3), 13–14.

Smith, J. (1986) The end of the beginning. *Senior Nurse*, **5**(1), 14–15.

Thomson, H. (1988) How to do research. *Nursing Standard*, **3**(9), 39.

Unsworth, D. (1990) In service to meet your research needs. The Index of Nursing Research Information Service. *Professional Nurse*, **6**(4), 213–16.

Webb, C. (1990) Partners in research. *Nursing Times*, **86**(32), 40–4.

Zelauskas, B.A., Howes, D.G., Christmyer, C.S. and Dennis K.E. (1988) Bridging the gap: theory to practice—Part II, research applications. *Nursing Management*, **19**(9), 50–2.

6

Primary nursing

Learning objectives

When the content of this chapter has been mastered, the learner should be able to:

Discuss methods of organizing nursing care.
State what is meant by primary nursing.
Discuss the roles of the primary nurse and associate nurse.
List the advantages of primary nursing.

Glossary

Accountability To be answerable for one's actions.
Associate nurse A nurse who is assigned to the primary nurse and assists with the care of her patients, assuming responsibility for those patients in the absence of the designated primary nurse.
Authority Power or right to make and implement decisions related to nursing care.
Autonomy Having the authority and being able to act upon it.
Comprehensiveness One nurse implementing all nursing care for a specific patient and family during a designated period of time.
Coordination The smooth flow of nursing care from one shift to the next.
Primary nurse An RGN who is accountable for the care planned and given to a patient from the time of admission through to discharge.
Responsibility Allocation and acceptance of making decisions related to the nursing care which is required.
Ritualistic Prescribed order for performance.

What is primary nursing?

Primary nursing is a style of organizing care whereby one nurse is responsible for the delivery of continuous coordinated care for a patient from the time of his admission through to discharge.

Primary nursing was first described by Manthey (1970, 1973) who introduced it to the University of Minnesota Hospital in the USA in the late 1960s.

Most of the early writings on primary nursing have stemmed from the USA but its successful development in other countries such as Australia, Japan and Europe is now being reported in nursing journals.

The essential elements which characterize primary nursing have been described by Wright (1987) as:
Accountability: to be answerable for one's actions.

Autonomy: having the authority and being able to act upon it—making decisions in relation to care.

Coordination: the smooth flow of nursing care from one shift to the next.

Comprehensiveness: each care giver gives all the nursing care required during the course of a shift, sometimes called "total patient care".

In recent years primary nursing has continued to gain popularity within the UK and appears to be the way in which nurses wish to organize care in the future. In order to understand why this is the case, it is important to consider the methods of organizing patient care which have gone before.

Task allocation

This method of organizing care was practised in the UK up until the mid 1970s. Lee (1979) thought of task allocation as being based on an industrial model of care, i.e. breaking down care into groups of tasks carried out by nurses according to their skill or status (e.g. "the back round" and "the observations round"). It appears that task allocation evolved in response to certain factors at the start of this century:

1. Increased hospital admissions.
2. An increase in medical technology and sophistication.
3. A higher patient turnover.

This method of organizing care was often accompanied by ritualistic habits of delivering care based on tradition rather than scientific research, e.g. the use of mercurachrome, honey or egg white and oxygen on pressure sores, depending on what the preference of the ward sister was. To assist with the ritualistic practice ward diaries, bowel books and bath books were readily available!

With task allocation came depersonalization of the patient; nurses were spending more time on the "tasks" to be completed rather than the individual needs of the patients. Often the tasks which related specifically to direct or total patient care were carried out by unskilled people such as student nurses or auxiliaries leaving the qualified staff free to undertake the supposedly more important tasks of doctors' rounds or medicine rounds.

It is clear that task allocation did little to develop the nurse-patient relationship and instead of individualizing care it fragmented it causing lack of continuity of care.

Numerous reports and studies have illustrated dissatisfaction of both nurses and patients using task allocation (Orton, 1981; Menzies, 1960). Menzies (1960) illustrated in her research that task allocation was a means of blocking nurses' communication with patients and thus reducing the nurses' stress and anxiety levels. Menzies felt that nurses found it stressful to form a rapport with sick people. This is not surprising in that nurse training did little to develop good communication skills and most nurses learnt by trial and error.

McLeod Clark's (1983) research supports the theory of nurses being poor communicators. She stated that the nurse-patient interaction was limited in both quantity and quality with nurses demonstrating minimal or no skills related to promoting good communication, but instead employing frequent blocking mechanisms.

However, nursing started to look towards a more meaningful approach to care. Concepts of patient centred care rather than task centred care were drifting across the Atlantic—the nursing process had landed in the UK.

Team nursing

The nursing process focused on the individual patient's needs and care was supposed to be delivered using a problem solving approach. Nurse training was also changing with nursing curriculums incorporating individual care and nursing models.

Team nursing was developed to allow patients to receive the optimal level of care encompassing the individual skills of the nurses within the team.

The team leader was usually a registered nurse with the relevant knowledge base of the patients' conditions which enabled her to plan and implement the care required alongside the other team members. The team leader was intended to act as a resource person and one who would supervise and support less experienced members of the team; e.g. student nurses.

This method of organizing care did provide some improvement on task allocation in that if the teams were constant there was improved continuity; at least patients had the opportunity to establish an improved rapport with the team nurses. It also provided nurses with the opportunity to develop leadership and management qualities, i.e. make decisions related to patient care rather than the ward sister having total control over the management of patient care.

One of the major disadvantages of team nursing

was highlighted by Pearson (1988) who stated that often within the team, task allocation was practised. He supports this argument with reference to work undertaken by Marram (1970) who stated "there was an over emphasis on supervision and task completion leading to a collapse of the concepts behind team nursing".

Patient allocation

This style of organizing care is one of the most popular, and consists of one nurse taking responsibility for a group of patients during the course of one single shift. This means she has to assess each patient's individual needs and then plan, implement and evaluate the care required. This is a good method of organizing care which promotes continuity and allows the nurse "to establish a positive nurse patient relationship", provided that the same nurse is allocated to the same group of patients on a day to day basis.

Although the allocation of staff to patient groups is organized by the ward sister who takes into account patient dependency levels and skill mix, care of patients in some instances is still being planned and implemented by untrained nurses. Lack of continuity using this method does occur in that it is unusual for the same nurse to care for the patient throughout his stay in hospital; instead, care is planned and implemented by several different nurses.

However, patient allocation has made the accountability of individual nurses more explicit in that the nurse cares for the patient in a more holistic manner—meeting his total needs rather than just undertaking a particular task, thus having to be answerable for the care which she gives.

Primary nursing

However, although patient allocation has improved the nurse-patient relationship, it still does not allow the nurse to develop as an autonomous practitioner working in partnership with the patient.

As stated earlier, the primary nurse plans and coordinates the patient's care throughout his hospital stay—the patient identifies his nurse in the same way as he might his doctor: the "my nurse", "my doctor" concept. In the absence of the primary nurse, an associate nurse assumes the care of her patients.

Primary nursing within the UK started to be used as an alternative method of organizing care in the early 1980s. Many different hospitals are now trying to adopt it and there are increasingly more reports and articles in the nursing journals which relate to its introduction in varying clinical settings.

The role of the primary nurse

The role of the primary nurse is to assess, plan, implement and evaluate nursing care for a named group of patients from the time of admission through to their discharge. To "prescribe" nursing care effectively, the primary nurse must possess the appropriate knowledge related to research and her clinical speciality. This is especially important in relation to the autonomy and accountability of the primary nurse; both to her patients and as a professional person.

The primary nurse is accountable to her patient and his family for the care that she implements and to her professional peers for maintaining standards of care within the area and speciality in which she works. Naturally she is also accountable to the professional code of practice and the law, and must adhere to and practise within its boundaries.

Although the primary nurse is accountable for the nursing care of her patient or patients over a 24 hour period, this does not mean that she is on continuous call 24 hours a day. In her absence the care of the patient is assumed by an associate nurse who cares for the patient in accordance with the care plan which has been completed by the primary nurse.

When considering autonomy and primary nursing it means that the nurse is able to make decisions related to nursing care and act upon them. This does not mean that the nurse fails to take any notice of other health professional decisions related to patient care, e.g. ignoring the doctors' orders, or not listening to the physiotherapist's opinion. This degree of autonomy promotes interdependence and cooperation not only among nurses working together but also with other health professionals.

The primary nurse is responsible for ensuring that the patient's care is coordinated. This means making sure that care is consistent and implemented smoothly. For this to happen, each person involved with the patient needs to know and understand his nursing requirements. This is especially important when associate nurses are caring for the patient in the absence of the primary nurse, therefore, accurate, up to date, clear and concise care plans are essential as well as good verbal communication between nursing staff.

The comprehensiveness of primary nursing can be seen in that although there may be three nurses caring for the patient in a 24 hour period, one will be the primary nurse who makes the decisions related to patient care. Each nurse then performs all the necessary nursing for her patient during a shift—this precludes any assignment of "tasks" or as Wright (1987) states, this is sometimes called "total patient care".

To be effective as a primary nurse, the nurse must possess a good knowledge base in relation to her clinical speciality and be well versed in relevant research. Some nurses, if inadequately prepared, may feel frustrated at not being able to meet the expectations of a primary nurse and perhaps not feel able to accept the aspects of accountability and autonomy encompassed within the role. It is vital that nurses are well prepared and supported when adjusting to the role of a primary nurse. It may not always be appropriate for a nurse who has just qualified to act as a primary nurse until she adjusts to her role as an RGN and gains confidence; in the meantime she may choose to act as an associate nurse.

There are two schools of thought which relate to enrolled nurses acting as primary nurses: those who say that the training and expected competencies of enrolled nurses do not allow for them to be truly accountable and autonomous practitioners, whilst others believe that if enrolled nurses have undertaken an ENB post basic course in relation to their clinical speciality then they will have acquired the necessary knowledge to be able to make decisions related to patient care. This second school of thought also feels that many enrolled nurses acquire patient management skills through experience. The criteria for who acts as a primary nurse and who does not vary from hospital to hospital but on the whole it is generally accepted that only RGNs should act as primary nurses and enrolled nurses as associate nurses.

The amount of patients allocated to a primary nurse is related to patient dependency levels. Watson (1978) recommends the following:

Two patients per primary nurse in a clinical care unit, e.g. intensive care.
Five patients per primary nurse in an acute ward.
Seven patients per primary nurse in a long term stay ward.

Alongside the above, Watson recommends that there should be 2.5 associate nurses per primary nurse.

To assist primary and associate nurses, support workers or health care assistants can also be added to the skill mix of a ward. These people work under the guidance and supervision of the trained nurses to assist with patient care.

Primary nursing and night duty

Where primary nursing is practised, the role of the night nurse must be considered. Normal staffing levels on night duty are less than those of day duty, this is because the majority of patient care required or investigations, etc. for the patient usually occur during the day. It is also generally accepted that the nurses on day duty have more contact with other members of the multidisciplinary team. For these reasons it makes it very difficult for the night nurse to act as a primary nurse planning the patient's care from the time of admission through to discharge. It seems more practical to have night nurses acting as associate nurses linked to one or more primary nurses on day duty. This can lead to increased satisfaction amongst night nurses in that they are allowed the opportunity to get to know their group of patients quite well, and they can report directly on their patients' progress to the appropriate primary nurse in the morning.

The role of the associate nurse

The associate nurse can be assigned to one or more primary nurses to assist with the care of patients. It is important that they are valued in their own right and not treated as "second class citizens". Instead, they must be made to feel part of the team and involved with discussions and decisions related to patient care. In clinical areas which promote an environment that values individual nurses, associate nurses can often be seen to act as speciality resource people; for instance, in areas related to wound care and pain control.

Associate nurses can be senior students, enrolled nurses, registered nurses or primary nurses who assume the role in the absence of a colleague. Burns (1988) suggests that "experience of the associate nurse role is almost a pre-requisite to becoming a primary nurse".

By assigning associate nurses to individual primary nurses, continuity of care for both the patient and

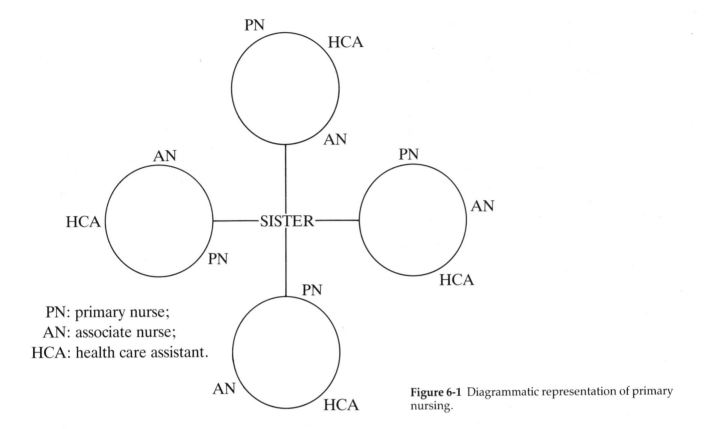

PN: primary nurse;
AN: associate nurse;
HCA: health care assistant.

Figure 6-1 Diagrammatic representation of primary nursing.

nurse can be maintained. This means that the associate nurse instead of caring for a different group of patients each day is able to care for the same group whenever she is on duty. Where assignment to a primary nurse is utilized, communication between the associate nurse and primary nurse is more effective and easier as they both have close contact with the same group of patients.

Associate nurses are accountable for their own practice, although the level of decision making expected of them is dependent on their qualifications and experience.

The role of the ward sister

With the introduction of primary nursing the role of the ward sister changes. Traditionally the ward sister used to plan the duty rotas, be able to answer all the doctors' questions about their patients, make decisions related to patient care and generally keep the ward running smoothly! Primary nursing means that many of these responsibilities are assumed by the primary nurse. This allows the sister to maintain her role as ward manager and coordinator, but the focus of her role is as a clinical leader and resource person, developing her educational, managerial and research input. The ward sister in some instances also acts as a primary nurse utilizing her clinical skills. As the clinical leader the sister is able to develop and support her staff. Whilst being sensitive to their needs and offering advice without undermining them, the ward sister can make her staff feel valued as individuals, working within the ward nursing team.

Changing to primary nursing

Introducing primary nursing may mean radical alterations in working patterns; therefore it is imperative that the change is managed appropriately.

Walsh (1989) identifies the need to consult all staff at different grades who will be involved in the change to primary nursing. Some nurses may not feel happy to undertake the role of a primary nurse in relation to the underlying principles it encompasses. It is vital that a comprehensive education programme is provided for all nurses concerned. Walsh recommends a preparation period of six months for staff wishing to implement primary nursing in their area.

Communication of the proposed changes should also extend to other members of the multidisciplinary team who are involved with the care and treatment of patients, so that they can liaise with the appropriate nurse responsible for individual patient care.

Off duty rotas may also need to be altered to ensure that each patient has at least one associate nurse on per single shift. This may result in the ward sister not being able to implement primary nursing in her ward area until she has the right skill mix within her team.

As discussed above, the role of the ward sister also changes; she has to abandon some of her traditional status and become more of a coordinator and clinical expert.

The above has only alluded to some of the main points concerned with changing to primary nursing. Perhaps the most important factors to remember are to ensure that all staff involved with the change move at the same pace, and that there is mutual support for each nurse provided from within the team. By doing this and proceeding carefully, change to primary nursing should be effective, with problems being overcome by the team as they are encountered.

Advantages of primary nursing

Although there has been little research done into how successful primary nursing is, in some areas quality assurance studies have been carried out before and after the introduction of primary nursing.

Binnie (1987) describes how the Oxfordshire Health Authority utilized Qualpacs, Phaneuf's nursing audit, to look at the quality of care. A study was carried out in 12 wards prior to the introduction of primary nursing, and then subsequently three months following its introduction. Although it was a relatively short time between the two studies there was a consistent improvement in the areas measured; this suggested that the quality of care would continue to improve as their project of introducing primary nursing progressively developed.

Although there is a need for more research into the effectiveness and advantages of primary nursing, quality assurance studies in different areas have shown that it improves the quality of patient care. Also nurses who are employed in primary nurse settings acknowledge an improved satisfaction with their role and a commitment to standards of care

and professional development. Steve Wright (1987) speaking at a primary nursing conference outlined the advantages of using primary nursing, as reported by nurses working in the Nursing Development Unit at Tameside General Hospital. These advantages are:

Increased nurse satisfaction.
Increased patient satisfaction.
The nurse's role is clearly defined.
Increased contact with patient and his family.
Improved learning environment for students.
The nurse is able to develop her role as a teacher.
Increased continuity of care.
Improved quality of care—knowledge base/
  research.
More effective use of resources.
Increased motivation and retention of staff.
Improved communication—patient problems
  solved more quickly.
Fewer patient complaints.

Primary nursing in different settings

Primary nursing is now being utilized in many different settings which are frequently reported in the nursing press. Implementing primary nursing in paediatric units has proved to be very successful, particularly where families are assuming more responsibility for their child's care whilst in hospital. This allows the nurse to develop a trusting and close relationship both with the family and the child. This proves beneficial in preparing children for surgery and allowing them with their parents to be active in their care. The role of the RSCN and her skills and knowledge can be employed to the maximum benefit. The value of primary nursing in paediatric care has been discussed by Fradd (1988).

Primary nursing is also an appropriate choice in psychiatric units where the importance of a one to one relationship based on mutual trust and respect is essential to meeting the needs of patients. This also helps to move away from the concept of labelling some patients "demanding" or "difficult" as shown by Stockwell's (1976) research. This point is highlighted by Gibbs (1988) who discusses primary nursing in psychiatric units. He stated that patients who were often labelled "demanding" found it helpful to have a designated nurse to approach who was more likely to deal with the factors motivating the demanding behaviour rather than treat the patient as unpopular. In this field of nursing where a patient's progress is dependent on good communication skills, the formation of a sound nurse/patient partnership through the principles underlying primary nursing can only endeavour to improve standards and quality of care.

The area of nursing where primary nursing continues to grow is care of the elderly. Many units now utilize primary nursing finding it to give much more satisfaction to both patients and nurses. The patients often have a photograph of their primary nurse and her name at the head of the bed. This enables patients, visitors and relatives to identify the primary nurse as well as other members of the multidisciplinary team. Practising primary nursing in care of the elderly allows for variety in the patient's day as care no longer becomes routine. It has been demonstrated in rehabilitation units, otherwise known as nursing development units, where primary nursing is used that patients progress more quickly and cope better when they return to the community.

Within this chapter the principles and benefits of primary nursing have been outlined in an attempt to show how it enhances care and the nurse-patient relationship in any environment and is establishing itself as the focus of nursing in the future.

References

Binnie, A. (1987) Primary nursing—structural changes. *Nursing Times*, **83**(39), 36–7.

Burns, S. (1988) The role of the associate nurse. *The Professional Nurse*, October, 18–20.

Fradd, E. (1988) Primary nursing—achieving new roles. *Nursing Times*, **84**(50), 39–41.

Gibbs, A. (1988) Primary nursing—an individual approach to patient allocation. *The Professional Nurse*, August, 443–6.

Lee, M.E. (1979) Towards better care—primary nursing. Occasional paper. *Nursing Times*, **75**(33), 133–5.

MacLeod Clark, J. (1983) An analysis of nurse patient conversations on surgical wards, in *Nursing Research. Ten Studies in Patient Care* (ed. J.C. Wilson Barnett), John Wiley, Chichester.

Manthey, M. (1970) Primary nursing—a return to the concept of 'my nurse' and 'my patient'. *Nursing Forum*, **9**(1), 65–83.

Manthey, M. (1973) Primary nursing is alive and well in the hospital. *American Journal of Nursing*, **73**(1), 83–7.

Marram, G.D. (1970) Incorporating supervised supervision in the graduate curriculum. *Nursing Outlook*, **18**(1), 46–7.

Menzies, I.E. (1960) Nurses under stress—a social system functioning as a defence against anxiety. *International Nursing Review*, **7**(6), 9–16.

Orton, H. (1981) *The Ward Learning Climate and Student Nurse Response*, Scutari, London.

Pearson, A. (1988) The role of the associate nurse. *Professional Nurse*, October, 18–20.

Pearson, A. (1988), *Primary Nursing*, Croom Helm, Kent.

Stockwell, F. (1976) *The Unpopular Patient*, Scutari, London.

Walsh, M. (1989) An introduction to primary nursing. *Nursing*, **3**(44), 25–7.

Watson, J. (1978) Patient evaluation of primary nursing project. *Australian Nurses' Journal*, **8**(5), 30–3.

Wright, S. (1987) Patient centred practice. *Nursing Times*, **83**(38), 24–7.

Futher reading

Biley, F. (1989) Who are you accountable to? *Nursing*, **3**(4), 30–45.

Bowers, L. (1989) The significance of primary nursing. *Journal of Advanced Nursing*, **14**, 13–19.

Campen, Y. (1988) Breaking new ground. *Nursing Times*, **84**, 38–40.

Grantham, G. (1988) Primary nursing; it really works. *Nursing Standard*, 1 October, 30–1.

Hunt, J. (1988) Primary nursing—the next challenge. *Nursing Times*, **84**(49), 36–8.

Lathean, J. (1988) Viable reality or pipe dream. *Nursing Times*, **84**(49), 39–40.

MacGuire, J. (1988) I'm yours nurse. *Nursing Times*, **84**(30), 32–6.

Malby, R. (1988) All you need is thought. *Nursing Times*, **84**(51), 47–8.

McMahon, R. (1989) One to one. *Nursing Times*, **85**(2), 39–40.

Remington, J. (1989) Night rites. *Nursing Times*, **85**(1), 30–1.

Singleton, P. and Gamlin, R. (1989) A primary change over. *Nursing Times*, **85**(4), 39–41.

Wills, G. (1988) Getting to know you. *Nursing Standard*, **3**(9), 32.

7

Legal implications of nursing

Learning objectives

When the content of this chapter has been mastered, the learner should be able to:

Describe the different types of law that affect the nurse.

Outline the effects of nursing legislation and the legal status of the Code of Professional Conduct.

Identify the main components of the law on negligence and its application to the nurse in carrying out her responsibilities.

Explore how the law safeguards the rights of patients.

Outline the legislation relating to drugs.

Describe how the law affects the nurse as student and employee.

Glossary

Assault Threat of violence against the person.

Battery Carrying out of violence against the person.

Bill Draft Act presented to Parliament.

Case law Judge-made law created by referring to previous similar cases.

Civil wrong A wrong perpetrated by one individual on another.

Common law Nonstatute law.

Consent Legal defence for trespass.

Contract Legal agreement.

Crime Offence committed against the state, punishable by the state.

Defamation To make public untrue and derogatory statements about an individual.

Defence A legal excuse for acting illegally.

Green Paper Consultative document on suggested legislation.

Judge Experienced legal person hearing cases in higher courts.

Libel Defamation in written form.

Negligence Act of causing harm to person to whom a duty is owed.

Precedents Previous cases that influence the interpretation of the law.

Statute Act of Parliament.

Statutory instruments, rules or orders System of delegated legislation.

Tort A civil wrong.

Trespass Invasion of personal territory.

Vicarious liability Legal responsibility of the employer for its employee's tort.

White Paper Document containing detailed proposals of suggested legislation.

Introduction

Both law and nursing are complex subjects to study, covering such a wide range of diverse material. One approach to the study of law is to see how it is made and from there to develop a framework for the application of law to nursing.

How law is made

Statute law. A major source of law is through Acts of Parliament. The legislative process can be complicated and lengthy (see Figure 7-1) and is often initiated by the publication of a Green Paper for discussion, followed by a White Paper containing more details of the Bill that will then be presented to Parliament. A Bill then goes through certain stages in Parliament and finally becomes an Act on receiving the Royal Assent. A Member of Parliament may on certain occasions present a Private Member's Bill as opposed to a Government Bill, but its chances of getting through Parliament are less likely than for a Government Bill. Because Parliamentary time is so limited, a number of statutes (Acts) enable certain named authorities to formulate Statutory Instruments, Rules or Orders which, when approved by the appropriate Secretary of State, become law through delegated legislation. For example, under the Nurses, Midwives and Health Visitors Act 1979, the UK Central Council can make various rules that control the nursing profession.

Reading an Act of Parliament may look daunting but if certain simple rules are followed the task becomes easier. Part of the Nurses, Midwives and Health Visitors Act 1979 is shown in Table 7-1.

Table 7-1. Extract from the Nurses, Midwives and Health Visitors Act 1979

Extract	Notes
Nurses, Midwives and Health Visitors Act 1979	This is the short title of the Act, together with its year of publication.
1979 Chapter 36	Each Act has an official citation and is given its own Chapter number for that particular year.
An Act to establish a Central Council for Nursing, Midwifery and Health Visiting, and National Boards for the four parts of the United Kingdom; to make new provision with respect to the education, training, regulation and discipline of nurses, midwives and health visitors and the maintenance of a single professional register; to amend an Act relating to the Central Council for Education and Training in Social Work; and for purposes connected with those matters.	This is the long title of the Act and gives some indication of the purpose behind the Act. However, it can be misleading and the law is that which is included in the main body of the Act.
(4th April 1979)	The Royal Assent was given on this date and the Bill became an Act. A statute becomes law on this day unless the Act says otherwise (see note at foot of column).
Be it enacted by the Queen's most Excellent Majesty, by and with the advice and consent of the Lords Spiritual and Temporal, and Commons, in this present Parliament assembled, and by the authority of the same, as follows:	This is the standard form of words to show that the Bill has been properly passed.

Continued

Table 7-1. *Continued*

Extract		Notes
The Central Council 1. (1) There shall be a corporate body known as the United Kingdom Central Council for Nursing, Midwifery and Health Visiting. (2) The council shall consist of the number of members, being not more than 45, prescribed by the Secretary of State by order. (3) Of the members of the Council— (a) the majority shall be members of the National Boards established by Section 5 below and be nominated by the Boards (in equal numbers) in accordance with Part 1 of Schedule 1 to this Act and (b) the other members shall be persons appointed by the Secretary of State.	Constitution of Central Council	The main body of the Act is broken up into sections and a marginal note by each section will give a short explanation of that section, thus making it easier for the reader to find his way through the Act. Each section may be further subdivided into subsections. S.1(1) is the quick way of referring to Section 1 subsection 1. Some Acts have additional schedules at the end which may contain further detailed provisions not found in the main body of the Act.
23.—(1) In this Act— "by order" means by order in a statutory instrument "the Central Council" and "the Council" mean the body established by Section 1(1).	Interpretation and summary	Within the Act will be sections that define and interpret words used.
24.—(1) This Act may be cited as the Nurses, Midwives and Health Visitors Act 1979.		The final section of an Act will repeat its short title.
(2) This Act, except Section 21(2) and this section (which shall come into force on the passing of this Act) shall come into force on such day as the Secretary of State may by order appoint: and different days may be appointed for different provisions of this Act.		The majority of this Act was not to come into force until the Minister authorized a commencement date.

Case law. Another important source of law is case law. This has developed as judges make decisions on the interpretation of nonstatute or common law within the court setting. Even with statute law it is often left to the courts to play a key role through the hearing of cases in clarifying such law. This case law is judge-made law. In order to make the law consistent, judges have to refer back to previous decisions involving similar cases, but it is only the decisions made in certain courts that are deemed to have the necessary authority to create legal precedents which are then binding on lower courts. Figure 7-2 shows the structure of the civil courts in England and Wales and which courts can make decisions that are binding on later cases. The nurse is more often involved in civil rather than criminal cases for a number of reasons. She may be the defendant being sued for damages or she may be called as a witness either of factual information or to give an expert opinion of professional practice.

The following example shows how judicial precedent and the hierarchy of the courts work in practice.

Mrs Gillick questioned the lawfulness of a DHSS circular which stated that in certain circumstances a doctor could lawfully prescribe contraception for a girl under 16 without the consent of the parents. The Area Health Authority (AHA) to whom she wrote responded by upholding this circular. Mrs Gillick then took the AHA and the DHSS to court that the notice was unlawful. The case was first heard in the High Court, where she failed. She then took it to the Court of Appeal, where she won. But the AHA and DHSS then took it to the House of Lords who

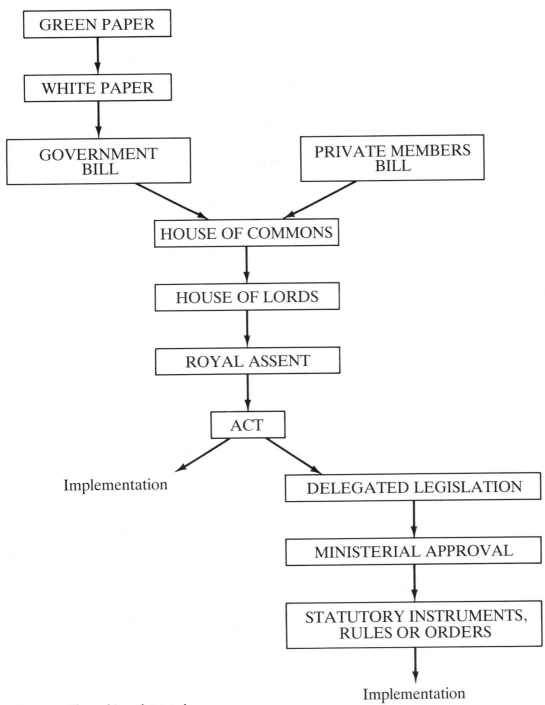

Figure 7-1 The making of statute law.

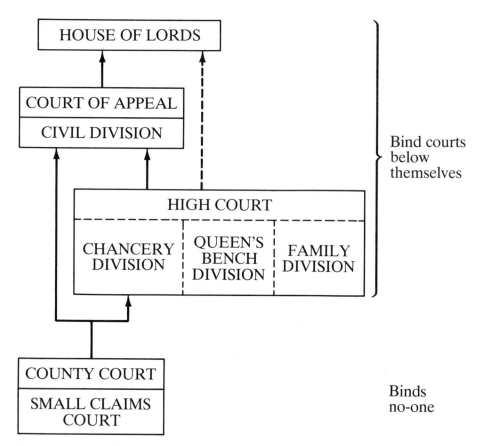

N.B. Both the court system and the law on precedents are different in Scotland.

Figure 7-2 Legal precedents and the civil courts in England and Wales.

decided against Mrs Gillick. As this is the highest court, that decision is binding on all other courts for future similar cases (Gillick v. West Norfolk and Wisbech AHA and the DHSS 1985).

EEC law. The European Economic Community also has a legal effect on the nursing profession. Since 1979, general nurse training and since 1983, midwifery training, have had to abide by EEC directives. These have included the provision of certain experiences as well as controlling the length of time spent on each speciality. To date, psychiatric and paediatric trainings have not yet been brought under the same umbrella.

In addition, the Single European Act which came into existence in 1987 and will be fully operational in 1992, has already had an influence on employment legislation. From 1992 it will also affect health and safety at work as well as standards of medical equipment and pharmaceuticals.

A UK subject dissatisfied with a decision in the UK can petition the European Commission of Human Rights. Such disputes may then ultimately be heard by the Court of Human Rights at Strasbourg.

Changes in the law

For the nurse to keep herself up to date as to what changes are occurring in the law, it is a good idea to scan the news items in the nursing journals on a regular basis. Lengthier commentaries are found in the *Times*, *Independent* and *Guardian* newspapers. Local public libraries and nursing libraries should both have small sections on legal issues, while a

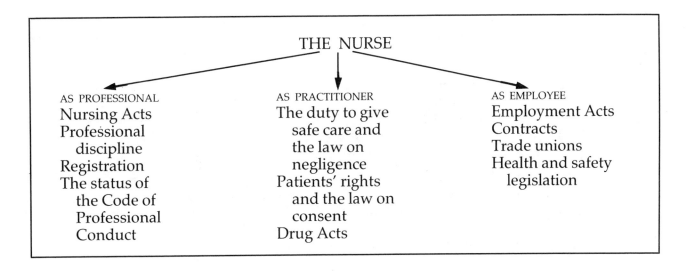

THE NURSE

AS PROFESSIONAL
Nursing Acts
Professional
    discipline
Registration
The status of
    the Code of
    Professional
    Conduct

AS PRACTITIONER
The duty to give
    safe care and
    the law on
    negligence
Patients' rights
    and the law on
    consent
Drug Acts

AS EMPLOYEE
Employment Acts
Contracts
Trade unions
Health and safety
    legislation

Figure 7-3 The application of law to nursing.

college library with a law department will of course have extensive reference material.

A framework for the application of law to nursing

In carrying out her work, a nurse fulfils a number of roles, for example professional, practitioner and employee. Each of these roles carries with it certain expectations and these in turn have legal significance. Figure 7-3 shows how the law may be linked to these roles.

In addition, the nurse may be a student and her inexperience and her need to be assessed also carry legal implications.

Unfortunately, because the law applicable to these various roles can be very different, there are times when conflicts can arise. For example, the nurse may be of the opinion that in order to act as a professional within the Code of Professional Conduct she must make decisions that conflict with her role as an employee. There may also be times when her own moral feelings (for example, regarding abortion) are at odds with her legal duties. Where such discrepancies seemingly arise, it is important that the nurse has a sound legal knowledge on which to base her decisions in order not to place herself on the wrong side of the law (and to justify the actions she takes).

The nurse as professional

The Nurses, Midwives and Health Visitors Act 1979 is the statute that sets up the legal framework in which the nurse operates. The United Kingdom Central Council (UKCC) and National Boards brought into being by this Act have a number of important functions.

The functions of the UKCC

1. To establish and improve standards of training and professional conduct for nurses, midwives and health visitors. A recent major development has been the setting up of Project 2000 trainings throughout the country. Government approval was given for this through the process of delegated legislation.
2. To determine the rules for registration and maintain the single professional register. Registration confers on the nurse the right to practise and it is illegal for a person to claim employment as a nurse if she is not on the register. There are 15 parts to the register as follows:
   Part 1   First level nurses trained in general nursing.
   Part 2   Second level nurses trained in general nursing (England and Wales).

Part 3   First level nurses trained in the nursing of persons suffering from mental illness.

Part 4   Second level nurses trained in the nursing of persons suffering from mental illness (England and Wales).

Part 5   First level nurses trained in the nursing of persons suffering from mental handicap.

Part 6   Second level nurses trained in the nursing of persons suffering from mental handicap (England and Wales).

Part 7   Second level nurses (Scotland and Northern Ireland).

Part 8   Persons trained in the nursing of sick children.

Part 9   Nurses trained in the nursing of persons suffering from fever.

Part 10   Midwives.

Part 11   Health visitors.

Part 12   Nurses qualified following a course of preparation in adult nursing.

Part 13   Nurses qualified following a course of preparation in mental health nursing.

Part 14   Nurses qualified following a course of preparation in mental handicap nursing.

Part 15   Nurses qualified following a course of preparation in children's nursing.

3. To provide guidance to the profession on standards of professional conduct. The UKCC has carried out this function by publishing a Code of Professional Conduct and some associated additional leaflets. However, the nurse should be aware this Code is published for the "guidance and advice" of the nurse and is *not* part of the law controlling nursing practice. It is reproduced in Figure 7-4. Although the Code

---

Each registered nurse, midwife and health visitor shall act, at all times, in such a manner as to justify public trust and confidence, to uphold and enhance the good standing and reputation of the profession, to serve the interests of society, and above all to safeguard the interests of individual patients and clients.

Each registered nurse, midwife and health visitor is accountable for his or her practice, and, in the exercise of professional accountability, shall:

1. Act always in such a way as to promote and safeguard the well being and interests of patients/clients.

2. Ensure that no action or omission on his/her part or within his/her sphere of influence is detrimental to the condition or safety of patients/ clients.

3. Take every reasonable opportunity to maintain and improve professional knowledge and competence.

4. Acknowledge any limitations of competence and refuse in such cases to accept delegated functions without first having received instruction in regard to those functions and having been assessed as competent.

5. Work in a collaborative and co-operative manner with other health care professionals and recognize and respect their particular contributions within the health care team.

6. Take account of the customs, values and spiritual beliefs of patients/clients.

7. Make known to an appropriate person or authority any conscientious objection which may be relevant to professional practice.

8. Avoid any abuse of the privileged relationship which exists with patients/clients and of the privileged access allowed to their property, residence or workplace.

9. Respect confidential information obtained in the course of professional practice and refrain from disclosing such information without the consent of the patient/client, or a person entitled to act on his/her behalf, except where disclosure is required by law or by the order of a court or is necessary in the public interest.

10. Have regard to the environment of care and its physical, psychological and social effects on patients/clients, and also to the adequacy of resources, and make known to appropriate persons or authorities any circumstances which could place patients/clients in jeopardy or which militate against safe standards of practice.

11. Have regard to the workload of and the pressures on professional colleagues and subordinates and take appropriate action if these are seen to be such as to constitute abuse of the individual practitioner and/or to jeopardize safe standards of practice.

12. In the context of the individual's own knowledge, experience and sphere of authority, assist peers and subordinates to develop professional competence in accordance with their needs.

13. Refuse to accept any gift, favour or hospitality which might be interpreted as seeking to exert undue influence to obtain preferential consideration.

14. Avoid the use of professional qualifications in the promotion of commercial products in order not to compromise the independence of professional judgement on which patients/clients rely.

Figure 7-4 The UKCC Code of Professional Conduct.

has many ethical facets (see Chapter 8), there are possible legal implications as pointed out below in relation to professional discipline.

4. To act, through the appropriate committees, to protect the public from unsafe members of the profession. This is carried out with the National Boards. Each Board has an investigating committee which acts as a sieve for the large number of incidents of possible misconduct. A high proportion of these are the result of nurses being convicted of certain crimes, the police being required to report certain convictions to the Board. Another large group of cases concern allegations of misconduct reported by colleagues or managers. If it is felt that the offence or allegation is serious enough, it is passed to the professional conduct committee of the UKCC. This committee has the power to remove a nurse's name from the register and the Code of Professional Conduct is used as a standard against which to judge a nurse's behaviour. It is ironical that reliance on a Code that does not have legal standing can result in an act of such legal significance as removal from the register. The UKCC also has a health committee which looks at cases where misconduct is due to illness, and a student conduct committee.

The following is a short transcript of a case coming before the professional conduct committee.

A 31-year-old RGN employed as a night community nurse in an inner city area, appeared before the professional conduct committee to face charges that she failed to visit a patient, and made a false entry in the report book purporting to have made such a visit.

The committee heard that the nurse had major difficulties in her personal life. She had a husband who drank very heavily as a result of which the financial burden of supporting the family (they had an eight-year-old daughter) fell almost entirely on her. Just before leaving to go on duty that night there had been a scene; she left the house not only feeling tired and unhappy but fearful for her daughter's safety, as her husband (under the influence of alcohol) was in a rather violent mood.

On her arrival at her patient's address the nurse got out of her car and made to approach the patient's flat which entailed going down a narrow passage. At the entrance to that passage there were two men who were obviously drunk and in a boisterous and threatening mood. The nurse explained that, after coming from a similar scene at home, she felt too distressed and frightened to risk trying to force her way past them to visit the patient. She returned to her car to make other calls. About an hour later she returned to try again, only to find the men again obstructing her path. She then took the step which in retrospect she realized was terribly wrong. She did not call her senior officer to indicate what had happened but made a false entry in the records.

At the hearing the nurse was distressed as she recalled the events of that night, and was obviously ashamed that she had failed her patient, who, without the normal assistance to return to bed, was found still in her chair in the morning by the day community nurse. It also emerged in evidence that it was the normal practice for night nurses in this area to work in pairs, but on this night there was a shortage of staff so she was alone.

On the basis of her recognized competence and normal high standards, she had not been dismissed from her employment. The committee learnt that her husband was attending Alcoholics Anonymous and that the nurse was hopeful that her personal life might now become easier.

The Committee decided not to remove her name from the register (Pyne, 1981, p. 122).

The functions of the National Boards

The four National Boards for England, Scotland, Wales and Northern Ireland have the following functions.

1. To arrange courses enabling people to qualify for registration and courses of further training meeting the requirements of the UKCC as to their content and standard.
2. To arrange for examinations to be held.
3. To carry out investigations of cases of alleged misconduct with a view to proceedings before the UKCC.
4. To work with the UKCC to promote and improve training methods.

In order to carry out some of these functions, the National Boards have education officers who have particular responsibilities for approving courses of training.

The nurse as practitioner

Probably the most important part of the law affecting the nurse is that known as the law of tort. This part of the law has its roots in common law (see p. 74) and is heard in the civil courts (see Figure 7-2). This means that if an individual sustains harm because of a wrong done to him by another, he can sue that person for damages and win a monetary award as compensation. Sometimes a civil wrong can be so severe that it can become a crime, for example gross negligence, or assault and battery. The commonest torts that the nurse must be aware of are negligence and trespass.

Negligence

The patient must feel assured that he will receive safe care from the professional and it is the law of negligence that particularly safeguards his wellbeing. For there to be negligence, there must be the following:

1. A duty of care.
2. A breach in that duty.
3. Harm as a result.

The nurse clearly has a duty of care to her patients, but she should remember that she also has a duty to avoid harming colleagues with whom she is working and any visitors that are on the premises. She should also be aware that even when off duty, the law expects her to show a greater duty of care to those around her than an ordinary member of the public, for example, when assisting at an accident. In this situation it may not be necessary for the person to admit to being a nurse unless legal proceedings are later commenced. On the other hand, a failure to give first aid could be seen as professional misconduct by the UKCC.

There are many situations where the nurse may be concerned that there has been a breach in her duty towards a patient by either doing something that she should not have done or omitting to do something that she should have done. The following case illustrates a breach of duty by the nurse.

A patient was prescribed 30 injections of streptomycin for boils. The sister failed to note on the treatment sheet when the prescribed course was completed. An additional four injections were given before the error was discovered. Damage to a cranial nerve (a known side effect of streptomycin) resulted and the sister was found to be negligent (Smith v. Brighton and Lewes HMC 1955).

Drug errors are unfortunately only too frequent, but omissions in care such as a failure to carry out relevant observations can also lead to negligence. In all these situations it is vital that care given or omitted is carefully documented. All nursing records are potentially legal documents. Any untoward incidents must be recorded, as should the outcome of care rather than just a record of what was done. For example, not only should it be recorded that pressure area care was carried out two hourly, but also a comment made as to the condition of the patient's skin. Abbreviations should be avoided, writing should be legible and all entries and documents should be dated and signed. Legal actions for negligence sometimes do not commence until several years after the negligent act or when the resultant harm became apparent. Thus a court case could well take place a number of years later and nurses have to be traced and memories refreshed in order for their evidence to be useful. It is likely that a number of cases have been won by patients, not because there was negligence by the nurses but because they had failed to make a useful record. If there is an element of doubt, the judge is more likely to find in the patient's favour.

It is difficult to avoid accidents to patients and there is often a concern that an accident may be regarded as negligence. The answer to this is that it depends on the circumstances of each situation. The law demands that reasonable care must be taken to prevent harm to the patient. In Bolam v. Friern HMC 1957, the judge stated "It is well established law that it is sufficient if (the doctor) exercises the ordinary skill of an ordinary competent man exercising that particular art". This rule is applicable to the nurse in the care she gives and acknowledges that she cannot be superhuman. For example, if a patient fell out of bed but at that particular moment the available nurses had been called to an emergency, then it may not have been reasonable to expect close supervision of all patients. However, if the patient was known to be confused and had already fallen out of bed before, then it may not have been reasonable to have left the patient unobserved.

Accidents can occur as patients are being rehabilitated prior to discharge from hospital. Here the law on negligence can help the nurse to assess the rate at which to encourage independence by looking at the risks involved in the various options open to her. For example, with a frail elderly person the risk of increasing mobility is a possible fall, but the risk of keeping the patient less mobile is the danger of chest infection, pressure sores and mental apathy. The benefits of either action can also be considered, independence versus safety, and the option chosen that presents the best outcome for the patient. The nurse can then argue that her actions were reasonable.

There can be negligence in the manner in which work is delegated. A nurse should only accept a delegated task if confident that she knows what she is doing (not to do so would also be professional misconduct, see p. 78). The delegating nurse also has a duty to check that the nurse has the knowledge and skill required by asking her about her experience, observing her carry out the task, and if necessary teaching her and supervising her until assured that she is safe in giving that care. This is particularly important when a student or unqualified person is giving the care.

The final component of negligence that has to be proved is that harm resulted from the breach of duty. This can be physical or psychological or a mixture of each. The causal link between the breach of duty and the harm may well be a major factor of the case and again good documentation is vital. A major criticism of the law on negligence is that there is no redress for harm sustained if that link cannot be proved. A "no fault" compensation system has been suggested. Such a scheme would provide financial recompense for damage without the need for an adversarial court case laying blame on medical or nursing staff. However, at present it seems unlikely that such a major change will be implemented.

Although it is quite possible for the nurse to be sued, it is more usual for the employer to be taken to court. This is because the employer has to be responsible for the actions of its employees by vicarious liability. However, it is possible for the employer to claim any damages back from the nurse, making it important for her to have proper indemnity insurance provided by a union or professional organization (see p. 85).

Trespass

Trespass is another tort that particularly affects the nurse in caring for a patient. Trespass can be to land, property or to the body and it is the last that is of major concern, as this is assault and battery. Assault is the threat of violence to another; battery, the actual carrying out of this physical threat, even if the touch is minimal. Thus nurses and doctors are potentially battering their patients all the time, except for the fact that there are certain "defences" in law to exonerate them.

A defence is a legal reason for being allowed to carry out a civil or criminal wrong. The commonest defence is that the patient consents to the touching. Another defence is that if the patient for some reason is unable to consent, there is such a degree of urgency and necessity to save life or prevent grave harm, it is acceptable to proceed without consent. The Mental Health Act 1983 allows certain treatment for mental illness to be given without consent if the patient has had to be formally admitted to hospital. A child can only give consent if he has the necessary understanding and it is usual for a parent or guardian to give consent for the child up to the age of 16 years.

Thus in most circumstances the nurse needs to gain the consent of the patient before proceeding with giving care, and even when the doctor has either prescribed or is carrying out treatment and therefore has the duty to gain consent, the nurse still has an important role to play. Consent may be gained orally or in writing, or can even be assumed in some instances, for example the patient rolling up his sleeve in order to have his blood pressure taken. Some degree of cooperation can also be expected from the patient who has agreed to hospital admission. Giving nursing care usually involves oral consent. Written consent is reserved for treatments or investigations carrying a risk of death or serious disability, for example general anaesthesia and any surgery, and is always the doctor's responsibility (see Figure 7-5 for sample consent form). In order for a consent to be valid, the patient must understand to what he is consenting and therefore an explanation of the procedure, the benefits and any material risks, must be given. Where this is the doctor's responsibility, the nurse may well check the consent form has been signed, that the patient has in fact understood the explanation and is happy to proceed with the treatment. Patients can misunderstand some of the words used by the doctor or may feel that they have little choice. The nurse may clarify what the doctor has said (bearing in mind that to give false information can be negligent) or ask the doctor to give further information to the patient. There are times when the nurse will need to help the patient formulate questions to ask the doctor as, although the law supports the doctor in deciding how much to tell a patient, he does have a duty to answer any queries put to him. How much information to give will vary

CONSENT FORM

For medical or dental investigation, treatment or operation

Health Authority .... Patient's Surname...............................

Hospital .... Other Names ....

Unit Number...................................... Date of Birth ....

Sex: *(please tick)*   Male ☐   Female ☐

DOCTORS OR DENTISTS *(This part to be completed by doctor or dentist. See notes on the reverse)*

TYPE OF OPERATION INVESTIGATION OR TREATMENT

I confirm that I have explained the operation investigation or treatment, and such appropriate options as are available and the type of anaesthetic, if any (general/regional/sedation) proposed, to the patient in terms which in my judgement are suited to the understanding of the patient and/or to one of the parents or guardians of the patient

Signature .... Date . . . / . . . / . . . . .

Name of doctor or dentist ....

PATIENT/PARENT/GUARDIAN

1. Please read this form and the notes overleaf very carefully.

2. If there is anything that you don't understand about the explanation, or if you want more information, you should ask the doctor or dentist.

3. Please check that all the information on the form is correct. If it is, and you understand the explanation, then sign the form.

I am the patient/parent/guardian *(delete as necessary)*

I agree	▪ to what is proposed which has been explained to me by the doctor/dentist named on this form.
	▪ to the use of the type of anaesthetic that I have been told about.
I understand	▪ that the procedure may not be done by the doctor/dentist who has been treating me so far.
	▪ that any procedure in addition to the investigation or treatment described on this form will only be carried out if it is necessary and in my best interests and can be justified for medical reasons.
I have told	▪ the doctor or dentist about any additional procedures I would <u>not</u> wish to be carried out straightaway without my having the opportunity to consider them first.

Signature   ....

Name   ....

Address   ....

(if not the patient) ....

....

NOTES TO:

Doctors, Dentists

A patient has a legal right to grant or withhold consent prior to examination or treatment. Patients should be given sufficient information, in a way they can understand, about the proposed treatment and the possible alternatives. Patients must be allowed to decide whether they will agree to the treatment and they may refuse or withdraw consent to treatment at any time. The patient's consent to treatment should be recorded on this form (further guidance is given in HC(90)22 *A Guide to Consent for Examination or Treatment*).

Patients

- The doctor or dentist is here to help you. He or she will explain the proposed treatment and what the alternatives are. You can ask any questions and seek further information. You can refuse the treatment.

- You may ask for a relative, or friend, or a nurse to be present.

- Training health professionals is essential to the continuation of the health service and improving the quality of care. Your treatment may provide an important opportunity for such training, where necessary under the careful supervision of a senior doctor or dentist. You may refuse any involvement in a formal training programme without this adversely affecting your care and treatment.

Figure 7-5 Sample consent form for investigation, treatment or operation (reproduced with permission of HMSO).

with circumstances. The more urgent the treatment, the less detail has to be given, and both nurse and doctor have to respect the wishes of the patient who wants only minimal information. The nurse should also be aware that the patient is entitled to change his mind at any time.

Assault and battery can also be a crime, in which case the police will become involved. An example of this is when a patient hits a nurse. However, very few of these cases go to court. A defence against this crime is lack of the necessary intention. If a patient is mentally confused by his illness or treatment, he may well not be aware enough to understand the implications of his actions and therefore to intend to harm the nurse. As this is not a defence in the civil courts, the nurse could sue the patient, but she may be loth to do so.

Other legal rights

The law provides a few other legal rights for the protection of the patient. Although the law has a limited amount to say about confidentiality (see Chapter 8), the Data Protection Act 1984 does safeguard any computerized records about the patient and a nurse could be prosecuted for failing to maintain confidentiality. The patient has the right to request a copy of information held about him on computer. However, there is a specific exemption clause in the Act concerning personal health data so that the doctor can block its release to the patient on the grounds that the information may be harmful to the physical or mental health of the applicant. Similar rights and safeguards regarding access to written medical records exist under the Access to Health Records Act 1990.

The patient is legally entitled to complain about any aspect of his care. In relation to hospital inpatients, outpatients or accident and emergency departments, the Hospital Complaints Procedure Act 1985 requires that any complaints should be investigated thoroughly, fairly and speedily by a designated officer. Complaints must be made in writing by the patient or someone acting on his behalf normally within six months of the incident. If a complainant is dissatisfied with the conduct or outcome of the health authority's investigation, the Health Service Commissioner (the Ombudsman) can investigate as long as the complaint is not being dealt with in a court of law or could be dealt with in this way, or where it concerns clinical judgement. A resume of a case investigated by the Commissioner is given below:

CARE OF AN INCONTINENT PATIENT

Summary of case

An elderly man was admitted to hospital for a hernia operation and was discharged a week later. His wife complained that the hospital failed to take adequate steps to manage his incontinence and that as a consequence he was incontinent when made to walk to the toilet two days after his operation. Further she said that his incontinence should have been resolved before he was sent home. She also complained that on two or three occasions she had found him sitting in a chair without trousers and covered by a blanket; that on occasions soiled clothing was left in her husband's bedside locker to be laundered at home; and that when he was discharged he had with him soiled items of clothing in a plastic bag. Finally, she complained about the circumstances of the discharge and in particular that although he was otherwise appropriately dressed, he had been sent home in a mini cab wearing pyjama trousers.

Findings

I did not consider that there was any question of the man being compelled to walk to the toilet shortly after his operation and I had no cause to doubt that his incontinence on that occasion was a mishap. However, I was concerned that this incident, and others when he was incontinent of faeces, had neither been recorded in the nursing notes nor reported to the ward sister. I was satisfied that the decision that he could be discharged, notwithstanding his incontinence, was taken solely in the exercise of clinical judgement which I could not question.

I upheld the complaint that the man was left sitting without pyjama trousers, which I found was due to inadequate arrangements for supplying these garments to the ward. I upheld the complaints about the laundering issue to the extent that the man's wife was not told she had to wash his clothes and that there were occasions when it was left to be taken home in an unacceptable state. I was not persuaded that the man had suffered undue hardship as a result of being discharged wearing pyjama trousers. But I considered it unacceptable to send home unaccompanied in a mini cab a 79 year old man who was confused at times and incontinent of diarrhoea.

Remedy

The Health Authority apologised for the shortcomings I identified and agreed to issue directions to their nursing staff to ensure that incontinence of the type revealed by this case is both recorded and brought to the attention of the nurse in charge (Health Service Commissioner, 1989).

Where a complaint involves health care outside the hospital setting, it can be directed to the health authority or the Family Practitioner Committee as appropriate. In any case, the local Community Health Council can assist and support the complainant. The private patient could also sue for a failure to provide care under the Supply of Goods and Services Act 1982.

Drug administration

The nurse is frequently involved in the administration of drugs and she should therefore have some knowledge of the legislation in this area. A failure to abide by the law in relation to drugs could lead to criminal prosecution. However most legislation is to do with the supply, storage and prescription of drugs, and only minimally with their administration. As already pointed out, wrong administration could be negligence (see p. 80) and in addition a drug error could lead to disciplinary action (see p. 79).

The Medicines Acts 1968 and 1971 control the manufacture, sale and supply of medical products. Included are substances for treating or preventing diseases, diagnosing disease, contraception and anaesthesia. The Poisons Act 1972 legislates over the supply, packaging, storage, transport and sale of a range of poisonous substances, both medicinal and nonmedicinal. The most important legislation for the nurse is the Misuse of Drugs Act 1971. In this certain drugs open to misuse are classified into five schedules. Schedule 2 is the most relevant to the general nurse as it contains the strongest pain killers available and these are all potentially addictive. The best known are morphine, diamorphine, papaveretum and pethidine and because of the strictness of the law in relation to these, they are known as controlled drugs.

Controlled drugs must be kept in a locked safe, cabinet, room or receptacle and the qualified nurse in charge of the ward is responsible for them. There are requirements as to how the doctor completes the prescription and a register must be kept of the amount kept on the ward and details of the controlled drugs administered. This register must be a bound, not a looseleaf, book and any entries must be in ink and may not be cancelled, obliterated or altered. Any correction must be made in the margin or at the foot of the page and dated.

The nurse will notice that the hospital also has local rules regarding drug administration which are in addition to the law. These policies must be followed, both for the safety of the patient and for her to avoid being in breach of her contract.

The nurse as student and employee

The law and the student

Although the student must be supervised by a qualified nurse during her clinical experience and therefore that nurse can be negligent in delegation (p. 81), the student should be aware of her own legal position towards the patient. Anyone giving care can be negligent and therefore the student is not protected by her inexperience. The law is clear that if an individual is giving care, the standard expected is that of a person qualified to do so. A judge in Wilsher v. Essex AHA 1986–1988 stated: "The law requires the trainee or learner to be judged by the same standard as his more experienced colleagues. If it did not, inexperience would frequently be urged as a defence to an action for professional negligence" (Tingle, 1988). Although this has only been tested in the courts in relation to medical care, there is little doubt that such a ruling would also apply to nurses. There must therefore be some responsibility on the student to check that she has the necessary knowledge and skills and to ask for further supervision if unsure.

All students will be assessed as to their competence. Each training programme will have a documented method of practical assessment. This must be seen to be fair and ensure that opportunities are given for improvement if performance is poor. For the student who is also an employee, relevant legislation in relation to dismissal must be taken into account. The law on defamation (another tort) should also be considered by the nurse compiling a report or completing an assessment on a student. Libel is when a statement is made in permanent form which exposes a person to hatred, ridicule or contempt. As long as the person writing adverse comments has evidence that they are true, and only divulges these comments to the student's tutor, then the student will have no grounds for suing for defamation.

The law and the employee

An employee has to have a contract of employment, and even the student who is supernumerary will need to have some kind of contract with the health authority in order to gain clinical experience. A contract involves offer and acceptance and the person must have the required capacity to fulfil the contract, for example adequate health and qualifications. Thus the student or employee will have to be screened medically prior to being offered a contract, and a student will need to meet the entry requirements of the National Board in order to commence training.

A certain amount of legislation protects the employee. For example, dismissal is unfair unless it follows the requirements of the Employment Protection (Consolidation) Act 1978 (Bercusson, 1979). Dismissal is fair if it is due to misconduct or incapacity which may include sickness. In order to interpret the legislation, various Codes of Practice have been developed and, although these are not the law, they do give sound guidance to the employer. Each health authority will also have developed local policies regarding discipline and sickness which must be followed. Even the student will be subject to discipline while working in the clinical area and she will also be bound by certain criteria regarding the amount of sickness leave that she can take prior to completing her training.

Employment legislation also controls the existence and functioning of trade unions. Nurses choose to belong to a trade union or professional organisation for several reasons. It provides legal protection, indemnity and advice, it plays a part in negotiating pay and conditions of service and it can assist in the settling of grievances. The law also limits the nature of industrial action that can be taken. However, the nurse is further limited by the Code of Professional Conduct (UKCC, 1984). The nurse taking industrial action could be in breach of clauses 1 and 2 of the Code (p. 78) and therefore have a case to answer for misconduct before the Professional Conduct Committee (p. 79).

Health and safety at work

Nurses are frequently working in areas where their health and safety are likely to be put at risk. Infection, radiation, fire and injuries due to lifting or equipment can all have serious consequences.

The Health and Safety at Work etc. Act 1974 is an important piece of legislation which, unlike the law on negligence, aims to bring about action before rather than after harm is sustained. Both employer and employee have certain responsibilities. The employer must give the employee information, training and supervision as well as providing and maintaining equipment and safe buildings. The employee must cooperate with the employer in health and safety matters, including the use of safety equipment provided, for example, hoists for lifting.

Additional legislation under this Act is implemented by means of regulations. The Reporting of Injuries, Diseases and Dangerous Occurrences Regulations 1985 (RIDDOR) ensures that a wide range of injuries and incidents have to be reported to the Health and Safety Executive, the enforcement body of the Health and Safety at Work Act. More recently, the Control of Substances Hazardous to Health Regulations 1988 (COSHH) have important implications in the assessment of and the prevention or control of employee exposure to a range of substances including microorganisms, certain drugs, anaesthetic gases and dust.

The implementation of the Act and its associated regulations are monitored by inspectors who have wide powers of enforcement. Trade unions are also allowed to appoint safety representatives. The nurse should find out the names and locations of any representatives in her area as they can give advice and direct matters of concern to management.

The employee is also protected to some extent by the law on negligence. The employer has a duty of care to ensure the safety of employees. For example, if a nurse injured her back due to a failure of the employer to provide proper lifting equipment, adequate training or sufficient staff, she may have grounds for suing for damages. She may also be able to claim industrial injury benefit. As with any involvement with the law, careful documentation of any injuries or accidents is extremely important.

References

Access to Health Records Act 1990, HMSO, London.

Bercusson, B. (1979) *The Employment Protection (Consolidation) Act 1978*, Sweet and Maxwell, London.

Control of Substances Hazardous to Health Regulations 1988, HMSO, London.

Data Protection Act 1984, HMSO, London.

Employment Protection (Consolidation) Act 1978, HMSO, London.

Health and Safety at Work, etc. Act 1974, HMSO, London.

Health Service Commissioner (1989) *Epitomes of Selected Cases November 1988–March 1989*, Department of Health, London.

Hospital Complaints Procedure Act 1985, HMSO, London.

Medicines Acts 1968 and 1971, HMSO, London.

Mental Health Act 1983, HMSO, London.

Misuse of Drugs Act 1971, HMSO, London.

NHS Management Executive (1990) *A Guide to Consent for Examination or Treatment*, HC(90)22, Department of Health, London.

Nurses, Midwives and Health Visitors Act 1979, HMSO, London.

Poisons Act 1972, HMSO, London.

Pyne, R. (1981) *Professional Discipline in Nursing*, Blackwell, London.

Reporting of Injuries, Diseases and Dangerous Occurrences Regulations 1985, HMSO, London.

Single European Act 1987, HMSO, London.

Supply of Goods and Services Act 1982, HMSO, London.

Tingle, J.H. (1988) Negligence and Wilsher. *Solicitors Journal*, **132**(25), 910–11.

UKCC (1984) *Code of Professional Conduct*, 2nd edn, United Kingdom Central Council, London.

Further reading

Bradney, A., et al. (1986) *How to Study Law*, Sweet and Maxwell, London.

Brazier, M. (1987) *Medicines, Patients and the Law*, Penguin, Harmondsworth.

Carson, D. and Montgomery, J. (1989) *Nursing and the Law*, Macmillan, Basingstoke.

Dimond, B. (1990) *Legal Aspects of Nursing*, Prentice Hall, London.

Eddey, K. (1982) *The English Legal Systems*, 3rd edn, Sweet and Maxwell, London.

National Consumer Council (1983) *Patients' Rights; A Guide for NHS Patients and Doctors*, HMSO, London.

Rogers, R. and Salvage, J. (1988) *Nurses at Risk; A Guide to Health and Safety at Work*, Heinemann, London.

Vousden, M. (1984) Sacked ECT nurse loses appeal. *Nursing Mirror*, **159**(18), 5.

Young, A.P. (1989) *Legal Problems in Nursing Practice*, 2nd edn, Harper and Row, London.

Young, A.P. (1991) *Law and Professional Conduct in Nursing*, Scutari Press, London.

8

Ethical implications of nursing

Learning objectives

When the content of this chapter has been mastered, the learner should be able to:

Discuss what is meant by ethics.

Consider various ethical theories and how they are encompassed in ethical codes.

Review how nurses can best prepare themselves to deal with ethical dilemmas, and what guidelines they can use to assist them when making ethical decisions.

Consider the ethical issues which are raised in relation to management and resources and transplantation.

Glossary

Autonomy The right or power to self govern.

Beneficence Doing good, actively kind.

Code of ethics A list of written statements describing ideal behaviour for a group of individuals.

Confidentiality An ethical term for the right of an individual to have personal information protected from public knowledge.

Constitution Form in which a "State" is organized; a system of laws and customs.

Deontological Considers moral principles of others as well as the anticipated outcomes as a guide to what action to take.

Dilemma A situation which leaves only a choice of two equally difficult situations.

Ethics A system of moral or philosophical principles that directs actions as being either right or wrong.

Informed consent Special permission given by one person to another based on acquired information or knowledge.

Justice Fairness—acting in an impartial way.

Morals Concerned with right or wrong conduct.

Nonmaleficence Not doing any harm.

Transplantation The therapeutic transplant of any organ or tissue to another person.

Utilitarian Cosiders the consequences of an action, seeking the greatest good for the greatest number of people.

Introduction

The word *ethics* comes from the Greek word *ethos*, meaning customs or modes of conduct. Ethics can be defined as the study of moral judgements which is based on the individual's values, beliefs and attitudes. Morals can be defined as the standard of behaviour that an individual practises.

Ethics involves identifying the rights of individuals, respecting those rights, and performing certain obligations, called duties, which protect rights. Ethics often arise from social customs and religious traditions.

There was a time when making decisions about ethical issues was quite simple. Today, certain issues present health practitioners with difficult decisions, primarily because of the increased use of sophisticated equipment, new techniques in health care, and a change in national values toward health care. Nurses may find themselves facing dilemmas when personal codes of conscience conflict with those being used as a standard. Examples of situations in which an ethical dilemma may arise include abortion on demand, test-tube fertilization and the prolongation of life with various types of equipment.

Codes of ethics

Various organizations representing nurses have developed ethical codes. A *code of ethics* is a list of written statements describing ideal behaviour for a group of individuals. It is difficult for codes of ethics to be enforced. Each nurse is expected to uphold and abide by the code. Enforcement depends more on one's conscience and heart than on law enforcement officials. Codes of ethics usually cover the following issues:

1. Duties to self and others.
2. Treatment of the individual.
3. Certain values such as honesty and integrity.
4. Cooperation with other people.

Ethics are based on various theories, no single ethic guides all our actions. Outlined briefly below is a summary of these ethical theories which people use to formulate the "right answer" or the correct line of duty for different ethical situations.

Utilitarian approach

This theory goes back as far as Aristotle, who felt that the test of human actions and moral principles was based on whether they were conducive to the greater happiness and good of mankind and society. This theory considers the consequences of an action and seeks the greatest good for the greatest number. It was expanded further initially by Jeremy Bentham (1748–1832) who believed in obtaining the maximum

amount of happiness for the greatest number of people (Rumbold, 1986). Mill (1867) considered the following modifications to this theory:

The good of the whole rather than the good of the part.

The need for a hierarchy of pleasures, i.e. discrimination between desirable and nondesirable pleasures.

The concept of good, which combined the value of the individual, and justice, thus promoting the common good of society.

Thompson et al. (1988) suggest that the utilitarian theory appeals to health professionals, due to their ability to predict outcomes of treatment or nursing care. They therefore believe that they know how the greatest benefit for the greatest number can be achieved.

"For the good of all" theory

This point of view suggests that no one should benefit unless everyone can. Rumbold (1986) suggests that Marxist ethics were based on this belief, and related to the whole population of the state. This theory aims to achieve an overall greater benefit than the utilitarian approach. It ignores the needs of the individual, and may lead to the violation of the interests of either the minority or the majority.

Formalist or deontological theory

This approach considers the moral principles of others as well as the anticipated consequences, as a guide to the appropriate course of action. Tschudin (1989) describes this approach under nonconsequentialism; she cites Jamerton (1984) who stated that every time someone is about to make a moral decision they should first ask two questions.

1. What is the rule authorizing the act they are about to perform?
2. Could it become a universal rule for all humans to follow?

This theory encompasses the concept of the will to do what one knows to be best.

Obligation theory

This looks at rules and actions in two ways:

1. Doing good.
2. Treating people fairly or justly.

This theory involves treating all men as equals and looks at the needs of the individual based on their individual values and beliefs. The obligation theory equates closely in nursing to the concept of individual care, i.e. the "nursing process".

Codes of ethics are intended to guide actions and most professional groups have their own "codes of conduct" which reflect different ethical approaches. The UKCC Code of Conduct (which has been reprinted in Chapter 7) and the International Council of Nurses' (1973) *Code for Nurses* are both examples of ethical codes.

The following ethical concepts applied to nursing were adopted by the International Council of Nurses (ICN) when they met in Mexico City in 1973.

1973 Code for Nurses

The fundamental responsibility of the nurse is fourfold: to promote health, to prevent illness, to restore health and to alleviate suffering.

The need for nursing is universal. Inherent in nursing is respect for life, dignity and rights of man. It is unrestricted by considerations of nationality, race, creed, color, age, sex, politics or social status.

Nurses render health services to the individual, the family and the community and coordinate their services with those of related groups.

Nurses and People

The nurse's primary responsibility is to those people who require nursing care.

The nurse, in providing care, respects the beliefs, values and customs of the individual.

The nurse holds in confidence personal information and uses judgment in sharing this information.

Nurses and Practice

The nurse carries personal responsibility for nursing practice and for maintaining competence by continual learning.

The nurse maintains the highest standards of nursing care possible within the reality of a specific situation.

The nurse uses judgment in relation to individual competence when accepting and delegating responsibilities.

The nurse when acting in a professional capacity should at all times maintain standards of personal conduct that would reflect credit upon the profession.

Nurses and Society

The nurse shares with other citizens the responsibility for initiating and supporting action to meet the health and social needs of the public.

Nurses and Co-Workers

The nurse sustains a cooperative relationship with co-workers in nursing and other fields.

The nurse takes appropriate action to safeguard the individual when his care is endangered by a co-worker or any other person.

Nurses and the Profession

The nurse plays the major role in determining and implementing desirable standards of nursing practice and nursing education.

The nurse is active in developing a core of professional knowledge.

The nurse, acting through the professional organization, participates in establishing and maintaining equitable social and economic working conditions in nursing (Anon, 1973).

The patient's rights

In addition to being familiar with codes of ethics, nurses should also be familiar with the patient's rights in relation to his health care.

In North America the legal system is based on a constitution; this, combined with the fact that the majority of Americans pay for their health care, led to the American Hospital Association publishing *A Patient's Bill Of Rights* in 1975. This is reprinted for interest, below. In the UK our legal system has no provision for a Patient's Bill Of Rights; however, advisory documents are available from the National Consumer Council and the Citizens Advice Bureau.

American Hospital Association Statement

A Patient's Bill of Rights

The American Hospital Association Board of Trustees' Committee on Health Care for the Disadvantaged, which has been a consistent advocate on behalf of consumers of health care services, developed the Statement on a Patient's Bill of Rights, which was approved by the AHA House of Delegates February 6, 1973. The statement was published in several forms, one of which was the S74 leaflet in the Association's S series. The S74 leaflet is now superseded by this reprinting of the statement. *The American Hospital Association presents a Patient's Bill of Rights with the expectation that observance of these rights will contribute to more effective patient care and greater satisfaction for the patient, his physician, and the hospital organization. Further, the Association presents these rights in the expectation that they will be supported by the hospital on behalf of its patients, as an integral part of the healing process. It is recognized that a personal relationship between the physician and the patient is essential for the provision of proper medical care. The traditional physician-patient relationship takes on a new dimension when care is rendered within an organizational structure. Legal precedent has established that the institution itself also has a responsibility to the patient. It is in recognition of these factors that these rights are affirmed.*

1. *The patient has the right to considerate and respectful care.*

2. *The patient has the right to obtain from his physician complete current information concerning his diagnosis, treatment, and prognosis in terms the patient can be reasonably expected to understand. When it is not medically advisable to give such information to the patient, the information should be made available to an appropriate person in his behalf. He has the right to know, by name, the physician responsible for coordinating his care.*

3. *The patient has the right to receive from his physician information necessary to give informed consent prior to the start of any procedure and/or treatment. Except in emergencies, such information for informed consent should include but not necessarily be limited to the specific procedure and/or treatment, the medically significant risks involved, and the probable duration of incapacitation. Where medically significant alternatives for care or treatment exist, or when the patient requests information concerning medical alternatives, the patient has the right to such information. The patient also has the right to know the name of the person responsible for the procedures and/or treatment.*

4. *The patient has the right to refuse treatment to the extent permitted by law and to be informed of the medical consequences of his action.*

5. *The patient has the right to every consideration of his privacy concerning his own medical care program. Case discussion, consultation, examination, and treatment are confidential and should be conducted discreetly. Those not directly involved in his care must have the permission of the patient to be present.*

6. *The patient has the right to expect that all communications and records pertaining to his care should be treated as confidential.*

7. *The patient has the right to expect that within its capacity a hospital must make reasonable response to the request of a patient for services. The hospital must provide evaluation, service, and/or referral as indicated by the urgency of the case. When medically permissible, a patient may be transferred to another facility only after he has received complete information and explanation concerning the needs for and alternatives to such a transfer. The institution to which the patient is to be transferred must first have accepted the patient for transfer. The patient has the right to obtain information as to the existence of any professional relationships among individuals, by name, who are treating him.*

8. *The patient has the right to obtain information as to any relationship of his hospital to other health care and educational institutions insofar as his care is concerned. The patient has the right to obtain information as to the existence of any professional relationships among individuals, by name, who are treating him.*

9. *The patient has the right to be advised if the hospital proposes to engage in or perform human experimentation affecting his care or treatment. The patient has the right to refuse to participate in such research projects.*

10. *The patient has the right to expect reasonable continuity of care. He has the right to know in advance what appointment times and physicians are available and where. The patient has the right to expect that the hospital will provide a mechanism whereby he is informed by his physician or a delegate of the physician of the patient's continuing health care requirements following discharge.*

11. *The patient has the right to examine and receive an explanation of his bill regardless of source of payment.*

12. *The patient has the right to know what hospital rules and regulations apply to his conduct as a patient.*

No catalog of rights can guarantee for the patient the kind of treatment he has a right to expect. A hospital has many functions to perform, including the prevention and treatment of disease, the education of both health professionals and patients, and the conduct of clinical research. All these activities must be conducted with an overriding concern for the patient, and, above all, the recognition of his dignity as a human being. Success in achieving this recognition assures success in the defense of the rights of the patient

(American Hospital Association, 1975. Reprinted with permission).

Ethical dilemmas

Decisions affecting health care are often guided by ethical or legal standards. However, there are situations in which an action considered legal may be ethical or unethical and an action considered ethical may be legal or illegal. In addition a choice may have to be made between two equally difficult alternatives on a purely ethical basis. Where the ethical codes used in the decision-making process are at odds with each other, this creates a dilemma.

Make sure that whatever is done is in the patient's best interest.

Promote the rights of the individual patient and act as their advocate.

Work cooperatively with the patient and other health practitioners.

Follow written policies, codes of conduct, and laws.

Follow your conscience.

An example of an everyday ethical dilemma which the nurse might be faced with is, should she be honest with the patient who has been diagnosed as having terminal cancer when the doctor has decided, for his own reasons, to withhold information from the patient regarding his prognosis?

When making ethical decisions, one suggested approach is that of a problem-solving method. This is described by both Tschudin (1989) and Thompson et al. (1988), who include in the four stages the following points for consideration:

Assessment

Has the patient expressed his point of view?

Who are the people involved?

Has a similar situation occurred before?

What conditions and factors exist that are relevant to the situation?

What relevant rules, principles and/or codes need to be considered?

What are the personal moral principles of the people concerned?

Planning

What are the possible solutions?

Who is going to benefit by each solution (anticipated outcomes)?

What ethical principles are involved with each solution?

Do conflicting values and loyalties exist?

Is a compromise possible or a direct line of action required?

Will anyone suffer from the chosen line of action?

Formulate action plan and if possible include a contingency plan.

Implementation

Have the courage, competence and confidence to carry out agreed plan. All involved must know what action to take and agree to cooperate.

Plan of action must be implemented.

Evaluation

Has the plan of action solved the problem? If not, consider why.

Were the predicted outcomes accurate?

How do the people involved feel about the outcome?

How will the outcome affect similar situations in the future?

Ethical issues

Conflicts that develop from ethical dilemmas are not always easily solved. How can nurses best deal with these situations? Certainly, the first obligation for a nurse is to be well informed about the issues that may arise and present personal controversy. Better understanding comes through study and discussion of ethics in a classroom. It also develops through understanding of one's own values. In addition, nurses benefit when ethical issues are openly discussed among them and when specialists in ethical and legal aspects of nursing are used as consultants.

Confidentiality. The foundation of any relationship is trust. *Confidentiality* is a principle that directs nurses and other health practitioners to prevent private information about a patient from becoming public. The patient may need to share sensitive information about his health. Any information that the patient confides should not be divulged without his written permission.

It requires that the nurse protect the patient's health history from others not only through overheard spoken communication but also by ensuring that patients' notes are safeguarded. There is a UKCC advisory paper available for nurses an confidentiality and the patient (UKCC, 1987). It is based on clause 9 of the Code of Professional Conduct and states, when defining confidentiality, the following:

To trust another person with private and personal information about yourself is a significant matter. Where the person to whom that information is given is a nurse, midwife or health visitor the patient/client has a right to believe in the expectation that it will be used only for the purposes for which it was given and will not be released to others without the consent of the patient/client.

The document continues by stating the ways in which information regarding patients/clients is disclosed, i.e.

1. With consent of the patient.
2. Without the patient's consent when disclosure is required by law or order of court.
3. By accident.
4. Without the patient's consent when disclosure is considered necessary in the public interest.

The document advises that when a nurse is faced with a decision about whether to disclose information without the patient's consent, she should seek advice from other practitioners or a professional organization.

Once the nurse has made her decision she should then document her reasons in either an appropriate record or special note which can be kept on file. This allows the nurse to justify her decision and be able to review it in light of future developments.

Two areas will be addressed in this chapter from an ethical perspective. Firstly, management and resource allocation, a topic not frequently discussed, but in light of the NHS and Community Care Act, April 1990, is perhaps an area which nurses might find themselves increasingly concerned with, when considering resource management and patient care.

The second issue, organ and tissue transplantation, has in recent times been the subject of much controversial discussion. It is for this reason that it has been selected as an ethical area to be addressed in this chapter.

Ethics committees

Some ethical decisions related to health care are extremely complex. They often involve individuals who are not capable of exercising their right to choose. Making a substituted judgement for another is a weighty responsibility. Committees of individuals with various backgrounds have been formed.

However, the role of ethics committees within the UK is limited—they are largely concerned with approving research involving patients.

Needless to say there are numerous ethical issues which relate to nursing which would be impossible to cover within the context of this chapter; the reader is therefore directed to both the reference and further reading lists at the end of this chapter.

Management and resource allocation

When we consider ethical dilemmas we tend to focus on the more obvious issues such as abortion and euthanasia; however, ethical situations also arise in relation to management of resources. An example of such a case is two patients requiring intensive care nursing when there is only one bed available. Which patient should be sent to the intensive care unit? What criteria are the patients to be assessed on? Who makes the decision about which patient should be transferred? These are all difficult questions to answer whilst guarding the interests and needs of each patient. In this instance the nurse manager might consider the following points:

1. Is there a patient who could be transferred out of the ICU to a high dependency unit or ward area?
2. What staff are available to nurse the patients concerned effectively elsewhere?
3. Can one of the new patients be transferred to another hospital's ICU without causing further harm?
4. Is an appropriate nurse escort available?

The above questions would be considered alongside the factors influencing ethical decision making as referred to earlier in the text; but to assist nurse managers the Kings Fund (1989) has issued a report called "Cost and Choice in Health Care—The Ethical Dimension". This report offers guidelines on what principles should be used to decide what care to provide and to whom. It identifies four principles:

1. Autonomy.
2. Nonmaleficence.
3. Beneficence.
4. Justice.

Autonomy. The report states that illness can impede an individual's autonomy, i.e. the ability to reason and decide what action to take. However, it warns health professionals about making decisions for elderly, frail or disabled people; stating that although an individual might not be able to take their decided action, their right of choice should still be respected.

Nonmaleficence. This means the patient should suffer no harm; a principle first expressed by Florence Nightingale—"Hospitals should do the patient no harm". Pownall (1989) gives an example of this in relation to vaccinations; these have associated risks for a few patients but for the majority of people the benefits to health are high, with no adverse effects.

Beneficence. Trying to achieve goals which will be beneficial to patients. The report warns against overwork by nurses and other health professionals.

Justice. The report states that health services should meet "reasonable needs". This also implies that the government has to decide what health needs should be met by the resources they provide.

Combined with the above the report also includes questions which health professionals can ask, to determine if they are acting ethically. These are stated below:

> Are all cases treated similarly, avoiding irrelevant criteria such as race, occupation and age?
>
> When dealing with individual patients are the needs of others considered and if so, in what ways?
>
> Are matters always explained clearly to patients and relatives, so that they can make an informed choice?
>
> Do the interests of specialist areas outweigh the overall interests of health care?
>
> What evidence supports the choice of therapy and care, and how is it evaluated?

This report, together with the UKCC Code of Professional Conduct (UKCC, 1992), can assist nurse managers to make decisions related to patient care and the allocation of resources, whilst treating all patients as both individuals and equals.

The ethics of organ transplantation

Transplantation refers to the therapeutic transplant of any tissue or organ to another person. For the sake of convenience the ethics concerned with transplantation will only be discussed in relation to heart, lung and kidney transplants.

Within the UK we have a donor card system whereby people who wish to donate any of their organs and tissues at the time of death can make their intentions clear by carrying a signed donor card.

Consent of the next of kin is a legal necessity. If at all possible the hospital authority must make "reasonable" attempts to contact them.

With advanced technology people can be kept alive much longer through the aid of life support machines. One ethical issue which arises from this is; should patients who have been diagnosed as "brain stem dead" be kept alive by the use of machines in order that their organs may be taken for transplant?

This also raises the issue of supporting distressed relatives who may find it difficult to accept that a person is dead, whilst a machine is breathing for him and he just appears to be sleeping. It might be at this difficult time that the doctor or transplant coordinator requests the organs and/or tissues of the patient. In this instance the nurse must come to terms with her own feelings and offer emotional support to the relatives. Sometimes it can be a comfort to relatives to know that the organs of a loved one are going to give life to another person.

Kidney transplants have been accepted for many years, both cadaveric (organs from a deceased person) and kidneys from live donors. In recent times ethical issues have been raised over kidneys that have been bought from foreign nationals to be transplanted into private patients. This resulted in one of the doctors concerned having his licence to practice withdrawn. The whole case raised a question mark over the use of live donor kidneys and the circumstances surrounding how they are obtained.

Satterwaite (1990) considered the ethical issues which are raised when looking at heart-lung transplants. A few years ago patients waiting for such a transplant would have been assessed as to their suitability; only those patients with the best chance of survival were offered the option of surgery, an option not offered to those patients who were considered too high a risk postoperatively. The advancement of technology shows that these high-risk patients do equally well postoperatively. Ethically it is important that all patients requiring this type of surgery are offered equal opportunity for transplant.

The Department of Health (1990) offers advice to doctors on another aspect of transplantation; that of testing donor organs and tissues for human immunodeficiency virus (HIV), prior to transplant. It recommends that the blood of live donors be tested for HIV infection with their specific consent, stating that results should be confirmed as negative prior to surgery taking place. Contained within the Department's circular is the advice of the Expert Advisory Group on AIDS who recommended that,

"In the case of tissues from living donors which may be stored prior to use, the tissue should not be transplanted until a second negative test at least ninety days later is obtained".

In relation to cadaver donors they advise that sensitive inquiry should be made of the relatives in order to exclude as far as is possible donors at high risk of HIV infection. The circular recommends that relatives are informed that assessing suitability of organs for transplant entails testing for certain infections, including HIV. Should a live donor be found to be HIV positive, it is the responsibility of the doctor to ensure that appropriate counselling and support are provided. Similar help should also be given to sexual partners and children of cadaver donors.

Ethical issues surrounding transplantation will continue to be debated alongside growing technology and man's ability to offer life to those people who would once have died. Who knows what organs and tissues we will be able to transplant in the future; but we can say that there are a lot of happy healthy people enjoying life as a consequence of having transplant operations.

References

American Hospital Association (1975) *A Patient's Bill of Rights*, Chicago, Illinois.

Anon. (1973) The ICN meets in Mexico City. *American Journal of Nursing*, **73**, 1351.

Department Of Health (1990) *HIV Infection, Tissue Banks and Organ Donation*, PL/CMO (90) 2, London.

International Council Of Nurses (1973) *Code For Nurses*, ICN, Mexico City.

Jamerton, A. (1984) *Nursing Practice; The Ethical Issues*, Prentice-Hall, Englewood Cliffs, NJ.

King's Fund (1989) Cost and choice in health care—the ethical dimension. Cited in Pownall, M. (1989) When care has to be rationed. *Nursing Times*, **85**(5), 16–17.

Mill, J.S. (1867) Cited in Tschudin, V. (1989) *Ethics In Nursing, The Caring Relationship*, 2nd edn, Heinemann Nursing, Oxford, p. 28.

Pownall, M. (1989) When care has to be rationed. *Nursing Times*, **85**(5), 16–17.

Rumbold, G. (1986) *Ethics In Nursing Practice*, Bailliere Tindall, London.

Satterwaite, H. (1990) When right and wrong are a matter of opinion. The ethics of organ transplantation. *Professional Nurse*, **5**(8), 434–8.

Thompson, I.E., Melia, K.M. and Boyd, K.M. (1988) *Nursing Ethics*, 2nd edn, Churchill Livingstone, Edinburgh.

Tschudin, V. (1989) *Ethics In Nursing, The Caring Relationship*, 2nd edn, Heinemann Nursing, Oxford.

UKCC (1987) Confidentiality—an elaboration of Clause 9 of the second edition of the UKCC's Code of Professional Conduct for the Nurses Midwives and Health Visitors, UKCC Advisory Paper, UKCC, London.

UKCC (1992) *Code Of Professional Conduct for Nurses, Midwives and Health Visitors*, 3rd edn, UKCC, London.

Further reading

Allen, D. (1988) The ethics of brain death. *Professional Nurse*, **3**(8), 295–8.

Craig, R. (1989) The nurse's role in ethical decisions. *Nursing*, **3**(36), 42–3.

Gray, J. (1989) A testing dilemma. *Nursing Standard*, **4**(4), 20.

Jones, C. (1989) Little white lies. *Nursing Times*, **85**(44), 38–9.

Lloyd, A. (1990) Ethics and health. *Nursing Times*, **86**(25), 36–7.

Mackie Bailey, S. (1990) Life and death—the moral dilemmas facing nurses. *Nursing Standard*, **4**(16), 37–9.

McLean, J. (1990) The placebo effect—drug trial considerations. *Nursing Times*, **86**(17), 28–30.

Melia, K. (1988) Everyday ethics for nurses, to tell or not to tell. *Nursing Times*, **84**(30), 37–9.

Sheehan, J. (1985) Ethical considerations in nursing practice. *Journal of Advanced Nursing*, **10**, 331–6.

Stewart, K. and Rai, G. (1989) Resuscitation: a matter of life and death. *Nursing Times*, **85**(35), 26–9.

Part 2

Nursing Skills for

Health Promotion

and Maintenance

9

The need for personal hygiene

Learning objectives

When the content of this chapter has been mastered, the learner should be able to

Define the terms appearing in the glossary.

List at least four reasons for bathing.

Identify methods of bathing a patient.

List three modifications of bathing.

Discuss the components of healthy skin, mucous membranes, nails, hair, vision and hearing.

Describe how to care for the patient's perineal area, teeth and mouth, including dentures and bridges, and for the eyes, ears, nose, fingernails, feet, toenails and hair.

Discuss the care of eyeglasses, contact lenses, artificial eyes and hearing aids.

List suggested measures for promoting personal hygiene in selected situations, as described in this chapter.

Summarize suggestions for patient teaching offered in this chapter.

Glossary

Acne A skin eruption due to inflammation and infection of oil glands in the skin.

Antiperspirant A preparation for reducing the amount of perspiration on the skin.

Bridge A dental appliance that replaces one or several teeth.

Callus A thickening of the outer layer of the skin.

Caries The decay of teeth with the formation of cavities.

Cerumen The waxlike substance found in the external canal of the ear.

Ceruminous glands Glands in the skin that secrete cerumen.

Chiropodist A specialist on care of the feet.

Decibel A measurement of sound.

Denture A dental appliance of artificial teeth that replaces the person's own upper, lower, or all teeth.

Deodorant A preparation to mask or diminish body odours.

Emollient An agent to soften, smooth and protect the skin.

Eye fatigue The discomfort experienced from poor lighting or prolonged focusing on an object.

Feedback The loud, shrill noise from a hearing aid that is not fitted snugly into the ear canal.

Field of vision The ability to see images in all directions.

Gingivitis Inflammation of the gums.

Halitosis Foul smelling breath.

Hygiene The establishment and preservation of well-being through personal care.

Integument A covering; refers to the skin.

Integumentary system The skin and its parts including mucous membranes, hair, and nails.

Mucus The slimy substance secreted by glands in the mucous membranes.

Perineal care Cleansing the genital and anal areas.

Periodontitis Severe inflammation of the gums and bone tissue around the teeth. Synonym for *pyorrhoea*.

Plaque A mass of bacteria covering teeth, causing cavities and gum disease.

Prosthesis A manmade object that replaces a natural body part.

Pyorrhoea Severe inflammation of the gums and bone tissue around teeth. Synonym for *periodontitis*.

Sebaceous glands Glands in the skin that secrete sebum.

Sebum A thick, fatty substance secreted by the sebaceous glands.

Visual acuity The ability to see words or objects that are near or far both clearly and comfortably.

Introduction

Hygiene deals with the establishment and preservation of well-being through personal care. This chapter discusses common practices that contribute to well-being through cleanliness, grooming, and care of vision and hearing. Roper et al. (1985) state that "hygiene habits are built into a routine which gives a pattern to the day, feelings of security and stability".

A person's health values and health perception can be associated with his degree of self-care including personal hygiene, dental care, and care of vision and hearing. People differ in their practices of personal health management. For example, some people prefer bathing to showering; some brush their teeth after every meal and others just in the morning and evening; some keep regular appointments when their vision or hearing becomes impaired, while others live with their losses.

A primary concern for nurses is that personal care be carried out in a manner that promotes health. Personal care does not have to be carried out in an identical fashion among all people. In fact, to do so would ignore the individuality among people in relation to their age, inherited characteristics and cultural background. The exact way it is done is less important than the fact that it meets the health needs of the individual. The nurse must become tolerant of personal preferences and adapt to the differences among people.

The nurse should reinforce and encourage appropriate hygiene practices among healthy individuals. There may be opportunities to teach patients and their families new or modified practices that may improve established hygiene patterns. For those who are ill, the nurse may substitute the care that a patient is unable to perform. The nurse may be one of the first to detect deficits in hearing and vision. Referrals may be made to other health practitioners who can help improve an individual's overall health and quality of life.

Structures and functions of the skin and mucous membranes

The word *integument* means a covering. The largest organ that covers the body is the skin. The main components of the *integumentary system* include the skin, its various parts such as hair and nails, and mucous membranes.

Within the skin there are specialized glands and cells that support the healthy functions of this system. *Sebaceous glands* secrete *sebum*, a thick, fatty substance that oils the skin and keeps it supple. Sebum also lubricates the hair. Sweat glands secrete perspiration. *Ceruminous glands* secrete *cerumen*, a waxlike substance found in the external canal of the ear.

The mucous membranes are continuous with the skin. They line body passages that open to the outside of the body. These passages include the digestive, respiratory, urinary and reproductive systems. The conjunctiva of the eye is also lined with mucous membrane. Goblet cells in the mucous membranes secrete *mucus*, which is the slimy substance that keeps the membranes soft and moist.

The skin has a variety of functions, including the following:

- It protects the body.
- It helps regulate body temperature.
- It assists with the body's fluid and chemical balance.

- It has nerve endings that are sensitive to pain, temperature, touch and pressure.
- It produces vitamin D with the help of sunlight, and the vitamin D is then absorbed from the skin into the body.
- It provides a basis for personal identification.

Assessment of skin and related structures

When assessing the patient's skin and related structures it is important that the nurse has a good knowledge base of how a healthy individual's skin, hair, nails, teeth, etc. should appear.

When talking to the patient the nurse should also establish how he usually cares for his hair and skin, what are his usual washing habits and his individual preferences in relation to meeting personal hygiene needs. By doing this the nurse can then assess how the patient's illness has interfered with his usual routine and also assess those areas in which the patient may require further health education.

Characteristics of healthy skin and mucous membranes. There are general features of the skin that are important to assess. One of the first concerns should be whether the skin is intact. Its very protective nature depends on this quality. The colour of the skin should be uniform and reflect the ethnic origin of the patient. The texture, or feel, to the skin should be warm, soft, smooth, and easily moved. Mucous membranes should be pink, moist and smooth.

Characteristics of healthy hair. Hair generally covers similar parts of each adult male or female. There are hereditary factors that may affect its distribution, colour, and texture. Some individuals may alter these characteristics cosmetically. The nurse should evaluate the cleanliness and lustre of hair when assessing the individual's personal hygiene.

Characteristics of healthy nails. Fingernails and toenails are hardened extensions of the skin. They should be thin, pink, and smooth. A free margin should extend from the end of each nail. The skin around the nail should be intact.

Characteristics of healthy teeth. Adults normally have 32 permanent teeth. The colour of teeth generally is a result of inheritance. Some drugs, food and beverages, and tobacco may discolour teeth. Teeth should be firm in the gums without open spaces. Any malposition, missing teeth, or offensive breath odour may reflect information about the oral hygiene of the patient.

Caring for healthy skin

One of the primary practices associated with personal hygiene is regular bathing. Cleansing the skin helps remove bacteria, oils, and dirt. These substances are responsible for body odour and the potential for infection. *Deodorants* mask or diminish body odour; *anti-perspirants* contain a chemical to close or clog pores, thus reducing perspiration on the skin. Bathing should always precede the use of any cosmetic product.

The following are examples of practices that protect unbroken and healthy skin. There may be times when the nurse will need to perform skills that meet the hygiene needs of a patient when the individual cannot do so independently.

Bathing. Bathing is an important part of hygiene whether accomplished in a bath or shower. It serves various purposes:

- The bath cleans the skin and gives a feeling of refreshment.
- The warmth of bath water and the massage associated with washing and drying the skin aid relaxation.
- Circulation of blood is stimulated as a result of the friction created by washing and drying the skin.
- The activity involved when giving a bath acts as a muscle toner and body conditioner. Sometimes, it may even help stimulate the appetite.
- The bath often helps improve self-image and morale.
- Discomfort is often relieved by bathing. Moist heat is soothing to sore muscles. Some medications can be added to bath water to treat skin conditions, skin dryness, or itching.

Planning and recording nursing care

Documenting the nursing care required to meet the patient's hygiene needs should always be signed by a trained nurse. Nurses in training can write on the patient's care plan but it must always be counter-signed by a trained nurse.

Providing for a bath or shower

All procedures should be explained by the nurse to the patient. The nurse should always begin and end each procedure with hand-washing. The equipment should be put away and the patient returned to a comfortable position.

Principles of Care 9-1. Providing a bath or shower

Nursing Action	Rationale
Clean the bath or shower.	Use of a common bath or shower is a way that bacteria can be transferred among patients.
Assemble supplies and clean garments near the shower or bath.	Organizing equipment prevents the patient from becoming tired or chilled once the bath has begun.
Use a nonslip bathmat in baths or showers. A bath towel may be used as a substitute if a mat is not available.	The floors of bath and showers are slippery. Modifying the surface may prevent falls.
Regulate the temperature of the water to from 40°C to 43°C (105°F to 110°F) or adjust water in the shower to the appropriate temperature. To prevent burning, do not turn on hot water while the patient is in the bath except with extreme caution.	The temperature of the water should be warm but not hot enough to burn the skin. Agitate the water well to equalize the water temperature.
Fill the bath approximately half full.	Water is displaced when the patient sits in a bath. Filling a bath half full prevents spilling, which could be a safety hazard.
Escort the patient to the shower or bath.	If the patient becomes weak, the nurse will be there for assistance.
Place a DO NOT DISTURB sign on the door.	The nurse is responsible for protecting the patient from invasion of privacy.
If necessary, help the patient into the bath or shower; place a chair next to the bath.	Supporting the weight of the patient helps provide stability for maintaining balance.
Have the patient ease himself from the chair to the edge of the bath, place his feet in the bath and then assist the patient to lower his body into the water.	Using slow, simple instructions will promote safety through the coordinated efforts of the patient and the nurse. More falls take place in the bathroom than any other location.
Encourage the patient to use handrails while in the shower.	Installed rails provide a permanent safety device that prevents falls.
A stool may be placed in the shower.	If the patient becomes tired or weak, the stool may be used for both comfort and support.
Remain with the patient if he appears weak, faint, or fearful.	The nurse may be held liable for any injury that may occur because of poor judgement or negligence.

Continued

When assisting a patient to have a bath or a shower the nurse should encourage as much independence and participation from the patient as possible not only in relation to hygiene but also with any care that is planned (Principles of Care 9-1).

Sometimes the patient cannot go to a bathroom, but can bathe most of his body at the bedside with a minimum of assistance (Principles of Care 9-2).

The bed bath. There may be times when the patient is too ill or weak to bathe by himself. In this instance the nurse may be required to give the patient a bed bath (Principles of Care 9-3). This should be carried out at a time which most meets the needs of the patient in terms of convenience and comfort. This may mean giving the patient a bed bath in the afternoon or evening.

Giving a bed bath offers the nurse an excellent time to become better acquainted with a patient and to

Principles of Care 9-1. *Continued*

Nursing Action	Rationale
Provide the patient with a means to summon the nurse.	The patient may appear capable of bathing without assistance but may develop problems later.
Adult patients may be left alone, but stay close at hand and check the patient every 3 or 4 minutes.	The nearer the nurse, the quicker assistance may be provided. Children should never be left alone in a bath or shower.
The nurse may make the bed while the patient is in the bath or shower if the patient can be left alone.	The patient may wish to go directly to bed following bathing. A bed with clean linen extends the feeling of refreshment from the bath.
Offer to assist the patient with bathing.	There may be some parts of his body, such as his back, that he cannot reach but would appreciate to have washed.
Assist the patient out of the bath or shower onto a dry bath mat.	Wet, slippery floors can lead to falls.
Help the patient, as necessary, with drying and putting on a gown or pyjamas.	Some patients may have used considerable energy in bathing and appreciate assistance with getting dressed.
Help the patient back to a clean bed and offer the patient a backrub.	A backrub can further contribute to a feeling of relaxation while at the same time it stimulates the circulation to the skin.
When the patient is comfortable, return to the bathroom, remove all soiled and wet linen, and restore the room for the next patient's use.	Leaving the bathroom in the same way it was found is one way that nurses work as a conscientious team.

work on developing a helping relationship with him. Other nursing contacts with the patient tend to be more brief than the time involved in giving a bath. Good opportunities for assessment and health teaching usually arise while bathing a patient. Giving a patient a bath demonstrates caring, an important aspect of the nurse-patient relationship.

Perineal care

There are times when the patient cannot wash his own genital and anal areas at the time of a bath, or this type of hygiene may require more skill than the patient can provide. The special care of this area is called *perineal care*. The nurse should not ignore or omit cleansing this area because many bacteria and secretions located there could lead to unpleasant odours or infection. Perineal care should be left to the patient's discretion. However, if the patient is unconscious, follow Principles of Care 9-4.

Shaving

A common hygiene routine for men is to remove, clean, or groom facial hair Most men prefer to be clean shaven. Women may shave the hair from their legs and underarms. Many prefer to shave at the time of bathing. The patient should be consulted about his preferences for this personal practice.

On the basis of the nurse's knowledge some modifications for shaving may need to be made. For instance, patients who have blood disorders or take medications that increase the tendency to bleed should use electric razors. Also, use of a razor with a blade by a confused or depressed person should be forbidden to prevent accidental or self-inflicted injury. Those receiving oxygen may use safety or battery-operated razors to reduce electrical hazards and the possibility of combustion.

The nurse may need to shave patients from time to time. Some patients may be unable to shave because

---

Principles of Care 9-2. *Assisting the patient to wash in bed*

Nursing Action	Rationale
Place the head of the bed to a sitting position or help the patient sit on the edge of the bed.	The patient will use less energy in reaching the equipment and parts of his body in this position.
Pull the curtains around the patient's bed.	This protects the patient's privacy and prevents chilling from draughts.
Assemble the following equipment: basin with warm water between 40°C to 43°C (105°F to 110°F), towels, bath blanket, soap, shaving equipment, mirror, oral hygiene supplies, cosmetics and clean bed clothes.	Organizing equipment prevents fatigue, delay and chilling during a bath.
Remove the top linens and replace them with a bath blanket.	A bath blanket absorbs water and is likely to provide more warmth than sheets.
Allow the patient to bathe himself; assist him as necessary.	Most patients prefer to be alone while bathing. There may be some areas of the body with which the patient may appreciate assistance, such as the back, buttocks, lower legs and feet.
Change the water frequently.	The water may become cool and soapy.
Remove the bath water and make the patient's bed.	Removing the water prevents any spilling on the floor. The patient will feel more refreshed with a clean change of linen.
Give the patient a backrub and leave the patient positioned comfortably in bed.	Following the activities of bathing and bedmaking with a backrub will restore a feeling of relaxation and rest.
Clean and put away all the patient's personal hygiene items to their proper place.	A sense of orderliness will contribute to relaxation, and the patient will know where to look for his bathing supplies when needed again.

Principles of Care 9-3. *Giving the patient a bed bath*

Nursing Action	Rationale
Preparing for the Bath	
Bring articles needed for hygiene and bedmaking to the bedside and arrange them in order of their use on the bedside table, overbed table or a chair. The bathwater should be comfortably warm, about 40°C to 43°C (105°F to 110°F). Include equipment for shaving and oral hygiene. If the patient uses a safety razor, he will need a basin of hot water, a mirror and a good light.	Bringing everything to the bedside conserves time and energy. Arranging items conveniently and in order of their use saves time and helps prevent stretching and twisting of the nurse's muscles. Warm water is comfortable and relaxing for the patient.
Pull curtains or shut the door.	The patient's privacy and warmth are maintained from unnecessary exposure.
Place an adjustable bed in the high position and remove the bed siderails.	Having the bed in a high position and removing the bed siderails prevent strain on the nurse's back.

Continued

Principles of Care 9-3. *Continued*

Nursing Action	Rationale

Preparing for the Bath

Loosen top linen where it is tucked under the mattress. Fold the spread and blankets individually from top to bottom and in half again (in quarters). Drape them over the back of a chair if they are to be reused. If not, discard into a linen basket or skip. Keep linens away from the uniform while handling them.	Folding linen in place and as it is removed avoids stretching of the arms and saves time and energy when putting it back on the bed later. Avoiding draughts while handling linens and keeping linens away from the uniform help prevent the spread of organisms.
Place a fanfolded bath blanket or large towel over the patient's chest and have the patient hold the top edge of the bath blanket or towel. Grasp the bottom of the bath blanket or towel and the top edge of the sheet; pull the sheet to the foot of the bed. Remove the sheet, fold it, and place it in a linen skip.	The patient is not exposed unnecessarily as the top sheet is removed. Avoiding draughts and keeping linens away from the uniform help prevent the spread of organisms.
Assist the patient to the side of the bed where you will work. Have him lie on his back.	Having the patient positioned near the nurse helps prevent unnecessary stretching and twisting of muscles.
Assist the patient with oral hygiene, as necessary.	Oral hygiene is an important part of helping to keep the mouth and teeth clean, healthy and comfortable.
Remove the patient's gown by slipping it off under the bath blanket. Remove all but one pillow and place the bed in a flat position.	Keeping the bath blanket in place avoids exposure and chilling. Having the patient flat in bed with one pillow is comfortable for most patients and convenient for the nurse.

General Techniques to Observe During the Bathing Procedure

Protect the bed linens with a towel while bathing each part of the body.	Keeping the linens protected with a towel prevents the patient from feeling uncomfortable in a damp or wet bed.
Expose, wash, rinse, and dry one part of the body at a time.	Exposing, washing, rinsing and drying one part of the body at a time avoids unnecessary exposure and chilling.
Fold the washcloth like a mitt on the hand so that there are no loose ends.	Having loose ends of cloth drag across the patient's skin is uncomfortable for the patient. Loose ends cool quickly and will feel cold to the patient.
Keep the washcloth wet enough to wash, lather and rinse well but not so wet that it drips.	Dripping water from the washcloth is uncomfortable for the patient and will dampen the bed. Too little moisture on the cloth makes thorough washing and rinsing difficult.
Wash, rinse, and dry the skin well. Change the water as necessary if becomes dirty or too soapy for thorough washing and rinsing.	Thorough cleaning removes dirt, oil and many organisms. Soap or moisture left on the skin is uncomfortable and may irritate the skin.
Do not leave the soap in the bathwater.	The soap will become soft and water becomes too soapy for good rinsing.

Continued

Principles of Care 9-3. Continued

Nursing Action	Rationale

General Techniques to Observe During the Bathing Procedure

Use firm but gentle strokes while washing and drying the patient. Use strokes as long as the body part allows.

Friction helps remove dirt, oil and organisms, and helps dry the skin well. Friction stimulates circulation and muscles. Too much friction may injure tender skin. Long, firm strokes are relaxing and more comfortable than are short, uneven strokes.

Pay particular attention to these areas: under the breasts; axillae; between fingers and toes; in any folds of the skin, such as in the groin or on the abdomen of a patient who is fat; behind the ears; and the umbilicus.

Organisms and dirt are lodged in areas where skin touches skin; if these areas are not washed, rinsed and dried well, they will become irritated, and injury to the skin will eventually occur.

Bathing the Patient

With no soap on the washcloth, wipe one eye from the inner part of the eye near the nose to the outer part near the forehead, as illustrated in Figure 9-1. Rinse or turn the cloth before washing the other eye. Bathe the patient's face, neck and ears, avoiding soap on the face if the patient prefers.

Bathing one eye and then the other prevents spreading organisms from one to the other. Soap is irritating to the eyes. Moving from the inner to the outer aspect of the eye prevents carrying debris toward the lacrimal duct, from which it may enter the nose.

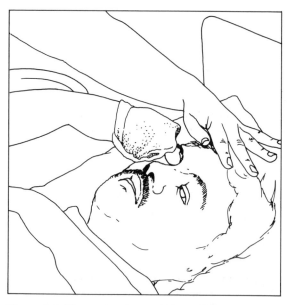

Figure 9-1 The patient lies near the side of the bed where the nurse works. The nurse washes the patient's eye by moving from the inner aspect of the eye outwards. Note that the washcloth is tucked into the nurse's hand.

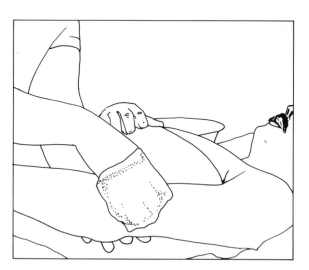

Figure 9-2 The nurse first washes the arm furthest away. A towel protects the bed.

Continued

Principles of Care 9-3. Continued

Nursing Action	Rationale

Bathing the Patient

Bathe the patient's arms, the one farther from the nurse and then the other as illustrated in Figure 9-2. The axillae may be bathed with the arms or with the chest, which is bathed after the arms and hands are finished.

If the nearer arm is washed first, water may accidentally drip on the clean arm as the nurse reaches to do the other.

If the patient is able, place his hands in a basin to wash them, as in Figure 9-3.

Placing the hands in the basin of water to bathe them is comfortable and relaxing for the patient and allows for a thorough washing of the hands and the areas between the fingers.

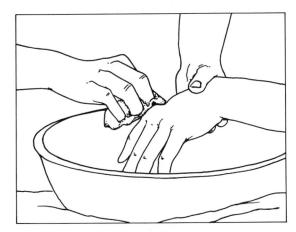

Figure 9-3 The patient's hand is washed in a basin of water.

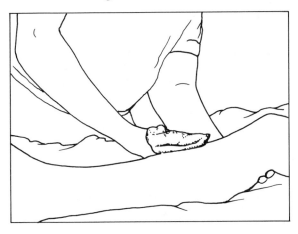

Figure 9-4 The leg furthest from the nurse is washed first. A towel protects the bed.

Bathe the leg, thigh, and groin area farther from the nurse first, as illustrated in Figure 9-4. The front of the thighs and the groin may be washed with the abdomen, and the back of the thighs with the back if desired.

If the nearer leg is washed first, water may accidentally drip on the clean leg as the nurse reaches across to do the other.

Leave the patient at this time, if safe, after placing the wash basin, washcloth and towel within easy reach so that he can wash the genital and anal areas. Discard washcloth, towel and water.

The washcloth, towel and water are considered highly contaminated after washing the genital and anal areas. Changing to clean supplies decreases the spread of organisms.

If the patient is unable to do this independently, assist him as necessary, ensuring the patient's dignity is maintained. Have the patient lie on his abdomen or on his side, facing away from the nurse. Tuck the clean towel under the length of the back. Wash the back of the neck, shoulders, back and buttocks. Expose and wash the upper back, if the patient is likely to become chilled.

Change the patient's bed linen and leave in a comfortable position.

Principles of Care 9-4. Providing individual perineal care

Nursing Action	Rationale
For Female Patient	
Bring equipment and supplies to the bedside, including soap or solution for cleaning, clean washcloths or cotton balls, and plain water for rinsing. The solution should be about 40°C (105°F).	Bringing everything to the bedside saves time and energy. A warm solution will be comfortable for the patient.
Place the patient on her back and cover with a bath blanket. Fanfold the top linens to the foot of the bed.	Proper draping prevents unnecessary exposure and chilling of the patient.
Place a towel beneath the buttocks or place the patient on a bedpan.	These measures provide for the collection or absorption of water.
Bend the patient's knees and spread her legs.	This exposes the area to be washed.
Wear disposable gloves.	Gloves act as a transmission barrier between any microbes and the nurse.
Separate the folds of the labia and wash from the pubic area toward the anal area. Use a clean area of the washcloth or a separate cotton ball for each stroke.	Care is taken to avoid introducing secretions and bacteria into the opening through which urine is released. This could cause a urinary tract infection.
Rinse the area, following the same steps described above, with a clean washcloth, cotton balls and water, or water may be poured from a height of 15 cm (6 in) over the area.	Rinsing removes loosened dirt, organisms and cleaning solution.
Dry the area well.	Drying prevents skin irritation and injury.
Turn the patient to the side. Wash away from the genital area. Rinse and dry well.	Cleaning an area where there are fewer organisms before an area with many helps prevent spreading them to cleaner parts of the body.
For Male Patient	
Follow the same general instructions described previously with the following modifications.	The differences in male and female genital anatomy call for some modifications.
Place a towel under the penis in addition to the one under the buttocks.	Male patients are generally not placed on a bedpan, and the extra towel will provide more absorption of the solution.
Clean around the penis and the scrotum thoroughly. In a patient who is not circumcised, gently pull back the foreskin and clean the area.	Secretions collect within the loose folds of the skin that covers the tip of an uncircumcised penis.
Rinse and dry the patient thoroughly and replace the foreskin to the original position.	Replacing the foreskin prevents injury to the penis.
Proceed with washing the anal area as described for a female.	

they are too ill or because an arm is immobilized in a cast or traction. Principles of Care 9-5 describes suggestions for shaving that the nurse may find helpful.

Making an occupied bed

It is usual to change linens at the time a patient is bathed. However, the bed may need to be remade

Principles of Care 9-5. *Providing a shave*

Nursing Action	Rationale
Determine the patient's usual shaving routine.	The nurse should attempt to follow the patient's grooming patterns as closely as possible.
Gather the equipment the patient prefers to use; modify any equipment for potential safety hazards.	The nurse may need to substitute safety, battery or electric razors in certain situations.
If possible, place the patient in a sitting position.	Being upright is a similar position to one a patient would assume himself. It also promotes eye contact and communication between the patient and nurse.
Wash the patient's face with warm, soapy water.	Removing oil helps to raise the hair shaft, promoting its removal. Soap removes bacteria that can enter tiny cuts from the razor.
Inspect the face for elevated moles, birthmarks or lesions.	Scraping or cutting can cause bleeding, irritation or infection.
Lather the face with shaving cream or soap.	Lathering softens the beard and helps the razor slide over the skin without nicking or cutting.
Using short strokes with the razor, shave in the direction of the hair growth as illustrated in Figure 9-5. Start from the upper face and lip and extend to the neck. The patient may tilt his head to help shave in hollow or curved areas.	Shaving in the direction of the hair shaft will produce a closer shave without irritating the underlying skin.
Use the hand without the razor to pull the skin below the area being shaved.	Pulling flattens and firms the skin surface, promoting uniform shaving.

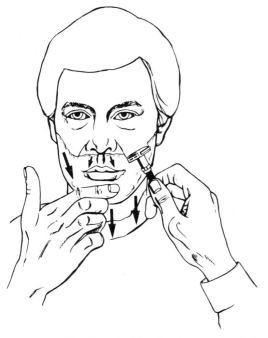

Figure 9-5 The direction for shaving a patient's face.

Continued

Principles of Care 9-5. *Continued*

Nursing Action	Rationale
Rinse the razor after each stroke.	Rinsing removes hair from between the blade and blade guard so the cutting edge remains clean.
Rinse and dry the face when completely finished.	Final rinsing removes remnants of lather and shaved hair.
Apply the patient's choice of lotion or cologne.	Most after-shave preparations contain scented alcohol. The alcohol acts as an antiseptic in any microabrasions. As the alcohol evaporates, it causes a cooling sensation that feels refreshing.
Return all shaving equipment to its proper location. Discard any dulled disposable razors or razor blades in a special safety container.	The nurse must take care that others will not be accidentally injured by sharp objects.

whenever it becomes wet or soiled. Principles of Care 9-6 describes how to make an occupied bed. An occupied bed is one in which the linens are changed with the patient still in bed. If the patient is able to be out of bed, the bed is made while unoccupied. Differences in details of bedmaking are less important than the patient's comfort, but the hospital procedures should be observed.

Caring for the teeth and mouth

General good health is important for keeping the mouth and teeth healthy. Unfortunately, dental diseases are common primarily because of poor oral hygiene, lack of dental care and general poor eating habits. Another point of concern to nurses is that many persons who observe good practices of oral hygiene when well often become careless and unmotivated in carrying out oral hygiene when ill.

Benefits of good oral hygiene. Howarth (1977) suggests that the principal objective of mouth care is to maintain the mouth in good condition; i.e. one which is comfortable, clean, moist and free from infection. This is for both physiological and psychological reasons. The following are some benefits of good oral hygiene:

- Most persons report that they enjoy the aesthetic effects of having the mouth and teeth well cared for and clean.
- Proper oral hygiene and the prevention of

mouth diseases help improve a person's self-image.
- Because the process of digestion starts in the mouth, sound practices of mouth and tooth care promote digestion.
- The pleasure of eating and the taste of food is improved when practices of oral hygiene are observed.
- Proper mouth and tooth care decrease various infections and the decay of teeth.

The decay of teeth with the formation of cavities is called *caries*. One of the leading contributors to dental caries is accumulated plaque. *Plaque* is a mass of bacteria that covers teeth, and it can extend to the roots of teeth, thus causing cavities and gum disease. Plaque can be removed with daily dental care. Figure 9-8 illustrates the chain of events that leads to dental caries. Breaking the chain with oral hygiene techniques can reduce their formation.

There are several commonly recommended ways to help prevent caries: cutting down on sweets, such as soft drinks, sweets, gum and pastries; brushing the teeth often and as soon after eating as possible; if brushing is not convenient, rinsing the mouth well with water after eating; using a toothpaste, powder or rinse containing fluoride; and visiting the dentist regularly, at least once or twice a year.

The major cause of tooth loss in adults is gum disease. *Gingivitis* is an inflammation of the gums; severe inflammation of the gums, including the bone tissue around the teeth, is called *periodontitis*, or *pyorrhoea*. Regular dental care and good oral hygiene are the best ways to prevent periodontitis.

Principles of Care 9-6. Making an occupied bed

Nursing Action	Rationale
Elevate the height of the bed.	To avoid back strain, the patient should be at waist level to the nurse.
Cover the patient with a bath blanket and remove the top bed linen.	A bath blanket provides warmth and prevents exposure while the soiled linen is removed and the bed is remade.
Help the patient to his side and to the far part of the bed, where a siderail is in position. (If a patient is confined to bed, and it does not have siderails, then two nurses should make it, thus maintaining a safe environment for the patient.) Loosen the bottom linens opposite the patient, roll them toward the patient, and tuck them as close to the patient as possible, as illustrated in Figure 9-6.	With the patient on the far side of the bed, the nurse is able to make half of the bed (bottom linens only). Rolling linen together with the cleaner side of the linens to the outside helps to prevent spreading organisms.

Figure 9-6 The nurse has the siderails in place opposite the work area so that the patient will not fall from the bed. The soiled linen is rolled close to the patient. The nurse has secured the bottom linen under the mattress and will roll all of it close to the soiled linen. Before moving to the opposite side of the bed, the nurse raises the siderail for the patient's protection.

Place a clean bottom sheet on the bed. Unfold it in place. Tuck the sheet under the mattress securely on the side opposite the patient. Fanfold the sheet and place it near the rolled-up linen at the patient's back. Unfold the drawsheet in place and tuck it securely under the mattress. Place the siderail in position on the side where you are working.	Opening linens by shaking them causes drafts that could spread organisms. Having linens free of wrinkles results in a more comfortable bed and reduces the risk of skin breakdown.
Assist the patient to roll over all linens to that half of the bed where the bottom linens are in place and secured under the mattress.	The nurse is now able to make the second half of the bed, bottom linens only.

Continued

Principles of Care 9-6. Continued

Nursing Action	Rationale
Move to the opposite side of the bed and lower the siderail. Loosen soiled linens and continue to roll them together and place them in the linen skip. Keep linens away from the uniform.	Avoiding stretching across the bed helps to prevent straining muscles. Keeping soiled linens rolled together and away from the uniform helps to prevent spreading organisms.
Pull the bottom sheet into place, as illustrated in Figure 9-7. Tuck it under the mattress. Do the same with the drawsheet. Be sure that linens are pulled and tucked firmly and securely.	Having linens free of wrinkles and well secured under the mattress results in a more comfortable bed and helps prevent the risk of skin breakdown.
Assist the patient to the middle of the bed and onto his back. Place the top linens in place and make the remainder of the bed. Slip the bath blanket out and fold it in place on the bed. Change pillow linens. Arrange the pillows comfortably for the patient. Put up the bed siderails as indicated.	

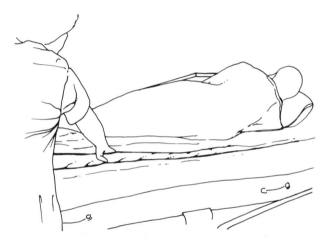

Figure 9-7 The siderail is in place on the side opposite the nurse's work area. After assisting the patient over the rolls of clean and soiled linen and removing the soiled linen, the nurse pulls the clean linen towards her and finishes placing all bottom linen securely.

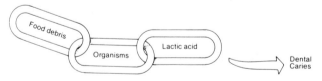
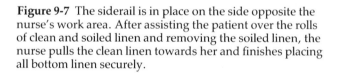

Figure 9-8 This chain illustrates events that lead to caries. Debris remaining in the mouth after eating (especially concentrated carbohydrates such as sweets) accumulates on and between the teeth. This debris is attacked by organisms in the mouth, which feed on it and produce lactic acid. Lactic acid destroys tooth enamel to cause cavities. Proper oral hygiene breaks the chain by removing debris and by breaking up colonies of organisms.

Brushing the teeth. A toothbrush should be small enough to reach all teeth. The bristles should be firm enough to clean well, but not so firm that they are likely to injure tissues. Many dentists recommend a soft-textured, multitufted toothbrush with a flat brushing surface. Others recommend brushes with widely spaced tufts. When tufts are widely spaced, the brush is easier to keep clean and dry. Electric or battery-operated toothbrushes have been found to be as good as hand brushes.

Principles of Care 9-7 describes an efficient method of brushing the teeth.

Principles of Care 9-7. Brushing the patient's teeth

Nursing Action	Rationale
Position the brush with the bristles at the junction of the teeth and gums.	This position helps clean debris away from the margin of the gums.
Move the brush in small circular and then upward movements over the teeth, paying particular attention to the junction between the teeth and gums.	This is the best direction and position for removing plaque and food particles from the outside surfaces of all teeth and the inside surfaces of the back teeth.

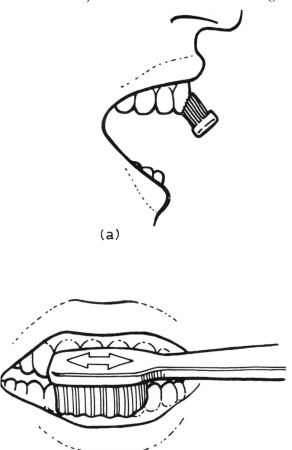

(a)

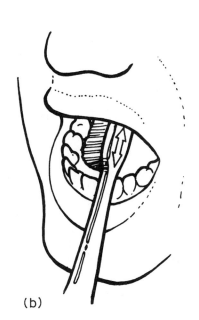

(b)

(c)

Figure 9-9 The toothbrush is positioned at a 45° angle to the gums (*A*). The outside and inside surfaces of the teeth should be brushed in the correct direction (*B*–*C*). Reproduced with permission from the Guide To Healthy Gums; published by the Health Education Authority, 1992.

Rinse the mouth with water.	This freshens the mouth and removes any food particles or plaque that have become dislodged. If the patient is unable to brush his own teeth it is recommended that the nurse brushes the front teeth up and down and the side teeth back and forth, whilst maintaining the brush at a 45 degree angle to the teeth (Bucholz, 1988).

Flossing the teeth. Many bacteria in the mouth become lodged between the teeth. The toothbrush cannot reach these areas well. Therefore, flossing twice a day is recommended (Principles of Care 9-8). The practice not only removes what the brush cannot, but also helps to break up groups of bacteria between teeth. There are no significant differences between the ability of waxed and unwaxed dental floss to remove plaque. Waxed floss is thicker than unwaxed, making it slightly harder to insert into narrow spaces. Unwaxed floss frays somewhat more

quickly. The choice of dental floss is a personal preference.

Oral irrigating appliances. Appliances that generate pulsating jet streams of water under pressure are available to assist with oral hygiene. They are particularly helpful for flushing debris that accumulates around stationary bridges and braces attached to the teeth. However, if too much pressure is used, damage to gum tissues may occur. Also, debris may be forced into tissue pockets, where a local infection can then develop. Because of these disadvantages,

Principles of Care 9-8. Flossing the patient's teeth

Nursing Action	Rationale
Wind dental floss around the middle fingers of each hand, keeping the fingers no more than about 4″ apart as illustrated in Figure 9-10A.	Threading the floss in this manner helps to control and advance areas of the floss.
Insert the floss without force between the teeth. Keep the thumb to the outside for upper teeth as shown in Figure 9-10B. Alter the way of holding the floss for lower teeth as in Figure 9-10C.	Controlled and gentle insertion prevents injury to the gums.

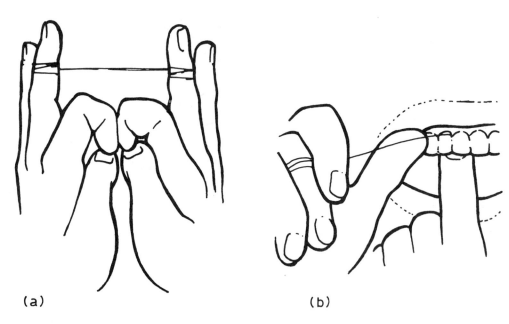

(a)   (b)

Figure 9-10 Flossing the teeth. Reproduced with permission from the Guide To Healthy Gums; published by the Health Education Authority, 1992.

Principles of Care 9-8. Continued

Nursing Action	Rationale
Gently saw the floss back and forth at the point where the teeth contact each other.	Advancing the floss gradually in this space helps it to slide gently into place at the junction of the tooth and gum.
With *both* fingers, move the floss up and down six times on the side of one tooth and then six times on the side of the other tooth until the surfaces are "squeaky" clean.	This movement cleans the area between two teeth.
Go to the gum tissue but not into it with the floss.	Stopping short of the gum prevents injury, which may cause discomfort, soreness or bleeding.
Turn the floss from one middle finger to the other after flossing between adjacent teeth.	Winding and unwinding the floss brings up a fresh section and prevents moving debris from one area of the gum line to another.
Rinse the mouth vigorously with water.	Water removes food particles and plaque that have been dislodged with the floss. Rinsing only after eating or using an oral irrigating appliance only after eating does not remove plaque and food particles well.

a dentist should be consulted before their use is recommended.

Providing oral hygiene. Measures for oral hygiene may need to be modified for certain patients (Principles of Care 9-9). If the patient is able to assist with his mouth care, he should be offered the necessary materials on awakening in the morning, before bedtime, after each meal and between meals, as indicated. If he is helpless, the nurse should give oral hygiene as often as necessary to keep the mouth and teeth clean and moist.

The care of dentures and bridges. Mouth care is equally important for a person with false teeth. The word *denture* refers to a dental appliance of artificial teeth that replaces the person's own upper, lower or all teeth. A *bridge* is a dental appliance that replaces one or several teeth. A bridge may be fixed to other teeth so that it cannot be removed, or it may be removable and fasten to adjoining teeth with a clasp. Dentures and removable bridges should be taken from the mouth and cleaned with a brush. There are commercial solutions available in which to soak dentures and bridges, if the patient prefers.

Many dentists recommend that dentures and bridges remain in place except while they are being cleaned. Keeping dentures and bridges out for long periods of time permits the gum lines to change, affecting the fit.

If the patient has been instructed to remove dentures or bridges while sleeping, a disposable, covered cup is convenient and easy to use. For aesthetic reasons, it is better not to use cups, drinking glasses or other dishes used for eating. Plain water is most often used to store dentures and bridges. Some persons add mouthwash to the water; this practice results in a pleasant taste when dentures and bridges are returned to the mouth.

Care should be taken when cleaning dentures and bridges. They are expensive, and damage or loss can create problems. They should be cleaned over a basin of water or a soft towel so that they will not drop onto a hard surface, should they accidentally slip from the nurse's hands. Warm water is used because hot water may warp the plastic material from which many dentures and bridges are made.

Care of the eyes and visual aids

It is not true that using one's eyes will lead to a decrease in the ability to see. As much as anyone may

Principles of Care 9-9. Providing oral hygiene

Nursing Action	Rationale
For cleansing use toothpaste or, if the patient prefers, a mouthwash solution. Plain water may also be used, although it does not have the cleansing ability that many other agents do. Additional cleansing agents are given below.	The choice of cleansing agents is largely personal, but the agent should be one that does not injure or irritate oral tissues.
Use a solution of half water and half hydrogen peroxide, especially if the patient has crustlike particles of mucus and secretions stuck on his teeth or around his lips.	Hydrogen peroxide releases oxygen and causes a froth that helps to break up dried and sticky particles.
Avoid the prolonged use of hydrogen peroxide (Shepherd et al., 1987).	Hydrogen peroxide may damage tooth enamel if used over a long period of time.
Consider using normal saline or a solution of sodium bicarbonate. Watson (1989) suggests the use of effervescent ascorbic acid as an alternative for removing debris from the mouth.	Normal saline and a solution of sodium bicarbonate are effective cleansing agents.
Use a toothbrush for cleansing the mouth and teeth. Run hot water over the tufts of the brush if they are stiff. The toothbrush is still the best tool to use to clean a patient's mouth of debris, even when the patient is unconscious. At one time a gloved finger with gauze wrapped around it was thought to be effective and comfortable for the patient. However, this method can push food particles into the corners of the mouth where they lodge and act as a source of infection (Shepherd et al., 1987). Gauze can also catch on the edges of the teeth and be left in situ.	A toothbrush is an effective device for cleansing the mouth and teeth. Hot water helps soften stiff tufts on a toothbrush, thereby decreasing the danger of injuring oral tissues.
Moisten the mouth and lips after cleaning all areas. Petroleum jelly or a cream can also be used to protect the lips. Oral tissues may be moistened with water or by having the patient suck ice chips if this is permitted.	The skin on the lips is very thin and evaporation of moisture from them occurs rapidly unless they are covered with a protective coating.
Remember that caring for the mouth and teeth is important for a patient's well-being and should be carried out as often as necessary to keep them clean and moistened.	Studies have shown that the procedure of cleansing the mouth and teeth appears more important than the agent used. The nurse is responsible for seeing to it that the patient receives proper oral hygiene.

protest, it is impossible to ruin the eyes from reading. It is true that certain factors can cause eye fatigue. *Eye fatigue* is the discomfort experienced from poor lighting or prolonged focusing on an object. To reduce eye fatigue, observe the following directives.

- Use adequate light such as daylight or a minimum of 75-watt light bulbs when reading.
- Adjust the light source so it comes from above rather than from the side of printed material.

- Lamps should be on while one watches television. There is too much contrast in a completely dark room.
- Glance about the room at frequent periods while reading or doing fine work. Muscles that must remain contracted to hold an image in focus become strained.

Ordinarily the eyes are so well protected naturally with eyelashes, tearing, and a split-second blink

Principles of Care 9-10. Providing eye hygiene

Nursing Action	Rationale
Tap water or normal saline should be warmed to near body temperature. For eyes that are extremely irritated or infected, the solution and its container may need to be sterile.	Warm water is soothing to the eye and promotes the patient's comfort. Sterile solutions prevent adding bacteria to the eye.
Wash hands well. If an infection is present, the nurse may need to wear sterile gloves for self-protection.	The hands contain many bacteria that could cause an infection in the eye. If an infection is already present, gloves act as a barrier for their transfer to the nurse.
Place a towel or a basin to the side of the patient's face.	The towel and basin will collect any solution that may drain downward and prevent having to change bed linen.
Position the patient on the side of the eye that will be cleansed, or the patient may sit and tilt his head to the side.	Water will flow downward due to gravity. Turning toward the side will prevent solution that may also contain some of the discharge material from flowing into the opposite eye or down the face.
Moisten cotton balls, which may also need to be sterile, in the solution. Wipe once with each cotton ball from the corner of the eye near the nose toward the other side near the temple.	The movement of the cotton ball toward the temple prevents solution from entering the nose through the lacrimal duct.
Use each cotton ball only once while cleansing the eye and then discard it.	This practice helps prevent carrying debris back over the eye.
Clean the other eye in a similar manner if necessary. If each eye is infected with different bacteria, all equipment, solutions and gloves will need to be changed.	Care must be taken to avoid transferring any organisms from one eye to the other.

reflex that they do not require special care. In spite of this, eyes occasionally become irritated. They may require special lenses to help focus images sharply, or they may become diseased or injured, thus requiring removal. The nurse may then need to provide special eye care skills. If a patient does not shut his eyes or blink, which is the case of some unconscious patients, the eyes need to be medicated, closed, and patched. They should be inspected and cleansed several times a day to make sure there are no signs of infection.

Cleansing the eyes. The eyes can become irritated from wind, smoke, dust, bacteria, or exposure to a source of allergy. In response to these irritants, the eyes increase mucus production and other secretions that trap and remove the irritating substances. This can lead to an accumulation of dried or liquid material. Discharges from the eyes should be removed carefully and as frequently as necessary to keep eyes clean (Principles of Care 9-10).

Care of spectacles. Many patients wear spectacles, which represent a considerable financial investment. They are not quickly or easily replaced. The nurse should use every effort to prevent glasses from being broken, scratched, or lost. Spectacles should be cleaned as follows:

- Work over a basin of water or a towel so that if the glasses accidentally slip from your hands they will not fall on a hard surface and break.
- Allow warm water to flow over the lenses and frames. Hot water may damage plastic lenses and frames. Use a little soap or detergent with the water if there is dried material on the glasses. Commercial glass cleaners may be used also.
- Rinse the glasses well. Soap or detergent is likely to streak the glasses if not rinsed off well.
- Dry glasses with a soft, clean cloth, such as a cotton handkerchief. Tissues are not recommended. They are made of wood pulp and

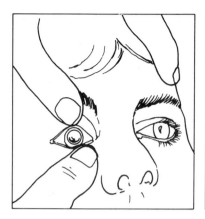

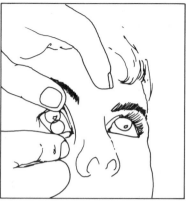

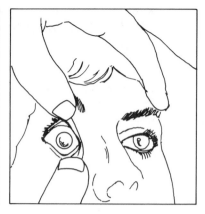

Directly over the cornea: This normal wearing position of the corneal contact lens is also the correct position for removing it. If the lens cannot be removed, however, slide it onto the sclera.

On the sclera only: Here the lens can remain with relative safety until experienced help is available; other white areas of the eye to the side or above the cornea might also be used. If the lens is to be removed, however, slide it to a position directly over the cornea.

After the eyelids have been separated and the corneal contact lens has been correctly positioned over the cornea, widen the eyelid margins beyond the top and bottom edges of lens (as shown).

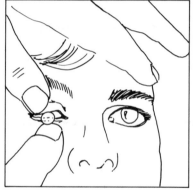

After the lower eyelid margin has been moved near the bottom lens edge and the upper eyelid margin has been moved near the top lens edge (as shown), move under the bottom edge of the lens by pressing slightly harder on the lower eyelid while moving it upward.

After the lens has tipped slightly, move the eyelids toward one another, thus causing the lens to slide out between the eyelids (as shown).

Figure 9-11 These drawings show how to remove hard contact lenses. A suction cup may also be used. Apply the cup to the lens and then lift it straight up and off the eye surface. A suction cup can be used only if the lens is visible in the eye. If the patient wears soft lenses, remove each one by grasping it near the lower edge between the fingers and thumb. The lens folds up with this manoeuvre and is then lifted from the eye. Clean soft lenses according to the manufacturer's instructions. Store them in a solution so that they do not dry and crystallize. Store hard and soft lenses in appropriate containers when not being worn, making sure that the left and right lenses are correctly inserted into containers that have been carefully marked.

have been found to scratch lenses, especially when the lenses are made of plastic material.

- Do not clean spectacles without washing them first. The dirt and dust on the lenses are likely to scratch when a cloth is wiped across dirty glasses.

Plastic lenses have become popular because they are considerably lighter in weight than are glass lenses. Plastic lenses have one disadvantage, however: they are very easily scratched. All glasses that are not being worn should be stored in a case or resting on the frame.

Care of contact lenses. Contact lenses are small plastic discs worn directly on the eyeball. The nurse will wish to know if her patient wears them. Ordinarily, the patient will insert, remove and take care of his own lenses. Some contact lenses are designed for extended wear and do not require removal at night. If a patient's condition is such that he cannot remove his contact lenses, it is best to seek assistance from someone familiar with the procedure. In emergency situations, the nurse should follow instructions as described in Figure 9-11. Hard contact lenses may cause damage to the cornea of the eye if left in place longer than the patient's customary wearing time, usually 12 to 15 hours, or if removed improperly.

Care of an artificial eye. Any man-made object that replaces a natural body part is called a *prosthesis*. An artificial eye, leg, and arm are examples of prosthetic devices. Artificial eyes are primarily plastic; rarely, the nurse may encounter an older prosthetic eye made of glass. Artificial eyes are custom made to match the patient's remaining eye.

Most people think that an artificial eye is round like a marble. Actually it is shaped like a shell as illustrated in Figure 9-12. An object called an implant is permanently inserted within the bony orbit at the time of the eye's removal. It is impossible to remove an implant.

An artificial eye is used strictly for cosmetic reasons; there is no way of restoring vision once the eye is removed. The artificial eye may need to be removed and cleaned from time to time. The patient wearing an artificial eye will generally wish to care for it himself. If the patient is unable to remove the eye, the nurse will need to do so using the following techniques:

- Have the patient lie down so that the artificial eye will not fall to the floor accidentally while it is being removed.
- Depress the patient's lower lid until the lower edge of the artificial eye slides out and into your hand.
- Clean the artificial eye well with soap and water by washing it with your fingers. Chemicals and alcohol are not used on an artificial eye because they are likely to damage its surface.
- Rinse the prosthetic eye before replacing it so that any remaining soap does not irritate the skin in which it rests.
- The cavity of the eye may be irrigated before reinsertion of the artificial eye.

Care of the ears and hearing aids

The outer ears are the collectors of sounds. The ability to hear sounds is important to survival and the appreciation of life. Too much sound or unpleasant sound has been referred to by some as "noise pollution".

The ability to hear decreases with age. The process can be speeded by exposure to loud sounds. Noise levels are measured in *decibels* (dB). Permanent damage to hearing begins to occur at 90 decibels according to the Environmental Protection Agency in the USA. Table 9-1 shows the decibel levels of various common sounds.

Healthy ears only need to be washed, rinsed, and dried when a patient is given a bath. No object should be placed into the ear canal because of the danger of injuring the eardrum. If the ear becomes

Figure 9-12 Front and side views of the shell-shaped artificial eye. The rounder device is the implant that is inserted permanently in the eye at the time of surgery.

Table 9-1. Common sound levels

Common Sounds	Decibel Level
Discotheque—1 m in front of loudspeaker	120
Pneumatic drill at 5 m	100
Heavy goods vehicle from pavement; powered lawnmower at operator's ear	90
Vacuum cleaner at 3 m; Telephone ringing at 2 m	70
Boiling kettle at 0.5 m	50
Refrigerator humming at 2 m	40
Threshold of hearing	0

Source: Bothered by Noise? DoE; reproduced with permission of the Controller of Her Majesty's Stationery Office.

plugged with cerumen, or wax, it may be necessary for a doctor to remove it. Nurses may irrigate the ear. Some nurses have found that using a pulsating stream of water produced by an oral irrigating appliance is useful to help remove wax and debris from the ear canal. When using this type of appliance, it is very important to be sure that the tympanic membrane is intact and that the stream of water is set at its *lowest* setting. This procedure is usually only undertaken by ENT specialist nurses.

Care for hearing aids. Some people require the use of a hearing aid, which increases the ability to hear sounds. These devices do not replace the complete quality of hearing but can be an adequate substitute for some people. They can be worn on the body, but more often they are fitted into spectacles, worn behind the ear, or placed completely within the ear. The nurse should know about hearing aids when caring for a patient who uses one. Note the following important information.

- Avoid exposing the hearing aid to extreme heat, water, cleaning chemicals or hair spray.
- The outside of a hearing aid should be cleaned with just a dry, soft cloth or tissue. Some hearing aids that are mouded to fit within the ear come with a special tool for removing any wax that may accumulate around the hearing aid.
- Turn the hearing aid off when not being worn to prolong the life of the battery.
- Store the hearing aid, when not in use, where it will not fall. A cracked case can cause variations in the sound level.
- Lack of sound or poor sound may indicate a need for a new battery. Use fresh batteries that are specific for each type of hearing aid. Old batteries can be recycled.

Most patients or their families are instructed on the care and use of hearing aids. They may continue to care for their hearing aid while being hospitalized for other reasons. If the nurse does need to help the

Principles of Care 9-11. Inserting a patient's hearing aid

Nursing Action	Rationale
Inspect the external ear and clean it if cerumen has accumulated.	Accumulation of cerumen can interfere with sound conduction.
Test the ability of the hearing aid to function by turning it on.	A functioning hearing aid produces a continuous whistle when not being worn.
Make sure the hearing aid is off and the volume is turned down before insertion.	A sudden loud level of sound can be annoying and uncomfortable for a patient who uses one.
Insert the hearing aid in the external ear. The earlobe should be pulled downward while pressing the hearing aid inward.	The hearing aid is custom moulded to fit snugly so that sound does not escape. *Feedback*, a loud, shrill noise, occurs when a hearing aid is not positioned correctly.
Turn the hearing aid on and gradually increase the volume.	The patient can best judge the volume that is most comfortable.
Turn the hearing aid off when it is removed from the ear.	The life of the hearing aid battery can be prolonged by turning the device off during periods of nonuse.

patient insert a hearing aid, suggestions in Principles of Care 9-11 may be helpful.

Care of the nose

The best way to clean the patient's nose is to have him blow it *gently* while allowing both nostrils to be open. Blowing while closing one nostril carries the danger of forcing debris into the eustachian tube. Occasionally, secretions may dry around the outside of the nose, especially when the patient is receiving oxygen or has a tube inserted through the nose. Washing with soap and water may be sufficient to remove these secretions. Cream, lotions, or ointments may be applied to the area to keep the skin moist.

Care of the fingernails

The nails are a structure of the skin. They are composed of flat, hard, keratin cells. Keratin is an insoluble protein material. The root of the nail lies in a groove where the nail grows and is nourished by the bloodstream. Nursing measures to care for fingernails include the following:

- Care for the nails at the time of the bath; this is usually convenient for the patient and the nurse. Soaking the nails before grooming will soften them and prevent injury.
- Groom the nails by filing or cutting. The nails should not be trimmed too far down on the side because of the danger of injury to the cuticle and the skin around the nail. Nail scissors should be used with great care to avoid injuring the skin. Cutting a patient's nails should be in line with district policy. The nurse must check this before proceeding to cut a patient's nails.
- After washing the hands, push the cuticle back gently to prevent hangnails, which are dried and broken pieces of cuticle. Once present, they may be removed with cutting. This should be done with great care to prevent injury to the cuticle.
- Clean under the nails with a blunt instrument, such as an orange stick or a nail file. The nurse will wish to be careful to avoid injuring the area under the nail where it is attached to the skin.
- Finish care by lubricating the hands with a cream or lotion to prevent drying and chapping of the skin. Massage the hands from the fingertips toward the wrists to help prevent congestion of blood in the hands.

Care of the feet and toenails

Patients who have diabetes or vascular diseases should have orders from a physician for cutting toenails. Many people, especially the elderly who may have diminished vision, strength, or coordination may utilize the services of a chiropodist. A chiropodist is an individual with special training in caring for feet.

The following neasures are important for proper foot care:

- Start foot care by cleaning the feet well. Ensure that the feet are well washed, rinse off the soap and dry thoroughly paying particular attention to between the toes.
- Use frequent bathing and foot powder when the feet tend to perspire freely. Odours can usually be controlled by these measures. Changing stockings regularly also helps keep the feet clean and dry. Shoes may be rotated on a daily basis to allow for moisture to evaporate.
- Trim straight across the toenails with scissors. Cutting or digging deeply at the sides of the nails predisposes the patient to ingrown nails and injury. Patients with ingrown toenails may need medical attention. The area under the toenails is cleaned in the same manner as that under the fingernails.
- Soak the feet of the patient before trimming brittle, thick toenails. If a basin of water is not convenient for soaking, the feet may be wrapped in damp cloths and each foot placed in a plastic bag for a period of time.
- Massage the feet with cream or lotion after trimming the nails. Begin with the toes and move toward the ankles to prevent congestion of blood in the feet. If the skin is not dry or if the feet are perspiring, use plain powder.
- Do not try to cut off a *callus*, which is a thickening of the outer layer of the skin due to pressure and friction. A pumice stone is frequently recommended to remove a callus if it becomes troublesome.
- Be aware of foot problems the patient may have, such as infections, inflammations, ingrown nails, breaks in the skin, corns, warts and

bunions. Such conditions require a doctor's attention.

Care of the hair

Hair grows on most parts of the body. Each hair has a shaft with its root in a hair follicle. There are small muscles attached to hair follicles that contract, causing the hair to stand on end (gooseflesh) when a person is shivering or very frightened.

Good general health is important for attractive hair. Cleanliness helps keep hair attractive. Poor nutrition and illness affect hair. Patients with elevated temperatures may need frequent care of the hair. Perspiration and sebum may mat the hair as the body attempts to regulate heat loss. Some drugs used for cancer treatment cause temporary loss of hair. The cancer patient may appreciate a creative nurse's efforts to design turbans or provide hats to compensate for the change in body image.

Grooming the hair. The following are recommended measures for grooming the hair:

- Try to use the hairstyle of the patient's preference. The patient feels more comfortable about his appearance when this is done.
- Brush the hair slowly and carefully to avoid damaging the hair follicles. Brushing keeps hair clean and distributes oil along the shafts. A comb cannot do this. Brushing also stimulates scalp circulation, which helps bring nourishment to the hair follicles.
- If the hair is tangled, use a wide-toothed comb and pull, starting at the ends of the hair rather than from the crown downward. Forcing and pulling on a tangled mass may break large numbers of hairs. Sometimes alcohol will loosen a tangle.
- Use a comb for arranging the hair after it has been brushed. Sharp and irregular teeth may scratch and injure the scalp and should be avoided. A large-toothed comb is recommended for very thick, curly hair.
- Wash the comb and brush periodically.
- Use oil on the hair if it is dry. There are many preparations on the market, but pure castor oil, olive oil and mineral oil are satisfactory. Coarse, curly hair tends to be dry, and, therefore, oil is usually necessary. If the hair is oily, more frequent shampooing is necessary.
- Do not neglect the hair of ill persons who may

beg to have their hair left undisturbed. This can become a problem, especially if the hair is long. If the patient's hair is not combed even for one day, hours of careful combing of small sections of hair will become necessary.

- If the patient does not object, braid the hair in two braids on either side of the head to prevent tangling or matting. The patient then does not have to lie on one heavy braid. Slides or hair clips should be avoided because they may injure the scalp.
- Be sure to obtain the patient's or family's permission if the hair is hopelessly tangled and cutting it seems advisable.

Shampooing the hair. Hair is exposed to the same dirt and oil as the skin. It should be washed as often as necessary to keep it clean. A weekly shampoo is sufficient for most persons but more or less shampooing may be indicated for others.

Shampooing the hair may be done in the shower when the patient bathes or in a basin in the bathroom if he is allowed out of bed. However, there may be circumstances in which the nurse will need to shampoo the patient's hair. The nurse may be responsible for shampooing the hair, especially when the patient cannot get out of bed (Principles of Care 9-12).

Cultural aspects of hygiene needs

Outlined below are some of the general considerations relating to hygiene needs for patients from three different cultural backgrounds. Within the context of this chapter it is not feasible to cover every cultural group. The three groups have been selected because of their large following within the UK; however, nurses may find themselves working in areas where the community is made up of patients from other multicultural groups. In this instance the nurse should endeavour to find out about the different cultures so that she can nurse patients from these groups as individuals, both in the community and the hospital setting.

Hindu patients

Physical cleanliness is extremely important to Hindus; most prefer to wash under running water, i.e. to have a shower as opposed to taking a bath. Hindus may also wish to wash their genital areas after using the lavatory. If a bidet is not available the

Principles of Care 9-12. Washing the patient's hair

Nursing Action	Rationale
Assemble the shampoo and towels near a source of running water if possible.	Being close to water will help to keep the water at a regulated, comfortable temperature of 40°C (105°F).
Remove the head of the bed and move the patient upward so that his head can be positioned over the mattress. Support the neck and shoulders with a pillow.	This enables the nurse to move behind the patient and place a bowl on a chair underneath the patient's head.
Protect the bottom sheets of the bed with moisture-proof pads or several thicknesses of towels.	The patient may become chilled and uncomfortable as water drips toward the back.
Use a plastic tray with a water trough such as the one illustrated in Figure 9-13 if available. Pad the lip of the tray before placing it under the nape of the patient's neck.	The water drains from the tray down the trough and into a receptacle on the floor.

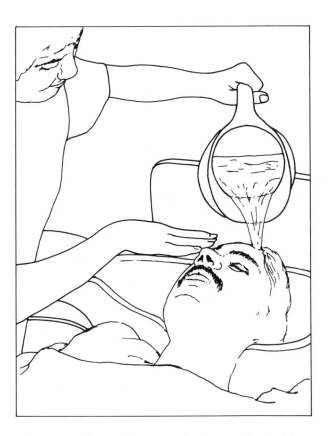

Figure 9-13 The nurse is using a plastic tray with a trough that carries water to a receptacle on the floor. Note how the patient's neck is supported with a towel on the edge of the tray.

Nursing Action	Rationale
Place a towel over the patient's chest and shoulders.	A towel can be used to wipe away any water that splashes the patient's face or ears.
Wet the hair thoroughly and apply shampoo.	The wet hair dilutes the shampoo, forming suds.
Work the shampoo into a lather.	The shampoo must be distributed throughout the hair to get it uniformly clean.

Continued

Principles of Care 9-12. Continued

Nursing Action	Rationale
Rinse the hair with clean, running water.	Shampoo that remains on the hair and scalp may cause irritation.
Wrap the head with dry towels.	Towels absorb water, beginning the process of drying while allowing the patient to assume a more comfortable position.
Fluff the hair with towels, and comb out the hair.	Loosening and combing the hair prepares it for styling.
Braid, blow dry, or set the hair.	Most prefer to work with the hair following a shampoo in order to make it more attractive.

nurse should offer the patient a jug and a bowl. Similarly for patients who are confined to bed, the nurse should offer them a wash following the use of a bedpan.

It is important, especially for Hindu women, that their modesty is maintained; this is in relation to their religious observance. They prefer to have their legs, breasts and upper arms covered. Hospital gowns may only be short and therefore cause embarrassment for the patient. In this instance the nurse should try to provide a long dressing gown, or the patient may prefer to wear her own clothes. Hindu men consider it important to be covered from the waist to the knees.

Prior to prayer, Hindu patients may wish to wash. If the patient is bedbound the nurse should offer the patient a bowl and jug. The nurse caring for the patient should ascertain at what time of day the patient would like to pray, so that she can provide washing facilities and privacy for him.

Muslim patients

Muslim people also prefer to have a shower as opposed to a bath. If this is not available the patient may wish to use a jug and bowl standing in the bath.

Muslim people also like to wash their genital area with water after using the lavatory. If a bidet is available the patient will use this; however, if it is not, then the nurse should provide a jug to fill with water which the patient can use to wash himself with. In the Muslim faith this is normally done using the left hand as the right hand is used for eating.

Modesty is very important to Muslim people. Women are usually covered from head to toe show-ing only their hands and faces. Hospital gowns may be very embarrassing for these patients, therefore the patient should be offered a long dressing gown or if possible allowed to wear their own clothes. The choice of dress for Muslim women will vary according to their country of origin. Many Muslim men wear Western clothes or else they usually wear long kaftan type garments.

Because of the importance Muslims attach to cleanliness, prior to prayer, which takes place five times a day, they wash their feet, hands and mouth. The nurse will need to communicate with the Muslim patient to allow privacy and provide the necessary washing facilities so that the patient, where possible, can follow his usual routine. If the patient is bedbound, a bowl and jug should be provided prior to the patient's prayer time.

Sikh patients

Physical cleanliness is very important to Sikh people. Similarly to Muslims and Hindus, they prefer to shower rather than have a bath.

Most Sikhs are accustomed to having water in the same room as the toilet. If a bedpan has to be used then a bowl of water should also be provided for washing.

Uncut hair and beards are traditional signs of Sikhism. Both men and women fix the hair on their heads in a bun which is kept in place by a small wooden or plastic comb, known as a "kangha". This should not be removed and should be kept with the patient at all times. Hair should be kept clean and never cut or trimmed without the permission of the patient or family (Sikhs believe the head to be the most sacred part of the body). If Sikhs do have their hair cut they will want to keep their kangha about their person at all times.

Underpants are also important in Sikhism to remind Sikhs of the duties of modesty and sexual morality. Devout Sikhs never take them off completely and refer to them as "kacchas". Sikh patients may prefer to leave at least one leg in their kaccha at all times. This is the method used for changing them. The patient will leave the dirty kaccha on one leg and put the clean one on the other leg before removing the soiled kaccha completely.

Sikhs also pray once or twice a day and usually prefer to wash if possible prior to this.

The above can only be used as guidelines for looking at hygiene needs of patients from different cultural backgrounds. The nurse should always consult each patient about their preferences as each patient is an individual.

Suggested measures for attending to hygienic needs in selected situations

When the patient is an infant or child

Remember that the skin and mucous membranes of an infant or child are easily injured. Therefore, offer personal hygiene while handling infants and children gently and with care.

Newborns have difficulty regulating their temperature. The temperature of the room should be increased and there should be adequate protection from drafts during bathing.

Until the umbilical cord of a newborn comes off, bathing should be restricted to sponge bathing. Use warm water, no hotter than 40°C (105°F). Soaps should be used sparingly and rinsed off well before an infant is dried because of the irritating effects of soap remnants.

Use appropriately sized tubs for bathing a newborn after the cord comes off and for bathing an infant. Be sure to hold the infant firmly across the back of the shoulders with one arm and hand so that the infant's head is well out of water.

Pat dry newborns and infants to prevent injury to the skin.

Check the temperature of water for an infant's or child's bath with a bath thermometer. These youngsters cannot indicate to the nurse when water is too hot or too cold. Children under 5 years of age are at the greatest risk.

Discourage the use of bubble baths for female children. The chemicals have been known to irritate the mucous membranes of the urinary system and cause burning when the child urinates.

Remember that children also need eye examinations and parents should be taught their importance. Many times, early detection of vision problems can prevent the occurrence of later problems that are more difficult to handle.

Infants should not be given bottles of milk or juice at night once the teeth have erupted. The sugar from the milk or juice remains in the mouth and can cause cavities. Water may be given or the mouth rinsed after a bottle of milk or juice.

Assist children under 3 years of age with oral hygiene. After about age 3, the youngster should be helped to learn how to perform his own oral hygiene.

Be sure to keep mouthwashes out of the reach of toddlers and young children. The colour and taste are appealing but some mouthwashes contain substances that, if swallowed in large amounts, could threaten a youngster's life.

Teach parents how to help prevent dental caries in children. A fluoride solution is used by many dentists who also recommend using a toothpaste containing fluoride. Some dentists recommend a fluoride supplement for all children up to about 14 years of age. Sealants may be applied by some dentists to cover uneven surfaces of teeth in order to prevent their decay.

When the patient is an adolescent

Help the adolescent who has *acne*, which is a skin eruption caused by inflammation and infection of glands in the skin. At present, acne cannot be cured or prevented, but teaching the adolescent the following hygienic skin care may help control it:

1. Wash the area where acne is present, usually the face, upper back, and chest, two to four times daily with soap or detergent and hot water to keep the skin clean and free of oils.
2. Shampoo the hair frequently to control oiliness.
3. Avoid using oily cosmetics.
4. Do not eat foods that make the condition worse. Other than avoidance of foods that

aggravate the condition, dietary restrictions have not been found helpful in the control of acne.

5. Use preparations available on the market for controlling acne according to directions, but do not use them if they irritate the skin.

6. Do not pick and squeeze pimples. Such practices cause scarring and spread of infection, making matters worse.

7. Teach that exposure to the sun tends to help control acne, but stress the importance of avoiding overexposure that may cause burning and predispose the patient to precancerous lesions.

8. Seek medical attention if these conservative measures are unsuccessful.

When the patient has diabetes mellitus

Teach diabetic persons the importance of observing good practices of hygiene, since they may encounter serious problems with healing when the skin and mucous membranes are irritated or injured.

Stress the importance of proper foot care. Because diabetics tend to have circulatory and nerve deficits, especially in the legs and feet, they should learn to take special precautions to help prevent injury and irritation. In addition to foot care measures described earlier in this chapter, these measures should also be observed and taught:

1. Inspect the feet daily. Use a mirror to look at the bottom of the feet if unable to lift and rotate them for inspection. Be sure to check between the toes for injury and infection.

2. See a chiropodist to remove corns and calluses. Do not try to remove them, and explain to the patient that he should not use commercial preparations or sharp instruments to remove them.

3. Refer the patient to a doctor when there is infection or inflammation on the skin of the feet.

4. Avoid cutting toenails with a scissors. Nails should be trimmed only with a file and with great care to prevent injuring the skin around the nails.

5. Teach the diabetic person to avoid placing heating pads or hot-water bottles at the feet. The patient often is unaware of burning until damage to the skin has occurred. Serious problems may arise when the feet have been burned.

6. Teach the patient to avoid stockings with elastic tops or round garters. Garters and elastic tend to decrease normal circulation in the legs and feet, which is often already impaired in persons with diabetes.

7. Recommend that the patient prop up his feet several times a day to encourage good blood return to the heart.

8. Recommend that a diabetic person not cross his legs at the knees when he is sitting down. This practice tends to decrease circulation to the lower legs and feet.

9. Teach the diabetic person that he should avoid going barefoot to prevent injury to the feet.

10. Instruct the patient to keep his feet dry and warm and to wear stockings and shoes that are clean and fit well. The diabetic person should be taught to break in new shoes gradually to avoid blisters and skin injury.

When the patient is elderly

Remember that the elderly person's skin is thin, has little elasticity, is wrinkled because of little subcutaneous fat, and is dry because of a decrease in the secretions of sebum. These characteristics make the skin easily susceptible to injury, and therefore all hygienic measures should be carried out with gentleness.

Take into account that the elderly have a decreased sense of temperature. Therefore, bathwater should be checked with a bath thermometer so that the skin is not burned. This is especially important for the patient who is mentally or physically handicapped.

Be sure to rinse soap or detergent from the skin *well*, including between fingers and toes. Remnants of soap or detergent are irritating to the skin.

Assist the elderly who take showers or baths. Be sure the water is of a proper temperature, obstacles over which they may fall are removed, and the light is of good intensity to help prevent accidents. Do not use bath oils in the water because they make the surfaces of baths and showers very slippery.

Use an *emollient*, which is an agent to soften, smooth, and protect dry skin. Cocoa butter, petroleum jelly and lanolin are often present in skin creams and lotions that serve as good emollients. Encourage the patient's fluid intake to help prevent dry skin.

Give careful foot care to the elderly person. In addition to measures described earlier in this chapter in relation to foot care, these measures should also be observed and taught:

1. Soak the feet for as long as 10 minutes and encourage the patient to wiggle and stretch his toes. Pat the feet dry, being careful to dry between the toes, and use an emollient when the skin is dry.
2. Refer the patient to a physician or chiropodist if the nails are deformed or corns or calluses are present.
3. Clean under the nails with great care to avoid injury. Bits of cotton may be placed under nails that tend to grow down and over the ends of the toes.

Be sure oral hygiene is used for the elderly who have dentures. Check the mouth for lesions and evidence of ill-fitting dentures and report abnormal findings.

Use a soft toothbrush to prevent injury to oral tissues when mouth care is given.

Use shampoos infrequently when the hair is dry. Brushing the hair regularly is recommended. Clean sections of hair by stroking them with cotton balls moistened in a mouthwash solution. This measure cleans the hair when a shampoo cannot be given and leaves the hair with a pleasant, clean smell.

Teach the dangers of overexposure to the sun, which may cause burning. The elderly are especially sensitive to overexposure to the sun. Some medications used for daytime sedation also increase sensitivity to sunlight.

High environmental temperatures and the diminished ability of the elderly to perspire predispose to heat stroke.

Encourage as much hygienic self-care as possible. This practice helps promote independence and improves morale.

Teaching suggestions for personal hygiene

Suggestions for teaching when carrying out measures of personal hygiene have been described in this chapter. They are summarized below:

Recommended measures that promote personal

hygiene should be included in patient care plans when the nurse notes that a patient is careless about hygiene, uses poor or incorrect techniques, or misuses products intended for personal hygiene.

The sketch in Figure 9-8 illustrates the chain of events that leads to the development of dental caries. It can be used to explain to patients and family members how the chain can be broken and cavity formation prevented through proper brushing and flossing of the teeth.

Teaching about oral care should include recommendations for regular dental care and emphasis on the importance of preventive dental care for persons of all ages. Patients with dentures and bridges need the continued services of a dentist.

The person with diabetes mellitus who is well educated about proper self-care is less likely to develop complications. Proper foot care is especially important for every diabetic, a point that should be stressed in a diabetic's teaching plan.

Families of patients being cared for at home should be taught how to carry out hygienic measures that the patient cannot manage on his own.

It has been rather clearly demonstrated that overexposure to the sun can lead to serious skin problems, such as skin cancer. If people wish to be or must be in the sun for long periods, they should use a good sun screen on the skin to help prevent damage.

References

Bucholz, K. (1988) When dental care is up to you. *Registered Nurse*, February, 42–4.

Health Education Authority (1991) *Guide to Healthy Gums*, HEA, London.

Howarth, H. (1977) Mouth care procedures for the very ill. *Nursing Times*, **73**(10), 354–5.

Roper, N., Logan, W. and Tierney, A. (1985) *The Elements of Nursing*, 2nd edn, Churchill Livingstone, Edinburgh.

Shepherd, G., Page, C. and Sammon, P. (1987) Oral hygiene. *Nursing Times*, **83**(19), 25–7.

Watson, R. (1989) Care of the mouth. *Nursing*, **3**(44), 20–4.

Further reading

Allbright, A. (1984) Oral care for the cancer chemotherapy patient. *Nursing Times*, **80**(21), 40–2.

Dealey, C. and Berker, M. (1986) Action speaks louder than words. *Nursing Times*, **82**(29), 37–9.

Geissler, P. and McCord, F. (1986) Dental care for the elderly. *Nursing Times*, **82**(20), 53–4.

Gooch, J. (1987) Skin hygiene. *Professional Nurse*, **2**(5), 153–4.

Hadley, A. and Sheiham, A. (1984) Smile please. *Nursing Times*, **80**(27), 28–31.

Lewis, I.A. (1984) Developing a research based curriculum: an exercise in relation to oral care. *Nurse Education Today*, **3**(6), 143–4.

Roberts, S. (1987) Getting to know you. *Nursing Times*, **83**(14), 36.

Wells, R. and Trostle, K. (1984) Creative hairwashing techniques for immobilised patients. *Nursing*, **14**(1), 47–57.

Wilson, M. (1986) Personal cleanliness. *Journal of Clinical Nursing*, **3**(2), 80–2.

10
The need for nutrition

Learning objectives

When the content of this chapter has been mastered, the learner should be able to:

Define the terms appearing in the glossary.

List examples of food and eating habits influenced by culture.

Describe the basic nutritional needs of man.

Identify two guides that may be used to plan well-balanced diets.

Discuss ways in which vegetarians remain healthy with the use of little or no animal protein.

List information that is useful for a nutritional assessment.

Describe suggestions for ways to gain or lose weight.

Discuss measures that may reduce or relieve anorexia and nausea, vomiting and stomach gas.

Describe actions the nurse could take when feeding patients, or when providing alternative nourishment through a nasogastric tube, a gastrostomy, or by hyperalimentation.

Discuss methods for inserting, maintaining, irrigating, and removing a nasogastric tube.

List suggested measures for promoting nutrition in selected situations, as described in this chapter.

Summarize suggestions for instructing the patient.

Glossary

Anorexia Loss of appetite or lack of desire for food.

Antiemetic Medication to relieve nausea and vomiting.

Aspiration The entry of fluid into the air passages and lungs.

Belching The discharge of gas from the stomach through the mouth. Synonym for *eructation*.

Cachexia A condition of extreme debility. The patient is emaciated with the skin loose and wrinkled from rapid wasting, but shiny and tense over the bones.

Calorie The amount of heat necessary to raise the temperature of 1 g of water 1°C.

Emesis Vomited contents from the stomach. Synonym for *vomitus*.

Flatus Intestinal gas released from the rectum.

Gastrostomy A surgical opening into the stomach through the abdominal wall.

Junk food Food that adds large amounts of calories without contributing much to nutrition.

Malnutrition A condition resulting from a lack of proper nutrients in the diet.

Metabolic rate The rate at which the body burns calories.

Nasogastric feeding Introduction of nourishment into the stomach with a tube inserted through the nose and oesophagus.

Nausea The feeling of sickness with a desire to vomit.

Nutrition The process whereby the body uses foods and fluids to reach and maintain health.

Obesity A condition in which there is an excess amount of body fat.

Parenteral hyperalimentation A method to supply all the necessary nutrients the body needs when other methods are no longer adequate. Synonym for *total parenteral nutrition*.

Patent A state in which a tube remains unobstructed.

Projectile vomiting Vomiting with great force.

Protein complementation The act of combining two or more plant proteins at the same meal in order to supply the same amino acids present in animal protein.

Recommended dietary allowance The average daily amount of a nutrient that is felt to be adequate to meet health needs.

Regurgitation The act of bringing the stomach contents to the throat and mouth without vomiting effort.

Retching The act of vomiting without producing vomitus.

Total parenteral nutrition A method to supply all the necessary nutrients the body needs when other methods are no longer adequate. Abbreviated TPN. Synonym for *parenteral hyperalimentation*.

Vegetarian An individual who avoids eating meat and meat products.

Vomiting The act of forcing the contents of the stomach out through the mouth.

Introduction

More and more information supports the fact that food intake, or the lack of it, influences health and well-being. Modifying and regulating food has been a standard technique used in the treatment of diseases. Now, there is an emphasis on improving nutrition in order to prevent diseases and improve a state of well-being. Healthy people in general are becoming selective about the quantity and quality of their daily food consumption. Nurses must be able to advise people about what to eat in order to meet normal needs, discourage food fads and unsafe dieting, and perform skills that affect the patient's nutrition and digestive processes.

This chapter primarily deals with nursing care that will help people maintain normal nutrition. It also provides suggestions for skills that may be necessary when normal nutrition or digestion is affected.

Culture and eating habits

Eating is one of man's basic needs. If an individual is deprived of food for a length of time, health will be affected or life may be endangered. Most eating habits are learned early in life and vary from culture to culture.

- Religious practices often influence eating habits. For instance, many Jews and Muslims avoid pork, and fasting is practised in certain religions. Some persons, because of religious or personal reasons, are vegetarians and eat no meat.
- Specific kinds of food are associated with certain nationalities. Hamburgers and hot dogs are associated with Americans; pasta, such as spaghetti, has been popularized by Italians; and baklava, a dessert, is a favourite among Greeks.
- Some people prefer the largest meal of the day at noon. Other prefer this meal in the evening.
- Family get-togethers are often centred around a holiday meal, such as Christmas or Easter.
- Certain beverages and foods are associated with festive occasions. Champagne is the traditional wedding beverage, turkey is served for Christmas and chocolate is a popular St. Valentine's Day gift.
- Eating utensils differ. The British use knives, forks and spoons; Far Easterners eat with chopsticks; and Arabs use bread to dip foods from serving containers.

Despite variations in preferred foods and eating customs, all humans have the same basic nutritional needs for health. The nurse should respect cultural differences while helping individuals meet nutritional requirements.

Outlined below are some of the variations in food and diet according to different cultural habits. The nurse should never assume that these guidelines always apply to people from these cultural backgrounds, as every person is an individual. Therefore the nurse should ascertain each patient's preference before making provisions for their diet.

Afro-Caribbean people. Caribbean cooking takes its influence from different countries including China and Europe. There can be variation between each island but certain foods seem to provide a common stable starch, e.g. yams, sweet potatoes and rice. Meat tends to be seasoned with herbs and spices. Afro-Caribbean patients may wish to have food brought in from home as they could find hospital food rather bland.

Seventh Day Adventists will not eat pork or pork products.

Rastafarians place great importance on food, believing it to influence the health of the body and soul. Many Rastafarians are vegetarian but some eat fish with scales and any meat except pork. Wine and any products of the vine are forbidden.

Chinese people. Chinese people also believe that food is important in relation to physical and emotional well-being. Rice is an essential source of nourishment and is considered necessary for every meal. During illness, herb teas, nourishing soups and tonics are taken. The emphasis is on eating foods to balance the yin and the yang; thus promoting a harmony between the physical and psychological aspects of the individual. Chinese patients may wish to have their food brought in from home as well as their eating utensils (chopsticks). Younger patients may be more familiar with English food and content to order from the hospital menu. The nurse should liaise with the dietician who can advise on suitable foods.

Greek people. Many Greek patients may find English food too bland. Soup and boiled chicken are traditional foods eaten during illness. Patients may wish their families to bring food in from home. The nurse should liaise with the dietician who can advise patients about different food on the menu.

Hindu people. Many Hindus do not eat meat and some will not eat eggs or anything made with them. Hindus that do eat meat avoid beef.

Strict Hindus in hospital may feel worried about contamination of food during preparation and may wish to only eat food prepared in their own home. Washing before and after every meal is very important.

Some Hindus, especially women, fast at regular periods, during which time they only eat certain foods, e.g. fruit and yoghurt for 24 hours.

Jewish people. Orthodox Jews have strict dietary laws eating only "kosher" food that is killed and prepared according to Jewish law.

Milk and meat are not eaten at the same meal by very orthodox Jews.

Meat is only acceptable from animals which chew the cud and have a cloven hoof, or from poultry. Pork, rabbit and shell fish are forbidden. Most hospitals can provide kosher food, but if not, then the patient may prefer a vegetarian diet or have food brought in from home.

Muslim people. Muslim people will eat meat provided it has been killed according to halal ritual which drains the meat of blood. Pork meat and carrion are always forbidden. Fish and eggs are allowed but must not be prepared where nonhalal meat has been cooked. Again, because Muslims use spices in their cooking they may find British food rather bland. Many Muslims whilst in hospital may eat a vegetarian diet as they are only allowed halal meat. The nurse and dietician should discuss dietary requirements with the patient. During Ramadan, which lasts one month, Muslims fast between sunrise and sunset, although those who are sick are not expected to fast.

Human nutritional needs

Nutrition can be defined as the process in which the body uses food and fluids to reach and maintain health. The science of nutrition has identified the body's needs for calories, water, proteins, carbohydrates, fats, vitamins and minerals.

Calories. Man has discovered that various substances can be converted into energy. Coal, oil, wood, steam and alcohol are energy sources for machines. Food is the source of energy for humans. It provides the means by which the body carries out its functions.

Energy sources can be measured; in this way their effectiveness as a fuel can be determined. This is done by comparing a certain volume or weight of the energy source with its ability to produce heat.

The energy equivalent of foods is measured in calories. A *calorie* is the amount of heat necessary to raise the temperature of 1 gram of water 1° centigrade. Protein, fats and carbohydrates have caloric value; they furnish energy to the body. Foods are usually combinations of proteins, fats, and carbohydrates. Water, vitamins, and minerals are not assigned a caloric value, though they are essential for health.

Needs for calories vary and depend on factors such as age, activity, body temperature and gender. Most average adults need between 2000 and 3000 calories per day.

Water. Approximately 45% to 75% of our body weight is water. The normal amount depends mostly on age. Infants have the largest amount and the elderly have the least in relation to body weight. Individuals can live longer without food than water. Water must be maintained at a fairly constant level to maintain health. Therefore, sufficient water intake is an essential part of health.

Proteins. The body uses proteins to build, maintain and repair body tissue. Protein can be used for energy. It provides 4 calories per gram. The body spares protein for energy use as long as calories are available from carbohydrates and fats.

Protein is constantly being formed or broken down in order to maintain a healthy state. The body cannot supply its own raw source of protein. Food sources of protein supply amino acids, the ingredients that the body refashions into types of proteins it requires. As long as the dietary intake of protein is adequate, the body can function at a fairly optimum level.

Proteins come from animal and plant sources of food. Animal sources of protein contain all the essential amino acids, or building blocks, the body needs for growth and repair. However, if certain plant sources are eaten together, each contributes some of these amino acids. *Protein complementation*, the act of combining two or more plant sources at the same meal, may supply the same total amino acids found in a single animal source. This will be discussed further in relation to vegetarian diets later in the chapter.

People who are poorly nourished almost always consume foods that are poor in protein content. The other extreme may also be unwise; diets that are exclusively protein are also dangerous. Protein food, especially from animal sources, is likely to be the most expensive nutrient in the diet. Individuals on low incomes who do not understand the principle of combining cheaper plant sources of protein are likely to be malnourished. *Malnutrition* is a condition resulting from a lack of proper nutrients in the diet. This is a common problem among people in poorer, developing countries. In Britain certain groups of people have a tendency to be undernourished; these include the elderly living on a fixed income, alcoholics, drug addicts and children from poor families. Even those who eat mostly convenience and fast foods may be marginally nourished.

The following are examples of protein foods: milk, meat, fish, poultry, eggs, legumes (peas, beans, peanuts), nuts and components of grains.

Carbohydrates. Carbohydrates are the chief component of most people's diets. Plants are the main source of carbohydrates; they are often referred to as sugars and starches. Carbohydrates supply 4 calories of energy per gram. Carbohydrates are used primarily as a quick energy source. They make the diet more tasty and attractive.

Carbohydrates, however, are important for more than just their calories. For example, the indigestible fibre found in the stems, skins and leaves of many fruits and vegetables gives the diet bulk that helps elimination. Some claim that various diseases can be prevented by increasing dietary fibre. Many people are now more health conscious and therefore have increased their consumption of fresh fruit and vegetables and whole grains in their diet.

The following are examples of good sources of carbohydrates: cereals and grains, such as rice, wheat and wheat germ, oats, barley, corn and corn meal; fruits and vegetables; molasses, maple syrup, honey and common table sugar.

Fats. Dietary fats come from both animal and plant sources. Fats have a higher energy value than other nutrients; they yield 9 calories per gram. This is 2½ times the amount of either proteins or carbohydrates. For this reason alone, their consumption should be limited especially by those who have a tendency to be overweight. Alcoholic beverages, though they are not fats, are also high in calories. Alcohol provides 7 calories per gram; these calories and the chemical, alcohol, are unnecessary and even damaging to the health of some people

Though fats are high in calories, they should not be totally eliminated. Fats provide energy and are necessary for many chemical reactions in the body. Some vitamins are absorbed with dietary fats. They add to the flavour of food and, because they leave the stomach slowly, they promote a feeling of having satisfied appetite and hunger.

The influence of fat consumption in relation to diseases is being studied. There seems to be a direct link between the intake of certain types of fat and heart disease.

The following foods are rich in fat: red meat, such as beef and pork; butter, margarine, and vegetable oils; egg yolk; whole milk and cheese, peanut butter; salad dressings; avocados; chocolate; and nuts.

Minerals. There are substances in food, other than the calories in nutrients, that are necessary for

Table 10-1. Common minerals needed by the body, their chief functions and dietary sources

Mineral	Chief Functions	Common Dietary Sources
Sodium	Maintenance of water and electrolyte balance	Table salt Processed meat
Potassium	Maintenance of electrolyte balance Neuromuscular activity Enzyme reactions	Bananas Oranges Potatoes
Chloride	Maintenance of fluid and electrolyte balance	Table salt Processed meat
Calcium	Formation of teeth and bones Neuromuscular activity Blood coagulation Cell-wall permeability	Milk Milk products
Phosphorus	Buffering action Formation of bones and teeth	Eggs Meat Milk
Iodine	Regulation of body metabolism Promotion of normal growth	Seafoods Iodized salt
Iron	Component of haemoglobin Assistance in cellular oxidation	Liver Egg yolk Meat
Magnesium	Neuromuscular activity Activation of enzymes Formation of teeth and bones	Whole grains Milk Meat
Zinc	Constituent of enzymes and insulin	Seafoods Liver

health. These substances are minerals and vitamins. Minerals are chemical substances, such as calcium, sodium, potassium, chloride, and so on. When these substances are dissolved in the body, they are called electrolytes. These chemicals do not supply the body with energy, but they are necessary ingredients of cells, body tissue, and body fluids. They play a role in the regulation of many of the body's chemical processes, such as blood clotting and the conduction of nerve impulses. Table 10-1 lists some of the major and trace minerals of the body, their chief functions, and common dietary sources.

Vitamins. Vitamins are unique chemical substances. They are not components of cells or tissue, but they are necessary in minute amounts for normal growth, maintenance of health, and functioning of the body. Many deficiency diseases have been associated with diets in which specific foods, rich in a source of a vitamin, have been lacking. For example, scurvy, a disease associated with vitamin C (ascorbic acid) deficiency, frequently occurred among British sailors who did not eat fresh fruits and vegetables. When limes were eaten while at sea, this disease did not occur. Hence, to this day British sailors are referred to as "limeys".

Vitamins were first named according to the sequence of letters in the alphabet. Numbers were subsequently added to some letters as more were identified. Chemical names are now replacing the letter-number system of identification.

Vitamins are dissolved in the water and fat of the body. The former require daily replacement because they are lost along with the water, which is eliminated from the body. The other fat-soluble vitamins are stored as a reserve for future needs. With the exception of vitamin K and biotin, vitamins

Table 10-2. Common vitamins needed by the body, their chief functions, and common dietary sources

Vitamin	Chief Functions	Common Dietary Sources
A (Retinol) Not destroyed by ordinary cooking temperatures	Growth of body cells Promotion of vision, healthy hair and skin, and integrity of epithelial membranes Prevention of xerophthalmia, a condition characterized by chronic conjunctivitis	Animal fats: butter, cheese, cream, egg yolk, whole milk Fish liver oil and liver Green leafy and yellow fruits and vegetables
B_1 (Thiamine) Not readily destroyed by ordinary cooking temperatures	Carbohydrate metabolism Functioning of nervous system Normal digestion Prevention of beriberi, a condition characterized by neuritis	Fish Lean meat and poultry Glandular organs Milk Whole grain cereals Peas, beans and peanuts
B_2 (Riboflavine) Not destroyed by heat except in presence of alkali	Formation of certain enzymes Normal growth Light adaptation in the eyes	Eggs Green leafy vegetables Lean meat Milk Whole grains Dried yeast
B_3 (Niacin)	Carbohydrate, fat, and protein metabolism Enzyme component Prevention of appetite loss Prevention of pellagra, a condition characterized by cutaneous, gastrointestinal, neurologic and mental symptoms	Lean meat and liver Fish Peas, beans Whole grain cereals Peanuts Yeast Eggs Liver
B_6 (Pyridoxine) Destroyed by heat, sunlight and air	Healthy gums and teeth Red-blood-cell formation Carbohydrate, fat and protein metabolism	Whole grain cereals and wheat germ Vegetables Yeast Meat Bananas Black strap molasses
B_9 Folic acid	Protein metabolism Red-blood-cell formation Normal intestinal-tract functioning	Green leafy vegetables Glandular organs Yeast

Continued

Table 10-2. *Continued*

Vitamin	Chief Functions	Common Dietary Sources
B_{12} Hydroxocobalamin	Protein metabolism	Liver and kidney
	Red-blood-cell formation	Dairy products
	Healthy nervous system tissues	Lean meat
	Prevention of pernicious anaemia, a condition characterized by decreased red blood cells	Milk
		Salt-water fish and oysters
C (Ascorbic acid) Readily destroyed by cooking temperatures	Healthy bones, teeth and gums	Citrus fruits and juices
	Formation of blood vessels and capillary walls	Tomato
	Proper tissue and bone healing	Berries
	Facilitation of iron and folic acid absorption	Cabbage
	Prevention of scurvy, a condition characterized by haemorrhagic condition and abnormal bone and teeth formation	Green vegetables
		Potatoes
D (Calciferol) Relatively stable with refrigeration	Absorption of calcium and phosphorus	Fish liver oils, salmon, tuna
	Prevention of rickets, a condition characterized by weak bones	Milk
		Egg yolk
		Butter
		Liver
		Oysters
		Formed in the skin by exposure to sunlight
E (Alphatocopheryl acetate) Heat stable in absence of oxygen	Red-blood-cell formation	Green leafy vegetables
	Protection of essential fatty acids	Wheat germ oil
	Important for normal reproduction in experimental animals (i.e. rats)	Margarine
		Brown rice
		Liver
		Egg yolk
		Milk
H (Biotin) Heat-sensitive	Enzyme activity	Egg yolk
	Metabolism of carbohydrates, fats and proteins	Green vegetables
		Milk
		Liver and kidney
		Yeast
K (Phytomenadione)	Production of prothrombin	Liver
		Eggs
		Green leafy vegetables
		Synthesized in the gastro-intestinal tract by bacteria

cannot be manufactured by the body. They are usually consumed within the food that is eaten. Cooking, processing, and lack of refrigeration can deplete the content of some vitamins in food.

Some prefer to take vitamin and mineral supplements, but they are not necessary for most people as long as they eat a well-balanced diet consisting of a variety of foods. Some foods have been enriched with vitamins and minerals to ensure that most individuals consume adequate daily amounts. Table 10-2 lists vitamins required by the body, their chief functions, and common dietary sources.

Consuming large amounts of vitamins, exceeding those considered adequate for health, can be dangerous. Some people with terminal diseases follow unconventional diets and take large doses of vitamins in a desperate attempt to restore their health. There is no conclusive evidence that this approach cures or helps their condition.

Basic food groups

Foods can be divided into four groups:
1. *Milk and Dairy Group*: milk; yoghurt; cheese.
2. *Meat Group*: meat; fish. Eggs, nuts and beans can be used as an alternative to meat and fish.
3. *Vegetable and Fruit Group*: all fruits; all vegetables.
4. *Bread and Cereal Group*: bread, plain biscuits; cereals; spaghetti. Rice and potatoes can be used as an alternative.

To constitute a healthy diet an individual should select two foods from each group every day. As individuals we all have varying tastes—but large amounts of fried foods, sugar and alcohol should be discouraged.

Public awareness of what constitutes a good diet has been greatly heightened in recent years especially by the Health Education Council's report—the NACNE (1983) report. Its findings and recommendations regarding nutritional guidelines in Britain were brought to the public's attention by the press and television. The Committee on Medical Aspects of Food Policy (1984) brought out a report termed the COMA report; this related to heart disease and diet.

Since the release of both these reports there has been an upsurge of health food shops and a heightened public awareness and demands for foods free from artificial additives and colourings. Similarly manufacturers now advertise the concept of whole foods and clearly label food packaging with lists of ingredients and any additives that may have been used in their preparation and manufacture.

Vegetarianism

Individuals who for religious or personal reasons do not eat animal sources of food are called *vegetarians*. A strict vegetarian otherwise known as a *vegan* is one who not only does not consume animal food, like meat, but also avoids eating any products from animals, such as milk or eggs. There are variations among the practices of vegetarians. Lacto-ovovegetarians eat milk and eggs; lactovegetarians drink milk and eat milk products but avoid eggs and meat. Because meat, eggs, and milk products are recommended sources of daily nutrients, deficiency diseases may be a potential nutritional problem. A strict vegetarian is wise to take vitamin B_{12} (hydroxocobalamin) supplements because the main sources of this vitamin are found in animal substances.

Those who omit eating meat as part of an organized religion or ethnic tradition, such as the Seventh Day Adventists and Muslims, usually have developed dietary substitutions for meat that are essentially healthy. There may be difficulty in obtaining appropriate foods or a variety of them while these individuals are patients. Nurses should make the effort to accommodate dietary choices rather than permit a patient to refuse eating. Family members are often willing to provide special food.

Those who arbitrarily choose to become vegetarians may need to learn how to combine plant sources to ensure that they are consuming adequate amounts of all the essential amino acids. Table 10-3 shows the types of second class proteins appropriate for protein complementation. All plant scources, if eaten daily with small amounts of dairy products or eggs, should be adequate for health.

Nutritional assessment

Because eating is a basic need, it is important for the nurse to identify any current or potential problems from inadequate nutrition. One place to begin is to obtain a diet history. The nurse should ask questions about the following:

- The amounts of specific foods eaten on an average day. The foods within the basic four

Table 10-3. Second class proteins

Source	Example	For the best complementation, choose:
Pulses	Peas, beans, lentils	
Nuts	Peanuts, walnuts, cashews	
Seeds	Sunflower, sesame	2–3 portions daily
Others	Soya products, Quorn, tofu, textured vegetable protein	

PLUS

Cereals	Wheat, barley, oats, couscous, bulghar wheat, rice	3–5 portions daily
Cereal products	Bread, pasta	

groups may be used as a guide. It may be helpful for the patient to use household measurements, such as a cup, glass or bowl, when describing the amounts.

- The amounts of non-nutritional foods eaten on an average day. Include sweets, soft drinks, snack foods, coffee and alcohol.
- Food likes, dislikes, and beliefs.
- Vitamin or mineral supplements that are taken routinely and why.
- Food supplements or restrictions and the reason for them.
- Current or previous special diets that have been medically or self-prescribed.
- Any problems with eating, digestion or elimination.

One of the easiest, though not always the most accurate, assessments related to an individual's nutritional state is body weight. There are various growth charts and height-age-sex graphs that may be used.

A more significant factor is the ratio of lean body mass to fat. Many an athlete weighs more than charts indicate is healthy, yet the body is composed primarily of lean, muscular tissue.

Cachexia is a condition in which there is general wasting away of body tissue. Most people in the UK do not manifest this except when extremely ill. More often the nurse is likely to find that individuals are obese. *Obesity* is a condition in which there is an excessive amount of body fat, usually over 20% of the ideal weight. Being able to "pinch an inch" is probably a good indication of excess weight. Measuring skin-fold thickness with a special instrument called calipers is a more objective measurement. This would also be a better method for comparing any future changes in the amount of body fat.

Other assessment also include the characteristics of healthy skin, mucous membranes, and hair and nails, as discussed in the previous chapter. Laboratory tests, such as haemoglobin and blood fat levels, also contribute information to the data base about nutrition.

Promoting weight gain or loss

It is important that individuals who are dissatisfied with their appearance actually have a need to lose or gain weight. A desire to change one's weight may be based on wanting to resemble an unrealistic cultural ideal. Individuals who are extremely underweight or overweight should be referred to a doctor to deter-

Measuring and recording fluid intake

An important means of identifying a potential fluid problem is to measure and record the amounts of all liquids consumed or instilled into the body. If fluid balance exists, the total intake should approximate the total output.

Hospitals generally have lists readily available to tell the nurse the amount of fluid contained in common serving dishes, glasses, cups and water containers. The unit of measure is a millilitre, abbreviated ml.

Hospitals tend to each have their own fluid intake/output charts whereby a patient's fluid balance can be recorded over a 24-hour period. The patient should be helped to understand why his intake and output are to be measured and recorded and why it is important to do so accurately. The amounts are usually totalled at 12 and 24-hour periods by the nurse. The nurse is responsible for evaluating the amounts. When communicating with others who will be responsible for the patient's care on other shifts, fluid intake and output are part of the information that is reported. Figure 10-1 is an example of a form used to record the patient's intake and output.

Accurate recording of a patient's fluid balance is an important nursing responsibility; mistakes or inaccurate recordings can lead to inappropriate treatment.

For home care, the nurse may need to teach an individual or a family member how to measure and record fluid intake. While using a common household measuring cup, the fluid content of that person's cup, glass, soup dish or other container used at home can be determined. Then it becomes an easy matter to measure and record the intake.

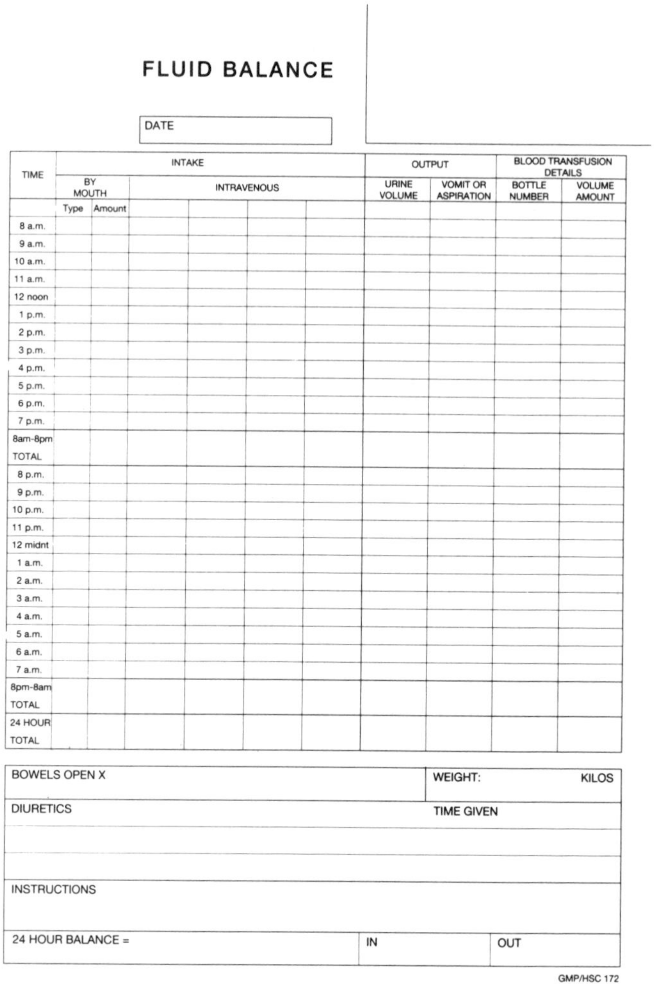

FLUID BALANCE

DATE

TIME	INTAKE						OUTPUT		BLOOD TRANSFUSION DETAILS	
	BY MOUTH		INTRAVENOUS				URINE VOLUME	VOMIT OR ASPIRATION	BOTTLE NUMBER	VOLUME AMOUNT
	Type	Amount								
8 a.m.										
9 a.m.										
10 a.m.										
11 a.m.										
12 noon										
1 p.m.										
2 p.m.										
3 p.m.										
4 p.m.										
5 p.m.										
6 p.m.										
7 p.m.										
8am-8pm TOTAL										
8 p.m.										
9 p.m.										
10 p.m.										
11 p.m.										
12 midnt										
1 a.m.										
2 a.m.										
3 a.m.										
4 a.m.										
5 a.m.										
6 a.m.										
7 a.m.										
8pm-8am TOTAL										
24 HOUR TOTAL										

BOWELS OPEN X	WEIGHT: KILOS
DIURETICS	TIME GIVEN
INSTRUCTIONS	
24 HOUR BALANCE =	IN OUT

GMP/HSC 172

Figure 10-1 An example of a form used to record oral intake and output.

Commonly prescribed diets

Most patients eat a well-balanced diet, selecting items of their choice from a menu card each day.

Some commonly ordered diets for patients are given in Table 10-4. Each is used to meet the specific needs of particular patients. The nurse should know the prescribed diet for each patient and why the diet was ordered. The patient needs to understand why he is receiving the diet. Care should be taken that the patient does not accidentally receive foods that are to be excluded.

Some individuals may need to continue a special diet or generally eat well-balanced meals when they leave the hospital. Local organizations in some areas provide food services both by home delivery ("meals on wheels") and at community centres. The nurse should be able to advise the individual on discharge from hospital how he can meet his nutritional needs at home to provide a well-balanced diet and one which is within his financial means.

Providing food for patients

Patients are usually served food at their bedside. Some hospitals have cafeterias for patients who are up and about. Nursing homes often have a large

Table 10-4. Common types and characteristics of prescribed diets

Type of Diet	Characteristics
Regular or standard	This diet is usually a selective diet and is allowed for persons who do not require a therapeutic diet. The basic diet provides about 1400 calories and foods usually selected by the patient are added as necessary to meet total caloric needs. This diet tends to be used for patients recovering from surgery.
Light or convalescent	This diet differs from a regular diet primarily in the method of preparing foods. The foods are simply cooked. Fried foods, rich pastries, fat-rich foods, gas-forming foods and raw foods are typically omitted. The diet may include all types of food served in soft and liquid diets.
Soft or puree	This diet contains foods that are soft in texture and liquids and semi-liquids. The diet is low in residue, is readily digested, contains few or no spices or condiments, and has fewer fruits, vegetables and meats than a light diet.
	This diet can be used for patients who have lost the ability to masticate, e.g. following a stroke, or patients who have an oesophageal stricture.
Full liquid	Fruit and vegetable juices are strained for this diet, and soups and gruels are strained or blended. Milk, ices, ice cream, jelly, junket, custards and usual beverages are included in this diet. This type of diet is suitable for those patients who have had their jaws wired.
Clear liquid	This diet consists of water, clear broth, clear fruit juices, plain gelatine, tea and coffee. Carbonated beverages may or may not be permitted. This diet is suitable for patients in the immediate postoperative period prior to the patient commencing a light diet.
Special therapeutic	There is a wide variety of therapeutic diets that are prepared to meet special needs. These are a few examples of therapeutic diets: high-caloric, low-caloric, diabetic, restricted-sodium, low-fat, low-protein, high-protein and low-roughage diets. The dietician should see the individual patient to explain why he is on the particular therapeutic diet and what food items he can eat.

dining room where patients eat together in small groups.

Nursing responsibilities in relation to food service vary among hospitals. Most hospitals have a dietician and centralized food service. However, nurses are still generally responsible for ordering and cancelling diets for patients, for assisting with serving of meals, for helping patients to eat and for recording information about how well the patient is eating.

Serving and removing trays. Nurses and dietary personnel must work cooperatively in delivering food to the patient (Principles of Care 10-1). The food should have been prepared in a clean, sanitary environment. It should be transported during delivery to the patient unit in such a way as to retain its appropriate serving temperature.

Principles of Care 10-2 gives suggestions for assisting patients to eat.

Alternative methods of providing nourishment

When patients are unable to take fluid or food by mouth, other methods are used to maintain nutrition. Giving solutions intravenously has already been mentioned. Other methods include feeding the patient through special tubes leading from the nose to the stomach, tubes inserted directly into a surgically made opening in the stomach, or special nutrient solutions instilled directly into the large blood vessels leading to the heart.

Nasogastric feeding

Nasogastric feeding means introducing nourishment into the stomach through a nasogastric tube. It is used when the patient has no disturbances of the stomach or small intestine. An example is the patient

Principles of Care 10-1. Serving and removing a patient's trays

Nursing Action	Rationiale
Be available when trays arrive from the dietary department.	Delay in serving food alters the serving temperature of food.
Clear the area where the patient will eat.	Clutter is likely to cause the tray or the patient's belongings to fall or become misplaced.
Check the general appearance of the tray for spilled liquids, missing items, or ordered food that is missing.	The tray should be complete, orderly and tidy so that eating can be enjoyed.
Compare the name on the tray with the name on the patient's identification bracelet.	A tray served to the wrong patient can be a serious error.
Make sure that patients who are undergoing special tests have food withheld or provided according to the test directions.	Some tests require that patients fast or eat specific types of foods, such as a fat-free meal.
Check to see that the patient is not being served foods to which he is allergic or cannot tolerate.	A patient's condition may be made worse by eating foods that his system cannot tolerate.
Place the tray so that it faces the patient, and remove the food covers.	Positioning the tray and removing covers allows easy access for the patient.
Open milk cartons and cereal boxes, butter toast, cut up meat and otherwise assist as necessary.	It may be difficult for the patient to do these simple tasks even if he is not disabled.
Serve trays that have been kept warm to those patients who need help with eating.	It is unappetizing and often annoying for the patient to have cold food waiting at his bedside.
Note the kinds and amounts of food the patient is not eating.	Substitutes for uneaten food may be ordered, or the nurse may need to solve other problems, such as loose dentures, which are interfering with eating.
Observe whether the patient feels satisfied with the amounts of food he is served.	Servings need to match appetites. Serving large portions to an individual with a minimal appetite may reduce food consumption.
Follow hospital policies about serving food brought from home. Be sure the food is covered, labelled and refrigerated or stored properly.	As long as the food is appropriate for the patient's diet, there usually is no problem. Spoiled or misplaced food offends those who made special efforts to prepare it.
Be considerate and visit the patient on a special diet who may be denied food he likes because of a health problem.	The patient needs the nurse's help, support and understanding with unwanted changes in lifestyle.
Encourage individuals to eat, but do not scold those who feel they cannot.	Insisting that the patient eat or implying that he is uncooperative is not a good nursing approach.
Remove trays as soon as possible, and restore the cleanliness of the eating area.	It is pleasant for the patient to be left clean and comfortable after eating.
Assist or offer the patient an opportunity to brush and floss his teeth.	Oral hygiene after eating helps prevent caries.
Record how the patient ate and enter the amounts of fluids consumed if appropriate.	Nurses need to evaluate if the nutritional and fluid needs of the patient are being met.

Principles of Care 10-2. Assisting the patient to eat

Nursing Action	Rationale
Complete or delay care that will interfere with eating.	Food should be eaten at its appropriate serving temperature.
Provide a period of rest or quiet before meals.	A tired or excited patient is usually in no mood to eat.
Offer the patient a bedpan or urinal before meal time.	It is uncomfortable for the patient to eat when he needs to go to the bathroom.
Provide the patient with an opportunity for handwashing and offer mouth care before eating.	Soiled hands can carry bacteria to the mouth. A fresh mouth improves the appetite.
Remove any soiled articles or clutter from the room.	An unattractive environment tends to decrease the desire to eat.
Make the patient comfortable for eating; use pain relief techniques if needed.	Food can be enjoyed more if the patient is comfortable.
Raise the head of the bed to a sitting position if possible.	The sitting or semi-sitting position usually makes swallowing easier and choking less likely than does the lying position.
Cover the patient's upper chest with a napkin or towel.	Use of an absorbent substance protects the bed-clothes and linen from becoming soiled.
Sit beside the patient. Avoid appearing rushed or hurried.	Tension interferes with chewing and digestion. The time spent should be relaxing and should provide an opportunity to gather more information or do informal teaching.
Encourage the patient to take part in his eating as much as possible and to the extent his condition permits.	Developing independence is a goal of nursing. Most adults feel childlike when they are fed by someone else.
Provide a flexible straw for patients unable to use a cup or glass.	A straw helps a patient direct liquids into his mouth at a pace and amount that match his ability to swallow.
Serve manageable amounts of food with each bite.	Even patients sitting up may choke when the amounts of food are too large.
For a stroke patient, direct the food toward the side of the mouth that is not paralysed.	The stroke patient is better able to chew and swallow food placed where he has feeling and muscle control.
Serve the food in the order of the patient's preference.	Feeding should simulate the manner in which a patient would eat by himself.
Give the patient time to chew thoroughly and swallow his food.	Chewing aids the first step of digestion by breaking up food and mixing it with saliva and enzymes in the mouth. Large pieces of food may obstruct the airway if swallowed.
Modify utensils and the texture of food if the patient must remain flat while eating. Use a baby's training cup or a large syringe with a flexible rubber tube. Puree or grind foods if necessary.	A flat position decreases the ability to control food in the mouth and increases the risk of choking.
If you have begun to feed a patient, do not leave until he has finished eating.	A meal should be uninterrupted. Food and beverages change temperatures with delays, thus making them unappealing.
Talk with the patient about pleasant subjects.	Eating is a social situation. Focusing on problems may interfere with the patient's appetite.

who has had extensive mouth or throat surgery. Occasionally, an unconscious patient is fed by a nasogastric tube. It is also used for patients too weak to eat or drink.

In some hospitals, a qualified nurse may be responsible for introducing a nasogastric tube into the patient's stomach (Principles of Care 10-3).

Guidelines for administering a nasogastric feed are given in Principles of Care 10-4. Two types of feeding may be used, intermittent or continuous. Principles of Care 10-5 gives suggestions for the management of a nasogastric feeding regime.

Intermittent tube feedings. Prescribed nourishment in liquid form is generally prepared by the dietary department of a hospital. Commercial preparations are also available. The nourishment consists of basic nutrient requirements. Intermittent feeds are usually administered every 2 to 4 hours depending on the volume and duration of each feed.

Continuous drip tube feedings. Another method for giving nourishment through a nasogastric tube uses a container or bag that will hold a pint or a specific volume of nourishment. The container is attached to the tube and hung on a standard at the patient's bedside. The nourishment is then given very slowly but continuously. The rate of introducing the formula is regulated with a clamp on the tube leading from the container. The nourishment may also be administered and regulated with an electrical infusion pump. These can be programmed to deliver a set rate, much the way intravenous fluids are regulated.

It is recommended that nourishment be given very slowly and at half strength, such as 50 ml per hour for about 24 hours. If the patient tolerates the nourishment well, the rate is increased by 25 ml per hour until the prescribed rate is reached. At that time, the nourishment is also started at full strength. Prewarming nourishment is not recommended. It will warm sufficiently before reaching the stomach.

The rate at which the nourishment is given is recorded, as is the total amount introduced in every 12-hour and 24-hour period. The nasogastric tube is ordinarily changed every 2 to 3 days for sanitary purposes.

The two main advantages of continuous feeding are that it saves nursing time and reduces the risk of gastrointestinal problems. However, its disadvantage is that mobile patients may feel restricted.

Common problems associated with nasogastric feeding are illustrated in Table 10-5.

Keeping a nasogastric tube patent. Nasogastric tubes and other kinds of tubes can get plugged. The nurse must assess whether the tube is remaining *patent*, or unobstructed. If a tube becomes plugged, it cannot serve its function for either instilling or draining fluids. Filling the nasogastric tube with water and clamping it after each tube feeding is a method to ensure its continued patency.

Nasogastric tubes used as drains have a tendency to become obstructed. Thick mucous secretions can collect within the tube. Giving a patient ice chips or small sips of water shortly before suctioning helps to dilute the secretions. Thinning secretions usually keeps the tube draining freely.

Occasionally, the nurse may need to instill solution through the tube to maintain its function. A doctor's order is always required. Some patients who have had recent stomach surgery should not have a tube irrigated.

Administering nourishment through a gastrostomy

A *gastrostomy* is a surgical opening into the stomach through the abdominal wall. A tube is placed into the stomach through the surgical opening. Nourishment is then given through the tube. Methods for giving gastrostomy feedings and the care and preparation of nourishment are the same as for nasogastric feeding. The amount of nourishment the patient receives is measured and recorded as intake. Patients who suffer from oesphageal obstruction are usually fed via a gastrostomy tube.

Patients who are fed through a gastrostomy are in need of special mouth care. The mucous membranes and lips should be kept lubricated. The skin around the wound on the abdomen where the tube is placed also requires care and attention.

Nourishing the patient by parenteral hyperalimentation

Still another way to provide a patient with nutrients is to use *parenteral hyperalimentation*, which is a way to introduce necessary nutrients of the body into the bloodstream when the patient cannot eat normally. The term *total parenteral nutrition* (TPN) is a synonym. Simple intravenous therapy supplies neither sufficient calories nor enough protein when alternative nutrition is needed quickly or for long periods. TPN supplies a concentrated solution of carbohydrate in the form of glucose, along with protein, vitamins,

Principles of Care 10-3. Nasogastric intubation

Nursing Action	Rationale
Explain the procedure to the patient.	To obtain the patient's consent and cooperation.
Arrange a signal by which the patient can communicate if he/she wants the nurse to stop, e.g. by raising his/her hand.	The patient is often less frightened if he/she feels able to have some control over the procedure.
Assist the patient to sit in a semi-upright position in the bed or chair. Support the patient's head with pillows. *Note*: the head should not be tilted backwards or forwards.	To allow for easy passage of the tube. This position enables easy swallowing and ensures that the epiglottis is not obstructing the oesophagus (see Figure 10-2).

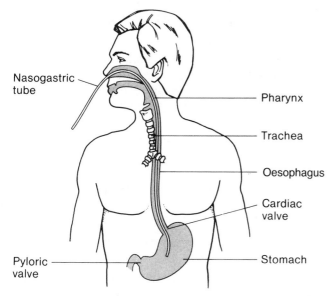

Figure 10-2 A nasogastric tube is inserted into the stomach via the nose and pharynx.

Tube Using a Guidewire

Select the appropriate distance mark on the tube by measuring the distance on the tube from the patient's ear lobe to the bridge of the nose plus the distance from the bridge of the nose to the bottom of the xiphisternum.	To ensure that the appropriate length of tube is passed into the stomach.
Wash hands and assemble the equipment.	
Either: Pour normal saline into the receiver and check that the guidewire is free from kinks. Pass the wire through the normal saline and insert it into the tube as far as the plastic safety stopper will allow (see Figure 10-3).	Lubrication of the wire promotes easy insertion and removal of the wire from the tube. The safety stopper prevents protrusion of the wire from the tube end, a potential source of trauma to the nasopharynx and oesophagus.

Continued

Principles of Care 10-3. Continued

Nursing Action	**Rationale**

Tube Using a Guidewire

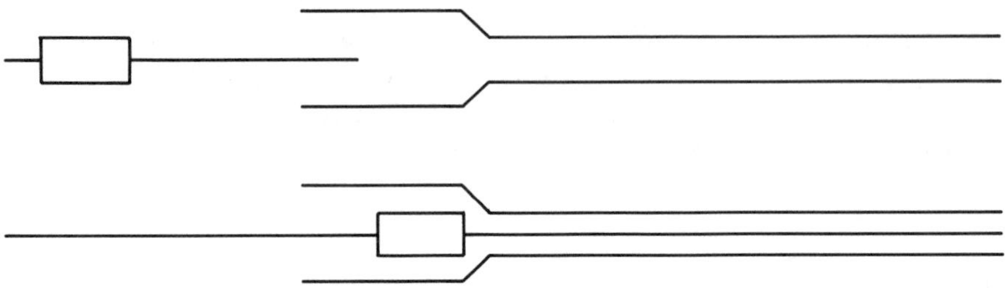

Distal   Proximal

Figure 10-3 Passing a nasogastric tube.

or:

For "silk" nasogastric tubes and others with guidewire packaged inside the tube: ensure wire is firmly anchored inside the tube. Flush tube with 10 ml of water. Dip proximal end of tube in water to activate hydrometer coat.

Contact with water activates hydromer coating inside tube and on the tip. This lubricates the tube assisting its passage through the nasopharynx and allowing easy withdrawal of the guidewire.

Check that the nostrils are clear by asking the patient to sniff with one nostril closed. Repeat with the other nostril.

To identify any obstructions liable to prevent intubation.

Insert the proximal end of the tube into the clearest nostril and slide it backwards and inwards along the floor of the nose to the nasopharynx. If any obstruction is felt, withdraw the tube and try again in a slightly different direction or use the other nostril.

To facilitate the passage of the tube by following the natural anatomy of the nose.

As the tube passes down into the nasopharynx, ask the patient to start swallowing and sipping water.

To focus the patient's attention on something other than the tube. A swallowing action closes the glottis, enabling the tube to pass into the oesophagus.

Advance the tube through the pharynx as the patient swallows until the predetermined mark reaches the point of entry into the external nares. If the patient shows signs of distress, e.g. gasping or turning blue, remove the tube immediately.

Distress may indicate that the tube is in the bronchus.

Remove the guidewire by using gentle traction. If the wire is difficult to remove, then remove the tube as well. Do not discard the wire.

If the wire sticks in the tube, it may indicate that the tube is in the bronchus. After use the guidewire should be cleaned carefully with an antiseptic solution, such as Savlodil, and dried thoroughly. Each wire may be used up to a maximum of five times.

Check the position of the tube to confirm that it is in the stomach by:

Aspirating 2 to 3 ml of gastric fluid through the tube and test with litmus paper (blue turns red).

The acid nature of stomach contents verifies the position of the tube.

Continued

Principles of Care 10-3. *Continued*

Nursing Action	Rationale
Tube Using a Guidewire	
or	
Introducing 2 to 5 ml air into the stomach via the tube and checking for bubbling sounds using a stethoscope placed over the epigastrium.	Air can be detected by a "whooshing" sound when entering the stomach.
or	
X-ray of chest and upper abdomen.	Radio-opaque tube shows up on the X-ray.
Secure the tube to the nostril with hypo-allergenic tape and to the cheek with an adhesive patch (if available). Spigot the tube.	To maintain the tube in place. To ensure patient comfort. Feeding via the tube must not begin until the correct position of the tube has been confirmed by one of the above methods.
Tube Without a Guidewire	
The tube should have been stored in a deep freeze for at least half an hour before the procedure is to begin.	Ensures a rigid tube that will allow for easy passage.
Mark the distance which the tube is to be passed by measuring the distance on the tube from the patient's ear lobe to the bridge of the nose plus the distance from the bridge of the nose to the bottom of the xiphisternum. Mark this distance with tape.	To indicate the length of tube required for entry into the stomach.
Wash hands and assemble the equipment.	
Check that the patient's nostrils are clear by asking him/her to sniff with one nostril closed. Repeat with the other nostril.	To identify any obstructions liable to prevent intubation.
Lubricate the tube for about 15 to 20 cm with a thin coat of lubricating jelly that has been placed on a topical swab.	To reduce the friction between the mucous membranes and the tube.
Insert the proximal end of the tube into the clearest nostril and proceed as described above for the tube with a guidewire (omitting stage regarding removal of the wire).	

Source: Pritchard and David, Royal Marsden Manual of Clinical Nursing Procedures; published by Blackwell Scientific, 1992.

and minerals. There are also solutions that contain fats.

It is usual for a pharmacy to prepare nutritional solutions for parenteral hyperalimentation if commercial preparations are not used. The solution is kept refrigerated and warmed to room temperature before administration. The needle or catheter used to introduce the solution is large in size to accommodate the solution. The needle or catheter is placed in a vein where blood flow is high so that the solution dilutes quickly in the blood. The preferred vein is the subclavian vein, which leads to the superior vena cava. Inserting the needle or catheter is the responsibility of a doctor. Nurses may assist with this procedure. Figure 10-4 illustrates the location of the catheter, common parts of the insertion equipment, and the dressings that are used for hyperalimentation.

Principles of Care 10-4. Administration of a nasogastric feed

Nursing Action	Rationale
Explain the procedure to the patient.	To obtain the patient's consent and cooperation.
Wash hands.	To minimize cross-infection.
Submerge the reservoir and airway, giving sets and connections in a tank of Milton solution until required.	To sterilize equipment.
Take the feed and tank containing necessary equipment to the patient's bedside. If the patient is capable of doing so, he/she should assist in the procedure.	To encourage feelings of independence.
Remove the reservoir from the tank and drain the fluid back into the tank (omit for continuous feeding). Do not rinse before use.	Rinsing may introduce infection and counteracts the cleansing effect of a solution such as Milton.
Remove the cap of the reservoir, and pour the prescribed feed into it (may be omitted if a prepacked bottled feed or a prefilled reservoir from the pharmacy is used).	
Replace the cap and insert the giving set. Close the airway. Hang the reservoir on the stand beside the patient. Run the feed through to the end of the tubing, collecting the waste Milton solution in a jug if necessary. Clamp the tubing firmly.	To prevent the feed escaping from the reservoir via the airway. Running the feed through the tubing removes excess solutions, such as Milton, and any air bubbles from the system and prevents them from reaching the stomach.
Check the position of the nasogastric tube by auscultation or aspiration (see Principles of Care 10-3).	To ensure that the tube is in the stomach before feeding begins.
Connect the giving set to the nasogastric tube using a three-way tap or an appropriate connector if required.	The three-way tap allows the addition of drugs or water for flushing without having to disconnect the system.
Open the airway and set the flow of feed at the prescribed rate. Pumps are commercially available for administering feeds at a constant rate.	The rate of feed must be regulated to meet the patient's need. If possible, the patient should control his/her own feeding rate.
Return periodically to check the patient's comfort and the rate of flow of the feed.	The rate of flow of the feed may alter suddenly, especially if the patient is mobile.
On completion of a feed, disconnect the giving set from the distal end of the nasogastric tube and flush the tube with 10 ml of water. Spigot the tube.	To remove particles of feed likely to block the tube.
Wash the reservoir and the giving set in hot water and a suitable detergent, rinse well (omit for continuous feeding).	Washing with detergent removes any feed left in the equipment. Thorough rinsing is required to prevent inactivation of Milton by the detergent.
Submerge the syringes, giving set and reservoir in the tank of Milton solution; leave them submerged until the next feed (omit for continuous feeding). The tank should be kept by the patient's bedside.	To sterilize this equipment. For both intermittent and continuous feeding, the Milton solution and equipment should be discarded every 24 hours. Feed reservoirs or bottles should be discarded according to manufacturer's guidelines.

Source: Pritchard and David, Royal Marsden Manual of Clinical Nursing Procedures; published by Blackwell Scientific, 1992.

Principles of Care 10-5. *Suggested management of a nasogastric feeding regime*

Nursing Action	Rationale
Starting the Regime	
This will vary depending on the following: 1. Nutritional requirements of patient. 2. Condition of the patient, e.g. has the patient been starved prior to starting the regime? 3. Type of feed being used.	
Gradually build up, over four to five days, volume and rate of feed to meet nutritional requirements.	Gradual increase in regimen allows the gastrointestinal tract to adjust to a liquid diet, thus reducing the risk of intolerance. Too rapid an administration may lead to nausea, distension and diarrhoea.
Timing of the Feed	
Preferably give a continuous drip feed over 24 hours.	Patients may find this restricting but it has the advantage of allowing a large volume of feed to be dripped in slowly over a long period of time, thus giving a high level of nutrition while keeping the osmotic load low.
Alternatively, give four or five feeds daily, the timing determined by convenience to patient and staff.	Patients may prefer intermittent feeds given throughout the day.
Duration of the Feed	
Decide the number of feeds and the drip rate in the light of patient requirements, condition and personal preference.	
Monitoring the Patient	
Fluid balance: measure daily input and output.	To monitor state of hydration.
Weight: weigh twice weekly (in same clothing and at same time of day).	To monitor weight changes which may be associated with a tube-feeding regimen.
Urine: daily urine analysis for glucose during first week of feeding. If glucose detected, check the urine throughout the whole period of tube feeding.	To ensure that the urine glucose level relates to the feed just given.
Bowels: check daily, by observation or by asking the patient about the frequency and nature of stools.	To detect and combat diarrhoea or constipation related to tube feeding.
Haematological investigations: test for urea and electrolytes and glucose levels once or twice weekly.	To monitor the patient's state of hydration. Nitrogen balance may be of value in some patients.
General condition: observe daily for thirst, lethargy, glycosuria and polyuria—all symptoms of dehydration.	To prevent the complication of end-state dehydration.

Table 10-5. Common problems associated with administering nourishment by nasogastric feeding

Problem	Common Cause/Usual Care
Irritation of oral mucous membranes	Oral mucous membranes often become dry and irritated when the patient is unable to take nourishment by mouth and is receiving nourishment by gavage. Frequent oral hygiene helps prevent this problem and should be administered at least four times each day.
Acute otitis media	Otitis media may occur when the nasogastric tube presses against the eustachian tube. This causes obstruction and oedema. It can best be prevented by turning the patient from side to side frequently, at least every 2 hours, and by using as small a nasogastric tube as possible.
Diarrhoea, nausea or abdominal distention	Nourishment introduced too rapidly, or nourishment is too concentrated. Usual care is to decrease the strength of nourishment and to administer it more slowly. An antidiarrhoea drug may be prescribed.
	Oral antibiotics; administer any medication prescribed for nausea or diarrhoea.
	Malabsorption due to enzyme depletion, villous atrophy following periods of starvation or inadequate nutrition; hyperosmolar feeds: dilute the feed or decrease the rate of feed. Inform the nutrition team.
	Lactose intolerance, especially in patients of African and Asian origin or severely debilitated patients: use a lactose-free feed.
	Contaminated feed and/or equipment: obtain a stool for bacteriological investigation. Take swabs from the equipment and any solutions used.
Weight gain is unsatisfactory and/or urea output high	Inadequate nutrition for patient's needs. Inform the nutrition team.
Dehydration	Inadequate water intake to meet patient's needs. Offer fluids. Inform the nutrition team.
Aspiration	Aspiration is best prevented by being sure the tube is in the stomach before introducing the nourishment and by keeping the head of the patient's bed elevated between about 30° and 45°. Suctioning of the mouth and throat may be used when regurgitation and vomiting are present.
Clogged tube	A clogged tube is prevented by keeping a constant flow rate when nourishment is given continuously and by flushing the tube well after single feedings. If irrigation does not relieve the obstruction, the tube may need to be removed and replaced.

Source: Pritchard and David, Royal Marsden Manual of Clinical Nursing Procedures; published by Blackwell Scientific, 1992.

The nursing care plan for a patient having parenteral hyperalimentation usually includes orders describing the following measures:

- Assessing the insertion site
- Regulating and maintaining the infusion
- Changing the dressing and tubing
- Carrying out urine tests to evaluate the metabolic effects of the infusion
- Weighing the patient
- Recording fluid intake and output
- Assessing for signs of high and low blood sugar

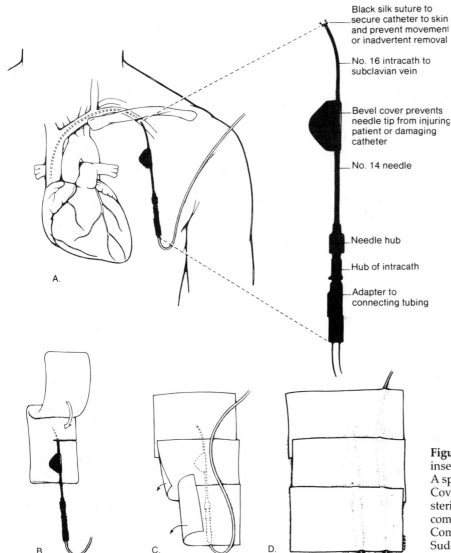

Black silk suture to secure catheter to skin and prevent movement or inadvertent removal

No. 16 intracath to subclavian vein

Bevel cover prevents needle tip from injuring patient or damaging catheter

No. 14 needle

Needle hub

Hub of intracath

Adapter to connecting tubing

A.

B.

C.

D.

Figure 10-4 Hyperalimentation. *A*: Note insertion of needle into subclavian vein. *B*: A split dressing accommodates intracath. Covering this split dressing is another sterile dressing. *C*: Adhesive dressings complete the occlusive dressing. *D*: Completed dressing. (Brunner and Suddarth, 1984. Reprinted with permission.)

- Administering insulin, ordered by the doctor, according to the results of urine and blood tests

Suggested measures to promote nutrition in selected situations

When the patient is an infant or child

Observe the same procedure for inserting a nasogastric tube in an infant as described earlier in this chapter, with these exceptions:

Use a small tube, a size 8 being common.

Place an infant's head over a rolled-up towel or napkin placed under the head. This positioning helps in the insertion of the tube by straightening the oesophagus.

Plan that it may be necessary to start the flow of nourishment by using a very gentle push on the syringe barrel or plunger. Then use gravity to continue the flow.

"Wind" the infant after giving nourishment to help remove air from the stomach, and then position him in a crib on his right side.

Offer an infant with a nasogastric tube a pacifier at regular intervals to satisfy his sucking reflex.

Infants born prematurely are often fed via a

nasogastric tube to conserve their strength until they have matured sufficiently to suck well.

Observe the following techniques when an infant has a cleft palate:

Follow hospital policy concerning the type of equipment to use for feeding. A medicine dropper, a small spoon, or a syringe may be used.

Hold the infant in a sitting position while feeding him to help avoid choking and aspiration.

Feed the infant very slowly to avoid choking and aspiration.

Wind the infant several times during and after feedings. A child with a cleft palate tends to swallow large quantities of air.

Be sure to check the temperature of formula before offering it to an infant. The formula should feel comfortably warm, but not hot, when a few drops are allowed to fall on the inner aspect of the nurse's wrist.

Alternate the sides on which the infant is held for bottle feedings, as with a nursed baby, to promote bilateral stimulation and coordination.

Hold an infant when he is nursing from a bottle. Do not prop a bottle. The infant needs the touch and cuddling offered while holding him, and he may choke on a bottle propped in place.

Offer finger foods to mature infants and toddlers up to about age 3. Then cut up food finely for them. Youngsters enjoy helping themselves to food but cannot manage utensils with ease. Unbreakable spoons are best when a youngster shows readiness to handle them.

Use small plastic cups partially filled with beverage for children learning to use a cup to help prevent spilling. Training cups are available and will also help prevent spilling when children are learning to use a cup.

Plan that, in terms of body weight, the infant or preschooler requires more calories than does the school-age child, whose body is growing at a slower rate. During adolescence, total caloric requirements increase because of a growth spurt.

Enlist the help of parents, when possible, for helping with feeding their children and also when children are on increased or restricted fluid intake. This helps parents feel that they can do something to help in the care of their infants and children. They can also help in the selection of menus for their children because they know what foods their children enjoy.

Offer the following items, which children generally enjoy, when fluids are to be encouraged:
Ice lollies of various flavours
Ice cream
Jelly—often especially attractive to children when moulded in various shapes and sizes
Soda pop and various fruit drinks

Place a stethoscope on a child and allow him to listen to the gurgling sound of liquids in his stomach. This technique often helps encourage drinking when children are to have a generous fluid intake.

Use game techniques to encourage fluid intake. For example, taping a picture on the bottom of a glass often interests a child in drinking so that he can see the picture. Also, stars may be placed on the side of a glass or cup as a reward for reaching certain levels.

Offer a child on restricted fluid intake an occasional ice lolly or a little jelly. These items help relieve thirst while still helping to keep the fluid intake low.

Use highchairs and small tables and chairs for children able to be out of bed. Children also like to eat in groups.

Use drinking tubes for children old enough to use them. If there is a problem with spilling, liquids can be placed in a bottle that is capped with a nipple; cut slits in the nipple in the form of an X, and place the drinking tube through the slit.

When possible, enlist the cooperation of children of school age to help with meal planning. This is a type of health teaching and also promotes interest in eating.

When the patient is pregnant or lactating

Note in a nursing history whether a pregnant or lactating woman is receiving sufficient calcium and iron in her diet. These two minerals are likely to be in short supply when the mother's diet is inadequate.

For most pregnant women, expect that the total number of calories necessary to support the developing foetus must be increased by approximately 300 daily.

For most lactating mothers, plan that several hundred additional calories per day are necessary to supply food for the infant. The lactating mother's diet should be rich in milk, in foods high in proteins, and in minerals and vitamins.

The lactating mother should have a generous daily fluid intake.

When the patient is blind or has his eyes patched

The suggestions given earlier in this chapter to help a patient eat should be observed when feeding a patient who is blind or whose eyes are patched. These additional techniques are recommended:

Tell the patient what you are offering him with each mouthful.

Use a system, such as a hand touch, to indicate when he is ready for more food or beverage or when there is another biteful ready for him.

If the patient can help, consider using dishes with rims if spilling is a problem. Place the food in identical positions for each meal. The place of food on his tray can be described by using a clock. For example, a beverage is placed in the position of 1 o'clock; a vegetable is placed at 3 o'clock; and so on.

When the patient is elderly

Remember that the elderly lose their sensitivity to taste and smell. Herbs and spices often help perk up a poor appetite. Foods and beverages with an aroma and flavours that are relatively intense often appeal more than bland foods. There appears to be a decrease in sensitivity to salty and bitter tastes but not to sweet and sour.

Remember also that the sense of temperature decreases with age. Therefore, be especially careful to avoid serving very hot foods with which the elderly could be burned without their realizing it.

Consult the elderly patient about supplemental vitamins if his eating habits are poor. The need for vitamins does not change with age, but vitamin intake is often relatively small. The vitamins most often lacking in the diet of the elderly include thiamine and vitamins A and C. Foods high in vitamin B, such as grain cereals, meat, poultry and fish, should be encouraged because vitamin B helps stimulate the appetite.

Take into consideration that the need for calories decreases with age, as people become more sedentary. As a general rule, the elderly person needs about one-third fewer calories than do young and middle-aged adults.

Take into account that the person with dentures or without teeth cannot chew well. Foods should be finely chopped or ground, as indicated.

If the patient has difficulty swallowing, hold his head slightly forward when offering foods and fluids and allow the head to go back gradually. This technique helps prevent choking and aspiration.

Position the patient in a low sitting position and place liquids under the tongue when the elderly person has trouble swallowing. This technique helps prevent offering fluids so rapidly as to cause choking and aspiration.

Consider using double-strength milk if the patient is undernourished. The protein and vitamin content of milk can be increased without increasing the fat content by reconstituting dry skimmed milk with whole milk.

Be sure that the elderly patient receives good oral hygiene. A clean, moist mouth, free of debris and irritation, helps improve the appetite and the desire to eat.

Be prepared to teach the elderly about common food fads. Many fad diets tend to make the elderly patient believe falsely that he will regain youth by using them.

Allow the elderly to dine in groups whenever possible. They ordinarily enjoy the social interaction and company of others when eating.

Teaching suggestions for promoting nutrition

The nurse should use opportunities to teach patients, their families, and the parents of children about the importance of proper nutrition. Including families in health teaching is especially important when the patient is a child or when he is elderly or too incapacitated to understand.

Patients requiring special diets need the nurse's help in learning how to select appropriate foods and why the special diet is important for health. A diet low in sodium content (low salt or salt free) is commonly prescribed. If the patient uses a salt substitute, the patient's potassium blood level should be monitored because many salt substitutes contain potassium. A high blood level of potassium can endanger health.

Advertising has been relatively effective in leading people to use fad diets and foods. The nurse can play an important part in helping patients understand the differences between fads or myths and facts through proper teaching.

There are various services available in most communities for serving meals. Some of these services bring meals to the home; others have programmes where people gather for meals served to them. The nurse should be familiar with these services and inform those who could benefit from them.

A variety of suggestions has been offered in this chapter to help patients meet nutritional needs, including suggestions in selected situations. These suggestions should be shared with patients and families as situations indicate.

References

Brunner, L.S. and Suddarth, D.S. (1984) *Textbook of Surgical Nursing*, 5th edn, J.B. Lippincott, Philadelphia.

Committee on Medical Aspects of Food Policy (1984) *Diet and Cardiovascular Disease*. DHSS report on health and social subjects no. 38, HMSO, London.

NACNE (National Advisory Committee on Nutrition Education) (1983) A discussion paper on proposals for nutritional guidelines for health education in Britain. Health Education Council, London.

Phylip Pritchard, A. and David, J.A. (1992) *Royal Marsden Hospital Manual of Clinical Nursing Procedures*, 3rd edn, Blackwell Scientific Publications, Oxford.

Further reading

Allen, D. (1984) Patient care in hyperalimentation. *Nursing Times*, **80**(18), 28–30.

Bewsher, C. (1984) Nutritional problems in the infant. *Nursing: The Add-On Journal*, **2**(22), 640–41, 644.

Bladen, L. (1986) Enteral feeding. *Nursing: The Add-On Journal*, **3**(8), 281–5.

Deakin, J. and Forrester, I. (1986) All change. *Nursing Times*, **82**(14), 47.

Dewar, B. (1986) Total parenteral nutrition at home. *Nursing Times*, **82**(28), 35, 37–8.

Dickerson, J. (1986) Nutrition in health and illness. *Nursing: The Add-On Journal*, **3**(8), 303–7.

Dickerson, J. (1986) Hospital induced malnutrition: a cause for concern. *Professional Nurse*, **1**(11), 293–6.

Dowding, C. (1986) Nutrition in wound healing. *Nursing: The Add-On Journal*, **3**(5), 174–6.

Francis, D. (1985) Foods, fats and facts for nutrition in children. *Nursing: The Add-On Journal*, **2**(39), 1149–52.

Goodinson, S. (1986) Assessment of nutritional status. *Nursing: The Add-On Journal*, **3**(7), 252–8.

Hadley, A. (1985) Vegetarianism—blowing the myths. *Nursing Times*, **81**(42), 27–9.

Hadley, A. (1986) Eat to your heart's content. *Nursing Times*, **82**(9), 18–19.

Holmes, P. (1985) The indigestible facts. *Nursing Times*, **81**(46), 46.

Holmes, S. (1985) The risk business. *Senior Nurse*, **2**(2), 20–3.

Holmes, S. (1985) Differing needs. *Nursing Times*, **81**(13), 35–6.

Holmes, S. (1985) Advice that's too hard to swallow? *Nursing Times*, **81**(38), 17–18.

Holmes, A. (1986) Food additives. *Nursing: The Add-On Journal*, **3**(8), 293–5.

Holmes, S. (1986) Nutritional needs of surgical patients. *Nursing Times*, **82**(19), 30–2.

Holmes, S. (1986) Determinants of food intake. *Nursing: The Add-On Journal*, **3**(7), 260–4.

Hunt, S. (1985) Below the breadline. *Community Outlook*, **19**, 21.

Jones, E. (1986) Changing our eating habits. *Nursing: The Add-On Journal*, **3**(7), 268–72.

Lask, S. (1986) The nurse's role in nutritional education. *Nursing: The Add-On Journal*, **3**(8), 296–300.

Lee, B. (1987) Total parenteral nutrition. *Nursing Times*, **83**(1), 33–5.

Shircore, R. and Baichoo, S. (1985) Understanding Asian diets. *Nursing Times* (Community Outlook supplement), **81**, 16–17.

Wood, S. (1986) Nutritional support: an overview of general principles. *Nursing: The Add-On Journal*, **3**(8), 301–2.

11

The need for activity and exercise

Learning objectives

When the content of this chapter has been mastered, the learner should be able to:

Define the terms appearing in the glossary.

Identify characteristics of good posture in a standing, sitting or lying position.

Identify principles of body mechanics that should be maintained using various activities as examples, such as ironing, gardening, carrying groceries and so on.

List seven benefits of exercise.

Discuss factors that indicate risks to certain individuals who impulsively begin an exercise programme.

Describe three types of information that are useful when assessing an individual's fitness.

Compare isotonic exercise with isometric exercise.

Describe ways that exercise may be performed safely.

List examples of exercises that are considered leisure-time activities.

List suggested measures to promote activity and exercise in selected situations, as described in this chapter.

Glossary

Active exercise A form of exercise performed by a person without the assistance of another.

Activity Movement that accompanies the activities of living.

Aerobic exercise A form of active exercise that challenges the heart and lungs.

Body composition The ratio of lean mass to fat mass.

Body mechanics The efficient use of the body as a machine.

Exercise Movement intended to increase strength, stamina and overall body tone.

Fitness An increased capacity to perform work with greater ease.

Flexibility The ability to move joints through their normal range of motion.

Isometric exercise A form of active exercise that alternates contraction and relaxation of skeletal muscles with little or no movement.

Isotonic exercise A form of active exercise that involves movement and work.

Musculoskeletal system The structures of the body used for support and movement.

Osteoporosis A condition in which the bones lose calcium and become less dense.

Passive exercise An exercise in which one person moves the body parts of another.

Posture The position of the body or the way in which it is held.

Range of motion The amount of movement that is possible in the joints of the body.

Stamina The ability to sustain effort.

Strength The potential for power.

Stress electrocardiogram A test that records the activity of the heart during exercise.

Tone The potential to respond when stimulated to work.

Introduction

Movement of the body is necessary for work and play. The need to move about is directly related to the quality of life. Roper et al. (1985) write that "physical activity is a basic human drive and is important throughout life, even in old age". Yet, science and technology continue to develop devices that decrease physical activity. What was once a long day's work at hard, manual labour has subsequently been lightened and reduced by time and labour-saving machines.

Though not everyone is destined to become an athlete, even maintaining good posture and using proper body mechanics to maintain normal musculoskeletal function will help individuals look and feel better.

There is currently a renewed interest and awareness of the importance of exercise. This has led many people to participate in some increased physical activity. The nurse can do much to identify the multiple physical and emotional benefits associated with a more active lifestyle. In addition, the nurse may be called upon to present methods to avoid exercise-related complications. This chapter may help the nurse assess the fitness of individuals and promote safe aspects of movement and exercise so that more people may find enjoyment and improved health through independent, group or team activities.

Basic terminology

Activity is movement that accompanies the activities of living. For most people, each day is filled with reaching, lifting, stooping, pulling, pushing, sitting, standing and so on. *Exercise* is movement intended to increase strength, stamina, and overall body tone.

Fitness is the result of exercise; it is an increased capacity to perform work with greater ease.

The *musculoskeletal system* of the body consists of structures that the body uses for support and movement. The manner in which these structures are used affects the efficiency with which the tasks are accomplished. A preliminary step to fitness is preventing strain and injury through the development of good posture and body mechanics.

Maintaining good posture

Posture refers to the position of the body or the way in which it is held. Posture requires energy to overcome gravity. Without this energy, the body would become entirely limp and fall to the floor.

Having good posture means positioning the body so that there is good body alignment and good balance. In this position, the musculoskeletal system can be used in the best way possible. Good posture makes it possible for other systems of the body to work more efficiently. For example, slouching when standing or sitting makes it difficult for the lungs to work their best. There is also a quality of attractiveness about a person when the body is positioned appropriately.

Standing. The following is a description of good posture in the standing position.

- Keep the feet parallel, at right angles to the lower legs, and about 10 cm to 20 cm (4 to 8 in) apart. Distribute weight equally on both feet. This position of the feet gives the body a good base of support.
- Bend the knees slightly. This position of the knees avoids the strain of "locked knees" and acts as a shock absorber for the entire body.
- Pull in the buttocks and hold the abdomen up and in. This position is often referred to as "putting on an internal girdle". It will help to keep the back straight by preventing swayback; this, in turn, keeps the spine properly aligned. This position supports the abdominal organs and reduces strain on both back and abdominal muscles.
- Hold the chest up and slightly forward and extend or stretch the waist. This gives internal organs, such as the lungs, the greatest amount of space possible for effective work. It also helps maintain good alignment of the spine by preventing a humped back. The shoulders may be relaxed but held back slightly.

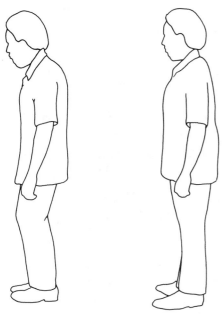

Figure 11-1 *Left*: Poor posture—the body is slouched over and abdominal muscles relaxed, leading to poor body alignment. *Right*: Good posture—the body is held upright, enhancing alignment.

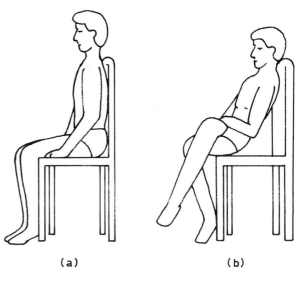

Figure 11-2 (A) Sitting with uncrossed legs improves circulation; good posture—back straight & head up. (B) Sitting slouched in chair with crossed legs—hinders circulation—puts strain on back & neck.

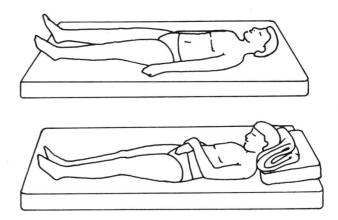

Figure 11-3 *Top*: The line of gravity passes through the body as though the person were standing. *Bottom*: Flexion of the neck and arms interferes with breathing and proper alignment.

- Hold the head erect with the face forward and with the chin in slightly. In a sense, the head is balancing at the top of the spine in this position. The position also helps keep the spine in good alignment by preventing a curve in the neck area. Correct and incorrect standing positions are illustrated in Figure 11-1.

Sitting. A good sitting position is like that just described for standing, except the buttocks and upper thighs become the base of support on the chair and the knees are bent. The legs should not be crossed at the knees when sitting because that position interferes with proper circulation of blood. The area under the knees, the popliteal area, should be free from the edge of the chair. Pressure in the popliteal area interferes with circulation in the legs and may cause damage to nerves in the area. Figure 11-2 shows poor and proper posture when sitting.

Lying down. It is also important to have good posture when lying down. The muscles are in a state of relaxation when resting or sleeping. Unless the parts of the body are properly supported, the body will respond to gravity and fall out of good alignment. Poor alignment makes it difficult for the body to function effectively. Correct and incorrect positions when lying down are illustrated in Figure 11-3.

The principles of body mechanics

Body mechanics is defined as the efficient use of the body as a machine. Using good body mechanics is as important to the nurse as it is for others. Basic principles of body mechanics are illustrated in this chapter, which uses the nurse as an example. However, the principles can be applied regardless of the worker or the task. Common terms used when

Table 11-1. Basic terminology of body mechanics

Term	Definition	Example
Gravity	A force that pulls objects toward the centre of the earth	The pull of gravity causes objects, such as an item dropped from the hand, to fall to the ground. It causes water to drain to its lowest level.
Energy	The capacity to do work	Energy is used to move the body from place to place. Energy is required to overcome the force of gravity.
Balance	Having a steady position with weight distributed equally on the base of support	A person falls when he is off balance as gravity pulls him out of position and to the ground.
Centre of gravity	The point at which the mass of an object is centred	The centre of gravity for a standing person is the centre of the pelvis and about halfway between the umbilicus and the pubic bone.
Line of gravity	An imaginary, vertical line that passes through the centre of gravity	The line of gravity in a standing person is a straight line from the head to the feet that passes through the centre of gravity of the body.
Base of support	The area on which an object rests	The feet are the base of support when a person is in a standing position.
Alignment	Having parts of an object in proper relationship to one another	The body is in good alignment in a position of good posture.

Figure 11-4 These illustrations show the effect of gravity and the type of base of support on balance. It can be seen that the wider the base of support and the lower the centre of gravity, the greater is the stability of the object.

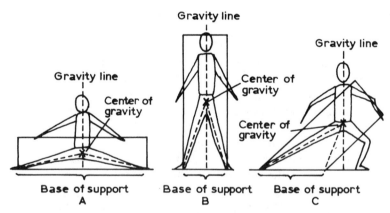

speaking of body mechanics are defined in Table 11-1. Figure 11-4 illustrates some of the terms.

General principles for good use of the musculo-skeletal system are described as follows.

- *Use the longest and strongest muscles to provide the energy needed for the task.* It is best to use the long and strong muscles in the arms, legs and hips whenever possible. Smaller, weaker muscles will strain and injure quickly if forced to work beyond their ability. One of the most common injuries affects the muscles in the lower part of the back. It is a painful injury and usually slow to heal, but it is preventable when proper body mechanics are used.

- *Maintain good posture.* This overcomes slouching and uses muscles properly to prevent strain and injury to the abdominal wall.

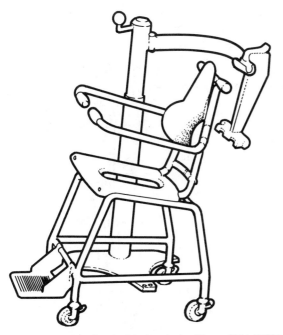

Figure 11-5 Mechanical hoist chair. (From BPA/RCN, 1987)

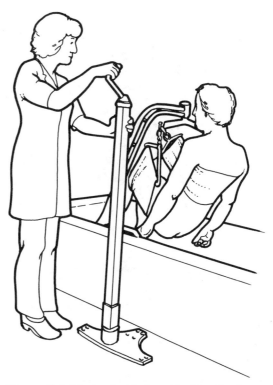

Figure 11-6 Mechanical hoist with sling: fixed type. (© Don Charlesworth)

- *Push, pull, or roll objects whenever possible, rather than lift them*. It takes more effort to lift something against the force of gravity. Use body weight as a lever to assist with pushing or pulling an object. This reduces the strain placed on a group of muscles.
- *Keep feet apart for a broad base of support*. If the feet are close together, weight is distributed over a small area. Balance can be upset in this position when there is even a slight tilt of the body.
- *Bend the knees and keep the back straight when lifting an object, rather than bending over from the waist with straight knees*. This position makes best use of the longest and the strongest muscles in the body. It also improves balance by keeping the weight of the object being lifted close to the centre of gravity.
- *Avoid twisting and stretching muscles during work*. These movements strain muscles and usually occur when there has been failure to bring the work as close to the body and its centre of gravity as possible. The result is that the line of gravity falls outside the body's base of support.
- *Rest between periods of exertion*. Muscles that are overused or misused build up chemicals that accentuate fatigue. Muscles work more effectively by resting them occasionally when working or exercising strenuously.

Nurses, because of the nature of their work, are particularly at risk of developing back pain and/or damage, especially if they do not adhere to the principles of body mechanics and correct lifting techniques.

One study undertaken by the Royal College of Nursing (RCN) in 1979 indicated that within the course of one hour, two nurses lifted the equivalent of two and a half tons in attending to patients' needs.

Other studies throughout the world have investigated the epidemiology of back pain in nurses. One such study in the UK (Stubbs et al., 1983), estimated that 40 000 nurses per annum had at least one day's absence from work due to pain. This same study estimated that the number of days lost by nurses because of back pain was 764 000 per annum.

To help reduce the risk of back pain and/or injury, the nurse should whenever possible employ the use of lifting aids such as mechanical hoists with appropriate chairs or slings as shown in Figures 11-5 to 11.8.

As well as using lifting aids it is important that the nurse assesses the individual mobility needs of each patient so that not only can she use the most

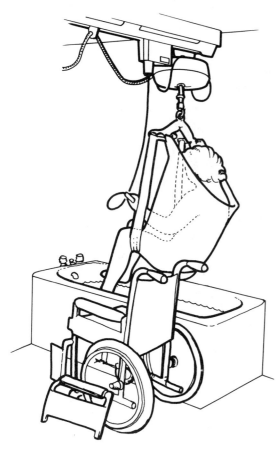

Figure 11-7 Mechanical hoist with sling: track type. (From BPA/RCN, 1987)

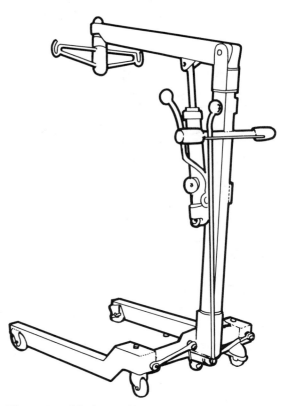

Figure 11-8 Mechanical hoist with sling: mobile type. (From BPA/RCN, 1987)

appropriate handling technique but also the patient knows what he can or should not do in relation to mobilizing (Roper et al., 1985).

Outlined in Figures 11-9 to 11-13 are some of the common lifting and handling techniques used by nurses to assist patients with varying degress of mobility. These techniques and more are described very clearly in *The Handling of Patients—A Guide for Nurses* (BPA and RCN, 1987).

If the principles of good posture and body mechanics are practised, the result will be good balance, increased muscle effectiveness, less fatigue or injury to the musculoskeletal system and an attractive appearance.

Benefits from activity and exercise

Besides feeling and looking better, increasing exercise can lead to many positive effects. Exercise has a holistic effect; both physical and emotional well-being are improved.

Improved cardiopulmonary function. The heart and the lungs work together to provide cells with oxygen and to remove wastes. The heart is a muscle. Any muscle that is exercised increases its tone. *Tone* is a term referring to the ability to respond when stimulated to work. Eventually the exercised muscle of the heart will be able to pump more blood with less effort. Athletes generally have low pulse rates, but their cells are adequately oxygenated. Similarly, the lungs take in more oxygen with each breath.

The circulation of blood is also improved with exercise. Blood in the veins of the legs, arms and lower body must travel back to the heart against gravity. Muscle movement helps to move blood out of these areas. People who sit or stand for long periods may experience swollen feet and ankles.

Improved muscle strength and stamina. The muscles of the body become strengthened. *Strength* is the potential for power. *Stamina* is the ability to sustain effort. Most people who exercise develop increased endurance. The *body composition*, the ratio

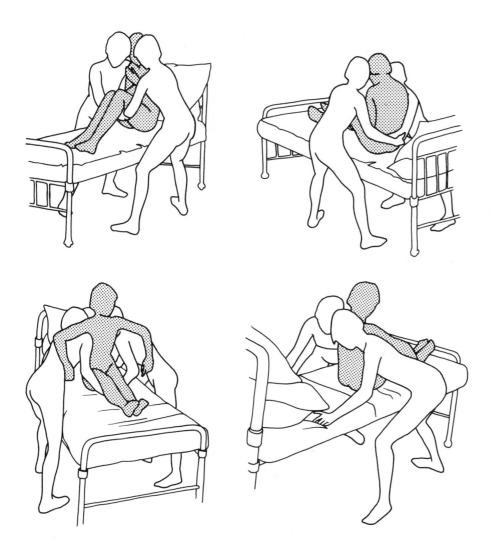

Figure 11-9. Two nurses lifting a patient in bed: orthodox lift. Source: Roper *et al.*, The Elements of Nursing, 2nd Edition; published by Churchill Livingstone, 1985.

Figure 11-10 Two nurses lifting a patient in bed: Australian lift. Source: Roper *et al.*

of lean mass to fat mass, also changes. Physically fit individuals appear sleek and coordinated.

Maintenance of joint mobility. Joints move in various directions. The amount of movement that is possible is called *range of motion*. The range that is available in each joint is referred to as *flexibility*. When joints are not moved, the normal range is reduced. Activity and exercise help promote the flexibility of joints. Table 11-2 describes and illustrates some of the common terms used to describe body positions when joints are flexible.

Increased bone density. One of the chief minerals that allows bones to be strong and compact is calcium. Activity and exercise promote the deposit and retention of calcium. A common problem for bedridden individuals and inactive elderly people is a softening of the bones called *osteoporosis*. Women are

at higher risk for this when they age, since a decrease in oestrogen, a female hormone, is thought to be a contributing factor. Figure 11-19 shows the difference in height due to a loss of bone density. The effects of this condition can be reduced by increasing the intake of dairy products or using calcium supplements, and by exercise.

Promotion of bowel elimination. Stool forms throughout the intestine as nutrients and water are absorbed. Gravity and muscle movement help move stool toward the rectum, from which it is eventually passed. Activity and exercise promote this process.

Aid to sleep. Fatigue is the body's signal for rest. Sleep restores the sense of well-being as a result of the stimulation from physical and mental activity.

Reduction of tension. Separating oneself from the usual daily stressors has been a technique frequently

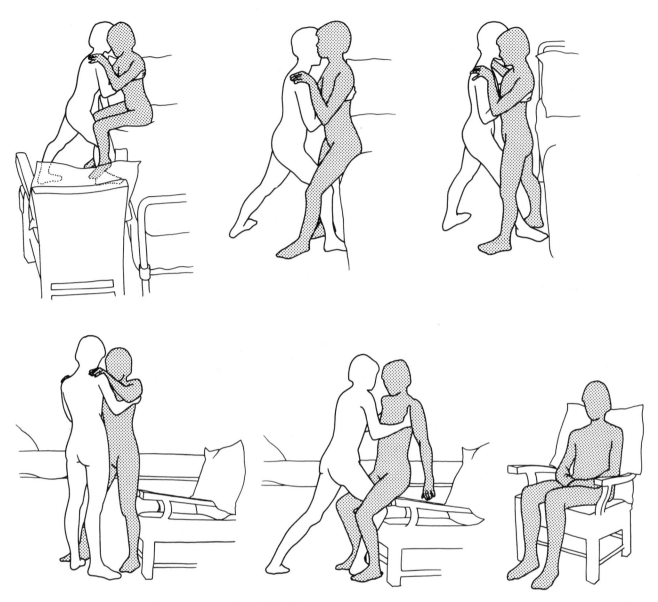

Figure 11-11 One nurse helping a patient from the bed to a chair. Source: Roper *et al.*, The Elements of Nursing, 2nd Edition; published by Churchill Livingstone, 1985.

used to reduce tension. Some do this by meditating; some participate in leisure-time activities; some exercise. Research suggests that during activity the body releases chemicals that elevate one's mood and promote a feeling of well-being.

Identifying risk factors

Even though most people are reasonably active, not all should make rash decisions to suddenly change their lifestyle by exercising. Caution should be used. Even some experienced athletes have died suddenly and unexpectedly during exercise. Factors that make some more prone than others to complications include:

- *Inactivity.* Those whose jobs require that they are stationary and those individuals whose leisure time is filled with sedentary activities such as playing card games or watching television may

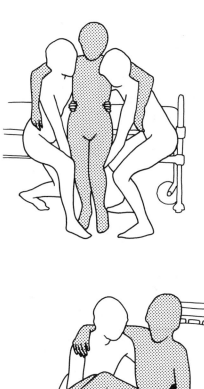

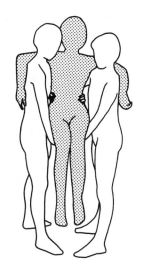

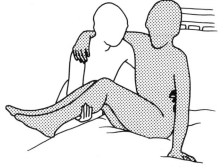

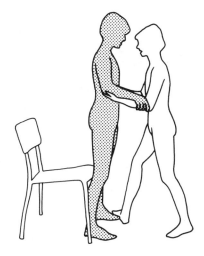

Figure 11-12 Two nurses helping a standing patient into bed. Source: Roper *et al*.

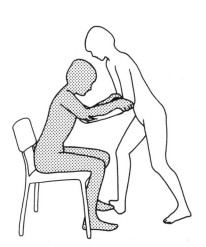

Figure 11-13 One nurse helping a seated patient to stand. Source: Roper *et al*.

Principles of Care 11-1. Using good body mechanics

Nursing Action	Rationale
Maintain good posture.	Good posture reduces strain and helps prevent injury to the musculoskeletal system. It helps maintain balance and keeps the body in good alignment.
When stooping, place one foot in front of the other; lower the body while bending the knees (Figure 11-14). Keep the body weight on the front foot and the ball of the back foot. Keep the back as straight as possible. Return to the standing position by lifting the body with the muscles in the thighs and hips.	These movements make use of the longest and strongest muscles of the body and reduce strain on the back. They provide for a good base of support, proper back alignment and balance.

Figure 11-14 *Left*: Reaching down to pick up a package. This results in poor body alignment and strain on back muscles. *Right*: Good body alignment, using strong muscles of the thighs to assist lifting.

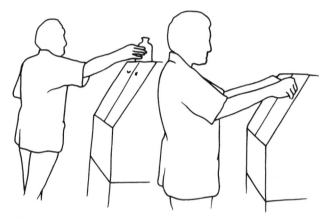

Figure 11-15 *Left*: Stretching and twisting place the body in poor alignment and strain muscles. *Right*: Keeping the work area close to the body minimizes stretching and twisting.

Keep the work area as close to the body as possible (Figure 11-15).	Stretching and twisting fatigue muscles quickly. When stretching or twisting, balance will be poor as the line of gravity falls outside the body's base of support.
Face the work area.	A position that requires twisting strains and tires muscles.
Pivot to turn the body. When pivoting, with the feet apart and the body weight on the ball of each foot (heels slightly raised), turn in the desired direction. Keep the body straight.	Twisting the body causes strain on the muscles. Turning is easier when the weight is off the heels and helps prevent twisting the knees.
Carry objects close to the body but without contaminating the uniform (Figure 11-16).	Carrying objects close to the body helps place the line of gravity within the body's base of support. Stretching the arms outward while carrying an object strains arm muscles.

Continued

Principles of Care 11-1. Continued

Nursing Action	Rationale

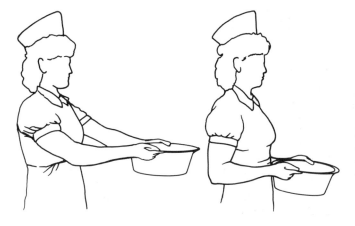

Figure 11-16 *Left*: The nurse strains the arms carrying the basin in this manner. The line of gravity is not within the base of support, which results in poor balance. *Right*: By bringing the line of gravity closer to the base of support, the nurse improves balance and reduces the strain on arm muscles.

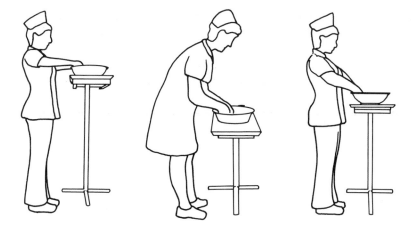

Figure 11-17 *Left*: The nurse's arms are stretched and the back thrown out of alignment by reaching to the work area. *Centre*: Bending over the work area strains back muscles. *Right*: Having the work area at a comfortable height prevents the strain of bending and stretching.

Keep the work area at a comfortable height, as illustrated in Figure 11-17.

Body alignment and balance are easier to maintain when the work is at a comfortable height. When the work area is too high, arm muscles are strained by stretching. When the work area is too low, back muscles are strained by bending over the work.

Lean toward objects being pushed and away from objects being pulled (Figure 11-18). Use the muscles of the legs as much as possible and use the internal girdle.

Body weight adds force to muscle action when pushing or pulling. Using the long and strong muscles of the legs relieves strain on the arms and back. Using the internal girdle protects abdominal organs and reduces strain.

Roll an object rather than lift it whenever possible.

Rolling an object requires less muscle work than does lifting an object.

Use the longest and strongest muscles of the body whenever possible.

These muscles are less likely to become strained and injured than smaller muscles.

Continued

Principles of Care 11-1. Continued

Nursing Action	Rationale

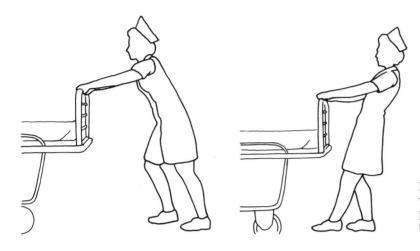

Figure 11-18 The nurse leans towards the bed while pushing it (*left*) and away from it while pulling (*right*). The body weight assists muscles to move the bed.

Use a sturdy stepping stool when obtaining articles out of easy reach.

Stretching causes strain on muscles. As the centre of gravity is raised while in the stretching position, the body is placed in poor balance.

Move muscles smoothly and evenly while working.

Jerky movements produce more strain on muscles and are uncomfortable for the nurse and the patient.

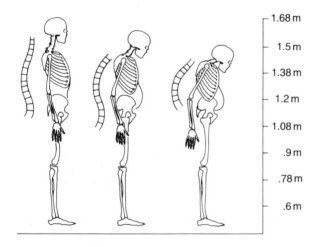

Figure 11-19 These figures show the potential change in height from middle age to old age as a result of the loss in bone density. Adapted by permission from Whitney *et al.*, Understanding Nutrition, 5th Edition; © West Publishing, 1990. All rights reserved.

not be able to adapt to the increased physical demands associated with exercise.

- *Obesity.* Those who are over 20% of their ideal weight are generally fat. Food that is not used for energy is converted to fat. A logical analysis is that fat people are inactive people.

- *Ageing.* As age increases so do changes in the functioning of vital organs such as the heart, lungs, and blood vessels. These organs may function adequately during rest and inactivity, but may not be able to meet the changes required during exercise.

- *Smoking.* The use of tobacco affects the heart and lungs, making an individual even more susceptible to exercise-related complications. Nicotine causes the heart rate to increase. The walls of blood vessels become smaller, thus elevating the blood pressure. This interferes with the circulation of oxygen-rich blood to cells.

Table 11-2. Terms commonly used to describe body positions and movements

Term	Description/Example	Term	Description/Example
Abduction (verb: abduct)	The act of moving a body part away from the centre of the body	Flexion (verb: flex)	The act of moving so that the angle between adjoining parts is reduced; bending

Abduction of arm

Term	Description/Example
Adduction (verb: adduct)	The act of moving a body part toward the centre of the body

Flexion of neck

Term	Description/Example
Hyperextension (verb: hyperextend)	The act of moving so that the angle between adjoining parts is made larger than its normal or average range, or more than 180 degrees

Adduction of arm

Term	Description/Example
Extension (verb: extend)	The act of straightening or increasing an angle that brings parts into or toward a straight line

Hyperextension of neck

Term	Description/Example
Rotation (verb: rotate)	The act of turning: the head is rotated when it is turned from side to side.
External rotation	The act of turning outward: the leg is rotated outward when the toes point outward.
Internal rotation	The act of turning inward: the leg is rotated inward when the toes point inward.

Extension of neck

Continued

Table 11-2.　Continued

Term	Description/Example	Term	Description/Example
Pronation (verb: pronate)	The act of positioning the forearm so that the palm of the hand faces downward; also, the act of positioning the body so that the person lies on his abdomen, as shown below		

Prone position

Pronation

Supination

Term	Description/Example	Term	Description/Example
		Distal	Farthest from the centre of the body: the foot is distal to the knee. The hand is distal to the elbow.
		Proximal	Nearest the centre of the body: the knee is proximal to the foot. The elbow is proximal to the hand.
Supination (verb: supinate)	The act of positioning the forearm so that the palm of the hand faces upward; also, the act of positioning the body so that the person lies on his back, as shown below	Active exercise	An exercise performed by a person without assistance: a person rotates his head without assistance. A person flexes and extends his elbows and knees without assistance.
		Passive exercise	An exercise in which one person moves the body parts of another: a person rotates another person's head. A person flexes and extends another person's elbows and knees.

Supine position

Mucus increases in lungs and makes it more difficult for gases to be exchanged. Long-term smoking causes even more serious, irreversible changes in lung tissue. One of the healthiest changes, even more healthy than exercise, is to stop smoking.

- *High blood pressure.* Elevated blood pressure usually means that the heart must work especially hard to pump blood through narrowed blood vessels. During exercise, cells need oxygen even more so than at rest. When a vital organ, such as the heart, cannot receive the oxygen it needs, life-threatening complications can occur.
- *Heredity.* Otherwise healthy individuals who have a family history of deaths or diseases associated with the heart should be careful. Some of these diseases may be so subtle that they do not cause obvious signs or symptoms until dangerously advanced. Exercise may trigger the first experience with symptoms, which may be so severe that they cause death.

Assessing fitness

There are ways that an individual's readiness for or response to exercise may be evaluated. It is best to use the results of several methods to be sure of the findings.

Measuring body composition. One of the better assessments is related to body composition. This information can be obtained by measuring skinfold thicknesses. Skinfold thickness is a measurement that indirectly reflects the state of fat throughout the body. It is measured with calipers at various parts of the body: the fleshy part of the upper arm, below the shoulder blade, in the lower abdomen and the upper thigh. Excess amounts are usually an indication of overeating or lack of exercise, or both.

Recording observations of pulse temperature, blood pressure and respiration. If these observations are above normal at rest, the individual may be unfit to exercise vigorously. Exercise usually will increase these measurements even more. Further testing and evaluation should be performed by a doctor. After a period of regular but modified exercise, a person may condition himself so that these measurements will become lowered.

Fitness tests. There are tests that are useful in evaluating an individual's current ability to exercise. These are important to assess the potential for life-

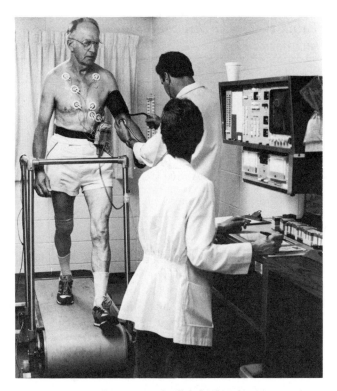

Figure 11-20 Walking a treadmill, which moves at a progressively faster pace while the heart activity is recorded, is a way of determining the heart's ability to adapt to increased work during exercise. (Courtesy of Borgess Medical Centre, Kalamazoo, MI.)

threatening complications associated with exercise after a period of inactivity.

A *stress electrocardiogram* is often recommended for middle-aged and older individuals. It is a test that records the activity of the heart during the time that an individual exercises. Figure 11-20 shows an individual undergoing a stress electrocardiogram. The heart rate, respirations, blood pressure and any symptoms such as chest pain are also recorded. Any irregularities or abnormal values may be reason to stop the test. Individuals can still exercise, but the level and length of time may require careful planning.

A test that requires less sophisticated equipment is the Three-Minute Step Test. Despite its simplicity, during the test life-threatening risks are still possible. The test should be used with caution and where medical assistance is available when an individual is middle-aged or older, has been inactive, or is overweight. If the person develops any discomfort or fatigue, the test should be stopped, and he should be checked by a doctor.

Table 11-3. The three-minute step test recovery index

	Cumulative Pulse Rate	
	Men	**Women**
Excellent	132 or less	135 or less
Good	150–133	155–136
Average	165–149	170–154
Fair	180–164	190–171
Poor	Above 180	Above 190

From Getchell (1983). Reprinted with permission.

When conducting the step test, the individual alternates going up and down two steps. The rate per minute should average approximately 26 to 27 steps. The pulse is counted at one-minute intervals after the exercise for three times. The rates for all three recordings are added. Values that reflect a state of fitness are listed in Table 11-3.

Types of exercise

The preferred type of exercise is *active exercise*. This is a form of exercise performed by a person without assistance. People who are ill may need the assistance of another to move. This would be considered *passive exercise*. Passive exercise and other forms of exercise that are considered therapy for patients are described in Chapter 16. There are several types of active exercise that healthy people may choose to perform.

Isotonic exercise. These exercises involve movement and work. One of the best examples is *aerobic exercise*, a type of active exercise that challenges the heart and lungs. Eventually these organs may perform at peak levels. To evaluate that the exercise is sufficient to accomplish this, certain guidelines must be met. An individual should exercise every other day for 20 minutes.

Exercise that is more frequent, less intensive, and of longer duration may also be beneficial.

Isometric exercise. These exercises involve contracting and relaxing muscle groups with little, if any, movement. An example of this type of active exercise is that used for weight training and body sculpting. These exercises increase the mass and definition of skeletal muscles, but they do not increase the capacity of the heart and lungs to perform.

Exercising regularly. When the resolution for exercise has been determined safe, the nurse may provide information that will reduce some of the risks. The object of exercise should be to promote health and well-being while avoiding injury or related complications. Principles of Care 11-2 gives suggestions for planning a safe exercise programme.

Leisure-time activities. Few people care to do one thing all day long; most enjoy some variety. Recreation and leisure-time activities can be more than just having fun. They can contribute to both physical and mental well-being.

Some spend a portion of their leisure time in exercise or sports activities. For various reasons many prefer group activities to solitary exercise. Fitness centres are now located in almost every city. The competition among them is resulting in attractive, affordable memberships. Many health clubs open early in the morning to enable people to attend exercise classes, swimming or work outs in a gymnasium before going to work.

Many annual races or walks are open to amateurs who gain sponsorship for charitable causes.

There are many opportunities to add exercise to one's life. Finding a leisure-time activity may open the door to developing a lifelong habit that is pleasurable and healthy.

Suggested measures to promote activity and exercise in selected situations

When the individual is an infant or child

Use toys and play activity to promote exercise and activity.

Select toys that are appropriate for the age of the child and choose them carefully with safety in mind. Toys with small, removable parts should be avoided because of the danger of their being swallowed. Also, toys with sharp edges or points should be avoided. Interesting and inexpensive toys can be made from common objects found in the home.

Select play activity with safety in mind. Play activity should be supervised at all times.

Select play activities that are appropriate for the age of the child. For example, young children may play next to each other but rarely play with each other. Activities involving groups of children become more appropriate among school-age children.

Principles of Care 11-2. *Planning a safe exercise programme*

Nursing Action	Rationale
Assess the level of fitness.	Serious complications can occur to individuals who are not able to adapt to the increased demands associated with exercise.
Find a partner who also exercises.	Exercising with someone can provide motivation and support when the best intentioned person loses interest or becomes discouraged.
Set a time during each day for exercise.	An activity that is scheduled is more often given priority.
Dress for the climate; wear layers of clothing. Clothing should be wind resistant and absorbent.	The body heats during exercise. Perspiration is a method for cooling. Being able to remove or replace clothing may prevent overheating or cooling.
If exercising in areas of traffic, wear reflective clothing. Walk or run against the traffic; cycle in the same direction as the traffic.	Reflective clothing is more readily seen by drivers. Following these directions reduces the potential for being injured.
Eat complex carbohydrates rather than high sugar food before exercising.	Foods such as oatmeal, or pasta take longer to digest and will sustain energy needs longer.
Drink or have access to a source of water or other liquids, such as orange juice.	The body loses water and electrolytes in perspiration. On days of high humidity there may be a problem in maintaining fluid balance.
Avoid drinking alcohol.	Alcohol dilates blood vessels. This contributes to the loss of body heat. It may also interfere with the good sense to rest or discontinue the activity.
Caution should be used when wearing radio headphones.	Music acts as a distraction from the effort of exercise, but it also reduces a person's awareness of the sounds that warn of danger.
Begin performing some mild form of exercise daily, such as walking.	The heart and other structures of the body need a period of conditioning to avoid injury.
Determine the target heart rate.	Exercising at less than maximum intensity still promotes cardiopulmonary performance while preventing overexertion.
Warm up for at least 5 minutes before attempting to reach the target rate. Stretch the muscles or walk at a progressively faster pace.	Gradually increasing the need for the body organs to perform avoids injury.
Use as many muscle groups as possible while exercising. Aerobic dancing, cross-country skiing, swimming, and brisk walking are several examples.	Using a variety of muscles promotes overall distribution of work. It also develops and strengthens the body uniformly.
Sustain the target rate for 20 minutes three times a week or every other day.	This level and frequency of exercise promotes many benefits for cardiopulmonary fitness.
Be attentive to body responses such as pain, difficult breathing, abdominal cramps or nausea, and feeling faint.	Exceeding one's tolerance or not compensating for weather conditions can lead to serious complications.
Cool down for approximately the same amount of time and in the reverse order of the warm-up routine. Fainting commonly occurs as the brain suddenly has a decrease in its blood supply.	The aim of the cool-down is help the body adjust gradually to the changing levels of activity.

Use television with discrimination for leisure-time activity. Watching television promotes minimal activity and does little to stimulate a child's imagination and ingenuity.

Plan activities with the knowledge that children have a short interest span and become bored easily when there is little variety.

When the individual is pregnant

Consult an obstetrician early in pregnancy in order that a realistic assessment of health and fitness may be obtained.

There is no common agreement on the effects of exercise during pregnancy, since research studies have not provided sufficient information.

Strenuous exercise is as unwise for the unfit pregnant woman as it is for any unfit woman.

A previous complication of pregnancy should be considered a risk factor for any extreme in behaviour, including exercise.

When the individual is elderly

Many elderly people have little opportunity to participate in exercise programmes. The nurse has an important opportunity and responsibility to initiate or encourage these kinds of programmes.

Some elderly persons are reluctant to participate in exercise and activity programmes. Gaining their cooperation often requires ingenuity, but concerted efforts are well worthwhile to prevent the serious complications of inactivity.

Take every precaution to prevent falls when promoting exercise and activity. Complications of falls are leading causes of death in the elderly. Safe walking shoes with nonslip soles, stable furniture, low beds, and an environment kept free of clutter are especially important.

Use rocking chairs as one means of promoting activity. Rocking a chair requires an activity most elderly persons can carry out with ease. Also, most enjoy using a rocking chair.

Work with the knowledge that elderly persons tend to have decreasing sensory perceptions. These factors make it especially important to plan exercises and activities that are appropriate and safe.

References

Back Pain Association and The Royal College of Nursing (1987) The *Handling of Patients—A Guide for Nurses*, 2nd edn, The Back Pain Association and The Royal College of Nursing, London.

Getchell, B. (1983) *Physical Fitness: A Way of Life*, 3rd edn, Macmillan, New York.

Royal College of Nursing (1979) *Avoiding Low Back Injury Among Nurses*, Royal College of Nursing, London.

Roper, N., Logan, W. and Tierney, A. (1985) *The Elements of Nursing*, 2nd edn, Churchill Livingstone, Edinburgh.

Stubbs, D.A., Buckle, P.W., Hudson, M.P., Rivers, P.M. and Worrington, C.J. (1983) Back pain in the nursing profession, epidemiology and pilot methodology. *Ergonomics*, **26**, 755–65.

Further reading

Baird, S.E. (1985) Development of a nursing assessment tool to diagnose altered body image in immobilized patients. *Orthopaedic Nursing*, **4**, 47–9.

Bennett-Canclini, S. (1985) The kinetic treatment table: a new approach to bed rest. *Orthopaedic Nursing*, **4**, 61–70.

Boyle, A.M. (1984) The adult hemiplegic patient—a functional approach. *Nursing: The Add-On Journal* **2**(32), 952–4.

Heeschen, S.J. (1989) Getting a handle on patient mobility. *Geriatric Nursing*, **10**(3), 146–7.

Jay, P. (1990) The role of community nurses. *Nursing*, **4**(4), 13–15.

Jones, A. (1988) A level of independence. *Nursing Times*, **84**(15), 55–7.

Lloyd, P. (1990) Handling techniques for nurses. *Nursing Standard*, **4**(25), 24–5.

Pugh, J. (1989) Nursing management for mobility: pre operative phase. *Surgical Nurse*, **2**(3), 24–7.

Pugh, J. (1989) Mobility in the perioperative phase. *Surgical Nurse*, **2**(5), 11–15.

Pugh, J. (1989) Mobility in the postoperative phase of care. *Surgical Nurse*, **2**(5), 15–19.

Tarling, C. (1984) Assessing the mobility needs of the dependent person. *Nursing: The Add-On Journal* **2**(32), 947–50.

Tyson, B. (1989) For want of a nail. *Geriatric Nursing*, **10**(2), 84–5.

Walsh, M. and Judd, M. (1989) Long term immobility and self care: the Orem nursing approach. *Nursing Standard*, **3**(41), 34–6.

12

The need for elimination

Learning objectives

When the content of this chapter has been mastered the learner should be able to:

Define terms appearing in the glossary.

Explain how urine is normally formed and eliminated from the urinary tract.

List and discuss alterations in the normal patterns of urinary elimination.

Describe normal and some abnormal characteristics of urine.

Describe how to toilet a patient. Include using the bathroom, a commode, bedpan and urinal.

List nursing measures commonly used when caring for patients with urinary incontinence and urinary retention.

List reasons for catheterization.

Demonstrate how to catheterize female patients.

Outline a teaching programme for helping a patient to learn intermittent self-catheterization.

Describe management techniques for caring for a patient with an indwelling catheter.

List nursing measures used when caring for a patient with a urinary diversion.

Describe how to collect urine specimens by using the following methods: voiding, clean-catch midstream, 24-hour collection, using a straight catheter, from a catheter that has been indwelling for some time, and from a urinary stoma.

Explain how to test a urine specimen for sugar and acetone, using the procedure of choice in the hospital in which care is being given, and explain how to determine the specific gravity of urine.

List and describe the functions of the structures involved with the elimination of stool.

List factors that affect bowel elimination.

Describe assessments that directly provide information about bowel elimination.

Discuss measures that promote and maintain bowel elimination.

Discuss alterations in bowel elimination; describe factors that contribute to their development and methods to help overcome them.

Describe how to insert a rectal suppository, and insert a rectal tube.

Discuss the differences between an ileostomy and a colostomy.

Demonstrate the application of an ostomy appliance.

Identify the purpose of a colostomy.

Discuss the differences in care when a patient has a continent ostomy.

Describe the general steps for collecting a stool specimen.

List suggested measures for promoting elimination from the urinary bladder in selected situations, as described in this chapter.

List suggested measures for promoting bowel elimination in selected situations, as discussed in this chapter.

Summarize suggestions for the instruction of patients that are offered in this chapter.

Glossary

Albuminuria The presence of albumin in urine. Synonym for *proteinuria*.

Anuria The lack of urine production.

Appliance A collecting bag that is placed over a stoma.

Bowel All the structures in the lower intestinal tract involved in the actual process of stool elimination.

Burning The feeling of warmth and local irritation occurring at the beginning of voiding and continuing throughout urination.

Catheter A tube for instilling or removing fluids.

Catheterization The act of introducing a hollow tube into a body structure.

Clean-catch midstream specimen A voided urine specimen collected under conditions of thorough cleanliness after the first 30 ml of urine are voided.

Cleansing enema An instilled solution used to empty the lower intestine.

Colostomy An opening into the colon.

Commode A chair with an opening in the seat under which a receptacle is placed to collect urine and stool.

Continence The ability to control elimination.

Continent ostomy An ostomy that allows an individual to control the release of liquid stool or urine. Synonym for *Kock pouch*.

Crede's method The application of light pressure over the lower abdomen and in a direction toward the urethra to aid in releasing urine.

Defaecation The act of eliminating stool from the bowel.

Diarrhoea The passage of watery, unformed stools accompanied by abdominal cramping.

Diuresis The excessive production and excretion of urine.

Dysuria Difficulty in voiding.

Enema The instillation of solution into the large intestine.

Enterostomal therapist A nurse who has been certified in skills for the care of ostomates.

Excoriation A condition that occurs from chemical injury to the skin.

Flatulence An excessive amount of gas within the intestinal tract.

Flatus Expelled intestinal gas.

Frequency Voiding at frequent intervals.

Gastrocolic reflex The automatic increase in peristalsis during the process of eating and drinking.

Glycosuria The presence of sugar in urine.

Haematuria The presence of blood in urine.

Haemorrhoids Distended veins in the rectum.

Hypertonic solution A mixture of water with a higher amount of dissolved substances than found in blood.

Ileostomy An opening into the ileum, a portion of the small intestine.

Indwelling catheter A catheter placed in the bladder and secured in place. Synonym for *retention catheter*.

Intestinal distention A condition that results when intestinal gas accumulates and is not expelled. Synonym for *tympanites*.

Kegel exercises Perineal exercises that help strengthen muscles that control voiding.

Kock pouch An ostomy that allows an individual to control the release of liquid stool or urine. Synonym for *continent ostomy*.

Lumen Space within a tube.

Meatus The external opening of a canal in a body structure.

Micturition The act of emptying the urinary bladder. Synonym for *urination* and *voiding*.

Nocturia The need to urinate during the night.

Oliguria The production and excretion of scant amounts of urine.

Ostomate A person who has an ostomy.

Ostomy A surgically created opening into a body structure.

Overflow The involuntary escape of urine associated with an extremely full bladder.

Peristalsis The rhythmic muscular contractions that move contents through the gastrointestinal tract.

Polyuria The excessive production and excretion of urine.

Port A self-sealing access into a closed piece of equipment.

Proteinuria The presence of albumin in urine. Synonym for *albuminuria*.

Pyuria The presence of pus in urine.

Residual urine Urine remaining in the bladder immediately after voiding.

Retention catheter A catheter placed in the bladder and secured in place. Synonym for *indwelling catheter*.

Retention enema An instillation of solution intended to be held within the large intestine.

Specific gravity The weight of a liquid substance compared with the weight of water.

Stoma An artificial opening in the body formed with natural tissue.

Straight catheter A catheter designed to be inserted and withdrawn following its use for some temporary measure.

Stress incontinence The escape of urine from the bladder during times of increased abdominal pressure.

Suppository An oval or cone-shaped solid substance designed for easy insertion into a body cavity.

Tympanites A condition that results when intestinal gas accumulates and is not expelled. Synonym for *intestinal distention*.

Urinalysis A laboratory study of urine.

Urinary incontinence The inability to retain urine in the bladder.

Urinary retention A condition in which urine is being produced by the kidneys but is not being excreted from the bladder.

Urinary suppression A condition in which the kidneys are not forming urine.

Urination The act of emptying the urinary bladder. Synonym for *micturition* and *voiding*.

Urine Waste solution released from the urinary system.

Urinometer An instrument for measuring the specific gravity of urine.

Valsalva's manoeuvre Forced exhalation against a closed glottis.

Voiding The act of emptying the urinary bladder. Synonym for *micturition* and *urination*.

Introduction

Elimination of excess water and wastes is a basic need for all forms of life. The urinary system eliminates excess fluid and toxic substances in a waste solution called urine. Components within food are digested, absorbed and eliminated by structures in the gastro-intestinal tract. Indigestible substances from food and some water are eliminated as stool or faeces. The process of eliminating intestinal and urinary waste is important for life and health.

In this chapter the process of urinary and intestinal elimination is briefly reviewed. Methods for assessing urinary and bowel function and promotion of elimination are also discussed. Nursing skills that may assist the patient with temporary or permanent alterations in elimination are also described.

Urinary elimination

Understanding urinary structures and function

The urinary tract is one of several routes from which wastes are excreted from the body. Other routes include the large intestine, lungs and skin. The urinary system consists of structures that produce urine, collect urine and transport it from the body.

The kidneys and ureters. The kidneys perform the major responsibility for maintaining the balance of water and other chemicals in blood and cells. The blood delivers these substances to microscopic structures called nephrons in the kidneys. The nephrons selectively remove excess water and substances for which the body has no need, thus forming urine. Urine is transported from the kidneys through the ureters to the urinary bladder. As long as this selective process takes place, the fluid and chemical content of the body remains relatively constant.

The urinary bladder. The bladder is a structure that temporarily collects and holds urine. It is made up of several layers of smooth muscle tissue. At the base of the bladder, a round ring of muscle tissue forms the internal sphincter, which guards the opening between the urinary bladder and the urethra.

As the volume of urine increases, the bladder expands and pressure increases within it. When the pressure becomes sufficient to stimulate stretch receptors located in the bladder wall, the desire to empty the bladder becomes noticeable. Usually this occurs in adults when about 200 to 300 ml of urine collect in the bladder.

The urethra. The urethra is the final passageway for urine as it is released from the bladder. In men, the urethra is a structure that also functions as a passageway for sperm. The male urethra is about 14 to 16.5 cm (5½ to 6½ in) in length. The female urethra is 4 to 6.5 cm (1½ to 2½ in long). It serves no reproductive function in the female.

Another sphincter, this one called the external sphincter, is located in the area of the urethra. It is under voluntary control; that is, one can contract and relax this muscle at will. When the sphincter is contracted, urine is held within the bladder. Upon relaxation of the external sphincter, urine is released.

The urinary meatus. The word *meatus* refers to an external opening of a canal in the body. The opening at the end of the urethra in both the male and female is called the urinary meatus. This is the terminal structure of the urinary system and the only part that can be seen with the eyes. *Urination*, the process of emptying the bladder, takes place when urine flows out the meatus. Synonyms for urination are *voiding* and *micturition*.

Factors influencing urinary elimination

A variety of factors influences the amount, contents, and characteristics of urine or its elimination:

- The amount of urine normally produced varies with fluid intake. The greater the amount of fluid intake, the larger will be the amount of urine, and vice versa. If large amounts of fluid are being excreted by the skin, lungs, or intestine, the amount formed by the kidneys will decrease.
- The contents and characteristics of urine are related to the individual's dietary intake and the chemical composition of body fluids. These conditions are in a constant state of fluctuation; yet, the kidneys maintain a relatively stable balance of all the constituents within blood and cells.
- The frequency of voiding depends on the amount of urine being produced. Since fluid intake is reduced during the night, less urine will be formed. Most healthy adults do not void during sleeping hours.
- The intervals at which individuals void generally is determined by habit. Everyone learns to respond to the impulse of a filling bladder on an individual basis. Some respond earlier than others to the urge to void. The intervals are insignificant as long as the overall total amount that is voided is adequate.
- Increased abdominal pressure—such as that which occurs during pregnancy and with coughing, sneezing and lifting heavy objects—

can increase the urge to void and even force urine through the external sphincter and meatus.

- Under certain conditions, it may be difficult to relax muscles sufficiently to void. For example, this may occur when a urine specimen is needed. It may also happen when a person is embarrassed or shy about using a bedpan or having to urinate in a public toilet.
- Women find it easier to void in a semi-sitting or sitting position than in the back-lying position. For the bedridden female patient, elevating the head of the bed and flexing the knees are helpful when permitted. If allowed, the patient may be assisted to a commode or to the bathroom. Men find it easiest to void when standing, and this position is preferred when the male patient's condition permits.

Assessing urinary function

The nurse uses assessment techniques to evaluate all the systems of the body. The process of assessment can be reviewed, and the specific techniques for physical assessment of the genitourinary system can be found in Chapter 4. The nurse can obtain a broad base of information when recording the patient's health history and assessing his patterns of elimination.

Identifying abnormal urinary patterns. There are certain terms that pertain to the signs and symptoms that may be assessed in relation to urinary function. The nurse should become familiar with the following common terms and their definitions:

Urinary suppression is a condition in which the kidneys are not forming urine. *Anuria* refers to the absence of urine. Because the kidneys do not produce urine, the bladder remains empty. Failure to produce urine can eventually lead to death. The nurse must use assessment techniques to determine if the absence of urine is due to nonproduction or the inability to release urine from the bladder.

Oliguria refers to the production of only scant amounts of urine. To excrete sufficient toxic wastes, an adult should eliminate at least 500 ml of urine in 24 hours. In some cases, even the output per hour is assessed to evaluate a trend that may be occurring. Anuria and oliguria are serious signs and should be reported promptly.

Urinary retention means that urine is being produced but is not being excreted from the bladder.

When a patient who is consuming normal amounts of liquid does not void for 8 or 10 hours, the abdomen should be palpated to determine if the bladder is distended. This condition should be reported promptly to restore elimination. Occasionally, when the bladder becomes extremely full, small amounts may leak from the patient as though he cannot control its collection in the bladder. This is referred to as retention with *overflow*.

Polyuria means an excessive production and excretion of urine in amounts significantly more than the amount consumed. Ordinarily, the amount of fluid that is consumed is nearly matched by the amount of urine eliminated. Certain fluids act as diuretics and cause a temporary increase in the production of urine. Examples include coffee, tea, and cocoa. Some drugs also produce diuresis. The cause of prolonged polyuria should be investigated, since it can lead to dehydration.

Residual urine is urine retained in the bladder after voiding. Normally all but 1 to 3 ml is excreted. Urine that is retained in the bladder can support the growth of organisms leading to an infection. Urinary in-fections can often be assessed by the accompanying subjective symptoms of frequency, dysuria, and burning. *Frequency* refers to voiding small amounts at frequent intervals. Urination should be painless and without effort. *Dysuria* means difficult voiding. It may be accompanied by *burning*. This term describes the feeling of warmth and local irritation occurring at the beginning of voiding and continuing throughout urination.

Urinary incontinence is the inability to retain urine within the bladder. Urine dribbles constantly. This can lead to skin irritation, offensive odour, and tissue breakdown. *Stress incontinence* is a condition in which small amounts of urine are released from the bladder only at times when there is increased abdominal pressure, such as when coughing and sneezing. This type of incontinence occurs more often in women than men because the structures that act to control urination may become stretched and weakened during pregnancy and childbirth.

Nocturia is present when individuals are repeatedly awakened during the night with the urge to void. This is especially significant when it is unrelated to

Table 12-1. Characteristics of normal urine in healthy adults

Item	Description
Amount	Approximately 1000 ml to 1500 ml of urine in each 24 hr period. The average is about 1200 ml.
Colour	Golden yellow to amber. If the urine is concentrated, such as early in the morning or after a period of little fluid intake, the colour will be darker. It will be lighter if the urine is dilute.
Clarity	Clear. Urine may turn cloudy on standing, owing to normal phosphate precipitation.
Odour	Faintly aromatic. Some foods, such as asparagus, and certain drugs cause a pungent odour.
Specific gravity	1.005 to 1.025. A wider range has been noted in some healthy adults.
Acidity	Average pH of 6 for persons on a standard diet. A range of 4.6 to 8 is within normal range. Vegetarians excrete slightly alkaline urine. A high-protein diet increases the acidity of urine. Certain drugs influence the acidity/alkalinity of urine.
Protein	Negative.
Glucose	Negative. Glucose may be found in the urine if the person has eaten concentrated sweets, such as boiled sweets.
Ketone bodies	Negative.
Sediment	Negative for red blood cells. Negative for white blood cells. Occasional epithelial cells. Occasional hyaline casts.

the intake of large amounts of fluid before retiring. As men age, the prostate gland enlarges. For some men, this interferes with the ability to empty the bladder completely. The excess volume of urine present in the bladder leads to nocturia.

Examining urine. Data about the functioning status of the urinary system may be obtained by collecting and examining urine. The nurse routinely assesses the colour, amount, clarity, and odour of urine. Table 12-1 is a summary of the normal characteristics of urine. Reviewing the results of laboratory tests performed on urine also can contribute assessment data. The techniques for collecting and performing specific urine tests are discussed later in this chapter.

Identifying abnormal characteristics of urine. Various terms are used to describe abnormalities in the contents of urine. These terms are formed by combining a common suffix referring to urine and a prefix that specifies a substance. Some of these terms include the following:

Haematuria refers to urine that contains blood. When blood is present in large enough quantities, the urine becomes reddish brown in colour; smaller amounts may make the urine appear smokey. The nurse must assess carefully to determine that the blood is coming from the urinary tract rather than from the rectum, or from the vagina of a menstruating female.

Pyuria means pus in the urine. The urine appears cloudy. Normal urine, when it stands and cools, may also become cloudy. The two should not be confused.

Albuminuria means that there is albumin in the urine. Albumin is a type of protein found in plasma. For this reason, the term *proteinuria* is sometimes used as a synonym. The nephrons should not permit albumin to filter through into urine. The presence of albumin may be an early indication of impaired kidney function.

Glycosuria refers to glucose, a type of sugar, in the urine. Glucose should be reabsorbed into the blood stream. When the amount of sugar in the blood exceeds the nephrons' ability to return it to the circulation, glucose is deposited in the urine. This may occur on occasions after an individual eats foods that contain great deal of sugar. It may even be associated with a period of emotional stress when the body requires a surge of glucose for additional energy. However, sustained glucose in the urine is one of the most common symptoms of diabetes mellitus.

Toileting a patient

To obtain a urine specimen or just provide for the patient's elimination, the nurse may need to assist the patient with toileting. Illness sometimes affects patients' strength and ability to eliminate normally. The nurse may be required to help the patient to the bathroom or to help with use of a commode, bedpan or urinal.

Assisting a patient to a bathroom. Some patients are able to use the toilet in a bathroom for elimination. The nurse's responsibilities depend on the patient's condition but, in general, include the following:

- Help the patient walk to the bathroom and stay with the patient if necessary. After being in bed, the patient is often weak and may faint.
- If it is determined that it is safe to leave the patient alone in the bathroom, be sure that the bathroom door is unlocked and a signal device is handy.
- Wait close by, ready to provide the patient with assistance.
- Help the patient clean the perineum of any residue from elimination if that is necessary.
- Observe the characteristics of the urine or stool before flushing the toilet.
- Provide the patient with the opportunity for handwashing before leaving the bathroom.
- Help the patient back to bed, leaving him clean and comfortable.
- Make the necessary notations on the patient's record.

Using a commode. A *commode*, a chair with an opening in the seat under which a receptacle is placed, is sometimes used for elimination at the bedside. This may be necessary when the patient is weak or when activity involved in walking to a bathroom is contraindicated. The patient can be helped from bed in the same manner as assisting a patient from a bed to a chair, described in Chapter 11. Some commodes are equipped with wheels, which allow the patient to be taken to the bathroom for more privacy during elimination. If that is the case, the opening in the seat can be placed over the toilet. Characteristics of the urine should be noted before flushing.

Using a bedpan. A bedpan can be used either for the elimination of urine or stool. Bedpans are made from stainless steel or plastic. One type, called a slipper pan, is more flat on the end that fits toward

Principles of Care 12-1. *Placing and removing a bedpan*

Nursing Action	Rationale
Bring the bedpan, toilet tissues and equipment for the patient to wash and dry his hands.	Having equipment on hand saves time by avoiding unnecessary trips to the storage area.
Warm the bedpan by rinsing it with warm water if the bedpan is made of metal.	A cold bedpan feels uncomfortable and may make it difficult for the patient to void.
Close the patient's room door (if appropriate) and pull the privacy curtains around the patient's bed.	The patient's right to privacy should be respected. Most are especially embarrassed about being observed during elimination.
Place an adjustable bed in high position.	Having the bed in high position promotes the nurse's good use of body mechanics.
Place the bedpan on the chair next to the bed or on the foot of the bed while preparing to position the patient.	To avoid spreading organisms, the bedpan should be placed in an area that is somewhat distant from clean articles.
Raise the top linen enough to determine the location of the patient's hip and buttocks.	This prevents unnecessary exposure while still allowing the nurse to place the bedpan.
Instruct the patient to bend his knees and press his weight downward on his heels.	Elevating the hips provides clearance for placing the bedpan.
Help the patient lift his buttocks by placing one hand under his lower back.	The nurse uses less energy when the patient can assist.
Slip the bedpan into place beneath the buttocks, as illustrated in Figure 12-1.	Proper placement ensures that soiling will not occur during elimination.

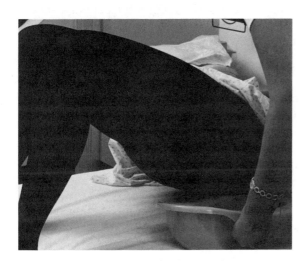

Figure 12-1 The model in this photo illustrates how a patient can help raise himself onto a bedpan. The nurse places one hand under the patient's lower back to help lift him and the other hand slips the bedpan underneath the patient.

If the patient is entirely helpless, two people may be required to place the patient on a bedpan.	Sharing the work reduces the possibility of injury when turning and positioning a helpless patient.
Place the helpless patient on his side while positioning the bedpan against the buttocks.	Turning a patient to the side takes less effort than lifting.
Roll the patient onto the bedpan, as shown in Figure 12-2.	Rolling takes less energy when positioning a patient.

Continued

Principles of Care 12-1. Continued

Nursing Action	Rationale
Look to see that the patient's buttocks rest on the rounded shelf of the bedpan, as is the case in Figure 12-3.	The weight of the patient should be supported, yet should allow sufficient room for elimination.

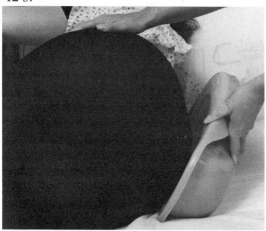

Figure 12-2 The model is in the side-lying position. Notice how the bedpan is tucked under the patient. The nurse then rolls the patient onto the bedpan.

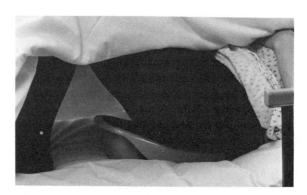

Figure 12-3 The bedpan is properly placed. The patient is sitting in such a way that soiling should not occur.

Nursing Action	Rationale
Raise the head of the bed slightly, if permitted.	This position generally makes it easier for the patient to eliminate and avoids strain on the patient's back.
Leave the signal device and toilet tissue within easy reach of the patient.	Falls can be prevented when the patient does not have to reach for items he needs.
Leave the patient if it is safe to do so.	Attending patients and using siderails help prevent falls or other accidents.
Return promptly to assist the patient with toileting hygiene.	Patients find sitting on a bedpan uncomfortable. Prolonged pressure can lead to skin breakdown.
Remove the bedpan in the same manner in which it was offered.	Proper lifting or turning helps prevent injury.
Place the patient on his side if he is not capable of removing residue that remains from elimination.	Cleaning the patient prevents offensive odours and skin irritation.
Wrap the hand with toilet tissue. Use one stroke from the pubic area toward the anal area. Discard the tissue and use more until the patient is clean. Spread the buttocks to clean the anal area.	Care must be taken to prevent introducing organisms into the urinary meatus. A principle of medical asepsis includes cleaning from an area that is less soiled to one that is more heavily soiled to prevent spreading organisms to cleaner areas.
Place soiled toilet tissue into the bedpan unless a specimen is required, in which case the tissue should be placed in a waxed paper bag or separate receptacle.	Toilet tissue mixed with a specimen makes laboratory examination more difficult. Tissue used for wastes contains organisms and should be disposed of properly.
Help the patient to a position of comfort and offer the patient supplies to wash and dry his hands, assisting him as necessary.	Handwashing is one of the most effective methods of controlling the spread of organisms.

Continued

Principles of Care 12-1. Continued

Nursing Action	Rationale
Assess the characteristics of elimination; collect a specimen; measure the urine if necessary.	The products of elimination may provide data that will aid in a medical or nursing diagnosis.
Do not discard contents of a bedpan if urine or stool appears abnormal in any way. Obtain a sample of the contents from the bedpan in a sealed container.	Disposing of abnormal urine or stool prevents having it analysed by the laboratory.
Record information according to hospital policy.	It is important to keep accurate records.
Empty the contents of the bedpan into the patient's toilet or flushable hopper in a dirty utility room.	Sanitary measures include disposal of urine and stool into a sewage treatment system.
Clean the bedpan and replace it in an area that is located separate from clean articles or possessions used by the patient.	Keeping items used for elimination separate from cleaner items helps prevent the spread of organisms.
Wash hands before performing any other nursing tasks.	Conscientious handwashing prevents the spread of organisms by health personnel.

the back of the buttocks. It is used for individuals who cannot sit or elevate their hips. Principles of Care 12-1 describes how to place and remove a bedpan.

Using a urinal. A urinal is a container designed just to be used during voiding Because of anatomical differences, it is easier for females to use a bedpan for urination. However, there are specially designed urinals that may be used by females under certain circumstances. In addition to the actions regarding privacy, hygiene and disposal of wastes described for using a bedpan, the following actions may be helpful when a male patient uses a urinal:

- To avoid wet linen, make sure that the urinal is empty before handing it to the patient or placing it in position.
- Warm the outside of a metal urinal in the same way that a steel bedpan is warmed, by running warm water over its surface.
- To assist a patient who cannot place the urinal himself, instruct the patient to spread his legs a short distance.
- Hold the handle of the urinal and direct it at an angle between the patient's legs so that the bottom rests on the bed.
- Lift the penis and place it well within the inside of the urinal.

Managing incontinence

Urinary incontinence may be either permanent or temporary, depending on its cause. It is a problem faced by many elderly persons. Family members often need the nurse's help on ways to deal with it in the home. The best approach is to assist with bladder retraining. This may not be possible or realistic for all incontinent patients. When total rehabilitation is not an option, other nursing skills may be implemented. These may include measures that help to reduce the frequency or limit the consequences of incontinence.

Assisting with bladder retraining. For some patients, a bladder retraining programme may be useful. However, to start this type of plan when there is little or no possibility of achieving results can be emotionally damaging to the patient. It can also affect the morale of the nursing team. Even if the programme of retraining is likely to succeed, the patient must be helped to understand that it will be a slow process and that the gains may be slight and very gradual. It will require the combined effort and dedication of all the nursing team as well as the patient and his family.

The following is a list of suggestions that may be developed into a more specific plan for bladder retraining:

- Assess for any regularities or patterns in the patient's period of dryness versus incontinence. Success is more likely if the nurse can adapt measures that correspond to the filling and emptying of the patient's bladder.
- Set realistic goals with the patient. The nurse may find that the patient desires so badly to regain control of his bladder that he sets un-

Principles of Care 12-2. Controlling incontinence

Nursing Action	Rationale
Explain to the patient that efforts will be made to help him.	Incontinence is a difficult problem psychologically and physically. The patient's morale and cooperation can be strengthened when he knows others support his desires.
Help the patient restore normal functioning if there is a possibility for success.	Urinary incontinence should not be a condition to which every patient becomes resigned.
Encourage the patient to establish a routine for attempting to void.	Voluntary efforts either to start or control voiding may be sufficient to help restore function for some patients.
Take chronically ill and elderly patients to a bathroom or offer a bedpan or urinal every 2 to 3 hours.	Providing frequent opportunities to void may decrease the accidental loss of urinary control.
Use hygienic measures to keep the incontinent patient dry, clean, and comfortable.	Accumulated urine forms ammonia, which can cause strong odours. Lying on wet linen can quickly irritate skin, leading to its subsequent breakdown.
Teach the patient Kegel pelvic floor exercises when possible. These exercises consist of contracting the muscles, simulating or actually halting urination.	*Kegel exercises* are perineal exercises that help strengthen muscles that control voiding. The patient should repeat at least 6 to 8 contractions as often as 20 to 15 times daily.
For a male, apply an external catheter that covers the outside of the penis.	Helping the patient remain dry improves a patient's sense of dignity. External catheters have not been found to be effective for incontinent women.
Use absorbent pads and waterproof undergarments for male or female patients.	Disposable briefs have been reported to function effectively and allow the patient freedom of movement without obvious soiling.
Keep a urinal in place if the incontinent patient is a bedridden male. Protect the skin from contact with the urinal by using stretch terry cloth wristbands, or a similar material, used by tennis players.	Protecting a urinal that is kept in place with terry cloth helps prevent irritation and chafing in the genital area, absorbs perspiration, and prevents the urinal from slipping out of place.
Obtain a doctor's order for inserting an indwelling catheter, as a last resort.	Because of the potential for infection, an indwelling catheter should only be used as a temporary measure or when the patient's psychological or physical comfort is at stake.
Demonstrate tact and understanding. Provide opportunities for the patient to express his feelings and concerns.	Discouragement and depression can be relieved by sharing the burden with an empathetic listener.

realistic and self-defeating goals. The nurse may have to help keep expectations within reason. Setting very limited, specific, short-range goals may promote more positive results.

- Plan a schedule with the patient for attempts to void according to the assessed patterns. For example, if it is noted that a frequent wetting time is 10:30 A.M., voiding could be attempted at 10:00 A.M. If night incontinence is a problem, awaken the patient and have him void. If no pattern is apparent, develop a schedule that meets the needs or desires of the patient, as long as they are realistic. An attempt to void should be made at least every 2 to 3 waking hours.

- Discourage strict limitation of liquid intake. The patient should have adequate amounts of fluids to keep urine diluted and prevent fluid imbalance. Also, when the patient's bladder is kept reasonably full, he is more apt to be successful when attempting to void.

- Everyone involved in the patient's care must be aware of the developed schedule and conscientiously carry it out. Unless everyone is dedicated to the plan, enthusiasm will be lost as goals remain unachieved.
- Teach the patient to take note of any sensation that precedes voiding. Examples include chilliness, perspiring, muscular twitching, and restlessness. Males may experience a spontaneous erection triggered by a full bladder. It is important that the patient recognize these signs and use them as indications for voiding.
- Encourage a relaxed atmosphere and as nearly normal circumstances for elimination. A toilet or a commode is preferable. However, simulating the positions for elimination can be done using a bedpan or urinal.
- Suggest that the patient bend forward in a slow, rhythmic manner. This increases abdominal pressure on the bladder. The nurse may also suggest that the patient use *Crede's method*. This involves applying light pressure with the hands over the bladder in the direction of the urethra.
- Experiment with the success of other measures that may stimulate urination, such as listening to running water or placing a hand in a basin of water. Whatever helps to accomplish a small goal can encourage individuals to persevere with the plan.

Limiting the effects of incontinence. Incontinence is a source of embarrassment for most individuals affected in this way. For many, it represents a loss of control similar to the dependency stages of infancy. In addition to the physical care of incontinent patients, nurses must be particularly dedicated to maintaining the individual's dignity. Principles of Care 12-2 provides suggestions that may improve bladder control or reduce the effects of involuntary urination.

Promoting urinary elimination

Rather than being incontinent, some patients may have difficulty releasing urine from the bladder. Such is the case of the patient with urinary retention. In the presence of urinary retention, the bladder may distend until it reaches the level of the umbilicus. The height of the bladder can be determined by palpating the lower abdomen with light pressure. Urine re-

tained in the bladder, for whatever reason, at the very least causes discomfort and, more significantly, increases the likelihood of infections and bladder stones.

The inability to void is often temporary. It is common following abdominal surgery, especially if the patient cannot be up and about. Any obstruction of the urethra or at the meatus can cause retention. Swelling at the meatus, which often occurs following childbirth, is an example. The following nursing measures often help a patient to void:

- Provide privacy while helping a patient to void. Relaxation is important and most patients cannot relax when trying to void if there is the potential that privacy may be invaded.
- Place a female patient in a semi-sitting or sitting position. Voiding may begin while sitting at the edge of the bed on a bedpan if use of a toilet or commode is not possible.
- Assist a male patient to stand at the bedside to void into a urinal. Standing is the natural position during male elimination. A commode or toilet may be used if walking is permitted.
- Warm the bedpan or urinal. Coming in contact with a cold surface may cause stiffening, which can interfere with the relaxation necessary to void.
- Offer the patient fluids. The urge to urinate is dependent on the pressure on stretch receptors as the bladder fills.
- Use the power of imagery and suggestion to help the patient void. This may be done by running water from a tap within hearing distance of the patient. Placing the patient's hand in warm water or running water over the perineal area may also be tried.
- Place the patient in a tub of warm water. The moist heat and relaxation may reduce tense, contracted sphincters and promote urination.

When all measures fail to promote urinary elimination, it becomes necessary for the safety of the patient to have a catheter inserted.

Utilizing urethral catheterization

A *catheter* is a hollow tube for instilling and removing fluids. *Catheterization* of the urinary bladder is the introduction of a catheter through the urethra into the bladder for removing urine.

The dangers of introducing a catheter into the bladder are injury and infection. An object forced through a narrowing, an irregularity, or a curve from the wrong angle can cause injury to mucous membranes. Microorganisms can enter the bladder by being pushed in as the catheter is inserted. The procedure of catheterization is used as infrequently as possible due to the hazards involved in their use. Only when the benefits outweigh the risks should the nurse propose insertion of a catheter. The nurse should also advocate its early removal.

Indications for catheterization. There are several common reasons for catheterizing a patient.

- Occasionally, a patient is catheterized to obtain a urine specimen entirely free of contamination. However, collecting a voided, clean-catch midstream specimen is now replacing the need to obtain a specimen by catheterization. This method will be discussed later in the chapter.
- Catheterization may be used before a surgical procedure to empty the patient's bladder completely. It is commonly recommended that the catheterization be performed in the aseptic conditions of the operating room to help prevent infections. Occasionally, a catheter is inserted before some abdominal or vaginal surgery to keep the bladder empty of urine. This permits the surgeon a better view and palpation of internal tissue. It also prevents accidentally injuring a full bladder with surgical instruments.
- Catheterization sometimes becomes necessary when, for whatever reason, a patient cannot void and nursing measures to induce voiding have failed.
- Catheterization is used when the amount of residual urine left in the bladder after voiding must be measured or to differentiate suppression from retention.
- Catheterization may be used to remove urine from a greatly distended bladder. It is generally agreed that gradual emptying of the bladder is a safer procedure than rapid removal of all urine. For patients with severe retention, if as much as 2000 ml is suspected, the bladder may be gradually emptied over a period of 24 hours or more. At other times, the nurse will need to use good judgment. Some believe that a conservative principle to follow is to remove no more than approximately 500 to 750 ml of urine at one time. Others feel that it is still within the range of safety to remove as much as 1500 to 2000 ml. When there is a conflict of opinion, it is best to observe the hospital's or doctor's preference.
- Catheterization may be used as a last resort to control incontinence. This should only take place if the patient has an open wound or his skin shows signs of breakdown. Frequent hygiene and changing linen present fewer risks than those that are potentially possible with the use of a catheter.
- A catheter may be inserted to monitor and accurately assess the fluid loss and replacement of critically ill patients.

Types of urethral catheters. There are many types of catheters that are manufactured for instilling or removing fluid from various parts of the body. Urethral catheters are intended to be inserted through the urinary meatus and progress up the urethra into the bladder. These catheters are manufactured in various diameters to correspond with the size of the meatus. For adults, sizes 14, 16, and 18 are generally used; the higher the number, the larger the diameter.

A *straight catheter* is a hollow tube that is intended to be inserted and withdrawn following its use for some temporary measure. An *indwelling catheter* is one that is placed into the bladder and secured there for a period of time. It is sometimes called a *retention catheter*. A drainage tube and collection device must be connected to this type of catheter.

The most commonly used indwelling catheter is called a Foley catheter. It has a balloon that can be inflated after the catheter is in place. The balloon prevents the catheter from slipping out of the bladder. An indwelling catheter is illustrated in Figure 12-4.

Although there are several types of indwelling catheters, the principles on which they operate are similar. The catheter has a double or triple lumen. A *lumen* is a space within a tube. When the word is applied to a catheter, it means that the catheter is made with channels that are separated from one another within the same tube. One lumen provides a passage for fluid that inflates the balloon. This portion of the catheter may be self-sealing or require a separate clamp. A second lumen is the channel through which the urine drains. A third lumen, available on some catheters, is made specifically for instilling irrigation fluid.

Preparing for catheterization. Sets are now available that contain the required equipment needed for catheterization. They are packaged in a manner that ensures that the equipment is sterile. Once the

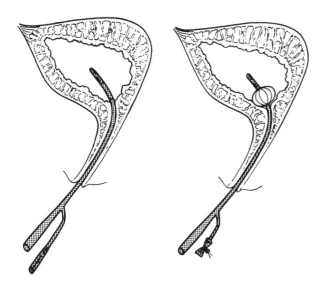

Figure 12-4 *Left*: An indwelling Foley catheter has been inserted into the urinary bladder. A straight catheter would appear similarly, except there would not be an extra projection from the end of the catheter where the lumen leading to the balloon is located. *Right*: The balloon is inflated to prevent the catheter from slipping from the urinary bladder. When the lumen is not self-sealing, it must be clamped to prevent solution from leaking, causing the balloon to empty.

contents of a catheterization set have been used, the set may be thrown away. Sets include the catheter, a drape, a receptacle to receive urine, materials to clean the area of insertion, a lubricant, a specimen container, and sterile gloves.

The preparation of a patient includes explaining that usually there is a sensation of pressure when the catheter is inserted rather than one of pain. Do not dismiss any report of pain, however, since introducing a catheter in swollen or injured tissue may cause discomfort. However, this experience should not necessarily be suggested to every patient who is to be catheterized.

Inserting a catheter. The technique for inserting a catheter for a femalt patient is described in Principles of Care 12-3. The skill can be adapted for use when either a straight or indwelling catheter is inserted. The main difference involves testing and inflating the balloon, which would not be done with a straight catheter.

Connecting a closed drainage system. An indwelling catheter is attached to a receptacle to collect urine. It is positioned lower than the bladder so that drainage occurs by gravity. A closed drainage system, as illustrated in Figure 12-13, is most commonly used. Urine follows a continuous sterile passageway from the bladder to the collecting container.

To ensure that the urine moves directly into the container, it must not become trapped within the tubing. The length of tubing from the bed to the collection bag cannot contain loops. Gravity controls the movement of fluid downward, not upward. If the tubing loops, fluid will be trapped and interfere with the continuous flow of urine. Some nurses use a plastic clip or safety pin to fasten the drainage tubing to the bed linen. This keeps the tubing hanging in a vertical line into the collection bag. When moving the patient or changing linen, these devices should be unfastened to avoid causing the patient discomfort or displacement of the catheter.

There is generally sufficient length of tubing to give the patient freedom to move about. However, it is important that the drainage tube does not become compressed by the weight of the patient's body. Placing it over the top of the patient's thigh is an acceptable common practice. Care must be taken that the siderails or other parts of the bed do not obstruct the flow of urine. Attaching the drainage bag midway to the bedframe generally avoids this problem.

The drainage bag should never be positioned higher than the bladder. The urine that has been collecting for a period of time could then flow back into the bladder, possibly carrying organisms with it. Occasionally, a patient must be transported in a wheelchair. It may be difficult to position the collection system and the tubing lower than the bladder. It is better in that situation to apply a clamp between the catheter and the bag until it is possible to reattach the drainage system to the bed. Before doing so, check to make sure that clamping the catheter for a brief period of time will not cause potential injury to the patient. For some patients, the catheter should never be clamped.

Many closed drainage systems have graduated markings on the collection bag that indicate the volume of drained urine. This helps in the routine assessment of urine. A port at the bottom of the drainage bag permits urine to be emptied without separating the connection between the catheter and the drainage tubing—hence the name closed drainage system. A *port* is an access area for instilling or removing fluid; some ports are self-sealing. To further avoid the need for separation, the drainage

Principles of Care 12-3. Inserting a catheter for a female patient

Nursing Action	Rationale
Assemble the equipment.	Sterile catheterization sets are used in most hospitals.
Obtain and position anglepoise lamp at the end of the patient's bed if the lighting in the room is poor and cannot be modified.	It is important that the light is sufficient for the nurse to locate and identify the urinary meatus.
Wash hands thoroughly. Some prefer to do this after the patient has been positioned and draped.	Handwashing is one of the best methods for removing organisms from the skin. The fewer items that are touched after handwashing, the more aseptic the conditions.
Provide privacy by closing the door and pulling the curtain surrounding the bed.	Pulling the curtains ensures a double protection for ensuring the privacy of the patient.
Position the female patient in a dorsal recumbent position with the knees flexed and the feet about 2 ft apart. If the patient cannot spread her legs, placing the patient on her side, as illustrated in Figure 12-5, can be tried as an alternative.	Good visualization of the meatus is an important aspect in successful catheterization.

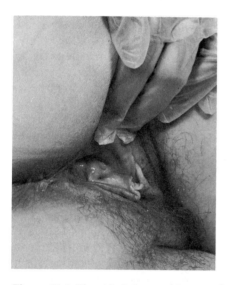

Figure 12-5 The side-lying position may be used when unusual circumstances prevent placing a female patient in a dorsal recumbent position. The photo illustrates that this position allows for good visualization of the meatus and surrounding area.

Figure 12-6 The patient has been properly draped while in a dorsal recumbent position, which is most often used.

Nursing Action	Rationale
Drape the female patient by covering the upper body and each leg, as shown in Figure 12-6. (Drape the male patient so that only the area around the penis is exposed.)	Embarrassment, chilliness, or tension can be avoided by proper draping.
If the patient is soiled, wash the area around the meatus with soap or detergent and water, then rinse and dry.	Having the area as clean as possible decreases the chance of introducing organisms into the bladder.
Place the catheter set between the female patient's legs.	Placing the equipment where it is close and convenient avoids having to reach over sterile items, possibly causing contamination.

Continued

Principles of Care 12-3. Continued

Nursing Action	Rationale
Remove the wrapper from the set and place it in an area close by but separate from the sterile set.	Eventually, the skin of the patient will be cleansed. The plastic wrapper provides a convenient waterproof receptacle for contaminated wastes.
Open the sterile set and don sterile gloves, following the principles described in Chapter 20.	All the equipment inside the set is sterile. To prevent contamination all equipment must be handled following the principles of surgical asepsis.
Open the lubricant container; add the antiseptic to the cotton balls.	All preparation of equipment involving the use of two hands must be done before touching the patient.
Test the balloon if the catheter will remain within the bladder. Fill it with the manufacturer's recommended amount, usually 5 ml to 30 ml, and replace the fluid back within the syringe.	It is best to determine if the balloon is defective before inserting the catheter. The balloon must be deflated prior to insertion.
Wrap the edges of a sterile towel around the gloved hands. Place the towel under the edge of the patient's buttocks as the nurse in Figure 12-7 is doing.	Wrapping the towel around the gloves prevents contamination. The towel provides a sterile field immediately below the working area.

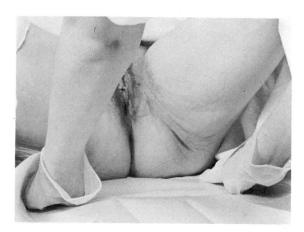

Figure 12-7 Notice how the nurse wraps the edges of a sterile towel around the gloved hands to protect them from contamination while tucking the towel under the edge of the patient's buttocks.

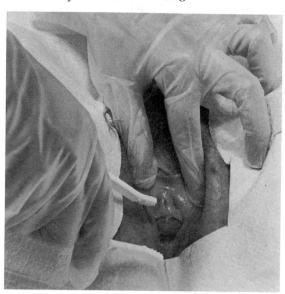

Figure 12-8 The labia minora are well spread and separated. This helps to expose the area for cleansing and for locating the urinary meatus. The nurse's forceps points to the meatus, which appears as a small dimple.

Lubricate the catheter used for a female for about 3.5 to 5 cm (1½ to 2 in).	Lubrication eases insertion.
To expose the meatus of a female, place the thumb and forefinger of the nondominant hand between the labia minora, spread and separate upward, as Figure 12-8 illustrates.	Separating the tissues provides the best condition for differentiating the urinary meatus from the vaginal meatus.
Consider the gloved hand that has touched the patient to be contaminated.	When a sterile area comes in contact with an unsterile area it is no longer sterile.

Continued

Principles of Care 12-3. Continued

Nursing Action	**Rationale**

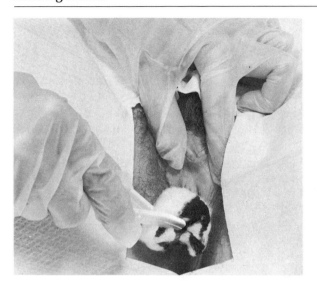

Figure 12-9 The nurse begins cleaning by starting the first stroke directly above the meatus.

Maintain the position of the contaminated hand until the urine is flowing well.

Allowing the labia to drop back into position may contaminate the surface of the catheter as it is advanced into the bladder.

Pick up the forceps and secure a cotton ball saturated with antiseptic solution, as shown in Figure 12-9.

Use of forceps prevents contamination of the remaining sterile glove.

Use one cotton ball for each stroke. Move the cotton ball from above the meatus down toward the rectum, as shown in Figure 12-10.

Thorough cleansing helps reduce the possibility of introducing organisms into the bladder.

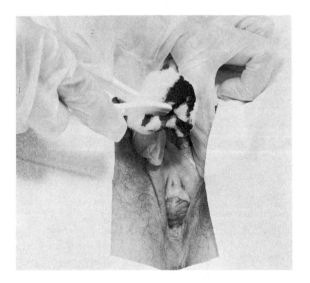

Figure 12-10 The first stroke is completed in a straight line ending well beneath the meatus. One cotton ball is used for each stroke. The areas to the sides of the meatus are also cleaned, while keeping the labia separated.

Continued

Principles of Care 12-3. Continued

Nursing Action	Rationale
Cleanse each side of the meatus with a separate cotton ball until all have been used. Do not go back over any previous area that has been cleansed.	Moving from an area where there is likely to be less contamination to an area where there is apt to be more helps prevent transfer of organisms into the cleaned areas.

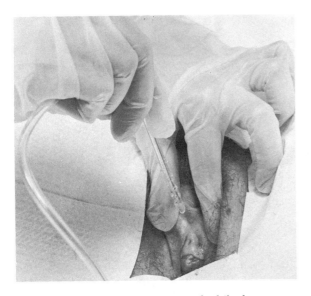

Figure 12-11 The catheter is inserted while the nurse continues to hold the labia apart.

Deposit each cotton ball in the plastic cover adapted for receiving contaminated material. After the last cotton ball is used, the forceps can also be added to the waste container.	Cotton balls used for cleansing are considered contaminated and should not be placed back with other sterile equipment or on the sterile field.
With the sterile gloved hand, pick up the catheter and insert it into the meatus a distance of 5 to 7.5 cm (2 to 3 in), as shown in Figure 12-11.	The female urethra is about 4 to 6.5 cm (1½ to 2½ in) in length. By advancing the catheter farther than this, the tip should be well within the bladder.
Do not force or push the catheter through the urethra into the bladder.	Applying force is likely to injure mucous membranes. Relaxation techniques may be useful for an apprehensive female patient.

Continued

system may also contain a special port through which specimens may be taken or irrigations may be instilled.

To reduce the potential that the collection device will become a reservoir of pathogens, the entire drainage system is changed whenever the patient's catheter is changed. It may be changed more frequently, but care must be taken that the end of the catheter is not contaminated when the connection is separated.

Stabilizing the catheter. A catheter that is not stabilized may pull on the internal sphincter, causing discomfort. Securing the catheter to the skin with some slack will prevent this from occurring.

For women the tubing should be anchored to the upper thigh, as illustrated in Figure 12-14. This

Principles of Care 12-3. Continued

Nursing Action	Rationale

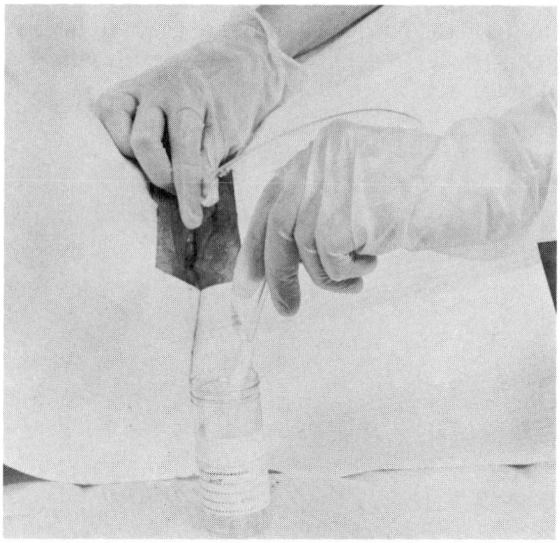

Figure 12-12 Once the urine is flowing, the nurse may allow the nondominant hand to hold the catheter securely in place while directing the urine into a sterile specimen container or the receptacle holding the catheterization equipment.

Nursing Action	Rationale
Discontinue the procedure if the female patient has unusual discomfort or if there is continued resistance to the insertion. Report the information promptly.	Force can cause damage to delicate structures within the urinary tract. Alternative methods may be necessary to remove urine.
Expect that urine will begin flowing when the catheter tip enters the bladder.	Once past the external and internal sphincters, if urine is present in the bladder, it will move out the catheter.
Place the outer end of the catheter within the catheterization set or the specimen container within the set, as shown in Figure 12-12.	Using a container helps prevent accidentally wetting the linen.
Hold the catheter securely while the bladder empties. Avoid advancing and withdrawing the catheter as the bladder drains, even if it may only be short distances.	Movements that cause the sterile surfaces of the catheter to come in contact with unsterile areas can increase the possibility of contamination.
Inflate the balloon when it has been determined that the catheter is well within the bladder, if the catheter is intended to remain for some time.	The balloon keeps the catheter located within the bladder.
Instill the amount recommended to fill the balloon plus 5 ml of extra fluid.	The additional amount ensures that the designated amount of fluid will totally fill the balloon and not be partially located in the lumen.
Withdraw the fluid if the patient describes any feelings of pain or discomfort.	Inflating the balloon within the urethra can cause injury to the mucous membranes.
Pull lightly on the catheter after filling the balloon.	Applying slight tension will indicate if the catheter is well anchored in the bladder.

Continued

Principles of Care 12-3. *Continued*

Nursing Action	Rationale

Figure 12-13 In a closed urinary drainage system, the collection bag is attached to the bedframe below the level of the bladder. The tubing coils on the bed but hangs straight into the bag to promote gravity drainage.

Nursing Action	Rationale
If the catheter is not needed for continued use, withdraw the catheter slowly about 1 cm (½ in) at a time, until urine barely drips, and then pinch the catheter while withdrawing the catheter tip.	Slow withdrawal aids a more complete removal of urine as the tip drains various levels of urine. Pinching prevents urine remaining in the catheter from dripping on the linen or patient.
Connect the end of an indwelling catheter into a drainage collection device. The specific techniques for attaching the drainage system and anchoring the catheter are described later in the text discussion.	A drainage bag provides for continuous collection of urine while the catheter is in place.
Remove the catheterization tray and make the patient comfortable in bed.	The nurse should replace the room in its original order.
Record the time of the catheterization, the amount of urine removed, a description of the urine, and the patient's reaction to the procedure.	An accurate record is important for validating and evaluating the patient's care.

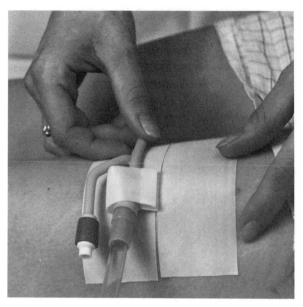

Figure 12-14 The nurse is securing an indwelling catheter on a woman's leg.

prevents the patient from lying on the tubing, yet allows freedom of movement without any pull on the catheter. For the male patient, the tubing can be secured in either of two ways. Both are illustrated in Figure 12-15. These methods of stabilizing the catheter for a male eliminate the pressure and irritation at the angle between the lower part of the penis and the scrotum.

Managing an indwelling catheter. Once a retention catheter has been inserted, the nurse is responsible for its daily care and maintenance. Special assessments and skills may be used to main-

tain its drainage and reduce the possibility of an infection from occurring. Principles of Care 12-4 describes the actions that may be utilized for managing an indwelling catheter.

Irrigating an indwelling catheter. A catheter that drains well does not need irrigating, except on rare occasions when the irrigation is used to instill medications. The usual purpose of an irrigation is to remove particles that are interfering with the drainage of urine. Seeing to it that the patient has a generous fluid intake, up to 2500 ml to 3000 ml daily, increases urine production and dilutes particles that may form in urine. This acts to irrigate the catheter naturally, avoiding any further invasive procedure.

However, irrigating an indwelling catheter with a syringe is sometimes necessary to keep the catheter free of debris. Blood clots and mucus are especially likely to plug the catheter. A doctor's order is necessary for irrigations in most instances.

Techniques for irrigating an indwelling catheter are described in Principles of Care 12-5. Sterile technique is followed, since the urine drainage system is opened when irrigation takes place. There are some types of catheters that allow irrigation without separation. The nurse should follow hospital policy when these are available.

The techniques for irrigation should be included in a teaching programme when the patient is being cared for at home. A method for home sterilization of equipment involves boiling equipment for 10 to 15 minutes at least once a day.

Removing an indwelling catheter. Catheters eventually must be removed either because their need no longer exists or because they require changing. Usually the nurse removes the catheter; how-

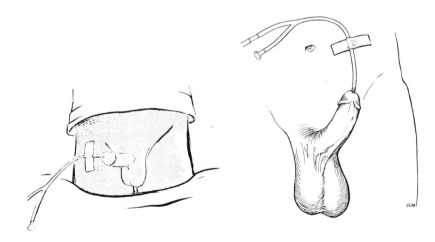

Figure 12-15 These two drawings illustrate acceptable methods for anchoring an indwelling catheter that has been inserted into a penis. Both eliminate pressure and irritation at the penoscrotal angle.

Principles of Care 12-4. Managing an indwelling catheter

Nursing Action	Rationale
Always perform handwashing whenever beginning care of a patient or after contact with heavy soiling.	Hands that contain organisms are one of the chief routes by which pathogens are spread.
Maintain a confident and reassuring attitude when caring for the patient. Handle equipment gently.	Most patients are fearful of having an indwelling catheter and may become upset and angry, especially if they think the nurse is mishandling equipment.
Clean the perineal area, and especially around the meatus, thoroughly at least two times a day and after each bowel movement.	Keeping the perineal area immaculately clean helps prevent organisms from entering the urinary system.
Use soap and water to clean the perineal area and rinse well. Many authorities recommend cleaning with an antiseptic, povidone iodine (Betadine) being a common one.	Thorough cleanliness and inhibition of bacterial growth around the meatus help prevent a urinary tract infection.
Use a separate area of the cloth for each stroke, as described for inserting the catheter.	Cleansing from an area of less contamination to one that is greater prevents the transfer of organisms.
Avoid using powders or lotions after cleaning.	Powders and lotions are likely to trap and retain organisms.
Provide a generous fluid intake; 2500 to 3000 ml daily is an appropriate amount for most patients.	A generous fluid intake keeps urine diluted and free-flowing. The prompt drainage of urine acts as a natural irrigation, preventing obstruction and infection.
Keep the tubing intact and free of kinks.	Any separation can provide an opportunity for contamination. The tubing should remain open and drain without interference.
Encourage the patient to be up and about as ordered. The collection container may be carried as illustrated in Figure 12-16.	Encouraging ambulation helps prevent complications due to immobility and promotes feelings of independence and well-being.
Instruct the patient on the use of a drainage bag attached to the leg. This appliance is especially handy when the patient is ambulating, and it is concealed well within normal clothing. A leg bag is illustrated in Figure 12-17.	Being able to ambulate and dress normally promotes feelings of independence and self-esteem.
Note the volume and characteristics of the urine regularly and record the observations. The urine can be observed through the transparent tubing and the collecting container, as shown in Figure 12-18.	Observing urinary output and characteristics of the urine aids early detection of signs of complications. Document assessments at least every 8 hours, though observations can be made more frequently.
Empty and measure the accumulated urine as the nurse in Figure 12-19 is doing. Usually this is done every 8 hours.	Removing urine periodically without separating connections minimizes the risk of introducing pathogens into the urinary tract.

Continued

Nursing Action   **Rationale**

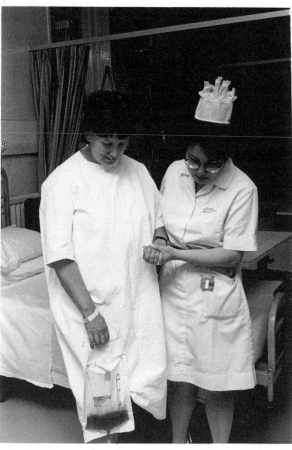

Figure 12-17 This shows a leg bag that can be worn when a patient has an indwelling catheter. It may also be used with an external catheter. This device allows an individual, male or female, to dress in usual clothing while disguising that a catheter is draining.

Figure 12-16 The patient is able to walk about while carrying the urine collection receptacle. Notice that the bag is held at a level lower than the bladder. (Courtesy Royal Marsden Hospital)

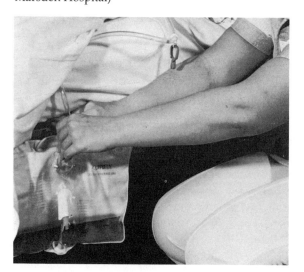

Figure 12-18 The nurse can examine the appearance of the urine through the transparent tubing and collecting bag.

Continued

Nursing Action

Rationale

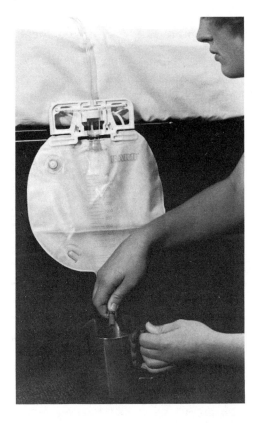

Figure 12-19 To empty the collecting bag the nurse opens the port at the bottom. This permits all the connections between the drainage device and the catheter to remain closed, yet permits the nurse to measure and dispose of accumulated urine.

Report any indications of possible problems. These may include a burning sensation and irritation at the meatus, leaking of urine around the catheter, cloudy urine, a strong odour, an elevated temperature, and chills. Also note whether the skin remains in good condition at the site where tubing is attached to it.

Early reporting facilitates implementing measures that may prevent or treat early complications associated with an indwelling catheter. The nurse is held accountable for responsible care and safety of the patient.

Promote the acidity of urine. Orange juice and other food sources of ascorbic acid, vitamin C, are usually used.

Keeping the urine acidic in character helps ward off bacterial growth.

Arrange for the patient to take a bath or shower, when permitted. The catheter should be clamped temporarily if the collecting container is higher than the bladder. In a bath, with the catheter clamped, the container may be hung over the side of the tub. In the shower, the collection container may be emptied and attached to the leg. Clamping is then usually unnecessary.

Using the bath or shower for personal hygiene promotes cleanliness, which, in turn, helps prevent infection. Self-care develops feelings of independence and well-being.

Teach the patient how the system works and how it is cared for.

A well-taught patient can help reduce potential complications by maintaining a well-functioning drainage system.

Continued

Principles of Care 12-4. Continued

Nursing Action	Rationale
Plan on changing an indwelling catheter as necessary or as specified by hospital policy. One indication that supports the need to change the tubing is that sandy particles are freed when the tubing is rolled between the thumb and fingers.	Any time an invasive procedure is performed, there is a risk of introducing pathogens. There should be an adequate reason for its change. The usual length of time between the need for catheter changes varies from 5 days to 2 weeks.
Use the following to predict the time when the next catheter change should take place. When the catheter is removed, if there is crusting at the tip, the catheter needs changing. When crusting is not present, subsequent catheters may remain in place a few days longer.	Crusting is an indication that substances in the urine are crystallizing and forming sediment. If this accumulates, it can interfere with the flow of urine. As long as no crusting can be noted, it can be assumed that the catheter was functioning well and others could continue in that condition for an additional period of time.

ever, sometimes the doctor will do so. The following techniques may be followed:

- Empty the balloon before removing the catheter. The balloon is emptied by cutting the tube extension used for inflating the catheter. Another method is to insert the barrel of a syringe and withdraw the amount of fluid that was used during balloon inflation. This is probably the safest method because the nurse can be assured that the entire balloon has been emptied.
- Gently pull on the catheter near the point where it exits from the meatus.
- Clean the perineum, following appropriate principles of medical asepsis.
- Inspect the catheter. Be sure no remnants have remained in the bladder, and report the situation promptly if that seems to be the case. Save the catheter for further inspection.
- Continue to assess the patient after an indwelling catheter is removed, focusing on the patterns of urinary elimination. The time and the amount of the first voided urine should be noted. Report any of the following: inability to void within 8 to 10 hours, frequency, burning, hesitation in starting the stream of urine, dribbling, cloudiness, or any other unusual colour or characteristic of the urine.
- Provide a generous level of fluids similar to that when the catheter was in place.
- Record according to hospital policy when the catheter is removed and by whom.

Urinary tract infections are one of the most common acquired infections. The invasive nature of a catheter is a logical explanation for this. The nurse can reduce accompanying risks by practising principles of medical and surgical asepsis, which includes keeping the patient scrupulously clean, especially in the area of the meatus. Seeing to it that the patient has a generous fluid intake also cannot be overemphasized.

Teaching intermittent self-catheterization. Some patients who need frequent catheterization can learn to do so themselves at home. These persons usually have irreversible disease or injury conditions that interfere with bladder functioning. Intermittent catheterization has an advantage in that the invasive equipment does not remain in place for very long at any one time. This reduces the potential for infection somewhat.

Catheterizations that are performed in hospitals follow principles of surgical asepsis. Self-catheterization is done following principles of medical asepsis. Experience indicates that this is entirely safe.

The procedure for self-catheterization is essentially the same as when a nurse inserts a straight catheter. The following are some differences and points to emphasize:

- It is important to stress that thorough hand-washing must be performed before self-catheterization. The catheter should be washed well in soap or detergent and water, rinsed, dried, and stored in a clean covered container. Some authorities recommend that the catheter be

Principles of Care 12-5. Irrigating an indwelling catheter

Nursing Action	Rationale
Gather sterile equipment: a bladder syringe, basin, tubing protector, and gauze moistened with antiseptic. Sterile normal saline is used as an irrigating solution unless otherwise specified.	The urinary bladder is a sterile cavity. Sterile equipment and techniques must be used to prevent infection.
Clean the area where the catheter and tubing join with antiseptic, as the nurse in Figure 12-20 is doing, and disconnect the catheter and tubing.	Wiping the immediate area of the connection removes organisms from the surface.

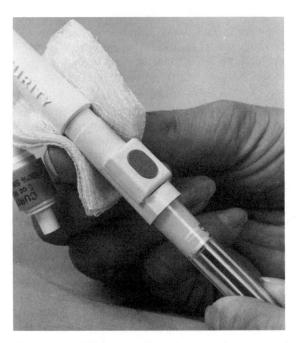

Figure 12-20 The nurse wipes the area where the catheter and the drainage tubing will be separated for irrigating purposes with sterile gauze moistened with antiseptic solution.

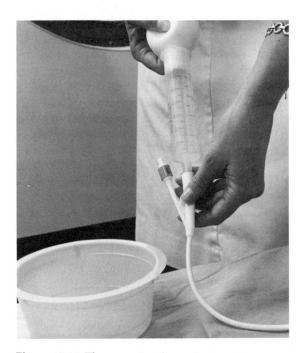

Figure 12-21 The nurse instils sterile normal saline into the catheter for irrigation. A sterile basin is ready to collect the solution, which will return by gravity once the syringe is removed.

Nursing Action	Rationale
Fill the syringe with 30 to 60 ml of solution and insert the syringe tip well into the end of the catheter.	A closely fitting connection allows fluid to move from the syringe through the catheter rather than leak onto bed linen or the patient.
Gently compress the ball of the syringe to instill the irrigating solution, as shown in Figure 12-21.	The flow of fluid helps to dilute and free sediment or debris within the lumen of the catheter.
Do not apply force. Remove and replace the catheter if it cannot be irrigated.	Using a great deal of pressure may injure tissue or cause the solution to leak out the connection.
Remove the syringe when it is empty of the solution.	Suction should be avoided because the mucosa of the bladder is easily injured. Removing the syringe breaks the vacuum suction.

Continued

Principles of Care 12-5. Continued

Nursing Action	Rationale
Allow the instilled solution to flow back by gravity into the basin. The catheter may be milked by holding and stretching sections of the catheter between the thumb and forefinger. Milk the catheter in a direction away from the bladder toward the open end of the catheter.	Milking creates slight negative pressure at periodic intervals that may facilitate the break-up of sediment that will allow free drainage. Milking away from the bladder prevents debris from being forced back into the bladder.
Connect the catheter and clean drainage tubing and assess for the drainage of urine into the collecting bag.	The urine should once again drain naturally by gravity.
Note the total amount of solution used for irrigating and measure the amount of solution returned in the basin.	The difference in these two amounts indicates the amount of urine that drained with the irrigating solution. In some cases there is less drainage than solution instilled. The amount that remains will eventually drain into the collection bag.
Record the fluid amounts accurately if a record is being kept. The total amount of fluid instilled is listed as intake; the solution drained is output.	When fluid balance is being assessed, both amounts must be recorded. Any amount that did not immediately drain will be calculated as output when the urine in the collecting bag is measured.
Discard the solution that has drained into the basin.	The nurse is responsible for maintaining the environment in a clean condition.
Replace or protect the irrigating equipment, depending on the frequency of irrigation.	Sterile equipment that has been opened may become accidentally contaminated. Unless the nurse can be assured of its sterile condition, it should not be reused.
Record the irrigation according to hospital policy.	Documentation provides a record of care and the patient's response so that evaluation can objectively take place.

boiled for 20 minutes between uses. Although sterile technique is not used, cleanliness and other practices of medical asepsis are important to prevent infection.

- The patient who can void should be encouraged to do so first—and then use the catheter if there is concern that the bladder has not been emptied. This may help promote at least some control over voiding. Certain patients may not be able to void, and this step can be eliminated.
- A man will find a standing or sitting position convenient for self-catheterization. A woman most often sits on a toilet seat.
- A good light is important for adequate visualization of the meatus. This is more difficult for the female than the male. While learning this

procedure, women find that using a mirror helps in locating the meatus. After the technique is well learned, a mirror may no longer be necessary.

- The perineal area is cleansed well with soap and water while using cotton balls in the same manner a nurse does during catheterization. The cotton balls are not sterile and the patient does not wear sterile gloves.
- The catheter is lubricated and inserted the appropriate distance, depending on the sex of the individual.
- The patient is taught Crede's method to remove as much urine from the bladder as possible before withdrawing the catheter.
- When urine flow stops, the patient pinches

the catheter and gently removes it. Pinching prevents leaking of urine that may be within the catheter.

- The frequency of self-catheterization varies. At first, every few hours may be necessary. Some patients eventually reach the point of self-catheterization only every 8 to 12 hours. The time interval between catheterizations depends on the amount of control the patient develops.

- Patients who self-catheterize should be taught the importance of maintaining the acidity of the urine as well as taking in a generous amount of fluids.

Eliminating urine from a surgical opening

At times patients require surgery to remove disease or restore function to the urinary tract. The elimination of urine may be altered in some manner. Temporarily, the surgeon may insert a catheter directly through the skin into the bladder or into the kidney. The patient may eliminate urine through the catheter as well as from the urethra. The characteristics and amounts of urine are assessed separately.

Another possible alternative means for providing for urine elimination occurs when permanent reconstruction must be done. This happens most frequently when the bladder is diseased and must be removed. The surgical technique is called a urinary diversion. A *urinary diversion* is a procedure in which the ureters are surgically implanted elsewhere. They may be brought through an opening in the abdominal wall onto the skin of the abdomen. There are other surgical variations as well. An artificial opening is called a *stoma*. A urinary stoma excretes urine.

Caring for this type of patient presents many physical, emotional, psychological, social, and spiritual challenges for the nurse. A means must be provided for collecting the urine that no longer is stored and released from the bladder. It is also necessary to care for the skin around the new surgical opening; it was never designed to be in constant contact with urine. These patients are often faced with life-threatening diagnoses; they question the meaning of life and death in a highly personal way. The changes in body image can affect the patient and others with whom he shares a close relationship.

Caring for a urinary stoma. Though the patient with a urinary diversion has multiple potential problems, the focus of this discussion will centre on the

Figure 12-22 Removing the protective cover exposes an adhesive patch on an appliance. The centre ring fits over the stoma. (Courtesy of Hollister Inc., Libertyville, IL)

care that is related to urine elimination. A patient with a stoma wears an appliance. An *appliance* is a plastic collecting bag. It has an opening that fits around the stoma and is attached to the skin with a special adhesive, as shown in Figure 12-22. The patient may wear a belt or use paper tape to hold the appliance in place. There can be a great deal of stress on the skin as the appliance becomes heavy with the weight of urine.

Some appliances have an opening at the bottom, to which drainage tubing can be attached. This permits drainage from the appliance during night hours. It eliminates the need for the patient to empty his collecting bag during sleeping hours.

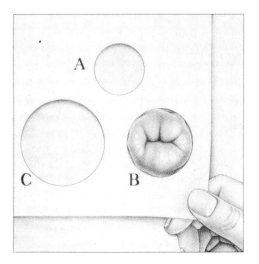

Figure 12-23 This stoma measuring card helps determine the size of the appliance that fits best. Accurate fit reduces injury to the skin and stoma, promoting extended comfort while the appliance is in place. (Courtesy of Hollister Inc., Libertyville, IL)

Nursing measures for caring for a patient with a urinary appliance include the following:

- Make sure that the opening fits the stoma. The stoma can be measured with a special tool, shown in Figure 12-23. There should be only about 1/16 to 1/8 of an inch of skin exposed around it. The less skin that is exposed, the less likely will be skin irritation around the stoma. The tissue of the stoma may be damaged if the opening is too small.
- Use a specially designed skin adhesive to attach the appliance to the skin around the stoma. A solvent is used to remove the adhesive when the appliance is changed. This reduces abrasion of the skin that could occur if the appliance were pulled free.
- Empty the collecting bag when it is one-third to one-half full. Urine can drain through a port provided for this purpose on the appliance. This reduces stress on the skin and avoids removing the entire appliance each time urine accumulates.
- Change the appliance only when it becomes loose or uncomfortable. As long as the skin and the stoma are unaffected, and the urine is draining well, frequent changing can lead to unnecessary trauma to the skin.
- When the appliance is changed, try to do so in the morning shortly after awakening. Urinary output is normally low at this time of the day. Changing is easier when urine is not dripping in high amounts onto the skin.
- Insert a tampon a short distance into the stoma or place a folded, sterile gauze square into the stoma when changing the appliance. This absorbs urine and helps keep the area dry so the adhesive will attach well.
- Clean a reusable bag with soap or detergent and hot water. Rinse well. A half-strength solution of white vinegar or household bleach may be used for soaking the appliance in order to control odours. Commercial liquid deodorants that may be instilled directly within the appliance are also available. Airing and exposing the appliance to sunlight may also help reduce odours. Some have found that inserting a crushed aspirin or tablet of activated charcoal may be helpful. Aspirin has been found to irritate the stoma of some individuals, however.
- Keep the skin dry and clean around the stoma. Antibiotic or steroid creams may become necessary if skin irritation occurs.

- Describe specific care techniques that have been successful on the nursing care plan. This ensures the continuity of care that is provided by other nurses.
- Be sure the patient has a generous fluid intake, at least 2000 ml or more daily. This helps keep urine diluted and free-flowing, and it removes organisms and debris that may accumulate in the urine or around the stoma.
- Help the patient make adjustments in his diet. For some patients, a diet with minimal amounts of certain minerals (e.g. calcium) is recommended to help prevent the formation of kidney stones. Asparagus is discouraged because it causes the urine to have a strong odour. Consuming foods high in vitamin C helps control infection because they keep the urine acid.
- Be sure the patient understands how his urinary diversion works and what care it needs. A well educated patient can learn to resume normal living and to care for himself safely and efficiently.
- Encourage the patient to return to his normal way of living. Clothing conceals the appliance well. Some patients benefit from talks with others who have had a similar operation and returned to their normal activities.
- Consult with other health personnel who have additional expertise in stoma care when perplexing problems occur.

Obtaining urine specimens

Urine can be tested for a great many substances. The general laboratory study of urine is called a *urinalysis*. It can provide a great deal of information about the condition of the patient. The nurse may obtain and examine a sample of urine from time to time. Various techniques may be used for obtaining a specimen for urinalysis. These include collecting a specimen directly from the patient as he voids and removing it from a catheter, or as it flows from a stoma. The skill and judgment that the nurse uses in collecting the specimen can affect the results of the analysis.

Collecting a voided specimen. A voided specimen can be obtained by assisting a patient to a toilet or using a bedpan or urinal. The urine is voided either directly into the container or into the bedpan or urinal. Some of the urine is then poured into the specimen container. Toilet tissue should not be discarded in a specimen container. Paper within the specimen makes urine difficult to examine. The container is properly labelled and sent to the laboratory.

Principles of Care 12-6. Collecting a clean-catch midstream specimen

Nursing Action	Rationale
Gather equipment cotton balls, antiseptic of the hospital's choice, and a sterile specimen container. Gloves must be used if the patient cannot collect the specimen.	Following proper cleansing and collection techniques, the sample of urine is considered a sterile specimen.
Assist the patient to the bathroom or have a clean bedpan or urinal handy.	Some of the urine must be voided before it is collected.
Position the patient either on the toilet with the legs well spread or in a manner in which cleansing the urinary meatus can be performed prior to voiding.	The labia and urinary meatus of a female are best cleansed in this position. A male patient may stand or lie on his back.
Separate the labia well on a female patient, or retract the foreskin of an uncircumcized male.	Organisms are present on the tissue around the urinary meatus. By holding the tissue away from the meatus, contamination of the specimen is prevented.
Clean the area at and around the meatus in the manner described for catheterization. Use each cotton ball that is saturated with antiseptic once. Cleanse away from the meatus.	Precautions are used to prevent infection and to prevent organisms at and near the meatus from being washed into the specimen. This cleansing technique prevents bringing organisms to the meatus.
Have the patient void about 30 ml into the toilet, bedpan, or urinal while continuing to hold the labia apart or the foreskin in a position of retraction.	The first voided 30 ml of urine are discarded. It is expected that any organisms still located at the meatus will have been flushed away. If the labia or the foreskin fall back into place, the area at the meatus becomes contaminated.
Hold the specimen container so that the edges of the opening are not touched.	Though handwashing is a good medical aseptic technique, all organisms are not removed. The specimen container should not be contaminated with these organisms.
Catch some of the urine in the container as it is being voided.	A sample of the urine that is released midway during voiding is the specimen that is meant for collection.
Allow the labia or the foreskin to fall back into place.	It is no longer necessary to position this tissue away from the meatus.
Instruct the patient to continue voiding into the toilet, bedpan, or urinal until the bladder is emptied.	It is unnecessary to fill the entire specimen container. Any urine remaining in the bladder after the specimen is collected can be voided and discarded.
Label the laboratory slip identifying that the urine was collected by the clean-catch midstream method and take it to the laboratory.	Urine should not be allowed to stand unrefrigerated once it has been collected.
Record on the patient's chart and on other areas of the hospital's forms that the specimen was obtained and taken to the laboratory.	Written communication avoids duplication of work by documenting completed actions.

A note should be made if the urine is contaminated with blood from a woman who is menstruating. Misinterpreting that the blood is from the urinary tract rather than from the reproductive tract can result in an inaccurate medical or nursing diagnosis.

Specimens of urine should not be allowed to stand at room temperature before they are sent to the laboratory. Bacterial growth is likely to occur as well as alter other results of the urinalysis. The usual procedure is to store a urine specimen in a refrigerator if it is not taken directly to the laboratory after it is collected. Specimens that are collected from multiple voidings are either refrigerated on the ward or placed in a container with a chemical preservative.

Collecting a clean-catch midstream specimen. A *clean-catch midstream specimen* is a voided specimen collected under conditions of thorough cleanliness and after approximately the first 30 ml of urine have been voided. The advantage to collecting a voided specimen in this manner is that if organisms appear in the urine, they are probably from structures such as the bladder or kidneys rather than just surface contamination. Cleansing removes organisms from the urinary meatus. Voiding moves any residual organisms present in the urethra out with the beginning stream of urine. This principle is similarly applied when a small amount of sterile solution is wasted before it is added to a sterile container, as described in Chapter 16. Catching the midstream specimen as it flows out cleaned structures provides a more accurate analysis regarding the presence of organisms. Techniques for obtaining this type of specimen are described in Principles of Care 12-6. Due to anatomical differences, the cleansing techniques differ somewhat, depending on whether the patient is a male or a female.

Collecting a 24-hour specimen. Some tests require that the entire volume of urine from a 24-hour period be collected. The procedure for ensuring that the test can be performed accurately is as follows:

- Instruct the patient about the importance of collecting *all* urine for a period of 24 hours.
- Have the patient void at the time when saving urine for the 24-hour specimen is to begin.
- Discard this urine because it has been formed in the urinary system before the study began.
- Save *all* urine for the 24-hour period; place each voided specimen into the larger container.
- Have the patient void at the hour that the specimen collection ends and include it with all the

other collected urine. This urine completes the total produced within the urinary system during the time the collection was in process.

Obtaining a specimen from a catheter. A specimen can be taken from a catheter at the time it is inserted. The catheter is sterile and the urine is considered sterile. Some modifications must be made if the catheter has been in place for some time.

Obtaining a sample of urine from a drainage bag that has held accumulating urine for several hours, or longer, is not considered the best technique for an accurate analysis. The urine in the collecting bag is not fresh; therefore, this technique is rarely recommended. Separating the collecting tubing from the catheter could be done. However, whenever there is a separation in a closed system, there is also an increased risk of introducing organisms. Pathogens may then travel through the tubing to the urethra and even possibly to the bladder, where an infection can occur.

The best technique for obtaining a fresh, sterile specimen from a catheter should include the following:

- Clamp off the drainage between the catheter and the drainage tubing, if it is not contraindicated, for approximately 15 minutes before collecting the specimen. This ensures that there will be a sufficient quantity of urine available for the specimen. About 5 to 10 ml should be collected for a urinalysis.
- Before the drainage system is entered, the *port*, a self-sealing access area, is cleaned thoroughly with an antimicrobial agent. This step is illustrated in Figure 12-24. Some catheters that do not contain a port must be entered through the catheter above its connection to the drainage tubing, as shown in Figure 12-25.
- A small sterile needle is inserted into the port of the catheter as shown in Figure 12-26. Urine will fill the syringe when the nurse pulls back on the plunger of the syringe. The urine can be placed directly into a sterile specimen container.

Collecting a specimen from a stoma. If a urine specimen is needed from a patient with a stoma, there are two methods that may be used. To obtain a fresh specimen, cleanse the area around the stoma. Hold the specimen container beneath the stoma and allow the urine to drip directly into it. Increasing the fluid intake just prior to the collection of urine is

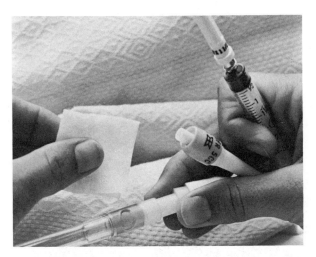

Figure 12-24 Before the closed urinary drainage system is entered to obtain a specimen, the area is thoroughly cleaned. This precaution helps decrease the chance of introducing organisms into the system.

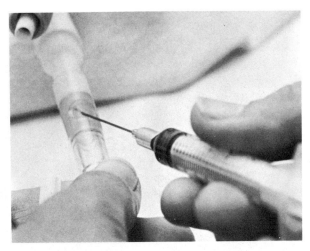

Figure 12-26 The needle is held at a slant when insertion is made through a port. A sterile 5 ml or larger syringe is used to aspirate the urine. The sample of collected urine is placed directly from the syringe into a sterile specimen container.

helpful when obtaining a specimen in this manner. Urine may also be collected from the appliance. Empty the urine that has collected in the last few hours. Then hold the container beneath the port used for draining the appliance. Since urine flows constantly from the stoma, it should not take long to collect 5 to 10 ml. This method avoids having to remove the appliance from the skin.

Performing common urine tests

The nurse may on occasions perform certain urine tests to detect abnormal substances. This assessment

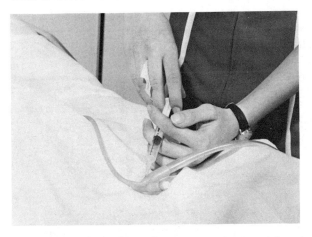

Figure 12-25 This catheter does not contain a special port through which specimens may be obtained. Instead, a small sterile needle, gauge 25, is introduced near the end to withdraw approximately 5 ml for a urine specimen. The needle hole is so small that leakage will not occur.

is done to add to the data base and provide current information about the patient's urinary function and overall state of health. These tests do not require the use of a microscope or complex methods of analysis. When they are performed on a routine basis, the order for testing is usually written by a doctor.

The results of the test are recorded in the patient's record or on a flow sheet. They are not recorded on a laboratory form.

Testing for sugar and acetone. The nurse may test the patient's urine for its sugar and acetone content. If a patient is a newly diagnosed diabetic, the nurse may teach the patient urine testing before discharge. More and more diabetics, however, are learning to perform home blood testing by obtaining a specimen from a pricked finger. This method provides more current and accurate information on the level of glucose within the body.

Several types of commercial testing kits are available. Some require using a tablet. A tablet is dropped into a sample of urine and water to test for glucose, and a drop of urine is placed onto a tablet to test for acetone. After a recommended period of time, the colour changes are compared with a chart provided by the manufacturer.

Others use a strip of treated paper, as illustrated in Figure 12-27. The strip is saturated with urine. Following a specified number of seconds, its colour is compared with a colour chart. The particular method for testing urine depends on the hospital's choice.

Strips may also be available to test urine for other

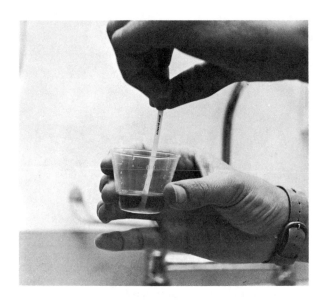
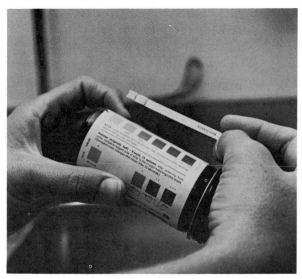

Figure 12-27 *Left*: The nurse places a specially treated strip into the urine. *Right*: After the specified time, the nurse compares the colour of the strip with a chart. This test measures sugar and acetone; other strips measure other substances. Be sure that the colour chart and the testing materials are not outdated. Also, commercial kits vary in how they are used. Be careful not to confuse one manufacturer's materials with another's.

substances, such as albumin, blood, bile, and so on. These tests are relatively simple and the manufacturer's instructions are easy to follow. However, *accuracy is essential*. Instructions must be followed with care.

Testing for the specific gravity. A nurse often tests urine for its *specific gravity*. This test provides a measurement of the weight of urine as compared with the weight of water. The amount of dissolved substances in urine contributes to its higher weight. The more concentrated the urine, the higher its specific gravity will be; the more diluted, the lower its specific gravity will be. The average normal range of specific gravity is between about 1.010 and 1.025, although even wider ranges have been observed in some healthy persons.

A *urinometer* is an instrument used to measure the specific gravity of urine. Urine is placed in a cylindrical container. The urinometer, which is calibrated, is placed in the urine. The more concentrated the urine, the higher the urinometer will rise in the urine. The reading on a urinometer should be taken at eye level, in this case at the bottom of the cup-shaped meniscus formed by the urine. This is illustrated in Figure 12-28.

Bowel elimination

Reviewing bowel elimination

All the structures of the gastrointestinal tract must function adequately to maintain bowel elimination.

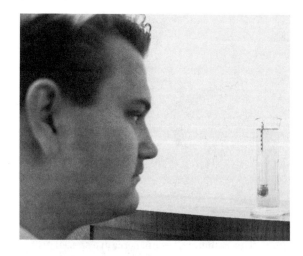

Figure 12-28 The nurse places a urinometer into a specimen of urine and reads the calibrated urinometer at eye level for an accurate determination of the urine's specific gravity.

The act of elimination involves the functioning of the structures collectively referred to as the *bowel*. These structures include the large intestine, the rectum, the anal canal, and the anus.

The large intestine. The large intestine, also called the colon, is composed of four parts. The function of the large intestine involves the collection and excretion of intestinal wastes. However, each one of the four substructures of the colon contributes to the overall purpose.

- The ascending colon absorbs up to 800 to 1000 ml of water from intestinal wastes daily. The absorption of water accounts for the formed, semi-solid nature of normal stool. When absorption does not occur properly, the stool remains soft and watery. If too much water is absorbed, the stool is dry and hard. Each area of the colon absorbs water. The water content of the stool decreases as stool moves through the bowel.
- The transverse colon transports wastes along the large intestine and continues to absorb water.
- The descending colon acts to collect forming stool.
- The sigmoid colon collects formed stool and retains it until it can be eliminated.

The rectum, anal canal and anus. The rectum acts as a passageway for faeces moving from the sigmoid colon to the anal canal. As the rectum distends with stool, pressure on nerves signals the need to have a bowel movement.

The anal canal provides a reservoir for stool prior to its elimination. It contains a ring-shaped band of muscles, called the internal sphincter. It controls filling from the intestine. The internal sphincter is not under voluntary control.

The anus is the terminal outlet of the rectum. This structure could be compared to the urinary meatus. An external sphincter is located at the anus. It can be voluntarily contracted or relaxed to control the elimination of stool from the body.

Defaecation. Defaecation is the act of eliminating stool from the bowel. It is facilitated by *peristalsis*, the rhythmic muscular contractions that move contents through the gastrointestinal tract. When the internal sphincter relaxes to allow stool to pass into the rectum and anal canal, the urge to have a bowel movement is recognized. The individual voluntarily relaxes the external sphincter to release stool. This process is facilitated by performing Valsalva's manoeuvre. This closes the glottis and increases ab-dominal pressure due to the contraction of pelvic and abdominal muscles.

Understanding factors affecting bowel elimination

A variety of factors influences normal intestinal elimination:

- The volume of the stool is affected by the amount of food that is consumed. A diet high in fibre and roughage produces a larger stool and promotes quicker passage through the intestinal tract. A diet low in roughage produces a smaller stool and tends to increase the time it remains within the bowel.
- The types of foods consumed also affect the characteristics of stool and associated aspects of elimination. Certain foods, such as red meat, can alter the colour of stool. Some foods, like beans, cucumbers, cabbage, and so on are called gas formers because they increase the volume of intestinal gas.
- Fluid intake influences elimination. A normal to above average consumption of liquids and watery foods helps keep the stool moist; a low fluid intake results in a drier stool.
- Most individuals experience an urge to defaecate in association with the gastrocolic reflex. The *gastrocolic reflex* is an automatic increase in intestinal peristalsis during the process of eating and drinking. It seems to be most active when consuming the first food of the day.
- Stool is usually eliminated in a cycling pattern. The frequency of having a bowel movement varies among healthy persons. Some have one or more movements a day; others normally defaecate less often. Many individuals eliminate at approximately the same time or times during their cycle.
- Patterns of bowel elimination and the characteristics of stool are influenced by drugs and other conditions in which stool is delayed or rapidly propelled through the gastrointestinal tract.
- Defaecation can be voluntarily controlled. Some delay defaecation despite the urge to eliminate by contracting the external sphincter. Others force elimination despite a lack of stimulation. Either of these two responses can lead to discomfort during elimination. Either can also promote the formation of haemorrhoids. *Haemorrhoids* are distended veins in the rectum. They are made

Table 12-2. Characteristics of normal stool

Item	Description
Amount	The volume depends on the amount and type of food a person eats, but the average adult daily stool weighs 100 g to 300 g, of which about 70% is water.
Colour	The stool is brown in colour. It darkens with standing.
Odour	The characteristic aromatic odour of the stool varies with its pH, which is normally neutral or mildly alkaline. The odour is caused by bacterial action in the gastrointestinal tract.
Consistency and shape	The stool is a formed, semisolid mass, which assumes the shape of the rectum.
Constituents	The stool contains wastes of digestion, bile pigments and salts, intestinal secretions, leucocytes that migrate from the blood, shed epithelial cells, bacteria, inorganic material (primarily calcium and phosphates) and very small amounts of undigested material (such as seeds and fibres).

worse by straining, which causes increased congestion of blood in the area.

- Nervous tension affects bowel elimination. For some, tension results in a state of increased muscle contraction. Digestion and elimination slow. For others, peristalsis becomes rapid and the individual may experience abdominal cramping and diarrhoea. Each individual usually responds consistently either one way or the other to stressful situations during life.
- An intact spinal cord and state of alertness affect bowel elimination. Unconscious individuals or those with lower body paralysis may not be able to control or release stool voluntarily.
- Gravity, movement, and exercise associated with an active lifestyle facilitates muscle tone and the ease of elimination.

Assessing bowel elimination

The nurse generally obtains certain basic information from the patient at the time of admission. Questions about the frequency, characteristics, and consistency of the stool are asked to identify the patterns of bowel elimination that are unique to the patient. The nurse usually inquires about the date of the last bowel movement and the use of any self-administered medications or techniques for promoting bowel function.

The nurse cannot order x-ray examinations of the gastrointestinal structures. However, the information from the results of those tests can help the nurse plan measures that will relieve any abnormal conditions that they identify.

Noting the characteristics of stool. While providing care the nurse has the opportunity to assess the characteristics of the patient's stool. This adds to the initial data base of information about bowel elimination. The volume, colour, odour, consistency, and shape of the stool are assessed. These characteristics are mentally compared with those of normal stool. Table 12-2 provides a description of the appearance and content of normal stool.

Tests are not routinely performed on stool. They are usually only ordered when the stool appears abnormal. A sample of any unusual stool should be saved in a covered container in case testing is necessary. There are some tests that the nurse may perform on stool, using colour-coded strips similar to those described for testing urine. They are used most often to detect blood that may be hidden in the stool. The results of any laboratory tests performed on stool add to the assessment information that may be used to identify a nursing or medical diagnosis.

Identifying and relieving common alterations in bowel elimination

Various definitions of common problems associated with bowel elimination are provided in Chapter 16 in a discussion of the disuse syndrome of inactive patients. These terms and their definitions, though not listed again in the glossary, will be given below to provide an introduction within the content of this chapter.

Constipation. Constipation is a condition in which the stool becomes dry and hard and requires straining in order to eliminate it. The frequency of stool passage is not always a factor. Some persons may be

Principles of Care 12-7. Promoting and maintaining bowel elimination

Nursing Action	Rationale
Explore the patient's patterns of elimination to validate that the symptoms are characteristic of constipation.	Misleading literature, advertisements and long-held beliefs have caused many individuals to be bowel conscious. Some may attempt to alter bowel elimination unnecessarily.
Consume a variety of foods, but especially include fresh fruits, vegetables, and whole grains. Limit eating highly processed and refined foods.	Bulk and residue that are made up of undigestible fibres produce more faeces and stimulate peristalsis.
Eat a nutritious breakfast that consists of good-sized portions.	The gastrocolic reflex is more often experienced following a period of fasting.
Avoid snacking as a substitute for eating a full meal.	Snack foods are likely to lack nutrition and be low in fibre. They relieve hunger and interfere with eating patterns that promote the formation and elimination of stool.
Drink an adequate amount of fluids, preferably between 2000 and 3000 ml daily.	Dietary liquids contribute to the moisture content of stool.
Consume fruit juices as part of the total fluid intake.	Fruit juices contain sugar and pectin, which act as natural laxatives by forming bulk and stimulating peristalsis.
Participate in some form of regular exercise.	Exercise and activity promote muscle tone and stimulate peristalsis.
A hospitalized patient should walk about the room and hallway, if possible.	The hospitalized patient who is as active as his condition permits tends to maintain normal patterns of elimination.
Respond to the urge to have a bowel movement when the stimulus is experienced.	Delaying defaecation causes the absorption of more moisture from the stool. It also may cause the bowel to become insensitive to the normal urge to defaecate.
Promote relaxation and privacy when there is a need to defaecate.	Stress and worry, using a public toilet or one located in an unfamiliar environment, and being rushed for adequate time may disrupt normal bowel elimination.
Assume a sitting position for bowel elimination. Provide support for the feet. A short person may need a footstool. Having a patient sit on a bedpan on the edge of the bed or on a commode simulates use of the toilet. A patient who cannot be in this position will usually find it best to have the head of the bed elevated and the knees somewhat flexed.	This aids gravity and relaxation of the external sphincter so that stool can be eliminated. Contraction of muscles and the use of Valsalva's manoeuvre increase abdominal pressure and aid expulsion of stool.
Use laxative medications infrequently and follow labelled instructions.	Frequent use of drugs that purge the system can cause the bowel to become sluggish in responding to natural stimuli.
Select medications that promote bowel elimination appropriately. *Laxatives* are preparations that induce emptying of the bowel. A drug that softens or lubricates stool may be a more desirable action.	Laxatives tend to act more harshly on the gastrointestinal system than stool softeners. Using medications without proper knowledge contributes to abuse and can increase problems associated with elimination.

Continued

Principles of Care 12-7. Continued

Nursing Action	Rationale
Avoid using enemas or suppositories on a regular basis, and never use them when abdominal pain, nausea, or vomiting is present.	Repeated use of enemas or suppositories can have the same effect as abuse of laxatives. Their use as self-treatment for disease symptoms can cause serious complications.
Teach the patient the signs and symptoms associated with significant alterations in bowel elimination and abnormal characteristics of stool. These include change in the shape of stool, altering periods of constipation and diarrhoea, and the presence of blood in the stool.	Changes in bowel elimination are significant signs of some diseases. Some changes should be reported immediately so that early diagnosis and treatment can occur. The signs described are early warnings of colorectal cancer. This is one of the leading types of cancer among men and women. Assuming these signs are due to something minor can delay the potential for cure.

constipated and yet have a daily bowel movement. Others who defaecate no more than three times a week are not necessarily constipated. The consistency of the stool and the effort associated with defaecation, rather than frequency, determine whether constipation is present.

The constipated patient sometimes complains of headache, lower abdominal discomfort, malaise, anorexia and so on. Relief of these symptoms is usually rapid following a bowel movement. These symptoms have been produced experimentally by packing the rectum with cotton. Therefore, the belief that the symptoms are caused from absorbing toxic substances from faeces is unfounded.

Identifying causes for constipation. One of the major responsibilities of the nurse, in addition to relieving constipation, is to determine its cause. Constipation can be prevented by understanding factors that interfere with the normal elimination of stool. The following list represents a variety of causes that contribute to constipation:

- Certain diseases or physical conditions that cause inactivity or immobility predispose to constipation.
- An inadequate intake of food or the intake of highly processed foods with little or no fibre are often associated with the prolonged collection of stool within the intestine. The longer stool remains in the bowel, the more water that becomes absorbed.

- An insufficient intake or excessive loss of water through sweating, vomiting, and so on can reduce moisture within the stool, making it dry and hard.
- Some drugs, such as morphine and codeine, slow peristalsis. Antacids that contain aluminium gel change the consistency of the stool.
- Abuse of laxatives and frequent enemas can decrease or eliminate the normal response of the bowel to natural stimulation for elimination.
- Conditions that limit the space for stool to pass through the large intestine can produce constipation. These may occur outside or inside the intestinal tract. For example, pregnancy or an abdominal tumour may interfere with stool passage. A mass growing within the bowel may delay the release of stool and also affect its shape and consistency.
- Ignoring the urge to defaecate is a common cause of constipation. Delaying elimination of stool can interrupt a regularly occurring cycle.
- Extended periods of stress can affect eating habits and patterns of bowel elimination.

Relieving constipation. When constipation occurs, it may require the combined efforts of the doctor and nurse to provide measures that restore bowel elimination. When no disease is present, the nurse can often help patients understand and utilize measures that overcome constipation. Normal patterns of elimination may take time to restore, but success has been observed among patients who desire to cooperate. Principles of Care 12-7 describes common measures to help promote bowel elimination when no disease or injury process is causing it.

Faecal impaction. Faecal impaction is the retention of an accumulation of faeces which forms a hardened mass in the rectum. The mass enlarges as more and more stool accumulates. The dry condition and increased volume make it impossible to pass normally. There is no specific length of time in which an impaction develops. Some have been known to form within 24 hours in certain individuals. The patient is likely to say he is constipated. Usually, he experiences a frequent desire to defaecate but is unable to do so. Rectal pain may be present due to his unsuccessful attempts to evacuate the bowel.

A patient with a faecal impaction may expel liquid stool around the impacted mass. For the inexperienced person, it may seem as though the patient is experiencing faecal incontinence. However, this symptom in combination with a lack of normal defaecation is almost a sure indication of an impaction. The nurse can easily confirm the suspicion by inserting a lubricated, gloved finger into the rectum. If the presence of hard formed stool is felt, the nurse should prepare to take measures that facilitate its removal.

Identifying causes for a faecal impaction. Various factors predispose a person to the development of a faecal impaction:

- Constipation usually precedes an impaction. Therefore, factors that cause constipation also may cause faecal impaction.
- Conditions that cause abdominal weakness can contribute to an impaction, since the individual may lack the strength to contract his abdominal muscles in an effort to expel stool.
- Barium used as a contrast medium during some x-ray examinations of the gastrointestinal tract contributes to the formation of an impaction when measures are not taken to clean the tract.
- Extremely fibrous foods, such as bran and fruit seeds, when consumed with an inadequate amount of fluid, have been known to cause an impaction.
- Some enteric-coated tablets have been noted to cause faecal impaction. These medications are covered with a material that prevents the active ingredient from dissolving in the stomach. It is intended that these drugs undergo delayed

breakdown when in the small intestine. However, some have been found to accumulate similarly to undigested substances.

Relieving a faecal impaction. Several measures may relieve a faecal impaction. The stool may be passed if sufficient moisture and lubrication are instilled into the rectum in the area of the stool. An oil retention enema is often prescribed to first provide lubrication to the mass and the mucous membrane that lines the rectum. A cleansing enema is frequently ordered following an oil retention enema. A discussion of enemas appears later in this chapter.

Intestinal distention. An excessive amount of gas within the intestinal tract is known as *flatulence.* Expelled intestinal gas is called *flatus.* When the gas is not expelled and instead accumulates, the condition is called *intestinal distention,* or *tympanites.*

Distention can be identified by inspecting and percussing a swollen abdomen. Gentle tapping with the fingers produces the drumlike sound of a tympanum instrument. The abdomen can be measured for more objective assessment and evaluation. Usually the patient will describe cramping pain. If distention is sufficient to cause pressure on the diaphragm and the chest cavity, shortness of breath and dyspnoea may also result.

Identifying causes of intestinal distention. The bowel normally accumulates and releases approximately 1000 ml of gas daily. Certain conditions predispose a person to form greater amounts or have difficulty in releasing it:

- Swallowing large amounts of air while eating and drinking can cause distention. Persons who are tense sometimes gulp air, especially when taking fluids or when breathing rapidly. Drinking through a straw also contributes to air swallowing. Consumption of carbonated beverages can increase gas accumulation.
- Gas-forming foods, mentioned earlier, can cause more than the usual amount of gas to be present in the intestinal tract.
- Inactivity tends to impair the movement of gas through the intestinal tract. Gas will generally pass from an area of higher concentration to one where it is lower. The atmosphere represents the area of lower concentration in comparison with the amount in the bowel. Due to the lack of movement, the gas remains trapped within the intestine.

Principles of Care 12-8. Inserting a rectal tube

Nursing Action	Rationale
Select a straight catheter according to the size of the individual. A size 22 to 32 is appropriate for an adult. A flexible hollow tube with openings along the insertion tip may also be used.	The anus is large enough to permit the insertion of a tube of this size without causing discomfort or trauma. A flexible tube prevents injury to the mucous membrane. The holes provide an opening through which the gas can travel.
Close the door and pull the privacy curtains.	If the patient is tense and embarrassed, it is likely to cause discomfort while inserting a rectal tube.
Position the patient on his left side.	The position helps to facilitate the passage of the tube past the sphincters and into the rectum.
Lubricate the rectal tube generously.	Lubrication reduces friction and eases insertion.
Separate the buttocks well so that the anus is in plain view and insert the tube for about 4 to 6 inches in an adult.	Positioning the tube well above the sphincters stimulates peristalsis and helps prevent the tube from slipping out of place.
Place the free end of the tube into a clean bowl of water.	
Leave the rectal tube in place for a period of no longer than 10 minutes.	The rectal tube can affect the ability to voluntarily control the sphincter if placement is prolonged.
Reinsert the rectal tube every 2 to 3 hours if the distention has been unrelieved or reaccumulates.	Reinserting the tube after a rest period allows gas to move in the direction of the rectum. Replacement acts to stimulate peristalsis and continues the release of gas.

- Some patients experience intestinal distention after surgery in which the bowel is handled. Peristalsis slows or temporarily stops while bacteria continue to form gas. When the patient can again pass flatus, it is a positive sign that intestinal functioning is restored.
- Drugs, such as morphine, tend to decrease peristalsis and thus cause distention.
- The presence of a mass that obstructs the passage of stool may also interfere with the ability of the intestine to eliminate gas.

Relieving intestinal distention. The following are suggested nursing measures to help bring relief from intestinal distention.

- Identify the cause, when possible, and treat the condition that has contributed to the gas accumulation.
- Have the patient move about in bed and walk to help promote the movement and expulsion of the gas.
- Have the patient assume various positions to

help move gas in the direction of the anus. Gas is lighter than fluids or solids, and hence will rise. Positioning the patient so that the rectum and anus are higher than the bolus of gas may help to distribute and expel the gas. These include lying prone, assuming a knee-chest position, lowering the upper body over the edge of the bed, and even a side-lying position may be effective. The nurse should use good judgment when considering positioning. The patient's comfort and safety must be primary concerns. Some consequences of these positions may be more damaging than the intestinal gas.

- Insert a rectal tube to help gas escape. The technique is described in Principles of Care 12-8. Gas will usually follow the path of least resistance. The inserted tube provides a channel through which the gas can travel despite a contracted sphincter.

Diarrhoea. *Diarrhoea* is the passage of watery, unformed stools accompanied by abdominal cramping. Although frequent bowel movements do not necessarily mean that diarrhoea is present, persons with diarrhoea usually have stools frequently. This condition tends to have a sudden onset and last only a short period of time. Other associated signs and symptoms include nausea and vomiting, and the presence of blood or mucus in the stools.

Identifying causes of diarrhoea. Various factors predispose to the development of diarrhoea:

- Diarrhoea may be a response on the part of the body to rid itself of some allergic substance within the intestinal tract. It may also be a natural defence for eliminating an irritating substance, such as tainted food or intestinal pathogens.
- Some individuals respond to stress with an increase in the rate of peristalsis. This shortens the time during which water can be absorbed from the stool.
- Certain dietary indiscretions cause diarrhoea. Rich pastries and coffee and excess consumption of fruits and alcoholic beverages may produce temporary diarrhoea for some persons.
- Intentional or accidental abuse of laxatives can cause diarrhoea. There seems to be an increased incidence of eating disorders, one of which involves purging the body with laxatives to reduce the effects of eating binges.
- Many digestive and intestinal diseases may be accompanied by diarrhoea. It occurs as a result of chemical and mechanical changes within the bowel from the disease condition. This type of diarrhoea may become chronic and is less easily relieved.

Relieving the effects of diarrhoea. The following nursing measures are recommended to help the patient who has diarrhoea:

- Take into consideration that diarrhoea is often an embarrassing and usually painful disturbance. Listen to the patient and give him opportunities to explore possible causes.
- Reduce or remove the cause of diarrhoea when possible. Explain the importance of avoiding foods and fluids that cause diarrhoea.
- Temporarily limit the consumption of food. Provide clear liquids until the number of stools and the consistency improve. Follow with bananas, apple sauce, and light foods. Avoid fried foods, highly seasoned foods, or foods high in roughage.

- Investigate the relationship between the side effects of medications and the occurrence of diarrhoea. Consult with the doctor when a prescribed drug may be a factor in diarrhoea.
- Remember that a person with diarrhoea often finds it extremely difficult to delay the urge to defaecate. When a patient has diarrhoea, the problem should be noted on the nursing care plan. The nursing orders should include instructions to watch for the patient's signal light and to answer it promptly. It may be necessary to place the bed pan within easy reach for the patient yet out of sight to prevent embarrassment and accidents.
- Use hygienic measures following each stool. Clean the patient well, and rinse and dry the area thoroughly. Use soft toilet tissues or cloths to avoid further injury to anal tissue. Apply a medicated powder or cream according to hospital policy. Friction, soap residues on the skin, and watery faeces irritate the skin and may lead to tissue breakdown.
- Count the number of stools that the patient is having. Frequent diarrhoea can lead to water and chemical imbalances. This can take place fairly quickly in the very young or debilitated patient.
- Consult with the doctor concerning the possible use of medications to control the diarrhoea or abdominal cramping.

Faecal incontinence. Faecal incontinence is the inability to retain stool within the bowel. *Continence* is the ability to control elimination. For the most part, patients with faecal incontinence are much more devastated psychologically than those with urinary incontinence. It is difficult to disguise when stool is expelled. Incontinent patients and their families require much support and understanding.

Identifying causes of faecal incontinence. Although faecal incontinence is not life-threatening, identifying its cause may help resolve the condition. By obtaining a complete history from the patient about his bowel habits, possible causes for the incontinence may be determined. There are some possible factors that should be considered:

- Usually the cause of faecal incontinence is a result of disease or injury. If these are progressive or permanent types of conditions, such as damage to the spinal cord or stroke, the outlook for restoring control is doubtful.

- Determine if a faecal impaction is present and, therefore, confusing the appropriate interpretation of the condition.
- Loss of bowel control may occur for only a temporary period, for instance when associated with diarrhoea. This presents less of a potential problem for eventual control.
- Some individuals may lose control of the bowel if they must wait to use a toilet.
- Taking an extremely harsh or large dosage of a laxative may result in such rapid peristalsis that loss of control is simply unavoidable.

Managing faecal incontinence. Nursing measures suggested for the patient with diarrhoea can be used if the incontinence is due to a temporary or reversible cause. Anal control is dependent ultimately on proper functioning of the anal sphincters. For some patients, functioning of impaired sphincters can be improved. When the incontinence is likely to be a continuous problem, the following actions may be helpful:

- See to it that the patient eats regularly and has a nutritious and well-balanced diet. Eating foods that are high in bulk and fibre can help keep the stool more formed. A formed stool is more easily controlled than one that is liquid.
- Note whether there are certain times of the day when incontinence is more likely to occur, such as after breakfast or another meal. This is when the gastrocolic reflex is more likely to be activated.
- Place the patient on a bedpan shortly before a time when the individual is likely to eliminate stool. If there is no pattern, place the patient on a bedpan at frequent intervals, such as every 2 to 3 hours. Do not allow the patient to remain on the bedpan for long periods of time. Pad the hard surface of the bedpan to avoid skin breakdown.
- Consult with the doctor about using a suppository or an enema every 2 to 3 days. If a pattern can be established by stimulating peristalsis and emptying the lower bowel with these aids, faecal incontinence may become controllable.
- Use moisture-proof undergarments and absorbent pads as necessary to protect bed linen and clothing when incontinence is frequent. Padding the patient should be avoided if possible to help preserve the patient's dignity and self-esteem.

Performing skills that empty the bowel. There are times when individuals may have alterations in bowel elimination, such as constipation, which must be relieved. There are also certain diagnostic examinations for which adequate inspection requires a clean bowel. The nurse may utilize skills for removing stool from the lower bowel.

Inserting a rectal suppository. A *suppository* is an oval or cone shaped solid substance designed for easy insertion into a body cavity. It is constructed to melt at body temperature. Because a certain amount of absorption takes place in the large intestine, some medications can be given by suppository. The most frequent use of the suppository is to administer a substance that will cause the expulsion of faeces and flatus.

A variety of suppositories with various actions is available. Some soften the faeces; some lubricate the anal canal; some stimulate peristalsis by chemical means. Others liberate carbon dioxide, thus increasing rectal bulk to stimulate defaecation. Principles of Care 12-9 describes how to insert a rectal suppository.

Administering an enema. An *enema* is the introduction of a solution into the large intestine. The most common type is the *cleansing enema*, which is used to empty the lower intestinal tract of faeces. The most frequently used solutions are soap and water, normal saline, and highly concentrated hypertonic solutions.

Instilling a hypertonic enema solution. A *hypertonic solution* is a solution in which there is a higher amount of dissolved substances than that found in blood. Hypertonic solutions act on the principle of osmosis. In other words, fluid moves from an area of low concentration of substances to one in which there is a higher concentration. This type of solution, since it is highly concentrated, will cause fluid to be drawn from body tissues into the bowel, eventually increasing the fluid volume in the intestine to more than the original amount that was instilled.

Hypertonic enema solutions are available in commercially prepared, disposable solution containers. The total amount of hypertonic solution that is instilled is about 120 ml. The solution also acts on the mucous membranes as a local irritant. Usually, the patient defaecates with good results after administering the enema. In many hospitals and in the home, these disposable administration sets have become the method of choice for cleansing the lower intestinal tract of faeces. They are less fatiguing and distressing to patients than are cleansing enemas that

Principles of Care 12-9. Inserting a rectal suppository

Nursing Action	Rationale
Close the door and ensure privacy by pulling the curtains surrounding the bed.	Individuals are likely to be tense if concerned about unexpected interruptions.
Position the patient on his left side and drape the patient to expose only the buttocks.	Proper positioning provides an adequate view and access to the rectal area. The left side position facilitates the use of the nurse's right hand. Reverse the position if the nurse is left handed.
Apply a finger cot or don a clean glove on the dominant hand.	The finger cot or glove acts as a barrier from contact with stool within the rectum.
Lubricate the length of the finger and the suppository.	Lubrication reduces friction and eases insertion.
Separate the buttocks so that the anus is in plain view and have the patient take several deep breaths.	Having the patient take deep breaths helps relax the anal sphincters and makes insertion more comfortable.
Introduce the suppository beyond the internal sphincter, about the distance of the inserted finger. The suppository should be in contact with the mucous membrane and not be embedded in stool.	The suppository should be placed well into the rectum, where its effect is desired. The medication must be absorbed by melting and contact with the mucous membrane. Placement in stool slows the desired action and effect.
Instruct the patient to retain the suppository until he has an urge to defaecate, usually in 15 minutes to 45 minutes.	Retaining the suppository for a period of time allows time for achieving maximum results.
Allow the patient to walk about if he is ambulatory.	Walking about often helps distribute the medication and stimulate peristalsis.
Request that the patient save the stool for examination.	The nurse should observe the amount and other characteristics of the stool to evaluate the effectiveness of the procedure.
Record the procedure and the results according to hospital policy.	The patient's chart contains a continuous record of care and the patient's response.

use a large volume of solution. They can be easily self-administered.

- The solution container comes with an attached prelubricated tip in the commercial sets; therefore, no additional equipment or supplies are needed.
- The entire container of solution can be warmed by placing it in another container of warm water. Some patients do not warm the container at all prior to self-administration. Since there is a low volume of solution, few experience any discomfort.
- The recommended position for the patient receiving a hypertonic enema is the left lateral position.

- The prelubricated tip is inserted completely within the rectum. Disposable hypertonic enema sets are also available for children. To ensure safety, the applicator tip is shorter and there is less volume.
- Apply gentle, steady pressure on the solution container, which collapses as the solution enters the intestine. It takes about a minute or two to instil the solution and about two to eight minutes to obtain results.

Administering a retention enema. A *retention enema* is an instillation that is intended to be held within the large intestine. Some are retained for a period of time; others are not expelled at all. Oils, such as mineral, arachis or olive oil, are usually used for retention enemas. The primary purpose of the oil retention enema is to lubricate and soften the stool so that it can be expelled more easily. Usually, 100 to 200 ml of oil are given slowly to avoid stimulating peristalsis and the desire to defaecate. The effectiveness of an oil retention enema varies. Often, it becomes necessary to follow an oil enema with a cleansing enema before defaecation occurs.

- Most hospitals have prepackaged oil retention enema sets that contain necessary supplies and equipment, including oil. Disposable oil retention enema sets may be similar in appearance to hypertonic enema solution sets.
- Oil is warmed only to body temperature to minimize the muscular stimulation caused by a warmer or colder solution.
- The patient is encouraged to retain the oil for at least 30 minutes before attempting to have a bowel movement. This provides time to soften and lubricate the faeces.

Teaching the patient to self-administer an enema. A common misunderstanding many people have is that the enema can be given successfully while sitting on a toilet. The enema solution cannot be distributed very well in this position unless a great amount of pressure is used to force the solution upward against gravity. The patient will usually experience a need to defaecate sooner because of the pooling of solution within the rectum. Overall there will be a less than desirable cleansing effect.

Reinforce that enemas should not be taken on a routine basis. The occasional use of an enema may not be harmful. Problems arise when a patient is concerned about not having a daily bowel movement and then takes an enema that empties the entire lower intestinal tract. The intestinal tract may not fill for several days. When no bowel movement occurs in a day's time, the patient then tends to repeat the cycle by taking another enema. Eventually the normal urge to defaecate is absent or markedly decreased. The bowel may become completely dependent on the need for enemas to eliminate faeces.

Advise patients to also refrain from automatically self-administering an enema when nausea, vomiting, or abdominal pain is present. Increasing the volume and pressure within the gastrointestinal tract may lead to severe complications of some conditions that are associated with these symptoms.

Eliminating stool through a stoma

When the suffix *ostomy* is attached to a root word, it describes a surgically created opening into a body structure. The prefix that is combined with ostomy indicates the location of the artificial opening. A *colostomy* is an opening into the colon or large intestine. The bowel is opened onto the surface of the abdomen. An *ileostomy* is an opening into the ileum, a portion of the small intestine. An ileostomy is similarly opened onto the abdominal wall. Figure 12-29 shows the locations of ostomies performed in various areas of the intestine. The word *ostomate*

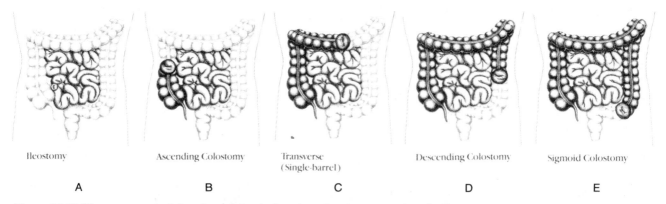

| Ileostomy | Ascending Colostomy | Transverse (Single-barrel) | Descending Colostomy | Sigmoid Colostomy |
| A | B | C | D | E |

Figure 12-29 These anatomical drawings show the location of various ostomies. An ileostomy (*A*) produces watery or pastelike stool almost continuously. An ascending colostomy (*B*) produces watery or semisolid stool, which may be expelled frequently. A transverse colostomy (*C*) expels pastelike or semisolid stool in an unpredictable frequency. A descending colostomy (*D*) and a sigmoid colostomy (*E*) are likely to release faeces that resembles normal stool. These may become regulated through colostomy irrigations. (Courtesy of Hollister Inc., Libertyville, IL)

refers to a person on whom an ostomy has been performed. Ostomates have unique problems and needs. All members of the health care team must participate in providing care that will meet each ostomate's optimum recovery.

Collecting stool from an intestinal stoma. There are no natural sphincters in a stoma. A fairly new surgical procedure is being performed in which a type of valve is fashioned to prevent the automatic expulsion of stool and urine. This type of ostomy requires siphoning liquid at periodic intervals. However, for most ostomates, retaining stool or urine within the body is impossible. Almost all intestinal ostomates wear an appliance to collect faecal wastes. It is fastened and worn in a manner similar to the one for a urinary diversion.

Stool that collects within an appliance can be emptied through an opening at the bottom without removing the appliance from the skin. Once the contents are rinsed from the appliance, it can be reclosed.

Changing an appliance. Ostomates learn to change an appliance before being discharged from the hospital. Some appliances may require daily changing while others may develop a pattern that only makes changing the appliance necessary every 3 to 7 days. Factors such as the location of the stoma, the consistency of the stool, and the condition of the skin affect the need for changing an appliance.

Prevention of skin breakdown is one of the biggest challenges in ostomy care. Enzymes in stool can quickly cause excoriation. *Excoriation* is the chemical injury of skin. It can be prevented by properly fitting the appliance and protecting the skin with substances that act as a barrier between the skin and faecal wastes. Barrier substances also help attach the appliance in a manner that prevents slipping. The nurse may follow the suggested actions in Principles of Care 12-10 when changing an appliance.

Irrigating a colostomy. The purpose of a colostomy irrigation is to remove formed stool and in some cases regulate the timing of bowel movements. It involves instilling solution through the stoma into the colon, similarly to administering an enema.

This procedure is usually only necessary for individuals who have a colostomy. The stool from a colostomy can range from semisolid to the formed consistency that is passed from the rectum during normal bowel elimination. The variation depends on the anatomical location of the ostomy along the length of colon. Once an individual recovers from the operative period, stool elimination from the colostomy may be released in a cycle similar to normal bowel movements. With regulation, a patient with a sigmoid colostomy may choose to omit wearing an appliance and may cover the stoma with only a gauze square.

An ileostomy is not irrigated, since the consistency of stool from this area of the bowel is liquid or similar to thin paste; its passage is rarely difficult. An ileostomy drains at frequent intervals and therefore regulation is not easily achieved. Some learn a degree of control, knowing that the release of stool is more apt to occur after meals.

Draining a continent ostomy. A *continent ostomy* is a surgically created opening in which the drainage of liquid stool or urine is controlled by the patient. This technique has only recently been used for a small, selective number of patients. It was first performed on patients who required an ileostomy; it is now also being used when a urinary diversion is performed. The continent ostomy is also referred to as a *Kock pouch* after the surgeon who developed the technique. The surgeon creates a reservoir out of the ileum that collects liquid stool or urine. Just inside the stoma, a valve made of tissue retains the collection of urine or faeces. The release of the liquid stool or urine takes place when the patient inserts a catheter and siphons the drainage from the pouch.

The advantage of this type of ostomy is that an appliance need not be worn. The disadvantage is that the patient must drain the accumulating liquid stool or urine about every 4 to 6 hours. A gravity drainage system can be used during the night.

If the patient has a continent ostomy, the following actions may be used in relation to its care:

- Place the patient in a comfortable sitting position.
- Insert a lubricated catheter, size 22 to 28, into the stoma.
- Expect resistance after the tube has been inserted approximately 2 inches; this is the location of the valve that controls the retention of liquid stool or urine. Instruct the patient to take deep breaths, cough, or perform Valsalva's manoeuvre at this time.
- Gently advance the catheter through the valve.
- As stool or urine begins to flow through the catheter, direct it into a container or toilet that is at least 12 inches below the patient's ostomy. Expect drainage of stool to take 5 to 10 minutes; urine should drain in less time. There may be

Principles of Care 12-10. Changing an ostomy appliance

Nursing Action	Rationale
Prepare to change the appliance when it is ⅓ full and no more than ½ full.	An appliance that is allowed to become extremely full may pull away from the skin due to its weight. It will also cause obvious bulges under clothing.
Assemble the replacement appliance and any solvents, adhesives, or skin care preparations that are necessary.	There are various choices available in ostomy appliances. Each type may require different substances for removal and attachment. The condition of the skin may require special treatment from time to time, depending upon its state of irritation.
Schedule the appliance change for a time of day when there is sufficient time and the activity of the ostomy is relatively quiet. Allow a minimum of 20 minutes if there are no unusual problems.	Rushing while changing an appliance can result in poor attachment or a poor placement on the skin. When there is less likelihood of stool being eliminated, the patient will feel less embarrassed and relaxed.
Remove the appliance from the skin, following the manufacturer's recommendations. Some possible methods include using a solvent, gently peeling the adhesive away from the skin in small sections, or loosening the adhesive with warm water.	Pulling adhesive from the skin can injure the tissue. Covering irritated skin with another appliance can compound the damage to the area. Taking sufficient time to do a proper job and being gentle will maintain the integrity of the skin.
Place the removed appliance into a waterproof bag.	Eventually the nurse will need to rinse the soiled appliance before disposing of it.
Wash the stoma in a circular manner with plain warm water or mild soapy water using a soft wash cloth or gauze. The patient may shower or bathe without an appliance.	The area around the stoma should be cleaned of stool, skin secretions, and adhesive before a new appliance is attached. Soap may be irritating to some; rinse well if soap is used.
Explain to the patient that it is normal for the stoma to appear red. Removal of mucus and slight bleeding from the surface of the stoma is also normal. Washing should not cause pain or discomfort in the stoma. Excoriated skin may be painful during washing.	The stoma is inverted bowel that normally has a rich blood supply. Its surface is mucous membrane, which explains the presence of clear, sticky material. The bowel does not contain sensory nerves. The patient may bathe or shower without the appliance.
Inspect the condition of the skin and the stoma. Report signs of excoriation or a very dark red, blue, or swollen appearance to the stoma.	Breakdown usually occurs under the stoma where the appliance attaches to the skin. Abnormal colour and size may indicate a problem with circulation of blood to the stoma.
Pat or fan the area completely dry.	Adhesive materials will not stick firmly to wet skin.
Measure and trim the opening of a disposable appliance to fit the size of the patient's stoma. Add ¹⁄₁₆ to ⅛ inch to the size of stoma hole when cutting the opening for the stoma.	Some appliance rings are custom made to fit individuals; disposable appliances must be adapted according to each patient's needs. The opening of the appliance should be just large enough to avoid pinching the stoma.
Peel the covering from the adhesive backing that will surround the stoma, as shown in Figure 12-30.	To preserve its ability to adhere to the skin, the protective cover should not be removed until ready for immediate use.

Figure 12-30 This type of appliance has a protective cover over the adhesive backing. The side strips allow the appliance to be handled while positioning the opening over the stoma. (Courtesy of Hollister Inc., Libertyville, IL)

Continued

Principles of Care 12-10. Continued

Nursing Action	Rationale
Have the patient stand or lie down in bed.	The skin should be taut when the appliance is applied. Sitting causes wrinkling of the skin.
Position the opening of the appliance over the stoma, as illustrated in Figure 12-31. Allow only a thin margin of exposed skin around the stoma.	The adhesive backing must be applied to skin, not the stoma itself. If too much skin is exposed, it may become excoriated from contact with faecal wastes.

Figure 12-31 The opening in the appliance is positioned over the stoma so that only a thin margin of skin is exposed. (Courtesy of Hollister Inc., Libertyville, IL)

Figure 12-32 The adhesive backing is smoothed to avoid wrinkles and air pockets. The adhesive strips on the sides can be removed once the inner area is in place. (Courtesy of Hollister Inc., Libertyville, IL)

Press the adhesive patch to the skin from the stoma outward while preventing wrinkles, as shown in Figure 12-32.	Uneven application may form air pockets or wrinkles if the edges are pressed before the centre areas. An appliance that is not uniformly applied may become uncomfortable or loose.

Figure 12-33 The bottom of the appliance is folded and sealed using a clamp. This type of clamp is curved to fit flatly against the natural curve of the body so that wearing an appliance is less obvious. (Courtesy of Hollister Inc., Libertyville, IL)

Fold and seal the bottom of the appliance with a special clamp, shown in Figure 12-33. Other types of appliances may be closed with a rubber band or other similar material.	The opening at the bottom of the appliance permits emptying without removing the appliance from the skin. Tight closure prevents leaking of the contents.

large variations in the amounts that drain in the early postoperative period. The pouch may eventually stretch to hold as much as 600 ml. The average amount that may be drained each time is between 200 and 250 ml.
- Remove the catheter and clean it with warm soapy water. Place it in a clean, sealable, plastic bag until its next use.

- Cover the stoma with a gauze square or a large sized bandaid.

Plugging of the catheter may become a problem. It may be due to thick stool or mucus that blocks the drainage holes in the catheter. Suggestions for clearing the tube include the following: (1) instruct the patient to perform Valsalva's manoeuvre, (2)

Principles of Care 12-11. Collecting a stool specimen

Nursing Action	Rationale
Obtain a waxed paper container that has a cover or use the appropriate container specified by the hospital.	Stool is moist and the container should not permit saturation and the deposit of faecal wastes onto the surfaces of work areas. A cover helps contain the odour and conceals the specimen.
Have the patient void into a toilet or separate receptacle before the stool specimen is collected.	Urine mixed with stool may interfere with the proper examination required for some tests.
Observe principles of medical asepsis when collecting stool.	Sterile technique is not necessary, since the stool already contains organisms. Principles of medical asepsis restrict and contain organisms preventing their transfer to cleaner areas.
Use a clean bedpan. Avoid taking specimens from a toilet bowl.	When stool becomes mixed with water its consistency changes. Water and urine may destroy some parasites and obscure proper diagnosis.
Lift a portion of stool approximately equivalent to 1 teaspoon to 2 teaspoons, with two clean tongue depressors.	Only a small sample of stool is usually necessary for analysis. Tongue depressors provide a convenient method for removing stool from the bedpan.
Place the faeces directly into the container. Discard the remaining stool.	The stool should not be allowed to remain in the bedpan where moisture may evaporate or other changes can occur.
Take care to avoid contaminating the outside of the specimen container with stool.	A clean outer surface prevents spreading organisms to individuals who handle and examine the specimen.
Wash hands thoroughly after collecting stool and handling the bedpan.	Organisms are spread easily when good handwashing is not practised.
Label and attach the appropriate laboratory form to the specimen.	Poor identification may result in having to repeat the collection and examination.
Take the specimen directly to the laboratory. Notify the laboratory personnel as to the contents of the specimen container and the requested test.	There may be differences in hospital policy or examination methods related to the need to refrigerate, keep the specimen at room temperature, or warm it until it can be examined.
Record the collection of the specimen, description of the stool, and the time it was taken to the laboratory.	Charting is a method for recording that diagnostic measures have been carried out.

rotate the catheter tip inside the stoma, and (3) milk the catheter. If these are not successful, the catheter should be withdrawn, rinsed, and reinserted. If repeated efforts do not result in any drainage, a doctor should be notified. Draining should not be delayed longer than 6 hours.

Obtaining stool specimens

Information acquired from the examination of a stool specimen can add to the nurse's data base assess-

ments. They may contribute data supporting a medical or nursing diagnosis.

Stool may be analysed to detect any number of abnormal characteristics or contents. For example, faeces may be examined for blood, bile, parasites, parasite eggs and so on. The nurse either instructs the patient in the collection of a specimen or personally obtains the specimen from a sample of the patient's stool. The technique for collecting a specimen of stool depends on the purpose of the test. Principles of Care 12-11 describes actions that pertain to any

Table 12-3. Special stool examination techniques

Purpose of Examination	Recommended Techniques
When examining for the presence of blood	Obtain only a small amount of stool when it is being tested for blood. One common method is to use a rectal applicator or a gloved finger to swab the stool. The stool on the finger or applicator is then placed directly onto a special slide.
When examining for the presence of pinworms	Use *clear* cellophane tape. Frosted tape makes examination difficult. Place the tape directly over the anal region, remove almost immediately, and place on a slide. Be sure to collect a specimen immediately in the morning, before the patient has had a bowel movement or a bath. Pinworms tend to come to the anal canal area during the night.
When examining for the presence of parasites	See to it that the patient does not have a laxative or enema because parasites may thus be destroyed. Include some blood or mucus, when present in the stool, because parasites tend to thrive in these media.
When collecting an entire bowel movement	Rinse a bedpan and then line it with plastic material that will stick to the damp surface. Have the patient defaecate, then twist and tie the plastic together and place it in an appropriate container. The above technique is also helpful when stools need to be weighed.
When collecting a specimen for culture purposes	Pass a sterile rectal swab beyond the internal sphincter, rotate it carefully, and place the swab in an appropriate container tube.
When collecting a specimen from a patient with a colostomy or ileostomy	Remove a portion of stool from the patient's collecting bag and place the stool directly into a specimen container.

collection of stool. Table 12-3 lists particular techniques that are indicated when specific information is needed.

Suggested measures for promoting urinary elimination in selected situations

When the patient is an infant or child

Expect that characteristics of normal urine for an infant and child resemble those of an adult, except that the total amount voided in each 24-hour period is smaller. Despite the smaller amount, infants and children excrete more urine in proportion to body weight than adults.

In general, the urine of infants and young children tends to be lighter in colour than that of an adult.

Anticipate that voiding will occur at more frequent intervals for infants and children. A child will feel the need to urinate when about 100 to 150 ml of urine collects in the bladder. The bladder holds even less in toddlers and much less in infants.

To assess the control of urinary elimination, use the following information as a guide:

18 months old	An infant is usually aware of having a wet nappy.
2 years old	A toddler begins to cooperate with toilet training.
2½ years old	Daytime control of urinary

Table 12-4. Characteristics of infants' stools

Ingested Substance	Appearance	Frequency
Amniotic fluid swallowed during the period before birth	Dark blackish green, sticky stool called meconium	Meconium is passed four to six times daily for 1 to 2 days after the baby is born.
Breast milk	Unformed, pastelike, bright or golden yellow	Frequency is unpredictable. Some pass stools once or twice a day and others at every feeding.
Cow's milk	Firmer consistency, yellow but not as bright as seen with breast milk	Infants fed cow's milk pass stools less often, usually one to three times a day.
Soft and solid foods	Formed, brownish colour	A bowel movement once a day becomes common as the infant approaches toddlerhood.

3 years old	elimination begins, although frequent accidents occur. Nighttime control of urinary elimination is possible for some, although accidents occur.

Expect that, despite control at home, many youngsters when hospitalized will revert to wetting clothing. This is a reaction to the stress of being separated from a familiar environment. Regression to more infantile behaviour can be considered normal unless other factors are present.

Use equipment of the hospital's choice when collecting a urine specimen from an infant or young child who cannot cooperate. Most hospitals have a plastic, disposable collection bag that contains an adhesive backing. It adheres to the perineal area. A nappy is placed over the collecting bag to prevent the child from dislodging the bag. Be sure that adhesive is applied to dry, clean skin. It has been found that for the male infant, it is easier when the penis and the scrotum are placed inside the collecting device. Some nurses use a finger cot over the penis of newborn males if a urine specimen is required.

Provide additional fluids that the child enjoys before collecting a urine specimen from children. This promotes urine production and often helps gain the child's cooperation.

When the patient is pregnant or in the early postpartal period

Expect that the characteristics of normal urine for a pregnant woman resemble those during non-pregnancy, except that the total amount voided in each 24-hour period increases and tends to have a lower specific gravity. Sugar in the urine during pregnancy is relatively common, but when present, the finding should be reported. Albumin in the urine is also a significant abnormal assessment to report.

Anticipate that a pregnant woman will void more frequently than usual when the enlarging uterus causes pressure on the bladder. This occurs early in pregnancy and continues until the uterus rises out of the pelvis and into the abdomen. It recurs late in pregnancy when, because of its size, the uterus again causes pressure on the bladder.

If a catheter is difficult to introduce into the bladder of a woman in labour, proceed slowly and gently and *never use force*. The difficulty is most probably due to the head of the foetus pressing on the lower bladder and urethra as the foetus descends through the birth canal.

Proceed with extreme care if a woman in the post-partum period requires catheterization. A good light is essential because the meatus may be difficult to find due to local swelling. Use care to avoid additional discomfort in the perineum.

When the patient is elderly

Keep in mind that, despite considerable reserve of the ability of the kidneys to produce urine, functioning in general tends to decline with age. As a result, the system may have lost its earlier level of effectiveness in maintaining the fluid and chemical balance of the body.

Assess the urinary function of elderly patients accurately. The elderly are more prone to urinary problems due to alterations in bladder control or retention of urine. This is especially true of women who experience stress incontinence and males with an enlarged prostate gland.

Remember that urinary incontinence, a relatively common problem among the elderly, has profound psychological effects on the patient and his family. Unfortunately, in many instances, efforts to correct the situation are impossible. The best the nurse can offer then includes emotional support and a type of care that minimizes dangers of complications, especially skin breakdown and infections, and promotes psychological and physical comfort.

Expect that the incontinent elderly patient is often depressed and frustrated when there is little hope for bladder control. The shame of being unable to control urination may result in isolation and other changes in the patient's social relationships. Incontinent patients require the nurse's ingenuity in providing methods for maintaining the patient's lifestyle while disguising the loss of control.

Teaching suggestions for promoting urinary elimination

Teaching opportunities are offered throughout the content of this chapter. Key points and additional information are summarized as follows:

Many people are unaware of how the urinary system operates and of the vital role of the kidneys in the proper functioning of the body. Sharing information with patients, especially those with alterations in urinary elimination, helps in gaining their cooperation and also helps them promote their own health and well-being.

Patients, too, should be familiar with the normal appearance of urine and with the relationship between fluid intake and urinary output so that they recognize abnormal conditions and seek prompt health care when indicated.

Incontinent patients should be instructed that limiting fluid intake is a dangerous method to control urination. It may have an overall effect of altering the body's fluid and chemical balance, a more life-threatening condition than incontinence.

Nurses should develop detailed teaching plans for

patients who will use self-catheterization, use an indwelling catheter after discharge from hospital or have a urinary diversion. Well-taught patients have fewer complications and enjoy physical and psychosocial well-being when they understand what has caused a problem, how it can be managed, and what self-care techniques are necessary to promote health.

Teach the family or patient to change the drainage tubing and collecting receptacle used with a catheter several times a week. The equipment can be washed thoroughly in hot, soapy water, rinsed well, and stored in a clean towel or covered container. Some prefer soaking the equipment in an antiseptic solution, but it should be rinsed well after soaking so that none of the antiseptic can reach the bladder.

Teach the patient with a stoma to be aware of weight gains or losses. This may change the size of the stoma and create an improperly fitting appliance. A decrease or increase of 5 to 10 lb may require refitting the external appliance.

Instruct the patient with a urinary diversion that sexual activity will not injure the stoma nor will pregnancy interfere with its functioning. The size of the stoma may change during pregnancy, but this may only involve a change in the size of an appliance and more frequent emptying.

Obtaining urine specimens and performing certain common tests can be carried out by most patients when they have been properly taught. Stress collecting the first voided specimen in the morning or a second voided specimen, depending on the purpose of the test. The patient may benefit from a set of written instructions for review at home.

Suggested measures to promote bowel elimination in selected situations

When the patient is an infant or child

Assess the characteristics of a normal stool according to an infant's age and diet. Use Table 12-4 as a guide.

Keep in mind that diarrhoea may rapidly become serious in infants and young children because they are especially susceptible to water and chemical imbalances.

Plan that infants and children with diarrhoea are often placed in isolation to help control the spread of causative organisms. Many children with diarrhoea may be placed within the same isolation room to facilitate their care. Isolation techniques are described in Chapter 20.

Compare and describe the characteristics of abnormal stool that a sick infant or child eliminates.

Be especially careful to keep infants and young children with diarrhoea clean and dry because their skin is very sensitive to irritation. Change nappies as often as necessary to prevent stool from remaining in contact with the skin. Rinse soap or detergent off the skin well because remnants are irritating to the skin. Protect the skin as indicated with an ointment of the hospital's choice.

Expect that rectal suppositories containing drugs are frequently prescribed for infants and children because they may have difficulty swallowing medications. Paediatric suppositories are smaller, and the dosage is reduced in comparison to adult drugs.

Use child-sized equipment for infants and children who have a colostomy or ileostomy. Skin care around a stoma is especially important because of the sensitivity of a youngster's skin to irritation and injury.

Be especially supportive of parents whose child has a colostomy or ileostomy. Surgery of this magnitude with its continued demands for care can be very devastating to parents. It has been found that if parents accept a child's colostomy or ileostomy, so will the child.

When the patient is elderly

Take into account that gastrointestinal motility, muscle tone, and digestive enzymes decrease with age. These normal ageing processes tend to predispose a person to constipation.

Obtain a health history that includes a careful assessment of the elderly person's elimination patterns. When possible, practices the patient uses to promote elimination should be included in his nursing care plan, if they are safe. For example, if the patient drinks hot water or prune juice before breakfast to promote elimination, follow this routine unless it is contraindicated.

Include a dietary history when assessing the patient's elimination patterns. Many elderly persons have diets low in fibre and bulk; they tend to eat processed convenience foods. Such diets predispose the patient to constipation.

Assess intestinal elimination patterns accurately. Many elderly persons become very bowel conscious and report a problem with constipation erroneously because they lack accurate information concerning elimination.

Use a teaching programme that includes bowel retraining for the elderly with constipation or incontinence. When possible, include the use of a commode, which is generally more acceptable to the patient than a bedpan, when helping to establish normal elimination patterns.

Advise against using routine enemas or laxatives. Fluid and chemical imbalances occur more easily in the elderly than in other adults.

Keep in mind that the skin of an elderly person is especially thin and sensitive to faecal matter. Use nursing measures to keep the patient meticulously clean and the skin well protected.

Teaching suggestions for promoting bowel elimination

Key suggestions for teaching described in this chapter to promote intestinal elimination are included in the summary below. Special information related to specific conditions that affect elimination has also been added.

Problems often arise because people lack knowledge about normal bowel elimination. Sharing accurate information with patients, especially those having problems related to elimination, helps promote health and well-being. Some areas include: how to prevent and manage constipation, diarrhoea, faecal incontinence, intestinal distention, and faecal impaction.

Although laxatives and enemas sometimes play a proper role in intestinal elimination, they are also very often abused. Teaching their proper use and the dangers of abuse is a nursing responsibility.

Individuals are often able to perform many self-care techniques when they experience alterations in bowel elimination. The nurse can use the same skill procedures described for inserting a suppository, administering an enema, ostomy care, and collection of a stool specimen when a patient needs to learn one of these skills.

The patient who has an ostomy should be told about various skin protection methods. One of the most common substances used is karaya. Tincture of benzoin may be sprayed or swabbed on the skin *if the skin is not already irritated.* It can also be used to create a tacky surface to enhance the adhesive quality of an appliance.

A plastic or paper cup placed over the stoma before spraying or swabbing the area protects the stoma and prevents faecal material from dribbling on the cleaned area.

Explain to an ostomate that odours can be controlled by keeping the appliance clean and deodorized. They may be washed between uses with soap and water and rinsed well. Commercial deodorants are available. Some are used in soaking solutions for the appliance; others may be placed inside while it is being worn.

Teach the ostomate the importance of a balanced and nourishing diet. Only foods that stimulate excessive peristalsis or cause gas should be avoided. Keep in mind that not all people are troubled by the same kinds of foods; some may choose to continue eating them occasionally despite the changes they cause in bowel elimination.

Instruct the ostomate patient that one way to release accumulating gas from an appliance is to prick pinholes at the upper end of the appliance. This provides a route for the escaping gas, yet prevents leakage of faecal wastes that may be accumulating at the bottom of the appliance.

Encourage the ostomate to construct coverings for the appliance that conceal its contents if this is a concern in relation to sexual activity. Bathing and emptying an appliance are also important in prior planning before sex.

For the patient with a continent ostomy, advise that a Medic-Alert tag be worn in case of a medical emergency. When a person cannot speak for himself, emergency medical personnel should be able to determine that an ostomy requires draining and continuous care.

Further reading

Anon. (1985) Altered image . . . a continent ileostomy. *Nursing Mirror*, **160**, 46–7.

Black, P. (1985) Stoma care: Selecting a site, *part 1. Nursing Mirror*, **161**, 22–4.

Black, P. (1985) Stoma care: The right appliance, *part 2. Nursing Mirror*, **161**, 34–5.

Black, P. Stoma care: Drugs and diet, *part 3. Nursing Mirror*, **161**, 26, 28.

Black, P. (1985) Stoma care: Rehabilitation and problem solving, *part 4. Nursing Mirror*, **161**, 34–6.

Black, P. (1985) Stoma care: Body image and reproduction, *part 5. Nursing Mirror*, **161**, 32–3.

Black, P. (1985) Stoma care: Stoma care in youth and old age, *part 6. Nursing Mirror*, **161**, 23–4.

Burns, P.A., Narecki, M.A. and Dittmar, S.S. (1985) Kegel's exercises with biofeedback therapy for treatment of stress incontinence. *Nurse Practitioner*, **10**, 28, 33–4, 46.

Fryer, S. (1985) Colostomy care: Smiles hide the truth, *part 1. Nursing Times*, **18**, 31–2, 34.

Gould, D. (1985) Management of indwelling urethral catheters. *Nursing Mirror*, **161**, 17–8, 20.

Jones, H. (1985) Colostomy care: Maintaining an active life, *part 2. Nursing Times*, **81**, 36, 38.

Macleod, E. (1984) Only when I cough . . . stress incontinence. *Nursing Mirror*, **159** (Clinical Forum), xvii–xviii, xx.

Norton, C. (1985) Incontinence in the elderly: Incontinence aids, *part 5. Nursing Times*, **81**, 17–20.

Tallis, R. (1984) Incontinence in the elderly: Treating the impairment, *part 2. Nursing Times*, **80**, 5–8.

Tallis, R. (1984) Incontinence in the elderly: Preventing the disability, *part 3. Nursing Times*, **80**(Suppl), 9–12.

Tallis, R. and Norton, C. (1984) Incontinence in the elderly: The rehabilitative approach, *part 1. Nursing Times*, **80**(Suppl), 1–4.

Tallis, R. and Norton, C. (1985) Incontinence in the elderly: Summary and conclusions, *part 6. Nursing Times*, **81**, 21–4.

13

The need for breathing

Glossary

Aerosolization The process of suspending droplets of water in a gas.

Airway The passages through which air from the atmosphere moves to and from the lungs.

Atomization The process of producing rather large droplets of water.

BP Blood pressure.

Cardiopulmonary Pertaining to the circulatory and respiratory systems.

Cardiopulmonary resuscitation A combination of techniques to open and maintain a good airway and provide artificial ventilation and circulation. Abbreviated CPR.

Crepitus A crackling sound heard coming from within tissue.

External cardiac compression The rhythmic administration of pressure on the chest wall as a substitute for normal heart contractions.

Heimlich manoeuvre The technique for administering abdominal or chest thrusts to clear an object from the airway.

Haemothorax A condition in which blood fills the pleural space.

Humidification Adding moisture to the air.

Hypoxaemia A condition in which there is a less than adequate level of oxygen in the blood.

Hypoxia A deficiency of oxygen in inspired air. It also describes a condition in which the tissues and cells are experiencing an inadequate supply of oxygen.

Intermittent positive-pressure breathing A mechanical means for administering gases or drugs above atmospheric pressure. Abbreviated IPPB.

Nebulization The process of transforming a liquid into a mist or fog of fine droplets.

Percussion A technique for loosening respiratory secretions by striking the chest with rhythmic gentle blows using a cupped hand.

Pneumothorax A condition in which atmospheric air enters the pleural space.

Postural drainage A technique for removing secretions from air passageways by placing the patient in various positions that utilize gravity.

Rescue breathing Artificial ventilation of the lungs using the rescuer's breath.

Semi-Fowler's position Sitting up with the head of the bed at an angle of 45 to 60 degrees.

Suctioning A procedure in which a catheter is used to clear the airway of secretions.

TPR Temperature, pulse and respirations.

Tracheostomy An artifical opening into the trachea.

Vibration A technique for loosening respiratory secretions using firm, strong, circular movements on the chest applied with open hands to produce wavelike tremors.

Introduction

The word *cardiopulmonary* refers to the circulatory and the respiratory systems. The act of respiration involves the exchange of gases: oxygen from inhaled air and carbon dioxide from cellular waste are exchanged. These two substances, along with other nutrients and wastes, are transported by the circulatory system. Cell life cannot exist without the coordinated functioning of the cardiopulmonary system.

This chapter describes various skills for promoting and assisting cardiopulmonary functioning. It includes emergency measures to use when these systems become impaired and, in some cases, fail.

Most measures described in this chapter will require a doctor's order and must only be carried out under direct supervision of a first level practitioner. Recording is done according to hospital policy and should include the patient's reaction to whatever type of intervention is used.

Clearing the airway

The airway includes the passages through which the air from the atmosphere moves to and from the lungs. Any situation that narrows the passageways can interfere with optimal ventilation and the transportation of oxygen to the blood and cells of the body.

The nurse can utilize various skills to keep the airway clear. Methods for encouraging coughing and deep breathing as techniques for promoting ventilation are discussed in Chapter 21. These measures should be reviewed since they are basic to maintaining cardiopulmonary functioning.

Liquefying secretions

The respiratory tract is lined with mucous membrane. This tissue keeps the passageways moist and sticky so that nongaseous particles are trapped before falling into delicate smaller structures within the lungs. Dry air or reduced volumes of body water can alter the moist condition within air passages. The mucous membrane can become dehydrated, causing mucus to become thicker than usual. Trapped particles will then tend to remain within the lungs because the mucus is too thick to be raised. The airway will not be easily cleared. This can lead to narrowing of the passageways and a decreased volume of exchanged gases.

To avoid this, the nurse may keep the patient well hydrated. This may be done by encouraging an adequate fluid intake. This will balance the body's needs with its supply. Mucus produced when the body is well hydrated ordinarily should be thin enough to be removed by clearing the throat or coughing if it accumulates.

Providing humidification

Measures are available for providing *humidification*, that is, adding moisture to the air that the patient breathes. *Atomization* refers to the production of rather large droplets. *Nebulization* is the production of a mist or fog. Suspending the droplets in a gas is called *aerosolization*. These processes have the effect of delivering and distributing moisture directly within the respiratory tract rather than indirectly through the processes of body fluid distribution.

Machines that add moisture to air may add humidity to the air within the room. They can be connected to hoods or tents, which deliver the moisture in the immediate area of the patient's nasal passages. They may also be connected directly to tubes within the airway.

Warmed air inhalation. Steam vaporizers are now virtually obsolete. These provide humidification by transforming water from a liquid state to a gas by boiling. Machines of this type always pose the potential for accidental scalding and tend to elevate temperature or interfere with its regulation.

However, the therapeutic effect of warmed, moist air is still desirable. Warm, moist air soothes inflamed and irritated mucous membranes and loosens respiratory secretions. The inhaled air, carrying minute droplets of water, brings moist heat to the respiratory tract. This produces the same results as when moist heat is applied locally to other parts of the body.

Hospitals now use various humidification techniques in which beads of moisture are produced without excessive heat being used to produce steam. Those that warm as well as moisten the air may be selectively controlled within a preset temperature range. Usually a setting close to body temperature is used. These machines now contain automatic regulators that turn the heating element on and off according to the desired levels. Alarms sound if overheating occurs. These humidifiers are far superior to the types that boiled water continuously.

Cool mist inhalation. For those who may not benefit from the warming of inhaled air, a mist humidifier may be prescribed. It aerates the water,

making fine droplets of moisture that the patient breathes along with the air in the atmosphere. Humidification is always necessary when the patient is receiving oxygen since increased percentages of oxygen dry the mucous membranes.

Humidification of this type is not warmed; in fact, it may be cooled with ice to an approximate temperature of 21°C or 70°F. The patient may become chilled and wet. The patient should be protected from draughts and from chilliness with appropriate coverings. Absorbent fabrics such as cotton bath blankets and towels may be used to collect condensation accumulating around the patient. Clothing and bed linen should be changed as it becomes necessary. The nurse should check the fluid and ice levels on each shift and refill as indicated.

Administering postural drainage

Postural drainage is a technique for clearing secretions from air passageways by placing the patient in various positions. Gravity is used to help promote drainage. It is often recommended for the patient with considerable heavy respiratory secretions who finds it difficult to raise the material by coughing only.

Using percussion and vibration

Many patients, especially those with chronic pulmonary diseases, may have difficulty raising mucus from the respiratory tract even with postural drainage. To enhance postural drainage, or if postural drainage does not seem effective, percussion and vibration may be ordered. *Percussion* is the technique of striking with rhythmic gentle blows using a cupped hand. *Vibration* is the technique of using firm, strong, circular movements with open hands to produce wavelike tremors. Both of these actions are intended to cause thick secretions to break loose from within the airway.

When percussion and vibration are performed, the patient is placed in various positions, such as the sides, back, and abdomen, so that all areas over both lungs can be percussed and vibrated. Percussion and vibration are continued for about 15 minutes if the patient tolerates the therapy well.

With the break up of mucus, the patient can more easily raise and expectorate it. Other procedures may be performed in conjunction with percussion and vibration to clear the airway effectively. Areas over the spine, liver, kidneys, abdomen, breasts, clavicle and sternum should not be percussed or vibrated because of the danger of injuring tissues. Postural drainage and percussion and vibration are techniques carried out by the physiotherapist. However, many nurses give valuable physiotherapy "back up" to patients in respiratory units but these techniques must only be used by experienced clinical nurses.

Suctioning the airway

Sometimes coughing may be inadequate or the patient too weak to expectorate or swallow raised mucus. *Suctioning* is a procedure in which a catheter is used to remove secretions from the airway. The nurse may use suctioning to remove secretions from the upper airway in the area of the oropharynx and nasopharynx or deeper within the trachea and bronchi. Suctioning the lower airway through a tracheostomy will be discussed later in this chapter.

Assembling suction equipment

The source of suction may be a wall unit or a separate portable machine. Usually a pressure of 100 to 120 mmHg using a wall unit or a low setting, usually 10 to 15 mmHg, using a portable suction machine is sufficient enough to remove secretions from an adult without damaging the tissue severely.

A suction catheter usually is made of flexible plastic or rubber. Catheters are available in a variety of sizes. The size selected should allow for the passage of air around the outside of the catheter. An adult is likely to require a size 14 to 18 while catheters in smaller sizes, indicated by lower numbers, should be used for children. Suction catheters have a series of holes located along the sides of the insertion tip. This design allows the removal of larger amounts of secretions during a short amount of time. A vent or Y-connector at the upper end of the catheter permits creation of a vacuum once the catheter is in its proper location. The secretions are pulled into the catheter and tubing and deposited within a receptacle attached to the suction unit.

Assessing the need for suctioning

Suctioning should never be performed routinely. This procedure can cause injury to respiratory passageways, remove oxygen as well as secretions, cause bradycardia and hypotension, and often causes the patient to feel apprehensive and frightened. Some criteria that indicate a need for suctioning include ineffective coughing and expectoration; dyspnoea; cyanosis of the skin, lips, and nailbeds; moist breath sounds heard on auscultation with a stethoscope; rattling sounds heard without a stethoscope; vibrations felt over areas where secretions are moved about during respiration; and tachycardia. The nurse should note these focus assessments before, during and after the suctioning procedure. Repeated suctioning should be avoided and frequent suctioning should only be performed after providing the patient with periodic rest and oxygenation (Allen, 1988).

Performing nasopharyngeal or oropharyngeal suctioning

The nurse may choose to suction the upper airway either through the nose or mouth or both. However, separate catheters should be used for each.

Hospitals differ as to the recommendation for medical or surgical asepsis when performing oropharyngeal and nasopharyngeal suctioning. One rationale is that if the tip of the catheter will not be passed further than the pharynx, a place where organisms are ordinarily found in larger numbers, the procedure may follow principles of medical asepsis or clean technique. Others feel that any patient who requires suctioning already is susceptible to infection. Therefore, it is better to be overly cautious when it comes to his protection. The nurse should follow the policies developed by the hospital.

Clean gloves may be worn as a transmission barrier to protect the nurse from pathogens present in the patient's secretions. If sterile gloves are used, they protect both the nurse and the patient from contact with pathogens. A basin of normal saline should be available for rinsing the lumen of the catheter. If the hospital procedure specifies that sterile technique be used, the solution and the basin should be sterile. The catheter may be dipped into the saline solution or coated with water soluble lubricant prior to insertion within the nose; it need not be lubricated, other than with saline, prior to insertion within the mouth.

Principles of Care 13-1 describes the actions involved in using suctioning for clearing the upper airway of secretions.

Collecting a sputum specimen

A patient who accumulates copious amounts of secretions within the respiratory tract, called sputum, will more than likely need to have it analysed by the laboratory of the hospital. The nurse is responsible for collecting the specimen. It is not uncommon for the doctor to request that three different specimens be obtained to ensure adequate test results.

A specimen is best obtained early in the morning

Principles of Care 13-1. Suctioning the upper airway

Nursing Action	Rationale
Assess the patient to determine the need for suctioning.	Suctioning should be done only when secretions are accumulating and the patient is not able to clear his own air passages.
Explain the purpose and plan for suctioning to the patient.	The patient who understands the measures that will be provided can tolerate and cooperate with the procedure.
Gather the equipment that will be needed for suctioning, such as catheter, extension tubing, suction unit, basin of normal saline, gloves, and lubricant.	The patient who cannot breathe well may be extremely anxious. Disorganization may tend to heighten the patient's anxiety.
Attach the suction machine to the wall outlet or power source. Set the pressure gauge, as the nurse in Figure 13-1 is doing, according to the age and size of the patient.	A wall unit may be regulated at 100 to 120 mmHg for an adult or a low setting, approximately 10 to 15 mmHg, using a portable machine. Follow hospital policy specifing pressure ranges for upper airway suctioning.

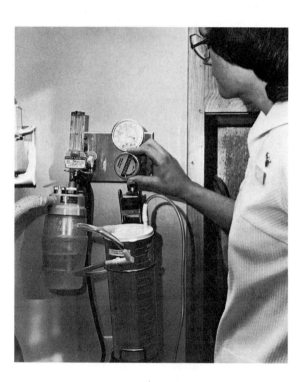

Figure 13-1 The nurse begins the suctioning procedure by turning on the suction machine and checking to see that it is working properly.

Provide privacy by closing the room door and pulling the cubicle curtains surrounding the bed.	The patient should be protected from the view of others when any procedure is carried out.
Protect the front of the patient's bed clothes and pillow with clean towels.	Towels are easily removed and laundered if secretions or droplets from suctioning, coughing or sneezing soil or contaminate the area.
Place the patient in a semi-Fowler's position or in a side-lying position if the patient is unconscious.	A semi-Fowler's position aids breathing and passage of the catheter. A lateral position may prevent aspiration.

Continued

Principles of Care 13-1. *Continued*

Nursing Action	Rationale
Inspect the condition of the nares if the catheter will be inserted through the nose.	The catheter is more easily passed through a nostril that is not narrowed or partially obstructed as a result of a deviated nasal septum.
Preoxygenate the patient with 100% oxygen for 1 to 2 minutes if advocated by hospital policy. Wash hands thoroughly.	This provides a potential extra reserve of oxygen within the blood to compensate for the volume of oxygen that will be removed during suctioning.
Open the package containing the catheter without touching the tip to any unsterile equipment or articles. Attach the catheter to the tubing that extends from the suction unit.	The suction tip should be kept as clean as possible, or sterile, prior to placing it within the patient.
Check to see that there is suction by placing a thumb over the vent, as the nurse in Figure 13-2 is doing.	When the vent is closed, the pressure gauge should register at the level previously set.

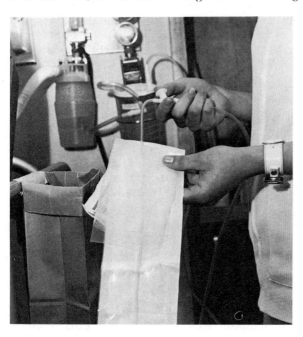

Figure 13-2 The catheter for suctioning is sterile when dispensed in its plastic bag. The top is turned down only sufficiently to connect the catheter with the suction machine. The nurse checks to see that there is suction by placing a thumb over the vent, as shown. When the thumb is off the valve, there will be no suction through the catheter.

Don a sterile or clean glove on the dominant hand.	The hand that will hold the catheter should be covered with a glove that acts as a transmission barrier.
Measure the distance from the tip of the nose to the tip of the patient's earlobe without actually touching the catheter to the patient's face.	The length between these two structures is approximately the distance internally to the pharynx.
Turn on the suction machine with the nondominant hand.	The hand that will be used during direct contact with the patient should not touch the pressure gauge, which is neither clean nor sterile.
Test the suction by pulling normal saline through the suction catheter.	It is better to identify mechanical problems before the suction catheter is inserted.
Lubricate the suction tip by coating it with water-soluble lubricant or wetting it with the rinsing solution.	Lubrication reduces friction and facilitates the ease of insertion. To avoid injury, the catheter should never be forced through a body structure.

Continued

Principles of Care 13-1. Continued

Nursing Action	Rationale
Follow the floor of the nose or the side of the mouth during insertion.	These techniques help to reduce the potential for sneezing or gagging during insertion.
Expect that the patient may cough. Encourage the patient to cough if this does not occur as a reflex action.	Coughing helps to break up and raise thick secretions to a level where they may be reached by the suction catheter.
Turn the patient's head to the side and stop the catheter insertion if it appears that vomiting may occur.	There is a danger of aspiration if the patient should vomit. Interrupting the insertion may allow time for the feeling to pass.
Occlude the vent or exposed tip of the Y-connector once the end of the catheter is in the desired location.	Suction should never be applied during insertion of the catheter . . . only during its removal.
Rotate or twist the catheter as it is being removed.	This helps to remove secretions from all the surface areas of the airway.
Release the finger from the vent if the catheter seems to resist removal. This is more likely to occur when suctioning structures deeper than the pharynx.	Spasms may occur. The patient should still be able to breathe when the suction is not being applied. Relaxation will eventually counteract the spasm and the catheter will be released.
Observe the patient's response during suctioning. An assistant may be required especially to assess the pulse of a patient who is elderly or has a history of heart disease. Watch the heart rate and rhythm on a cardiac monitor, if that is in use.	Temporary reduction of oxygen levels within the blood as well as stimulation of the vagus nerve during the insertion of the catheter can cause bradycardia or other dangerous arrhythmias.
Complete the process in no more than 15 seconds from the time of the insertion of the catheter to its removal.	Suctioning that extends beyond this period of time may remove significant amounts of oxygen needed by the cells and tissues of the body.
Rinse the secretions from the tubing by inserting the catheter in the basin of normal saline and applying suction.	The protein in mucus may become dry and interfere with further use of the tubing for subsequent suctioning.
Repeat suctioning if assessments indicate that secretions are still present, but allow a 2 to 3 minute rest period and reoxygenation in between.	Repeated attempts at suctioning are fatiguing to the patient and can lower the amount of oxygen in the blood to dangerous levels.
Pull the glove on the dominant hand inside out over the catheter and dispose of both when suctioning is completed.	Enclosing the contaminated catheter within the soiled side of the glove helps to control the spread of microorganisms.
Turn off the suction machine.	The suction machine need only be operational during the time of the procedure.
Reassess the patient.	The nurse should collect data similar to that gathered before suctioning to evaluate the response of the patient to the procedure.
Provide mouth care.	Oral hygiene measures will remove unpleasant tastes and mouth odours related to the cleared respiratory secretions.
Record pertinent assessments and a description of the suctioning procedure in the chart.	The permanent record should reflect the quality and standards of care provided for the patient as well as his unique responses.
Empty the container that holds the suctioned secretions immediately or at least at the end of the shift.	The container holding suctioned secretions supports the growth of pathogens and is aesthetically unpleasant to observe.

because a higher volume of secretions is likely to have accumulated throughout the night. Another time that may provide a better opportunity for collecting specimens would be following respiratory therapy treatments, postural drainage, and percussion and vibration.

The patient should be instructed that the specimen consists of material coughed up from the respiratory tract and not saliva that is present in the mouth. Special mucus traps are available for use with suction catheters if a specimen must be obtained using the suction catheter.

The following techniques are used to collect a sputum specimen:

- Encourage the patient to have a generous fluid intake and have him breathe humidified air when possible. These measures help to prevent the sputum from becoming sticky and difficult to raise.
- Use a large-mouthed sterile container that has a secure cover and have the patient expectorate directly into it.
- Avoid contaminating the inside of the container by exposing it to air unnecessarily or touching it.
- Avoid collecting a specimen after the patient eats. Food particles in the specimen make examination difficult.
- Assess the volume and other characteristics of the sputum that will be sent to the laboratory. Some sputum specimen containers are calibrated, making measurement easy. Another technique is to fill an identical container with water to the level of the sputum expectorated and then measure the amount of water.
- Handle sputum specimens carefully and observe aseptic techniques to avoid spreading organisms to the hands, linens, and personal care items. Sputum should be considered highly contaminated.
- Provide the patient with the opportunity for mouth care following the raising of sputum.
- For best results, label and send the sputum specimen to the laboratory within an hour of collecting it.

Relieving airway obstruction

The airway may be occluded suddenly by an aspirated object or food. Cardiopulmonary function may also become compromised if the tongue or swelling closes off the passageway for air through the trachea and bronchi. Various measures may be used to promote air exchange.

Assisting the individual with a blocked airway

Certain measures are helpful in an emergency to assist a victim who is choking on a foreign object. In adults, the foreign object is most often a piece of food. In children, in addition to food, the object may be a large piece of gum, buttons, marbles, deflated balloons, removable parts from toys and so on.

Signs of sudden airway obstruction. The nurse should be able to determine if the patient is experiencing distress due to an airway obstruction or a heart attack since the symptoms are somewhat similar. If the symptoms occur at the time of eating, aspiration of food into the airway is a real possibility. The following signs are typical when a victim is choking on a foreign object:

- Grasping for the throat with the hands.
- Spontaneous efforts to cough and breathe.
- Producing a high-pitched sound while inhaling indicates that air passageways are almost totally blocked.
- Turning pale and then blue.
- Being unable to speak, breathe, or cough indicates a total block.
- Collapsing and becoming unconscious. The victim will die unless the foreign body is removed to allow for air exchange in the lungs.

Dislodging an object from the airway. If it is determined that the victim is indeed choking and there is poor or absent air exchange, action should be taken immediately to dislodge the foreign object. A series of manual thrusts are recommended to remove a foreign object on which a victim is choking. For infants under the age of 1, a combination of back blows and chest thrusts is advised. The sequence of recommended actions for an adult are described and illustrated in Principles of Care 13-2.

Caring for the patient with an artificial airway

Various tubes and hollow devices may be inserted into the nose or mouth of an unconscious or critically ill patient to maintain an open airway. Simpler types, like the oral airway shown in Figure 13-8, hold the tongue forward so that it cannot obstruct the air

Principles of Care 13-2. *Dislodging an object from the airway*

Nursing Action	Rationale
Ask if the patient can speak.	Speech is only possible when air moves from the lower areas of the lungs through the vocal cords. If the victim can speak, either the airway is only partially occluded or something else is causing the symptoms.
Encourage forceful coughing.	Coughing increases intrathoracic pressure and can sometimes force a foreign object into a large air passage so that breathing can resume.
Avoid attempts to assist the victim as long as there is adequate air exchange.	Attempts to assist may lead to unnecessary injury to the victim.
Call for emergency assistance if the victim continues to be unsuccessful in his efforts to relieve a partial obstruction.	The assistance of emergency personnel may become necessary if the situation becomes prolonged or progresses to a complete obstruction.
Review the "Suggested Measures to Promote Cardiopulmonary Functioning in Seclected Situations" at the end of this chapter if the victim is an infant under the age of 1.	Altering the position of infants and administering back blows are additional techniques used to dislodge an object from the airway of victims under the age of 1.
Prepare to perform the *Heimlich manoeuvre,* also called abdominal thrusts, if the victim has an ineffective cough, increased respiratory difficulty, or cannot exchange any air.	The Heimlich maneouvre must be performed when the victim's own efforts to relieve the obstruction are unsuccessful.
Stand behind the victim and allow him to lean over with his head lower than his chest, as illustrated in Figure 13-3.	This positioning increases intrathoracic pressure and allows gravity to help in the removal of an aspirated object.

Figure 13-3 The rescuer positions herself behind the victim.

Continued

Principles of Care 13-2. Continued

Nursing Action	Rationale
Alternatively, get behind the victim who is sitting in a chair.	This alternative position may be used when the weight of a victim cannot be supported by the rescuer.
Bring the arms around the victim's abdomen.	The hands must be below the lungs in order to elevate the diaphragm.
Make a fist, the thumb tucked inside, with one hand and grab the fisted hand with the other, as shown in Figure 13-4.	Using a fist and the combined effort of the strong muscles of the arms helps to provide enough pressure to force out air trapped below the object.

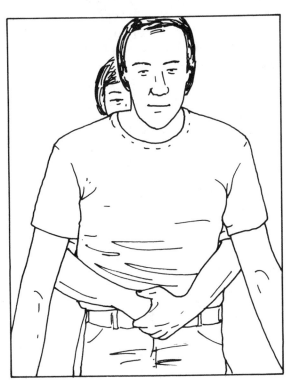

Figure 13-4 The rescuer administers the first of what may be several abdominal thrusts needed to dislodge an object obstructing the victim's airway.

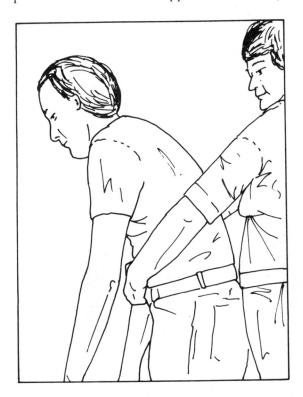

Figure 13-5 This side view shows the proper positioning of the hands of the rescuer for delivering abdominal thrusts to the victim.

Nursing Action	Rationale
Place the flat side of the clasped fist against the victim's abdomen between the lower end of the sternum and above the navel, not on the lower sternum or the rib cage. This is illustrated in Figure 13-5.	Proper hand placement is necessary to prevent injury to abdominal and thoracic organs.
Press the clasped fist into the victim's abdomen with a forceful thrust. Do not squeeze, but rather carry out the manoeuvre in an upward direction.	With sufficient force, the trapped air may cause enough pressure to dislodge the object from the airway.
Repeat this action 6 to 10 times until there is restoration of breathing or the victim becomes unconscious.	Efforts should be continued even if they are not successful the first time.

Continued

Principles of Care 13-2. Continued

Nursing Action	Rationale
Follow by sweeping the throat, administering rescue breaths or cardiopulmonary resuscitation as described in the following section and in more detail in Principles of Care 13-7 when a victim cannot breathe and the heart has stopped beating.	When the conscious victim becomes unconscious, further actions are necessary to help restore breathing and circulation.
When the Victim Is Unconscious:	

Nursing Action	Rationale
Place the victim in a supine position.	A supine position is the preferred position for an unconscious victim in order to place the hands properly and administer abdominal thrusts.
Kneel over the victim placing one leg on each side of the victim's hips facing toward the head.	Working directly over the victim provides the best use of the rescuer's body mechanics and strength.
Place the hands on top of each other in the midline between the victim's rib cage and navel and administer a forceful upward thrust with the heel of the bottom hand.	Positioning the hands in this manner facilitates applying force to the centre of the abdomen without encircling the victim's abdomen.
Perform 6 to 10 repeated abdominal thrusts if the object does not become dislodged.	Continuing efforts must be made to restore breathing despite initial unsuccessful attempts.
Open the unconscious victim's mouth and sweep the throat as illustrated in Figure 13-6. Take care to avoid driving the object deeper within the airway.	If the object is not too low in the respiratory tract, a sweeping action with a finger will sometimes help to bring it to the mouth for removal.

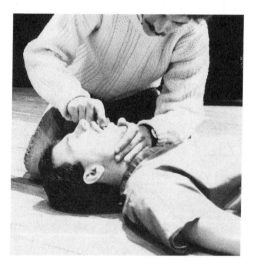

Figure 13-6 A hooked index finger can be used to sweep a foreign object lodged in the mouth or throat.

Nursing Action	Rationale
Tilt the head upward and lift the chin to open the airway.	Adjusting the position of the head will move the tongue from the airway and may permit partial air exchange.
Administer two rescue breaths into the victim's mouth and observe if the chest rises during the ventilation attempts. If no artificial airway is available, use nose to mouth resuscitation. Use clean gauze or handkerchief to cover nose.	Seeing the chest rise provides evidence that air is passing through the airway and filling the lungs.

Continued

Principles of Care 13-2. Continued

Nursing Action	Rationale
Continue with rescue breathing, administering one breath every 5 seconds on anyone over 8 years of age. Faster rates, listed in Table 13-2, must be administered to infants and children.	Efforts must continue to revive the patient when no spontaneous breathing is occurring.
Begin cardiac compressions at a rate of 80 to 100 per minute with two breaths administered between every 15 compressions on victims who are 8 years old or older when a pulse cannot be felt.	When there is no pulse, the rescuer must include cardiac compressions to provide resuscitation.
Continue with resuscitation efforts until the victim responds or the rescuer becomes exhausted.	Resuscitation efforts should be continued while waiting for assistance.
When the Patient Is Obese or Pregnant:	
Stand behind the victim with arms under the victim's axillae. Place the clasped fist on the middle of the victim's sternum, not at the lower end of the sternum or at the edge of the rib cage, as illustrated in Figure 13-7.	This position helps prevent injury to the sternum, ribs, and organs located within the thoracic cavity.

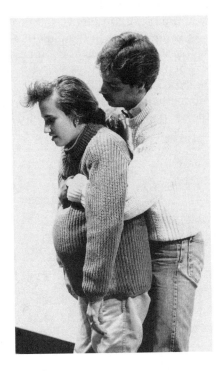

Figure 13-7 These two people demonstrate how to position the arms and hands when the victim is pregnant or obese.

Administer 6 to 10 chest thrusts rather than abdominal thrusts.	Chest thrusts provide an alternative method for relieving an obstruction from a victim with an enlarged abdomen without injuring a foetus or enlarged abdominal organs.
Continue with resuscitation efforts, as described earlier and in Principles of Care 13-7 if the victim fails to breathe spontaneously and has no pulse.	Additional measures must be performed when attempts to free an object from the airway prove unsuccessful.

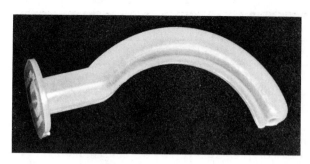

Figure 13-8 A plastic disposable airway may be inserted through the mouth, following the contour of the mouth and upper respiratory tract. When in place properly, the oral airway holds the tongue so that it cannot drop back and into the throat. It can be suctioned easily should secretions accumulate.

passages. An oral airway or nasopharyngeal airway, placed in upper airway structures, may be inserted by a qualified nurse. An endotracheal tube, inserted into the trachea using a laryngoscope as a guide, is generally the responsibility of a doctor, nurse, anaesthetist, or certified critical care personnel. The doctor usually inserts a tracheostomy tube, which is introduced through an incision in the lower neck.

Inserting and maintaining an artificial upper airway. An artificial airway may be placed within the patient's nose or mouth to maintain an open upper airway. The nurse may use the following description as a guide for inserting and providing care for the patient with an oral airway device. Modifications that apply to a nasopharyngeal airway are found at the end of the discussion.

- Position the patient on his back with his neck hyperextended, if this is not contraindicated.
- Insert the thumb and index finger into the patient's mouth to separate the teeth and spread the jaw.
- Use a tongue blade as an additional measure, if needed, to open the mouth and depress the tongue.
- Hold the airway so that the curved tip points upward toward the roof of the mouth.
- Guide the airway to the back of the mouth while keeping the tongue forward and below the oral airway.
- Turn the airway within the mouth until it is positioned over the top of the tongue following its natural contour.
- Secure the flange of the exposed end of the air-

way to the skin in the area of the lips using tape.
- Perform oropharyngeal or nasopharyngeal suctioning as necessary to clear secretions from the natural and artificial airway.
- Remove the oral airway briefly every 4 hours.
- Assess the condition of the mouth and tongue.
- Provide mouth care and skin care to the taped area and lips.
- Rinse and clean the oral airway.
- Reinsert the oral airway if the patient remains unconscious.

A nasopharyngeal airway may be used rather than an oral airway. It is inserted similarly to a nasopharyngeal catheter; however, the airway is secured in place rather than removed. The alternate nostril should be used when a nasopharyngeal airway is removed, cleaned, and reinserted every 8 hours.

Caring for the patient with a tracheostomy

A *tracheostomy* is an artificial opening into the trachea. A hollow device is inserted into the opening and the patient breathes through it. The tube has an inner and an outer cannula or, more simply, a tube within a tube. The outer cannula rests in the patient's trachea and the inner cannula fits into the outer cannula to form one opening, through which the patient breathes. This type of tracheostomy tube is made of silver and noncuffed and used on a permanent basis for those patients who have undergone

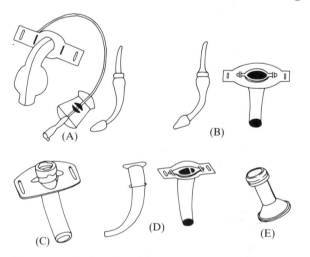

Figure 13-9 Tubes for permanent tracheostomies. (*A*) Portex cuffed tube. (*B*) Colledge silver tube. (*C*) Shiley's laryngectomy tube. (*D*) Shaw's laryngectomy tube. (*E*) Stoma button. Pritchard and David, Royal Marsden Manual of Clinical Nursing Procedures, 3rd Edition; published by Blackwell Scientific, 1992.

Principles of Care 13-3. Suctioning secretions from a tracheostomy

Nursing Action	Rationale
Assess for evidence of mucus accumulating in the patient's respiratory tract, such as noisy, moist, and laboured respirations, and increased pulse and respiratory rates.	Noisy, moist, and laboured respirations indicate that mucus is accumulating in the respiratory tract, putting extra stress on the cardiopulmonary system.
Help the patient into a Fowler's position, if permitted.	The patient can ventilate more fully in this position.
Encourage and help the patient to cough up respiratory secretions, to see whether this will clear the respiratory tract.	Suctioning, which is irritating to mucous membranes, should be avoided when the patient can successfully cough up secretions.
Wipe away secretions coughed out through the tracheostomy tube.	The secretions below the tracheostomy tube will not be expectorated from the mouth.
Use wipes that are free of lint around the tracheostomy opening.	Inhaled lint irritates the respiratory passages and may cause undue coughing.
Give the patient 100% oxygen for 1 to 2 minutes before suctioning if advocated by hospital policy.	Giving oxygen before suctioning prevents depletion of the supply to the cells since suctioning removes oxygen, as well as debris, from the respiratory tract.
Attach a sterile catheter to the tubing leading from the suction source. The catheter should be about half the diameter of the tracheostomy tube.	If the catheter is too small, suctioning will be ineffective. If the catheter is too large, it may injure tissue and totally obstruct the airway.
Don a sterile glove on the dominant hand. Touch the catheter only with a sterile, gloved hand.	Sterile technique is used to help prevent introducing organisms into the patient's respiratory tract.
Lubricate the catheter with fresh, sterile, normal saline for each pass of the catheter. Bacteriostatic water is usually not recommended.	Lubricating the catheter decreases irritation to mucous membranes. The preservative used in bacteriostatic water is irritating to mucous membranes.
Test the catheter with the saline to be sure it is patent and working properly.	Potential mechanical difficulties should be identified before inserting the suction catheter.
Instill 4 to 5 ml of fresh, sterile normal saline into the tracheostomy tube with a syringe if mucus is sticky and crusty material is present. Be sure there is no needle on the syringe used to introduce the saline.	The normal saline helps liquefy sticky mucus and thus makes it easier to remove it with the suction catheter. A needle on a syringe may come off and fall into the tracheostomy.
Insert the catheter carefully and slowly about 15 to 25 cm (6 to 10 inches) into the inner cannula and into the respiratory passage without covering the vent on the tubing.	Respiratory membranes can be easily injured when a catheter is inserted carelessly. Having suction on while inserting the catheter removes valuable amounts of oxygen unnecessarily.
Have the patient turn his head to the side opposite where the catheter is to be located. To suction the left bronchus, instruct the patient to turn his head to the right, and vice versa.	Turning the head will provide easier access for placement of the catheter within one or the other bronchus.
Occlude the vent and gently rotate the catheter 360 degrees, as the nurse is doing in Figure 13-10, while removing it slowly from the respiratory tract.	Rotating the catheter improves the removal of the secretions from the circular surfaces of the air passages.
Apply suction for only 10 seconds and never more than 15 seconds at one time. Then allow a rest period of 2 to 3 minutes between suctions, and preoxygenate the patient again.	Suctioning removes oxygen as well as secretions from the respiratory tract. The patient suffers an insufficient supply of oxygen when suctioning is prolonged.

Continued

Principles of Care 13-3. Continued

Nursing Action	Rationale

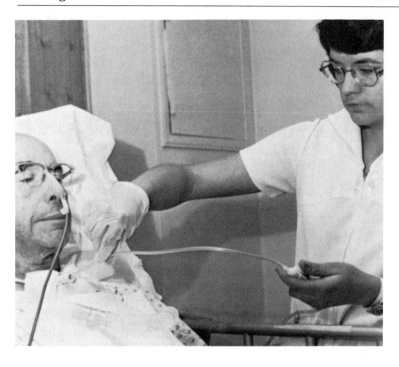

Figure 13-10 After donning a sterile glove, the nurse handles the sterile catheter as she suctions. The catheter is inserted without occluding the vent. The nurse regulates the suction with her thumb. The catheter should be inserted carefully and slowly without forcing it so as not to injure mucous membranes in the respiratory passage. Suctioning should not be administered for more than 10 to 15 seconds. Suctioning removes oxygen as well as secretions; hence, longer periods of suctioning will result in severe oxygen deprivation for the patient and may cause arrhythmia.

Nursing Action	Rationale
Flush the catheter with sterile normal saline between passes with the catheter.	Rinsing the catheter prevents inefficient application of suction from partially obstructed tubing.
Suction the inner cannula as often as necessary to keep it open and free of mucus. This may be as often as every 5 to 10 minutes when the tracheostomy has been performed recently but it *may* be no more often than three or four times every 24 hours.	Suctioning must be performed as often as necessary to keep the respiratory tract clear and open. Excessive suctioning irritates mucous membranes.
Oxygenate the patient after suctioning has been completed.	Giving the patient oxygen after suctioning restores the depleted supply within the blood.
Dispose of the glove and the catheter after suctioning.	To maintain sterile technique, this equipment must not be reused.
Restock additional sterile gloves and suction catheters as the supply is used.	A tracheostomy may require frequent and, in some cases, immediate suctioning to maintain adequate ventilation.

laryngectomy. The more common type of tube used in hospital immediately after surgery or for maintaining an airway is usually disposable. It comprises a nonirritant curved tube approximately four inches long, with an inflatable cuff (Allen, 1987). One is illustrated in Figure 13-9. The cuff is filled with air so that secretions from the upper air passages cannot pass around the cannula and be aspirated. The cuff also helps hold the cannula in place. It prevents oxygen that the patient may be receiving from leaking out rather than being delivered to the lungs. Unless the cuff is of a type that is very pliable and soft, it should be deflated at regular intervals. If this is not done, the cuff may cut off blood circulation to the area and cause injury to tissue cells. An experienced nurse is ordinarily responsible for inflating

Principles of Care 13-4. Providing tracheostomy care

Nursing Action	Rationale
Assemble equipment, which generally comes already prepared, with various items that will be needed.	Disorganization will interfere with completing tracheostomy care within a minimal safe period of time.
Obtain a waterproof receptacle for holding contaminated and soiled items.	Care must be taken to keep items containing organisms separate from clean and sterile areas within the work space.
Open the tracheostomy care set or dressing pack following the principles of surgical asepsis described in Chapter 20.	Contamination of the contents of the set could lead to the spread of organisms within the patient's respiratory tract.
Add sterile hydrogen peroxide to one basin and sterile normal saline or sterile water to a second basin within the set.	These solutions must be added before sterile gloves are donned to avoid contaminating the hands.
Remove the dressing from around the stoma and place it within the container for soiled items.	A soiled dressing contains pathogens and should be suitably contained to control the spread of organisms.
Wash hands thoroughly and don sterile gloves.	Even though the hands were washed prior to opening the equipment set, they must be rewashed after handling the soiled dressing.
Clean around the stoma with a sterile swab moistened with sterile hydrogen peroxide. Follow with a second swab moistened in the saline.	Cleaning the stoma removes secretions and organisms that could cause an infection.
Discard both swabs with the soiled dressing following their use.	Each swab should be used only once to avoid reintroducing organisms into a cleaned area.
Remove the inner cannula by unlocking it from its position within the outer cannula, as the nurse in Figure 13-11 is doing.	Most twist free for removal; however, individual manufacturers may vary in the methods used for securing the two tubes.

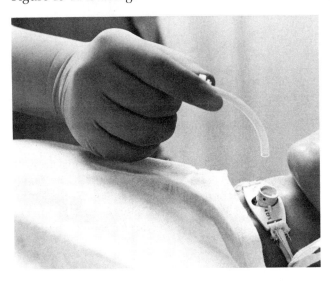

Figure 13-11 The nurse removes the inner cannula only for regular cleaning. The outer cannula remains in place within the tracheostomy. Note that the tracheostomy ties have been secured at the side of the neck where they are less likely to cause pressure from the knot or bow.

Deposit the inner cannula in the basin of hydrogen peroxide.	Hydrogen peroxide is an antimicrobial agent and also loosens protein substances. It is an ideal solution for removing secretions from the surfaces of the cannula.

Continued

Principles of Care 13-4. Continued

Nursing Action	Rationale
While holding the cannula, insert a brush or sterile pipe cleaner through the centre of the cannula. Scrub the outer surfaces also.	The bristles help to mechanically remove debris that the peroxide may have been unable to loosen chemically.
Rinse the cannula in the basin of sterile normal saline or sterile water.	Rinsing removes remnants of undiluted hydrogen peroxide that may irritate the tissue within the respiratory tract.
Drain or dry the cannula using a gauze square and reinsert it within the outer cannula.	The inner cannula should be replaced within 5 minutes of being removed.
Secure the inner cannula in place.	If the cannula is not secured, it could be expelled if and when the patient coughs.
Place a sterile dressing over the stoma incision and under the exposed areas of the tracheostomy tube.	Special dressings that resemble miniature pants protect the incision from organisms and absorb secretions.
Fold a gauze square to fit over the stoma incision using material that does not fray, if special tracheostomy dressings are not available.	Fibre particles that may fall into the respiratory tract can irritate the tissue.
Remove the gloves and deposit them in the container holding the soiled dressing and swabs.	The contaminated gloves and other soiled articles may be discarded for eventual burning to destroy any pathogens that may be present.
Thread clean tracheostomy ties through the slits on each side of the outer cannula before removing the soiled ties.	The tracheostomy tube is only held in place by the ties. Removing one set before the other is secure creates a potential for displacement.
Seek the assistance of another person who will stabilize the tracheostomy tube while one set of ties is removed and replaced with another.	With the help of another person, the tube can be held in place when the ties are removed. This provides more room for threading the clean ties.
Secure the ties in place at the side of the neck.	A knot at the back of the neck may cause pressure and irritation.
Check to see that the ties allow adequate blood flow.	The ties should not be so tight that they impair the circulation of blood.
Remove all soiled equipment from the room to designated areas in a utility room.	A new sterile equipment tray should be obtained each time tracheostomy care is provided.

and deflating a tracheostomy cuff. These tubes have a standard 15 mm connection point to permit secure attachment to ventilatory equipment.

Removing secretions from a tracheostomy. Secretions may accumulate within the lower respiratory air passages. To remove these secretions, suctioning may be performed by inserting a suction catheter through the tracheostomy tube. This procedure *must* be performed following the principles of sterile technique. Many factors affect the potential for infection in a patient with a tracheostomy, such as the extended presence of an artificial object in the trachea, altered skin integrity due to the incision and opening for the tracheostomy tube, and the limited

ability of the patient to remove the build up of secretions naturally (Mapp, 1988).

The procedure for removing secretions from a tracheostomy is somewhat similar to the skills involved in suctioning the upper airway. Principles of Care 13-3 describes and illustrates the special adaptations that may be performed when suctioning a tracheostomy.

Providing tracheostomy care

Immediately following tracheostomy patients will have a disposable tracheostomy tube in situ. This is usually sewn into position and care of the stoma is all that is warranted for the first five to six days following surgery. However, on a more permanent basis a silver tracheostomy tube will be inserted and this will need the inner cannula to be cleaned regularly to help prevent infection. Most hospitals specify that cleansing should be performed at least once every 8 hours. The inner cannula must be removed in order to clean it. Cleansing should be performed in a short amount of time since secretions may accumulate and dry on the surface of the outer cannula, which remains in place. This may interfere with the ability to reinsert the inner cannula. It may ultimately require replacement of the entire equipment within the surgical opening or risk endangering the patient's life. A duplicate set of sterile equipment should be kept at the patient's bedside so that everything is in readiness if the tracheostomy tube must be replaced.

When the inner cannula is cleaned, the stoma is also cared for, the dressing around the stoma is changed, and the ties securing the tracheostomy tube are changed as well. Dressings and tapes are a source of infection when they are not properly cared for and should be changed whenever they become soiled or damp. Principles of Care 13-4 provides a description of the actions that may be followed when providing tracheostomy care using both disposable and permanent tracheostomy tubes.

Many nurses feel distressed at the thought of caring for a patient with a tracheostomy. An interesting study carried out by De Carle (1985) highlights the areas for concern and offers an ideal model of care for the patient with a tracheostomy.

Restoring cardiopulmonary functions

Heart diseases and pulmonary diseases are two of the leading causes of disability and death in the UK. Measures must often be implemented that either temporarily or permanently help to restore the functions of the cardiopulmonary system when it becomes impaired or ceases to operate. This may be done by administering prescribed inhaled medications, providing oxygen, maintaining water-seal drainage, and administering cardiopulmonary resuscitation.

Administering inhaled medications

Drugs that help to restore cardiopulmonary functions can be given by any of the routes discussed in Chapter 16. However, some that are particularly useful directly to the pulmonary system, and indirectly to the heart, are administered by inhalation. Much of the absorption occurs on the surfaces of lung tissue. Because of the large surface area in the lungs, absorption after inhalation generally is rapid. Drugs commonly used are antibiotics, expectorants, and those that help to dilate the bronchioles and bronchi.

Before drugs can be inhaled, they must be vaporized to permit entry into the body with each inspiration. Drugs intended for administration by inhalation are added to a vehicle such as water. The mixture is then processed into droplets. The finer the particles, the farther they will travel into the respiratory tract.

Using a hand-held nebulizer. There are several ways in which a spray may be produced. When a hand-held nebulizer is compressed, air is forced through the container holding the drug in solution. The increased pressure in the unit then forces solution into a narrow channel. The force with which the solution is made to move through this stricture to leave the container is sufficient to break the larger droplets of fluid into a fine mist. The mist is inhaled

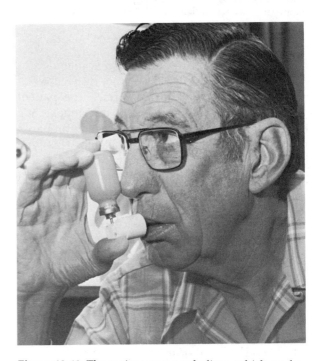

Figure 13-12 The patient uses a nebulizer, which can be purchased in most chemists with a doctor's prescription. He is about to place the mouthpiece into his mouth. Then, by pressing his fingers and thumb together on the nebulizer, the drug in solution will be nebulized and inhaled into his respiratory passage.

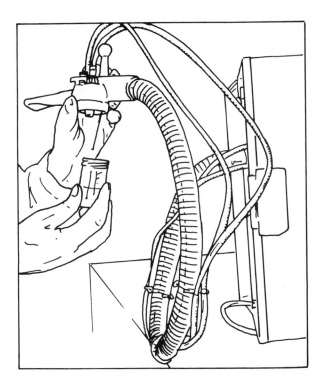

Figure 13-13 A drug in solution can be placed in the small container near the mouthpiece. The pressure created by the machine produces nebulization while the patient gives himself therapy.

through the mouth. If the inhalation is intended to produce effects in the nasal passage as well as in the remainder of the respiratory tract, the patient closes his mouth while he breathes and inhales the substance through his nose. Commercially prepared nebulizers with medications are available. This type is being used by the patient in Figure 13-12.

Using a mechanical nebulizer. Nebulization can also be accomplished using a machine that forces oxygen or compressed air through the drug in solution in a nebulizer. A device of this kind is shown in Figure 13-13. This method of administration is valuable for patients who may be required to inhale a drug for several minutes frequently each day. Using a hand nebulizer for the specified amount of time would prove to be fatiguing; a machine may be used as an alternative.

A common means of administering oxygenated air and a nebulized drug using a machine is by *intermittent positive-pressure breathing*, usually abbreviated IPPB. Using this method, a machine provides a specific amount of air and medication under increased pressure. IPPB forces deeper

inspiration by positive-pressure inhalation and permits the patient to exhale normally. The amount of pressure varies according to the patient's tolerance and needs. Usually, IPPB therapy is ordered to be used two to four times daily for 15 to 20 minutes each time.

There are many models of IPPB machines on the market. The one illustrated in Figure 13-14 is portable and especially useful for home use. In many hospitals, respiratory technicians are responsible for administering IPPB therapy. The nurse will wish to become familiar with the machine used in each hospital so as to understand the exact nature of the therapy the patient receives.

Providing oxygen therapy

Oxygen is essential for life. When the body is deprived of adequate amounts of oxygen, hypoxia and hypoxaemia can occur within a relatively short time. *Hypoxia* is defined as a deficiency in the amount of oxygen in inspired air; it has also come to mean a condition in which cells and tissues are experiencing an inadequate supply of oxygen. *Hypoxaemia* is a condition in which there is a less than adequate level of oxygen in the blood.

Oxygen therapy is very frequently provided when the cardiopulmonary system is functioning poorly either because ventilation is inadequate or the circulatory system is impaired, or both. For example, when the lungs are diseased, oxygen is added to inhaled air so that the blood receives sufficient oxygen. Certain heart conditions impair the ability to circulate blood through the lungs. Oxygen therapy is then used to ensure that the tissues will be adequately supplied. The higher concentration of oxygen compensates for the limited transfer of oxygen to the blood.

Basic guidelines for administering oxygen. Certain basic guidelines should be observed when administering oxygen therapy (Clark Mims, 1987; Allen, 1989).

- Oxygen therapy is given as prescribed by the doctor, except in certain emergency situations when experienced nurses are permitted to use independent judgement. The doctor's order will specify the method of administration and the percentage of oxygen to be given along with the flow rate. The nurse administers oxygen just as cautiously as administering a medication, observing the same precautions and attention to accuracy as when giving a drug.

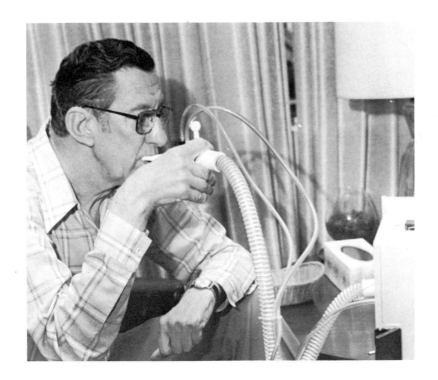

Figure 13-14 The patient holds the mouthpiece securely between his lips as he gives himself intermittent positive-pressure breathing therapy. The pressure forces deep inspirations but allows the patient to exhale normally.

• Patients suffering from insufficient oxygen often feel as though they are suffocating and are unable to breathe. They are usually restless, worried, and frightened. Respirations are char-·acteristically achieved with great effort. It is a terrifying experience to be unable to breathe adequately. The patient needs support and the comfort of feeling that all that is possible is being done.

• Oxygen therapy must sometimes be instituted with such speed that there is little time for explaining procedures to the patient. However, some concurrent instruction is generally possible. After the patient is out of immediate danger, he should be told about the equipment and measures being used in his care.

• The patient's responses to oxygen therapy are most accurately determined by laboratory examinations of the patient's arterial blood. Observations of the patient are also important for judging responses prior to and concurrent with oxygen therapy. These observations should include changes in the colouring of the patient's skin and nailbeds, changes in the vital signs and the nature of respirations, and level of consciousness.

• Oxygen becomes progressively toxic at high concentrations. Signs of oxygen toxicity include a dry cough that may eventually become moist as lung damage occurs, chest pain felt beneath the sternum, nasal stuffiness, nausea and vomiting, and restlessness. The lungs and brain may become damaged, but unfortunately signs of injury to these structures may not be identified as early as other signs.

• Oxygen supports combustion and, hence, must be used with great care. The following recommendations are offered to help avoid fires:

"NO SMOKING" signs should be placed in prominent places and the patient and his visitors should be taught the importance of this regulation.

Electrical devices, such as razors, radios and television sets, should be removed or checked *carefully* to be certain they are not sources of any sparks. All electrical equipment used with the patient's care, such as suctioning equipment, should be in good working order and properly earthed.

Electrical signal devices should be checked for safety or removed from the room. A simple hand bell may be used instead.

Oil and alcohol for backrubs are generally not used because of the fire danger they present. Lotions are used instead. No petroleum products should be used for lubricating the lips.

Oil and grease should not be used near oxygen gauges and outlets because of the danger of their igniting spontaneously.

There should be no open flames in the presence of oxygen. For example, candles may not be used during religious ceremonies for the sick when oxygen is in use.

Fire extinguishers should be readily available wherever oxygen is being used and personnel should be familiar with their use.

If oxygen is delivered from a cylinder, the cylinder should be secured properly to its stand to prevent accidents.

Precautions should be used concerning static electricity. Fabrics that generate static electricity should not be used in the presence of oxygen. Some hospitals require nurses working around oxygen to wear cotton uniforms and undergarments to help avoid static electricity.

- Oxygen is delivered to the respiratory tract artificially under pressure. Therefore, excessive drying of mucous membranes lining the respiratory tract occurs unless the oxygen is humidified. Because oxygen is only slightly soluble in water, it can be passed through solutions with little loss. Tap or distilled water is generally used for this purpose. Some authorities recommend that the solution be warmed to between 52 and 54°C (125 to 130°F) to improve the humidification of the oxygen. The exact method of moisturizing oxygen depends on the hospital's equipment.

Figure 13-15 shows the colour code used for British gas cylinders.

- In most hospitals, oxygen is piped into each patient unit and is immediately available from an outlet in the wall. The oxygen is supplied from a central source through a pipeline, usually at 50 to 60 lb per square inch of pressure. A specially designed flowmeter is attached to the wall outlet. The flowmeter opens the outlet and a valve makes regulation of the oxygen flow possible. Oxygen is compressed and dispensed from a cylinder when oxygen is not piped into the room.

Handling an oxygen cylinder. A few hospitals and nursing homes may provide oxygen by cylinder rather than by piped wall units. Many are utilizing small individual cylinders of oxygens for those patients who require it. However, when a large cylinder is the only source of supply, the nurse must be aware of its potential hazards when handling the equipment.

Cylinders of oxygen are delivered with a protective cap to prevent accidental force against the cylinder outlet. When a standard, large-sized cylinder is full, its contents are under more than 2000 lb of pressure per square inch. Force accidentally applied to a partially opened outlet could cause the cylinder to take off like a rocket, with disastrous results. The cylinder should be transported carefully while strapped onto a wheeled carrier.

When oxygen is dispensed from a cylinder, the cylinder should be handled as follows:

- Check to see that the cylinder contains oxygen. Gases other than oxygen are used in many hospitals. Administering the wrong gas is a serious error!

Name of gas	Symbol	Valve end colour	Body colour
Oxygen	O_2	White	Black
Nitrous oxide	N_2O	Blue	Blue
Cyclopropane	C_3H_6	Orange	Orange
Carbon dioxide	CO_2	Grey	Grey
Helium	He	Brown	Brown
Nitrogen	N_2	Black	Grey
Oxygen and carbon dioxide	O_2+CO_2	White and grey	Black
Oxygen and helium mixtures	O_2+He	White and brown	Black
Air (medical)	AIR	White and black	Grey
Oxygen and nitrous oxide mixture	O_2+N_2O	White and blue	Blue

Figure 13-15 British standard cylinder colour code. Source: Carrie, L.E.S. and Simpson, P.J., Understanding Anaesthesia; published by Heinemann, 1982.

- Attach a humidifier to the cylinder and fill it with water according to the manufacturer's directions.
- Check to see that the cylinder is stabilized at the patient's bedside in a properly fitting stand so that there is no danger of the cylinder's tipping and possibly causing injury. The equipment is now ready to deliver oxygen to the patient.

Methods for delivering oxygen. There are several ways in which oxygen can be delivered to a patient. The oxygen may be administered with a nasal cannula, nasal catheter, mask tent and even into a tracheostomy. The doctor will indicate the method for delivering the oxygen. Basically all facilitate providing the oxygen directly to structures involved in breathing. Some methods of delivering oxygen are more efficient in providing higher concentrations of oxygen to the patient than others. This may become a critical criterion for selecting a particular delivery method when the patient is severely hypoxaemic.

Using a nasal cannula. The simplest way to administer oxygen is through a cannula. A cannula is a hollow tube. A nasal cannula is a disposable plastic flexible tube with protruding prongs for insertion into the patient's nostrils. The tube is then positioned over the ears and under the chin. The cannula can be self-adjusted to fit the patient comfortably without occluding the supply of oxygen. The patient in Figure 13-16 is receiving oxygen by nasal cannula. A cannula's advantage is that it allows the patient to eat and talk normally.

A nasal cannula is often used by a patient receiving oxygen at home. A relatively small cylinder of oxygen is held in the hand, strapped to the back, or fastened to a cylinder holder that can be pulled about easily.

Using an oxygen mask. Various types of masks for administering oxygen are available. One type is a simple, plastic disposable one, Hudson or MC. It allows some room air to enter the mask. The air mixes with the oxygen so that dangerously high levels of oxygen are not inhaled by the patient. They are used in the short term only.

Another type is the Venturi mask, shown in Figure 13-17. It allows air to enter the mask and exhaled carbon dioxide to leave the mask at special ports. It can supply up to 40% oxygen; the level of oxygen in the atmosphere is nearly 20%.

Two types of masks have a reservoir bag. The patient breathes oxygen from the bag through the mask. One is the partial rebreathing mask, which provides a moderately high concentration of oxygen because of its design. It allows some room air to enter the device but eliminates carbon dioxide so that the patient does not rebreathe his own exhaled carbon dioxide. The partial rebreathing mask is most often used for patients who are seriously ill and in need of fairly high concentrations of oxygen. An example is a patient acutely ill with pneumonia.

The second type of mask with a reservoir bag is a nonrebreathing mask, which provides the patient with the highest concentration of oxygen. It allows

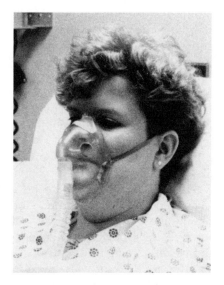

Figure 13-17 This shows a disposable oxygen mask in place. Most patients find the elastic strap to be most comfortable when placed just above the ears and around the back of the head.

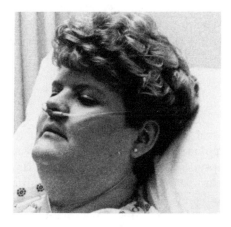

Figure 13-16 This shows how a nasal cannula is secured so that the prongs remain in the nostrils.

little or no air to enter the reservoir bag and exhaled air leaves the mask. A nonrebreathing mask is most often used for patients with smoke inhalation or carbon monoxide poisoning who require very high concentrations of oxygen, up to 90 to 100%.

A disadvantage of all oxygen masks is that they do not allow the patient to eat and talk normally. If a patient is taking nourishment by mouth, the mask needs to be removed and a cannula or catheter used while the patient eats.

In general, masks are uncomfortable for most patients. They tend to irritate the skin where they rest on the face. Another disadvantage is that they often aggravate feelings of claustrophobia (fear of small enclosed areas). Despite its other disadvantages, however, a mask is best suited for a patient who breathes through the mouth.

Using an oxygen tent. An oxygen tent is a light, portable structure made of clear plastic and attached to a motor-driven unit. The motor circulates air in the tent. A thermostat in the unit keeps the tent at a comfortable temperature for the patient. The tent fits over the top part of the bed so that the patient's head and chest fit inside of it. Oxygen is supplied to the tent through a special opening.

The tent is seldom used now for adults because other methods for delivering oxygen have been found to be more efficient, very handy and less cumbersome. However, the nurse may still find tents being used with children, who are less likely to keep a cannula, catheter, or mask in place. Tents may also facilitate the combination of oxygen and humidification therapy for children with croup, bronchitis and other respiratory conditions. The tent permits unrestrained movement and is less likely to cause excessive dryness of mucous membranes. A face tent or face hood may be placed over the head of small infants and children who are not likely to move about in bed.

Using a tracheostomy collar or T-piece. Several devices, like the T-piece shown in Figure 13-18, permit oxygen and humidification to be delivered directly to a tracheostomy. It is common for the water used for humidification to condense within the tubing. Therefore, these devices need to be removed, drained, and cleaned frequently.

Principles of Care 13-5 provides a summary of the care that should be provided when the patient receives oxygen therapy by various common methods of delivery. Whenever implementing the actions that are described, it is assumed that the nurse will have

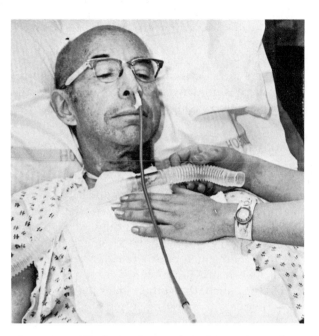

Figure 13-18 The large plastic tubing fastened over the tracheostomy is called a T-piece. It supplies moistened air or oxygen to the patient. The tube in the patient's nostril is a nasogastric tube, used for giving this patient nourishment and oral medications.

provided an explanation of its use and implemented safety precautions related to the environment and the source of the oxygen supply.

Maintaining water-seal drainage

There may be times when a lung partially or completely collapses. When this happens, the pleural space fills with air, called a *pneumothorax*, or it fills with blood, called a *haemothorax*. It is possible that both may be present at the same time.

The lung collapses due to the loss of negative pressure within the pleural space. The atmospheric air, which is higher in pressure, moves into and remains within the pleural space. The lung is no longer able to expand completely during each inhalation. Gas exchange is severely impaired.

Water-seal drainage may be instituted to remove the accumulated air or blood and gradually re-expand the collapsed lung. When water-seal drainage is used, the nurse must understand the equipment and the measures necessary for maintaining its care.

Many types of commercially manufactured systems, such as the one in Figure 13-19, are being used now for water-seal drainage and have replaced the

Principles of Care 13-5. Administering oxygen

Nursing Action	Rationale
Observe practices of medical asepsis.	The upper respiratory passages are not considered sterile.
Assist the patient into a position of comfort, usually a variation of a Fowler's position.	Fowler's position reduces the effort of breathing by promoting more area for lung expansion.
Check the flow meter and level of fluid for humidification frequently during the course of time that the patient receives oxygen therapy.	The nurse must administer the prescribed amount of oxygen while ensuring its proper humidification. Administering too little or too much oxygen may endanger the patient's life.
Provide special hygiene measures for the nose and mouth that keep the tissues moist, lubricated, fresh and clean during the course of therapy.	Oxygen is drying to mucous membranes. The patient may mouth breathe and be too fatigued to take adequate fluids or initiate hygiene measures independently.

Care When Using a Nasal Cannula

Attach the nasal cannula to the humidified oxygen source. Start the oxygen at the rate that will deliver the prescribed percentage of oxygen.	Starting oxygen and making certain that the apparatus is functioning properly are less frightening, safer, and more comfortable for the patient than starting oxygen after the cannula is in place.
Determine that the oxygen is flowing by placing the prongs of the cannula in a glass of water.	The oxygen should form bubbles when the prongs are submerged in water.
Dry the cannula well before applying it to the nose.	Large droplets of inhaled moisture may cause choking. A wet cannula next to the skin is likely to feel uncomfortable.
Place the prongs of the cannula in the nostrils. Secure the cannula in place.	Oxygen is delivered from the tips of the prongs into the nose efficiently when the cannula is in a good position on the patient.
Instruct the patient to breathe through his nose.	Oxygen may be lost and never reach the lungs in sufficient therapeutic amounts when the patient mouth breathes.
Move the cannula slightly from time to time. Use small gauze squares to pad areas where the cannula tends to create pressure and irritate the skin.	While still having the cannula in place, changing the position and cushioning help relieve pressure and aid absorption of moisture from next to the skin.
Remove and clean the cannula every 8 hours or more often if indicated.	A soiled cannula is uncomfortable and unpleasant for the patient.
Cleanse the nostrils around the cannula as necessary.	Accumulated secretions at the nostrils are uncomfortable for the patient and will irritate the skin and mucous membrane.

Continued

use of glass bottles. Regardless of what type is used, the nurse can expect that one or two large-sized catheters will extend from the upper or lower chest of the patient. The catheter(s) will drain into a collection chamber. The system is designed to prevent atmospheric air from re-entering the pleural space by partially filling one of the chambers in the drainage device with water; hence the term water-seal drain-

Principles of Care 13-5. Continued

Nursing Action	Rationale
Care Using a Face Mask	
Attach the tubing from the face mask to the source of oxygen.	Oxygen must be humidified; moisture may be present from the patient's exhalations into the mask, but humidity is also usually added.
Turn on the oxygen to prescribed rate of flow.	When the mask is placed over the patient's face, the patient can feel fearful of suffocating unless sufficient levels of oxygen are immediately available.
Adjust the mask in place to cover the nose and mouth. Fill open spaces between the skin and the mask with gauze.	More accurate concentrations of oxygen can be delivered when a mask conforms to the face and potential sites for leakage are sealed.
Check the flow of oxygen is at the prescribed rate once the mask has been in place for several minutes.	The administration of oxygen must continue at the prescribed rate once a sufficient level has been achieved.
Use a mask with a reservoir bag to deliver oxygen ordered above 60% concentration.	It is difficult to achieve an oxygen concentration above 60% without using a reservoir bag.
Encourage the patient to breathe normally and help him to relax if he seems to struggle while receiving oxygen.	Support and instructions from the nurse may relieve anxiety and restore a more normal pattern to breathing.
Assess that the reservoir bag used for delivering oxygen does not collapse more than halfway during inspiration.	Oxygen flows directly into the bag and sufficient amounts may not be available at the time of each breath.
Remove and clean the mask at least every 8 hours, or more often as indicated.	Moisture may accumulate within the mask, making it uncomfortable and unpleasant to the patient.
Wash the face and dry it well each time the mask is removed.	Evaporation is reduced in the area where the mask is applied. Skin care is essential to remove accumulated secretions and maintain cleanliness.
Care When Using an Oxygen Tent	
Inspect the tent for tears, nonfunctioning zippers, or ports in need of repair.	Oxygen will escape from the tent through any opening.
Place the tent over the upper portion of the bed.	Only the nose and mouth must be exposed to the oxygen. Covering the upper body provides room for movement and lessens feelings of claustrophobia.
Flood the tent with oxygen to achieve the desired level prescribed.	Each time the tent is opened, it will take an increased volume of oxygen to restore the concentration to its prescribed amount.
Tuck all the edges of the tent securely beneath the mattress. Use a bath blanket to enfold the edge of the tent that covers the upper body of the patient.	Oxygen can leak out through open spaces.
Check the level of oxygen in the tent using an oxygen analyser. Fill and maintain the liquid used for humidification. Regulate the temperature setting that will be maintained within the tent.	Enclosing an individual can be hazardous if the amount of oxygen, the humidity and environmental temperature within the tent are not adequate for safety.
Supply the patient with a device for summoning the nurse.	The patient may feel anxious within the tent and must know that it is possible to call someone to come to his assistance.

Continued

Principles of Care 13-5. Continued

Nursing Action	Rationale
Using a Tracheostomy Collar or T-Piece	
Attach the device to the neck so that it covers the tracheostomy opening.	An individual with a tracheostomy does not breathe through his nose or mouth, but through the stoma.
Regulate the flow rate of oxygen.	The flow rate must be set at the amount necessary to deliver the percentage of oxygen prescribed by the doctor.
Regulate the temperature of the humidified gas.	Warming the nebulized fluid increases the amount of moisture present in the oxygen.
Use large-sized tubing from the oxygen source to the patient.	Condensation occurs less rapidly when the diameter of the tubing is increased.
Assess frequently for the accumulation of condensation within the tracheostomy collar or T-piece.	The fine mist droplets in the nebulized fluid tend to become larger as condensation occurs.
Remove the collar or T-piece frequently to drain and clean the tubing.	Moisture can be aspirated. The wet condition within the tubing can support the growth of pathogens.
Suction the tracheostomy and provide tracheostomy care as frequently as necessary when moisture accumulates.	The moisture increases the potential for such complications as aspiration, skin breakdown and infection.

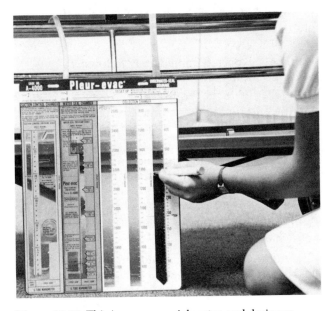

Figure 13-19 This is a commercial water-seal drainage system. This model contains chambers for drainage, water-seal, and suction.

age. A vent will be located in the system to permit air from within the pleural space to escape. As the air and blood drain from the pleural space, the lung will gradually re-expand. Suction may or may not be applied. When suction is used, it can speed the evacuation of fluid or air.

Principles of Care 13-6 provides suggested actions for maintaining water-seal drainage.

Administering cardiopulmonary resuscitation

Cardiopulmonary resuscitation, commonly abbreviated CPR, consists of techniques to open and maintain a good airway and provide for artificial ventilation of the lungs and circulation of the blood. It is performed on a person who has suffered sudden and unexpected failure of the cardiopulmonary system. The term rescue breathing is sometimes used for artificial ventilation. It means using the rescuer's breath to revive someone who is unable to breathe for himself. *External cardiac compression* is the rhythmic administration of pressure on the chest wall as a substitute for normal heart contractions.

The ABCs of basic life support. The procedure of cardiopulmonary resuscitation is often described as the ABCs of basic life support.

A is for Airway
B is for Breathing
C is for Circulation

Principles of Care 13-6. Maintaining water-seal drainage

Nursing Action	Rationale
Place the patient in Fowler's position or turned somewhat toward the side on which the chest tube has been inserted.	Gravity will help to move secretions in the direction of the drainage tube.
Assess the patient's lung sounds, TPR and BP, colour and effort of breathing.	A baseline of assessments can be used to mark the progress of the patient's response to treatment.
Expect that no lung sounds will be heard over the areas in which the lung is deflated.	Air will only be moving in the functioning areas of the lung.
Inspect all connections to determine that they are secure and air tight. Tighten or tape connections, as the hospital policy indicates.	Air must be prevented from entering the system or the lung will continue to remain collapsed. Connections may be taped to ensure that they will not separate.
Inspect the fluid level in the water-seal chamber and keep it filled to the 2 cm level.	Water must be present to prevent atmospheric air from entering the drainage system. It may slowly evaporate.
Pinch off the tubing leading to the suction control chamber, if it is being used, to inspect the level of water. Keep the water level at 20 cm.	When suction is operating there may be so much bubbling that it may be difficult to assess the water level.
Check the pressure level of the suction gauge.	Suction should be adjusted to produce constant gentle bubbles in the fluid in the suction control chamber.
Observe the nature and amount of drainage in the collection chamber.	The characteristics of the drainage indicate the volume and type of drainage being removed from the pleural space.
Report bright red bleeding or a volume that exceeds 100 ml per hour.	Bleeding is expected immediately following insertion, but it should be dark red and the volume should gradually decrease.
Mark the levels of drainage on the collection chamber. Initial, date, and mark the time of the levels.	Marking and timing the drainage level aids objective assessment and promotes accurate recording and calculation of fluid output.
Do not empty the collection container routinely.	Emptying the collection chamber increases the risk that air will enter the pleural space when the equipment is disconnected.
Observe that the level of water in the water-seal chamber rises and falls in synchrony with the patient's respirations.	As the pressures within the thorax change with breathing, the level of the water will coincide with those changes.
Become concerned if the fluid fails to rise and fall within the water-seal chamber during ventilation.	Failure of the water to fluctuate can be a welcome sign that the lung is expanded. Or, it may mean that the tubing is occluded.
Report constant bubbling in the water-seal chamber.	Constant bubbling may mean that an air leak is present. Periodic bubbling may occur as a result of the suction pulling air through the water-seal fluid.
Clamp the tubing for an instant using a haemostat close to the chest insertion site if constant bubbling is observed in the water-seal chamber.	If bubbling continues, the air leak exists below the level of the clamp.

Continued

Principles of Care 13-6. *Continued*

Nursing Action	Rationale
Release and reclamp the haemostat at increasing increments down the length of the tube until the bubbling stops.	When the bubbling stops, it can be assumed that the air leak is between the clamp and the last location that was assessed.
Tape the tubing in the area of the air leak.	The tape will seal the air leak and re-establish the full function of the water-seal drainage system.
Keep the drainage device level below the area of the chest. Chest tubes may be curled on the bed but should hang straight into the collection chamber.	Straight gravity drainage helps maintain continuous movement of fluid into the collection chamber.
Avoid kinks in the drainage tube(s) or obstruction from the body weight of the patient.	If the tubing is occluded, drainage will not occur and pressure will build within the pleural space.
Encourage coughing and deep breathing at least every 2 hours.	Coughing and deep breathing aid in removing secretions from the upper airway and help force more air and drainage out from between the pleural space.
Encourage the patient to move about in bed, ambulate if allowed, and exercise the shoulder on the side of the drainage tube(s).	Inactivity should be avoided. Patients have a tendency to hold their shoulder rigid on the side of the chest tube(s). Exercise maintains the joint's range of motion.
Assess the skin area around the insertion site. Feel and listen for air crackling in the tissues.	Air may escape into the tissue around the insertion site rather than through the tubing. The crackling sound is called *crepitus*.
Milk the tubing only if absolutely necessary to remove secretions that interrupt drainage.	Stripping the tubing creates a dramatic increase in negative pressure that may injure pleural membranes. This action should never be performed routinely.
Do not clamp the tubing for an extended period of time. Temporary clamping may be indicated when the entire drainage device will be changed, but this should be accomplished within 2 minutes.	When air in the pleural space has no route for escape, it can compress the re-expanding lung causing increased tension within the pleural space.
Insert an accidentally disconnected chest tube into a container of water rather than clamping the tubing.	A partial pneumothorax is better than a tension pneumothorax.
Disconnect the tube leading to the suction source to transport a patient. Keep the drainage collector below the level of the patient.	Drainage will be temporarily removed by gravity only.
Continue to assess lung sounds, vital signs and the effort of breathing throughout the time that water-seal drainage is used.	Periodic documentation should record the progress of the patient and the effectiveness of the treatment.

The letter A means that the respiratory tract must be opened so that air can enter and leave the victim's lungs. The letter B means that if the victim does not start to breathe spontaneously after the airway is opened, artificial ventilation must be started.

The letter C means that if the victim is pulseless, artificial circulation must be started along with rescue breathing.

The carotid artery is recommended for checking the pulse of an adult. It is an easily accessible artery when

Principles of Care 13-7. Performing cardiopulmonary resuscitation

Nursing Action	Rationale
Two Rescuers	
Place the victim on a flat, firm surface, such as the floor, ground, or a wooden board. The legs may be slightly elevated.	During cardiac compression, the firm surface on which the victim lies prevents dissipation of pressure on the sternum. There will be inadequate blood flow to the brain if the victim is in a vertical position. Lying flat with the legs slightly elevated promotes blood flow to the brain.
Place one rescuer on one side of the victim's head; this rescuer will provide artificial ventilation. Place the second rescuer on the victim's opposite side near his chest; this rescuer will provide artifical circulation, if it is needed.	Having the rescuers positioned as described allows for maximum efficiency when assessing the victim and administering artificial ventilation and circulation.
First Rescuer	
Attempt to arouse the victim by shaking and shouting.	Stimulating the patient may restore consciousness.
Send someone to notify emergency personnel if the victim does not respond.	Advanced life support techniques may be needed if basic efforts to restore breathing and circulation are ineffective.
Tilt the victim's head backward as far as possible by placing one hand on the victim's forehead and one under the neck. Lift up with the hand under the neck and press down with the hand on the forehead. This is illustrated in Figure 13-20.	Tilting the victim's head backward opens the airway by extending the neck and lifting the tongue from the throat.
—or—	
If the airway does not open with the above manoeuvre, the jaw thrust method should be used. Move to the top of the victim's head and place the fingers behind the victim's jaws. Push the jaw forward. This may be followed by slightly tilting the head backward; use the thumbs to retract the lower lip. This is illustrated in Figure 13-21.	This technique may be attempted secondarily when tilting the head and lifting the jaw does not open the airway; it should be the method of choice when the victim has a possible neck injury.

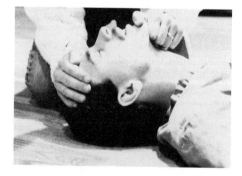

Figure 13-20 The rescuer opens the victim's airway by tilting the head backwards.

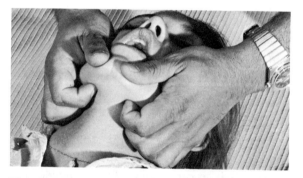

Figure 13-21 In this case, the rescuer opens the victim's airway by pushing the jaw forward while tilting the head back.

Remove any objects or vomited substances within the mouth.	Loose objects or liquid substances can be forced further within the airway as resuscitation efforts continue.

Continued

Principles of Care 13-7. *Continued*

Nursing Action	Rationale

First Rescuer

Nursing Action	Rationale
After the airway is open and cleared, listen for breathing and watch to see whether the chest or abdomen is rising and falling.	If the patient is breathing, there is no need to administer artificial ventilation.
While keeping the head tilted backward with one hand under the victim's neck and one on the forehead, pinch the victim's nose shut with a finger and thumb from the hand that is on the victim's forehead, as illustrated in Figure 13-22.	Keeping the head tilted backward helps maintain an open airway. Pinching the nose shut allows maximum ventilation with no loss of air through the nostrils.

Figure 13-22 The rescuer is ready to blow breath forcefully into the victim's mouth. Notice that the rescuer has pinched the nose shut so that air does not escape.

Nursing Action	Rationale
Prepare to administer two rescue breaths into the mouth of the victim.	Air delivered from the rescuer to the victim has an adequate amount of oxygen to sustain life.
Take a deep breath, seal your lips around the victim's widely open mouth, and blow a forceful breath lasting 1 to 1½ seconds. Lift your face away from the victim and allow him to exhale passively. The chest should visibly rise and then fall.	The force of rescue breathing needs to be sufficient so that the chest visibly rises when air is forced into the victim's mouth and then visibly falls with the victim's passive exhalation. The rescuer will note resistance in his own airway and can hear and feel air leave the victim when rescue breathing is given properly.
Repeat the above procedure once more.	Giving breaths that last 1 to 1½ seconds after taking the time for a full breath will prevent distention of the stomach with air, which could lead to vomiting and aspiration of vomitus.
—or—	
Cover the victim's nose with your mouth and administer the ventilations, if it is impossible to develop a good seal around the victim's mouth. Open the victim's lips between rescue breaths to allow the escape of air.	This technique may be used on an adult when the rescuer cannot develop or maintain an airtight passage into the respiratory tract.
Feel for a carotid pulse by lightly pressing two fingers into the groove between the trachea and the muscles at the sides of the neck.	The carotid artery is a large vessel and is likely to produce more obvious pulsations than could be felt at other peripheral sites on an adult.
Continue with one rescue breach every 5 seconds, each lasting 1 to 1½ seconds, as long as the adult victim shows respiratory inadequacy.	A minimum of 12 regularly spaced rescue breaths per minute has been found to supply any victim over the age of 8 with sufficient oxygen to maintain cell integrity.
Continue to tilt the victim's head backward during all artificial ventilation.	Keeping the head tilted throughout artificial ventilation helps maintain an open airway.

Continued

Principles of Care 13-7. Continued

Nursing Action	Rationale
First Rescuer	
Check for the presence of a pulse every few minutes. If the victim is pulseless, prepare to coordinate administering ventilations with cardiac compressions.	Resuscitation must provide ventilation and circulation when the victim's own cardiopulmonary system no longer functions.
Second Rescuer	
Place the width of the heel (the part near the wrist) of one hand over the long axis of the lower half of the sternum, but about 3.75 cm (1½ inches) from the xiphoid process.	Keeping pressure off the xiphoid process at the tip of the sternum prevents possible liver injury and internal haemorrhaging.
Place the second hand over the first hand; the fingers should interlock. Bring the shoulders directly over the hands and keep the elbows and arms straight. This is illustrated in Figure 13-23.	Interlocking the fingers helps keep them off the victim's ribs, where pressure may cause fractures. This position, with the elbows and arms straight, allows for best exertion of pressure on the sternum over the heart.

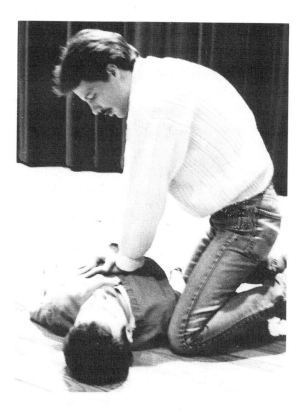

Figure 13-23 The rescuer compresses the victim's chest wall so that blood is forced from the heart and into the vascular system. Note that the rescuer's fingers are interlocked, his elbows are straight and his shoulders are positioned over the victim's chest for most effective compression.

Exert pressure on the sternum by rocking forward slightly so that pressure is applied almost vertically downward. Depress the sternum a minimum of 4 to 5 cm (1½ to 2 inches) on anyone over the age of 8 and then relax pressure immediately, but without using a bouncing movement.	The depression of the sternum with pressure causes the heart to be compressed and forces blood into the aorta and pulmonary arteries. Relaxation of pressure allows the heart to expand and refill.

Continued

Principles of Care 13-7. Continued

Nursing Action	Rationale
Second Rescuer	
Keep the hands in proper position and on the victim's chest wall between compressions while applying no pressure, so that the heart can fill with blood.	Keeping the hands in place over the sternum helps to administer regular and even compressions.
Allow a pause after each 5 compressions to permit the administration of a rescue breath that lasts 1 to 1½ seconds.	A brief pause during ventilation further prevents the possibility of inducing vomiting or aspiration.
Continue with compressions and relaxations at a rate of 80 to 100 per minute as long as the victim's heart does not beat spontaneously.	A compression rate of 80 to 100 per minute will maintain adequate blood pressure and flow to maintain cell integrity for all victims except infants up to 1 year of age. A faster rate, identified in Table 13-2, is necessary for infants.
Check the effectiveness of CPR after the first minute and then regularly every few minutes by noting whether the pupils respond to light, whether there is pulsation at the carotid artery, and whether the victim shows improvement in skin colour.	When pupils constrict in the presence of light, adequate blood flow with oxygenated blood is reaching the brain. The carotid artery is large, centrally located, and ordinarily readily accessible. Colour and pulsation will return spontaneously when the victim's heart begins to beat on its own.
Enlist assessment assistance from the rescuer providing ventilations or a third person so that CPR is never interrupted for longer than 7 seconds.	CPR should be performed without interruptions in order to facilitate the maximum oxygenation and circulation for the victim.
One Rescuer	

The procedure of CPR is as described above when there is only one rescuer to perform artificial ventilation and circulation, *except*:

When no one is available to assist, the rescuer should begin resuscitation efforts for a full minute and call for emergency assistance. If circumstances are such that this is impossible, resuscitation should be uninterrupted.

Administer two rescue breaths after each 15 cardiac compressions. Repeat this pattern for a total of 4 cycles per minute. The same rates of compression apply whether CPR is performed by one or two rescuers.

clothing about the neck is removed. Also, arteries in the extremities may be pulseless when a pulse can still be felt at the large carotid artery, even when the heartbeat is of poor quality. A femoral artery is satisfactory but is ordinarily not as accessible as the carotid.

Indications for cardiopulmonary resuscitation. When no breathing or pulse can be felt and signs of death are not pronounced, resuscitation efforts are made. However, it is not generally administered when prolonged cardiac arrest is suspected, such as when the person has been found dead, and signs indicate that he has been dead for some time.

Dilemmas occur when it is established that a person is terminally ill. If the person is a patient in a hospital, it is more than likely that there will be technology and personnel available at the time of death to revive the patient successfully. The choice as to whether cardiopulmonary resuscitation will be performed, in this situation, is usually discussed with the patient and the family. The wishes of the individuals involved are recorded on the patient's permanent record and on the nursing Kardex so that all personnel are aware of the directives concerning resuscitation.

Performing cardiopulmonary resuscitation. Principles of Care 13-7 describes and illustrates CPR for

Table 13-1. Common errors during cardiopulmonary resuscitation

Error	Effect
The airway is not patent.	Air cannot enter the lungs in sufficient quantity to sustain life when the airway is not open.
The head is tilted back too far and with too much force when a cervical injury is present.	The head tilt may cause damage to the victim's spinal cord in the area of the injury. A modified jaw thrust is recommended, in which the head is maintained in a neutral position rather than tilted backward.
The seal made by the rescuer's mouth over the victim's mouth or nose is broken.	Sufficient air will not enter the victim's lungs when the seal formed by the rescuer's mouth is not secure.
The rescue breaths are of insufficient force to cause the victim's chest to rise with each one.	When the victim's chest does not visibly rise and fall with each complete rescue breath, sufficient air for adequate ventilation is not entering the lungs.
Artificial ventilation is too forceful or it is administered when there is an airway obstruction.	There will be distention of the stomach if artificial ventilation is too forceful. This occurs more commonly in children than in adults. The danger is that distention tends to cause vomiting and predisposes the patient to aspiration, and it causes the diaphragm to rise and interfere with proper artificial ventilation and circulation.
The fingers of the rescuer who is placing pressure on the sternum rest on the ribs of the victim during compression.	Pressure on the rib cage caused by the fingers of the rescuer may result in fractures of the ribs.
The xiphoid process is depressed during cardiac compression.	Depression of the xiphoid process may rupture the liver and cause internal haemorrhaging.
Some pressure is maintained between cardiac compressions on the victim's chest wall.	When complete relaxation after each cardiac compression is not maintained, the heart cannot adequately fill with blood.
The sternum is depressed less than the recommended distance.	Blood flow and pressure will be insufficient to maintain cell integrity.
The rescuer administering cardiac compression is not properly positioned directly over the victim and/or has his elbows bent.	The thrust of compression will be ineffective when the rescuer is improperly positioned. Also, the rescuer will tire more quickly.
Sudden, irregular, or jerking movements are made during cardiac compressions.	Sudden, irregular, and jerking movements tend to cause injuries and are ineffectual for maintaining good blood flow and pressure.
CPR is interrupted for more than 7 seconds. If a victim *must* be intubated or moved, the interruption should not exceed 15 seconds.	Ventilation and circulation quickly become inadequate, and cell integrity suffers, when CPR is interrupted.

adults using either one or two rescuers. Administering CPR can be tiring and, when possible, it is better to have two rescuers who can switch responsibilities from time to time.

Before starting cardiac compressions, it is particularly important to be sure the victim is pulseless.

If a pulse is present and compressions are given, the victim may develop a potentially fatal cardiac arrhythmia. Table 13-1 lists common errors when giving CPR and the effects of these mistakes on the victim. Various modifications in CPR techniques should be made depending upon the age of the

Table 13-2. Differences in CPR among infants, children and adults

Technique	Infant (to 1 year)	Child (1 to 8 years)	Adult (8 years + older)
Rescue breaths			
Initial:	2 breaths	2 breaths	2 breaths
Subsequent breaths:	1 every 3 seconds	1 every 4 seconds	1 every 5 seconds
Rate:	20/minute	15/minute	12/minute
With chest compressions:	1 breath to 5 compressions	1 breath to 5 compressions	1 breath to 5 compressions
Duration:	1 to 1½ seconds	1 to 1½ seconds	1 to 1½ seconds
Compressions			
Location:	In the midline, one finger's width below the nipples.	Two finger widths above the tip of the sternum.	Two finger widths above the tip of the sternum.
Hand use:	Two fingers (or, in neonates, encircle the infant's chest with both hands and compress the sternum using both thumbs)	Heel of one hand	Two hands
Rate:	At least 100 per minute	80–100/min.	80–100/min.
Depth:	½" to 1"	1" to 1½"	1½" to 2"

Adapted from American Heart Association (1986).

victim. The differences are listed in Table 13-2.

Using a self-inflating breathing bag and mask. Several self-inflating breathing bags and masks are on the market. A popular example is the Ambu bag, shown in Figure 13-24. It is used in emergency situations for artificial ventilation of the lungs and, in such instances, replaces giving mouth-to-mouth ventilation. The bag is compressed by the rescuer to force air into the lungs. It self-inflates during the time the rescuer releases pressure, allowing exhalation to occur. Oxygen need not be used but, in many situations, it is added to enrich the air.

The recommended procedure for using a self-inflating breathing bag and mask is as follows:

- Stand at the head of the patient if he is on a bed, or kneel at his head if he is on the floor. This positioning makes handling the bag and mask convenient.
- Place the mask firmly over the patient's nose and mouth with the rescuer's thumb placed near the patient's nose and the index finger near the patient's chin. The other fingers should be used

Figure 13-24 This is a self-inflating breathing bag and mask. The mask is made of transparent plastic so that the rescuer can better observe the victim.

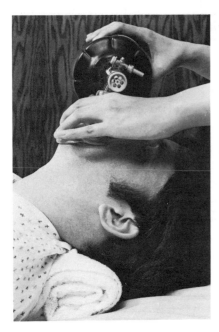

Figure 13-25 The mask is properly applied over the victim's nose and mouth, and the rescuer is ready to use the right hand to compress the bag. Note that the victim's head is placed over a rolled towel to help keep his airway open.

to hold the patient's chin up and back to keep an open airway. Otherwise, place the victim's head over a rolled towel to hyperextend the neck. Proper patient positioning, hand placement and application of equipment are illustrated in Figure 13-25.

- Spread the edges of the mask laterally if there is difficulty in getting the bag to fit tightly. When the mask returns to its normal shape, the victim's tissues will be gathered into the mask on his face and the seal will usually be tighter.
- Do not use straps to keep the mask in place. They get in the way if the victim vomits or needs to be suctioned because of accumulated mucus.
- Squeeze the bag to force inhalation and quickly release pressure on the bag to allow for exhalation.
- Compress the bag at the average normal respiratory rate unless the victim's condition indicates otherwise. This means between 16 and 20 ventilations a minute on the average for adults, faster for children, and up to 40 to 60 ventilations a minute for newborn infants.

Discontinuing cardiopulmonary resuscitation. CPR is discontinued when a person begins breathing

Figure 13-26 An infant rests on the forearm of the rescuer while his head is supported on the rescuer's hand to administer a back blow.

and his heart starts beating. If the victim does not respond to resuscitation, remains unconscious, and has pupils that are dilated even in the presence of light for as long as 30 minutes, further resuscitation efforts will probably be to no avail. However, the final decision about futher resuscitation efforts is left up to the doctor or the leader of the resuscitation team. In the meantime, the victim is given resuscitation until the rescuer is exhausted and cannot continue. Some persons have been reported to have survived without permanent brain damage even after signs of death were present for as long as an hour or two. This has been found to be the case especially

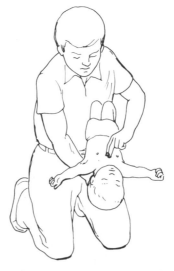

Figure 13-27 This illustrates how to administer a chest thrust to an infant.

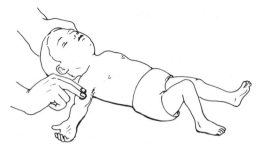

Figure 13-28 This illustrates how to obtain a pulse rate at the brachial artery of an infant.

with children involved in cold water drownings and others suffering from hypothermia.

Suggested measures to promote cardiopulmonary functioning in selected situations

When the patient is an infant or child

Assess infants and small children carefully for the need for oxygen therapy because they cannot communicate in the same manner as an adult. Flaring of the nostrils, a grunt on exhalation, restlessness, and poor skin colour are typical signs of a need for oxygen in youngsters.

Be prepared to use an isolette or oxygen hood when an infant needs oxygen therapy. An isolette fits over the cot. It is transparent, permitting the infant to be seen. Portholes are provided through which care and therapy are given. Warmed oxygen and humidity can be easily supplied to an isolette. An oxygen hood provides similar therapy but only covers the infant's head.

Be prepared to use a croupette for youngsters requiring humidified air for inhalation. A croupette has a metal frame, over which a tent is constructed with plastic sheets and linen and into which humidified air is supplied. In some instances, oxygen may also be added to the humidified air in a croupette.

Place infants and young children in the various positions for postural drainage while holding them on the lap over the thighs when they cannot maintain proper positioning in bed.

When percussing the chest wall of an infant, con-sider using a nursing nipple instead of a cupped hand. The rim of the nipple is petalled with adhesive tape in the same manner as a cast is petalled, as described in Chapter 16. The petalling provides sturdiness to the rim. Some nurses have found that a tennis ball cut in half is effective for percussing the chest wall of a young child.

When vibrating the chest wall of an infant or young child, consider using the handle of an oscillating electric toothbrush rather than the hands.

Take sufficient time to explain about a tracheostomy that is to be performed on an infant or child. Having a tracheostomy can be an extremely frightening experience for parents as well as for children.

Plan to have someone in attendance with infants and children who have a tracheostomy because they cannot signal for help and may try to remove the cannula. Restraining the elbows may be necessary in some situations but restraining does not replace the need to stay with young patients at all times.

When the victim is an infant or child, use emergency measures to relieve choking as described earlier in this chapter, with the following important differences:

For evidence of choking, note whether a child too young to speak can cry. If the airway is open, the child will be able to cry; if the airway is obstructed by a foreign object, the child will not be able to cry.

Place an infant on his abdomen while he is resting on the rescuer's forearm. Position the head of the victim lower than the rest of the body to administer four back blows with the heel of the hand between the shoulder blades when the victim is under 1 year of age, as illustrated in Figure 13-26. Otherwise, a young child can be placed crosswise over the rescuer's thighs with the head lower than the rest of the body. Having the head lower than the rest of the body permits gravity to assist in removing a foreign object from the respiratory tract.

When an infant is on his back or on the rescuer's thighs with the head lower than the rest of his body, administer chest thrusts to the middle of the sternum at about the level of the nipples, well away from the lower end of the sternum. The thrusts are administered with two fingers, as illustrated in Figure 13-27.

Avoid using abdominal thrusts in infants and children because of the danger of injuring internal organs. Use chest thrusts instead.

Give CPR to infants and children in the same manner as for adults, applying the modifications listed in Table 13-3 and the following suggestions:

Use a brachial artery to check for the pulse on an infant, as illustrated in Figure 13-28. This site is recommended by the American Heart Association. The apical pulse, which can be heard with a stethoscope or felt with a fingertip at a point under the nipple line and just to the left of the sternum, is recommended by some authorities. It is suggested that hospital policy be observed if there is a question about where to obtain a pulse rate on an infant.

Tilt the head of an infant or young child backward to open the airway very gently and without exaggeration. The neck of the very young is pliable and can be injured with relative ease.

If the child is small, the rescuer should cover both the mouth and nose with his mouth when administering artificial ventilation. Some authorities recommend covering the mouth of the rescuer with a handkerchief while administering rescue breathing.

Use rescue breaths smaller than those for an adult but deep enough to make the chest wall rise.

Teaching suggestions for promoting cardiopulmonary functioning

Teaching suggestions for helping patients promote cardiopulmonary functioning are summarized below:

Patients using oxygen at home should be taught to use safety precautions, as described in this chapter, to prevent accidents with fire. Oxygen is safe to use when its characteristic of supporting combustion is respected at all times.

Patients using oxygen at home should have careful instructions about safe amounts to use. Many persons are likely to think that if a small amount

is helpful, larger amounts may be even more helpful. The dangers of using other than prescribed amounts should be carefully explained.

Steam vaporizers may still be used in some homes. Patients and parents of children should be taught about the dangers of burns because steam humidifiers become very hot.

Some patients are discharged with a tracheostomy in place. The home care of a tracheostomy is similar to care given in a hospital. If a reusable inner cannula is used, the patient should be instructed to have several on hand so that, while cleaning one, another one is in place.

A patient with a tracheostomy who uses a reusable cannula should be taught how to clean it and maintain his care as follows:

Use a small brush or pipe cleaner while scrubbing the cannula with soap or detergent and water.

Rinse the cannula well after scrubbing it and boil it for 8 to 10 minutes, or place it in 70% alcohol for disinfection for 20 minutes or longer. Be sure to rinse the cannula well with sterile water because alcohol is irritating to mucous membranes.

Clean cannulas are best stored in a sterile, covered jar.

The patient with a tracheostomy should be instructed about reporting symptoms that indicate he may be developing a complication, such as an infection. He should also be taught the urgency of obtaining immediate medical attention if the outer cannula becomes obstructed or is dislodged.

Many lives are saved when persons at the scene of an emergency are familiar with how to administer CPR and how to relieve choking on a foreign object. Nurses are looked to as examples and sources for information. They should teach people the importance of enrolling in classes, now offered by a variety of community organizations, to learn proper techniques.

It is better to prevent choking than to have to handle an emergency when it occurs. In addition to helping people learn how to remove a foreign object from respiratory passages, the following measures should be taught concerning how best to prevent choking and how to signal for help when choking:

Do not talk or laugh with food in the mouth.

Cut food into small pieces and chew it well.

Make sure dentures fit well to prevent choking on them.

Do not drink alcoholic beverages in excess. Choking is more common when the alcohol blood level is excessive.

When choking, grasp the throat with both hands to signal for help.

Take special precautions with infants and children to prevent choking. Keep small objects, such as small toys or parts of them, coins, safety pins, nuts, popcorn and so on, away from infants and small children. Their natural curiosity often leads to emergency situations because they tend to place objects in the mouth without realizing the dangers of choking.

References

Allen, D. (1987) Making sense of tracheostomy. *Nursing Times*, **83**(45), 36–8.

Allen, D. (1988) Making sense of suctioning. *Nursing Times*, **84**(10), 46–7.

Allen, D. (1989) Making sense of oxygen delivery. *Nursing Times*, **85**(18), 40–1.

American Heart Association (1986) Standards and guidelines for cardiopulmonary resuscitation and emergency cardiac care. *Journal of the American Medical Association*, **255**, 2841–3034.

Carrie, L.E.S. and Simpson, P.J. (1982) *Understanding Anaesthesia*. Heinemann, London.

Clark Mims, B. (1987) The risks of oxygen therapy. *Registered Nurse*, July, 20–6.

De Carle, B. (1985) Tracheostomy care, occasional paper. *Nursing Times*, **81**(6), 50–4.

Mapp, C.S. (1988) Trach care—are you aware of the dangers? *Nursing (US)*, **18**(7), 34–42.

Phylip Prichard, A. and David, J.A. (1992) *Royal Marsden Hospital Manual of Clinical Nursing Procedures*, 3rd edn, Blackwell Scientific Publications, Oxford.

Further reading

Goodwin, R. (1988) Cardiopulmonary resuscitation. *Nursing Times*, **84**(34), 63–8.

Goodwin, R. (1988) Cardiopulmonary resuscitation in children. *Nursing Times*, **84**(35), 48–51.

Harkrigg, J. (1987) Rehearsing for the real thing. *Nursing Times*, **83**(45), 57–9.

McKirdy, M. (1985) Resuscitation of a collapsed patient. *Nursing Mirror*, **161**(17), 23.

Newbold, D. (1987) The physiology of cardiac massage. *Nursing Times*, **83**(25), 59–62.

Newbold, D. (1987) External chest compression—the new skills. *Nursing Times*, **83**(26), 41–3.

Openbrier, D.R., Hoffman, L.A. and Wesmiller, S.W. (1988) Home oxygen therapy—evaluation and prescription. *American Journal of Nursing*, February, 192–210.

Sloman, M. (1988) Paediatric cardiopulmonary resuscitation. *Nursing Times*, **84**(43), 50–2.

Thom, A. (1988) Who decides? *Nursing Times*, **85**(2), 35–7.

Wynne, G. and Marteau, T. (1987) Race against time. *Nursing Times*, **83**(30), 16–17.

14

The need for relaxation and sleep

Learning objectives

When the content of this chapter has been mastered, the learner should be able to:

Define terms appearing in the glossary.

List some examples of situations that can interfere with a person's biorhythms.

Discuss facts that are associated with the characteristics of sleep.

Outline the stages of sleep.

Discuss at least five factors that influence sleep.

Describe the effects of sleep loss.

Discuss the information that is essential for assessing an individual's rest and sleep.

Describe nursing measures that may be useful for promoting sleep.

List and describe five common sleep disorders.

List suggested measures for promoting comfort, rest, and sleep in selected situations as discussed in this chapter.

Summarize suggestions for instructing the patient.

Glossary

Biorhythms Body functions that occur in cycles.

Circadian rhythm Events that are repeated every 24 hours.

Endorphins Natural chemicals in the body with properties similar to morphine.

Enuresis A type of sleep disorder in which there is nightly bedwetting.

Hypnosis A technique to produce a subconscious state through suggestion by a hypnotist.

Infradian rhythm Events that repeat monthly.

Insomnia A sleep disorder characterized by difficulty in falling or remaining asleep.

Mantra A Hindu word for a sound that is repeated during prayer and meditation.

Meditation A relaxation technique in which a person excludes disturbing thoughts for those that have a calming effect.

Narcolepsy A condition characterized by an uncontrollable onset of sleep.

Nightmares A childhood sleep disorder in which the child seems to be awake and in a state of panic, yet has no memory of having had the experience.

Nonrapid eye movement A broad category referring to four distinct stages of sleep in which little movement, including eye movement, can be observed. Abbreviated NREM.

Pain A sensation of physical and/or mental suffering and hurting that causes misery or agony.

Rapid eye movement The dream stage of sleep that is associated with characteristic darting of the eyes beneath the eyelids. Abbreviated REM.

Relaxation A state in which the body is less rigid and tense.

Rest A decreased state of activity that results in a refreshed feeling.

Sleep A state of relative unconsciousness.

Sleep apnoea Periods that occur during sleep when a person does not breathe.

Somnambulism A sleep disorder characterized by sleepwalking.

Ultradian rhythm Events that repeat several times within a 24-hour period.

Yoga A special type of relaxation exercise involving bending and stretching of the body.

Introduction

Adequate sleep and relaxation is vital to the individual's feeling of well-being. Usually, having slept soundly most people awake feeling refreshed and relaxed. Although we all require approximately 7–9 hours sleep in 24 hours, the way we sleep and individual preferences vary.

- Some people prefer a duvet to a blanket.
- Some people wear night attire, whereas others prefer to sleep naked.
- Some people like to have the window open.
- Others enjoy a bedtime night cap, which can range from a milky drink to a glass of brandy.

The list is endless; from this we can see that although sleep and relaxation is a need common to all, the environment and preparation for each individual can be totally different. Fordham (1988) states that sleep can be defined in two ways: firstly as a discrete state and secondly as a continuous cycle whereby changes in the level of consciousness occur. The significance of these points to patients in hospital is that some patients have a problem with the state of sleep, whereas others have a problem with the scheduling of sleep; alternatively patients may have a "problem" with sleep related to both these points.

Just as much of our understanding of sleep and sleep patterns has grown in the last decade so has our interest in the need for relaxation.

Alternative therapies are much more in vogue now—many people incorporate massage, relaxation techniques or yoga, etc. as part of their everyday living to reduce stress and increase feelings of well-being. The public are much more aware of the hazards to health associated with tranquillizers and sleeping tablets.

Other people find they can relax by reading, going to the theatre or taking up some other hobby such as gardening or pottery.

Being able to reduce stress and tension is vital and the nurse should be able to advise the patient on how to reduce tension and forms of relaxation which he can incorporate easily into his life. Stress is one of the main factors which interferes with sleep. From this we can see that if an individual is able to relax he is more likely to be able to have a good night's sleep.

The nature of relaxation, rest and sleep

For rest or sleep to occur, an individual must be in a relaxed state. *Relaxation* is a state in which the body becomes less rigid and tense. *Rest* is a state in which the body and mind are in a decreased state of activity that produces a refreshed feeling. *Sleep* is a state in which an individual is seemingly unconscious, yet is easily aroused. During sleep, a person's perception and activity are reduced.

Promoting relaxation

Relaxation is necessary in order to feel rested. It facilitates sleep. If relaxation is achieved for even brief periods during the day, it may be sufficient to restore an individual's mental and physical resources. A person may be better able to deal with the responsibilities of life and the physical work associated with it. Principles of Care 14-1 describes some techniques that may be useful in achieving a relaxed state. *Yoga*, which is a special type of relaxation exercise, involves bending and stretching of the body. It is often combined with *meditation*, in which a person excludes disturbing thoughts for those that have a calming effect.

Biological cycles

The patterns for sleep and some other physical functions seem to reoccur in rather predictable cycles. The physical cycles often correlate with cycles in nature. They are collectively referred to as *biorhythms*. Phenomena that reoccur every 24 hours are said to be

---

Principles of Care 14-1. A simple relaxation technique

Nursing Action	Rationale
Find a room that is not associated with work or tension and that will be free from momentary distractions.	Relaxation involves altering one's state of consciousness. Decreasing stimuli helps in the transition from heightened awareness to one that can be described as peaceful.
Assume a relaxed position.	Allowing an object, such as a chair or the floor, to support the body frees a person from the muscle activity needed to overcome gravity.
If a quiet room is unavailable, close the eyes and consciously focus within oneself or think about a relaxing location.	Blocking visual stimuli and using the imagination may compensate for the inability to change one's location.
Listen to soothing music or the sounds of nature that produce a personal calming effect. Some hum a repetitive sound called a *mantra*.	The functions of the body tend to become synchronized with the slow, repetitive sounds.
Breathe slowly and deeply through the nose; concentrate on the rising and falling of the abdomen.	Tension restricts breathing. As the breathing becomes slower with concentration, the heart and other muscles will tend to follow the pattern.
Let the muscles of the body loosen as though becoming weightless. Focus on relaxing each limb and body part from the toes to the head.	Any effort to hold the muscles in a state of contraction inhibits total body relaxation.
Enjoy the feeling which relaxation produces.	Training oneself to recognize how a relaxed state feels, may help to promote the same effect again with less effort.
At the end of the period of relaxation, gradually increase movement and awareness.	The calming effect should produce an increase in the ability to cope mentally and perform physically.

---

cycling in a *circadian rhythm*. The sleep-awake pattern is an example that corresponds to the cycling of night followed by day. Events that repeat monthly, like menstruation, are on an *infradian rhythm*, similar to the monthly cycling of the moon. *Ultradian rhythm* is the term given for those physical occurrences that take place frequently in a repeated sequence during a 24-hour period. For instance, scientists now know that there are sleep cycles that reoccur in repeated patterns during sleep. The stages during sleep will be described later in this chapter.

When biorhythms become disturbed, people often feel poorly. Situations that can disturb these cycles include working the night shift and rapidly changing from one time zone to another, which produces "jet lag". Patients in intensive care units who are exposed to constant artificial light and monotonous noise may experience disturbed sleep patterns. Some develop emotional problems. These disappear when the natural pattern of sleep is restored.

Biological cycles can work to an individual's advantage. Some people can predict the time of day, or month, during which they are at the peak of productivity. Research is being carried out on plotting biorhythms to promote health.

Characteristics of normal sleep
The need for sleep varies throughout life at various ages. Table 14-1 shows the various amounts of sleep required during different stages within the life cycle. Other facts about sleep follow:

- The exact purpose and mechanism of sleep are not clearly understood. However, the importance of rest and sleep for well-being is clearly established.
- Rest and sleep generally occur best when a person is relaxed and relieved of tension and worry. One can relax without sleeping. However, sleep rarely occurs until one relaxes.

Table 14-1. Age variations in total sleep needs

Age	Total Sleep Needs
Neonate (Up to 1 month)	16–20 hours
Infant (Up to 1 year)	10–12 hours plus 2–3 naps
Toddler (1–3 years)	10–12 hours plus 1–2 naps
Preschooler (3–5 years)	9–11 hours plus 1 nap or rest period
School-age child (6–12 years)	9–11 hours
Adolescent (13–18 years)	9–11 hours
Adult (over 18 years)	7–8 hours

Reproduced by permission from Bellack and Bamford, Nursing Assessment; © Jones and Bartlett Publishers, 1984.

- The depth of unconsciousness during sleep varies. During certain periods of sleep, the person can be awakened easily. During others, it is difficult to do so. The depth of unconsciousness for the sensory perceptions also varies. For example, the sense of smell is the least perceived of the sensory experiences during sleep. This may explain why home fires gain headway because sleeping occupants do not smell the smoke. Pain and sounds seem to be easily perceived. This explains why ill persons experience sleeplessness when pain is present. Strange noises may disturb the sleep of hospitalized persons. Parents tend to wake easily to the cries of their children. Alarm clocks use sound to wake most individuals from sleep.

- Eight hours of sleep daily is generally recommended for well adults, yet some people need more to feel refreshed and some require less. Factors such as metabolic rate, age, physical condition, type of work, and amount and kind of exercise influence the amount of sleep people need. Despite such differences, healthy adults average 7 to 9 hours of sleep daily.

- Refreshing sleep can occur during any period of the day or night. Most people work during the day and sleep during the night. However, many night-time workers learn to sleep well during the day. Some people tend to work best during early morning hours; others prefer working later. There is no indication that any one of these patterns is better than another.

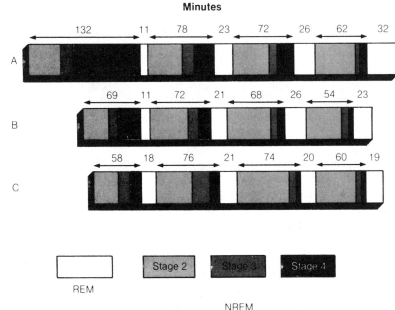

Figure 14-1 These graphs illustrate sleep patterns during the first four cycles that were identified among sleep research participants. They show variations according to age. Pattern A was found among children; pattern B was associated with young adults; pattern C occurred in normal elderly people. Note that dreaming, which occurs during REM sleep, lasts longer as sleep cycles progress. (Wolff et al., 1983.)

Stages of sleep

The total numbers of hours are spent cycling through various stages. Sleep is broadly separated into two major stages described as *nonrapid eye movement*, abbreviated NREM, and *rapid eye movement*, abbreviated REM.

There are four stages within NREM sleep. The first two stages consist of light sleep. During the third and fourth stages, the person sleeps deeply, hardly moving. Ordinarily, more sleep occurs in the fourth stage of NREM sleep in the first half of the night, especially if the person is tired.

During REM sleep, dreams take place. The eyes appear to dart about beneath closed lids. The person appears close to being awake because there is a great deal of body movement. However, it is more difficult to awaken a person during REM sleep than during NREM sleep. The cyclic patterns of the stages of sleep are illustrated in Figure 14-1. Oswald and Adam (1983) also suggest from their research that we sleep in cycles lasting approximately 90–100 minutes. During the individual's normal sleep period, four to six sleep cycles may occur. These encompass the REM and NREM stages which are now generally recognized. Professor Oswald's work at the University of Edinburgh has led to a greater understanding about sleep cycles and the nature of sleep.

Additional characteristics of NREM and REM sleep are summarized in Table 14-2.

Factors that influence sleep

The amount and quality of sleep can be affected by various factors.

Age. The amount of sleep required for well-being varies with age. The younger the person, the more sleep is required, until adulthood, when the amount of sleep necessary for well-being remains quite constant for the rest of life.

Activity. Activity, especially exercise, increases fatigue and the need for sleep to restore well-being. It appears that activity increases both REM and NREM sleep, but especially the deep sleep of the fourth stage of NREM.

Environment. Most people sleep best in their usual home environment. Certain habits that develop and conditions associated with bedtime seem to contribute to sleep. Preferences for sleepwear, the type of pillow, the numbers of blankets, room temperature and ventilation, and even lighting are factors that promote sleep. Individuals even tend to adapt to the unique sounds of their residence, like traffic, trains,

Table 14-2. Stages of sleep*

Stage	Characteristics
Sub-Stage I	This stage is a transition stage between wakefulness and sleep.
	Great relaxation is present.
	Muscle jerking may occur and awaken the person.
	The stage lasts only a few minutes.
	Arousal is easy.
Sub-Stage II	A state of sleep exists.
	Arousal is relatively easy.
Sub-Stage III	The depth of sleep increases.
	Arousal becomes increasingly difficult.
Sub-Stage IV	This stage is one of deep sleep.
	Arousal is difficult.
	Brain waves are slow, pulse and respiratory rates are decreased, blood pressure decreases, metabolism slows and body temperature is low.
REM Stage	Dreams occur during this stage.
	Respirations are irregular; apnoea may sometimes be present.
	The pulse rate is rapid and occasionally irregular.
	The blood pressure increases or fluctuates.
	Gastric secretions, metabolism and body temperature increase.
	Arousal is difficult.

*Normally, persons are observed to go through four or five sleep cycles each night, and each cycle lasts approximately 90 to 100 minutes.

and the hum of appliance motors. When these conditions are changed, as they may be if a person goes on holiday or is hospitalized, the ability to fall asleep and feel rested may be affected.

Motivation. When there is no particular reason to stay awake, sleep generally occurs easily. But if the desire to remain awake is strong, such as when a person wishes to participate in something interesting or important to him, sleep can be delayed.

Emotions. The level of awareness and the ability to sleep are influenced by many naturally occurring chemicals released as a result of emotional stimulation. Those that interfere with sleep are generally produced as a result of worry over problems that may be occurring. However, even anticipating a pleasant future event, such as a holiday, may stimulate production of these chemicals, which will cause sleeplessness.

Food and fluids. A constituent in protein (L-tryptophan), found especially in milk and other dairy products, is believed to promote sleep. A diet lacking in sufficient protein may interfere with normal sleep. Alcoholic beverages, in moderation, appear to promote sleep in some people. Excessive amounts reduce normal REM and deep sleep. Beverages containing caffeine, which is a central-nervous-system stimulant, tend to cause wakefulness. Beverages containing caffeine include coffee, tea, chocolate and most cola drinks.

Illness and drugs. The stress and anxiety commonly associated with illness disturb sleep, as does the pain that accompanies many illnesses. In the hospital many conditions interfere with the sleep of patients. These include the noise from equipment, which tends to be constant and monotonous; being interrupted with nursing and medical measures; unfamiliar sounds associated with hospital activity, such as lifts, food and tea trolleys, and housekeeping equipment. Interrupting the rest and sleep of a hospitalized person may seem unimportant when the patient appears to have little to do except rest and sleep; however, it represents poor-quality care because it interferes with well-being.

Sleep is influenced by certain drugs other than just caffeine and alcohol. Most drugs used to promote sleep, relieve anxiety, and overcome depression interfere with REM sleep. The individual may sleep but not feel rested.

The effects of sleep loss

Most individuals can lose sleep on occasion without experiencing ill effects. However, if sleep loss occurs regularly, or when an individual is totally deprived of sleep over an extended period of time, serious physical and emotional changes occur. Some of the facts that have been identified with sleep loss include the following.

- The feelings of pleasantness, reassurance and buoyancy that occur with adequate sleep are replaced by diminished energy and enthusiasm. Judgement becomes dull and normal performance of activities of daily living fades. There are lapses in attention, memory and the ability to concentrate.
- Unpleasant sensations, such as blurring of vision, itching of the eyes, nausea and headache are common signs of tiredness.
- There may be an attitude of not caring what happens and of feeling irritable and depressed, with fatigue.
- Inability to recognize reality, even experiencing hallucinations, is likely when sleep loss is prolonged. There is research being done to determine if the chemicals that become imbalanced during sleep loss are the same ones that may contribute to certain mental illnesses such as schizophrenia. They symptoms are remarkably similar.
- A person normally attempts to "catch up" on the sleep that has been lost. The fourth stage of NREM sleep generally tends to be extended when sleep occurs following sleep loss.
- When REM sleep is reduced, as occurs with the use of some drugs, the dream stage is shortened. These individuals tend to have an increased sensitivity to pain, poor judgement and increased irritability. Normal relationships with others suffer and depression becomes common. When REM sleep finally recurs, the body appears to try to make up for its losses with excessive dreaming. Nightmares are also reported among those who dream after REM sleep deprivation.

Assessing rest and sleep

The need for sleep can vary from person to person. Before planning and providing measures to promote rest and sleep, it is important to obtain information that is particular to the individual person. The following are types of information the nurse should gather and interpret:

- Learn the person's usual sleep pattern. Ask about his usual times for retiring and arising. Inquire about napping and the type of environment the patient prefers for sleep.
- Determine the individual's bedtime habits. For example, some like a snack before bedtime; others may prefer a beverage. Reading, listening to a radio or watching television can be a re-

laxing activity. For many, preparations for sleep include brushing the teeth, washing the hands and face, and going to the bathroom. A bath or shower may be preferred by some at night rather than in the morning.

- Ask about relaxation techniques the individual has found to promote sleep. Inquire about what activities of daily living, such as dietary habits and daily exercise, influence his sleep.
- Determine whether the person is experiencing any sleep disorders. Various disorders are described later in this chapter.
- Learn if and how often the person uses drugs, including alcohol, to promote sleep. Determine the name of the products used.
- Observe the person's energy level. There may be other information than this required to validate that a person is experiencing insufficient sleep. However, this plus other signs associated with fatigue, such as short concentration, yawning and "nodding off" to sleep, may be characteristics associated with sleep loss.
- If the individual is hospitalized, the nurse can determine how the patient's sleep may be influenced by his illness, medications and therapy.

Nursing measures to promote rest and sleep

As the nurse begins to know and appreciate the importance of sleep and the problems that can result with sleep loss, there should be a great deal of effort to help promote rest and sleep (Principles of Care 14-2).

Within the ward environment it can be extremely difficult for patients to sleep undisturbed. Factors which affect this are the drug rounds, phones which still ring at night, the emergency admission and nurses doing observations on patients.

A study undertaken by Goodemote (1985) demonstrated the following main points which affected patients' sleep:

- Time of settling the patients at night.
- Early waking in the morning, 5.30 A.M. on average.
- Quantity of work in relation to the number of staff on duty.
- Noise from staff carrying out work, staff "chatter", unavoidable admissions, movement

of patients and other procedures, machinery and other patients.

Based on the above points, Hill (1989) undertook a study of patients' sleep disturbance on a neuro-medical ward, a neurosurgical ward and an acute neurosurgical ward. Her results were similar to Goodemote's. From this, the following changes in the ward were proposed:

- Only essential care and observations to be carried out.
- No early morning tea unless specifically requested by the patient.
- Alterations in timing of drug rounds.
- Provision of a high care area to isolate noise which is largely unavoidable from the majority of patients.
- Alteration in nasogastric feeding to coincide with timing of other care which the patient might require.

The above is a good example of how we can organize nursing care to meet the need of patients rather than the need of the ward.

Common sleep disorders

Some unusual patterns of sleep only annoy those whose sleep is affected. They are not necessarily dangerous to the person. Others are quite serious sleep disorders and require that individuals receive special treatment. Some sleep disorders that occur with some frequency in the general population are discussed here in more depth.

Insomnia. Difficulty in falling asleep, waking during sleeping hours and early awakening from sleep describe *insomnia*. The condition may lead to such distress that further wakefulness occurs. There are some physical conditions that cause wakefulness, but insomnia is usually noted to occur during a period of personal stress and when the person is a worrier.

Having a patient keep a sleep diary is helpful to assess insomnia. Studies have shown that insomniacs tend to underestimate the time they sleep and overestimate the time it takes them to fall asleep. However, these findings do not relieve the distress that most insomniacs suffer. When a person says he has insomnia, steps to promote rest and sleep should be taken.

The following are recommended for helping overcome insomnia:

Principles of Care 14-2. *Promoting rest and sleep*

Nursing Action	Rationale
Assess the individual's sleep pattern.	Sleep is a basic need. An individual's customary sleep routine, if adequate, should be maintained in order to promote well-being.
Simulate, as much as possible, the person's usual sleep environment and rituals.	Human beings are creatures of habit. Slight deviations from personal routines may result in a disturbed sleep pattern.
Respect the person's usual time for retiring regardless of how it differs from one's own.	The time for retiring is not as critical as the total amount of sleep. Interfering with a personal biorhythm may cause sleeplessness.
Provide the person with a glass of milk or other dairy product.	Milk is a source for L-tryptophan, a component of a chemical within the body that promotes sleep.
Avoid any excess intake of foods or beverages that contain caffeine. Diet medications should also be taken with caution.	Drugs such as caffeine and those found in appetite control medications are stimulants. They may interfere with the ability to sleep.
Help the person assume a comfortable position in bed.	Good posture in a lying position and support for the musculoskeletal system facilitate comfort.
Use techniques that promote relaxation (Principles of Care 14-1).	Relaxation is a preliminary step to sleep.
Use measures to relieve pain, if that is a problem for the individual.	Pain causes anxiety. An aroused state is associated with worry, tension, and fear.
Give prescribed medications for sleep when other measures have failed.	Medications should be used with good judgement and not as a substitute for good nursing care.
Advise those individuals, such as hospitalized patients, who have sleep medications ordered that it is available if needed.	Knowing that a medication is available may provide enough reassurance that relaxation and sleep occur naturally.
Be conscientious about controlling loud or unfamiliar noises.	Sleep may be interrupted most easily through the sense of hearing.
Use every effort not to awaken or disturb an individual who is sleeping.	It is important that the stages of the sleep cycle occur in an uninterrupted fashion.
Evaluate the quality of the person's sleep by asking questions that reflect the night that just passed.	Nurses must be careful not to assume that a person is asleep just because his eyes are closed.
Discuss alternative courses of action that may promote sleep if other measures have failed.	Involving a person contributes to an individual's sense of personal control.
If the nurse is caring for a hospitalized patient, write any helpful directions that promote sleep on the nursing orders.	Specific communication promotes continuity of care. Other nurses and the patient benefit from successful prior experiences.
Consult other health personnel for help when it seems that current efforts are insufficient to promote rest and sleep.	Some people suffer from sleep disorders that may require elaborate testing and complex treatment in order to restore natural sleep.

- Advise the person to lie down for sleep only when he feels sleepy, not when he feels wakeful.
- If sleep does not occur within 20 minutes of retiring, suggest that the individual get up and do something to keep himself busy and occupied until he feels sleepy.
- Instruct the person to try to wake up and get out of bed at the same time every morning and to take no naps during the day.
- Avoid using the bed for other activities, such as reading or sewing. The bed should be used only for sleeping.
- Recommend daily exercises, but not before bedtime.

Many insomniacs tend to self-medicate themselves with drugs that do not require prescriptions. Temporary relief may be obtained, but prolonged use of these drugs may not prove beneficial. Some may go from doctor to doctor accumulating prescription drugs that they take in amounts other than directed. Caution must be advised about the dangers of substance abuse and misuse associated with this classification of drugs.

Somnambulism. *Somnambulism* is sleepwalking. It is seen more commonly in children than in adults. The danger of this disorder is that the person may suffer injury. Measures to provide safety include having secure locks on doors. If a sleepwalker is admitted to the hospital, a record should be made of this and proper precautions taken to prevent injury. The cause of sleepwalking is unknown but it has been found that certain medications taken at bedtime, such as those to control depression, most tranquillizers, and some antihistamines may lead to sleepwalking.

Snoring and Sleep Apnoea. A person who snores is a noisy nuisance to anyone sharing the same room. Snoring occurs most commonly when the person lies on his back with his head tipped forward. This position causes a narrowing of the air passageways, which, added to complete relaxation of the soft palate and uvula, results in the snoring sound.

Snoring itself is not a disorder, but sleep apnoea, which often accompanies it, is a disorder. *Sleep apnoea* refers to periods during sleep when a person does not breathe. It is most common among overweight, middle-aged men. During long periods of apnoea, the patient's body suffers from lack of sufficient oxygen and an accumulation of carbon dioxide. Then, starved for air, the patient usually resumes breathing with snoring. Sleep apnoea may be repeated hundreds of times a night in some people. For some, it can become life-threatening and fatal if the apnoea is not interrupted. Awakening the person will restore breathing.

Sleep talking. From observations, it appears that almost everyone talks in his sleep at some time. It rarely presents a problem unless the talking disturbs persons sharing the same room.

Narcolepsy. *Narcolepsy* is a neurologic disorder. Its primary symptom is an uncontrollable onset of sleep. The danger is that the person with the condition may fall asleep while carrying out potentially dangerous activities, such as driving a car or swimming. Persons with narcolepsy need close watching so that they do not suffer injury. Fortunately, drugs that cause wakefulness have been used effectively for controlling the condition. However, the drugs must be taken faithfully throughout an affected person's lifetime to avoid a return of symptoms.

Suggested measures related to pain, rest and sleep in selected situations

When the individual is an infant or child

Use distraction when caring for an infant or child in pain. Using mobiles over a crib and encouraging play with favourite toys often distract attention from pain. Singing, tapping a homemade instrument, or clapping with a song may also be tried.

As soon as a child is old enough to understand, explain when something will hurt. Saying that a procedure will not cause pain when it will is deceptive. A youngster will quickly lose confidence in his care takers.

Tell a child that it is all right to cry if he hurts. This technique often relieves tension and makes the youngster feel that he is being accepted even though he cries.

Expect that newborns and young infants sleep most of the time. It is best to rotate their sleeping position from side to side. It is difficult for regurgitated and vomited material to leave the mouth when the infant is in the back-lying position. It is generally recommended that an infant not be placed on his abdomen for sleep unless he is old enough to raise his head. This prevents danger of suffocation. Pillows are not recommended for infants because of the danger of suffocation.

Expect that the amount of sleep children require decreases with age. Children ordinarily take naps until about school age.

Newborns and infants may manifest sleep apnoea, which some believe is a factor in infant cot deaths. Sleep monitors are available for children who have sleep apnoea. These monitors sound alarms if the child stops breathing.

Cuddle and rock infants and toddlers to promote relaxation and sleep.

Some children experience nightmares. Parents may find that avoiding stories or television programmes that are apt to suggest fears to the child are helpful in preventing nightmares. *Nightmares* are a type of childhood sleep disorder in which the child seems to be awake and in a state of panic. The child does not seem to respond to questions by concerned family members trying to soothe the child. The child generally has no memory of the episode. It is more frightening to the family than to the child.

Enuresis is involuntary urination and is often called bed-wetting. Because enuresis occurs at night, it is commonly considered a disorder of sleep. Children who experience frequent bed-wetting should always be examined by a doctor to make sure that no urinary problems are the cause. The greatest problem with bed-wetting is the damage that can occur to a child's self-esteem. Enuresis is an uncommon disorder among adults.

When the individual is elderly

Carefully observe the elderly person whose sense organs may have diminished with age. This person may have tissue damage without the usual sensation of pain.

Be aware that the sleep patterns of the elderly vary widely but that they tend to sleep less at night and do more napping than younger adults. Some persons state that elderly persons require less sleep than younger persons because of less activity and exercise.

Take into account that elderly people typically require more time to fall asleep, find it more difficult to change sleep patterns, are awake more often during sleeping hours, retire and awaken earlier, and show more concern about sleep than do younger adults.

Assess an elderly person's diet in relation to protein when sleep is poor. A combination of a low-protein intake and the poorer absorption of food nutrients in the elderly may account for unsatisfactory sleep.

In planning, remember that the elderly prefer a warmer room in which to sleep than do younger adults. Use extra covers as necessary for their comfort.

Teaching suggestions related to pain, rest and sleep

Summarized below are some suggestions to promote sleep and rest in those patients suffering from pain.

Very few people understand pain. Therefore, an important responsibility for nurses is to explain its cause and the reasons behind measures used to relieve it. From an understanding of pain, people are in a better position to help cooperate in its control.

Many remedies are available to help control pain. Unfortunately, most people turn to the use of medications immediately. Nurses have an important role in helping people explore other measures to relieve pain.

Sleep also is poorly understood by most people. As with pain, teaching about sleep helps individuals cooperate more fully when using measures to promote rest and sleep. This type of teaching will also facilitate an understanding of normal changes in sleep patterns so that people do not become unduly concerned when there are sleep changes during the life cycle.

There are many measures to help promote relaxation and sleep. Individuals should be taught about alternative ways to overcome sleeplessness so that they are less likely to use medications unnecessarily.

It is a fallacy that everyone needs 8 hours of sleep every night. The fact is that sleep is a highly individual matter. It has been demonstrated that for some, more or less than 8 hours of sleep promotes well-being.

A great variety of medications for relieving pain and sleeplessness is available. Sleeping medications have been observed to lose their effectiveness after a week or two of use. Using medications that do not require a prescription may delay a person from seeking medical attention.

15

Admitting, transferring and discharging the individual

Learning objectives

When the content of this chapter has been mastered, the learner should be able to:

Define terms appearing in the glossary.

Describe current trends in health care.

Describe at least four common emotional reactions that occur during hospitalization.

Discuss ways that a nurse can reduce or eliminate the emotional effects associated with admission to hospital.

Identify the nurse's responsibilities during admission to a hospital.

Discuss the nursing actions that are important during the transfer of a patient within a hospital or to another hospital.

Discuss the purpose of a referral and typical information included in a referral.

Describe how a nurse should prepare a patient for discharge, and the actions associated with discharging a patient.

Indicate the usual procedure the nurse should follow when a patient chooses to leave a hospital against advice.

List suggested measures for admitting and discharging patients in selected situations, as described in this chapter.

Summarize suggestions for instructing the patient.

Glossary

Admission The process of entering a hospital for care and treatment.

Community health care Care provided by nurses and allied professionals within a person's home or community health centres.

Continuity of care Providing uninterrupted care among various health practitioners, whether within the hospital or community, and without disrupting a patient's progress.

Discharge A process that occurs when a patient leaves a hospital.

Orientation The act of providing a person with new information.

Outpatient A person who travels back and forth to a hospital for testing or treatment.

Personal space The invisible area around one's body in which an individual feels safe.

Referral The process of sending or guiding someone to another place for assistance.

Separation anxiety The uncomfortable feeling associated with leaving familiar people and surroundings.

Transfer The process of discharging a patient from one unit or hospital and admitting him to another.

Introduction

Unfortunately, everyone experiences at some stage in their lives changes in health. Some people become ill suddenly; some sustain an injury; others may have felt poorly for some time. All may need some form of care and treatment for their needs. This care may require admission into a hospital or a nursing home.

Most nurses are employed by health authorities that care for sick people. Illnesses or injuries that require admission to a hospital are likely to cause a person to feel overwhelmed. The nurse faces a challenge to carry out hospital procedures for admission, transfer, referral, or discharge while helping an individual maintain his dignity and sense of control.

The information in this chapter is intended to help the nurse understand and respond to typical reactions that occur when a person is admitted to a hospital.

Trends in health care delivery

People being admitted to hospital require skilled treatment now more than ever before. There are various options available to reduce the amount of time an individual must be away from home while receiving health care. Creative alternatives for the services commonly associated with hospital care are being established. The trend is to provide care in the most economical way possible giving patients more choice with higher standards and better quality of care (Working for Patients White Paper, 1989). Even when hospitalization is necessary, the amount of time spent there is brief. There has been a decrease in the use of acute facilities and a move towards outpatient and community care in recent years primarily due to economic constraints. The cost-effectiveness of many of these new programmes is due to the manner in which nurses are applying their knowledge and skills.

Outpatient services

An *outpatient* is a person who continues to live at home but travels back and forth to a hospital for testing or treatment. Outpatient services have been available for laboratory testing, physical therapy and respiratory therapy for some time. Many types of surgery are now being performed on this model commonly called day surgery (Royal College of Surgeons, 1985). Nurses play a major role in teaching and preparing a person for the procedure. They monitor the immediate postsurgical period for several hours until the person can safely go home. Finally, nurses phone or reexamine the person the next day to ensure that all is progressing well.

Community health care

Community health care is the care provided by nurses and allied professionals or community health centres within a person's home. Some individuals may only need temporary or brief assistance with technical procedures. Providing nursing services within the home may prevent admission to a hospital or nursing home, or it may shorten the time spent recovering in the hospital. This extension of the nurse's knowledge and skills maintains a person's independence and helps control health care costs.

Common reactions to hospitalization

Despite methods to prevent or reduce the time spent away from home when a person is ill, admission to a hospital may be inevitable. The need to leave home for care compounds the stress of physical illness. The physiological response to stress is well documented (Montague, 1980) and its relation to organic disease is illustrated by MacKenzie Stuart (1980). The exact effects of admission to hospital are unique to each individual, but some common reactions can be anticipated.

Helping patients to cope with the stress of hospital admission combined with illness is probably one of the most vital functions a nurse fulfils. It is necessary that she understands the feelings and anxieties that a patient may experience and prevents or alleviates possible stressors (Wilson Barnett, 1980, 1988).

Separation anxiety

Separation anxiety is the uncomfortable feeling associated with leaving familiar people and surroundings. The need for love and belonging are higher level needs described by Maslow (1943). Children and parents are mutually sensitive to being separated. The child in Figure 15-1 would be much more frightened if his mother and father were not with him. Elderly people may become depressed, con-

Figure 15-1 A child needs the support of parents when entering a strange world.

fused, and disoriented when they must leave home. The nurse must be aware of the effects on all of the people who are involved—not just the patient.

Loneliness

Loneliness occurs when an individual misses the company of others. Individuals can feel lonely even if they are surrounded by other people. The nurse can never take the place of those who are significant to a patient. However, the nurse can spend time with lonely patients. Many hospitals have liberal visiting hours to counteract loneliness. Age restrictions are also being lifted in order to allow children to visit sick relatives. Parents are encouraged to stay with their sick children. Passes may also be allowed for brief visits away from the hospital.

Insecurity

The hospital environment and routine are generally unfamiliar to most people. Fear of the unknown creates insecurity and anxiety. The nurse may relieve some of the patient's anxiety by orienting the patient

to the ward. A simple explanation of the time for meals, visiting hours, and equipment within the room is important when a person is first admitted for care.

Decreased privacy

Humans establish real and imaginary boundaries for themselves and their possessions, creating an area that identifies ownership and provides a feeling of safety. There is a tendency to protect and defend this territory when it becomes threatened. When a person is admitted to a hospital, a new territory must be established. Closed doors or pulled curtains indicate that a person wishes to be alone; the nurse should always knock or ask permission to enter.

There is even an invisible body area that an individual considers private. For most, it is just beyond an arm's length. Entry into this area, called one's *personal space*, may cause an individual to feel threatened. This space often becomes invaded in the course of health care and treatment. Nurses should respect the individual's personal space by explaining what will be done during a procedure, especially when it involves close contact with the person's body. The patient should also be protected from the view of others when care is given.

Loss of identity

All people have a need for esteem and recognition. It is enhanced by objects, such as clothing, and personal honours that have been achieved. When a person is admitted to a hospital, the symbols of his identity may be left behind. Providing patients with institutional gowns increases an impersonal attitude toward the person. It may even be some time before all the staff are familiar with a new patient's name. The nurse should always learn and call the patient by name. First names should only be used if the patient asks that this be done. Efforts should be made to display the patient's family pictures or other personal objects that reinforce the unique aspects of each individual's life.

Hidegard et al. (1981) suggest that severe anxiety debilitates and curtails normal behavioural responses. The severity of stress experienced by an individual is thought to be dependent on five factors:

- Predictability of events.
- Control during events.
- Cognitive evaluation of the event.
- Feelings of competency during the event.
- Social supports during the event.

It is extremely important that the nurse incorporate these five factors into her nursing intervention whilst recognizing the individual's reactions to hospitalization.

Preparing for admission

Admission is a process that takes place when a person enters a hopsital for care and treatment. Each hospital has a procedure and follows certain policies when a patient is admitted, transferred, referred, and discharged. The hospital has its own forms on which health practitioners enter information about the patient. The duties of a nurse for admitting, transferring, referring and discharging a patient, and for record keeping depend on the policies of the hospital.

The admission office

Most hospitals have an admission office where clerical personnel begin to gather information. The patient's record is started in the admission office. Forms are prepared with the patient's name, age, date of birth, home address and telephone number, religion and type of employment plus name of next of kin or significant other and their address and telephone number. This information is used primarily by the hospital's admission office for record keeping.

Preparing an identification bracelet for the patient is one of the first components of the admission routine. Someone in the admitting department types identifying information on the bracelet, such as the patient's name and age, the patient's identification number, the name of the doctor caring for the patient, and the ward. The bracelet is usually applied by someone in the admitting department. An identification bracelet is illustrated in Figure 15-2. It is important for the patient's safety that the bracelet remain on throughout his time in the hospital. The patient is then escorted to the ward where he will be cared for.

Preparing the patient's bed

When the nurse learns that a patient will be arriving, the bed should be prepared. The patient should feel that everyone on the nursing unit is prepared and ready for his admission. If the patient feels that he is unexpected or is an inconvenience to the personnel, it is likely to make a unsettling first impression.

Before the patient is escorted to the ward, the nurse should check the bed and replace any missing items from the bedside locker. If the patient is known to

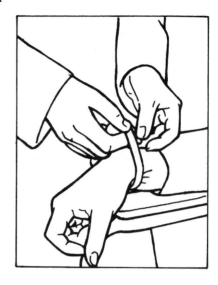

Figure 15-2 An identification bracelet.

need special equipment, such as oxygen, it should be at his bedside upon his arrival.

The bed should be in a low position if the patient can walk. If the patient is arriving by stretcher, the bed is placed in a high position to facilitate moving the patient onto the bed. Moving helpless patients is described in Chapter 16. The patient may require a hospital gown or may choose to use his own nightclothes.

Admitting a patient

Nursing responsibilities that are common with these routines will be discussed, but it is recommended that the policies and procedures of each hospital be followed. Porter et al. (1977) discuss many of the needs of the patient on admission to hospital. One of the most important steps in the admission procedure is to make the patient feel welcome. Being treated as an expected guest helps put the patient at ease.

Orienting a patient

Orientation is the act of providing a person with new information. To help the patient feel more secure, several explanations should be made. The nurse should point out the following locations: the nurse's work area in relation to the patient's ward or room; the toilet; the shower or bathing area if not located with the toilet; and any lounge area that may be used by the patient and his family.

Within the room, the nurse who is admitting the patient should explain:

- How to contact a nurse. This may be done with a buzzer or a bell. If an intercommunication system is available between the nurse and the patient, this should also be explained and demonstrated.
- Directions for changing the position of the bed. Any position that is restricted should be explained.
- How phone calls may be made or received.
- The use of remote controls for operating a television, if available.

The daily routine and activities that will affect the patient should also be explained. The nurse should identify the times for meals, when the doctor may be expected, when surgery is scheduled, and when laboratory tests or x-rays may be performed. Some hospitals provide booklets with general information for newly admitted patients. Many patients are anxious when they are admitted. Anxiety interferes with the ability to remember. A booklet acts as a reminder for what was explained. Booklets, however, should never take the place of the nurse's explanations.

Handling a patient's valuables and clothing

It is preferable for admitting personnel to give the patient's valuables, such as jewellery and money, to family members to take home. If this is not possible, admitting personnel may place the patient's valuables in a safe. There should be a note made on the patient's record about how valuables were handled.

When the nurse is responsible for handling the patient's valuables and clothing, *the hospital policy must be carefully observed*. Losing personal items belonging to a patient can have serious legal implications for both the nurse and the health authority. The patient may sue, claiming his belongings were lost or stolen because they were handled carelessly. It is best to have a second nurse or a representative from the hospital's administrative staff present when a nurse receives valuables for safekeeping. An inventory must be made. The nurse and the patient may cosign the inventory. One copy is given to the patient, while another is attached to the patient's notes. Problems occur when in the course of hospitalization other valuable items are brought in without subsequent documentation. Figure 15-3 illustrates one type of clothing and valuables checklist used by hospitals.

Most hospitals have facilities in the ward or in the patient's room for the storage of street clothing. The nurse should also note any supplies or equipment the patient brings with him, such as glasses, crutches, a wheel chair, or other items. Items that are similar to those owned by the hospital should be labelled with the patient's name. This identification will help if the items become mixed with hospital equipment.

Assisting a patient to undress

There will be times when a patient is unable to undress without the nurse's help. A method for helping the patient is as follows:

- Provide privacy.
- Have the patient sit on the edge of the bed, which has already been lowered.
- Remove the patient's shoes.
- Assist the patient to turn on the bed and help him into the lying position if he is weak and tired.
- Slip off the patient's clothing in a manner least disturbing to him after fasteners, such as zippers and buttons, are opened. For example, fold or gather a garment in your hands as you work it up the body. Have the patient lift his hips, if he can, to slide clothes up or down.
- Lift the patient's head so garments can be guided over the head.
- Roll the patient from side to side to remove clothes that fasten up the front or back, after removing arms from sleeves.
- Cover the patient with a bath blanket after removing the outer clothing.
- Gather a stocking, sliding it down the leg and over the foot.
- Put on the patient's gown after he is undressed.

Gathering information

At the time of admission, the nurse begins the nursing assessment by collecting information (McFarlane and Castledine, 1982). Assessment skills are discussed in more depth in Chapters 15 and 17. The nurse ordinarily measures and records the patient's temperature, pulse and respiratory rates, and blood pressure. The patient is weighed on the hospital's scales. A specimen of urine may be obtained. Observations of the patient's general condition are made. All known allergies are noted. Collecting

CLOTHING LIST:
(Please check articles of clothing with patient and describe.)

Dress_____   Pants_____
Slip_____   Shirt_____
Bra_____   Undershirt_____
Panties_____   Undershorts_____
Hose_____   Socks_____
Girdle_____   Tie_____
Slippers_____   Shoes_____
Nightgown_____   Pajamas_____
Suit_____   Robe_____
Sweater_____   Coat_____
Slacks_____   Truss_____
Blouse_____   Backsupport_____
Shorts_____   Belt_____
Skirt_____   Hat_____

Other items not listed:

_____
_____

Check valuables below and describe if necessary:

Watch_____   Earrings_____
Medals_____   Ring - Type & Number_____
                             _____
Other jewellery_____

Dentures - Yes_____No_____   Prosthesis - Yes_____No_____
Contact Lenses - Yes_____No_____ Glasses - Yes_____No_____
         Removed - Yes_____No_____ Hearing Aid - Yes_____No_____

Wallet_____Colour_____With Pt._____In Safe_____To Family or Friend_____
Purse_____Colour_____With Pt._____In Safe_____To Family or Friend_____
Cash_____With Pt._____In Safe_____To Family or Friend_____
Cheques/Cheque Book_____With Pt._____In Safe_____To Family or Friend_____

The above list is correct:

Patient's signature_____Witness_____

Clothing taken home by_____

Relationship_____

Witness_____

Received by on Nursing Unit_____

Figure 15-3 This form is commonly used in hospitals for listing the patient's clothing and valuables. It is completed at the time the patient is admitted.

specimens and measuring and recording temperature etc. are discussed in subsequent chapters.

The doctor is ordinarily notified when a patient for whom he is caring has been admitted. The doctor may have sent forms with the patient. In some cases, doctor's orders and a copy of a medical history and physical examination are brought with the patient's forms from the admitting department. The nurse should check to determine whether there are orders that are to be carried out at the time of admission.

Principles of Care 15-1 describes a summary of the steps in admitting a patient to a hospital ward. More specific details depend largely on the patient's condition and hospital policies. A description of the admission and initial assessment information must be entered on the patient's record within the first 24 hours.

Transferring a patient

When a patient's condition changes, for better or worse, he may need to be transferred. A *transfer* involves discharging a patient from one ward or hospital and admitting him to another.

Principles of Care 15-1. Admitting a patient

Nursing Action	Rationale
Greet the patient and relatives. Introduce yourself to the patient and the patient to his neighbours.	Calling the patient by name, extending common courtesies, and welcoming the patient and relatives often help them feel at ease and less frightened.
Check the patient's identification bracelet to be sure it contains complete and accurate information.	The safety of the patient often depends on being accurately identified before tests are performed or medications are given.
Explain use of the bathroom and of hospital equipment, such as the call system, adjustable bed, television, telephone and so on. Explain hospital routines, such as mealtimes, visiting hours and so on.	Explaining hospital routines and how to use equipment helps put the patient at ease. Knowing how to use equipment helps prevent anger, frustration and accidents.
Make provisions for privacy. Ask the patient if he wishes relatives to remain or leave while the rest of the admission procedure is carried out.	Providing privacy shows respect and interest in the patient as a person. The patient often wants his family present as a source of security and emotional support.
Help the patient to undress and to get into a comfortable position.	Helping the patient to undress conserves his strength, can prevent accidents such as falling, and prepares the patient for receiving care. It also gives the nurse an opportunity to assess his skin and ability to move.
Take care of the patient's clothing and valuables. Follow hospital procedure.	Losing items is upsetting to the patient and can result in serious legal problems.
Place the buzzer/bell and other equipment so that it will be convenient for the patient to use.	Being unable to call for help is unsafe and can result in accidents. When equipment is handy for patients, accidents are less likely to occur.
Measure and record the patient's temperature, pulse and respiratory rates, and blood pressure. If indicated, obtain a urine specimen at a time that is convenient during the admission procedure.	Collecting this information is an important part of the patient's initial assessment.
If the patient's relatives left earlier, indicate that they may return to the patient's bedside.	Relatives have worries and fears too. They usually feel better when they know the patient is admitted, settled, and comfortable.
Do necessary recording on the patient's charts, following hospital policy.	The information is an important part of the permanent record. It is the description of the beginning of the patient's care.

The move usually provides some advantage to the patient. It may locate the patient on a unit where nurses and staff have special experience and skills in caring for particular types of patients. Examples include the intensive care unit, cardiac care unit, high dependency unit or surgical unit.

A transfer is similar to an admission and discharge. A patient is received on the new unit or ward in a manner much the same as that used for his admission. Principles of Care 15-2 describes general suggestions for transferring a patient. Also, the patient does not dress in street clothes.

Referring a patient

A *referral* is the process of sending or guiding someone to another place for assistance. A patient may be referred by a nurse in a hospital to a community service that provides community health care. A school nurse may refer a student who does not see well to an

Principles of Care 15-2. *Transferring a patient*

Nursing Action	Rationale
Be sure the patient and his family receive information about the transfer.	Communication promotes cooperation when dealing with the changes in a patient's condition.
Be sure that the patient has all his personal belongings.	Carelessness can lead to loss of the patient's clothing or valuables.
Notify receiving-unit personnel that arrangements are being made for a patient transfer.	Other personnel should be allowed time to plan and adjust their schedules so the transferred patient will feel welcome and unhurried.
In a brief summary to new personnel, list significant information, such as medical diagnosis, treatment, nursing diagnoses, care, tests, and medications.	New personnel may not have time to read the chart thoroughly before assuming responsibility for the patient's care.
Review the current written nursing and medical orders with the nurse taking over the patient's care.	Reviewing the patient's current records together avoids overlooking aspects of the patient's care. Serious errors have occurred when there was insufficient communication between nurses during a patient's transfer.
Explain procedures, policies, and equipment that will be new to the patient.	Surroundings that are new to the patient may continue to cause fear and worry.
Introduce the patient to those who will be caring for him, as well as to his new neighbours.	Learning the names of other patients and personnel conveys a feeling of belonging.
Take the patient, if his condition permits, on a tour of the new ward.	Not all hospital words are exactly similar.
Record the circumstances and condition of the patient when transferred. The nurse who assumes care for the patient should also record a brief summary of assessments about the condition of the patient upon his arrival.	The chart is a record of all the care and responses of the patient throughout the care given during hospitalization.
Notify other departments within the hospital of the patient's change in location.	Services such as mail and phone calls will need to be redirected. Other personnel will experience less delay in their schedules when they must locate the patient.
Visit the transferred patient from time to time.	It is a courteous and thoughtful gesture to remain in contact with a patient. This promotes a feeling of self-esteem and recognition of their personal worth.

eye-care specialist. An example of a referral form used when a patient was moved from one hospital to another appears in Figure 15-4.

Thinking about a referral is often a part of good discharge planning. The nurse should begin to anticipate what kind of care the patient may require before it is time for him to leave. Planning, coordination, and communication take time in order to ensure that patients receive *continuity of care*. This term means that a patient's care is uninterrupted among various health practitioners, whether within the hospital or community, and avoiding disruption to any progress that has been made.

Discharging a patient

A *discharge* is a process that occurs when a patient leaves a hospital. Preparing a patient for discharge actually should begin when he is admitted. The purpose of his stay is to help him reach an improved state of health, and this begins at the time of admission.

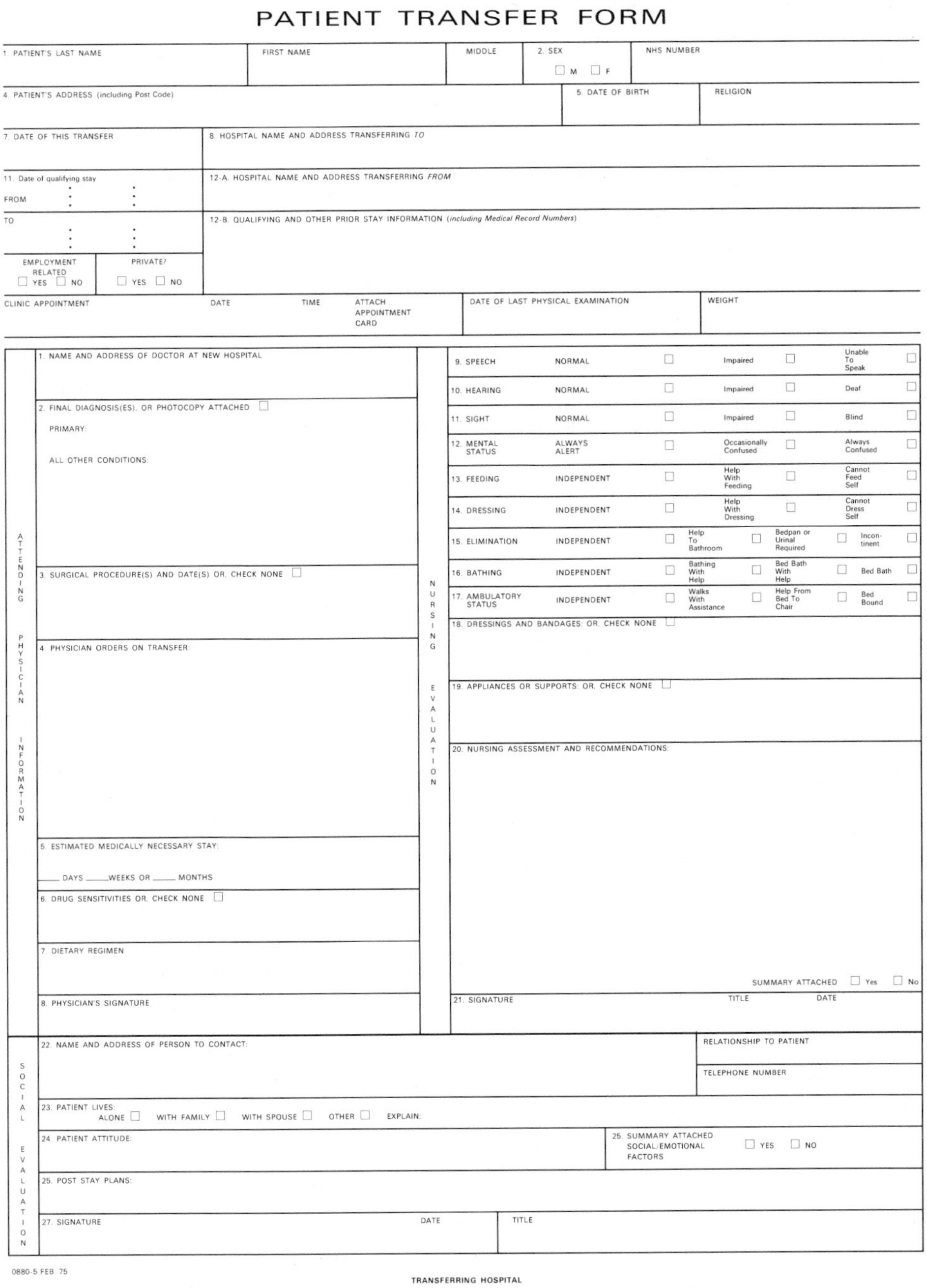

PATIENT TRANSFER FORM

1. PATIENT'S LAST NAME | FIRST NAME | MIDDLE | 2. SEX ☐ M ☐ F | NHS NUMBER

4. PATIENT'S ADDRESS (including Post Code) | 5. DATE OF BIRTH | RELIGION

7. DATE OF THIS TRANSFER | 8. HOSPITAL NAME AND ADDRESS TRANSFERRING *TO*

11. Date of qualifying stay FROM : : TO : : | 12-A. HOSPITAL NAME AND ADDRESS TRANSFERRING *FROM*

12-B. QUALIFYING AND OTHER PRIOR STAY INFORMATION (*including Medical Record Numbers*)

EMPLOYMENT RELATED ☐ YES ☐ NO | PRIVATE? ☐ YES ☐ NO

CLINIC APPOINTMENT | DATE | TIME | ATTACH APPOINTMENT CARD | DATE OF LAST PHYSICAL EXAMINATION | WEIGHT

ATTENDING PHYSICIAN INFORMATION

1. NAME AND ADDRESS OF DOCTOR AT NEW HOSPITAL

2. FINAL DIAGNOSIS(ES), OR PHOTOCOPY ATTACHED ☐
PRIMARY:
ALL OTHER CONDITIONS:

3. SURGICAL PROCEDURE(S) AND DATE(S) OR CHECK NONE ☐

4. PHYSICIAN ORDERS ON TRANSFER:

5. ESTIMATED MEDICALLY NECESSARY STAY:
____ DAYS ____ WEEKS OR ____ MONTHS

6. DRUG SENSITIVITIES OR CHECK NONE ☐

7. DIETARY REGIMEN

8. PHYSICIAN'S SIGNATURE

NURSING EVALUATION

9. SPEECH	NORMAL ☐		Impaired ☐		Unable To Speak ☐	
10. HEARING	NORMAL ☐		Impaired ☐		Deaf ☐	
11. SIGHT	NORMAL ☐		Impaired ☐		Blind ☐	
12. MENTAL STATUS	ALWAYS ALERT ☐		Occasionally Confused ☐		Always Confused ☐	
13. FEEDING	INDEPENDENT ☐		Help With Feeding ☐		Cannot Feed Self ☐	
14. DRESSING	INDEPENDENT ☐		Help With Dressing ☐		Cannot Dress Self ☐	
15. ELIMINATION	INDEPENDENT ☐	Help To Bathroom ☐		Bedpan or Urinal Required ☐		Incon-tinent ☐
16. BATHING	INDEPENDENT ☐	Bathing With Help ☐		Bed Bath With Help ☐		Bed Bath ☐
17. AMBULATORY STATUS	INDEPENDENT ☐	Walks With Assistance ☐		Help From Bed To Chair ☐		Bed Bound ☐

18. DRESSINGS AND BANDAGES OR CHECK NONE ☐

19. APPLIANCES OR SUPPORTS OR CHECK NONE ☐

20. NURSING ASSESSMENT AND RECOMMENDATIONS:

SUMMARY ATTACHED ☐ Yes ☐ No

21. SIGNATURE | TITLE | DATE

SOCIAL EVALUATION

22. NAME AND ADDRESS OF PERSON TO CONTACT: | RELATIONSHIP TO PATIENT | TELEPHONE NUMBER

23. PATIENT LIVES: ALONE ☐ WITH FAMILY ☐ WITH SPOUSE ☐ OTHER ☐ EXPLAIN:

24. PATIENT ATTITUDE: | 25. SUMMARY ATTACHED SOCIAL/EMOTIONAL FACTORS ☐ YES ☐ NO

25. POST STAY PLANS:

27. SIGNATURE | DATE | TITLE

0880-5 FEB 75

TRANSFERRING HOSPITAL

Figure 15-4 This form is used when patients are referred from one hospital to another. It illustrates the type of information the receiving hospital needs to make continuity of care possible.

Planning for a patient's discharge requires that the specific needs of a patient be identified. Figure 15-5 provides a checklist to help the nurse assess a patient's discharge needs.

A group of nurses, who emphasized a need for a good teaching plan to prepare patients for discharge, used the acronym METHOD as a guide.

M—Medications. The patient should have thorough knowledge of the medications he should continue taking after discharge.

1   Initiate planning for discharge when patient is admitted.
2   Consider any self-care needs:
- Does patient need to be taught to change dressing/administer medications/change appliance/use prosthesis/prepare special diet?
3   Does patient have an acute or long-term illness with:
- more than one medical or surgical problem?
- need for community nurse?
- need for support from community health team?
- need for recurrent admission to hospital?
4   Is there altered body function/changed body image?
- Can patient benefit from a self-help/support group?
- Does patient need a supply of a special appliance, e.g. stoma bag, breast or limb prosthesis?
5   Is patient terminally ill?
- Would patient benefit from community/specialist support, e.g. Macmillan or Marie Curie nursing?
6   What are the home circumstances?
- Does patient live alone?
- Does patient live in nursing home/sheltered accommodation?
- Does patient require support from a social worker?
- Is patient already known to Social Services?
- Is patient a single parent?
- Does patient have a disabled partner/dependent relatives?
7   Is patient drug/alcohol dependent?
8   Does patient have emotional psychological problems?
9   Does patient need a supply of medication?
10 Does patient need a follow-up appointment/return admission booking?

Figure 15-5 This form provides a checklist to help the nurse assess a patient's specific needs so that discharge planning needs can be better met.

E—Environment. The environment to which the patient will be going after discharge from a hospital should be safe. The patient should also have whatever services are necessary for continuing care in that environment.

T—Treatments. The nurse should be sure that treatments to be continued after discharge can be carried out by the patient or a member of his family. If this is not possible, arrangements should be made so that someone can come into the home to give skilled care.

H—Health teaching. The patient being prepared for discharge should be taught how to maintain well-being. This includes which signs and symptoms indicate that additional health care is required.

O—Outpatient referral. The patient should be familiar with services from the hospital or other community agencies that will promote his continued care and progress.

D—Diet. The patient should be taught about any restrictions in his diet. He should be able to select an appropriate diet for himself.

As is true when a patient is admitted (Connolly, 1981), there are certain policies that are carefully observed when he is discharged. Principles of Care 15-3 describes discharging a patient from a hospital.

The importance of communication between health professionals cannot be overstated in the process of discharging a patient. Parnell (1982) highlights some of the problems associated when information is either incomplete or not sent, messages are left with a third person and feedback is insufficient.

Leaving against medical advice

There are times when a patient leaves a hospital against medical advice. In such instances, he is asked to sign a special form, which states that he is leaving without being discharged by his doctor. It indicates that the individual will not hold the doctor, the hospital, or hospital personnel responsible for anything that may happen to him as a result of his leaving. If the patient refuses to sign the form, he may not be detained from leaving. The refusal should be noted within the patient's hospital record.

The nurse responsible for the patient's care should be sure the doctor is notified and aware of the patient's wishes to leave. Unsuccessful attempts to locate the doctor should be noted on the patient's record. The hospital's nursing supervisor may also be notified. Health practitioners should share information with the patient about the risks his decision involves, but the patient cannot be forcefully detained when he is a rational adult. The only exception to this is the case of a patient admission that has been ordered by a judge. This usually only occurs when a patient has a mental illness. It may also occur if the patient has a contagious disease and has refused measures that would prevent its spread among other susceptible people. In all other cases, detaining a patient against his wishes invites serious legal problems. A health practitioner and the hospital could be sued for false imprisonment.

Cleaning the room and equipment

Cleaning a patient's room and equipment after discharge is ordinarily a housekeeping responsibility. However, in some instances, a nurse may be required to do this job. The nurse is referred to Chapter 20, in which recommended techniques for cleaning, disinfection and sterilization techniques are discussed.

Suggested measures when admitting and discharging patients in selected situations

When the patient is an infant or child

Bear in mind that a hospital admission is a difficult experience for most children and their parents. No admission to a hospital is routine for them. Therefore, every effort should be taken to offer explanations, give emotional support, and orient both the child and his parents to the hospital environment.

Parents of very young, hospitalized infants often require more nursing support than the patient. Their protective and nurturing role is threatened, and they feel helpless.

Permit a parent to help undress a child and help with other admission and hospital procedures as much as possible. This practice helps reduce a child's fears and anxieties.

Parents should be told if a hospital permits rooming in, a service that allows a parent to share a room with their child. It has been found that hospitalization and separation from parents are extremely difficult for young children, especially if the child is under 4 or 5 years of age. Lewer and Robertson (1983) state that all paediatric wards should have accommodation for families to be resident, for when rooming in is permitted, children can be saved from much emotional trauma.

When a child is very young, obtain information about a child and his illness from a parent. The nurse should also ask a parent to describe how the child may feel about his illness. It is best to interview parents out of the child's hearing. This protects the child from hearing something he cannot understand, which may be extremely frightening to him.

If the child is old enough, ask the child to explain how he feels and how his illness is affecting him. Ignoring that a child can participate in the conversation conveys a message to the child that his contributions are not important.

Preschool children can often cope with the experiences of hospitalization by using dolls. The dolls may represent models of themselves and other hospital personnel. Playing provides an opportunity for acting out conflicts and a means to their resolution.

Principles of Care 15-3. Discharging a patient

Nursing Action	Rationale
Check to see that the patient is for discharge.	It is the doctor's responsibility to discharge the patient.
If the patient is leaving without a doctor's consent, request that the patient sign pertinent hospital forms.	The patient cannot legally be held in hospital against his wishes except in certain circumstances. Having the patient's signature on a form identifies that the patient assumes responsibility for the consequences of leaving the hospital.
Notify the family or responsible person who will provide transportation from the hospital.	A discharged patient should not sit in the lobby or wait for a long period of time for someone who will drive him home.
Check to see that the patient or a relative has had discharge instructions, such as instructions about diet or medications.	The patient or a relative will be able to continue with necessary care safely after discharge when properly instructed.
Check to see that all necessary equipment and supplies, such as prescriptions and dressings, are ready for the patient to take with him. Locate missing items.	Having equipment and supplies ready saves the time and annoyance of having to wait for them when the patient is ready to leave.
Write down the date, time, and location of the next appointment with the doctor on an outpatient appointment card.	Some patients may be unfamiliar with the office locations of doctors who have provided care. Writing down appointment information will help the patient maintain continued follow-up.
Check the patient's belongings with the clothing and valuables list. Some hospitals require that the patient sign the form if he agrees that he can account for all the items that were listed.	Following the hospital policy may help to avoid legal problems in the future.
Help the patient to dress and to pack his belongings. Some disposable hospital equipment may be taken home by the patient.	Assisting the patient conserves his strength. Such assistance is courteous and helps the patient feel that personnel are interested in his welfare.
Transport the patient and his belongings to a car and help him into the car if neccessary.	Hospital personnel are responsible for the patient's safety until he has left the hospital grounds. The hospital is liable for any personal injury that occurs on its property.
Record essential information on the patient's chart.	Information concerning discharge is important because it indicates the patient's condition at the time of his release on the permanent record.

Encouraging the early school-age child to draw a picture about the hospital and discuss it may help the nurse assess the significance of hospitalization to a child.

Be sure that the parents are aware when a child is to be discharged and that they have been properly instructed about continuing care after discharge.

When the patient is elderly

Do not misjudge an elderly patient as being senile when he is admitted to a hospital until you have sufficient evidence. Very often, the elderly person is so concerned about a physical problem with which he is trying to cope that he becomes confused and sometimes disoriented, especially when admitted to the strange environment of a hospital.

Be prepared to expect that an elderly patient may be fearful of discharge from a hospital and may wish to stay (Haug, 1985). Many are very concerned about their care after discharge, especially if they live alone or with a spouse who has limited ability to give necessary care. The nurse should work toward helping the elderly patient become as self-sufficient as possible during hospitalization so that he can better cope with his care at home.

Allow a patient to display personal items by the bed. This promotes a feeling of security and familiarity within a strange environment.

Expect to repeat information about the daily routine and names of staff and other patients. Anxiety may temporarily interfere with remembering.

Teaching suggestions for admitting and discharging patients from a hospital

The following summary offers suggestions for teaching about admitting and discharging a patient from a hospital:

The patient should be taught about the hospital environment, his ward, hospital policies and procedures, and so on upon his admission to a hospital. This type of explaining should also be done when a patient is transferred within a hospital.

The patient should be well prepared for discharge through a planned teaching programme, as described in this chapter. A programme should include information about medications, treatments and diet restrictions ordered for the patient and about any other factors influencing his health and well-being. Included in discharge planning should be instructions about when to call a doctor if problems arise.

References

Connolly, M.L. (1981) Organize your workday for more effective discharge planning. *Nursing 81*, **11**, 41–7.

Haug, M.R. (1985) Home care for the elderly. Who benefits? *American Journal of Public Health*, **75**, 127–8.

Hidegard, E., Atkinson, R.L. and Atkinson, R.C. (1981) *Introduction to Psychology*, Harcourt Brace Jovanovich, San Diego.

Lewer, H. and Robertson, L. (1983) *Care of the Child*, The Essentials of Nursing Series, Macmillan, London, p. 71.

MacKenzie Stuart, A. (1980) Stress and organic disease. *Nursing*, 1st Series, February, 437–8.

Maslow, A. (1943) A theory of human motivation. *Psychological Review*, **50**, 370–90.

McFarlane, J. and Castledine, G (1982) *A Guide to the Practice of Nursing using the Nursing Process*, Mosby, St Louis.

Montague, S. (1980) The physiological basis of the stress reaction. *Nursing*, 1st Series, February, 422–5.

Parnell, J. (1982) Continuity and communication. *Nursing Times*, **78**(9), 33–40.

Porter A. et al. (1977) Patient needs on admission. *American Journal of Nursing*, **77**, 112–13.

Royal College of Surgeons of England Commission on the Provision of Surgical Services (1985) *Guidelines for Day Case Surgery*, Royal College of Surgeons of England, London.

Wilson Barnett, J. (1980) Prevention and alleviation of stress in patients. *Nursing*, 1st Series, February, 432–6.

Wilson Barnett, J. (1988) Patient teaching or patient counselling? *Journal of Advanced Nursing*, **13**, 215–22.

Working for Patients, White Paper, London, HMSO, January 1989.

16

The comfort and safety needs of the individual

Learning objectives

When the content of this chapter has been mastered, the learner should be able to:

Define terms appearing in the glossary.

Describe a comfortable, attractive and practical ward area for a patient in terms of space, furniture, personal care items, decor, temperature, humidity and ventilation.

List equipment ordinarily found in a patient's ward area and indicate how each type is used to fit the patient's needs.

Describe the steps in making an unoccupied bed.

Describe how a patient's privacy can be protected and ways to control noise and odours in a patient's ward area.

Describe methods to promote sensory stimulation.

List items that could be considered when helping to make a patient's environment safe and discuss common practices that ensure safety in each case.

Explain steps to take when an accident occurs.

List suggested measures for promoting a safe and comfortable environment in selected situations, as described in this chapter.

Describe signs or symptoms associated with disuse syndrome.

List positioning devices used for the safety and comfort of patients confined to bed and explain the purpose of each.

Demonstrate how to turn and move patients safely.

Demonstrate how to position a patient on his back, side, and abdomen, and in a sitting position.

Identify the purpose and demonstrate range of motion exercises.

Describe exercises that help prepare a patient to walk.

Demonstrate how to transfer a patient to a stretcher and chair and back to bed again.

Identify the manner in which a cane and walking frame should be used.

Describe ways in which a patient is prepared for crutch walking.

Describe or demonstrate basic gaits for crutch walking.

List suggested measures to prevent inactivity and promote safety in selected situations, as described in this chapter.

List general purposes for mechanical immobilization devices.

Identify types of splints and indicate the reason for their use.

Describe the technique for applying a splint in an emergency and measures that should be included with its use.

Demonstrate the application of a triangular sling.

Identify types of casts and the body areas they generally enclose.

List advantages and disadvantages of materials used for constructing a cast.

Describe the nurse's responsibilities when assisting with the application of a cast.

Discuss methods for supporting and ensuring thorough drying of a wet plaster cast.

Describe the initial assessments that should be made after a cast has been applied.

Discuss the immediate and continuing care of a patient with a cast.

Identify measures that may be utilized to keep a cast clean, repair cast edges and maintain cast structure when a window has been cut.

Discuss methods for removing a cast.

Describe potential changes in a body part that may be expected when a cast is removed and methods for assisting the patient to adjust to those changes.

Describe observations that the nurse may use to determine that traction is being properly maintained.

Describe the care that should be provided for a patient in traction.

List suggested measures that apply to the care of certain patients requiring mechanical immobilization, as described in this chapter.

Summarize suggestions for patient teaching offered in this chapter.

Glossary

Abduction The act of moving a body part away from the centre of the body.

Accident report A written report that describes an accident or error. Synonym for *incident report*.

Active exercise An exercise performed by a person without assistance from others.

Adduction The act of moving a body part toward the centre of the body.

Alignment Being positioned in a straight line.

Ambulatory Able to walk about, not confined to bed.

Asphyxiation Suffocation caused by lack of oxygen in the blood.

Atelectasis An incomplete expansion or collapse of a portion of lung tissue.

Atony Decreased muscle tonus.

Atrophy The wasting away of body tissue.

Axillary crutches Crutches that fit under the upper arms into the axillae.

Bivalved cast A cast that has been cut into two separate pieces.

Body cast A rigid mould that encircles the trunk of the body.

Brace A device designed to support weakened body structures during weight bearing.

Cast A solid mould of a body part.

Circumduction Movement in a circular direction.

Closed reduction Realignment of broken bone ends without making a surgical incision.

Comfort An inner sense of well-being.

Constipation A condition in which stool becomes dry and difficult to pass.

Contracture A fixed decrease in a joint's range of motion.

Cravat binder A piece of cloth folded into a strip of a desired width.

Cross ventilation The movement of air that occurs as a result of opening windows that face each other but are located on opposite walls of a room or building.

Cylinder cast A rigid mould that encircles an arm or leg.

Dangling The position in which a person is sitting on the edge of the bed with his legs and feet over the side of the bed.

Decubitus ulcer Breakdown of skin as a result of prolonged pressure over a bony prominence. Synonym for *pressure sore*.

Disuse syndrome The collective signs and symptoms that develop as a result of inactivity.

Dorsiflexion Movement of the foot at the ankle so that the toes point toward the kneecap.

Embolism A sudden blockage of an artery by material that has been brought to the site by the blood stream.

Embolus A blood clot that is no longer stationary but moves from one blood vessel to a smaller one. Plural is emboli.

Environment All that surrounds and influences life and development.

Environmental psychologist A psychologist whose

specialty is the study of how the environment affects behaviour.

Extension The act of straightening or increasing an angle that brings parts into or toward a straight line.

External rotation The act of turning outward.

Faecal impaction A condition in which stool becomes so dry that it cannot be passed.

Faecal incontinence The inability to control the release of stool.

Faeces The product of intestinal elimination, also called stool.

Flexion The act of moving so that the angle between adjoining parts is reduced; bending.

Foot drop A common condition associated with inactivity in which the foot cannot assume a position of dorsiflexion.

Fowler's position A sitting position.

Fracture A break in the continuity of a bone.

Gluteal setting Isometric exercises in which the muscles of the buttocks are alternately tensed and then relaxed.

Hip spica cast A rigid mould that encircles one or both legs and the lower trunk.

Humidity The amount of moisture in the air.

Hyperextension The act of moving so that the angle between adjoining parts is made larger than its normal or average range.

Hypostatic pneumonia An inflammation of the lungs due to decreased ventilation and retained secretions.

Immobilizer A cloth or foam splint used to limit movement and pain in an injured body part.

Incident report A written report that describes an accident or error. Synonym for *Accident report*.

Inflatable splint An immobilizing device that produces its effect by surrounding an injured body part with air. Synonym for *pneumatic splint*.

Internal rotation The act of turning inward.

Lateral position A position in which a person lies on his side.

Manual traction Pulling on a part of the body using an individual's hands and muscular strength.

Mechanical immobilization Restricted movement as a result of the application of a splint, cast or traction.

Moulded splint A plastic immobilizing device that is bent to fit the contour of a body part.

Neutral position A joint's normal position of alignment.

Open reduction Realignment of broken bone ends through an incision.

Passive exercise An exercise in which one person moves the body parts of another person.

Petals Strips of adhesive tape used to repair rough or crumbling edges of a cast.

Phlebitis An inflammation of a vein.

Plantarflexion Movement of the foot so that the toes point in a direction away from the head.

Platform crutches Crutches on which the patient bears his weight on his forearms.

Pneumatic splint An immobilizing device that produces its effect by surrounding an injured body part with air. Synonym for *inflatable splint*.

Pressure sore Breakdown of skin as a result of prolonged pressure over a bony prominence. Synonym for *decubitus ulcer*.

Prone position A position in which a person lies on his abdomen.

Protective restraints Devices that limit a person's movement to prevent harm.

Quadriceps setting Isometric exercises in which the muscles in the front of the thigh are alternately tensed and then relaxed.

Reduction Repositioning of a broken bone into its proper alignment.

Relative humidity The ratio between the amount of moisture in the air and the greatest amount of moisture the air could contain at the same temperature.

Rotation The act of turning.

Sensory alteration Difficulty in processing information because of an excess or insufficient amount of stimuli.

Sensory deprivation A state in which a person receives less than optimal amounts of stimuli for well-being.

Sensory overload A state in which a person receives more than optimal stimuli for well-being.

Skeletal traction Pulling effect applied directly to the skeletal system by attaching wires, pins or tongs into or through the bone.

Skin traction Pulling effect applied indirectly to the skeletal system by attaching equipment and weight to the skin.

Sling A muslin binder that elevates and supports an injured area.

Spasticity A sudden, continuous and involuntary muscle contraction.

Splint A device that immobilizes and protects an injured part of the body.

Stimulus A change in the environment sufficient to cause a response. The plural of the word is stimuli.

Stockinet Stretchy fabric that is knitted into a tube.

Supine position A position in which a person lies on his back.

Syndrome A group of signs and symptoms that occur together.

Temperature The measurement of heat.

Thrombophlebitis Inflammation of a vein accompanied by a thrombus.

Thrombus A stationary blood clot. Plural is thrombi.

Tonus The normal, slight, continuous contraction of muscles.

Traction Equipment attached to the bed and patient to produce pull and counterpull on a particular part of the body.

Traction splint Metal immobilizing device that also applies a pulling effect on an injured body part.

Transfer To move a person from one place to another.

Trapeze A triangular piece of metal hung by a chain over the head of a bed.

Urinary incontinence The inability to control the release of urine.

Valsalva's manoeuvre The use of efforts to force exhalation against a closed glottis.

Ventilation Movement of air.

Window A square piece removed from a cast.

Introduction

Comfort is an inner sense of well-being. It is the result of physical and mental equilibrium. This state is in constant fluctuation. A variety of stimuli or emotions can cause a change that people readily identify as discomfort. Examples of factors that can create discomfort are pain, fatigue, hunger, extreme environmental temperatures, worry, tension, and so on.

The environment

The word *environment* refers to all of an individual's natural and man-made surroundings. The environment influences life and human development. When the environment is safe, clean, comfortable and attractive, it can contribute to a sense of well-being.

The patient's ward area is the environment in which the nurse carries out the most personal kind of care. This may be in a hospital, in the home, in a clinic—wherever the person receives care. A unit is an area in a hospital where patients with similar conditions are housed.

Many things in a patient's ward area or in a hospital unit cannot be changed by the nurse. However, sometimes the nurse can make modifications in the environment that do not involve major alterations. This chapter discusses nursing measures that help make the patient's environment more comfortable, safer and more pleasant.

The patient's ward area

All individuals have a need to possess an area they can call their own. The characteristics of that area appear to vary among people. The city dweller may be content within a small efficiency apartment, whereas a farmer may feel a need for a barn and utility buildings on acres of property. Regardless of its characteristics, having and controlling a personal territory contributes to one's self-concept and self-esteem.

It has been observed that people will defend the area they have. Usually, the smaller the area, the more an individual will fight for it. Individuals often zealously claim and guard their seat on a park bench, for example.

The nurse should be aware of the importance of the patient's need for a personal area. Some may even refer to an assigned room as "my room". A person in a nursing home, for example, may feel offended if another sits in his usual chair for meals. Some occupy the same place whenever there are planned activities. The nurse shows respect for the patient's feelings by seeing to it that other patients, who may be confused, do not wander into another's room or ward area. The nurse should see to it that a person's personal items are not taken, lost, or damaged. What may seem as having litttle value to the nurse may be extremely valuable to the patient.

Walls and floors

It is no longer the practice for hospitals to appear bare and sterile. Plain, white walls and imposing equipment are being replaced by more colourful furnishings within a functional decor. Floors and walls are more tastefully decorated. There is a new speciality within the field of psychology. An *environmental psychologist* is a specialist who studies how the environment affects behaviour. Information is being accumulated on ways to alter a ward and its furnishings to produce a particular mood or feeling. The use of colour and design is being used in careful planning of a patient's environment.

Bright and stimulating colours are often annoying. Research indicates that various colours, such as blue and green, promote feelings of coolness and relaxation. These colours are being used to promote well-being in environments, like hospitals, that are associated with anxiety and tension. Most patients prefer a modest, simple decor. Many patients have been disturbed by wall coverings with large and distinct designs because they can create the illusion of faces and other objects. Pictures, bedspreads and curtains may have the same effect if not selected carefully. Some patients feel dizzy when they look at floor or wall coverings with small designs, parallel lines or tiny squares. Carpeting is now being used in areas within hospitals. This reduces noise and promotes a more homelike atmosphere.

When hospitals construct new patient care units, nurses are being consulted on their functional design as well as decor. Nurses may provide advice about equipping a patient's room for care in the home. It would be well to consider some of the points about walls and floors already discussed to promote the patient's comfort while still keeping the decorating pleasant.

Lighting

Good lighting, both natural and artificial, is important both to patients and to health workers. Light bulbs, shades and lamps usually are easily adjusted so that good lighting is generally available. Many hospitals are now being built with large windows or sliding glass doors that can be shaded as needed. In addition to providing much more natural light, they make it pleasant for patients to enjoy looking or being outdoors.

Looking into light, seeing glare from artificial lights, and seeing light reflected from linens may be uncomfortable for patients and workers. In particular, older persons and those wearing glasses are bothered by glaring lights. Often moving furniture a bit and adjusting shades on lights will help to decrease glare.

Although light that brightens the entire room may be best for health workers, it may not be satisfactory for the patient when he wishes to read. A bedside lamp that is adjustable for brightness and for different angles is best.

Most persons prefer that a ward be darkened when they rest and sleep. This can usually be accomplished with ease by adjusting shades and draperies and by turning off artificial lights.

At night, a dim light is a valuable comfort and safety measure. Newer hospitals are installing night lights at the base of the floor and in hall areas. These lights illuminate the environment yet do not shine in the patient's eyes.

Humidity, temperature and ventilation

A patient's comfort often depends on regulating environmental factors such as humidity, temperature, and ventilation. *Humidity* is the amount of moisture in the air. Relative humidity is the ratio between the amount of moisture in the air and the greatest amount of moisture the air could contain at the same temperature.

Temperature is the measurement of heat. Most people are comfortable in a room maintained in a temperature range of 20°C to 23°C (68°F to 74°F) and a relative humidity of 30% to 60%. Illness may influence the patient's comfort, and he may feel too warm or too cold even when the temperature and humidity are within average normal ranges.

Most hospitals have airconditioning units that regulate temperature and humidity. In climates or buildings where humidity is very low, measures that add moisture to the air may be helpful. This may be done with the use of humidifiers or machines that produce steam or a fine mist of water.

Ventilation refers to the movement of air. A room with fresh air is comfortable, but a room with stale air is almost always uncomfortable. Air-conditioning units help keep the air fresh and clean. Windows may be used for ventilation when weather permits. Open windows that face each other, but are located on opposite sides of a room or building, promote cross ventilation. *Cross ventilation* is the movement of air in one opening and out the other. When ventilating rooms, take care to prevent draughts that could circulate microorganisms carried on air currents.

Furnishings within the patient's ward area

Manufacturers of hospital furnishings attempt to combine equipment that is both attractive and serves a utilitarian purpose. The items within a patient's ward area must be safe, durable, and comfortable.

The bed

For the convenience of health practitioners and patients, most hospitals have adjustable beds, which can be raised and lowered, usually with an electric motor or a hand crank. When the patient is ambulatory, the height of an adjustable bed is lowered so that he can get in and out of bed with ease. The head and foot may be elevated independently. The family may wish to consider renting or borrowing a hospital bed for a person who will need home care. A standard bed at home can be raised on solid blocks of wood for the convenience of care givers. Beds designed for particular patient needs are discussed later in this chapter.

The comfort of the patient while in bed is related to the quality of the mattress. Other comfort factors include the cleanliness and smoothness of the linen. Principles of Care 16-1 describes a method for making an unoccupied bed. This type of bedmaking can be performed for patients who are ambulatory. An *ambulatory* patient is one who is able to walk and be out of bed. The actions that are described for making

Principles of Care 16-1. *Making an unoccupied bed*

Nursing Action	Rationale
Bring a linen rounder and a clean chair to the bedside if there is no bedmaking rack attached to the bed.	Having equipment on hand saves energy by avoiding trips to obtain necessary equipment.
Place an adjustable bed in the high position and lower the bed siderail.	Having the bed in the high position and the siderails down reduces musculoskeletal strain on the nurse.
Remove equipment attached to bed linens and check for personal items the patient may have dropped in the bed, such as a watch or dentures.	Equipment attached to the bed may be lost or ruined if it is accidentally sent to the laundry. It may be costly or impossible to replace lost or broken items.
Starting at the head of the bed, loosen all linen while moving around the bed.	Loosening linens helps prevent tugging and tearing. Moving around the bed while loosening linen reduces strain caused by reaching across the bed.
Remove pillowcases by slipping them off while the pillows lie on the bed.	Not lifting the pillows reduces draughts that may spread organisms and lessens strain on the nurse's arms.
Fold reusable linens, such as blankets, in place on the bed in quarters, and hang them over a clean chair.	Folding saves time and energy when reusable linen is replaced on the bed. Folding linens while they are on the bed reduces strain on the nurse's arms.
Snugly roll all the soiled linen inside the bottom sheet and place it directly into the linen rounder. Do *not* place it on the floor or on furniture.	Rolling linens snugly and placing them directly into the linen rounder helps prevent the spread of organisms. The floor is heavily contaminated; soiled linen will further contaminate furniture.
Keep all soiled linen away from the front of the uniform.	The nurse must go from patient to patient. Organisms from a patient's soiled laundry, which are transferred to the nurse's uniform, could spread disease to the nurse or other patients.
Wash hands thoroughly after stripping a bed before making a clean bed.	Hands contain organisms from soiled laundry. Handwashing reduces their transfer to the clean linen.
Bring necessary clean linens to the bedside.	Having linens on hand saves nursing time by preventing unnecessary trips to the linen storage area.
Place linens on a clean chair or on the overbed table in the same order in which they will be placed on the bed.	Having linens in the order in which they will be used saves nursing time.

Continued

Principles of Care 16-1. Continued

Nursing Action	Rationale
Place the mattress pad on the bed in position so that, as it is unfolded, it will be in the proper place.	Opening linens by shaking them causes movement of air. Air currents can carry dust and organisms about the room. If linens were held with the arms extended, the nurse's arms would be strained.
Place the bottom sheet on the bed and unfold it.	Opening linens by shaking them causes air currents that may spread dust and organisms about the room.
Position the bottom sheet with its centre fold in the centre of the bed and the hem of the sheet even with the lower edge of the mattress. The seam should be on the underneath side.	Positioning the sheets in this manner allows for sufficient fabric to be tucked in at the top and sides of the mattress. Placing the seam underneath prevents the raised edge from irritating the skin of the patient.
Tuck the bottom sheet securely under the head of the mattress on one side of the bed, making a corner according to hospital policy. A mitred corner is shown in Figure 16-1.	Having bottom linens free of wrinkles results in a comfortable bed. Making a mitred or square corner makes the bed look neat and prevents linen from becoming loose and wrinkled.

Figure 16-1 *Left*: To make a mitred corner, the nurse folds the sheet back on the bed and holds her right hand to form the corner. *Centre*: The nurse tucks the bottom of the sheet, forming the corner under the mattress. *Right*: The nurse places a hand at the side of the mattress to hold the corner in place and with the other hand brings the sheet down over the corner. She is then ready to tuck the entire length of the sheet under the mattress.

If a waterproof sheet is used, place it over the bottom sheet so that it will be under the patient's chest-to-knee area. Place the cotton drawsheet in the same manner over the waterproof drawsheet.	When a patient soils his bed, drawsheets can be changed without requiring that the entire bed be re-made.
When pulling bottom sheets tightly, hold the hands with the palms downward so that pull is produced by the large muscles of the arms and shoulders. Bend the knees. Spread the feet as though to walk backward and rock back so that the weight of the body helps produce the force needed, as illustrated in Figure 16-2.	The longest and strongest muscles in the nurse's arms are at work in this position. Bending the knees and spreading the feet produce a wide base of support. Rocking backward uses the body's weight as a force. The nurse uses the body efficiently throughout these movements to reduce the effort of work.

Continued

Principles of Care 16-1. Continued

Nursing Action   **Rationale**

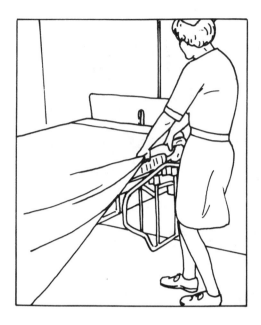

Figure 16-2 The bottom sheet on the opposite side of the bed is already tucked in securely. Note the position of the nurse as the sheet is pulled tightly before tucking it under the mattress. The nurse faces the work area. The feet are separated and the knees are flexed. The sheet is grasped with the palms of the hands held downwards.

Tuck the linens from the bottom sheet, the waterproof sheet, and the drawsheet under the mattress. Move to the other side of the bed and do the same.

Making the bed on one side and then completing the other side saves time.

Place the top sheet on the bed with its centre fold in the centre of the bed and with the top of the sheet placed so that the hem is even with the head of the mattress.

Opening linens by shaking them spreads organisms and dust on air currents.

Make a toe pleat by making a small horizontal or vertical fold in the top sheet near the bottom of the bed, as shown in Figure 16-3, or slightly gather the linen before tucking it under the mattress. Place the blanket and the spread about 20 cm (8 in) from the top of the bed in the same manner as the top sheet.

Providing room for the patient's feet prevents top linens from forcing the patient's feet into an uncomfortable position.

Tuck top linens, blanket and the spread securely at the foot of the mattress and make corners according to hospital policy.

Securing bed linens well, but without placing pressure on the patient's feet, results in a bed that is comfortable.

Turn the top of the sheet down over the spread and blanket.

Folding the sheet over the blanket and spread protects the patient's chin and face from irritation.

Place the pillow on the bed. Unfold the pillowcase in the same manner as that used for the other linen. Gather the pillowcase as you would gather hosiery, and slip the case over the pillow, as illustrated in Figure 16-4.

Opening linens by shaking them causes organisms and dust to be carried about on air currents. Covering the pillow while it rests on the bed reduces strain on the nurse's arms.

Continued

Principles of Care 16-1. *Continued*

Nursing Action	Rationale

Figure 16-3 A vertical toe pleat is being made. For a horizontal toe pleat, the nurse would fold the top sheet so that the pleat would lie across the bottom of the bed rather than on the vertical plane.

Figure 16-4 The nurse places protectors and cases on a pillow by gathering them first and then sliding them one at a time over the pillow.

Figure 16-5 The nurse, in preparing the bed for the patient, 'piefolds' the top linen.

Figure 16-6 The nurse attaches the signal device to the bottom bed linen so that the device will remain in place and be handy for the patient's use.

Principles of Care 16-1. *Continued*

Nursing Action	Rationale
Place the pillow at the head of the bed with the open end away from the door and the seam of the pillowcase toward the top of the bed.	The enclosed end of the pillow presents a neat and tidy view of the patient's bed. The seam can create a source of pressure and discomfort as the patient lies in bed.
Fanfold or prefold the top linens, as illustrated in Figure 16-5, to the lower part of the bed.	Having linens folded to the bottom of the bed makes it more convenient for the patient to get into the bed.
Secure the signal device on the bed according to hospital policy, as shown in Figure 16-6.	Having the signal device handy for the patient makes it possible for him to call for assistance as necessary.
Adjust the bed to the low position.	Having the bed in the low position makes it easier and safer for the patient to get into bed.

an unoccupied bed promote good body mechanics and prevent the transmission of bacteria and dust. These practices contribute to the safety and comfort of both the nurse and the patient.

The mattress

A good mattress adjusts to the shape of the body sufficiently to permit the body to be in good position. A mattress that is too soft allows the body to sag and the patient may become uncomfortable and suffer backaches.

The covering of the mattress should be of good quality so that it will not tear or separate easily. It is not general practice to sterilize mattresses between patient uses. Most hospitals use mattresses with a special waterproof coating. These mattresses can be washed after each patient use. A plastic drawsheet is unnecessary, although mattress pads are still used.

Pillows

Pillows may be filled with various materials and vary in comfort. Foam-rubber pillows are often used by persons who are allergic to kapok, feathers and other commonly used materials. They are not easily moulded, and, therefore, are often difficult to arrange in the most comfortable position for the patient. Also they tend to absorb and retain heat, causing the patient to perspire.

Most persons use pillows under the head for comfort. Nurses also find pillows helpful in aiding the patient to maintain a comfortable position in bed. This is discussed further in this chapter.

Pillows are generally not sterilized between patient uses, but it is general practice to protect them in some way. Certain pillows are made from material that is resistant to dirt and moisture; this is a great help in keeping them clean. Others require a separate cover to protect them. Plastic covers are commonly used. Their disadvantages include being slippery and hot. The patient is always welcome to bring his own pillow from home if that would provide more comfort. The nurse should take care to identify and safeguard it from loss.

The bed table

Bed tables are conveniently used by patients for eating, reading, writing and performing personal hygiene. They can also be used to support the patient in a forward leaning position while he rests the upper part of his body on the table (Figure 16-7). Health practitioners also find bed tables convenient for holding equipment used for some procedures. Most bed tables are designed so that they can be lowered for the patient while he is in a chair. There is sometimes a portion of the table that can be tilted and will support a book or newspaper. Some have mirrors on the back of the tilt portion; these are convenient for the patient to use when combing hair, shaving or applying makeup.

The bedside locker

A bedside locker is used for storing the patient's personal care items. Although lockers may vary among hospitals, certain features are handy for both patients

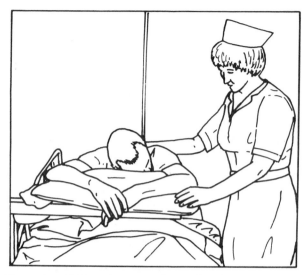

Figure 16-7 This patient is made comfortable by being supported on the bed table in a forward leaning position. The patient often welcomes this position after lying in bed for some time.

and health personnel. The patient can handle the locker with greater ease when it is mounted on wheels. A drawer in the table usually is used for the patient's personal possessions. The inside of the locker is used for the storage of items such as a washbasin, oral hygiene equipment, soap dish, bedpan, urinal, bath blanket and so on. It is an important safety practice to keep the utensils used for elimination clean and separate from other items. This helps to control odours and the transmission of microorganisms present in stool.

Chairs

A straight chair with good arm and back support is comfortable for most patients. For very short patients, a footstool can be placed under the feet. Having chairs without arms available is desirable. For instance, these chairs are more suitable when patients must be lifted out of bed and into chairs, because there are no arms to get in the way of those who are lifting.

Upholstered chairs are often very comfortable but are not practical for patients who find it difficult to raise themselves out of them. Elderly patients and those with limited movement usually find upholstered chairs difficult to use.

Personal care utensils

The following items are basic equipment needed for giving personal care:

Bedpan	Soap dish
Drinking glass	Wash basin
Vomit bowl	Water container
Mouthwash cup	Urinal

Disposable personal care items are in common use. Glass breaks easily; metal is noisy when handled; and enamel chips, making it hard to keep clean. Reusable items are cleaned and sterilized before being supplied to another patient as described in Chapter 20.

Most patients bring combs, brushes, shaving equipment, toothbrushes and toothpaste with them when they are hospitalized. In some hospitals, kits containing these items are available.

Diversional items

Most hospitals have television sets and telephones for the use of patients. Although these items offer patients diversion and convenience, the nurse will wish to remember that they can also be hazardous in the ward. Wiring on the floor, loose plugs, frayed cords and television stands in doorways are some of the dangers they can present.

The patient may bring diversional items to hospitals when admitted, such as handicraft work and books. If a patient brings an electrical item, such as a tape player or radio, the same precautions mentioned above should be used. Also, the nurse should check hospital policy concerning which types of electrical items are allowed.

Modifying the environment

It is easy for health personnel who work each day in the same environment to be unaware of things that may be offensive to a patient. Some factors may be controlled, making the patient's stay in hospital more comfortable.

Controlling noise

Many patients complain of noises that often seem to be a part of every hospital. Much money and effort have gone into the design of buildings and into the use of carpeting, curtaining and acoustic ceilings to help reduce noise. Yet, many patients complain of the hospital's noisy environment. Two of the most common complaints from patients are that people allow telephones to ring and that people speak loudly when conversing on the phone. Patients and visitors find frivolous chatting and laughing by personnel difficult to accept and consider it an annoyance.

Controlling odours

Illness tends to alter the sense of smell and may make mild odours that are usually pleasant become disagreeable. For example, the smell of good cooking is pleasant for a well person but may cause nausea in an ill person. There are various air deodorants on the market, but in general they seem to do little more than substitute one odour for another. However, they are frequently the only help when odours are hard to control and ventilation is insufficient. Removing soiled articles and opening privacy curtains may help to control odours in the patient's immediate area. The nurse should avoid using highly scented colognes, deodorants, or cosmetics. It is important for the nurse to be clean and free of offensive body odour.

Providing privacy

Anyone who is being interviewed, examined or cared for has the right to privacy. The nurse will want to remember that certain legal problems may develop when the patient's privacy is invaded, as Chapter 7 described. Patients also enjoy privacy when they have visitors. If a procedure, which may be embarrassing to the patient, cannot wait to be performed, visitors should be shown where they may wait until the care is finished. If the patient requests that a family member remain while the care is given, his wish should be respected. It is a thoughtful gesture to notify visitors or family, who have momentarily left a patient's bedside, when the care has been completed. Table 16-1 offers suggestions to help control noise and odours and provide privacy.

Table 16-1. Suggestions for controlling noise and odours and providing privacy

Controlling Noise	Controlling Odours	Providing Privacy
Handle equipment as carefully as possible. Dropping articles and bumping things cause unpleasant noises.	Discard waste and refuse promptly.	Use cubicle curtains or screens when caring for patients on wards or who share rooms.
Handle dishes, silverware and trays to prevent rattling them about.	Remove old flowers and stagnant water promptly.	Close doors when giving care to patients in private rooms.
Answer the telephone promptly and speak in a normal tone of voice.	Empty bedpans, urinals and vomit bowls promptly and clean them properly.	Drape patients carefully when giving care.
Avoid calling down corridors; go to people to whom you wish to speak.	Remove leftover food from rooms promptly.	Allow the patient privacy when using the bedpan or urinal, if it is safe to leave the patient.
Avoid laughing and social chatting in corridors and patient lounges.	Remember that patients find it offensive to receive care from nurses who are in need of deodorant, whose perfume is strong or who have been smoking recently.	Knock before opening a closed door. Identify your presence outside the privacy curtains.
Limit reporting about patients to the nurses' station and conference rooms. In addition to causing noise, overheard conversations may be misinterpreted by patients.		Help visitors find the patients they wish to visit so that they do not enter a stranger's room.
Try to keep television sets and radios at a low volume. Remind patients courteously to keep the volume low. Have them use ear receivers if possible.		

Sensory alteration

There may come a point at which environmental stimuli, or the lack of it, become harmful to a patient. A *stimulus* (plural is *stimuli*) is a change in the environment sufficient to cause a response. For example, an unexpected, loud noise is a stimulus that may cause a person to respond with fear. Stimuli are received through various senses (i.e. sight, hearing, touch, smell and taste).

When normal stimuli are absent or decreased, when their quality is poor, or when they are above normal in amount, well-being suffers. The person may experience a *sensory alteration*. This means a person is experiencing an excessive or insufficient stimulation, making it difficult to process information appropriately. Patients in hospitals and nursing homes are especially at risk for this. Patients typically show signs of loneliness and a variety of unusual states, such as fear and panic, depression, inability to concentrate, boredom and the like when sensory alteration is present.

Some nurses use two additional terms when speaking of sensory alteration. *Sensory deprivation* is receiving less than optimal amounts of good quality stimuli for the person's well-being. This includes monotonous or repetitive stimuli; the stimuli are present, but lack the variety to be noticed. *Sensory overload* means receiving more than optimal amounts of stimuli for well-being. Interestingly enough, the signs are similar when the patient suffers from either too many or too few stimuli over a period of time.

The most desirable amount of stimuli for well-being varies among people. For example, the noise in a crowded disco is tolerated well by some, while others find the noise intolerable. Also, the quiet and the slow pace of country living may be uncomfortable for the city dweller who is used to noise and bustle.

Knowledge of sensory alteration has implications for nursing. The actions described in Principles of Care 16-2 suggest ways and reasons for promoting sensory stimulation in a hospital or the home. With experience, the nurse will find still other measures for helping to prevent sensory alteration. Efforts to adjust stimuli within a patient's environment are evidence of quality nursing care.

Ensuring the patient's safety

It will never be possible to prevent accidents completely. However, there are ways that injuries can be reduced. The nurse must take various safety precautions to limit the potential for accidents that may harm patients.

Signalling for assistance

Hospitals use a signal system so that patients can call for assistance. A device, usually with a push button, is placed on the bed near the patient. It may be attached to the bed linen with a clasp. When the patient pushes the button, a light or bell signals the nurse. Some devices have an attachment that, when activated, sounds a loud buzzer, indicating that an emergency exists and help is needed immediately. Some hospitals use intercom systems for patients to communicate with the nurse. Signal devices are usually placed in bathrooms, lounge areas and other places where patients gather.

It is very important to make certain that a signal device is convenient for the patient's use and that it is in working order. Nursing personnel must respond to the patient's signal promptly. Health practitioners can be held negligent when accidents occur because a patient cannot reach his signal device or does not know how to use it, or if the signal is ignored.

In the home, a bell placed at the patient's bedside can be used. Individuals with health problems who are at home should have a telephone within easy reach so that they can call for help if necessary. Some communities use the emergency assistance number, 999 or 111, which is easily remembered and can be dialled quickly. There are phones that dial specific numbers, such as the ambulance or fire department, automatically.

Identifying the patient accurately

It is important to check the patient's identification bracelet before giving nursing care, so that treatments and medications are not given to the wrong patient. As important as an identification bracelet is, the nurse should also ask an unfamiliar patient to state his name before giving care. A very ill, hard of hearing, or confused patient may respond even if the nurse calls him by the wrong name. Asking the patient to state his name is particularly important when caring for patients in clinics, nursing homes and in home care, where identification bracelets may not be used. Legal problems may be very serious when health practitioners confuse one patient with another.

Principles of Care 16-2. Promoting sensory stimulation

Nursing Action	Rationale
Move the bed to various places in the room. Rearrange the furniture and change the curtains occasionally. Use items such as pictures, flowers and plants to vary what the patient sees.	Any stimulus becomes monotonous if it is not changed periodically.
Change the location of the patient so that he may look out windows that provide a change of scenery.	Changing the scenery and the activity in an area prevents boredom.
Encourage family members and friends to visit the patient as much as possible and in accordance with the policies of the hospital.	A change in the faces and voices of people breaks monotony.
Encourage the patient to telephone relatives and friends when face-to-face visits are not possible.	The phone can be a substitute for personal visits. It helps stimulate individuals and provides a means for checking on their safety.
Speak to the patient. Make conversation about what is happening in the world or community.	Giving explanations about nursing care is not enough in itself to prevent sensory alteration.
For the patient who is unconscious, tune and change radio stations and talk to the patient during the day.	An unconscious patient may still hear. Stimulating him through this sense may help the person gain consciousness.
Vary sounds as much as possible, especially when the patient must listen to the continuous sound of equipment.	Changing the position of equipment, even slightly, often changes its sound and adds some variety.
Encourage as much physical activity as permissible. Help the patient leave his room for visits to lounges and cafeterias.	This increases the variety of stimulation a patient experiences.
Use touch appropriately and frequently. For example, give a back rub or hold the patient's hand.	Touch is a means for both communication and sensory stimulation.
Encourage the use of leisure-time activities. Provide reading and handicraft materials as alternatives to television and radio.	Using more than one sensory organ at a time, or varying its pattern of use, may divert the patient's interest to something new.
Be sure patients using spectacles or hearing aids have them available. Read to patients whose sight is limited or absent. Provide books, magazines and calendars with large print and numbers for those with poor vision.	The nurse must make special efforts to compensate for those who have limitations of their sensory organs.
Help the patient to be aware of the time and date. Place a clock and a calendar nearby.	Patients who are not necessarily confused may lose track of the time and date if they lack the usual reminders.
Offer a variety of foods that provide different flavours, temperatures and textures.	Varying the sensations associated with taste can provide another source of stimulation.
Relieve discomfort and sleeplessness as much as possible, using the nursing actions discussed in Chapter 14.	Prolonged pain and fatigue can contribute to an inability to interpret and respond to stimuli appropriately.

Preventing falls

Falls are among the most frequent causes of accidents for people of all ages. It has been estimated that 75% of accidents in hospitals result from falls. Most are due to slipping, sliding, fainting, tripping or falling from a bed, wheelchair, toilet or commode. Patients who are most often likely to fall include those with neurological disorders, such as a brain tumour, mental deterioration, or a stroke; those with debilitating illnesses, such as heart diseases; and those who have difficulty walking, are depressed or confused, or have sensory impairments, such as blindness.

Siderails on the bed help prevent patients from falling out of bed. Most hospitals have policies stating that siderails are to be up at all times except when care is being given. Patients sometimes complain of siderails and ask that they be removed. Often an explanation of why they are there will satisfy the patient. If the patient refuses to have the siderails raised on his bed, most hospitals require that he sign a release form that frees the hospital and the health practitioners of responsibility if an accident occurs.

Sometimes, visitors ask to have siderails down and say they will watch the patient. It should be remembered that the nurse, not the visitor, is responsible for the patient's safety. Therefore, extreme caution must be used before leaving siderails down. The supervising nurse should be consulted when the slightest doubt exists.

Preventing electrical injuries

Hospitals and homes today contain a great variety of electrical equipment that can be extremely dangerous if used improperly. The danger of accidents from electrical shocks and from fires is always present unless precautions are taken.

Preventing fires

Despite fire regulations and the use of much fire retardant material, fires still occur. Most hospitals have regular fire drills so that all health practitioners, including student nurses, know exactly what to do in case of fire.

Preventing poisoning

Poisoning is a threat to the hospitalized patient because there are many poisonous substances in a hospital environment. Special precautions need to be observed, particularly in relation to various chemicals such as those used for cleaning purposes. Safety associated with the administration of medications is discussed in Chapter 18.

Preventing scalds and burns

A hospital environment exposes some patients to the potential for scalds and burns. Equipment that provides heat as a therapeutic agent creates the possibility for hazards and injuries of this nature. Ill persons often become unable to handle items that they previously used with ease, such as hot coffee, tea and soup. Many hospitals have thermostats to regulate the temperature of hot water from taps. This precaution has helped reduce burns that have been caused when patients or personnel have carelessly used very hot water for baths and showers.

Preventing drowning and asphyxiation

Asphyxiation means suffocation because of lack of oxygen. Dangers of drowning and asphyxiation are relatively minimal among healthy persons, but they are a threat for many ill patients, especially those taking baths without supervision.

Preventing the spread of infections

Chapter 20 discusses ways to prevent the spread of microorganisms. Observing practices presented in that chapter means a safer environment for everyone.

Table 16-2 offers more suggestions on helping to provide a safe environment for the patient as well as for health practitioners.

When accidents occur

Despite efforts to prevent accidents, they unfortunately still occur. Human errors are sometimes made. In addition to possible harm to the patient, serious legal problems can be caused by accidents. Therefore, it is especially important to handle each accident with great care. The following steps are recommended when an accident occurs:

1. Check the patient's condition immediately. Note his condition and be ready to describe it accurately.
2. Call for help to assist you. For example, seek help in the event of a fall because sufficient help is almost always necessary to move a patient so that injuries are not made worse.
3. Do *not* move a patient who has fallen until it is considered safe to do so. If a bone has been

Table 16-2. DOs and DON'Ts for providing a safe environment

Do	Don't
Helping to Prevent Falls	

Do	Don't
Place adjustable beds in the low position when patients are getting in and out of bed. Have a patient use a sturdy step stool when the bed is high and not adjustable.	Do not use equipment and supplies for anything but their intended purposes. For example, chairs are dangerous step stools!
Use nonslip mats or strips in baths and showers to prevent the patient from falling on slippery shower floors and baths.	Do not allow patients to use floppy, high heeled, soft or loose fitting shoes when walking. The patient should wear good walking shoes with low heels to help prevent falling.
Use bath and shower stools and sturdy handrails in bathrooms. Figure 16-8 illustrates several bath safety features.	Do not allow items such as books, magazines, handicrafts, shoes and so on to be placed on floors and stairways. Litter on floors and stairways can easily cause tripping and falls.

Figure 16-8 This photo illustrates several safety features. The support on the side of the bath helps the patient get in and out, several hand bars provide extra support, a mixer tap controls water temperature, nonslip strips are affixed to the bottom of the bath, and a call cord is conveniently placed next to the bath.

Do	Don't
Have patients in wheelchairs use wide doorways, ramps, and lifts so that they are not tempted to try to walk stairways.	Do not leave spilled liquids on the floor until some one else wipes them up. Mop or wipe up promptly. Also, see to it that signs are posted and warn patients and visitors when floors are wet and slippery after being scrubbed.
	Do not use throw rugs that slip easily or rugs that are torn or curled at the edges. Throw rugs are hazardous.

Continued

Table 16-2. *Continued*

Do	Don't
Helping to Prevent Electrical Injuries	
Use earthed plugs and outlets when possible. These plugs have three prongs and will fit only into outlets with three-prong sockets.	Do not stand in water or wear wet shoes and then handle electrical equipment. Water conducts electricity well.
Remove a plug from a wall socket by grasping the plug. Pulling on the cord to remove the plug may damage both the plug and the wire.	Do not kink cords. The fine electrical wires inside a cord may break.
Use equipment for its intended purpose only. Using a hot plate, for example, is a dangerous way to warm a chilly room.	Do not use frayed or broken electrical cords or overload an electrical outlet. Overheating may occur and cause a fire.
Keep all electrical equipment in good working order and in good repair.	Do not use an appliance that overheats, produces a shock, or gives off an odour while being used.
Keep television sets, telephones, radios, hair dryers and so on away from baths and sinks.	Never use faulty pieces of equipment. Test electrical equipment before use.
Helping to Prevent Fires	
Know where there are emergency exits. Know where fire extinguishers are kept and how to use them.	Do not allow a confused, sleepy or drugged patient to smoke unattended. Stay with the patient if he wants to smoke and take care of the cigarette for him when he has finished. Keeping cigarettes and matches out of his reach will prevent his using them when alone.
Know the hospital's policy and plan for fire and evacuation of patients.	
Remember that oxygen supports combustion. The smallest flame or a live cigarette can become a torch in the presence of concentrated oxygen. When a patient is receiving oxygen as part of his treatment, be sure the patient, his visitors and his neighbours know of the fire dangers. Post signs to show that oxygen is in use and that smoking is prohibited.	Do not store materials saturated with solutions that could lead to spontaneous combustion unless they are in an airtight metal container. Certain cleaning solutions and acetone are offenders in this regard.
Be sure smoking regulations are enforced. When patients and visitors are allowed to smoke, provide safe ashtrays, preferably ones from which a burning cigarette cannot fall. Many fires have started when wastebaskets were used for ashtrays.	
Helping to Prevent Poisoning	
Be sure you know where emergency instructions on how to handle poisoning are posted in the hospital where you study or work. Having such instructions handy in the home is also important.	Do not remove poisonous substances from their original containers and place them in another container. A poisonous substance may be mistaken for something entirely different because of the appearance of a container that ordinarily contains nonpoisonous contents. For example, poisonous cleaning solutions have been mistakenly drunk when the solution has been placed in a soft drink bottle.
Be sure that poisonous substances are conspicuously labelled.	
Put poisonous substances away immediately after use and store them where patients cannot get at them.	

Continued

Table 16-2. Continued

Do	Don't
Helping to Prevent Poisoning	
	Do not place medications anywhere except where they are normally to be stored. Chapter 18 discusses further safety precautions when handling medications.
Helping to Prevent Scalds and Burns	
Place hot liquids, such as coffee and tea, in a place that is convenient for the patient. The nurse should plan to help a patient if he is unable to handle liquids safely on his own.	Do not add hot water to a bath in which a patient is bathing without agitating it as you add the hot water. The patient may be burned by hot water that is not being mixed with the cooler water.
Check the temperature of water being used by patients in baths and showers. This is especially important if there is any doubt about whether the patient can safely regulate the temperature of water.	Do not use hot water bottles and heating pads without checking hospital policy. Many do not allow their use because of the danger of burning patients. Hot water bottles and heating pads are discussed further in Chapter 22.
Helping to Prevent Drowning and Asphyxiation	
When helping a patient eat, offer small bites of food and give him sufficient time between mouthfuls to chew food well. Offer fluids carefully also, especially if the patient must remain flat on his back or has trouble swallowing.	Do not leave a patient while he is in the bath if there is any danger of drowning.
Use dentures for patients if available. Have food pureed or coarsely ground for those who lack teeth or can't chew.	Do not leave a patient to feed himself if he requires help.
Place an unconscious patient on his side or abdomen.	Never "prop" a bottle against an infant and leave him unattended during feeding.

broken, moving the patient without proper support may cause further injury to bone and surrounding tissues.

4. Report the accident to the proper person promptly. Usually this is the supervising nurse, who will then notify the doctor.

5. Comfort and reassure the patient. Explain that help is available and proper care will be taken. Indicate concern for the patient who is in discomfort. Experience has shown it is particularly important to maintain a helping nurse-patient relationship whenever an accident occurs. Feelings expressed by the patient, such as anger and fear, can be handled best when the patient is helped to feel that personnel are sorry that the accident occurred, that care will be provided for

him and that prompt measures will be taken to prevent future accidents.

6. Do not offer explanations if you were not involved with the accident or without authorization to do so. It is best to consult a supervising nurse about explanations when an accident occurs.

7. Be *sure* to record exactly what happened in the patient's record after you have finished caring for the patient. The patient's record is discussed in Chapter 4.

8. After the patient is properly cared for and the doctor has been notified, prepare an *incident* or *accident report*. All information related to the accident is entered on the form (Fig. 16-9) which is signed by those persons completing the form.

INCIDENT REPORT

HOSPITAL:

Accident Book ☐
Copy Legal Dept. ☐

| SECTION A: | COMPLETED BY: |
| | POSITION: | DATE: |

INJURED PARTY
Name: ....
Address: ....

....

....

Age: ....Sex: M / F   Hospital Reference No: ....
Status: (e.g. Staff, Visitor, Patient) ....
If Patient, name of Consultant: .... Consultant informed: YES/NO

INCIDENT
Date: .... Time: .... Place: ....
How was Hospital/Unit made aware of incident: ....
Nature: (If employee, state work being carried out at time)

....

....

....

Incident Cause/Contributing Factors: ....
....
Apparent Result to injured party: ....
....
....

Witnesses
Name(s): ....

Address(es): ....
....
....

Occupation(s): ....
If no witness, who reported incident: ....
and to whom: ....

| SECTION B | TO BE COMPLETED BY R.M.O. |

Injury: ....
....
....
....
Follow up
Treatment: ....
....
Signed: .... Date ....

SECTION C:
Hospital Director and/or Director of Nursing Comments:
....
....

| SECTION D: | TO BE COMPLETED BY HEAD OF DEPARTMENT OR WARD SISTER |

Date Incident entered in Accident Book: ....
Date Legal Department notified: ....
Follow Up Action ....
....
Reported to Health & Safety Officer : ....
....

SECTION E:
SIGNATURES
Person completing form: .... Date ....
Head of Department: .... Date: ....
Hospital director/
Unit Manager: .... Date: ....

Figure 16-9 This is an example of an incident or accident report form.

These guidelines apply when any accident occurs within the hospital, regardless of the type (e.g., errors in giving medication or a fall from a bed). Accident reports may be required even if visitors or personnel are injured. This form does not become part of the patient's permanent record; it is used to examine the circumstances surrounding the accident and prevent future accidents of a similar nature.

Suggested measures to promote a comfortable and safe environment in selected situations

When the patient is an infant or child

Use mobiles over an infant's cot to add variety to the environment. Use objects that are safe for the infant who is able to grasp things in his hands.

Take into account that young infants respond best to colours with a high contrast, such as black and while. Older infants appear to prefer cool colours, such as blue and green. By the time they are toddlers, children like brilliant colours, such as red and yellow. These findings have resulted from studies that looked at the effects of environmental factors in stimulating development.

Keep small objects away from children who frequently place them in their mouths and may choke. Examples include safety pins, marbles, small balls and broken pieces from toys. Check stuffed animals for parts that may come off. For

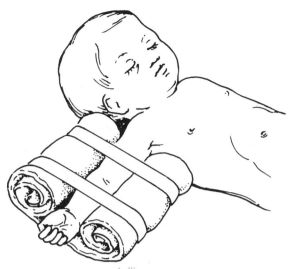

Figure 16-10 This illustrates a method of restraining an infant's arm. The restraint is made with a nappy and secured with pieces of tape.

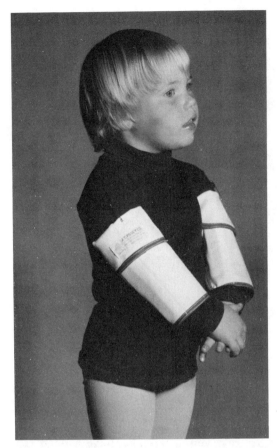

Figure 16-11 These elbow restraints have ties that may be fastened to the child's clothing if necessary. (Courtesy J.T. Posey Co., Arcadia, CA)

example, the eyes on stuffed animals may be dangerous if they can be removed.

Fasten plastic sheeting well on a young child's bed. Keep plastic bags away from units housing youngsters. Accidents from suffocation have occurred when a child's face has accidentally become covered with plastic material.

Keep cot sides up except when giving an infant or young child care. Keep a hand securely on a child when the siderails are lowered. Also, secure youngsters in high-chairs to prevent their falling.

Use restraints judiciously, as described earlier in this chapter. Various types are available for youngsters, such as a crib net, a bubble top, a control jacket, and a papoose or restraining board. Several additional ones are illustrated in Figures 16-10 to 16-12.

Explain to the child when he is old enough to understand, as well as to his parents, why restraints are needed.

Use safe and sturdy furniture and equipment for children. Be sure windows are well secured, electrical equipment is out of reach and unused electrical outlets are covered. Serious shocks and even death have occurred when children have placed things, such as items made of metal, into an electrical outlet.

Know where every child is at all times. Children who play together in hospital rooms should be under adult supervision.

Group together children with similar degrees of illness. For example, grouping children who are convalescing from illness often provides them with good company for one another.

Keep the environment as flexible as possible so that children who are not acutely ill can be near friends and watch activity. These measures help prevent loneliness and sensory deprivation.

Never leave a child alone in a bath because of the danger of drowning.

Recommend gate guards or half-doors to close off the nursing work area, utility room, and medication room from curious children.

Figure 16-12 These restraints restrict a child's fingers and hands without restraining arm movements. They are particularly useful when a youngster scratches or picks. (Courtesy J.T. Posey Co., Arcadia, CA)

Remember that youngsters also have a need for their own personal area. Personal playthings are very important to a child. A place should be provided for playthings and none should ever be thrown away without consulting the child or his parents.

Expect that a children's ward is not likely to be as tidy as an adult ward. Use large containers that will give the children easy access to toys and will provide ample storage space, thus promoting neatness.

When the patient is helpless

Seek ways to provide a safe calling device for a helpless patient, such as one who is paralysed. Several devices are available to help patients who cannot use a typical push button to call for assistance. One type has a plastic tube that is placed near the patient's mouth; when the patient puffs air into the tubing, the call system is activated. Another type has a switch in a large sponge and can be activated when slight pressure is made on it by any part of the body. Still another uses a highly sensitive touch plate.

Check a helpless patient at frequent intervals to be sure that he is not in danger.

When the patient is elderly

Expect that the effects of being in a strange environment develop more quickly in an elderly person than in a young adult. The effects include confusion, disorientation and anxiety. These observations illustrate the decreased ability in the elderly to adapt to change.

Take into account that older persons generally prefer a warmer room and usually are more sensitive to draughts than are young people.

In addition to a night light, provide an elderly patient with a torch, as indicated, to help orientation at night. Also, placing fluorescent tape at light switches and on door knobs helps the patient orient himself to his environment.

Allow elderly persons to keep personal items close to them, even on their bed, if the items present no danger. Examples include spectacles, a purse, a sweater, or a blanket or pillow of their own. Familiar items close at hand help the elderly feel more secure and comfortable in a strange environment.

Be especially alert to sensory alteration among elderly persons. They tend to show the effects of sensory overload and sensory deprivation relatively quickly.

Teaching suggestions for promoting a comfortable and safe environment

The alert nurse will find many opportunities to teach patients how to prevent accidents. Safety measures apply to the home as well as to a hospital.

The nurse may teach by setting a good example. When care is given and the nurse expresses concern and interest in safety measures, patients will learn. Also, the patient is quick to realize when a nurse is not observing safety measures and will soon lose confidence.

The inactive patient

Research has shown that activity is essential for health. Therefore, patients confined to bed or those with physical limitations require care that includes movement and exercise. Procedures to turn, move, position, exercise and promote mobility to prevent complications associated with inactivity are described below.

Dangers of inactivity

Though many individuals are not active enough to improve their level of health, some are so inactive that their health deteriorates. Multiple complications can and do occur among individuals whose activity and movement are limited.

It has been demonstrated that a person needs only about 2 hours of activity in every 24 hours to prevent many problems. The dangers of inactivity illustrate the importance of a nursing care plan that includes activity and exercise for the patient. The following discussion deals with these effects.

The muscular system

Muscular weakness develops quickly with inactivity. When inactivity is prolonged, muscle weakness may become so severe that the effects are more damaging than the original illness.

Tonus refers to the normal, slight, continuous contraction of muscles. Decreased muscle tonus, called *atony*, develops with inactivity. In time, there is the development of *atrophy*, which is the wasting away of muscle cells.

Most patients experience backaches after being in bed for several days. Poor posture in bed and a soft mattress most frequently are responsible for

Figure 16-13 *Left*: Dorsiflexion. *Right*: Plantarflexion, the position of foot drop.

backaches that are caused by the stretching of back muscles and failure to support them properly in bed.

The skeletal system

One problem associated with the disuse syndrome commonly affecting the skeletal system is osteoporosis, which was also discussed in Chapter 11. This is a condition characterized by loss of minerals, especially calcium, from the bones. The result is that the bones become less dense. When this condition occurs, the bones are brittle, fracture easily and often become deformed. The calcium leaves the bone and is eliminated through the urinary tract. This predisposes the inactive patient to kidney stone formation.

Poor alignment also affects structures of the skeletal system. *Alignment* refers to arranging the body or its structures in a straight line. Allowing joints to be bent and unmoved for long periods of time can limit their range of motion.

Inactivity may eventually lead to a *contracture*, which is the decrease in a joint's range of motion due to the shortening of a muscle, disuse of a joint, or improper positioning. A joint can become fixed within a matter of days unless preventive measures are used. Patients often refer to a contracture at a joint as a "locked" or "frozen" joint.

Ordinarily the foot can easily be moved from a position of plantarflexion to dorsiflexion. *Dorsiflexion*, shown in Figure 16-13, means the foot is in a position in which the toes point upward. It is important to position the feet of an inactive person in dorsiflexion. This is the joint position that is necessary for walking. In a normal standing position, the foot is at a right angle to the leg, with the toes pointing straight forward. When a person takes a step the heel strikes the floor, followed by the toes.

Plantarflexion, also shown in Figure 16-13, means the foot is in a position that allows the toes to point downward. When the patient is in bed on his back, the foot tends to assume the position of plantarflexion. If this position is maintained for a period of time, a condition known as foot drop occurs. *Foot drop* is a type of contracture that results from prolonged plantarflexion, lack of movement of the ankle joint, and shortening of muscles at the back of the calf. This condition makes walking difficult or impossible since the heel and foot cannot be placed flat on the floor. In order to prevent permanent disuse, the foot must be kept in dorsiflexion and exercised.

The cardiovascular system

Normally, when muscles contract during activity, they squeeze veins, helping to move blood back to the heart. Lack of activity reduces this circulatory assistance. It contributes to sluggish circulation with pooling of blood in the veins. This can lead to several circulatory complications.

The flow of blood may be so slowed in the lower legs that a clot forms. A *thrombus* is a stationary blood clot. It frequently causes a slowing or block in the flow of blood through a blood vessel. A thrombus is often accompanied by an inflammation of the vein in the area in which it is located. The suffix ''itis'' refers to the presence of an inflammation. When combined with the root word for vein, ''phleb'', it forms the word phlebitis. *Phlebitis* is an inflammation of a vein. A *thrombophlebitis* is a condition in which a thrombus lies within an inflamed vein.

An embolus can develop from a thrombus. An *embolus* is a blood clot that is no longer stationary. It moves from a larger blood vessel to a smaller one. The sudden blockage of an artery or vein with material, such as a blood clot or other substance, is called an *embolism*. If the thrombus or embolus lodges in a blood vessel supplying a vital organ, like the arteries that supply the heart muscle, the lungs or the brain, the life of the patient could be in danger. If the blockage is not promptly relieved, the embolism may prove fatal. Periodic movement, especially of the lower extremities, can reduce the risk of cardiovascular complications associated with inactivity.

The respiratory system

Inactivity and poor posture cause a decrease in the movement of the thorax and a loss in tonus of the muscles of respiration. As a result, the exchange of oxygen and carbon dioxide is diminished and the normal chemical balance of the blood may be placed in jeopardy.

Inactivity causes a pooling of respiratory secretions. The patient tends to lose the ability to raise and expectorate them. This predisposes the patient to respiratory infections and a poor exchange of oxygen and carbon dioxide. *Hypostatic pneumonia* is a condition associated with inactivity that results from retained secretions.

Still another possible result of inactivity and poor posture is *atelectasis*, which is an incomplete expansion or collapse of small areas of lung tissue.

Secretions that gather in the respiratory system block air passageways and predispose the patient to the condition.

The urinary system

A reduction in the passage of urine, urinary tract infections and urinary stone formation are the most common urinary complications that result from inactivity. There are many reasons that explain why an inactive person is predisposed to these complications associated with the disuse syndrome.

Pressure from the accumulation of urine within the bladder signals a person that he should urinate. When a person is in a reclining position, the amount of pressure on sensitive muscles is reduced. The bladder continues to fill. As urine remains in the bladder, organisms can grow and multiply, leading to an infection. Substances normally dissolved in urine can crystallize as urine is retained for longer periods of time within the bladder. The crystals eventually form stones if the urine is not kept dilute and frequently passed. As the muscles that control urination are used less often, their tone decreases. *Urinary incontinence*, the inability to control the release of urine, may develop as a further complication.

The gastrointestinal tract

Anorexia is often associated with inactivity. When the patient is eating poorly, ensuring that he has a well-balanced and nourishing diet becomes a problem.

The movement of food in the gastrointestinal tract and proper intestinal elimination also become problems with inactivity. Gravity acts along with abdominal muscle movement to propel food and stool through the intestinal tract. Gravity is more effective in a standing position. As stool remains in the intestinal tract for longer periods of time due to inactivity, more and more water is absorbed from the stool. The stool becomes dry and difficult to pass. This is known as *constipation*. It is a common symptom associated with the disuse syndrome.

Faeces is another word for stool. A *faecal impaction* is a further complication of constipation. This is a condition in which the stool becomes so dried that it cannot be passed. When an inactive person acquires a faecal impaction, liquid stool from above the hardened mass is sometimes released around the dry faeces. It may seem that the patient is experiencing *faecal incon-*

tinence, the inability to control stool, or has diarrhoea; the actual problem may be just the opposite.

The integumentary system

The skin's response to inactivity is ordinarily easy to see and it occurs rapidly. As a result of diminished blood supply caused by pressure from an inactive person's body weight, decubitus ulcers form. A *decubitus ulcer*, also called a *pressure sore*, is a condition in which areas of skin are actually destroyed. This is a common problem that occurs when a person sits or lies in the same position for prolonged periods of time. The formation of a decubitus ulcer is even more likely to occur when the patient is also incontinent of urine or stool. When that is the case, pressure plus the moisture and organic substances in the waste products of elimination contribute to the breakdown of skin. The prevention and care of a pressure sore is discussed in greater detail in Chapter 22.

Changes in metabolism

The metabolic rate decreases when patients are inactive because the body requires less energy to function. Body temperature is lowered; there is a decrease in hormonal secretions. In fact, most of the body's processes are carried out at a reduced capacity.

Sleep pattern disturbance

Sometimes inactive individuals sleep as a result of boredom rather than to compensate for fatigue. Frequent naps change the cycles of REM and NREM sleep.

Psychosocial changes

It is normal to be up and about, to work, to exercise and to enjoy outlets for recreation and diversion. When a patient cannot participate in these normal activities because of illness or physical handicaps, his mental attitude and motivation generally suffer. Feeling depressed is common and the person often loses interest in carrying out activities of daily living. Anger may occur as a result of the frustration of feeling dependent on others.

Inactive persons may become more self-centred, since their "world" is confined to the immediate environment around themselves. They may appear impatient and demanding to others whose lives include varied activities, social and professional obligations.

Helping to prevent disuse

When a patient is inactive, the nurse must carry out measures that prevent disuse. This may involve performing passive exercises. *Passive exercise* is an exercise in which one person moves the limbs of another. The patient may have to be encouraged to do active exercises. *Active exercise* is an exercise performed by a person without assistance from others.

Policies about orders for and recording of exercise and activity vary. A doctor's order may be necessary in some situations. In others, the primary nurse or nursing team leader takes responsibility for writing nursing orders for the patient's activity and exercise. It is recommended that the nurse follow orders on the nursing care plan and consult the supervising nurse if there are any questions.

It is self-defeating to both the patient and the nurse to write unrealistic orders for activity. A more practical approach is to evaluate the patient's present abilities and maintain them. The nurse can then consult with the patient about mutually agreed upon expectations and methods for increasing levels of activity and exercise.

Several of the following nursing approaches can be used to avoid the dangers of limited activity that accompanies most illnesses:

- Teach the patient the importance of activity. This should include explaining that activity and exercise are a part of prescribed care.
- Encourage and supervise active exercises as much as is possible and safe for the patient. The nurse can build on the patient's abilities and encourage efforts he can take on his own.
- Carry out passive exercises as indicated and gradually help the patient move toward active exercising.
- Change the helpless patient's position every 1 to 2 hours and use different positions to promote comfort, variety and exercise.
- Demonstrate patience and understanding when the patient seems uninterested, fearful or opposed to activity and exercise.

Various devices and nursing measures that are commonly used to prevent the disuse syndrome through positioning, exercise and mobility, are now discussed.

Using positioning devices

Some patients' activity and exercise may be limited to moving within a bed. The nurse may be required to use many skills for positioning, musculoskeletal support, movement and exercise that some patients are independently unable to carry out.

It is just as important for the body to be in good alignment and posture when a person is lying down as it is when he is standing or sitting. There are many devices that help to maintain good body alignment in bed and to prevent discomfort or pressure on various parts of the body. It should be remembered that any position, no matter how comfortable or anatomically correct, must be changed frequently.

Pillows

The primary purposes of pillows are to provide support and elevation of a body part. A pillow under the arm of a patient in the semi-sitting position helps prevent pulling the shoulders downward and into a poor posture. Small pillows are ideal for support or elevation of the head, extremities, shoulders or incisional wounds. Specially designed, heavy pillows are useful to elevate the upper part of the body when an adjustable bed is not available as, for example, in the home.

Mattress

For a mattress to be comfortable and supporting, it must be firm but have sufficient give to permit good body alignment. A nonsupportive mattress promotes an unnatural curvature of the spine.

Bed board

If the mattress does not provide sufficient support, a bed board may help to keep the patient in better alignment. Bed boards are usually made of plywood or some other firm material. The size varies with the needs of the situation. If sections of the bed such as the head and foot can be raised, it may be necessary to have the board divided and held together with hinges. For home use, full bed boards can be purchased or they can be made from materials on hand.

Adjustable bed

The adjustable bed was described earlier in this chapter. In the high position, this bed is helpful for the nurse when giving care. When it is in the low position, it enables the patient to get in and out of bed with greater ease. Raising the head of the bed helps the bedridden patient see and look about without twisting and bending his neck. Also, he is in a nearly vertical position without the effort of standing, which helps make more effective use of gravity and prepares him for the day when standing and walking will begin.

Rocking bed

The rocking bed is mounted on a special frame rather than on the usual bedstead and, by means of an electric motor, it can be made to rock rhythmically up and down in seesaw fashion. It has a footrest to help keep the patient from sliding and also to help keep the feet in good alignment. The bed ordinarily is adjusted to rock at the same rate as the patient's respirations. By shifting the abdominal organs, the rocking bed aids respirations for the patient having difficulty with breathing.

Chair bed

Another type of bed is one that can be placed into a chairlike position. These beds are designed primarily for patients who have certain heart conditions. They are sometimes called cardiac beds.

Stryker and Foster frames

A Stryker frame, illustrated in Figure 16-14, has two canvas covered frames. The patient is securely sandwiched between them with safety belts. He is then turned to his back or onto his abdomen. After the patient is in the desired position the upper frame is removed.

The frame on which the patient lies when on his back has an opening for a bedpan and a support to prevent foot drop. The frame on which he lies when on his abdomen has an opening between the forehead and shoulders so that his face is exposed. He can then see objects placed under this area, such as reading materials, food, fluids and so on. The canvas ends at the ankles so that it cannot cause pressure on the patient's toes when he lies on his abdomen. Bed linen covers the canvas pieces and is pinned under the frame. A Foster frame is similar to a Stryker frame except that it is larger and sturdier.

Patients are placed on Stryker or Foster frames when they are to be immobilized so that healing may occur, such as in the patient whose spine has been fractured. They also are used by patients who are paralysed, such as patients who have paraplegia (paralysis of both lower extremities) or quadriplegia (paralysis of all four extremities).

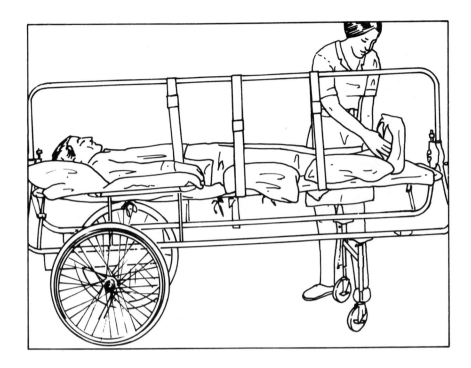

Figure 16-14 The patient is positioned on his back on the Stryker frame. Note the support for the feet to prevent foot drop. The knees are kept free of pillows to prevent pressure on blood vessels and nerves in the posterior area of the knees. The arms and hands are positioned in good alignment.

Circular bed

A circular bed operates with an electric motor. It has a 6- or 7-ft frame with a platform for body support runnng across the diameter of the frame. The patient can be placed in any number of positions, and this helps prevent the dangers of immobility. Two frames are used in the same manner as the Stryker and Foster frames. This type of bed is used most often for a patient who is completely helpless. The circular bed is illustrated in Figure 16-15.

Footboard and foot block

Footboards and foot blocks are used primarily to keep the feet in the normal walking position (i.e. the feet held at right angles to the legs and the toes pointed straight up when the patient is lying down). This position prevents foot drop, which is illustrated in Figure 16-16. The board is placed between the foot of the bedstead and the mattress. If the patient is short and cannot reach the board, a foot block can be used. The block may be an improvised sturdy box or wooden block padded with linen. On some commercial footboards, there are supports that hold the foot in dorsiflexion as well as prevent outward rotation of the foot and lower leg. Another type fastens to the sides of the mattress with a clamp. It can then be placed on the mattress at the appropriate

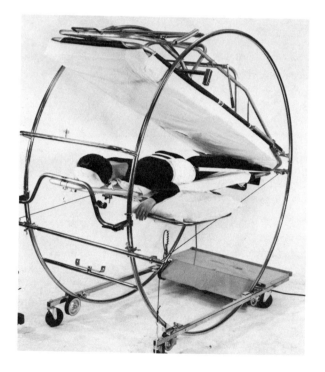

Figure 16-15 In this photo, the bed has been turned so that the patient lies in the prone position. (CircOlectric bed, courtesy Stryker Corporation, Kalamazoo, MI)

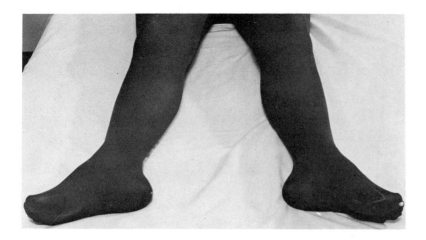

Figure 16-16 This is a typical position of the legs and feet when they are not properly supported in bed. The toes point downward and the legs rotate outward.

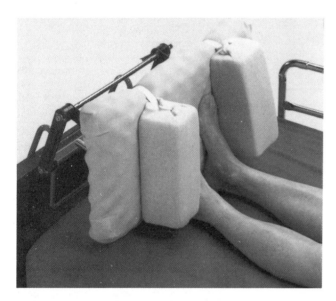

Figure 16-17 This foot support can be fastened at any level along the sides of the mattress. Special supports help prevent the feet and legs from rotating outward. (Courtesy J.T. Posey Co., Arcadia, CA)

place for the patient. A foot board is illustrated in Figure 16-17. Some nurses have found that having the patient wear ankle-high tennis shoes in bed will also help prevent foot drop. The shoes must be removed regularly, and proper foot care should be given.

If a foot block or footboard is not readily available, a temporary foot support can be made with a pillow and large sheet. The pillow is rolled in the sheet, and the ends of the sheet are twisted before being tucked under the mattress. The tucked ends should be placed under the mattress at an angle toward the head of the bed to help keep the pillow in place. A pillow support does not provide the firmness of a board or block and, therefore, should eventually be replaced as soon as possible with something more sturdy.

Cradle

Tight linen over the toes can contribute to foot drop. Recall that a toe pleat or fold in the top sheet is used to avoid this. A high footboard may also be used to help keep the bed linen off the patient's feet or legs. A cradle is a frame that is usually made of metal and constructed so that it can be secured well to the mattress. It forms a shell over the patient's lower legs. It is often used for patients with burns, painful joint disease and fractures of the leg.

Sandbags

Sandbags are used when an extremity needs firm support, such as to keep the foot or leg from turning outward. When sandbags are properly filled, they are not hard or rigid, but rather pliable enough to be shaped to fit body contours. To promote proper alignment and positioning, sandbags can be placed along the outer surface of the leg from the hip to the knee or ankle. They should be placed so that they do not create pressure on bony prominences, such as the bony area of the hip, knee or ankle. They should be covered with absorbent material, such as a sheet or bath blanket, to avoid accumulation of moisture next to the skin. These precautions help prevent the development of a decubitus ulcer. Sandbags are available in various sizes.

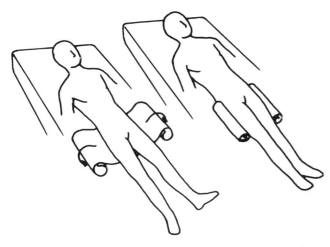

Figure 16-18 These sketches illustrate how trochanter rolls are made and used to support the patient's legs so that they do not rotate outward.

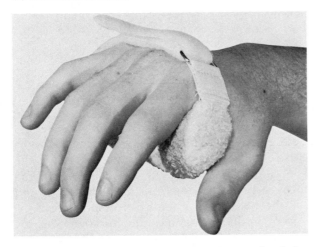

Figure 16-19 This is an example of a palm grip that helps prevent contractures of the fingers and thumb. (Courtesy J.T. Posey Co., Arcadia, CA)

Trochanter rolls

Trochanter rolls prevent the legs from turning outward. They received their name from anatomical landmarks of the femur. The femur is the long, large bone in the thigh. The trochanters are bony ridges at the head of the femur near the hip. The top of the femur and the depression into which it fits within the pelvis form the ball and socket joint of the hip. This type of joint permits the leg to be moved in multiple directions, one of which is outward rotation. Placing a positioning device at the area of the trochanter helps to keep the leg from rotating out-

ward. Trochanter rolls are illustrated in Figure 16-18. They can be made and used in the following manner:

- Fold a sheet lengthwise in half or in thirds and place it under the patient so that it extends from the hips to about the knees.
- Place a rolled-up bath blanket or two bath towels under each end of the sheet that extends on either side of the patient. If the roll is too short, the leg will have very little support.
- Roll the sheet around the blanket so that the end of the roll is underneath. In this way, it cannot unroll itself and the weight of the patient will hold it securely. The patient will be lying on a section of linen that has a large roll on either side of him so that his legs cannot turn outward.
- Fix the rolls close to the patient and firmly against the hips and thigh on each side.

Hand rolls

The most important function to preserve in relation to the hand is the ability to grasp and pick up objects. If positioning of the hands is overlooked, they will become so contracted that they may no longer be useful. To preserve their function, the thumb is held away from the hand slightly and at a moderate angle to the fingers. A rolled washcloth or a ball secured in the hand can be used to maintain this position. There are several commercial hand supports available, like the one in Figure 16-19, that are especially helpful if the patient needs hand and thumb support for extended periods of time.

Positioning should always be accompanied by periodic movement and exercise. Positioning the hands alone will not prevent contractures from forming, but if they occur, the thumb and figers will still be in a position for some use.

Bed siderails

Bed siderails are a valuable self help device to aid patients in changing their own position, moving about and exercising while in bed. For example, with siderails in place, the patient can safely roll himself from side to side and sit up in bed. These activities help patients maintain or regain muscle strength and joint flexibility after periods of time when they have had to lie in bed.

Trapeze or monkey pole

A *trapeze* is a triangular piece of metal hung by a chain over the head of the bed. The patient grasps a trapeze and can then move himself about and to a sitting position in bed. Unless arm movement or lifting is undesirable, a trapeze is an excellent device to help and encourage a bedridden patient to be active. A trapeze is illustrated in Figure 16-20.

Turning and moving a patient

Before learning to position a patient the nurse must learn skills for turning and moving a patient. These skills are important to prevent injury to the nurse and the patient. Many of the principles of body mechanics are related to the techniques for turning and moving an individual whose weight may equal or exceed that of the nurse. Principles of Care 16-3 and 16-4 describe and illustrate the suggested actions when the patient requires turning and moving.

Positioning a patient confined to bed

The proper positioning of the patient in bed is essential to promote comfort and provide for proper body alignment. Changing positions in bed may be the only exercise some patients are allowed. An inactive patient's position should be changed at least every two hours and more frequently if any signs or symptoms of disuse have been assessed. When the position of the patient is changed, it presents a good opportunity for providing whatever measures may be necessary to prevent decubitus ulcer formation. Techniques for skin care are described in Chapter 22.

The supine position

The *supine position* is one in which the person lies on his back. There are two primary concerns when using the supine position. One concern is pressure on the back of the body where pressure sores commonly develop, especially in the area at the end of the spine. The second is toe pressure from linens, which, when combined with gravity, forces the feet into the foot drop position.

The lateral position

A *lateral position* is one in which an individual lies on his side. Foot drop is of less concern in this position because the feet are not being pulled down by gravity as they are when the patient lies on his back. However, there is concern when using this position if the upper shoulder and arm are allowed to rotate forward and fall out of alignment. This tends to interfere with proper breathing.

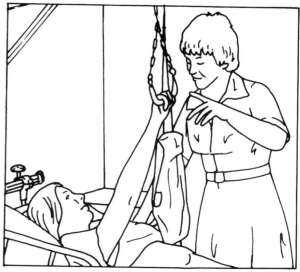

Figure 16-20 The nurse explains how the patient can lift herself and move about in bed by using the trapeze.

The prone position

A *prone position* is one in which an individual lies on his abdomen. Lying on the abdomen is a comfortable and relaxing position for many patients. It is helpful for the person with pressure sores or one who is likely to develop them when lying on his back or side. The position also provides for good drainage from bronchioles, stretches the trunk and extremities, and keeps the hips in an extended position. However, the prone position is often contraindicated when the patient has respiratory distress or heart disease, since it interferes with chest expansion. It may be uncomfortable for patients with recent abdominal surgery or those with back pain.

Fowler's position

Fowler's position is a sitting position. With the head of the bed elevated 45 to 60 degrees, it is referred to as a semi-Fowler's position; a 90-degree elevation is a high Fowler's position. This position is especially helpful for patients with dyspnoea. It causes abdominal organs to drop away from the diaphragm, relieving pressure on the chest cavity. This allows the lungs and heart to fill efficiently. It also makes eating, conversing and looking about easier than from a lying position.

Principles of Care 16-5 illustrates and describes how to position a patient properly in the supine, lateral, prone and Fowler's positions.

Principles of Care 16-3. Turning a patient

Nursing Action	Rationale

Turning the Patient From His Back Onto His Side

Turning the Patient Toward the Nurse
Raise the bed to the high position.

The nurse needs to maintain adequate balance and prepare to centre the patient's weight over the widest base of support.

Have the patient flex his knees and place his arms across his chest.

This positioning helps prevent the patient from rolling back, partially prepares him for lying on his side, and prevents him from rolling onto his arm.

Place one hand on the patient's shoulder and one on the hip on the far side.

The heaviest part of the body is centred in the pelvis. Using the arms and hands in this way will help move the patient most efficiently by distributing the weight more evenly.

Spread the feet, flex the knees, place one foot behind the other, and while rocking backward, gently roll the patient towards you, as illustrated in Figure 16-21.

This provides a wide base of support for balance. It makes use of the longest and strongest muscles. Rocking provides momentum and uses the nurse's own body weight to reduce the effort required to move the patient.

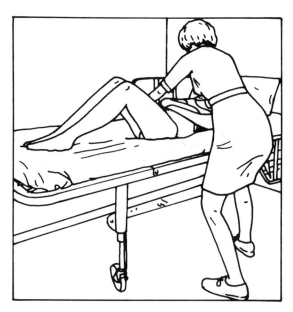

Figure 16-21 Note the nurse's position as she prepares to rock backward while turning the patient from her back to her side.

Raise the bed siderails on the working side and move to the other side of the bed.

Having siderails in place prevents the patient from rolling out of bed.

Turning the Patient Away From the Nurse
Raise the bed to the high position.

The nurse needs to maintain adequate balance and distribute the patient's weight over the widest base of support.

Place a hand under the patient's shoulders, spread the feet, flex the knees, place one foot behind the

This position creates momentum and uses the nurse's body weight to assist with moving the

Continued

Principles of Care 16-3. Continued

Nursing Action	Rationale
other, and, while rocking backward, gently pull the patient to the middle of the bed.	heaviest parts of the patient while distributing the bulk of the mass over the widest base of support.

OR

Nursing Action	Rationale
Stand at the patient's shoulder area. While using the same foot positions, place the arms under the patient's shoulders and move the shoulders to the centre of the bed. Move parallel to the patient's hips. Use the same actions to move the hips.	To prevent a personal injury, an alternative technique may be used if the nurse is slight, the patient is extremely heavy, or cannot help in any way. It involves moving portions of the patient's body in separate actions. This dual manoeuvre is shown in Figure 16-22.

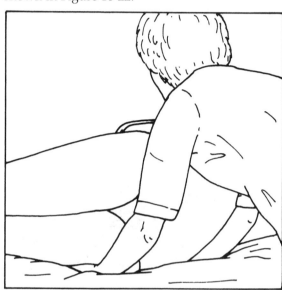

Figure 16-22 The lightweight patient can be moved to the centre of the bed in one manoeuvre. For most adults, it is best to move the shoulders first (*left*) and then the hips (*right*).

Nursing Action	Rationale
Continuing to spread the feet and flex the knees, the nurse can roll the patient away by pushing at the shoulder and hip areas of the patient, as shown in Figure 16-23.	Lowering the nurse's centre of gravity, distributing weight over a wide base, and using the longest and strongest muscles facilitate moving a patient while avoiding personal injury. Rolling requires less effort than lifting because it avoids overcoming gravity.

Turning the Patient From His Back Onto His Abdomen

Nursing Action	Rationale
Turning the Patient Toward the Nurse Place the patient's arm nearest you under his buttock with the palm up. Bring the far leg over the leg nearest you, and turn the patient's face away from you, as illustrated in Figure 16-24.	This position secures the patient's arm and leg so that he does not injure or roll onto them and prevents him from turning onto his face.
Grasp the patient's far hand with one hand and his far hip with the other hand. The nurse's feet should	This positioning will roll the heaviest parts of the patient's body comfortably. The nurse's positioning

Continued

Principles of Care 16-3. Continued

Nursing Action	Rationale

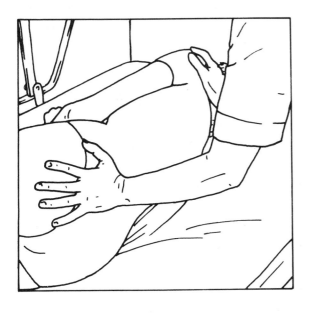

Figure 16-23 While lying on her back, the patient is asked to flex her knees. The nurse then gently pushes the patient at the hip and shoulder to roll her away from the nurse and from her back onto her side.

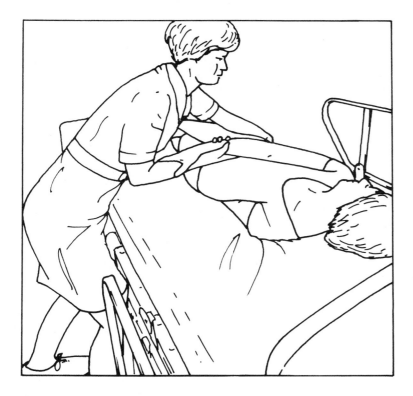

Figure 16-24 The nurse grasps the patient's far hand and hip and prepares to rock backward to turn the patient from the back-lying to the face-lying position.

Continued

Principles of Care 16-3. *Continued*

Nursing Action	Rationale
be spread, the knees flexed and one foot should be behind the other. Gently pull on the arm while rolling the hips toward you, turning the patient onto his abdomen, as shown in Figure 16-25.	gives stability by providing a wide base of support and lowering the centre of gravity. The body weight of the nurse is used to assist the nurse's arms while rolling the patient.

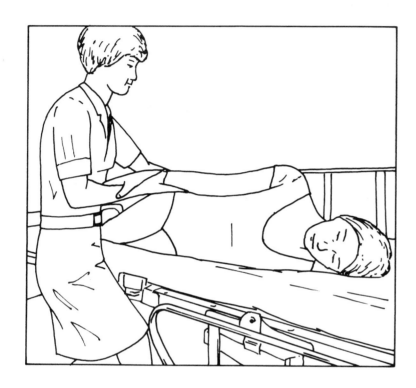

Figure 16-25 As the nurse rocks backward, she brings the patient from her back to her abdomen while gently pulling on the far arm and hip to roll the patient towards her.

Nursing Action	Rationale
Move the patient to the centre of the bed.	Centring the patient provides sufficient area to position the head, arms and legs properly.
Turning the Patient Away From the Nurse Raise the siderails on the opposite side of the bed.	The raised siderail will prevent the patient from accidentally rolling out of bed.
Stand at the side of the bed with the lowered cotsides and move the patient toward you.	Bringing the patient toward the nurse avoids stretching and allows room to accommodate the patient's body after it is turned.
Place the patient's arm that is most distant from the nurse under the buttock, with the palm up. Bring the near leg over the far leg, and turn the patient's head toward you, as illustrated in Figure 16-26.	This positioning helps prevent the patient from rolling onto his face and arm and secures his leg for comfortable rolling.
Place one arm under the patient's upper leg with an elbow at the level of the patient's buttock. Place the other arm under the patient's shoulders with a hand on his lower shoulder.	This positioning will help move the heaviest parts of the patient's body comfortably.

Continued

Principles of Care 16-3. Continued

Nursing Action	Rationale

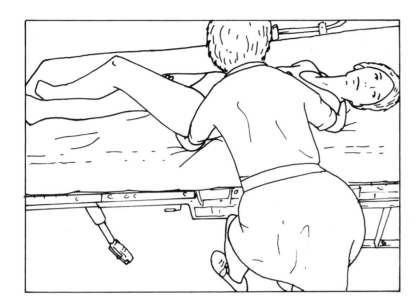

Figure 16-26 The nurse and patient are ready so that the nurse can roll the patient from her back to her abdomen. The patient will roll away from the nurse.

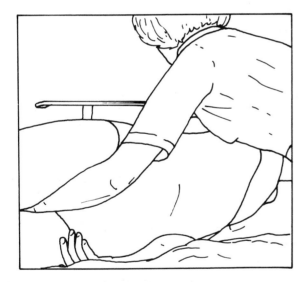

Figure 16-27 The nurse straightens her arms and the patient rolls away from the nurse from her back to her abdomen.

The feet of the nurse should be spread, and the knees should be flexed.

This positioning gives stability by providing a wide base of support and balance.

Pull by straightening the arms. This will gently roll the patient onto his abdomen, as illustrated in Figure 16-27. With this manoeuvre, the patient is centred on the bed.

The strongest muscles in the arms are used to roll the heaviest parts of the patient's body. Pulling, pushing and rolling use less effort than lifting.

Continued

Principles of Care 16-3. Continued

Nursing Action	Rationale

Turning the Patient From His Abdomen Onto His Back

First Technique

Place the patient's hand that is most distant from the nurse under the thigh on the same side. Cross his near leg over his far leg, and turn the patient's face toward you.

This positioning secures the patient's arm and leg so that he does not injure or roll on them and prevents him from turning onto his face.

Grasp the patient's far hand by reaching under the patient. Place the other hand on the patient's uppermost hip, as illustrated in Figure 16-28.

This positioning will prepare the nurse for pulling and rolling the patient.

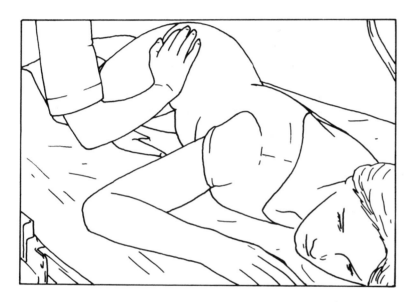

Figure 16-28 The nurse grasps the patient's far hand and prepares to push on the near hip to make the patient roll from her abdomen to her back.

Spread your feet and flex both knees.

This positioning gives stability by providing a wide base of support and balance.

Pull the patient's hand while pushing on his hip and gently roll him away onto his back, as illustrated in Figure 16-29.

This motion uses the strong muscles of the arms to roll the heaviest parts of the patient's body. Pulling and rolling require less effort than lifting.

Second Technique

Place the patient's far hand under his far thigh, cross his near leg over his far leg, and turn the patient's face towards you. One arm of the nurse should be inserted between the patient's legs to a level where the elbow is even with the patient's knee. The nurse's hand should be on the patient's thigh. The other arm is placed under the patient's chest with that hand on his far shoulder.

This positioning secures the patient's arm and leg so that he does not injure or roll on them and prevents him from turning on his face. This positioning will prepare the nurse to pull and roll the patient.

Continued

Principles of Care 16-3. Continued

Nursing Action	Rationale

Turning the Patient From His Abdomen Onto His Back

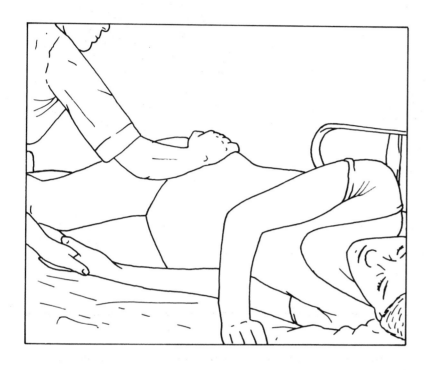

Figure 16-29 The nurse pulls on the patient's far hand and pushes on the near hip as the patient rolls away from the nurse from her abdomen onto her back.

Nursing Action	Rationale
Spread your feet and flex the knees.	This positioning gives stability by providing a wide base of support and balance.
Pull, using both arms, and use the momentum gently to roll the patient onto his back.	This motion uses the strong muscles of the arms to roll the heaviest parts of the patient's body. Pulling and rolling require less effort than lifting.

Turning the Heavy Patient Onto His Back, Using Two Nurses

Nursing Action	Rationale
One nurse should stand at the patient's head with one arm under the patient's upper chest with the hand on the far shoulder. The patient's face should be turned toward the nurse.	This technique uses two people, each of whom moves an area that involves the heaviest parts of the patient's body.
The second nurse should place the patient's hand at his side with the palm up. One arm is inserted between the legs of the patient grasping the hand of the patient. The second hand is placed on the near hip. The positions of the two nurses prior to turning can be seen in Figure 16-30.	The second nurse will be helping to move the lower area of the body as the first nurse moves the upper body. The patient is positioned in such a way that injury will not occur during rolling.

Continued

Principles of Care 16-3. Continued

Nursing Action	Rationale

Turning the Heavy Patient Onto His Back, Using Two Nurses

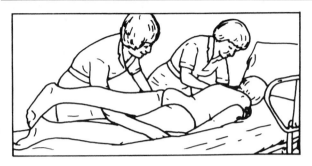

Figure 16-30 Nurses with a slight build may need to work together to turn a heavy patient. Each nurse is in the proper position to turn the patient.

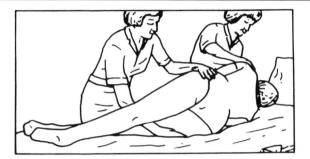

Figure 16-31 The coordinated efforts of two nurses share the work of turning a patient from the abdomen onto the back.

The nurse at the upper area of the body pulls on the lower shoulder while pushing on the upper one. The second nurse pulls the patient's hand and pushes on the patient's hip. Figure 16-31 shows the patient being gently turned from the abdomen onto his back.

The opposing movements serve to roll the patient onto his back. Pulling, pushing and rolling require less effort than lifting.

Principles of Care 16-4. Moving a patient up in bed

Nursing Action	Rationale

One-Person Technique When the Patient Can Assist

First Technique
Remove the pillows from under the patient's head and place one against the headboard.

The pillow at the head of the bed prevents having the patient accidentally hit the headboard as he is moved.

Have the patient flex his knees and place one arm under the patient's shoulders and the other under his hips, as illustrated in Figure 16-32.

The patient flexes his knees so that he can assist by pushing with the strong muscles of his legs. The nurse uses the strong muscles of the arms to move the heaviest part of the patient's body comfortably.

Assume a position of hugging the patient.

It is easier to move a heavy object when it is close to one's centre of gravity.

Spread your feet, flex the knees and rock toward the head of the bed while the patient pushes with his feet.

Such positioning and motion give the nurse stability by providing a wide base of support and balance. Rocking creates momentum that combines with the nurse's body weight to assist the muscles of the upper arms to move the patient up in bed.

Continued

Principles of Care 16-4. Continued

Nursing Action	**Rationale**

One-Person Technique When the Patient Can Assist

Figure 16-32 The nurse hugs the patient by grasping her under the buttocks and shoulders to move her up in bed. Notice that a pillow protects the headboard.

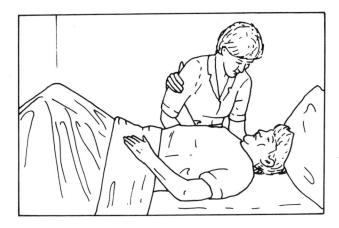

Figure 16-33 The nurse and patient lock hands so that each can share in the work of moving upward in bed. The knees of the patient are flexed to help push as the nurse pulls the patient's upper body.

Second Technique
Repeat positioning the pillow and flexing the patient's knees as described before.

The nurse should stand facing the head of the bed. The patient and the nurse should lock arms. This is done when the nurse grasps the patient's shoulder while the patient grasps the nurse's elbow. The nurse's opposite arm should be placed under the patient's shoulder, supporting the head and neck as shown in Figure 16-33.

Spread your feet by placing one foot in front of the other, and flex the knees.

Rock back and forth, putting weight on one foot and then on the other while counting 1, 2, 3. Explain to the patient that on the count of three, which will coincide with the forward rocking motion, the patient should push with his legs as the nurse pulls the locked arm.

Care must be taken to avoid injuring the head of the patient. The patient will use the strong muscles of his legs to help move his body.

Locking arms doubles the arm strength for moving. Utilizing mutual strength, along with the strong muscles in the patient's lower legs, produces movement with ease.

Placing one foot in front of the other forms a wide base of support and balance. Flexing the knees helps use the strongest muscles of the legs more efficiently.

Momentum, using strong muscles, and coordinated effort help move the weight of the patient up in bed with the least amount of effort.

Continued

Principles of Care 16-4. Continued

Nursing Action	Rationale

Two-Person Technique

When the Nurses Slide the Patient
Protect the headboard with a pillow, as described
and explained before.

The nurses, who are facing each other on opposite
sides of the bed between the patient's hips and
shoulders, join hands under the widest part of the
patient's shoulders and hips.

This positioning facilitates moving the heaviest parts
of the patient's body comfortably and provides for
the best use of the nurses' arm muscles.

The nurses should spread their feet, flex their knees,
and lean close to the patient by locking hands with
each other under the patient's buttocks and
shoulders, as illustrated in Figure 16-34.

This positioning provides a wide base of support
and balance and moves the weight of the patient
into the nurses' centre of gravity.

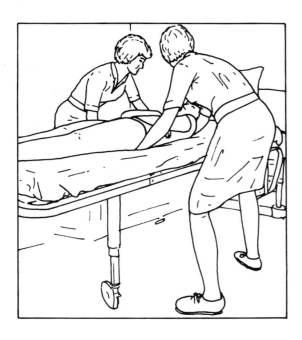

Figure 16-34 These nurses are properly positioned to rock
as they move the patient up in bed.

Rock in unison toward the head of the bed. Upon a
previously agreed signal, move the patient up in
bed. The patient may even assist by flexing his
knees and pushing when the signal is given.

Momentum, and using the coordinated strength of
each person's muscles, will help move the weight of
a patient with ease. Rocking, pushing and pulling
require less effort than lifting.

When the Nurses Slide the Patient, Using a Drawsheet
Protect the headboard with a pillow, as described
and explained above.

Continued

Principles of Care 16-4. Continued

Nursing Action	Rationale

Two-Person Technique

Place a drawsheet under the patient so that it extends from the patient's head to below his buttocks and roll the sides of the sheet up close to each side of the patient's body.

The sheet will act as a sling to help carry and slide the patient up in bed.

The nurses, who are facing the foot of the bed on opposite sides near the patient's chest and waist, take a firm grip of the rolled drawsheet on each side, as illustrated in Figure 16-35.

This positioning prepares the nurses to use their arm muscles and the weight of their bodies to slide the patient, using the drawsheet.

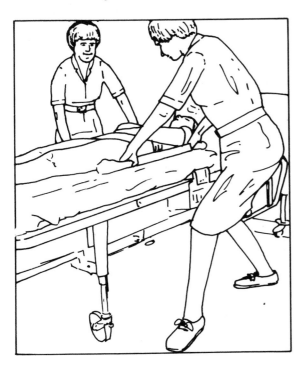

Figure 16-35 The nurses grasp the rolled drawsheet and prepare to rock to move the patient up in bed.

The nurses spread their feet, place the leg nearest the bed behind them, flex their knees and rock backward. Upon reaching a given signal that coincides with a backward motion, the nurses slide the patient up in bed.

Such positioning and motion give the nurses stability by providing a wide base of support and balance. They use their own weight, momentum and the strongest muscles in the arms and legs to slide the patient. Sliding requires less effort than lifting.

At the completion of the rocking motion, each nurse has the elbow nearest the patient on the mattress.

If the technique has been performed correctly, the elbow will rest on the mattress to counteract the shift in the centre of gravity.

This same procedure can be performed with the nurses facing the head of the bed.

Some nurses prefer to observe the face of the patient and the progress of movement toward the head of the bed. However, the work seems easier when the backward rock is used, perhaps because different combinations of muscles are used.

Principles of Care 16-5. Positioning a patient

Nursing Action	Rationale
The Supine Position	
Remove all pillows and positioning devices used in the current position.	Positioning devices interfere with the movement of the patient.
Move the patient to the centre of the bed.	Centring the patient provides sufficient area to properly position the head, arms, and legs.
Place a *small* pillow under the upper shoulders, neck, and head so that the head and neck are held in proper alignment.	The position of the head should appear similar to one if the patient were standing. The chin should not be pressed into the neck, nor should the head tilt backward.
Bring the patient's arms out to the side, bend the elbows, and place the forearms on pillows so the palms face downward.	Slight flexion and pronation of the joints in the upper extremity promote comfort.
Place handrolls within the patient's hands, if necessary.	Handrolls help maintain the position for potential use of the fingers and thumb.
Elevate the wrists above the level of the elbows, and the elbows above the shoulder. This may be accomplished by compressing the pillow more at one end, or by overlapping two pillows.	Elevation helps drain blood from the distal areas of the body back to the heart.
Place a *small* roll just above the patient's knees, *not* directly under them. The knees should be bent only 5 to 10 degrees.	Hyperextension of the knees must be avoided. Slight flexion is preferred. If the roll is placed under the knees or if they are bent more than 10 degrees, the pressure may slow circulation through blood vessels or cause pressure and damage to nerves in the area.
Use a footboard to hold the patient's feet at right angles to his lower legs.	Maintaining the feet in a position of dorsiflexion will help to prevent foot drop.
Place sandbags or trochanter rolls alongside the hips and thighs. Figure 16-36 shows a patient who has been placed in a supine position.	Trochanter rolls help prevent permanent external rotation, which can also interfere with the ability to walk normally.
Arrange top linens, using a toe pleat, or spread them over a high footboard or cradle.	Relieving pressure on the toes helps prevent footdrop.

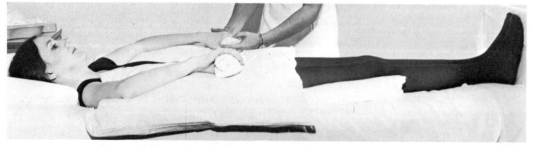

Figure 16-36 This illustrates the supine position. A trochanter roll conceals a very small roll, just above the knees, used to prevent hyperextension of the knee joint.

Continued

Principles of Care 16-5. Continued

Nursing Action	Rationale

The Lateral Position

Remove all pillows and positioning devices used in the current position.

Positioning devices interfere with the movement of the patient.

Centre and move the patient to the outer side of the bed.

There must be room for the arms and legs, which will extend from the midline of the body when using this position.

Place a *small* pillow under the patient's head and neck.

This prevents rotation of the neck, which may lead to a contracture or at the very least, some discomfort.

Place the arm on the side on which the patient is lying straight out from his body; bend the elbow about 90 degrees so that it is resting alongside the pillow at the patient's head. This may be observed in Figure 16-37, which shows a person in a lateral position.

The patient should not lie on his arm. This can interfere with circulation. Pressure on nerves may cause the hand to feel tingly and numb. It can cause discomfort from the pressure of body weight.

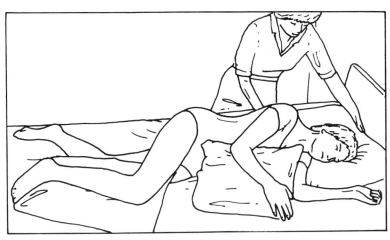

Figure 16-37 The patient has been properly placed in a lateral position.

Place a pillow under the uppermost arm.

The pillow holds the arm in such a way as to prevent inward rotation and interference with respirations.

Use handrolls, if needed.

If the patient does not move one or both hands, handrolls may help prevent permanent loss of finger and thumb function.

Slightly bend the knee on the side on which the patient is lying.

Slight flexion promotes comfort for the patient.

Bring the top leg forward and slightly bend that knee also. Place pillows under the thigh, leg and foot.

Supporting the upper leg in this manner prevents it from falling onto the bed and causing internal rotation and adduction of the femur.

Pull the hip on which the patient is lying slightly backward.

The hip is stabilized with this movement, thus preventing the patient from rolling forward.

Continued

Principles of Care 16-5. Continued

Nursing Action	Rationale

The Lateral Position

Cover the patient with the linen and blankets that are desired.	The pressure and weight from linen is less likely to contribute to foot drop in this position than in others.

The Prone Position

Remove all pillows and positioning devices used in the current position.	Positioning devices interfere with the movement of the patient.
Move the patient down in bed so that when he is turned, his feet can be positioned over the edge of the mattress or be supported on pillows just high enough to keep the toes from touching the bed.	A prone position can contribute to foot drop unless the feet are positioned correctly. If a pillow is used, the knees should not be bent more than a few degrees to avoid contributing to a knee flexion contracture.
Place the arms on either side of the head, either straight up in bed with the elbows only slightly flexed, or at the side of the body with the elbows flexed about 90 degrees.	This prevents the patient from lying on his arms, which would interfere with comfort and circulation.
Use handrolls as indicated.	Handrolls help maintain functional use of the fingers and thumb.
Place a very *small* pillow under the patient's head if he wishes, or the head may rest directly on the mattress. The person in Figure 16-38 has been properly placed in a prone position.	A pillow supports the head and prevents flexion of the neck.

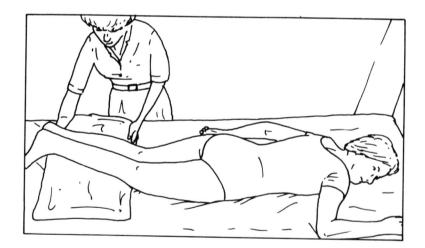

Figure 16-38 The nurse has placed this patient in a prone position.

Slip a small pillow into the space at the lower end of the ribs and the upper abdomen if the patient is thin.	This type of support prevents hyperextension of the back and facilitates breathing.

Continued

Principles of Care 16-5. Continued

Nursing Action	Rationale

Fowler's Position

Remove all pillows and positioning devices used in the current position.	Positioning devices interfere with movement of the patient.
Centre the patient on his back so that when the head is elevated, the break in the bed will be at the hips.	The back should be straight. Flexion at any point in the spine will cause discomfort from poor alignment and interfere with ventilation.
Raise the head of the bed to the desired height.	The height of elevation may be adjusted according to the doctor's order, the comfort of the patient, or the activity the patient may perform.
Allow the patient's head to rest against the mattress, or support it with a small pillow.	The neck should not be flexed or hyperextended.
Support the forearms on pillows so that they are elevated sufficiently to prevent a pull on the patient's shoulders.	Pulling on the shoulders contributes to stress on the joint and discomfort.
Support the hands on pillows so that they are in line with the forearms and slightly elevated in relation to the elbows.	This positioning prevents a contracture at the wrist and promotes circulation through the hands.
Use handrolls if the patient is extremely inactive.	Handrolls help to maintain the fingers and thumb in a functional position.
Elevate the knees for brief periods only. Figure 16-39 shows a person being placed in Fowler's position.	Flexion of the knees promotes comfort, but it may slow the circulation of blood from the legs and put

Figure 16-39 The patient is in Fowler's position. Notice that the break in the bed is at the hips so that the back is in proper alignment.

Continued

Principles of Care 16-5. Continued

Nursing Action	Rationale
Fowler's Position	
	pressure on nerves. Patients who have had blood clots or who are at risk for developing them should never have the bed broken at the knees. Prolonged flexion of the knees that is not alternated with periods of extension can cause contractures that interfere with standing and walking.
Support the feet at right angles to the lower legs using pillows, a footboard, or a foot block.	Keeping the foot in a position of dorsiflexion will prevent foot drop.

Transferring a patient

In this chapter, the word *transfer* refers to moving a patient from place to place. For example, the patient is transferred when he is moved from a bed to a chair and back to bed, or to and from a stretcher. The patient assists in an active transfer; that done entirely by others or by mechanical means is a passive transfer.

Basic guidelines when transferring a patient

Certain techniques are used when transferring a patient to help prevent injury to the patient as well as to the nurse. The following are basic recommended guidelines:

- Know the patient's diagnosis, capabilities, weaknesses and any movement he is not allowed. For example, patients who have had surgery on bones or joints may not be permitted full weight bearing or certain movements.
- Put on braces and other devices a patient may use before getting him out of bed.
- Plan exactly what will be done while transferring a patient so that the appropriate techniques will be utilized. Without planning, the nurse or the patient may acquire an injury.
- Explain what will be done to the patient. Then, use his ability to assist as much as possible to reduce the work.
- Remove obstacles that may make transferring more difficult. For example, see to it that furniture, such as chairs, bedside tables and overbed tables, is not in the way.
- Elevate the patient's bed as necessary so that the

work is being done at a safe and comfortable level.
- Lock the wheels of the bed, wheelchair or stretcher so that they cannot slide about as the patient is moved.
- Observe sound principles of body mechanics so that muscles are not strained and injured. It is a good idea to review these principles in Chapter 11 before transferring a patient.
- Be sure to keep the patient in proper alignment during transfer procedures so that the patient is also protected from strain and muscle injury.
- Support the patient's body, especially near the joints. Avoid grabbing and holding an extremity by the muscles, which will injure tissues and often put unnecessary strain on joints.
- Avoid causing friction on the patient's skin. Roll or push the patient when possible rather than pull him across bed linens. Friction can be reduced by sprinkling powder on the patient's skin and linens.
- Use smooth rather than jerky movements when transferring the patient. Jerky motion tends to put extra strain on muscles and joints and is uncomfortable for the patient.
- Use mechanical devices whenever they are available for transferring patients. Many hospitals have them and some persons also have such devices in their homes. Have a thorough understanding of how the device operates; be sure the patient is properly secured and is informed of what will occur. Patients who do not understand or are afraid may not be able to cooperate and may suffer injury as a result.
- Be realistic about how much you can safely

do without injury. Two small-statured women cannot safely lift and carry a patient weighing 250 pounds without straining their muscles.

Transferring a patient to and from a stretcher

Considerable care must be taken to prevent injuring the patient and the nurse when transferring a patient to and from a stretcher. If he is unconscious or helpless, the extremities and the head must be supported especially well.

The most convenient way to move a patient is to place a sheet under him and then pull carefully on the sheet to slide the patient from one surface to another such as from a bed to a stretcher and from a stretcher back to bed. When the patient must be lifted and carried, a three-carrier lift is recommended. It is described and illustrated in Principles of Care 16-6.

Principles of Care 16-6. Transferring a patient to and from a stretcher

Nursing Action	Rationale
Place the stretcher at a right angle to the foot of the bed with the brakes locked.	This places the stretcher out of the way when the carriers pivot from the bed, yet close enough so that the patient will only need to be lifted and carried a short distance.
Arrange the carriers according to height, with the tallest person at the patient's head.	The tallest person usually has the longest arm grasp, making it easier to support the patient's head and chest.
Stand facing the patient while sliding arms under him. The arms of the middle carrier are placed under the patient's waist and buttocks. One arm of the carrier at the head is under the patient's head, neck, and shoulder area and the other arm is directly against the middle carrier's arm at the bottom of the patient's chest. The carrier at the patient's feet has one arm against the middle carrier's lower arm and the other arm under the patient's legs and ankles, as shown in Figure 16-40.	The greatest weight is in the middle of the body. Having the middle carrier's armspread smaller than that of the others and supported by the other two carriers helps prevent strain on this person.

Figure 16-40 The patient has been moved to the edge of the bed and the carriers are positioned to lift him.

Slide the arms under the patient as far as possible and slide the patient to the edge of the bed.	Moving the patient near to the carriers at the edge of the bed helps position the mass of the patient within the nurses' centre of gravity. This makes it easier and safer to lift the patient.

Continued

Principles of Care 16-6. Continued

Nursing Action	Rationale
Spread the feet and flex the knees.	The position provides a wide base of support and balance. It prepares for using the leg muscles more effectively.
Place the arms further underneath the patient and logroll him onto the chests of all three carriers at the same time the patient is being lifted from the bed. During logrolling, the patient's head should turn with his shoulders. Figure 16-41 illustrates the position of the carriers and patient when he is lifted from the bed.	Rolling reduces the effort of lifting. Keeping the patient's head and shoulders straight places the back in correct alignment.

Figure 16-41 The patient has been logrolled onto the chests of the three carriers. Notice that the patient's back and head are straight and in proper alignment.

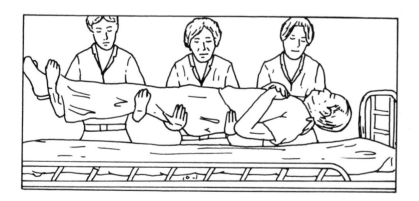

Figure 16-42 On a signal, the patient is gently lowered onto the stretcher.

Pivot and move to the stretcher. On a signal, bend the knees, as the body of each carrier is lowered with that of the patient, as shown in Figure 16-42.	The manoeuvre reduces the strain on the back muscles of the carriers while letting the large leg and arm muscles do the work of lowering the patient.
Secure additional persons if the patient is extremely heavy, has a large cast, or in some other way presents special problems.	Nurses are responsible for the safety of the patient and will be held accountable should an injury occur.

Continued

Principles of Care 16-6. Continued

Nursing Action	Rationale
From a Stretcher to a Bed	
Lift and move the patient from the stretcher, as was described when transferring him from the bed to the stretcher.	The same techniques are applicable in either situation.
Place the patient on the bed but near the edge when carrying him from the stretcher.	Trying to place the patient in the middle of the bed after carrying him from the stretcher causes strain on the backs of the carriers. Also, the patient is likely to be dropped onto the bed if an attempt is made to place him in the middle of the bed.
Have one carrier support the patient at the edge of the bed.	One person supports the patient so that he will not fall from the bed.
Have the other carriers go to the opposite side of the bed and place their arms underneath the patient in preparation for sliding him to the centre of the bed.	Sliding the patient to the middle of the bed requires less energy than lifting the patient.
Measures should be taken to reduce friction during sliding.	Friction can injure the patient's skin.
At a given signal, the carriers should use one of the techniques described earlier for moving or sliding the patient up in bed.	Cooperative efforts by all carriers reduce the possibility of straining back muscles or acquiring other injuries.

Transferring a patient from a bed to a chair and back to bed

The Chair. A correct sitting position was described in Chapter 11. The chair in which a patient sits should make it possible for him to maintain good posture. Figure 16-43 illustrates ways in which necessary adjustments may be made when the chair does not accommodate a patient well.

In general, upholstered chairs should be avoided. The patient tends to sink into an upholstered chair, making it difficult for him to maintain good posture and to get into and out of it.

When a patient can assist with the transfer. If a patient can assist and stand while he is being transferred from a bed to a chair or wheelchair, the following techniques are used:

- Use equipment with firm and stable surfaces. If the mattress is soft and the patient sinks into it, place a bedboard under it before transferring the patient to a chair or wheelchair.
- Take the patient's condition into account. For example, if the patient is weaker on one side of his body than on the other, or if he has a leg or arm that is weaker than the other, transfer him to his stronger side. This means placing a chair or wheelchair alongside the bed on the patient's stronger side.
- Make the distance for transferring as short as possible. Place the chair or wheelchair parallel to and near to the head of the bed. Be sure the wheels of a wheelchair are locked and the foot supports are in the up position.
- Place short bed rails in the up position so that the patient can grasp a rail to sit up in bed and steady himself as he moves. This is illustrated in Figure 16-44.
- Stand at the side of the bed on which the patient will be moving. Do not reach across the bed to assist the patient. Help the patient to a sitting position.
- Allow the patient to sit a few seconds until you are sure he is not feeling faint.
- Pivot the patient a quarter of a turn by supporting his shoulders and legs.
- Dress the patient appropriately, as he sits at the side of the bed. If he is going to walk, help him put on shoes and stockings. Hard-soled and

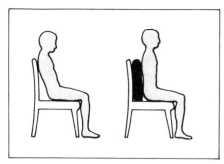

If the chair is too deep, place a pillow or cushion at the patient's back.

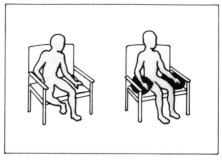

If the chair is too wide and the patient tends to lean to one side, place a cushion or pillow on each side.

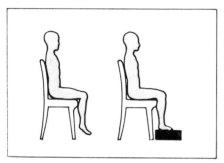

If the chair is too high, support the patient's feet to promote good posture and relieve pressure on the back of the knees.

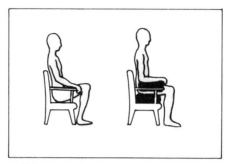

If the chair is too low, place a cushion on the seat and, if necessary, pad the arms of the chair.

Figure 16-43 This figure illustrates how to adapt a chair to fit the patient's needs. (After Talbot (1981); used with permission)

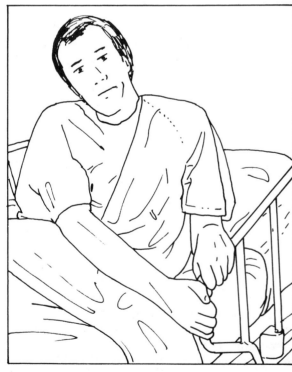

Figure 16-44 This illustrates how a patient can use siderails to help move in bed.

well-fitting shoes will give him more support than will loose, floppy slippers.

- Place the bed in the low position or have a footstool handy on which the patient can stand as he gets out of bed.
- Face the patient, spread the feet to provide a wide base of support and balance, put one foot forward between the patient's feet, and flex the knees to provide stability and the most effective use of the strong leg muscles. The patient puts his hands on the nurse's shoulders, while he is held in the axillary areas. Grasping the patient on his chest wall is uncomfortable and restricts breathing. Helping the patient out of bed is illustrated in Figure 16.45.
- As the patient's upper body is lifted, ask the patient to lift himself from the bed. If a footstool is used, assist the patient off of it while continuing to hold him.
- Maintain a wide base of support while pivoting with the patient so that his back is toward the chair.
- Bend the knees and keep the back straight as the patient is lowered into the chair or wheelchair, as illustrated in Figure 16-46. Have the patient

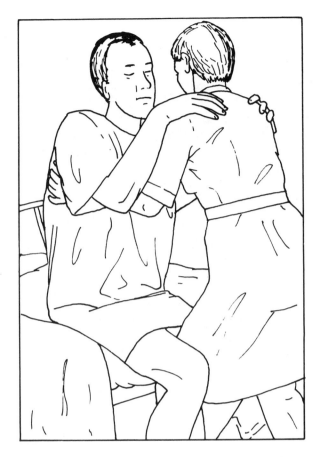

Figure 16-45 The nurse assists the patient out of bed. Notice the placement of the nurse's and patient's hands. Some nurses prefer to lock arms to assist the patient to a standing position.

Figure 16-46 After helping the patient to his feet, the nurse assists him to a chair. A chair with arms would provide another means for the patient to help support and guide himself into the chair.

assist by holding onto armrests on the chair or wheelchair if they are available as he is being lowered into it.

Sometimes a patient may end up sitting too far from the back of a wheelchair. An easy way to move him back is to place a folded towel in the wheelchair before placing the patient in it. Have one end of the towel hanging out the back of the wheelchair and the rest of it on the seat. Once the patient is seated, it becomes relatively easy to move the patient back by standing behind the wheelchair, bracing the feet and pulling on the towel from the back of the chair. This technique avoids friction on the patient's skin and requires less energy than lifting him back into the chair.

The same techniques are used, but in reverse order, when transferring the patient from a chair back to bed.

When a patient cannot assist with the transfer. If a patient cannot stand before he sits in a chair, it is best to have two persons lift the patient from the bed into a chair. However, one person can do so unless the patient is simply too heavy for one nurse to handle. The single-person technique is handy for home use and in situations when only one person is available. It is described in Principles of Care 16-7.

Maintaining joint mobility

Each joint in the body has a range of motion; that is, it has the capacity to move in certain directions. The direction of movement differs at various joints and depends on the shape and structure of the bones

Principles of Care 16-7. Moving a patient to and from a chair

Nursing Action	Rationale
Place a chair parallel with and against a point near the patient's buttocks.	Having a chair as close as possible decreases the distance to which he must be moved.
Place arms under the patient's head and shoulders and slide the upper portion of the patient's body to the edge of the bed. Move the lower portion of the patient's body by pulling with arms placed under the waist and beneath the buttocks. A rocking motion created by placing one foot in front of the other with the knees bent will help to move the weight of the patient.	Positioning the patient near the edge will reduce the energy required for transferring the patient. The more lifting that must be done, the more strain on the nurse's muscles.
Place arms well under the patient's axillary areas from the rear. The patient's head and shoulders may rest on the nurse.	Supporting the upper portion of the patient's body increases the mass over the nurse's own centre of gravity where there is more support.
Move to the back of the chair while pulling the patient into the chair. Lean against the back of the chair to keep it from moving and to provide a base for support. Rock back while pulling the patient into the chair. This is illustrated in Figure 16-47.	Pulling and sliding require less effort than lifting. Rocking creates momentum that supplements the effort of the strong muscles in the nurse's arms and legs that are used to move the patient.

Figure 16-47 With the chair near the bed and while supporting the patient from the back, the nurse gently moves the helpless patient onto the chair. The nurse has a wide base of support, bends her knees and rocks back as the patient slides to the chair.

Flex knees, grasp the chair near the seat, rock back and pull the chair with the patient away from the bed until the patient's feet are on the edge of the bed.	Sliding the chair that supports the weight of the patient reduces the effort for the nurse.

Continued

Principles of Care 16-7. Continued

Nursing Action	Rationale
Bend from the knees rather than from the waist while supporting and lowering the patient's legs and feet to the floor.	When the knees are flexed to lower the body, rather than bending from the waist, the nurse uses the musculoskeletal system more effectively and avoids personal injury.
To move the patient back into the bed, slide the chair directly alongside the bed with the patient facing the foot of the bed.	Sliding the chair with the patient on it requires less energy than lifting. If the floor has a polished surface, the chair may be slid on a small rug or cloths.
Flex the knees and pivot the patient's legs onto the edge of the bed.	Using the strong muscles of the legs rather than weaker muscles of the back helps reduce strain on the nurse.
Go behind the chair, grasp the patient in the axillary areas from the rear, and roll him onto the bed, as illustrated in Figure 16-48. Have a wide base of support and rock to move the patient onto the bed.	Rolling rather than lifting the patient, having a wide base of support, and rocking reduce the strain on muscles.

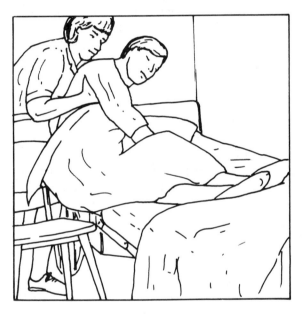

Figure 16-48 The nurse places the patient's legs and feet onto the bed first as she rolls him off the chair and onto the bed.

Slide the chair away using a foot. The nurse's body should be braced against the bed to prevent the patient from falling out of bed.	The nurse must clear away objects that interfere with controlling and supporting the patient.
Help the patient into a position of comfort, such as on his side, back, or abdomen.	A patient's position should be changed frequently. A Fowler's position is too similar to the position of the patient in a chair. Pressure should be relieved from the buttocks and heels. The hips should be extended after being flexed for a period of time.

forming the joint. For example, the joint at the shoulder allows movement of the arm in a complete circle; it is a ball and socket joint. The joint at the elbow moves like a hinge. The amount of movement, or the joint's range, can be measured.

An active patient generally uses all his joints in the process of performing activities of daily living. However, an inactive patient may be unable to perform a variety of activities. The joints eventually sustain reduced range of motion and can become totally nonfunctional. The nurse should carry out certain measures, in addition to changing the patient's positions in bed, to ensure that the inactive patient's joints remain flexible.

A good exercise for the inactive patient is to move each joint through its full range of motion by purposefully exercising each one to the extent its structure allows. Range-of-motion exercises may be carried out by the patient as active exercises or by the nurse as passive exercises, or the patient may do some of them on his own while the nurse assists with or carries out others with him.

Basic guidelines using range-of-motion exercises

The following are basic guidelines when the patient is helped to put joints through their full range of motion:

- Know the patient's diagnosis and why range-of-motion exercises are to be used. This knowledge helps the nurse in determining what exercises are needed and which ones may be contraindicated.
- Teach the patient what exercise is being undertaken, why, and how it will be done. Using a show-and-tell technique is recommended. A patient at ease and relaxed about exercising can more actively take part in it.
- Use ROM exercises twice a day and do the exercises regularly to maintain or increase joint flexibility. Each exercise is carried out two to five times. Many exercises can be carried out when the patient is being bathed. Routine tasks, such as eating, dressing, self-bathing and writing, also help to put certain joints through their full range of motion and should be encouraged.
- To conserve energy and to avoid strain and injury, use good body mechanics when placing a patient through the exercises.
- Avoid overexertion and using exercises to the

point at which the patient experiences fatigue. The purpose of moving the joints is not to exhaust or tax the patient. Certain exercises may need to be delayed until the patient's condition allows, such as those that require a standing position.

- Follow a pattern to avoid omitting any joint of the body. Begin at the head and move progressively down the body or vice-versa.
- Start gradually and work slowly. All movements should be smooth and rhythmic. Irregular, jerky movements are uncomfortable for the patient.
- Support the joint being exercised. Use a firm but comfortable grip when holding the patient's joints. This technique gives the patient a feeling of adequate support. Grasping muscles or tendons is likely to cause injury or discomfort.
- Move each joint until there is resistance but not pain. Movements should not be forceful. Uncomfortable reactions should be reported and exercises halted until further instructions are obtained. Excessive stretching of joints may lead to injuries and even bleeding into joints. When the patient cannot speak, watch for nonverbal signs, such as facial expressions, to judge discomfort.
- Place each joint in its *neutral position*, that is, its normal position of alignment, when beginning and finishing each exercise.
- Stop the exercises if *spasticity*, which is sudden, continuous and involuntary muscle contraction, occurs. Gentle pressure on an extremity tends to cause the muscle to relax. Moving a joint more slowly often helps prevent spasticity.
- When moving extremities, keep friction to a minimum to avoid injuring the skin. Some hospitals use powder boards to assist when exercising the legs. The boards are made of smooth material, such as fibreboard, and spinkled with powder to reduce friction.
- Expect that the patient's respiratory and heart rates may increase within the upper limits of normal during exercise, which is good. These rates should return to the resting rate within a few minutes. Otherwise, the exercises are probably too strenuous for the patient.
- Use passive exercises as necessary. When the patient is able to do for himself, encourage active exercises to move joints through their range of motion. Family members can be taught to perform the exercises with patients. Exercises

should continue at home after a period of hospitalization if the individual continues to be inactive.

Principles of Care 16-8 describes and illustrates the actions that should be carried out when performing range-of-motion exercises.

Preparing a patient for walking

When patients are confined to bed for short periods of time, preparing them for increased activity may be simply a matter of assisting them out of bed and helping them to walk. However, there are some patients who may require special preparation, es-

---

Principles of Care 16-8. Performing range-of-motion exercises

Nursing Action	Rationale
Place one hand beneath the neck of the patient and the other on the patient's forehead, as the nurse in Figure 16-49 is doing. Lift the neck while the forehead is gently pushed down.	Joints must be supported during range-of-motion exercises. This action moves the joints of the cervical spine in a position of hyperextension. *Hyperextension* is the act of moving so that the angle between adjoining parts is made larger than its normal or average range, or more than 180 degrees.

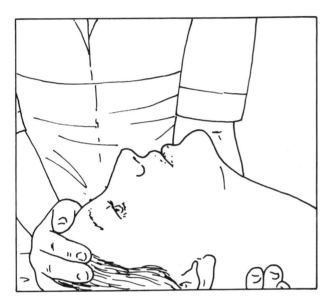

Figure 16-49 Hyperextension of the neck.

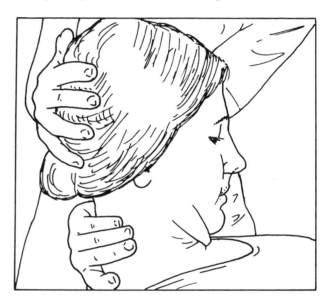

Figure 16-50 Flexion of the neck.

Repeat each joint exercise between two and five times at least twice a day.	Repeated and frequent exercise of joints helps to maintain and restore a joint's flexibility.
Place one hand under the neck and one under the back of the head, as shown in Figure 16-50. Move the head so the chin is in the direction of the chest.	This action puts the joints of the cervical spine into a position of flexion. *Flexion* is the act of moving or bending so that the angle between adjoining parts is reduced.
Place a hand on either side of the head and turn the head from side to side, as the nurse in Figure 16-51 is doing.	This action puts the joints of the cervical spine through rotation. *Rotation* is the act of turning.

Continued

Principles of Care 16-8. *Continued*

Nursing Action	Rationale

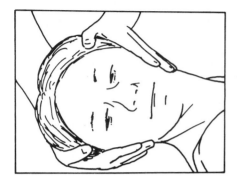

Figure 16-51 Rotation of the neck.

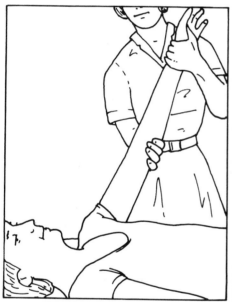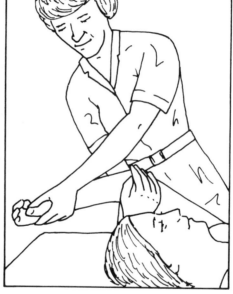

Figure 16-52 *Left*: Extension of the shoulder. *Right*: Flexion of the shoulder.

Grasp and support the elbow and wrist of either arm. Bring the arm straight up and over the head to across the back of the head as far as possible, as shown in Figure 16-52.

When the patient is on his abdomen or is able to sit the arm can be moved beyond its neutral position toward the back, as shown in Figure 16-53.

The inactive patient usually maintains this joint in position of extension. *Extension* is a position that brings parts into or toward a straight line. The action described moves the joint of the shoulder to a position of flexion.

This action moves the shoulder to a position of hyperextension.

Continued

Principles of Care 16-8. Continued

Nursing Action	Rationale

Figure 16-53 Hyperextension of the shoulder.

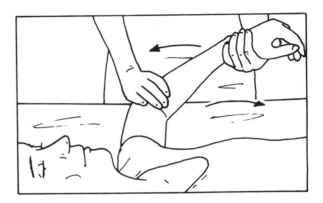

Figure 16-54 The shoulder is in external rotation when moved towards the head. It is in internal rotation when moved towards the feet.

With the patient on his back, stabilize the elbow and move the forearm first to a position in which the hand is above the head and then brought down to the side. Follow the direction of the arrows in Figure 16-54.

This movement puts the shoulder through external and then internal rotation. *External rotation* is the act of turning outward; *internal rotation* is the act of turning inward.

If the patient is able to stand or sit on the edge of the bed, support the elbow and wrist while moving the shoulder joint in a full circle, as illustrated in Figure 16-55.

This exercise moves the shoulder through circumduction. *Circumduction* is circular movement. Confinement in a bed generally prevents this exercise from being performed.

Bring the arm so it rests in neutral position at the side of the body. Stabilize the arm above the elbow and bend the forearm toward the head as shown in Figure 16-56.

This position puts the elbow joint into a position of flexion.

Return the arm to neutral position. Support the wrist and elbow and bring the arm outward from the body and then across the chest, as is being done in Figure 16-57.

These movements exercise the elbow and shoulder joints, facilitating first abduction and then adduction. *Abduction* is movement away from the body; *adduction* is movement toward the centre of the body.

Prepare to exercise the wrist and fingers by supporting the joint at the hand and at the lower forearm. The bed can be used to support the arm.

Support of the joint prevents injury and promotes control during exercise.

With the hand held straight, bend the wrist first toward the inner forearm and then toward the outer forearm, as the nurse is doing in Figure 16-58.

This action moves the wrist from a position of extension, flexion and then hyperextension.

While stabilizing the forearm, move the hand in a twisting movement first in one direction and then in the other, as the nurse in Figure 16-59 is doing.

This action moves the wrist through external and internal rotation.

Continued

Principles of Care 16-8. Continued

Nursing Action	**Rationale**

Figure 16-55 This movement exercises the shoulder joint through circumduction.

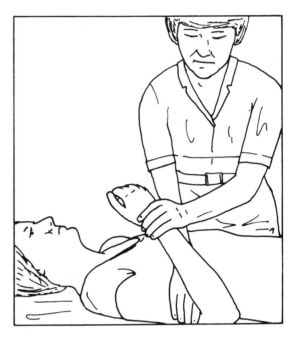

Figure 16-56 Moving the forearm towards the head produces flexion of the elbow joint.

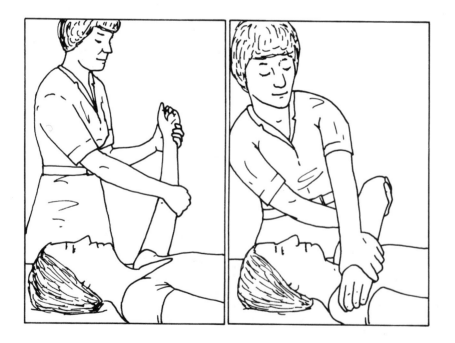

Figure 16-57 The arm is brought out to the side (*left*) into a position of abduction, and the arm is then brought across the chest (*right*) into a position of adduction.

Continued

Principles of Care 16-8. Continued

Nursing Action	Rationale

 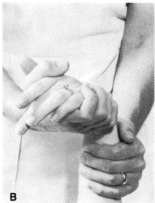 

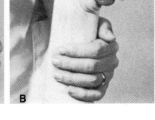

Figure 16-58 The wrist is extended (*left*), flexed (*centre*), and hyperextended (*right*).

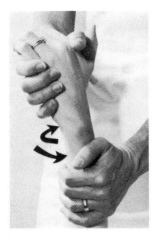

Figure 16-59 Turning the wrist moves the joint through rotation.

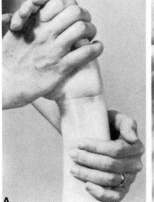

Figure 16-60 Bending the wrist away from the body (*left*) produces abduction, bending the wrist towards the body (*right*) produces adduction.

Bend the thumb side of the hand toward the wrist and then away from the wrist, as is shown in Figure 16-60.

This moves the wrist through abduction and then adduction.

Support the wrist and bend the thumb and fingers into the palm of the hand as shown in Figure 16-61. This should be followed by straightening all the fingers and the thumb.

This exercise places the joints of the fingers in a position of flexion followed by extension. An inactive patient may eventually acquire a permanent flexion contracture. Exercise that promotes extension helps maintain flexibility of the fingers.

Turn each finger and thumb, as illustrated in Figure 16-62.

Turning exercises the joints of the fingers and thumb through rotation.

Continued

Principles of Care 16-8. *Continued*

Nursing Action	Rationale

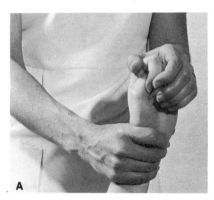 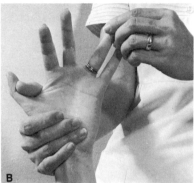

Figure 16-61 The joints of the fingers are flexed (*left*) by bending them and are extended (*right*) by straightening them.

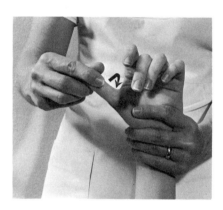

Figure 16-62 Exercising the thumb and then each finger by moving them in a twisting motion puts the joints through rotation.

With the patient flat in bed, support the knee and ankle while moving the leg out to the side and then back toward the centre of the body, as the nurse in Figure 16-63 is doing.

This position moves the leg into positions first of abduction and then adduction. The hip joint of an inactive patient is usually frequently moved from flexion to extension when his position is changed from a lateral and Fowler's position to a prone and supine position.

Support the knee and ankle and turn the leg outward, as shown in Figure 16-64, then inward.

This exercise alternates the position of the hip from external rotation to internal rotation.

With the patient on his abdomen, lift the leg backward, shown in Figure 16-65, as far as is comfortable while supporting the knee and ankle.

This exercise moves the hip joint to a position of hyperextension.

When the patient is able to stand, have the patient transfer his weight to one leg, lift the opposite leg, and turn it in a circular motion as shown in Figure 16-66.

This exercise moves the hip joint through circumduction.

Continued

Principles of Care 16-8. *Continued*

| **Nursing Action** | **Rationale** |

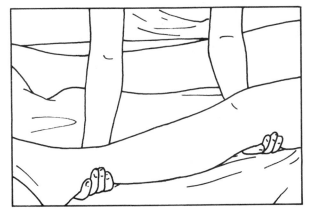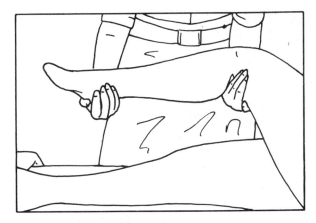

Figure 16-63 Hip abduction occurs when the leg is moved away from the centre of the body (*left*). Bringing the leg across and toward the midline of the body produces adduction of the hip (*right*).

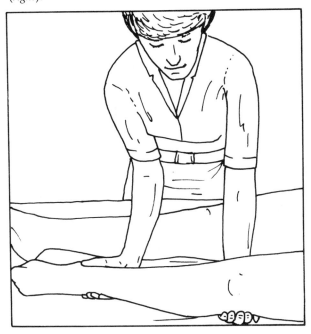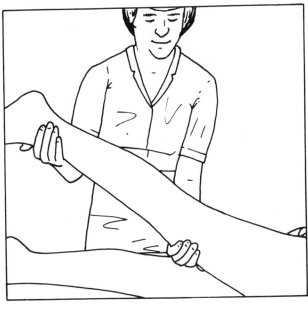

Figure 16-64 Turning the leg outwards produces external rotation of the hip.

Figure 16-65 Hyperextension of the hip.

With the patient lying in a supine position, place one hand beneath the knee and one under the ankle. Bend the knee in the direction of the head. These actions are shown in Figure 16-67.

When the knee is straight, the joint is in extension; when the knee is bent, the joint is in flexion. Sitting and bending the knees place the knees in flexion. Positions of flexion should be alternated frequently with periods of extension.

Continued

Principles of Care 16-8. Continued

Nursing Action	Rationale

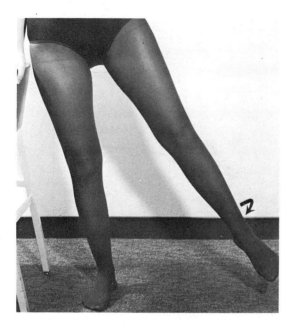

Figure 16-66 A method for maintaining joint mobility of the hip by moving it in a circular pattern called circumduction.

 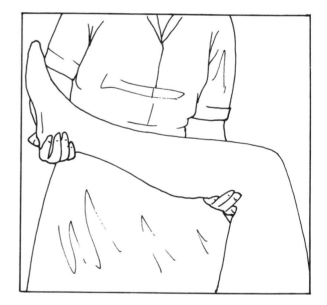

Figure 16-67 The leg is brought off the bed (*left*) with the knee extended. Bending the knee (*right*) flexes the knee and hip joints.

Prepare to exercise the ankle by using one hand to support the heel and the other to support the lower leg, leaving the ankle free to move.	Grasping the muscle of the calf can cause discomfort or injury to the patient.

Continued

Principles of Care 16-8. Continued

Nursing Action	Rationale
Pull as though stretching the heel so that the toes point in the direction of the head. Follow this by stretching the foot so that the toes point downward, as shown in Figure 16-68.	This exercise alternates dorsiflexion with plantarflexion. Positioning and exercising the ankle to maintain dorsiflexion can help maintain an inactive person's ability to eventually stand and walk.

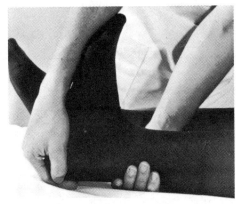

Figure 16-68 The foot is brought up (*left*) into a position of dorsiflexion and then down (*right*) to a position of plantarflexion.

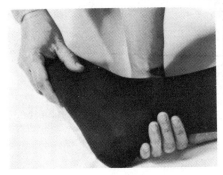

Figure 16-69 The ankle is rotated in an inward direction (*left*) and an outward direction (*right*).

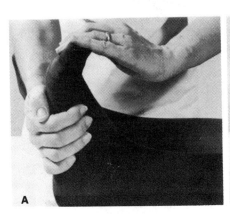

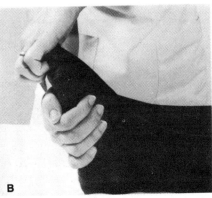

Figure 16-70 The joints of the toes are straightened to a point of hyperextension (*left*) and then bent to produce flexion (*right*).

Continued

Principles of Care 16-8. *Continued*

Nursing Action	Rationale
Support the ankle and turn the foot to the middle of the body and then to the outside of the body, shown in Figure 16-69.	This exercise alternately moves the ankle from internal to external rotation.
Let the bed support the foot. Hold the foot at the arch area, bend and then straighten the toes, as the nurse in Figure 16-70 is doing.	This movement causes the joints of the toes to become flexed and then extended.
To exercise the remaining areas of the spine, help the patient assume a curled-up position while sitting, as shown in Figure 16-71.	Bending the spine causes the joints to be placed in a position of flexion.

Figure 16-71 The back is curled to move the joints of the spine into a position of flexion. This movement could also be achieved with the patient lying on her side.

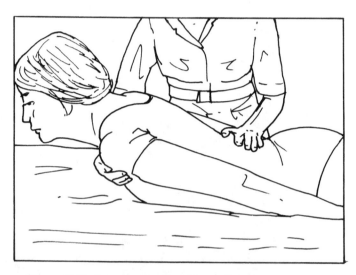

Figure 16-72 Bringing the shoulders off the bed while lying on the abdomen produces hyperextension of the spine.

With the patient lying on his abdomen, help him to arch his back by bringing the shoulders off the bed, as the person is doing in Figure 16-72.	With the back straight, the spine is in a position of extension. Arching changes the position of the spinal joints to hyperextension.

pecially those who have been in bed for long periods of time. In addition to the positioning and joint movements, certain other exercises and activities can be done that will help prepare the musculoskeletal system for weightbearing and activity.

Assisting with isometric exercises

Isometric exercises were discussed in Chapter 11. They are exercises that involve contracting and relaxing muscle groups with little, if any, movement.

Patients who perform these exercises must be taught to avoid using them with a closed glottis. The glottis is closed when one tries to stifle a sneeze or cough or when one grunts with a strain. Using effort to force exhalation against a closed glottis is called *Valsalva's manoeuvre*. Avoiding Valsalva's manoeuvre is especially important for patients with heart diseases. The straining against a closed glottis tends to raise blood pressure and can cause the heartbeat to become irregular. When performing isometric exercises, the patient should understand that the muscle contraction should be followed by muscle relaxation every few seconds. Patients tend to misunderstand and think they should keep the muscles in a contracted state for long periods of time. This tires and strains muscles rather than exercises them.

Quadriceps setting. *Quadriceps setting* is an isometric exercise in which the muscles on the front of the thigh are alternately tensed and relaxed. These muscles are some of the strongest of the leg muscles. Their tone must be maintained so the inactive patient can eventually stand and support his body weight. They also help in moving the leg during walking. They are exercised as follows:

1. Have the patient contract the quadriceps femoris muscles by pulling the kneecaps toward the hips. The patient will feel that he is pushing his knee down into the mattress and pulling his foot upward.
2. Contract the muscles for several seconds and then relax them for an equal amount of time.
3. Count slowly to four with each contraction and relaxation to establish a rhythm.
4. Contract and relax the muscles two to three times each hour but not to the point of fatigue.

Gluteal setting. The muscles in the buttocks are also important for body support and moving the legs in various positions. To perform gluteal setting exercises, the patient pinches the buttocks together and then relaxes. The guidelines for performing gluteal setting are the same as those for quad setting. Strengthening these muscles helps prepare the patient for walking as well as for climbing stairs.

Assisting with push-ups

Push-ups strengthen muscles of the shoulders and arms. These muscles are important for holding onto a chair as the patient begins to walk again. Also, they are needed for patients who must learn to walk with crutches or with a cane. Push-ups are done as follows:

Have the patient sit up in bed without support for one type of push-up exercise:

- Have the patient lift his hips off the bed by pushing down with his hands on the mattress. If the mattress is soft, a block or books are placed on the bed under the patient's hands.

Have the patient lie on his abdomen for another type of push-up exercise:

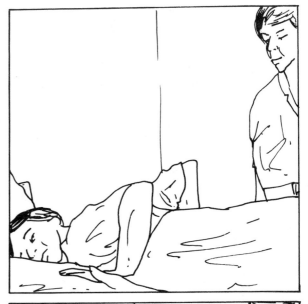

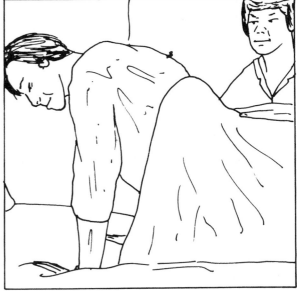

Figure 16-73 *Top*: The patient is in position to begin push-ups. *Bottom*: He lifts himself off the bed as he straightens his elbows, then lowers himself by flexing his elbows to return to his original position.

- Have the patient place his hands near his body at approximately shoulder level, palms down on the mattress, with the elbows sharply flexed.
- Have the patient straighten his elbows while lifting his head and shoulders off the bed, as illustrated in Figure 16-73.

Push-ups can be done when a patient sits in an armchair. He places his hands on the arms of the

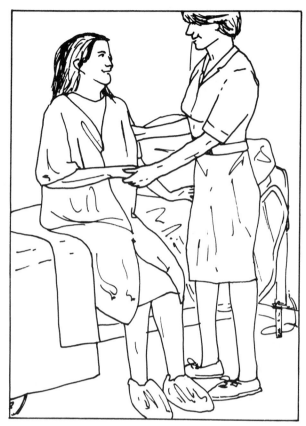

Figure 16-74 The patient dangles in preparation for getting out of bed. The bed is in the low position to allow the patient's feet to rest on the floor. The nurse remains ready in case the patient should feel weak or faint.

chair and then raises his body out of the seat. Push-ups are usually done three or four times each day.

Assisting the patient to dangle

Another exercise that helps prepare the patient for being out of bed is referred to as *dangling*. The patient is placed on the side of his bed with his feet on the floor or on a footstool, as shown in Figure 16-74. The exercise is carried out as follows:

1. Place the patient in Fowler's position for a few minutes to accustom him to the sitting position. This reduces the possibility for injury should he feel faint from a drop in blood pressure associated with a change in position.
2. Stand at the side of the bed and assist the patient to the edge of the bed.
3. Place the bed in low position or have a footstool handy on which the patient can rest his feet.
4. Pivot the patient a quarter of a turn by sup-

porting his shoulders and legs. Swing the patient's legs over the side of the bed. The patient may wish to place his hands on the nurse's shoulders for support.
5. Rest the patient's feet on the floor or on a footstool.
6. Remain with the patient and be ready to put him into a lying position if he feels faint or if his pulse rate is significantly affected by sitting on the edge of the bed.

Assisting the patient to walk

Despite strengthening exercises, some patients may still need progressive assistance to eventually take steps independently. There are several possible devices and techniques that provide support and assistance with walking.

Parallel bars. Some hospitals have parallel bars that help a patient begin to walk. The patient grasps a bar on either side of him and starts to walk as he supports himself on the bars. When parallel bars are not available, almost any two *stable* pieces of furniture can be used. Examples include the backs of two heavy chairs, the footboards of two beds or a hall rail and a chair. Figure 16-75 illustrates this technique, using two sturdy chairs and a chair and doorknob.

Walking belts. A walking belt is helpful for some patients. One is illustrated in Figure 16-76. The patient has the security of support until he feels ready to walk on his own. The nurse also has a method of anticipating that the patient is losing his balance and can prevent injuries associated with an uncontrolled fall.

Walking with a nurse. The nurse should walk

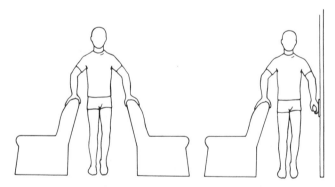

Figure 16-75 This illustrates how a patient can use two sturdy chairs, or a chair and a doorknob, for support as he prepares to walk.

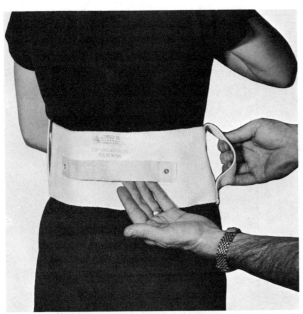

Figure 16-76 This is an example of a walking belt. Handles on the sides and in the back give firm grips for the person assisting the patient. (Courtesy J.T. Posey Co., Arcadia, CA)

alongside the patient who is just beginning to ambulate, keeping an arm under his in an arm-in-arm manner. If the patient begins to feel faint, the nurse can quickly slide an arm up and into the patient's axillary area. By placing one foot out to the side to form a wide base of support, the patient can then rest on the nurse's hip until additional help arrives to assist. This is illustrated in Figure 16-77.

Using aids for ambulation

There are several devices that may be used for support and safety. These may be used temporarily or permanently to assist with ambulation.

Canes

Canes may be used to help a patient walk. One type is a straight walking stick with a rubber cap on the end to help prevent the cane from sliding along the floor. A cane should be placed about 10 cm (4 in) to the side of the foot. It should be held in the hand on the uninvolved side. If the nurse helps the patient, support and assistance should be provided on the involved side. The patient should assume an erect position when walking with a cane. Leaning over a cane results in poor body posture.

Another type of cane, the quadripod or "quad" cane, has four legs, which give extra support for the patient. A patient may use one cane or two, depending on the amount of support he needs.

Walking frames

A walking frame is one of the most stable forms of ambulatory aids. It is used by patients who require considerable support and assistance with balance. Patients who are learning to walk again after prolonged periods in bed or following hip surgery often use a walking frame. The patient should hold onto the handgrips at the side of the walking frame. He should flex his elbows about 30 degrees and keep his feet apart, about 15 cm to 20 cm (6 in to 8 in), for a wide base of support while he walks. To maintain good posture, the patient should hold himself straight and look ahead, not at the floor. Figure 16-78 illustrates a patient using a walking frame.

Crutches

Crutches require considerable physical strength and balance to use. There are many safety hazards involved with their use. For this reason most elderly or inactive patients are supplied with a walking frame as an ambulatory aid.

Types of crutches. *Axillary crutches* fit under the arm into the axillary area. Most patients learn to use this type of crutch in the beginning of ambulation and when the use of crutches is a temporary measure.

There are crutches with no axillary support. One type is called *elbow crutches*. They are illustrated in Figure 16-79. This type of crutch has a frame or metal cuff that extends beyond the handgrip for the lower arm to help guide the crutch. These crutches are generally used by well experienced patients who need permanent assistance with walking.

Another type of crutch is called the *platform crutch*. It is especially useful for patients unable to bear weight on their hands and wrists. Many patients with arthritis use them. As Figure 16-80 illustrates, the patient's weight is distributed over the entire forearm.

Measuring a patient for axillary crutches. There are two common methods for measuring a patient for axillary crutches. With the patient in bed on his back and wearing shoes, the nurse measures the distance from the fold at the axillary area to the feet and adds 5 cm (2 in), or the distance from the fold at the axillary area to a point 15 cm to 20 cm (6 to 8 in) away from the patient's heel. The measurement of crutch length

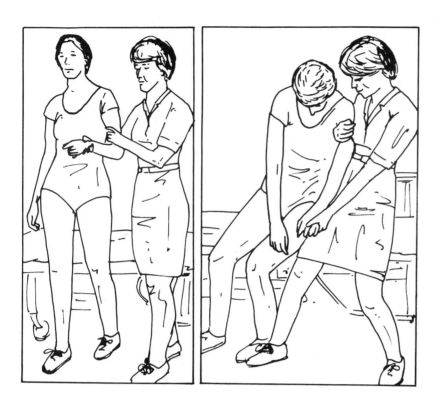

Figure 16-77 Note that the nurse walks hand in hand with the patient (*left*). When the patient slumps (*right*), the nurse slips her arm into the patient's axillary area, puts the foot closest to the patient out to one side to provide a wide base of support, and supports the patient on her hip until help arrives.

includes the axillary pads and crutch tips. The handgrips are adjusted so that with the patient standing, the elbows are slightly bent (about 30 degrees) and the wrists are bent backward (hyperextended) slightly. There should be room for two fingers in the space between the top of the axillary bar of the crutch and the fold of the axilla when the patient stands. Safety rubber suction tips on the ends of crutches prevent slipping. It is important to be sure the tips are clean and not worn.

Preparing for crutch walking. Several exercises help a patient prepare for crutch walking. Push-ups help strengthen the arm and shoulder muscles. The muscles in the hand can be strengthened by squeezing a ball 50 times or so a day. Handgrips can be purchased that are also used for this purpose.

The following recommended techniques help a patient prepare for using axillary crutches:

1. Assist the patient into a chair that is close to a wall when he is ready to get out of bed.
2. Help the patient stand against the wall with the crutches placed in his hands.
3. Have the patient sway from side to side on his crutches while standing slightly away from the wall. This helps the hands and arms become used to weight bearing.

4. Have the patient lean against the wall and pick up one crutch to about 15 cm (6 in) from the floor and then place it back down on the floor. He should do the same with the other crutch and repeat this exercise several times. It helps the patient learn how to manage his crutches. He is ready to start to walk after he has shown that he can handle his crutches with ease and comfort.
5. Have the patient assume a posture with the crutches that allows the line of gravity to go through a wide base of support. The crutches should be placed about 10 cm to 20 cm (4 to 8 in) in front and about the same distance to the side of the feet, forming a triangle for good balance.
6. Teach the patient he is to support himself on the crutches with his arms and hands. If he supports himself by placing his weight on the axillary area, he may irritate the skin. Also, the weight tends to cut off circulation and places pressure on nerves to the arms and hands, which may result in permanent paralysis.
7. Cover the place where the patient rests his hands with adhesive or moleskin if the patient's hands tend to slip on the hand supports, which will give the patient a feeling of unsteadiness.

Crutch-walking gaits. In many hospitals, a

Figure 16-78 This elderly lady is using her walking frame properly, despite her normal stoop. Some walking frames have rear extension legs to provide extra sturdiness for those who tend to fall backward.

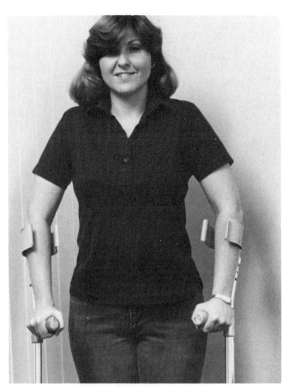

Figure 16-79 Elbow crutches.

physiotherapist teaches the patient how to use crutches. However, it is important for the nurse to observe that the patient uses his crutches properly. The nurse is often required to provide assistance after the initial teaching has been done. Also, the nurse may be responsible for teaching patients how to use crutches in some hospitals and in the home.

Table 16-3 describes several basic crutch-walking gaits. Some use the term *point* in their name. Point refers to the number of supports being used during ambulation. For instance, during a two-point gait a crutch and one leg represent the support that is utilized as one leg and the other crutch are picked up and moved forward; in a three point gait, two crutches and one leg act as supports and so on.

Using recreation for exercise

The concept of exercise need not be limited to dull routines that many find tedious and boring. Patients can be encouraged to move about while enjoying leisure-time activities.

Arts and crafts can often be a rewarding use of leisure time. Activities such as painting, clay modelling, knitting, and using a saw or sander in woodworking are examples of recreation that exercises the fingers, hands, wrists, elbows and shoulders. Family members are often eager to provide materials that the patient will enjoy while gaining therapeutic benefits.

At one time, patients helped each other and assisted with the unskilled work within hospitals when such work did not interfere with their recovery. However, using patients as workers is uncommon today. In hospitals where this system has been used carefully, the results have been impressive. For some patients, being able to help is gratifying. It gives them a feeling of personal accomplishment, relieves their boredom and provides exercise and activity. A few examples of things patients can do to help include making telephone calls for others confined to bed, writing letters for others, making beds, sorting laundry or supplies, delivering flowers and so on.

Figure 16-80 Platform crutches allow the patient to distribute weight bearing on the forearms.

Suggested measures to prevent inactivity in selected situations

When the patient is an infant or child

Most infants and children enjoy bathing and the freedom for movement it allows. Use water play as a means of promoting activity and exercise.

Mobiles hung above an infant's bed can be a source of sensory stimulation and can provide motivation for hand activity.

Soft foam action toys such as footballs, basket-balls and frisbies can be used safely inside to promote large muscle movement among children.

Many songs for children can be used along with actions to provide an enjoyable means for exercise.

Pet therapy can help children exercise by providing an opportunity for stroking, walking and playing with an animal.

Children may enjoy riding stationary bicycles as a means of indoor activity.

Using scissors to cut out colourful pictures from magazines or used greeting cards can provide a pleasurable activity as well as hand exercise. Children often enjoy pasting the cut-out pictures into a scrapbook.

Periodically assess the measurement of a child's ambulatory aid, such as canes and crutches, so that they remain appropriate for the growth of the child.

Inspect the rubber tips of crutches or other ambulatory devices. The tips should be replaced if they are worn. They must be cleaned to remove dust and dirt that build up.

When the patient is elderly

Consider disuse syndromes as serious threats to the elderly and work conscientiously to help prevent them.

Balance periods of activity with periods of rest.

The elderly often have arthritis. Expect that it will take the patient some extra time in the morning before he can gradually resume activity.

Elderly patients may enjoy the stimulation and activity associated with playing board games and card games.

Puzzles with large-sized pieces can be used as a means of solitary activity.

Remove any objects that may present an obstacle or hazard to the use of a walking frame or cane so that further injury is avoided. Common problems are water on the floor, throw rugs, electrical cords and chair legs.

Teaching suggestions for preventing inactivity

Suggestions for preventing and counteracting inactivity have been described in this chapter. They are summarized below:

Table 16-3. Common crutch-walking gaits

Gait	Condition for Use	Method for Use
Two-Point Gait	The patient must be able to bear some weight on each leg.	The patient bears weight on both feet. The right crutch and left foot are moved forward. Then, the left crutch and the right foot move forward. It resembles a normal walking pattern.
Three-Point Gait	Weight bearing is allowed on one leg. The other foot cannot bear weight or can bear only limited weight.	Both crutches and the leg that cannot bear weight move forward and then the foot permitted to bear weight comes through. The crutches are brought forward immediately and the pattern is repeated. The gait is illustrated in Figure 16-81.

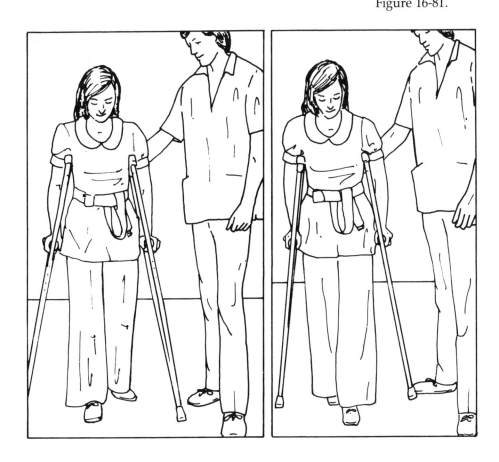

Figure 16-81 When using the three-point gait (*left*), one foot (in this case the patient's left) is permitted to bear weight. The patient is placing both crutches and her right foot, which can bear only limited weight, forward. After shifting her weight from her left foot to her crutches and right foot, she then brings her left foot through and in front of her to receive her weight (*right*).

Continued

Table 16-3. *Continued*

Gait	Condition for Use	Method for Use
Four-Point Gait	Weight bearing must be permitted on both feet; however, those using this gait may need to move slower because they lack balance, are weak or have limited ability to move.	Only one point is moved forward at a time in a sequence like this: left crutch, right foot, right crutch, left foot. Some may progress from this gait to a two-point gait as their condition improves. The patient in Figure 16-82 is using a four-point gait.

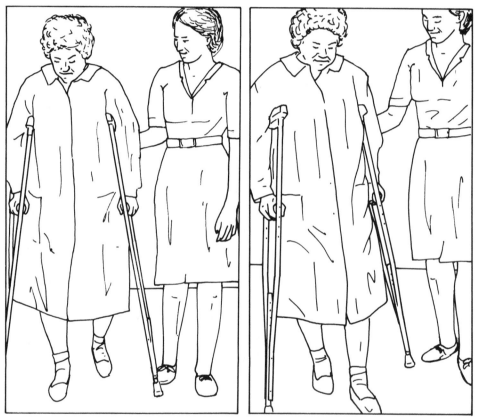

Figure 16-82 This patient is using the four-point gait for crutch walking with axillary crutches. *Left*: The left crutch is placed forward first, and the patient moves her right foot forward in position to receive weight. *Right*: The right crutch is then placed forward and the patient's left foot is brought forward in position to receive weight.

Swing Through and Swing to Gait	In this gait, one or both legs are involved. Usually, a patient using this gait has leg braces or a cast. The gait produces rapid	The crutches are advanced together. The body weight is shifted from the legs to the hand grips. The legs are swung either slightly beyond the

Table 16-3. Continued

Gait	Condition for Use	Method for Use
	movement, but it does not resemble normal walking.	crutch tips or just parallel with them. The person in Figure 16-83 is using a swing-through gait.

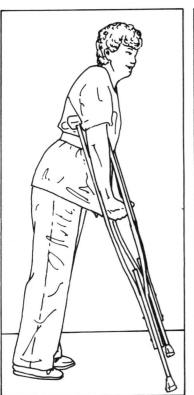 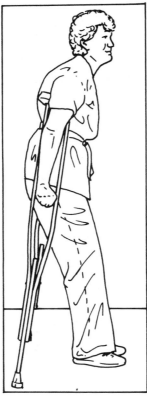

Figure 16-83 This patient demonstrates a swing-through gait used by someone with involvement of both legs. *Left*: Both crutches are brought forward. *Right*: After shifting the body weight to the handgrips, the patient swings her legs forward through the space between the crutches. Some patients, for instance those with a leg cast, use this gait while supporting their weight on one leg.

Few people are aware of the dangers of inactivity. Most seem to believe that complete bedrest during illness is essential to regain health and they are reluctant to return to activity. Bedrest is often very important for patients, but without some planned activity the patient is likely to develop serious complications. Therefore, it becomes important for the nurse to teach patients the many dangers of inactivity and to gain their cooperation to return to activity as soon as possible.

It is important to explain what is going to be done, and why, when transferring patients and when performing exercises. When patients have this information, accidents are less likely to occur.

Most patients assume a "coffin position", which is similar to the supine position, unless properly taught the benefits of other positions in bed. Teaching the patient the benefits of changing positions in bed is important, especially when this may be among the few activities allowed.

It is important to use necessary precautions when transferring patients and when helping them walk—and to teach why precautions are necessary. Patients often do not recognize their limitations or the state of weakness that follows a period of inactivity. Accidents are likely to occur when teaching has been inadequate. Although certain patients need to be encouraged to engage in activity and exercise, others may tend to take on more than is safe.

Patients need repetitive teaching about the use of crutches, canes and walking frames. Using these devices improperly can lead to accidents and injury.

Mechanical immobilization

Some patients are inactive and physically immobile due to an overall debilitating condition. The patient who is mechanically immobilized is in a somewhat different situation. *Mechanical immobilization* is the restriction of movement as a result of the application of a splint, cast or traction. Any apparatus of this type temporarily confines or limits otherwise active individuals.

These forms of treatment cover, attach to and confine areas of the body for varying periods of time. For these reasons, they require specialized skills in care to accomplish their intended purpose yet avoid injury to body structures during their use. Techniques required to care for individuals who require mechanical immobilization are now described.

General purposes for mechanical immobilization

Most individuals for whom mechanical immobilization is used have sustained trauma to the musculoskeletal system. These injuries are painful and do not heal as rapidly as those of the skin or soft tissue. They require a period of inactivity during the time that new cells are restoring the integrity of the damaged structures.

Splints, casts, traction and similar devices in this category may be applied to accomplish any one or a combination of the following:

Relieve pain and muscle spasm.
Support and align damaged tissues.
Reposition injured and healing musculoskeletal structures.
Maintain functional positions until healing is complete.
Allow activity while restricting movement of an injured area.
Prevent further structural damage and deformity.

Using splints

Splints are devices that immobilize and protect an injured part of the body. They come in a variety of designs depending upon the need for their use.

Ambulances stock *inflatable splints*, also called *pneumatic splints*, which become rigid when filled with air. The injured body part is inserted into the deflated splint. The splint moulds to fit the injured part and prevents movement when inflated. These splints also control bleeding and swelling by virtue of the pressure they exert. Emergency vehicles also carry traction splints made of metal. They are not as easily applied as an inflatable splint. They require special instruction prior to their use to avoid injuring structures even further. A *traction splint* is applied in such a way as to immobilize and pull on muscles that are in a state of contraction. Both pneumatic and traction splints are intended for very brief periods of use immediately after an injury occurs, until some other form of treatment can be provided.

Cloth and foam splints, called *immobilizers*, are used frequently to limit motion in the area of a painful but healing injury, such as in the neck and knee. This type can be removed for brief periods allowing for dressing and hygiene needs. Velcro or buckle closures permit them to be adjusted to fit a body part of almost any shape and size.

Moulded splints are made from plastic, like the one shown in Figure 16-84. They are used by patients with chronic injuries or diseases in whom prolonged support and inactivity are necessary to prevent further damage and pain. They maintain the body part in a functional position to prevent contractures and muscle atrophy during the period of disuse.

Applying an emergency splint

Whether one is using a manufactured splint or an improvised splint made from common articles in an emergency, several important techniques should be followed:

- Avoid changing the position of an injured part of the body even if it appears grossly deformed. Moving damaged structures can increase the severity of the injury.
- Leave a high top shoe or a ski boot in place if an injured ankle is suspected. The footwear can act as a splint to limit movement of the ankle and reduce pain and swelling.
- Select a splint or substituted splint material that

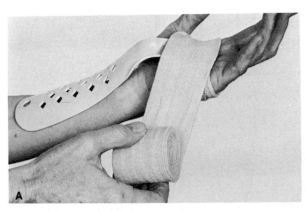 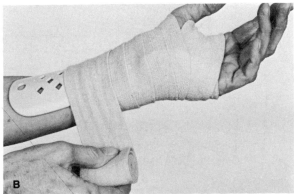

Figure 16-84 *Left*: This patient is securing a moulded plastic splint that spans the hand, wrist and forearm. Notice that the bandage anchors the splint with a circular turn on the palm of the hand. *Right*: The patient proceeds to unroll the bandage up the forearm.

will not permit movement of the body part once it is applied. Examples that may be adapted for use include flat boards of timber, tree limbs, broom handles, rolled layers of newspaper, rolled blankets, or pillows.

- Apply the splinting device so that it spans the injured area from the joint above the injury to beyond the joint below the injury. For instance, if the lower leg has been injured, the splint should be long enough to restrict movement of the knee and ankle.
- Inflate a pneumatic splint to the point that it can be indented only 1.3 cm (½ inch) with the fingertips. Avoid inflation longer than 30 to 45 minutes, or circulation in the area may be affected.
- Use an uninjured area of the body adjacent to the injured part if no other sturdy material is available. For example, an injured arm can be immobilized to the chest; one finger can be secured to the one beside it.
- Cover any open wounds with clean material to absorb blood and prevent the entrance of dirt and additional pathogens.
- Apply soft material over any area of the body that may be subject to pressure or rubbing by areas on an inflexible splint.
- Use tape or wide strips of fabric in several areas to confine the injured part to the splint so it cannot be moved. Narrow cord can create a tourniquet effect, especially if it encircles swelling tissue.
- Assess the colour and temperature of fingers or toes to evaluate if blood flow is adequate.

Loosen the attached device if the digits appear pale, blue or cold.
- Elevate the entire length of the immobilized part, if that is possible, so that the lowest point is higher than the heart. Elevation will reduce the rate of swelling.
- Provide for the individual's warmth and safety and seek assistance in transporting the injured person to a hospital.

Using supportive devices

While injured body structures are healing, supportive devices are used, thus enabling an individual to move about with less pain and without the need for a more confining device.

Braces

Braces are designed to support weakened structures during weight bearing. For this reason they are made of sturdy materials, such as metal and leather. When custom-made for the leg, they are incorporated into a shoe. Some back braces are cloth with metal staves, or strips, that are sewn within the fabric of the brace. The nurse must take care that a back brace is not applied upside down. Any improperly applied or ill-fitting brace can cause discomfort, deformity and pressure sores.

Slings

Slings are muslin binders that elevate and support an injured area. They are frequently used to position an arm across the chest, but they may also be used to suspend a leg when a patient is confined to bed.

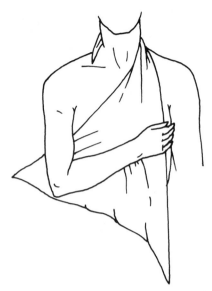

Figure 16-85 The points of a triangular piece of fabric are positioned in these locations prior to fashioning a sling.

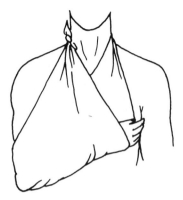

Figure 16-86 When a sling has been properly applied and fastened, the knot is at the side of the neck, the hand is elevated higher than the elbow, and all loose ends have been secured.

Commercial arm slings are available, but they are more costly than triangular pieces of muslin cloth. Slings come in various sizes. A common size for an adult triangular sling is made by cutting a 1 metre (36 to 40 inch) square in half diagonally.

A triangular sling used to support the arm is applied as follows:

- Place the open triangle on the patient's chest with the base of the triangle along the length of the patient's chest on the unaffected side, as shown in Figure 16-85.
- Place the upper end of the base of the triangle around the back of the neck on the unaffected side.
- Place the apex or point of the triangle under the affected arm.
- Place the lower end of the base of the triangle across the affected arm.
- Tie the two ends of the base of the triangle in a knot at the side of the neck, as illustrated in Figure 16-86. A knot should not be tied over the cervical spine at the back of the neck because it may create pressure on the bony prominences and cause discomfort to the spine.
- Be sure the hand is higher than the elbow in the sling to prevent swelling in the hand.
- Fold and secure the material at the elbow on the affected side neatly. A pin may be used, behind

the sling so that it is out of sight, to secure the material.

A triangular sling is a versatile item. It may be converted into a cravat binder, shown in Figure 16-87, and used in several different ways. A *cravat binder* is a piece of cloth folded into a strip of a desired width. It may be used as a temporary measure to support a sprained joint, used as a tourniquet to control severe bleeding, or as a binder around the head.

Casts

A *cast* is a solid mould of a body part. It is used to immobilize an injured structure that has been placed in correct anatomical position. Casts are used chiefly when an individual has sustained a *fracture*, which is a break in the continuity of a bone. The broken ends of the bone are repositioned when the doctor performs a procedure called a *reduction*. A *closed reduction* means the bone is realigned without making a surgical incision. During an *open reduction*, an incision is made and the bone ends are repositioned under the doctor's direct view. In addition to the use of a cast, sometimes repositioned bone is held in place internally with the use of metal devices, such as nails, wires, screws, pins or rods.

Types of casts. There are basically three types of casts. They are classified according to their shape and the area in which they are applied. They are categorized into cylinder casts, body casts and hip spica casts. The materials and principles involved in cast applications permit many variations in the three general types.

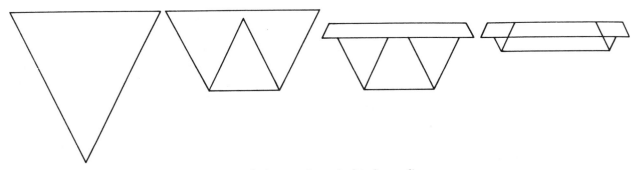

Figure 16-87 Left to right, a cravat is being made from a triangular binder or sling.

A *cylinder cast* is a rigid mould that encircles an arm or leg, leaving the toes or fingers exposed. It can be applied to enclose varying lengths of an extremity, such as a short leg cast, a long leg cast and so on. However, following the initial reduction, the cast will extend to include joint areas above and below the broken bone. This prevents movement of the repositioned bone ends to that healing will take place with the bone in correct alignment. As healing progresses, the cast may be trimmed or shortened.

A *body cast* is simply a larger form of a cylinder cast. Instead of encircling an extremity, a body cast encircles the trunk of the body. It generally extends from the nipple line on the chest to the hips. For some individuals with spinal problems, the body cast may extend from the occiput and chin areas to the hips with modifications made for exposing the arms. This type of cast may be cut in two and worn like a clam shell. This design permits one half of the cast to be removed while the patient is lying either prone or supine so that bathing and skin care can be provided.

A *hip spica* is a type of cast that encircles one or both legs and the lower trunk. It is usually used when a fracture has occurred in the femur close to the hip joint. A hip spica may be strengthened by attaching a bar spanning a cast area on one leg to a cast area on the other leg. This type of cast is trimmed in the anal and genital areas to provide room for the elimination of urine and stool. Despite this, the patient is unable to sit during elimination. The nurse must protect the cast from soiling using plastic wrap and a fracture bedpan. A hip spica cast is very heavy, hot and frustrating because it limits movement and changing positions.

Cast construction. At one time casts were made only from plaster of Paris embedded into gauze strips and rolls which hardened as it dried. There have always been disadvantages in using this material.

Though plaster casts are inexpensive and become rigid eventually, they are heavy, dry slowly and soften if they become wet.

Technological advancements have now created alternative substances that are being used as cast materials. Casts are being made of fibreglass and also polyurethane. They are marketed under a variety of names. The chemical substances in these cast materials are incorporated within widely woven rolls that become more porous than plaster letting air in and moisture out.

These newer cast materials tend to be strong, are lighter in weight, dry within 5 to 15 minutes and will not soften when wet. Some have mistakenly interpreted this to mean that they could swim and shower with a synthetic cast. Unfortunately the cast will not decompose but the person's skin underneath may, because the moisture does not evaporate easily. Each of these two materials used in cast construction is more expensive than plaster. For some, the advantages of their use may outweigh the added cost.

Applying a cast. The nurse prepares the patient and assists the doctor when a cast is applied. The patient should be informed by the doctor that a cast is necessary. If a choice of cast materials is possible, the doctor may permit the patient to select the type that will be used.

Preparing the skin. Since the skin will be covered for weeks or months, it is important that the skin is clean and protected. The nurse may prepare the skin in the following way:

- Remove clothing that will interfere with the cast application.
- Provide the patient with prescribed pain medication if he is experiencing discomfort.
- Wash the area thoroughly with warm water and soap or detergent. Some hospitals use special

antimicrobial cleansers to reduce the number of surface organisms.

- Wait to cleanse the area if the patient is uncomfortable and will be eventually anaesthetized.
- Note any cuts or abrasions that may become infected once the cast is applied. Under the cast it will be warm, dark and moist . . . a perfect environment for pathogen growth.
- Cover the skin with *stockinet*, stretchy fabric that comes knitted in a tube. The purpose of the stockinet is somewhat analogous to wearing stockings inside shoes. It protects the skin and absorbs moisture. Cut the stockinet much longer than the intended length of the cast. It will eventually be folded back making a smooth, cushioned edge at each end of the cast.
- Smooth any wrinkles in the stockinet and make sure it is not too tight.
- Cut thick pieces of felt for placement over and around bony prominences, such as the ankle, knee, elbow, wrist and so on.
- Wrap the entire area with cotton padding.
- Explain that as a plaster cast is applied, the sensation of heat will be felt. Steam or heat waves may even be seen rising from the surface of the wet cast.

Assisting with application of the cast. The nurse should have the following items ready for the doctor: strips and rolls of cast material, a source of water for wetting the cast material, gloves if the doctor prefers, and knife or scissors. The doctor may wish to help himself to the cast materials, wetting them as needed while the nurse maintains the body part in position.

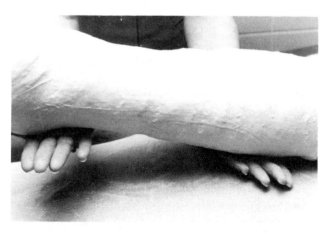

Figure 16-88 A damp cast should be handled with the palms of the hands to help prevent dents and flat spots.

At other times special tables with supports and slings may be used to maintain the patient's position. This frees the nurse to anticipate and provide the doctor with wetted cast materials. Synthetic cast materials dry so quickly that once the cast application begins everyone must work quickly and in a coordinated manner.

The nurse must take care when disposing of the water used to wet the plaster rolls and strips. Since the plaster in the water can ruin plumbing pipes, the water should be emptied in a sink that contains a special trap.

Handling and drying a wet cast. Casts made of the newer synthetic materials dry quickly. Drying of fibreglass casts may be facilitated with the use of a special ultraviolet lamp. These casts become rigid so quickly that the patient may bear weight within 15 to 30 minutes after application.

On the other hand, plaster casts may remain wet for 24 hours to 48 hours depending upon the level of humidity in the air. During this period the cast is vulnerable to becoming misshapen. At worst this could change the alignment of the repositioned bone. At the least, indentations can eventually rub internally and form pressure areas on the skin underneath.

Any wet plaster cast should be supported on pillows so that it is cushioned rather than pressed against a firm surface. The nurse should only use the palms of the hands to move and reposition the cast while it is wet. This technique can be seen in Figure 16-88.

Ordinarily, the air circulation in the room is adequate for drying the layers of plaster. A fan may hasten drying. To facilitate air drying, the cast should not be covered with bed linen or clothing. The patient's position should be changed every few hours to dry all the surfaces and depths of the cast. Plastic liners on pillows protect the pillow from becoming moist and musty, but may interfere with evaporation of water from the cast.

Using heat to dry the cast is not generally advisable. However, if a form of heat is applied, such as with a light within a cradle, it should not be covered nor used for an extended period of time. These precautions should be followed so that the patient will not become burned. Often attempts to use heat to dry the cast result in drying the surface but not the inner areas. This can lead to cracking of the plaster material.

Assessing the patient who has a cast. Because most

casts are applied after an injury and surgical procedure, the nurse may expect that the area will swell and bleed. These are the two immediate problems about which the nurse must be concerned. Swelling is especially serious since the cast is rigid and will not expand as the area within the cast becomes larger. The cast can create a tourniquet effect. If tissue becomes damaged due to a lack of adequate blood supply, amputation may be necessary. Nerves may also be damaged by a constricting cast. However, neurologic signs are not likely immediately after the cast has been applied. Neurological assessment is discussed later in Principles of Care 16-9.

Assessment is somewhat difficult because the nurse will be unable to see directly beneath the cast. However, certain physical assessment techniques may be used to detect early complications in the area where the cast has been applied.

Evaluating swelling and circulation. One assessment technique for determining the extent and effects of swelling and circulation involves performing the blanching test, as the nurse in Figure 16-89 is doing. Swelling affects blood flow. The nurse compares the information on the appearance and sensation in the fingernails or toes to determine if circulation is impaired. A radial or pedal pulse may or may not be palpated depending upon the length of the cast. In most cases, the area in which these arteries are located will be covered by the cast. All assessments are compared with duplicate assessments on the same area on the opposite side of the body, if that is possible. If that cannot be done, the nurse must mentally compare the assessment information with similar assessments performed on other individuals who have had casts. This assessment is performed at least every hour, or more frequently, for the first 24 hours after the cast application and then every 4 hours for another 2 to 3 days. After that, assessments should be made at least once on each shift throughout the patient's stay within the hospital. Performing this technique is discussed further in Principles of Care 16-9.

Detecting and evaluating bleeding. Since cast materials are constructed of porous gauze rolls, strips or tape, it is logical that the cast will absorb blood and other drainage. The volume and the rate of the drainage may be evaluated by inspecting all surfaces of the cast. It is more likely that bleeding will be evident in the area of a surgical incision. However, blood may drain toward the lower surfaces of a cast under the influence of gravity.

Figure 16-89 The nurse uses the blanching test to evaluate the adequacy of blood flow. The nail is compressed and the rate of colour return is noted. The nail in an uncasted area is also assessed and the two are compared. (Farrell, 1986)

The nurse should inspect all surfaces of the cast. Venous and capillary bleeding is characterized by a reddish brown appearance. When blood is observed on the cast, the nurse should circle the drainage on the cast. The circled margin is dated, the time indicated, and the initials of the nurse should appear on the cast. A description of the assessed size of the drainage area should also be noted in the patient's record with related information, such as the patient's blood pressure, pulse rate and level of consciousness. This information adds to the basis for evaluating the significance of the blood loss.

At 1- to 3-hour intervals, the nurse should inspect the previously circled margin and draw another line if the bleeding has extended beyond the previous line. A comment should follow in the nurse's notes as to whether the bleeding line remains the same or has changed.

The nurse should never hesitate to notify a doctor if swelling or bleeding continues to increase. In fact, the nurse would be held accountable and more than likely negligent if these observations went unreported and the patient experienced complications. A cast may need to be cut or removed if the patient's safety or life is endangered.

Caring for a patient who has a cast

In addition to the requirement that nurses meet the individual needs of the patient, special skills must be utilized when the patient has a cast. Principles of

Principles of Care 16-9. Providing basic cast care

Nursing Action	Rationale
Remove residue of plaster from the skin with a wet wash cloth.	When plaster is used, it is likely that it may drip and stick to various areas of the skin. It is especially annoying to a patient when it remains between toes, where it often cannot be reached.
Elevate the extremity in a cast, as one authority states, "the higher the better". Each distal joint should be higher than the preceding one. Pillows with a waterproof covering or a sling, like the one illustrated in Figure 16-90, may be used to help elevate a cast.	Elevating an area in a cast helps promote venous circulation and prevent problems of tissue oedema and pressure caused by swelling under the cast.

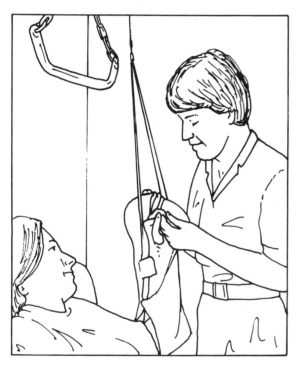

Figure 16-90 Slings may be used to suspend and elevate extremities that have been placed in a cast. This cast is supported within a sling with self-adhering closings. Notice that the sling is fastened to a pulley. A weight hangs over the head of the bed. The pulley and weight keep the arm well elevated at a comfortable height and allow the patient some degree of movement in bed.

Nursing Action	Rationale
Place ice bags next to a wet cast, especially over the area of an incision, to help control swelling and bleeding.	Cold causes vasoconstriction, which reduces the loss of fluid from within capillaries into the tissue spaces.
Expose the cast directly to the air.	A cast produces heat as it dries. If the cast is covered, moisture accumulates and evaporation is delayed.
Do not allow anything to rest on a wet cast and do not allow a wet cast to be placed on a flat, hard surface. Pillows are used under a cast, allowing it to dry on a soft surface. Bed linens should be supported off of the cast. A wet cast should be handled with the palms of the hands, not the fingers.	A wet cast dents and flattens easily. This is likely to cause pressure on tissues under the cast in dented and flattened areas. Handling a wet cast with the fingers causes dents in the cast.

Continued

Principles of Care 16-9. Continued

Nursing Action	Rationale
Support bed linens over a cradle or high footboard if the patient with a leg cast feels chilled. Linens can also be supported on straps extended from opposite sides of the bed between side rails.	Linens may become moist when they are in contact with a wet cast. As long as linens do not interfere with air circulation around the cast, the nurse may cover the patient.
Change the patient's position every 1 to 2 hours.	Repositioning helps to expose all the surfaces to air in order to dry the cast evenly and completely.
Use heat to facilitate drying a plaster cast only in rare circumstances. *Do not overdo.* Cradles with lights should not be covered with linens in this situation.	The heat may dry the surface but not the interior, leading to cracking. The skin under the cast may burn if too much heat is used. Covering a cradle over a wet cast may not allow moisture and heat to evaporate easily.
Watch for signs and symptoms of excess pressure on tissues under the cast.	A cast is a hard, rigid object that can interfere with blood flow, nerve function and skin integrity.
The following assessment techniques should be used frequently:	Frequent assessments help in identifying problems before they escalate.
1. Use inspection and palpation to test for swelling, paleness, cyanosis and coolness of the skin.	These signs and symptoms are typical of poor circulation to a part. It could be due to a cast that is too tight if the opposite area of the body does not appear similar.
2. Pinch the nailbeds and then release the pressure to test for the return of blood flow into the nail. Perform the same assessment on the opposite hand or foot.	The colour in the nailbeds should go from white to pink immediately when circulation is good. The colour change in patients with dark skin is less pronounced but observable.
3. Take pulse rates near casted areas to the extent the cast permits.	If no pulse can be felt, the cast may be interfering with arterial flow, which must bring oxygen to cells and tissue.
4. Ask the patient if there is sensation in the fingers or the toes. Ask the patient to describe any unusual feelings, such as numbness or tingling. Touch the exposed skin areas with objects of varying temperatures and textures if the patient describes unusual changes. This helps validate the ability of the patient to identify and discriminate sensations.	Pressure on nerves, cells deprived of oxygen, or tissue spaces filled with fluid may dull or alter the sensations a patient feels.
5. Ask the patient to move each finger and toe to test for movement. It is insufficient to check only a few fingers or toes or for him just to be able to wiggle them. The nurse in Figure 16-91 is assessing the patient's ability to move all the fingers on the arm that has been placed in a cast.	Normally, all toes and fingers should move with ease. The patient should be able to flex and extend the fingers or toes. If not all move or the movements are not normal, there could be pressure on one or more nerves that could result in permanent deformity.
Watch for spots on the cast due to bleeding. Venous blood normally is dark red, then turns brown and stops within a relatively short time.	Some bleeding can be expected after an open reduction. The nurse uses assessment to determine if the patient is losing arterial blood or if the blood loss is excessive.

Continued

Principles of Care 16-9. Continued

Nursing Action	Rationale

Figure 16-91 The patient is asked to demonstrate motion in all fingers and to extend them. Report the situation immediately if the patient cannot do so or has numbness or pain when moving the fingers or toes. In an arm fracture, observations just described help determine whether there is sufficient blood circulation and nerve innervation in the hand. If not, a serious deformity could result.

Nursing Action	Rationale
Draw a ring around an area of drainage on the cast and add the date, time and initials.	Encircling a stain on a cast with a line makes it simple to compare findings when drainage continues.
Feel for hot spots over the surface of the cast.	When inflammation is present from phlebitis or a pressure sore, the cast generally feels warmer than other parts of the cast.
Inspect for drainage, other than blood, due to an infection or necrotic tissue from an advanced pressure sore. Sniff the cast edge if an odour is not obvious. If an infection or sloughing tissue is present, the drainage is more likely to be brownish in colour and will have a foul odour.	An infection can lead to serious weakening or delayed healing if it extends to the depth of the bone. A pressure sore may extend more widely and deeply if the cast remains in place. The earlier these signs are detected and treated, the better the outcome will be.
Perform and document all these assessments regularly. A patient with a new cast should be assessed at least every hour for 24 hours and then every 4 hours for another 2 to 3 days. After that, the cast should be checked several times a day. Less frequent checking of a cast may be safe in *some* situations. Report *promptly* when abnormal signs and symptoms are noted.	Nurses are legally responsible for monitoring the condition of a patient in a cast. The consequences of delaying or not reporting significant assessments are too serious to allow one to take that responsibility lightly.
Change a casted patient's position frequently. Even patients with small casts tend to move little and must be encouraged to move about as much as permitted.	Encouraging mobility helps to prevent the many problems that are associated with disuse, as described previously in this chapter.
Turn a patient to his unaffected side when moving him. Support a dry cast under joint areas.	Handling a cast under a joint gives good support and helps to prevent cracking the cast if it is wet or weak.

Continued

Principles of Care 16-9. Continued

Nursing Action	Rationale
Use range-of-motion exercises for unaffected joints, and use a trapeze on the bed when possible to promote activity. Isometric exercises may be used for strengthening muscle groups under a cast.	Exercising not only promotes well-being but is also important to keep muscles in shape for eventual ambulation or activities of daily living.
Elevate the head of the bed on blocks when a patient is in a body cast. Provide prism glasses to help him read.	Elevation helps breathing, facilitates digestion and elimination, and helps him to be stimulated by activity in the environment. Prism glasses permit a patient to read while lying flat.
Inspect the edges of the cast for rough areas or chipping plaster.	Rough areas can cause skin abrasion or breakdown. Crumbs of plaster can fall into a cast and cause discomfort and itching.
Apply petals of tape to rough or crumbling cast edges in the manner described in Principles of Care 16-10.	*Petals* are trimmed strips of tape inserted over the edges of a cast to smooth and repair cast edges temporarily to protect the integrity of the skin.
Rub skin areas near the edge of the cast with alcohol. Apply lotion sparingly to exposed areas if the skin appears dry. Caution the patient not to insert objects, such as straws, eating utensils, hairpins, combs, tooth brushes and coat hangers when the skin itches.	Alcohol helps to keep the skin clean and in good condition. Lotion tends to build up and become sticky. Objects inserted under a cast may fall inside or cause an alteration in the integrity of the skin.
Remove crumbs and debris within the cast with a vacuum cleaner hose, hair dryer hose on a cool setting, or with a bulb syringe.	Air may be used to blow particles out or move them so that the patient does not experience as much discomfort or itching. Air will not damage the skin.
Protect the cast from becoming wet when tending to hygiene needs such as bathing or elimination. Use plastic wrap in the perineal area.	When a plaster cast absorbs moisture, the cast becomes soft. Plastic and plastic wrap are barriers to water and other forms of liquid, such as urine.
Provide general nursing care that is conducive to well-being, such as providing stimuli, movement, personal hygiene, nourishing diet with abundant sources of calcium for healing, sufficient fluids, comfort, and adequate rest and sleep.	Keeping the body in good physical condition promotes healing and helps to reduce the potential for complications.

Care 16-9 describes nursing measures that may be used during the time that a cast is applied.

Maintaining a cast

A cast must continue to remain intact and rigid during the full time it is applied. Plaster casts are more likely to weaken, crack and crumble. At times the only alternative for maintaining a cast will be adding more strips or rolls of plaster or a complete cast change. The nurse can use various techniques that will maintain the cast or repair it temporarily.

Keeping a cast clean. Most casts are either white or semiclear in appearance. Many people, especially children and adolescents, use the cast medium to display signatures, graffiti and drawings.

With wear, casts are bound to appear soiled. Those who are concerned about the appearance of a soiled cast may be helped by using various measures. Wetting the plaster can weaken the cast. However, the cast can be cleaned with a damp cloth and a little cleanser. It can be whitened with shoe polish used sparingly. An oversized knee sock, leg warmer or narrow tube knit fabric can be used to cover a cast and add fashion to its appearance.

Repairing cast edges. Cast edges may become sharp and cause skin abrasions or pressure sores. If a cast edge begins to crumble, it can irritate the skin within the cast. This may tempt the patient to insert objects for scratching. The nurse can repair cast edges by applying petals made from tape. The steps for petalling a cast can be found in Principles of Care 16-10.

Replacing a cast window. Sometimes it may become necessary to cut a square piece, called a *window*, out of a cast. A window facilitates inspection of an area without removing the entire cast. An example of a window is shown in Figure 16-94. A window may also permit various treatments, such as application of medication or a dressing, to be performed.

Once a window has been cut, the piece of plaster should not be thrown away. It should be replaced in its original site and secured with tape or a length of roller bandage. If the windowed area remains open, the tissue inside has a tendency to bulge through the window. This may lead to uneven pressure on the skin, possible skin breakdown, or pressure on nerves.

Removing a cast

A cast may need to be removed or split as an emergency measure if swelling becomes severe. The cast may also be removed when it will be replaced by another or when sufficient healing has occurred.

The doctor usually uses an electric cast cutter to separate and remove the cast. In an emergency, the nurse could wet the cast and cut through the softened areas with sturdy scissors. In some hospitals, there may be a written policy approving the use of a cast cutter by a qualified nurse.

A cast cutter is a noisy instrument that can be frightening to a patient. There is a natural expectation that an instrument sharp enough to cut a cast would be sharp enough to lacerate several layers of skin and tissue. However, when used properly, an electric cast cutter should leave the skin intact.

When the cast is removed, the cutter is moved along medial and lateral sides of the cast in order to bivalve it. A *bivalved cast* is one that has been split in two. After one half of the plaster shell has been removed, the stockinet and whatever padding was used prior to the cast application can be cut away with scissors.

Care following cast removal

The patient should be prepared for the expected change in the appearance of the body part that has been enclosed as well as the potential decrease in functional use. Many assume that the body part will look the same and be capable of its previous motion and strength. That, however, is rarely the case.

The muscle will usually have become smaller and weaker with the period of disuse. The skin will be pale and waxy looking. It may contain scales or patches of dead skin. The joints may be limited in their range of motion.

The skin may be washed as usual with soapy warm water but the semiattached areas of loose skin should not be forcibly removed. Lotion applied to the skin may add moisture and prevent rough edges from catching on clothing.

The area may swell once the support of the cast has been removed. Therefore, the patient may need to elevate a leg periodically or continue to wear a sling while upright. Crutches, a cane or a brace may be needed until muscle strength and joint movement return with gradual progressive exercise or physiotherapy.

Caring for a patient in traction

Traction is the application of equipment to the body to provide pull and counterpull on a particular part of the skeletal system. The pull is achieved by using weights in the form of sandbags or metal discs; the counterpull is almost always produced exclusively by the patient's own body weight.

Traction is usually applied and used while a patient is confined in bed. Occasionally it may be possible to apply traction within the construction of a cast. This is the exception rather than the rule. Traction is generally applied by using slings, ropes, pulleys and weights. The nurse must be aware of the various types of traction, the principles for maintaining their effect, and measures that will ensure that the patient receives proper nursing care.

Types of traction

There are three general types of traction: manual traction, skin traction and skeletal traction.

Manual traction is the pull on a body part using an individual's hands and muscular strength. This type of traction is most often used during the reduction of a fracture. It may also be used when replacing a dislocated bone end into its original position within a joint.

Skin traction is a pull applied indirectly to the skeletal system by attaching equipment and weight to

Principles of Care 16-10. Petalling a cast edge

Nursing Action	Rationale
Trim any frayed areas from the edge of the cast.	Loose and hanging pieces will not feel comfortable even if covered by petals of tape.
Stretch the stockinet from under the cast so that it extends higher above the cast edge.	The stockinet should not be allowed to slip beneath or become wrinkled inside the cast.
Fold the stretched stockinet over the trimmed cast edge and secure it in place temporarily with a strip of tape.	The stockinet may slip back within the cast if it is not secured in place.
Cut several strips of 1 or 2 inch wide adhesive tape.	Adhesive tape is structurally tougher and more durable than other types of tape.
Trim the end of the strips to form curves or points, as shown in Figure 16-92. Some nurses prefer to trim both ends of the tape.	The trimmed end(s) will fit the contour of a circle more easily without wrinkling than a flat edge on the tape. It is more important that the inner side of the tape does not wrinkle than the part that will extend over the outside of the cast.

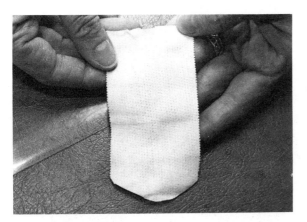

Figure 16-92 A petal has been shaped from a strip of adhesive.

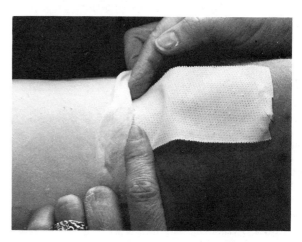

Figure 16-93 The rounded edge of the petal is placed under the cast's edge. The opposite end is brought up over the edge of the cast.

Slip half of the trimmed end of the tape on the inside of the cast with the sticky side facing the stockinet as the nurse is doing in Figure 16-93.	The side that contains the adhesive must be applied to the cast and not the skin.
Press the tape to make contact with the inner side of the cast. Take care that it remains smooth.	If the tape does not remain flat, it can cause irritation, discomfort, and even contribute to forming a pressure sore.
Hold the inserted end in place while bringing the opposite half end over the edge of the cast. Press it into place.	Secured tape will be less likely to come loose.
Repeat using as many strips as necessary next to one another to cover the entire cast edge or just the rough and crumbling areas.	This technique acquired its name because when finished, the tips of the tape resemble the petals of a flower extending from its centre.

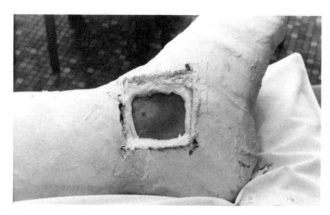

Figure 16-94 A square window has been cut from a cast so that the skin underneath can be assessed. (Farrell, 1986)

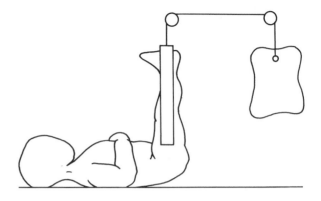

Figure 16-96 A child in Bryant's (Gallows) traction. Reproduced with permission from Taylor, I., Ward Manual of Orthopaedic Traction; published by Churchill Livingstone, 1987.

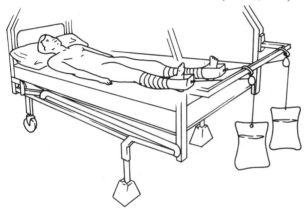

Figure 16-95 Completed Buck's traction. Reproduced with permission from Taylor, I., Ward Manual of Orthopaedic Traction; published by Churchill Livingstone, 1987.

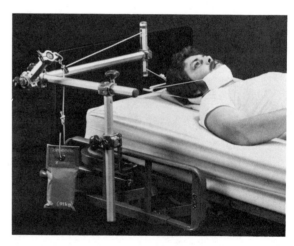

Figure 16-97 A cervical halter, a type of skin traction, is being used here. Any use of a pillow or elevation of the top end of the bed frame must be specified by the doctor in a written medical order. (Courtesy Zimmer Patient Care Division, Dover, Ohio)

the skin. There are various names for commonly applied forms of skin traction. Figure 16-95 shows a leg in Buck's traction. A child who does not weigh very much could not provide much counterpull with this type of skin traction. To compensate for that factor, an infant or young child may be placed in Bryant's traction, shown in Figure 16-96, to take advantage of the additional influence of gravity. Figure 16-97 shows another type of skin traction. It is applied to the skin at the chin and back of the neck but its effect is intended for the musculoskeletal structures around the cervical vertebrae.

Skeletal traction is a pull applied directly to the skeletal system by attaching wires, pins or tongs into or through the bone. Figure 16-98 shows tongs inserted into burr holes within superficial layers of the cranium. They are not deep enough to enter the area of the meninges beneath the cranium. Figure 16-99 is an example of skeletal traction in which a wire has been inserted through a bone in the lower leg.

The numbers of ropes, pulleys and weights may appear frightening to the patient, his family and even the nurse. However, most of this equipment, with the exception of what is attached to the bone, is being used to suspend the leg and balance the pull when the patient moves horizontally or vertically in bed.

A traction trolley, similar to a dressing trolley, is usually available on wards. It contains the various equipment that would be needed when assisting with the application of traction.

Figure 16-98 These tongs are located within burr holes in the cranium. If they should become displaced, the nurse should apply manual traction to the head and neck to prevent motion until assistance arrives and a replacement can be made. (Courtesy Zimmer Patient Care Division, Dover, Ohio)

Maintaining traction

The nurse must make various focus assessments to determine that the pull and counterpull are being maintained. The nurse should:

- Evaluate if the directions of the pull and the counterpull are in opposite but straight lines.
- Check that the patient or other objects are not interfering with the ratio of pull to counterpull.

This may occur if the patient rests his weight against the lower area of the bed frame. Bed linen or blankets may also get caught in the traction line and interfere with the ratio of pull to counterpull.

- Examine all the ropes to determine that they move freely through the pulleys.
- Inspect the weights to determine that they are the amount ordered by the doctor and that they hang free from the floor.

The patient in traction is relatively immobile because he is confined to bed. The nurse must provide care while maintaining the mechanical equipment. Various observations and actions must be carried out to ensure that complications do not occur. Principles of Care 16-11 may be used as a general guide for the care of patients in traction.

Suggested measures related to mechanical immobilization in selected situations

When the patient is an infant or child

Assess an infant or small child closely who has just had a plaster cast applied. The heat produced by a drying cast can alter a small individual's body temperature in a short amount of time.

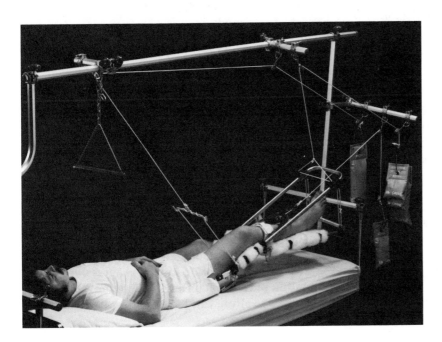

Figure 16-99 Skeletal traction is applied into or through a bone. A wire has been inserted through this patient's proximal tibia. The insertion site serves as a potential port of entry for pathogens. (Courtesy Zimmer Patient Care Division, Dover, Ohio)

Principles of Care 16-11. Caring for a patient in traction

Nursing Action	Rationale
Inspect the mechanical equipment used for the application of traction.	All the equipment should be in good repair and applied securely to the bed and the patient.
Provide a trapeze if the type of traction allows the patient to raise his body weight.	A trapeze may facilitate exercise, self-care and nursing care.
Position or reposition the patient so that his body is in the centre of the bed and the body part in traction is in the same line of pull.	The body must be maintained in good alignment and provide adequate counterpull in relation to the pull of the traction.
Avoid tucking top sheets, blankets, or bed spreads beneath the mattress.	Coverings can interfere with the pull produced by the traction equipment.
Instruct the patient and assigned nursing personnel as to the length of time the patient must be attached to the traction equipment	Traction is almost always meant to be applied continuously. Exceptions may be made when a patient in skin traction receives physiotherapy.
Identify the positions the patient may assume.	Most patients must lie flat and cannot even roll to either side without changing the direction of pull.
Wash the posterior areas of the body and rub bony prominences by depressing the mattress enough to insert a hand.	The patient should not turn to the side. Some types of traction may permit the patient to raise himself off the bed by using a trapeze.
Make the bed by removing bottom sheets from the head to the foot of the bed. Remake the bed by applying the linens in the reverse direction.	The technique for making an occupied bed must be modified since the traction patient cannot roll from side to side.
Use some type of pressure-relieving device on the bed, such as one of the examples discussed in Chapter 22.	Being restricted to a supine position creates the potential for pressure sores over the scapulae and coccyx.
Apply elbow and heel protectors, if necessary.	Friction and shearing forces may be reduced, thereby decreasing the potential for skin breakdown.
Omit using a pillow if the patient is in neck or head traction, unless specifically ordered by the doctor.	Elevating the head may alter the line of pull.
Use a fracture bedpan for bowel elimination if elevating the hips alters the line of pull.	A fracture bedpan can be inserted without appreciably raising the patient's hips off the bed.

Continued

Protect a cast well, when it extends to the perineal area, with plastic material to help keep the cast clean, dry and free of odours when the child cannot control elimination.

Help children adjust to wearing a cast by making it attractive. Most children enjoy drawing or colouring pictures on the cast.

Check a child in traction frequently. His smaller body weight and increased activity level may lead to improper positioning.

Provide and change mobiles or other visual stimuli frequently to reduce sensory deprivation.

Help parents to select safe toys that will stimulate and hold a child's attention. Pull-string toys that randomly reproduce sounds or words are examples that may be useful.

Take special precautions when assisting a child who is immobilized to eat. A supine position can interfere with swallowing and digestion. Aspiration of food is also a potential risk.

Caution children who begin progressive ambulation once a cast or traction is removed to do so slowly. Falling can lead to reinjury.

Principles of Care 16-11. Continued

Nursing Action	Rationale
Encourage active range-of-motion and isometric and isotonic exercise as much as possible.	Body areas that are unrestricted by traction should be kept flexible and in good tone. Isometric exercises may be performed on the areas where motion is restricted.
Encourage frequent dorsiflexion of any unrestricted lower extremities.	It may be impossible to provide a footboard because it may interfere with the ratio of pull to counterpull.
Inspect the skin where pins, wires or tongs have been inserted. Look for redness, tenderness, swelling and drainage.	Piercing the skin alters the skin's barrier to organisms. Pathogens may begin colonizing open skin areas and can then extend into the bone.
Cleanse the skin areas around the insertion points of skeletal traction using soap or an antimicrobial solution.	Cleansing removes the numbers of organisms present around an open area. Antimicrobial agents interfere with pathogen growth.
Apply and change dressings around skeletal traction insertion sites.	Dressings may be used to cover open areas and maintain antimicrobial agents next to the skin.
Cover any sharp points on traction equipment, such as the ends of pins, wires or tongs, with pieces of cork, eraser, or folded gauze squares.	Sharp points may scratch or puncture care givers, or tear clothing and linen.
Assess the colour, temperature and mobility of all areas where traction is applied.	If applied improperly, traction may interfere with the function of nerves and circulation of blood.
Insert padding material inside slings if they become wrinkled.	A wrinkled sling may occlude blood flow through an area or lead to skin breakdown. Padding helps to cushion and distribute the pressure.
Record the frequency of bowel movements and request an order for a stool softener or other measure to assist with bowel elimination when necessary.	Immobility and embarrassment about using a bedpan can easily lead to constipation.
Allow the patient to schedule his own activities and decorate the room with assorted items. Be flexible in enforcing rules regarding visitors.	When a patient feels some control over his life and lifestyle, depression may not be quite so severe.

When the patient is elderly

Selectively group patients of similar ages. Long-term confinement can be emotionally distressing when there are extremes in interests or lifestyles among those who must share a room.

Implement preventive measures to maintain skin integrity early during the period of mechanical immobilization. Skin breakdown is more easily prevented than treated.

Encourage an elderly person to perform as many of the activities of daily living as possible. Ageing individuals are especially depressed by continuing losses of independence.

Provide a variety of methods for orienting patients, such as large numbered calendars and clocks. When one day is so similar to the next, a patient may become temporarily disoriented to the date and time.

Maintain arm strength by encouraging various upper extremity exercises. The elderly may become extremely weak with prolonged immobilization, which may slow eventual ambulation efforts.

Anticipate that an elderly person may require home care, delivered meals or extended care in a nursing home. Begin discussing referrals early if the family cannot provide the care following discharge.

Teaching suggestions during mechanical immobilization

All patients should understand the purposes of the treatment and the methods for maintaining the equipment. Many teaching suggestions have already been described throughout this text. When the patient will be leaving the hospital and providing self care, the importance of comprehensive teaching becomes a priority for preventing complications.

Identify foods that are a source of complete protein. Indicate the type and amounts of foods that will supply at least three servings from the milk group each day, and foods that are sources of vitamin D. Bone healing requires additional nutrients and calcium. Vitamin D is needed to utilize calcium.

Discourage patients from snacking frequently on high calorie foods. It is easy to add additional weight while physical activity is restricted. Weight gain can cause a body cast to become tight. Added weight may increase the stress on weak joints, muscles or healing bones once mobility is possible.

Patients who are discharged wearing casts need written and oral instructions about how to keep the casts clean and dry. They should be taught very carefully about symptoms they can expect to experience and which ones should be reported *promptly* if they occur. Patients sent home with wet casts are especially in need of instructions about how to detect evidence of excessive pressure from casts and how to care for their casts.

Teach the patient to avoid getting his cast wet. Good protection from rain and from water may be obtained by placing waterproof material around the cast. A hair dryer on a warm setting works well when a small part of the cast accidentally becomes wet.

Provide phone numbers for the patient or family members. Explain that they should call promptly if any untoward signs or symptoms appear.

References

Farrell, J. (1986) *Illustrated Guide to Orthopedic Nursing*, 3rd edn, J.B. Lippincott, Philadelphia, p. 61.

Talbot, D. (1981) *Principles of Therapeutic Positioning: A Guide to Nursing Action*, Sister Kenny Institute, Minneapolis, p. 12.

17

Measurement and recording of the individual's vital signs

Learning objectives

When the content of this chapter has been mastered, the learner should be able to.

Define terms appearing in the glossary.

Summarize briefly how the body functions to maintain normal body temperature, pulse and respiratory rates, and blood pressure.

List factors that influence body temperature, pulse and respiratory rates, and blood pressure.

List average normal ranges for persons of various ages for body temperature, pulse and respiratory rates, blood pressure and pulse pressure.

Describe characteristics of a normal and abnormal temperature, pulse, respirations and blood pressure.

Describe how the measurements are obtained, including obtaining body temperature using three different sites, pulse rate using six different sites and blood pressure using two different sites.

Describe the following pieces of equipment and explain how each is used properly: a glass clinical thermometer, an electronic thermometer, a heat-sensitive thermometer, a sphygmomanometer and a stethoscope.

Discuss the frequency with which measurements are ordinarily obtained from hospitalized patients.

Demonstrate how to document on to the patient's record.

Explain how to clean a glass clinical thermometer.

List suggested measures for obtaining the TPR and BP in selected situations, as discussed in this chapter.

Summarize suggestions for instructing the patient.

Glossary

Adventitious sounds Abnormal breath sounds.

Apical rate The number of heart beats that occur in one minute as heard over the apex of the heart with a stethoscope.

Apical-radial pulse rate The pulse rate obtained by two persons when one obtains the radial pulse rate while the other obtains the apical rate.

Apnoea A period during which there is no breathing.

Arrhythmia An irregular pattern of heartbeats, and consequently an irregular pulse rhythm. Synonym for *dysrhythmia*.

Arteriosclerosis Loss of elasticity in arterial walls.

Atherosclerosis Narrowing of the inside of arteries due to deposits of fat.

Axilla Armpit.

Axillary temperature A measure of body heat obtained by placing a thermometer in a dry axilla.

Basal metabolic rate The minimum amount of energy required to maintain body functions during periods of inactivity. Abbreviated BMR.

Blood pressure The force of blood within the arterial walls.

Bounding or full pulse A pulse that feels full and strong to the touch and is not particularly easy to obliterate with mild pressure.

Bradycardia A heart rate below 60 beats per minute in an adult.

Bradypnoea A below-average or slow respiratory rate.

Celsius scale The original scale used in the centigrade thermometer.

Celsius thermometer An instrument having 0° for the temperature at which water freezes and 100° for the temperature at which water boils. Synonym for *centigrade thermometer*.

Cheyne-Stokes respirations A gradual increase and then gradual decrease in depth of respirations, followed by a period of apnoea.

Constant fever A fever that continues, is consistently elevated and fluctuates very little.

Crisis A rapid return of an elevated body temperature to normal.

Diaphragmatic respiration Respirations performed primarily by the diaphragm.

Diastole The time during which the heart muscle relaxes.

Diastolic pressure The least amount of pressure present in arteries when the heart muscle is in a state of relaxation.

Dyspnoea Difficult and laboured breathing.

Dysrhythmia An irregular pattern of heartbeats, and consequently an irregular pulse rhythm. Synonym for *arrhythmia*.

Exhalation The act of breathing out. Synonym for *expiration*.

Expiration The act of breathing out. Synonym for *exhalation*.

External respiration The process of exchanging oxygen and carbon dioxide between the lungs and the blood.

Fahrenheit thermometer An instrument having 32° for the temperature at which water freezes and 212° for the temperature at which water boils.

Febrile Having a fever.

Feeble, weak or thready pulse Descriptions of abnormal pulse volume that require much effort to feel and are easy to obliterate with pressure.

Fever Above normal body temperature.

Hypertension An abnormally high blood pressure.

Hyperthermia An abnormally high body temperature.

Hyperventilation Abnormally prolonged, rapid and deep respirations.

Hypotension An abnormally low blood pressure.

Hypothermia A body temperature that is below the average normal range.

Hypoventilation A condition in which a reduced amount of air enters the lungs.

Inhalation The act of breathing in. Synonym for *inspiration*

Inspiration The act of breathing in. Synonym for *inhalation*.

Intermittent fever A fever broken by periods of normal or subnormal temperature.

Intermittent pulse Periods of normal pulse rhythm broken by periods of irregular rhythm.

Internal respiration The process of exchanging oxygen and carbon dioxide between the blood and body cells. Synonym for *tissue respiration*.

Korotkoff sounds Sounds heard through a stethoscope while obtaining the blood pressure.

Lysis The gradual return of body temperature to normal.

Meniscus The curved surface at the top of a column of liquid in a tube.

Onset The period when fever begins.

Oral temperature A measure of body heat obtained by placing the thermometer in the mouth under the tongue.

Orthopnoea A condition in which breathing is easier when the patient is in a sitting or standing position.

Palpitation Awareness of one's own heartbeat.

Peripheral pulses Those pulse sites, located distant from the heart, which can be assessed with relative ease.

Postural hypotension A fall in blood pressure when a person assumes an upright position too quickly.

Premature contraction or bigeminal A pulsation that occurs sooner than has been the previous pattern.

Pulse A wave set up in the walls of the arteries with each beat of the heart.

Pulse deficit The difference between an apical and radial pulse rate.

Pulse pressure The difference between the systolic and the diastolic blood pressure.

Pulse rate The number of pulsations felt per minute.

Pulse rhythm The pattern of the pulsations and the pauses between them.

Pulse volume The quality of the pulsations felt.

Pyrexia Above-normal body temperature.

Radial pulse rate The pulse rate obtained by placing the fingertips on the radial artery at the wrist.

Rales Noncontinuous crackling sounds heard with a stethoscope caused by moisture in respiratory passageways.

Rectal temperature A measure of body heat obtained by placing a thermometer in the rectum.

Remittent fever A fever that fluctuates several degrees but does not reach normal between fluctuations.

Respiration The act of breathing.

Rhonchus A low-pitched, continuous sound heard with a stethoscope as air moves across narrowed respiratory passageways.

Rub A grating sound caused by friction as two structures move against one another.

Sinus arrhythmia An irregular pulse rhythm characterized by slowing when an individual breathes out and accelerating upon breathing in.

Sphygmomanometer An instrument used to measure the pressure of blood within an artery.

Stertorous respirations A general term referring to noisy breathing.

Stethoscope An instrument that carries sounds from the patient's body to the ear of the examiner.

Stridor A harsh, high-pitched sound heard on inspiration in the presence of an obstruction in larger airways, such as the larynx.

Systole The time during which the heart muscle contracts, causing blood to be pumped into the circulation.

Systolic pressure The maximum pressure exerted within arteries when the heart muscle contracts.

Tachycardia An abnormally rapid heart rate, between 100 to 180 beats per minutes in an adult.

Tachypnoea A respiratory rate that is more rapid than normal.

Thermometer An instrument used to measure the temperature of something; a clinical thermometer measures body temperature.

Thoracic respiration Respirations performed primarily by the intercostal and other thoracic muscles.

Tissue respiration The process of exchanging oxygen and carbon dioxide between the blood and body cells. Synonym for *internal respiration*.

Training effect Slowing of the heart rate, which results from regular, aerobic exercise.

Wheeze A high-pitched sound that occurs repeatedly during breathing as air is forced through narrowed respiratory passages.

Introduction

Changes in the way the body is functioning are often reflected in the body temperature, pulse and respiratory rates, and blood pressure. The body mechanisms that regulate them are very sensitive and respond quickly to changes in health. They are commonly abbreviated to TPR and BP. Because these signs serve as important indicators of the patient's condition, obtaining them is serious business—not just a routine task. The trend in the patient's measurements should be analysed each time they are taken by comparing the current measurements with those previously obtained.

Body temperature

Body temperature normally remains within a fairly constant range as a result of a balance between heat production and heat loss. This process is regulated in the brain's hypothalamus. Heat is produced primarily by exercise and by the body's metabolism of food. Heat is lost from the body primarily through the skin, the lungs and the body's waste products. When more heat is produced than is lost, the body's temperature will be above normal, or elevated. Conversely, when more heat is lost than produced, the body's temperature will be below normal, or subnormal. Figure 17-1 illustrates how heat loss and heat production determine the body's temperature.

The clinical thermometer. An instrument used to measure temperature is a *thermometer*. A clinical thermometer is used to measure body temperature. The thermometer is placed in the mouth to obtain an *oral temperature*. It is placed in the anal canal to obtain a *rectal temperature* and in the *axilla*, or armpit, to obtain an *axillary temperature*.

Body temperature is measured in degrees of Celsius, abbreviated °C. The Celsius thermometer has a scale at which 0°C is the temperature at which water freezes and 100°C is the temperature at which water boils. Although the Celsius scale is used extensively in hospitals, patients may still be using Fahrenheit thermometers at home. The nurse must be able to convert from one scale to another. Therefore Table 17-1 gives comparable Celsius and Fahrenheit temperatures and explains how tempera-

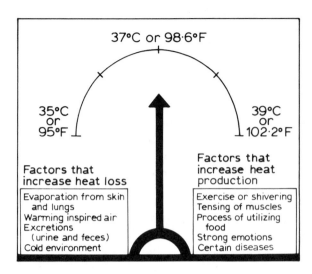

Figure 17-1 This illustrates the balance between factors that increase heat loss and factors that increase heat production.

Table 17-1. Equivalent centigrade and Fahrenheit temperatures and directions for converting temperatures from one scale to another*

Centigrade	Fahrenheit	Centigrade	Fahrenheit
34.0	93.2	38.5	101.3
35.0	95.0	39.0	102.2
36.0	96.8	40.0	104.0
36.5	97.7	41.0	105.8
37.0	98.6	42.0	107.6
37.5	99.5	43.0	109.4
38.0	100.4	44.0	111.2

* To convert centigrade to Fahrenheit, multiply by $\frac{9}{5}$ and add 32. To change Fahrenheit to centigrade, subtract 32 and multiply by $\frac{5}{9}$.

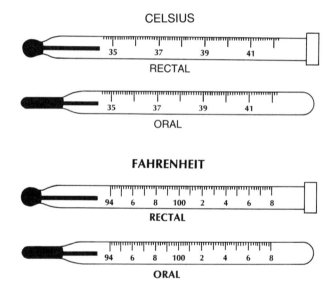

Figure 17-2 The two thermometers on top use the Celsius scale to measure temperature, the two on the bottom use Fahrenheit. Note the blunt bulbs on the rectal thermometers and the long thin bulbs on the oral thermometers.

tures can be converted from one system to another.

The glass clinical thermometer. The glass clinical thermometer most commonly used to measure body temperature contains mercury. It has two parts: the bulb and the stem. Mercury is a liquid metal and will expand when exposed to heat, causing it to rise in the stem of the thermometer. The stem is marked in degrees and in tenths of degrees. The range is from about 35°C to about 43.5°C. Fractions of a degree are recorded in even numbers, as 0.2, 0.4, 0.6 and 0.8. If the mercury appears to reach a bit more or less than an even tenth of a degree, it is usual practice to report the temperature to the nearest tenth. Figure 17-2

illustrates examples of glass clinical thermometers.

An *oral thermometer* has a long slender mercury bulb that provides a larger surface for contact with tissues under the tongue or in the axilla. A *blunt-bulb thermometer* is used to obtain a rectal temperature; the shape of the bulb helps prevent injury to or puncture of tissue when it is being inserted. Structurally, the design of the tip of an oral thermometer is weaker

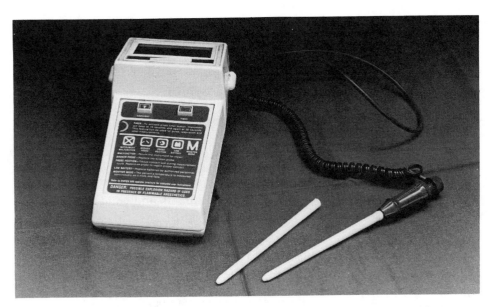

Figure 17-3 An electronic thermometer showing plastic probe covers. (Courtesy Royal Marsden Hospital)

than the more uniformly shaped bulb of the rectal thermometer. Considering that an oral thermometer has a greater potential for breaking within the body cavity being measured, it is dangerous to use it for obtaining a rectal temperature.

When using a thermometer in the home or anywhere else, check to see whether it is oral or rectal. Some thermometers have this printed on them, but others do not.

Some authorities recommend that an oral thermometer be used for obtaining an axillary temperature. Others recommend a rectal thermometer. It is best to observe hospital policy about which thermometer is best for obtaining an axillary temperature.

The electronic thermometer. The electronic thermometer measures body temperature in a matter of seconds. Reports in the literature indicate that these thermometers are accurate and their use saves considerable nursing time (Stronge and Newton, 1980). Figure 17-3 illustrates an electronic thermometer.

Heat-sensitive paper, patches and tape. Still another type of thermometer indicates body temperature by colour changes registered on heat-sensitive paper. This type of thermometer is used orally. Heat-sensitive patches and tapes are also available. They are applied on the skin and are most often used on normal newborns. All thermometers in this category are disposable. They are used for one patient only, register quickly and are nonbreakable.

Some studies have indicated that heat-sensitive

paper, patches, and tapes are not very reliable. Therefore, they should be used only when hospital policy is being followed. A glass clinical thermometer should be used to check the temperature if the patient's clinical condition does not seem to compare with the temperature registered on heat-sensitive substances.

Common factors influencing body temperature

A variety of factors normally influences body temperature.

Age. Newborns, infants and young children normally have a slightly higher average temperature than that of adults. Elderly people tend to have a slightly lower than average adult temperature. The body temperatures of infants, young children and the elderly are often influenced by environmental conditions. For example, the young and the elderly ordinarily require more clothing and bed covers than do young and middle-aged adults to maintain normal body temperature in a cool or cold environment.

Sex. Women demonstrate a slight rise in body temperature of about 0.6°C (1°F), rectally, when ovulating. This is most probably because of hormones that affect metabolism or tissue changes occurring in the body. The temperature returns to normal before menstruation.

Exercise and activity. The minimum amount of energy required to maintain body functions during periods of inactivity is called the *basal metabolic rate*, abbreviated BMR. Exercise and activity increase the need for energy. The body responds by increasing the metabolic rate. A by-product of metabolism is heat production. Certain disease conditions, one being an overactive thyroid gland, can also increase the metabolic rate and, consequently, cause a rise in body temperature.

Time of day. The vital signs normally fluctuate in circadian rhythm. For example, the body temperature is ordinarily about 0.6°C (1°F) lower in the early morning than in the late afternoon and early evening. This variation, which is considered normal, tends to be somewhat higher in infants and young children. An inversion of this cycle has been observed in persons who routinely work at night and sleep during the day.

Emotions. Persons having strong emotional experiences, such as fear and anger, are likely to have a higher than average temperature. Conversely, persons experiencing apathy and depression are likely to have a lower than average body temperature.

Illness. A deviation from normal, either above or below normal, is often an indication of a disease process. An elevated temperature is commonly associated with infections and other disease conditions; a lower than average temperature is a characteristic of certain others. Elevated and subnormal temperatures are discussed later in this section.

Normal body temperature

The range of normal body temperatures in well adults is between 36°C and 37.5°C. If the temperature goes above 37.5°C it can be regarded as an abnormally high temperature and is called pyrexia. If it goes below 36°C it can be regarded as an abnormally low temperature and is called hypothermia.

The average normal temperatures for well adults in various body sites are as follows:

Temperature Scale	Oral Site	Rectal Site	Axillary Site
°C	37.0°	37.5°	36.4°
°F	98.6°	99.5°	97.6°

Elevated body temperature (pyrexia)

A person with a *pyrexia*, or *fever* can also be called *febrile. Hyperthermia* refers to an abnormally high body temperature.

The following are commonly associated with a fever:

- Pinkish, red (flushed) skin that is warm to touch
- Restlessness or, in others, excessive sleepiness
- Irritability
- Thirst
- Poor appetite
- Glassy eyes and a sensitivity to light
- Increased perspiration
- Headache
- Above-normal pulse and respiratory rates
- Disorientation and confusion (when the temperature is high)
- Convulsions in infants and children (when the temperature is high)

A patient is considered to be in danger when his temperature reaches beyond 41°C (105.8°F). An individual rarely survives when his temperature reaches 43°C (109.4°F).

The *onset* of a fever may begin suddenly or gradually. A chill with shivering usually occurs before a rapid onset of fever. The skin is pale, due to constriction of small blood vessels in the skin, and the patient may state that he feels cold.

Fever and the manner in which it subsides may take a variety of courses. These courses are described and illustrated in Table 17-2. A fever that recurs following a period of normal body temperature may be a sign of relapse or complications; therefore, temperature should be reported promptly and will need continued frequent checking.

Subnormal body temperature (hypothermia)

The following are commonly associated with hypothermia:

- Pale, cool skin
- Listlessness
- Slow pulse and respiratory rates
- Decreased ability to solve problems
- Diminished ability to feel pain or other sensations

Death usually occurs when the temperature falls below approximately 32°C (89.8°F). However, cases of survival have been reported when body temperature has fallen considerably lower. Sometimes the body temperature is lowered below normal for therapeutic purposes. There are some illnesses in which the patient typically has a subnormal temperature. Therefore, it is important to observe a patient just as closely when the body temperature falls below normal ranges as when it is elevated.

Table 17-2. Courses and resolutions of fever

Course or Resolution	Definition	Illustration
Constant fever	A fever that continues, is consistently elevated and fluctuates very little	
Remittent fever	A fever that fluctuates several degrees but does not reach normal between fluctuations	
Intermittent fever	A fever broken by periods of normal or subnormal temperature	
Crisis	A rapid return of an elevated body temperature to normal	
Lysis	A gradual return of an elevated body temperature to normal	

Selecting a site for obtaining body temperature

Hospital policy guides the nurse in selecting the site at which the body temperature is to be obtained. The oral site is ordinarily used for most persons, although the axillary site is being recommended more often than it was in the past.

An axillary temperature has been thought to be a relatively poor indicator of body temperature. However, the axillary temperature is an accurate reflection of body temperature when it is obtained correctly. It may be the preferred site for a patient who has had oral surgery or facial injuries.

The following are advantages often cited for obtaining an axillary temperature:

- The axilla is readily accessible in most instances.
- It is a safe site to use.
- There is less danger of spreading microbes when compared with obtaining an oral or rectal temperature.
- Using the axillary site is less disturbing psychologically than using the rectal site for most patients.

For many years, it was believed that a rectal temperature was the most accurate reflection of the body's internal, or core, temperature. The exact placement of the thermometer, a lag in a change in the rectal temperature when blood temperature changes and the effect of stool in the rectum have been shown to influence the accuracy of a rectal temperature. Hence, the rectal site is probably no better than the oral or axillary site. Some persons are beginning to advocate that the rectal site be used only when the oral and axillary sites cannot be used.

Further guidelines for selecting the site at which to obtain the body temperature in selected situations are given later in this chapter.

Keeping clinical thermometers clean

Health personnel are aware of a responsibility to protect patients from acquiring infection. Use of disposable or individual-use equipment is becoming more common. However, nurses should know how to clean and disinfect thermometers, especially when caring for patients in a clinic or office, in a school or in a patient's home. If a nurse is unsure or questions the sanitary condition of a thermometer, or if there are no services for caring for thermometers between uses, the nurse should follow the suggested actions in Principles of Care 17-1 for cleaning a glass clinical thermometer.

There are thin, flexible, plastic sheaths available, such as Steritemp, that cover a glass clinical thermometer. They are intended to maintain the cleanliness of one thermometer being used on multiple patients. The sheath is applied over the thermometer before insertion and disposed after one use. This decreases spreading infections and cleaning chores. However, it has been found that some brands of sheaths may perforate before or with use; other brands are very sturdy. Nurses and individuals who use protective coverings on thermometers should inspect them carefully. The product must be of sufficient quality to keep the thermometer clean in

Principles of Care 17-1. Cleaning a glass thermometer

Nursing Action	Rationale
Use a soft clean tissue to wipe the thermometer.	Material on the thermometer interferes with disinfection. Soft material comes into close contact with all surfaces of the thermometer.
Hold the tissue at the stem part of the thermometer near the fingers and wipe down toward the bulb, using a firm twisting movement.	Cleaning from an area where there are few organisms to an area where there are numerous organisms minimizes the spread of organisms to cleaner areas. Friction helps loosen material on the thermometer.
Clean the thermometer with soap or detergent solution, again using friction.	A soap or detergent solution and friction loosen material on the thermometer.
Rinse the thermometer under cold, running water, and dry.	Cold water prevents breaking the thermometer. Rinsing helps remove material loosened by washing.

order to control the transmission of microorgainsms from one patient to another. Any thermometer that is soiled must be cleaned between uses.

Electronic thermometers are generally protected with hard, plastic, disposable probes. A separate probe is applied over the temperature sensor each time another patient's temperature is assessed. The probes can be attached and released without touching the area that is inserted in the patient. This method has also proven satisfactory in maintaining the cleanliness of thermometer equipment and preventing the spread of organisms.

Obtaining the body temperature

Principles of Care 17-2 describes how to obtain the body temperature when using the oral, rectal and axillary sites. All skills should begin and end with handwashing. Patients should always be prepared with proper explanations.

There have been many studies into the use of glass or electronic thermometers, the length of placement time and choice of placement area. The studies undertaken by Campbell (1983), Close (1987), and Davies et al. (1986) must be considered prior to obtaining a patient's temperature.

The pulse

Each time the heart beats, it forces blood into the aorta and then into smaller arteries. This causes the arterial walls to expand and distend. It produces a wave that can be felt as a light tap by the fingertips. This sensation is called the *pulse*.

Normal pulse rates

The *pulse rate* is the number of pulsations that occur in a minute. Normal pulse rates vary at different ages in life. Some common rates are listed in Table 17-3.

Common factors that influence pulse rates. A variety of factors can influence pulse rate.

Age. Pulse rate varies with age. It is relatively rapid at birth and gradually diminishes from birth to adulthood. It tends to be increased above the average adult's pulse rate in old age. For example, the approximate average pulse rate of an adult is 80, but an elderly person may exhibit a pulse rate that tends always to be higher than this.

Time of day. As is true of body temperature, the pulse rate is lowest in the morning on awakening and increases later in the day.

Gender. On awakening in the morning, the pulse rate of the average man is approximately 60 to 65 beats per minute. The rate for women is slightly faster, by about 7 to 8 beats per minute, than for men.

Body build. Tall, slender persons usually have a slower pulse rate than do short, stout persons.

Exercise and activity. The pulse rate increases with exercise and activity. This reflects the heat's effort to increase blood circulation and oxygen distribution necessary for proper cell functioning. However, with regular aerobic exercise, a *training effect* can be observed. This means that the heart can adequately supply cells with oxygenated blood with fewer beats. Those who are physically fit exhibit a slower pulse rate even during exercise.

Stress and emotions. Stress increases the pulse rate. When a person is experiencing strong emotions, such as anger, fear and excitement, the pulse quickens. Pain which is stressful especially when it is moderate to severe, can trigger a faster heart rate.

Body temperature. The body's need for energy is influenced by the body temperature. The body temperature may change due to illness, disease or exposure to an environment that is either hot or cold. When body temperature is elevated the pulse rate increases to supply nutrients and oxygen to cells. When body temperature is low, cells have reduced requirements. The heart will not need to work as rapidly to meet the cells' needs; the pulse rate will be slower.

Blood volume and components. Excessive blood loss causes the pulse rate to increase. When there are decreased red blood cells or inadequate haemoglobin to distribute oxygen to cells, the heart rate accelerates in an effort to keep cells supplied.

Drugs. Certain drugs influence the heart rate. Some are intended to restore an abnormal rate to one that is normal. For example, digitalis preparations typically slow the heart rate. Some drugs alter the heart rate unintentionally. Sedatives slow the heart rate though they are given to promote rest. Caffeine and nicotine increase the heart rate.

Abnormally rapid pulse rates

An abnormally rapid pulse rate is called *tachycardia*. An adult has tachycardia when the pulse rate is 100 to 180 beats per minute. The condition is usually a compensatory mechanism and occurs when there is a need to improve or increase blood circulation to the body's cells. Pulse rates can occur at rates higher than 180 beats per minute; very rapid heart rates may not

Principles of Care 17-2. Measuring the body temperature

Nursing Action	Rationale

Oral Method

Nursing Action	Rationale
Locate the type of thermometer used to measure temperatures in the particular hospital.	Some hospitals use glass clinical thermometers; some use flexible plastic sheaths to cover glass thermometers; some use electric thermometers with disposable probes.
Wipe from the bulb toward the fingers with each tissue.	Wiping from an area where there are few or no organisms to an area where organisms may be present minimizes the spread of organisms to cleaner areas.
Read the thermometer by holding it horizontally near eye level and turning it slowly between the fingers until the mercury line can be seen clearly, as illustrated in Figure 17-4.	Holding the thermometer near eye level makes reading it easier. Turning the thermometer will help to place the mercury line in a position where it can be read best.

Figure 17-4 The nurse reads the thermometer by holding it at eye level and rotating it until the mercury line is clearly seen.

Nursing Action	Rationale
Grasp the stem of the thermometer firmly between the thumb and forefinger and, with a snapping wrist movement, shake the thermometer until the mercury is well into the bulb end below the lowest markings.	The mercury will not drop below the level of the previous temperature reading unless the thermometer is shaken forcefully.
Cover the thermometer with a sheath, if that is hospital policy. Attach a disposable probe to an electric type and turn on the battery operated machine.	Coverings promote sanitary conditions. They reduce the need to cleanse the thermometer between uses.
Ensure the patient has not just had a hot drink or a cigarette.	A false reading will be obtained if the patient's mouth has recently been warmed.

Continued

Principles of Care 17-2. Continued

Nursing Action	Rationale

Oral Method

Nursing Action	Rationale
Place the mercury bulb of the thermometer under the patient's tongue and in the right or left posterior pocket at the base of the tongue.	When the bulb rests in a pocket where there is a rich supply of blood, and the mouth is closed, an accurate measurement of body temperature can be obtained.
Instruct the patient to hold the thermometer in place with his lips, and to avoid biting it.	Room temperature is lower than body temperature. Unless the thermometer is maintained within the mouth, the measurement may be inaccurate.
Leave a glass thermometer in place no less than 3 minutes. An electronic thermometer will register in less time. An audible signal indicates when an electronic thermometer has measured the body temperature.	Allowing sufficient time for the thermometer to reach maximum temperature results in an accurate measurement of body temperature.
Remove the thermometer and any plastic sheath that was used on the glass thermometer. Wipe it from the fingers down toward the bulb using a firm twisting motion. Discard tissues in a container for waste. A disposable probe covering an electric thermometer may also be placed in a waste container.	Mucus on the thermometer may make it difficult to read. Cleaning from an area where there are few organisms to an area where organisms may be abundant minimizes the spread of organisms to cleaner areas. Friction from the twisting motion helps to loosen matter.
Read the level at which the mercury expanded within the thermometer. Digital figures display the recorded temperature on electric thermometers.	The calibrations on the glass thermometer or the digitally displayed figures on the electric thermometer indicate the patient's temperature.
Follow hospital policy for handling the thermometer and record the patient's temperature.	Thermometers are generally kept in a certain location so that personnel may find them available when needed. Some nurses record the temperature directly on the patient's chart; others write it on a general sheet to be recorded later by a clerical assistant.

Rectal Method

Nursing Action	Rationale
Prepare the thermometer as suggested in the procedure for obtaining an oral temperature.	
Place lubricant on a paper tissue and lubricate the lower tip over about a 2.5 cm (1 in) length.	Placing lubricant on a tissue prevents contaminating the lubricant supply. Lubricant reduces friction and helps to insert the thermometer, thereby minimizing irritation or injury of the mucous membrane in the anal canal.
Provide privacy around the bed.	The patient's body should be protected from the view of others.
With the patient on his side, fold back bed linens and separate the buttocks so that the anal opening is seen clearly.	If the thermometer is not placed directly into the anal opening, the bulb may injure tissue at the opening. Separating the buttocks well makes the anal opening easy to see.
While instructing the patient to breathe deeply, insert the thermometer about a distance of 3.5 cm (1½ in) in	Breathing deeply promotes relaxation of the round sphincter muscle in the anus and rectum. The

Continued

Principles of Care 17-2. Continued

Nursing Action	Rationale
Rectal Method	
an adult. Do not use force to advance the thermometer.	thermometer may injure rectal tissue if force is applied.
Permit the buttocks to fall into place. Hold onto the thermometer. Leave a glass thermometer inserted 2 to 3 minutes. An electric thermometer will record in less time.	Maintaining a hold on the thermometer will prevent it from being expelled before the temperature is recorded.
Remove the thermometer and wipe it as described earlier so that the numbers may be observed. Dispose of any sheaths or probe covers.	Faecal material and lubricant on the thermometer make it difficult to read.
Wipe away any excess lubricant or stool from the patient. Assist him to a comfortable position.	The patient is apt to feel soiled and uncomfortable if lubricant and residue of stool remain at the anus.
Care for equipment and record the temperature as hospital policy directs.	Glass rectal thermometers are usually kept separate from oral thermometers to prevent accidentally mixing their use.
Axillary Method	
Prepare the thermometer as suggested in the procedure for obtaining an oral temperature.	
Follow hospital policy concerning whether to use a rectal or an oral thermometer.	Most often an oral thermometer is used for maximum contact with skin folds.
Place the bulb of the thermometer well into the axilla. Bring the patient's arm down close to his body and place the forearm over the chest toward the opposite shoulder. Stay with the patient so that the thermometer remains properly placed.	When the bulb rests against the superficial blood vessels in the axilla and skin surfaces are brought closely together to reduce air surrounding the bulb, an accurate measurement of body temperature can be obtained.
Leave the thermometer in place for at least 10 minutes, or longer.	Allowing sufficient time for the thermometer to reach its highest temperature results in an accurate measurement of body temperature.
Follow hospital policy regarding thermometer equipment and for recording the patient's temperature.	

---

oxygenate cells adequately. They may overwork the heart if sustained for very long.

The term *palpitation* means that the person is aware of his own pulse rate without having to feel for it over an artery. The pulse rate is ordinarily unduly rapid when palpitations are noted.

Abnormally slow pulse rates

The term used to describe the pulse rate when it falls below 60 beats per minute in an adult is called *bradycardia*. A slow pulse rate during illness is less common than a rapid pulse rate, but, when present,

bradycardia should be reported promptly. The following are conditions in which bradycardia is likely to be present:

- In heart block, when the atria may beat at one rate while the ventricles beat slower.
- When the brain has increased pressure.
- In athletes whose heart muscles have become well developed and efficient.
- In patients who are developing a toxicity to the medication digitalis, or one that is similar in action.

The rhythm of the pulse

The *pulse rhythm* is the pattern of the pulsations and the pauses between them. The pulse rhythm is normally regular; that is, the beat and the pauses occur similarly throughout the time the pulse is being obtained.

An irregular pattern of heartbeats, and consequently an irregular pulse rhythm, is called an *arrhythmia*. It may also be called a *dysrhythmia*. Some common patterns of irregular rhythms include the following:

- One that slows when a person breathes out and speeds up when a person breathes in. This type is not considered dangerous and is often seen in some children and young adults. It is called a *sinus arrhythmia*.

- A pulsation that occurs sooner than the regular beats that have previously been noted. This is called a *premature* beat or bigeminal pulse. It is usually less intense than the regular beats. If several premature contractions occur in succession, or happen frequently in a minute, it could be a warning of a potentially dangerous situation.

- An *intermittent pulse* is one that has a period of normal rhythm broken by periods of irregular rhythms. It may be a serious sign, such as in certain heart diseases, or it may be a simple response to being upset or frightened.

Any arrhythmia should be reported promptly. More details about arrhythmias and their causes can be found in clinical textbooks.

The volume of the pulse

The *pulse volume* refers to the quality of the pulsations that are felt. The volume is usually related to the amount of blood pumped with each heartbeat. This amount usually remains fairly constant under normal conditions. Normal volume results in the ability to feel a pulsation easily and requires mild pressure on an artery with the fingertips to stop the feel of the pulse wave. These two characteristics are used to evaluate the volume or quality of the pulse. Some common abnormal observations in pulse volume include:

- A *feeble, weak or thready pulse*. This term is used when the blood volume is small, making the pulse difficult to feel and, once felt, very easily stopped with pressure. A patient with a thready

Table 17-3. Normal pulse rates per minute at various ages

Age	Approximate Range	Approximate Average
Newborn	120–160	140
1 month to 12 months	80–140	120
2 years	80–130	110
2 years to 6 years	75–120	100
6 years to 12 years	75–110	95
Adolescence	60–100	80
Adulthood	60–100	80

pulse usually also has a rapid pulse. A rapid, thready pulse is usually a serious sign and should be reported promptly.

- A *bounding* or *full* pulse. This occurs when a large blood volume produces a pronounced pulsation that is not easy to stop even with mild pressure.

Another way to describe the volume or quality of the pulse involves the use of numbers. This numbering system and its corresponding descriptions can be found in Table 17-4. It is best to follow hospital policy when describing the volume of the pulse.

Selecting a pulse site

The rate, rhythm and volume of the pulse may be assessed by compressing an artery against an underlying bone with the tips of the fingers. The arteries that are most often used are those located close to the skin surface. Most, but not all, are named for the bone to which each is adjacent. They include: the temporal, carotid, brachial, radial, femoral, popliteal, dorsalis pedis and posterior tibial arteries. They are collectively called *peripheral pulses* because they are distant from the heart. The location of these sites is illustrated in Figure 17-5.

Usually the radial artery is the site commonly used for assessment. It is located on the inner, thumb-side, of the wrist. Figure 17-6 shows its location and the position of the fingertips during assessment using this site.

Obtaining the radial pulse rate

The pulse rate obtained at the wrist is called the *radial pulse rate*. The actions described in Principles of Care 17-3 describe the technique that may be used to

Table 17-4. Identifying pulse volume

Number	Definition	Description
0	Absent pulse	No pulsation is felt despite extreme pressure.
1+	Thready pulse	Pulsation that is not easily felt. Slight pressure causes it to disappear.
2+	Weak pulse	Stronger than a thready pulse. Light pressure causes it to disappear.
3+	Normal pulse	Pulsation is easily felt. Moderate pressure causes it to disappear.
4+	Bounding pulse	The pulsation is strong and does not disappear with moderate pressure.

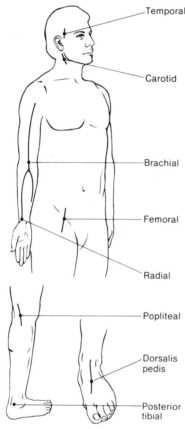

Figure 17-5 This diagram shows peripheral pulse sites. They may be used to assess the pulse characteristics of rate, rhythm and volume. An absent, thready or weak peripheral pulse may mean that there is an insufficient blood supply to that part of the body.

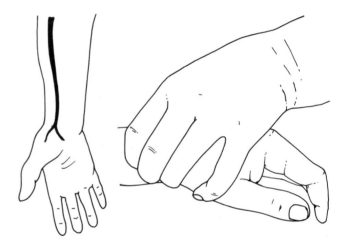

Figure 17-6 *Left*: The location of the radial artery. *Right*: The nurse's fingertips and the patient's hand should be positioned as here when assessing the radial pulse.

obtain the radial pulse rate. The other characteristics of the pulse should also be assessed at the same time.

The apical rate

If the radial pulse is irregular or difficult to count, the apical rate may be assessed. In the adult, the apical rate is counted by listening at the chest rather than feeling an artery. The heart beats are best heard at the apex, or lower tip, of the heart as illustrated in Figure 17-7. The nurse places a stethoscope, described and illustrated later in this chapter, slightly below the level of the nipple on the chest to the left of the breastbone. The nurse listens for the "lub/dub"

Principles of Care 17-3. Assessing the radial pulse

Nursing Action	Rationale
Help the patient to a position of comfort. If he prefers lying down, have him rest his arm alongside his body with the wrist extended and the palm of the hand downward. The arm may rest on his abdomen if this is comfortable. If the patient prefers sitting, have him hold his forearm at about a 90-degree angle to his body and rest his arm on a support with the wrist extended and the palm of the hand downward. It is common to assess the pulse rate while the body temperature is being obtained.	These positions are usually comfortable for the patient and convenient for the nurse. An uncomfortable position for the patient may influence the heart rate.
Place the first, second and third fingertips along the radial artery and press gently but firmly to compress the artery against the bone at the wrist.	The fingertips are sensitive to touch and will feel pulsation of the patient's radial artery. Using the thumb may result in feeling one's own pulse. This may result in an inaccurate assessment.
Gradually release the pressure while still feeling the pulsation. Note its rhythm and volume.	Too much pressure will shut off the pulse. If too little pressure is applied, the pulse will not be felt. The nurse should become aware of the feeling produced by the pulsation and the pattern of beats and pauses. The rate is not the only characteristic of the pulse that is assessed.
If the pulse is regular and feels normal, use a watch with a second hand, count the number of pulsations felt for half a minute. Multiply this number by two to obtain the rate for one minute.	A watch with a sweep second hand provides an accurate method for determining when half a minute has passed.
If the pulse is abnormal in any way, count the rate for a full minute. Repeat counting if necessary to determine an accurate rate and assessment of the rhythm and volume.	When the pulse is abnormal, a minimum of a full minute of counting is necessary to obtain a valid assessment of the rate, rhythm and volume.
Use good judgement to gather more information about the pulse by assessing the pulse at other peripheral pulse sites or by listening to the heart beats at the apex of the heart.	Nurses who detect abnormalities in the pulse or observe other signs that indicate that the patient may have cardiovascular problems may order or obtain more data, which will help in identifying a nursing diagnosis or collaborative problem.
Record the pulse rate according to hospital policy.	The rate of a pulse is often transferred and plotted on a graph. The characteristics of the rhythm and volume may be described in the patient's record.

sound. These two sounds equal one pulsation that would be felt at a peripheral site. The rate should be counted for one minute. The rhythm may also be evaluated. The heart rate obtained in this manner is called the *apical rate.*

The apical-radial pulse rate

Comparing the radial pulse rate with the apical heart rate may provide important information to health personnel. The rates should normally be equal, but for some patients they are not. Obtaining the *apical-radial pulse rate* requires two persons. One listens at the apex of the heart while the other feels the pulse at the patient's wrist. They use one watch placed conveniently between them, decide on a specific time to start counting, and count for a full minute. If a difference is noted in the two pulse rates—and the rates have been counted accurately—the findings

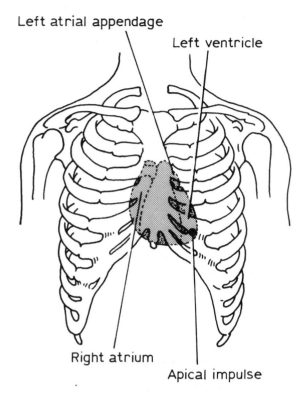

Left atrial appendage

Left ventricle

Right atrium

Apical impulse

Figure 17-7 This shows the location of the heart in the chest cavity and the area where the impulse for the apical pulse is normally found.

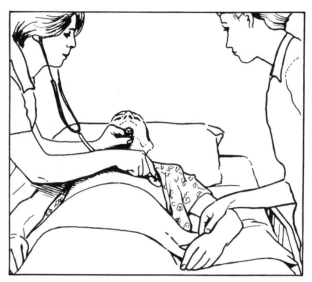

Figure 17-8 Obtaining an apical-radial pulse requires the simultaneous efforts of two nurses. Note that the patient's chest wall is exposed so that clothing does not interfere with hearing the apical pulse. It is best to warm the diaphragm of the stethoscope in the palm of the hand before placing it on the chest wall. A cold instrument placed on the patient could alter the pulse and respiratory rates.

should be reported promptly. The difference between the apical and radial pulse rates is called the *pulse deficit*. Figure 17-8 shows two nurses obtaining an apical-radical pulse rate.

Respiration

Respiration is the act of breathing. *Inhalation*, or *inspiration*, is the act of breathing in; *exhalation*, or *expiration*, is the act of breathing out. One act of respiration consists of one inhalation and one exhalation. Through the act of respiration, the body takes oxygen from the air and gets rid of carbon dioxide. The process of exchanging oxygen and carbon dioxide between the lungs and the blood is called *external respiration*. The process of exchanging oxygen and carbon dioxide between the blood and body cells is called *internal respiration* or *tissue respiration*.

The respiratory centre in the medulla and specialized sensing tissue in the carotid arteries are very sensitive to the amount of carbon dioxide in the blood. These structures carry out a coordinated effort to adapt respirations to the body's needs without the person having to think about breathing. Nevertheless, breathing can be controlled voluntarily to a certain extent. For example, a person automatically controls his breathing when talking, singing, laughing, crying, eating and so on. He can purposely take deep or shallow breaths. There are limitations, however, on how long a person can voluntarily hold his breath. When the body becomes desperate for lack of oxygen and for getting rid of carbon dioxide, the person will have to breathe sooner or later. A new mother, not realizing this, may panic when her child has a temper tentrum and holds his breath. The child will eventually breathe whether he wants to or not.

Normally the lungs fill and empty through pressure changes from the contraction and relaxation of various muscles. Infants and young children use the diaphragm to a large extent. This is called *diaphragmatic respiration*. Adults primarily use their intercostal (between the ribs) muscles when breathing. Though the diaphragm is also used, this breathing is called *thoracic respiration*.

Table 17-5. Normal respiratory rates at various ages

Age	Average Range
Newborn	30–80
Early childhood	20–40
Late childhood	15–25
Adulthood	
Male	14–18
Female	16–20

Normal respiratory rates

Table 17-5 identifies normal respiratory rates for various ages. Respiratory rates have been observed to vary considerably in well people, although the table of rates offers a good guide for evaluating respiratory rates. Factors that usually influence the pulse rate generally also affect the respiratory rate. The faster the pulse rate, the faster the respiratory rate, and vice versa. The relationship between the pulse and respiratory rates is fairly consistent in normal persons. The ratio is one respiration to approximately four or five heart beats.

Abnormally rapid respiratory rates

An above-average or rapid rate of respiration is called *tachypnoea*. A rapid respiratory rate may be observed with an elevated temperature because the body is attempting to rid itself of excess heat. Also, the body's metabolic needs are increased at this time. Cells require more oxygen, thereby triggering increased respirations. Rapid respirations are common when diseases affect the cardiac and respiratory systems. *Hyperventilation* is a term that describes prolonged, rapid and deep respirations. In an adult, a rate above 40 per minute, in the absence of exercise, is cause for alarm and should be reported promptly.

Abnormally slow respiratory rates

A below-average or slow respiratory rate is called *bradypnoea*. Certain drugs, such as morphine sulphate, will slow the respiratory rate. Slow respirations are also observed in the patient who has a brain tumour.

Hypoventilation is a term that describes a less than normal amount of air entering the lungs. This condition may occur when a person is taking shallow or slow breaths, or it may occur when an obstruction in the airway prevents a sufficient amount of air from reaching the lungs.

A respiratory rate of less than 8 per minute in an adult is cause for alarm and should be reported promptly.

Characteristics of breathing

Breathing is normally automatic. Respirations are relatively noiseless and effortless. The amount of air exchanged with each respiration varies widely among different people. Athletes generally have an increased capacity to exchange oxygen and carbon dioxide with each respiration. The depth of respirations is referred to as shallow or deep, depending on whether the volume of air taken in is below or above average for that person. Periodically, each person automatically inhales deeply, filling the lungs with more air than inhaled with the usual depth of respiration.

Certain terms are used to describe the nature and depth of respirations. *Apnoea* refers to periods during which there is no breathing. This is a serious situation in which brain damage and death can occur if breathing or blood circulation is suppressed for more than 4 to 6 minutes. *Dyspnoea* is difficult or laboured breathing. Dyspnoeic patients usually appear to be anxious and worried as they experience the inefficient work of breathing. The nostrils flare (widen) as the patient fights to fill his lungs with air. Abdominal and neck muscles may be used to assist other muscles in the act of breathing. When observing the patient, it is important to note how much and what type of activity brings on dyspnoea. For example, walking to the bathroom may bring on dyspnoea in a patient who may not be distressed by sitting in a chair.

Some respiratory patterns have descriptive names. *Cheyne-Stokes respirations* refer to breathing that consists of a gradual increase in the depth of respirations followed by a gradual decrease in the depth of respirations, and then a period of apnoea. Dyspnoea is usually also present. The observation of Cheyne-Stokes respirations is a serious sign often occurring as death approaches.

Orthopnoea is a characteristic in which breathing is facilitated by sitting up or standing. Dyspnoeic patients frequently find it easier to breathe in this manner. The sitting or standing position causes organs in the abdominal cavity to fall away from the diaphragm with gravity. This gives more room for the lungs in the chest cavity to expand, taking in more air with each breath.

Several terms are used to describe the nature of sounds that can be heard with the ear as a patient breathes. *Stertorous* breathing is a general term used to refer to noisy respirations. *Stridor* is a harsh, high-pitched sound that is heard on inspiration when there is a laryngeal obstruction. Infants and young children with croup often manifest stridor when breathing.

The nurse may listen to respirations throughout the chest with a stethoscope. The purpose of this assessment is to listen to the sounds of air moving through the large and small air chambers and lobes of the lungs. *Adventitious sounds* are abnormal breath sounds, such as the following:

- *Rales* are noncontinuous crackling sounds caused by moisture in respiratory passages. They are usually heard during inspiration and change in character with coughing. The sound heard as hair is rubbed between the fingers and thumb beside the ear simulates the sound produced by rales.
- A *rhonchus* is a continuous sound produced by air moving across narrowed respiratory passageways. A rhonchus (plural is rhonchi) is a low-pitched sound. It may occur during inspiration, expiration, or both. It may change with coughing.
- A *wheeze* is a high-pitched sound that is repeated during respirations as air is forced through narrowed respiratory passages. During an asthma attack, a wheeze is often heard during expiration. It may even be heard without a stethoscope at this time.
- A *rub* is a grating sound made as structures move against one another. When the membrane surrounding the lungs creates friction as it moves over the lung tissue, it is referred to as a pleural friction rub. Ordinarily there is a thin layer of moisture that helps this membrane glide noiselessly over the lung.

Assessing respirations

The nurse frequently observes respirations. Not only is the rate important, but also the effort, pattern of breathing, and sounds associated with breathing are important. Principles of Care 17-4 suggests techniques to use when obtaining the respiratory rate.

Principles of Care 17-4. Examining respirations

Nursing Action	Rationale
Observe the rise and fall of a patient's chest at a time when the patient is somewhat unaware that an effort is being made to count his breaths. A convenient approach is to count the respirations while appearing to concentrate on counting the pulse.	Counting the respiratory rate while presumably still counting the pulse keeps the patient from becoming conscious of his breathing and possibly changing his respirations. Altering the characteristics of normal, automatic breathing may cause data to be inaccurate.
Note the placement of the sweep second hand of a watch or clock. Count each rise and fall of the chest.	A complete respiration consists of one inspiration and one expiration.
If the respirations appear regular, even, and unlaboured, count the number that occur for half a minute. Multiply this number by two to obtain the rate for one minute.	Sufficient time is necessary to observe the rate, depth, and other characteristics of the patient's respirations. Counting the respirations for as little as 10 or 15 seconds allows too much room for error when working with numbers as small as the respiratory rate.
If the respirations are abnormal in any way, count them for a full minute and repeat if necessary for an accurate assessment.	A full minute of counting respirations and repeating the count if necessary allows time to collect and identify valid data.
Record information about the respirations according to hospital policy.	Respiratory rates are often graphed in order to analyse any trends. Descriptions about other characteristics of the respirations are made in the patient's record.

Blood pressure

Blood pressure is the force produced by the volume of blood pressing on the resisting walls of arteries. The arterial walls are normally elastic and expand as each new supply of blood is added to that which is already present.

Blood is pushed forward into the arteries during systole. *Systole* is the phase during which the heart works. It contracts and pumps blood out into the circulation. The pressure increases during this time. It is called the *systolic pressure*. The pressure is lower during *diastole*, the heart's resting phase. During that time the heart is filling with blood, which will be pumped out during the next systole. The pressure within the arteries that exists while the heart is at rest is called the *diastolic pressure*.

Blood pressure is commonly abbreviated BP. Its measurement is expressed as a fraction. The numerator is the systolic pressure and the denominator is the diastolic pressure. The pressure is expressed in millimetres of mercury, abbreviated mm Hg. Thus, an observation recorded as BP 140/80 means the systolic blood pressure was measured at 140 mm Hg and the diastolic blood pressure was measured at 80 mm Hg.

Measuring the blood pressure helps to assess the efficiency of the circulatory system. The following are examples of information that blood pressure findings directly reflect:

- Ability of the arteries to stretch and fill with blood
- Efficiency of the heart as a pump
- Volume of circulating blood

Common factors influencing blood pressure

Various factors listed below influence blood pressure.

Age. Blood pressure rises with age. As individuals age, changes occur in the arteries. They lose their elasticity and become more rigid. This condition is called *arteriosclerosis*. Arteriosclerosis results in an even greater resistance to the heart's effort to fill arteries with blood. Arteries may also fill with deposits of fat, a condition called *atherosclerosis* that interferes with the amount of blood that can be contained within the arteries. Both conditions contribute to increasing blood pressure. The rate at which these conditions occur with ageing depends on one's heredity and life-style habits associated with diet and exercise. Normal blood pressure readings at various ages are listed later in this section of the chapter.

Time of day. As is true of other vital signs, blood pressure tends to be lowest in the morning, on awakening, and highest later in the day and early evening.

Gender. Women usually have a lower blood pressure on the average than have men of the same age.

Exercise and activity. Blood pressure rises during periods of exercise and activity. Regular exercise can result in maintaining the blood pressure within normal levels.

Emotions and pain. Strong emotional experiences and pain tend to cause blood pressure to rise.

Miscellaneous factors. As a rule, a person has a lower blood pressure when lying down than when sitting or standing, although the difference in most people may be insignificant. It has also been observed that blood pressure rises somewhat when the urinary bladder is full, when the legs are crossed, and when a person uses tobacco, drinks a caffeinated beverage, or is cold.

Normal blood pressure

Studies of healthy persons show that blood pressure can fluctuate within a wide range and still be normal. Because individual differences can be considerable, it is important to analyse the usual ranges and patterns of blood pressure measurements for a particular person. If there is a rise or fall of 20 mm Hg to 30 mm Hg in a person's usual pressure, it is significant, even if it is well within the generally accepted range for normal. Table 17-6 offers a guide for average normal and upper limits of normal blood pressure measurements for persons of various ages.

Abnormally high blood pressure

High blood pressure is called *hypertension*. It exists when the systolic pressure, or diastolic pressure, or both, is sustained at levels above the normal level for a person's age. Occasional elevation does not necessarily mean a person has hypertension. Data should be recorded and continue to be gathered to determine if a trend or pattern exists when an isolated elevated measurement is obtained. Hypertension is not diagnosed until either of the following situations occurs.

- The average of two or more diastolic measurements on at least two different but subsequent visits exceeds the normal limit.

Table 17-6. Average and upper limits of blood pressure according to age

Age	Average Normal Blood Pressure	Upper Limits of Normal* Blood Pressure
1 year	95/65	Undetermined
6–9 years	100/65	119/79
10–13 years	110/65	124/84
14–17 years	120/80	134/89
18+ years	120/80	139/89

*From report published in Nurse Practitioner, 10(7), 1985 by the 1984 Joint National Committee on Detection, Evaluation and Treatment of High Blood Pressure.

• The average of multiple systolic measurements on two or more subsequent visits is consistently greater than the normal limit.

The 1984 Joint National Committee on Detection, Evaluation and Treatment of High Blood Pressure (JNC, 1985) considers a systolic pressure of 140 mm Hg or greater in adults 18 years or older, and a diastolic pressure of 90 mm Hg or greater, to be abnormally high. Other terms used to describe various adult blood pressure measurements can be found in Table 17-7. Not all health practitioners accept these figures and classification terms. The nurse is advised to check with the patient's doctor when a question arises about whether hypertension may be present.

Some feel that an abnormally elevated diastolic reading is more indicative of a potentially dangerous condition than an abnormally elevated systolic reading. Certain recommendations concerning the evaluation and care of adult patients with blood pressure measurements at various levels are described in Table 17-8.

The following are examples of conditions commonly associated with hypertension:

Obesity
Arteriosclerosis and atherosclerosis
Stroke
Heart failure
Kidney diseases

Table 17-7. Classification of adult blood pressure measurements

Blood Pressure (mm Hg)	Category*
Diastolic	
<85	Normal blood pressure
85 to 89	High normal blood pressure
90 to 104	Mild hypertension
105 to 114	Moderate hypertension
≥115	Severe hypertension
Systolic When DBP <90 mm Hg	
<140	Normal blood pressure
140 to 159	Borderline isolated systolic hypertension
≥160	Isolated systolic hypertension

* A classification of borderline isolated systolic hypertension (SBP 140 to 159 mm Hg) or isolated systolic hypertension (SBP ≥160 mm Hg) takes precedence over a classification of high normal blood pressure (DBP 85 to 98 mm Hg) when both occur in the same individual. A classification of high normal blood pressure (DBP 85 to 89 mm Hg) takes precedence over a classification of high normal blood pressure (SBP <140 mm Hg) when both occur in the same person.

(Classification terms and measurements from the 1984 Joint National Committee on Detection, Evaluation and Treatment of High Blood Pressure (JNC, 1985)).

Abnormally low blood pressure

An abnormally low blood pressure is called *hypotension*. It exists when the blood pressure measurements are below the systolic normal values for the individual's corresponding age.

Having a consistently low pressure, 96/60 mm Hg

for example, seems to cause no harm. In fact, low blood pressure is usually associated with efficient functioning of the heart and blood vessels. However, a low reading should be compared with the person's usual blood pressure to evaluate its significance.

Table 17-8. *Recommended follow-up for first-occasion elevated blood pressure measurement*

Blood Pressure (mm Hg)	Recommended Follow-up*
Diastolic	
<85	Recheck within 2 years
85 to 89	Recheck within 1 year
90 to 104	Confirm promptly (not to exceed 2 months)
105 to 114	Evaluate or refer promptly to source of care (not to exceed 2 weeks)
≥115	Evaluate or refer immediately to a source of care
Systolic When DBP <90 mm Hg	
<140	Recheck within 2 years
140 to 199	Confirm promptly (not to exceed 2 months)
≥200	Evaluate or refer promptly to source of care (not to exceed 2 weeks)

* If recommendations for follow-up of DBP and SBP are different, the shorter recommended time period supersedes, and a referral supersedes a recheck recommendation.

(Recommendations apply to adults age 18 or older as determined by the 1984 Joint National Committee on Detection, Evaluation and Treatment of High Blood Pressure (JNC, 1985)).

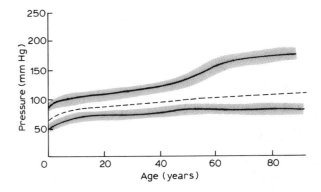

Figure 17-9 Changes in systolic, diastolic and mean arterial pressures with age. The shaded areas show the normal range.

The following are examples of common conditions with which hypotension may be observed:

- Sudden changes in position, such as when a person rises to an upright position too quickly following periods of lying down or sitting. This is called *orthostatic hypotension* by some and *postural hypotension* by others.
- Shock due to blood loss or the inability of the heart to pump blood efficiently.
- Dilation of peripheral blood vessels, which may occur with severe allergic reactions or with drugs that are used to treat hypertension.

Pulse pressure

The difference between systolic and diastolic blood pressure measurements is called the *pulse pressure*. It is computed by subtracting the smaller figure from the larger. For example, when blood pressure is 126/88 mm Hg, pulse pressure is 38. A pulse pressure between 30 and 50 is considered to be in a normal range, with 40 being average in health.

The mean arterial pressure. The mean arterial pressure is the average pressure throughout the pressure pulse cycle. The mean arterial pressure is slightly less than the average of systolic and diastolic pressure as is evident in Figure 17-9.

Equipment used to obtain blood pressure

Blood pressure is usually measured by a sphygmomanometer and stethoscope, which will be described shortly. It is possible to palpate a blood pressure using only a sphygmomanometer. Only the systolic reading can be determined with this method. In critical care areas, the blood pressure can be monitored with a probe placed directly within the artery.

The sphygmomanometer. A manometer is an instrument used to measure the pressure of a gas or liquid. A *sphygmomanometer* is used to measure the pressure of blood within an artery. It consists of a manometer and a cuff. The two types in common use are illustrated in Figure 17-10.

One type of sphygmomanometer uses a mercury gauge. A mercury gauge measures pressure with the use of liquid mercury within a column calibrated in millimetres. When using a sphygmomanometer with a mercury gauge, the manometer must be positioned vertically with the gauge at eye level. Before the blood pressure reading can be obtained, the mercury must be even with the 0 level at the base of the

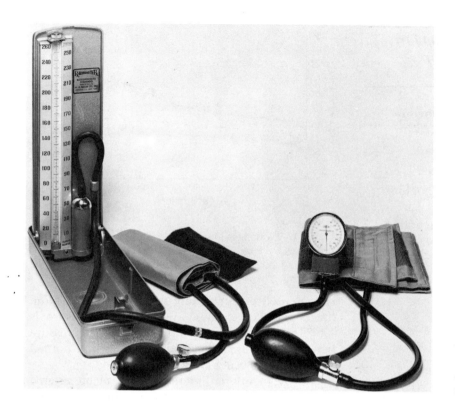

Figure 17-10 This photo shows a mercury manometer (*left*) and an aneroid manometer (*right*). One tube connects to the manometer, the other connects to the bulb. The screw above the bulb controls the air in and out of the bladder within the cuff. The cuffs on these two sphygmomanometers are self-securing.

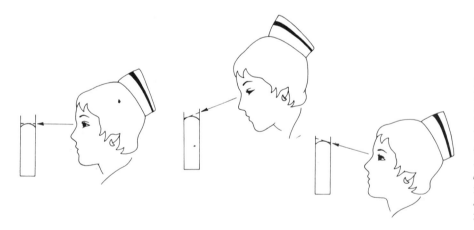

Figure 17-11 The surface of any liquid within a container tends to form a curve, called the meniscus. The curve may appear as an inverted bowl, as seen here, or it may appear cup-shaped. *Left*: The meniscus, and a reading made at eye level. *Centre and right*: How blood pressure readings could vary when the eye is at different levels in relation to the meniscus.

calibrated column. The surface of the column of mercury is slightly curved, like an inverted bowl. The curved shape is called the *meniscus*. The nurse notes the top of the meniscus while listening for certain sounds. If the meniscus is observed at a height above eye level, the pressure reading will appear higher than it really is. Conversely, if the meniscus is below eye level, the pressure reading will appear lower than it really is. Figure 17-11 illustrates the correct and incorrect observations of the meniscus.

The other type of sphygmomanometer uses an aneroid gauge. This type contains a needle that moves about a dial that is also calibrated in millimetres. The needle must be positioned initially at 0 to ensure an accurate recording. Either type of gauge, provided it is working properly and used correctly, can be used to measure blood pressure accurately. The readings obtained with one type of gauge are comparable to those obtained with the other.

The cuff contains an inflatable bladder, to which two tubes are attached. One is connected to the manometer, which registers the pressure. The other is attached to a bulb, which is used to inflate the bladder with air. A screw valve on the bulb allows the nurse to fill and empty the bladder of air. As the air escapes, the pressure is measured.

The cuff should be of a size appropriate for the patient. A common guide is that the cuff should be 20% wider than the diameter of the arm or leg on which it is to be applied. The cuff should not cover more than two thirds of the length of the upper arm. If the cuff is too large, the blood pressure reading will be falsely low. If the cuff is too small, the blood pressure reading will be falsely high.

The stethoscope. A *stethoscope* is an instrument that carries sounds from the body to the examiner's ears. The tip of the stethoscope magnifies sounds. Some stethoscopes have a cupped tip, called a bell; others have a flat disc tip, called a diaphragm; some have a tip that combines a bell and a diaphragm. The bell of the stethoscope is preferable when measuring blood pressure. The nurse obtains the blood pressure by noting the numbers on the gauge while listening for characteristic sounds. The parts of a stethoscope are shown in Figure 17-12.

If stethoscopes are used by various people, the eartips should be cleaned to avoid transferring organisms. Common practice is to clean the tips with gauze or cotton balls dampened with alcohol. Individually owned stethoscopes also need cleaning to keep the eartips free of earwax and dirt. Lint and other debris allowed to collect in the tubing or behind the diaphragm will distort sound. Scrubbing stethoscopes regularly with a germicide is recommended.

Electronic blood pressure meters. There are electronic blood pressure meters on the market that transform blood pressure measurements into audible sounds or a digital display of numbers, making a stethoscope unnecessary. They are helpful for patients who wish to obtain their own blood pressure and also have been found useful by some to measure blood pressure on infants. Because of their delicate instrumentation, electronic machines should be recalibrated more than once each year. Patients using

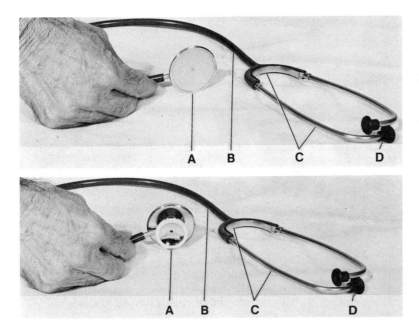

Figure 17-12 *A*: The chest piece on this stethoscope contains both a diaphragm (*top*) and a bell (*bottom*). The diaphragm is used for listening to high-pitched sounds. The bell is better for detecting low-pitched sounds. *B*: The tubing may be either rubber or plastic. Unnecessarily long tubing decreases good sound conduction. A length of about 50 cm (20 in) seems best. *C*: The brace and binaurals are the metal portions connecting the tubing and the chest piece. The binaurals should clear the examiner's face. The brace prevents the tubing from kinking. *D*: The eartips are rubber or plastic and should fit snugly but comfortably into the ears. They should be placed so that they are directed downward and forward. If the eartips are not properly positioned in the ear canal, sound quality will be poor, and in measuring the blood pressure, a falsely low systolic and high diastolic pressure are likely to be obtained.

these devices for home use should also have their blood pressure checked periodically by health personnel.

Korotkoff sounds

The nurse listens for a series of sounds when obtaining blood pressure. These sounds are called Korotkoff sounds. Changes in sounds indicate the pressures that exist within the artery. These sounds are described in Table 17-9. Figure 17-13 is a diagram of the changes occurring in the brachial artery when Korotkoff sounds are assessed.

The first sound heard in phase I represents the systolic pressure. It is recorded as the first number in the fraction. The diastolic pressure, the second number, is the level at which a change in the sound is first noted. Two figures are sometimes used to record the diastolic pressure. One is the first changed sound occurring in phase IV. The other is the last sound that can be heard, the beginning of phase V. An example of this type of recording would be BP 120/80/76. The number 76 indicates the point at which all sound disappeared. If sound is heard down to zero, this would be recorded as 120/80/0. If all sounds disappear when the diastolic pressure is noted, the blood pressure is recorded as 120/80/80.

Obtaining blood presssure

Principles of Care 17-5 describes how to measure the blood pressure on the arm. Blood pressure may also be obtained on the thigh with a larger cuff than used

Table 17-9. Korotkoff sounds

Phase	Description
I	This phase is characterized by the first appearance of faint but clear tapping sounds, which gradually increase in intensity. The first two consecutive tapping sounds represent the systolic pressure.
II	This phase is characterized by muffled or swishing sounds. These sounds may temporarily disappear, especially in hypertensive persons. The disappearance of the sound during the latter part of phase I and during phase II is called the auscultatory gap and may cover a range of as much as 40 mm Hg. Failing to recognize this gap may cause serious errors of underestimating systolic pressure or overestimating diastolic pressure.
III	This phase is characterized by distinct and loud sounds as the blood flows relatively freely through an increasingly open artery.
IV	This phase is characterized by a distinct, abrupt muffling sound with a soft, blowing quality. The first of muffled sounds is considered to be diastolic pressure.
V	The last sound heard before a period of continuous silence. The second diastolic pressure reading is noted for adults when this occurs.

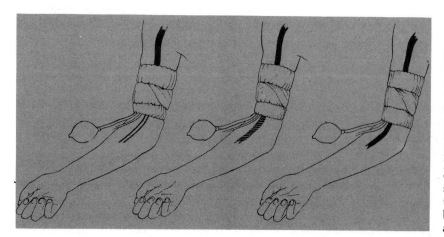

Figure 17-13 *Left*: When the cuff has been inflated sufficiently, it will prevent the flow of blood into the forearm. No sound will be heard through the stethoscope. *Centre*: When pressure in the cuff is reduced sufficiently for the blood to begin flowing through the brachial artery, the first sound is recorded as the systolic pressure. *Right*: As the pressure in the cuff continues to be released, the muffled sound heard through the stethoscope is the diastolic pressure. At this time, the blood flows freely through the brachial artery.

Principles of Care 17-5. Measuring the blood pressure

Nursing Action	Rationale
Select a blood pressure cuff of an appropriate size for the patient.	A cuff that is too large or too small will produce a false reading.
Delay obtaining the blood pressure if the patient is emotionally upset, is in pain, or has just exercised, unless it is urgent to obtain the blood pressure.	Factors such as emotional upset, exercise, and pain will alter usual blood pressure readings.
Have the patient assume a comfortable lying or sitting position with the forearm supported at the level of the heart and the palm of the hand upward.	This described position places the brachial artery on the inner aspect of the elbow so that the bell of the stethoscope can rest on it easily.
Expose the area of the brachial artery by removing garments, or move a sleeve, if it is not too tight, above the area where the cuff will be placed.	Clothing over the artery interferes with the ability to hear sounds and may cause inaccurate blood pressure readings. Tight clothing on the arm causes congestion of blood and possibly inaccurate readings.
Centre the inflatable area of the cuff over the brachial artery, approximately midway on the arm, so that the lower edge of the cuff is about 2.5 to 5 cm (1 to 2 in) above the inner aspect of the elbow. The tubing should extend from the edge of the cuff nearer the patient's elbow.	Pressure in the cuff applied directly to the artery will give the most accurate readings. If the cuff gets in the way of the diaphragm, readings are likely to be inaccurate. A cuff placed upside down, with the tubing toward the patient's head, will give a false reading in most instances.
Wrap the cuff around the arm smoothly and snugly, and fasten it securely or tuck the end of the cuff well under the preceding wrapping. Do not allow any clothing to interfere with the proper placement of the cuff.	A smooth cuff and snug wrapping produce equal pressure and help promote an accurate measurement. A cuff too loosely wrapped will result in an inaccurate reading.
Check that a mercury manometer is supported in a vertical position. The mercury must be within the 0 area with the gauge at eye level. If an aneroid gauge is used, the needle should be within the 0 mark.	Tilting a mercury manometer, inaccurate calibration or improper height for reading the gauge can lead to errors in determining the pressure measurements.
Palpate the brachial pulse by pressing gently with the fingertips in the antecubital space.	The location of the pulse is the area that is likely to produce the most audible sounds during the assessment of the blood pressure.
Tighten the screw valve on the air pump.	The bladder within the cuff will not inflate with the valve open.
Inflate the cuff while continuing to palpate the artery. Note the point on the gauge where the pulse disappears.	To identify the first Korotkoff sound accurately, the cuff must be inflated to a pressure above the point at which the pulse can no longer be felt.
Deflate the cuff and wait 15 seconds.	Allowing a brief pause before continuing allows the blood to enter and circulate through the arm.
Assume a position that is no more than 3 feet away from the gauge.	A distance of more than about 3 feet can interfere with accurate readings of the numbers on the gauge.
Place the stethoscope earpieces in the ears properly.	The eartips should be directed downward and forward to fit the shape of the ear canal.
Place the bell of the stethoscope firmly but with as little pressure as possible over the artery where the	Having the bell directly over the artery makes more accurate readings possible. Having the bell firmly

Continued

Principles of Care 17-5. Continued

Nursing Action	Rationale
pulse is felt. Do not allow the stethoscope to touch clothing or the cuff.	placed on the skin away from clothing and the cuff prevents missing sounds. Heavy pressure on the brachial artery distorts the shape of the artery and the sound.
Pump the pressure 30 mm Hg above the point at which the pulse disappeared.	Increasing the pressure above where the pulse disappeared ensures a period of time before hearing the first sound that corresponds with the systolic pressure. It prevents misinterpreting phase II sounds as phase I.
Loosen the screw on the valve. Slowly release the air at a rate of 2 to 4 mm Hg per second.	If air is released too slowly from the cuff, there will be congestion in the extremity, causing a false reading. If air is released too rapidly, sounds may not be accurately noted.
Note the point on the gauge at which there is an appearance of the first faint, but clear, sound, which slowly increases in intensity. Note this number as the systolic pressure.	Systolic pressure is the point at which the blood in the artery is first able to force its way through the vessel at a similar pressure exerted by the air bladder in the cuff. The first sound is phase I of Korotkoff sounds.
Read the pressure to the closest even number.	It is common practice to read blood pressure to the closest even number.
Do not reinflate the cuff once the air is being released to recheck the systolic pressure reading.	Reinflating the cuff while obtaining the blood pressure is uncomfortable for the patient and may cause an inaccurate reading. Reinflating the cuff causes congestion of blood in the lower arm, which lessens the loudness of Korotkoff sounds.
Note the pressure at which the sound first becomes muffled. Also observe the point at which the last sound is heard. These may occur separately or at the same point.	The point at which the sound changes corresponds to phase IV of Korotkoff sounds and is considered the first diastolic pressure reading. The point at which the last sound is heard is the beginning of phase V and is recorded in some hospitals as the second diastolic pressure.
Allow the remaining air to escape quickly. Repeat any suspicious readings but wait at least 15 seconds between readings to allow normal circulation to return in the limb. Be sure to deflate the cuff completely between attempts to check the blood pressure.	False readings are likely to occur if there is congestion of blood in the limb while obtaining repeated readings.
If it is difficult to hear sounds when checking the blood pressure, raise the patient's arm over his head for 15 seconds just before rechecking the blood pressure.	Raising the arm over the head helps relieve congestion of blood in the limb, increases pressure differences, and makes the sounds louder and more distinct when blood enters the lower arm.
Inflate the cuff while the arm is elevated and then gently lower the arm while continuing to support it.	Supporting the arm while it is lowered prevents altering the pressure in the manometer by as much as 20 to 30 mm Hg.

Continued

Principles of Care 17-5. *Continued*

Nursing Action	Rationale
Position the stethoscope and deflate the cuff at the usual rate while listening for Korotkoff sounds.	The techniques used throughout the remaining assessment of blood pressure do not require any further modification.
Remove the cuff, clean and store the equipment.	Equipment that must be shared among personnel should be left in a manner ready for use.
Record the patient's position, the arm that was used to obtain the blood pressure and the pressures that correspond to the systolic and diastolic readings.	Circumstances for assessing the blood pressure should be consistent for future comparisons.

on the arm. The patient lies on his abdomen and the cuff is applied with the bladder over the back side of the middle of the thigh. The stethoscope is placed over the artery in the back of the knee. This is called the popliteal space. The systolic pressure usually is a little higher when measured on the thigh than when measured on the arm, but the diastolic pressure has been found to be about the same.

If it becomes necessary to repeat obtaining a blood pressure, the nurse should make sure all the air has escaped from the cuff. Waiting at least 15 seconds before reinflating the cuff permits circulations to return to normal.

If a patient is to have frequent blood pressure readings and the cuff is left in place, it is necessary to check to see that it has not rotated out of position before taking the next reading. It is important to *make certain that the cuff cannot be inflated accidentally between readings.* When circulation is cut off for a long period of time, damage or death of cells in the patient's extremity will occur.

Frequency of measurement and recording of the vital signs

Obtaining a patient's temperature, pulse, respirations and blood pressure is part of most admission procedures. Hospital policies about how often measurements are to be obtained after admission vary. For example, if a patient has a body temperature above normal, usual policy is that his measurements, with the possible exception of blood pressure, are to be checked every 4 hours. For patients who have had surgery, most hospitals require that blood pressure be checked every 15 to 30 minutes for 2 to 3 hours and then every 4 hours, along with the other measure-

ments, for a period of time. Policies may require daily or even less frequent checking for patients who care for themselves or who are chronically or mentally ill. Blood pressure is often measured more frequently when a heart or blood vessel disease is present. All adults should have their blood pressure routinely checked at least every two years.

Whatever the hospital's policy about the frequency of measuring and recording signs, there are times when the nurse must use judgement. Measurements should be double-checked in the following circumstances:

- A change in the measurements is noted and a trend is developing. For example, a gradual increase in the pulse rate is noted.
- Findings are very different from previous recordings. For example, a patient's measurements may have been essentially normal and then an increase or decrease in one or all is noted.
- The measurements are not in keeping with the patient's condition. The patient's condition suggests that all should be normal and they are elevated, or just the opposite condition is present. Faulty equipment may be the cause. Reassess, using other equipment or sites for subsequent examinations.
- The measurements could possibly be fraudulent. Occasionally, a patient may produce fraudulent signs, especially in relation to body temperature. Patients have been known to cause a thermometer to register falsely high readings by placing it on a light bulb or by rubbing it on bed clothing to create heat from friction. Conversely, they have been known to remove the ther-

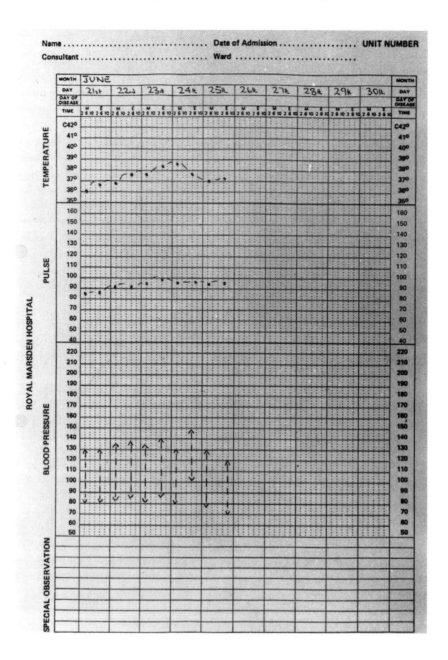

Figure 17-14 This graph illustrates how the vital signs are usually recorded. Plotting the figures on a graph helps to compare findings to determine any trends that may be occurring.

mometer before it registers properly. In these instances, the measurements are also not in keeping with the patient's condition. The nurse should remain with the patient while obtaining the temperature, etc. when fraudulence is suspected.

Recording the vital signs

The manner in which vital signs are recorded depends on the hospital's policies. Different hospitals use different forms and the nurse will use what is provided. Figure 17-14 is an example of a form used to record temperature, pulse respiration and blood pressure. Thompson (1981) has shown that there are discrepancies in measuring and recording blood pressure. It is therefore vital that all nurses are competent in the procedures.

If anything unusual is observed, it should be recorded and reported. For example, observations may be described in the patient's record. Many terms used to describe the measurements were defined in this chapter. Although it is important to be familiar with these terms, it is recommended in some hospitals that a particular observation be described rather than labelled with a term. Doing so tends to avoid confusion. For example, the nurse would record that a patient is breathing very deeply rather than noting that the patient has hyperpnoea.

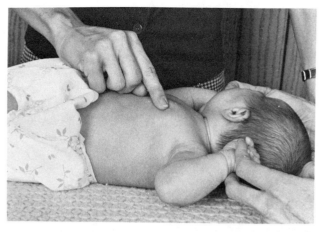

Figure 17-15 The index finger placed under the nipple and to the left of the sternum is the location for feeling an infant's apical pulse. The thin wall of an infant's chest makes this assessment possible. The apical pulse rate of an adult is obtained by listening to the heart.

Suggested measures for obtaining measurements in selected situations

When the patient is an infant or child

Obtain infants' and young children's pulse and respiratory rates when they are quiet. It is best to obtain pulse and respiratory rates before obtaining the temperature because placing the thermometer often causes the youngster to cry.

Palpate an apical heart rate on children under 2 years of age for greatest accuracy. Obtaining the pulse rate at the radial artery is usually satisfactory after about age 2. Palpating an apical rate from an infant is illustrated in Figure 17-15.

Observe an infant's or young child's abdomen to obtain the respiratory rate because respirations early in life are predominantly diaphragmatic.

Count the respiratory and pulse rates for a full minute when the patient is an infant or young child for greatest accuracy. A young child's pulse and respiratory rates normally tend to fluctuate more than an adult's rates.

Obtain the first temperature on a newborn rectally if this does not contradict hospital policy. This technique helps assess whether the anus is patent. Do not force a thermometer if insertion is difficult.

Position an infant on his side or abdomen, not on his back, while obtaining a rectal temperature. Positioning the infant on his side or abdomen reduces the danger of puncturing and injuring rectal tissues with the thermometer.

Lubricate the bulb of a rectal thermometer *well*

and insert the thermometer only slightly beyond the mercury bulb, about ½ to 1½ inches, when obtaining a rectal temperature on an infant or child. The manner in which the thermometer is handled and inserted is important in preventing injury to rectal tissues.

Obtain an axillary temperature from infants and young children unless hospital policy indicates otherwise. Experienced nurses have found that obtaining an axillary temperature is safer and less disturbing to youngsters than is obtaining a rectal temperature. Also, studies have shown that there appears to be little, if any, difference between axillary and rectal temperatures obtained on infants and young children, especially when they are not seriously ill.

Hold an infant or young child in the arms while obtaining an axillary temperature, as the mother of the child in Figure 17-16 is doing. This technique is comforting for the youngster and promotes relaxation while obtaining the temperature.

Be *sure* the size of the blood pressure cuff is appropriate when obtaining blood pressure readings from infants and children.

Obtain blood pressure readings from children when they are quiet, and in a quiet room, for most accurate readings.

Allowing an infant or young child to see, and possibly handle, the stethoscope before obtaining the

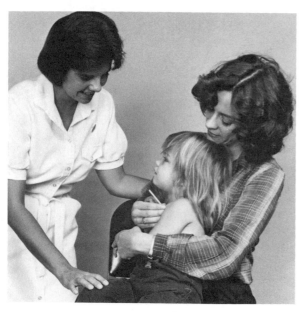

Figure 17-16 The nurse is teaching a mother how to obtain her youngster's axillary temperature. Note the correct placement of the thermometer.

blood pressure often helps decrease the youngster's fear of the equipment and procedure. The procedure should be explained to children old enough to understand.

When the patient cannot cooperate

Obtain a rectal or axillary temperature from a patient who is subject to seizure activity or from patients who are unconscious, combative, irrational or confused. A thermometer is likely to break in the patient's mouth if he cannot cooperate while an oral temperature is taken.

Locate the anal orifice digitally while using a lubricated finger cot or glove when the patient cannot be turned onto his side to obtain a rectal temperature. This technique avoids probing with the thermometer, which may injure local tissues. The technique also helps prevent placing the thermometer in a woman's vagina accidentally.

When the patient's activity or emotional status is likely to influence the measurement

Allow the patient to rest for a few minutes before obtaining measurements when he has been active or exercising. Activity and exercise tend to increase the pulse and respiratory rates and the blood pressure.

Except when necessary, avoid obtaining measurements when the patient is experiencing strong emotions, because they tend to increase readings. Examples of such emotions include fear, anger and excitement.

Wait for 15 to 30 minutes before obtaining an oral temperature if the patient has recently had hot or cold fluids. This allows time for oral tissues to return to normal.

Wait about 5 minutes before obtaining an oral temperature if the patient has been smoking or has been chewing gum. This allows time for oral tissues to return to a normal temperature. One study showed that a patient's oral tissues had dropped to normal in about 3 minutes after chewing gum. It suggested that the exercise of oral muscles could falsely elevate a temperature take during or immediately after chewing gum.

Delay obtaining an axillary temperature if the axilla has just been washed. The water and friction created by drying the skin may influence the temperature.

When the patient is elderly

Count the pulse and respiratory rates of an elderly patient for a full minute for greatest accuracy. The rigidity of arterial walls that often occurs in the elderly results in a faster than normal pulse rate. The respiratory rate is often irregular due to certain chronic conditions frequently observed in the elderly.

Delay obtaining measurements, unless necessary, when the patient has been under stress or has been more active than usual. It has been observed that it may take as long as several hours for signs to return to normal when an elderly patient has experienced psychological stress or more than usual exercise and activity.

When certain other conditions are present

Avoid taking a rectal temperature from a woman in labour. The thermometer may injure the head of the infant passing through the birth canal.

Avoid obtaining a rectal temperature when the patient has had rectal surgery or has diarrhoea. The thermometer is likely to injure tissue or increase the diarrhoea.

Avoid obtaining an oral temperature when the patient breathes through his mouth. Examples of patients who usually are mouth breathers are those with respiratory tract diseases and obstructions in the nasal passages and those who have had oral or nasal surgery.

Observe hospital policy about obtaining a rectal temperature when the patient has had a heart attack. It is thought by many that the thermometer may stimulate the vagus nerve causing the heart to slow to dangerous levels in some patients. However, one study to test this belief raised doubts and suggested that vagal stimulation may not be as harmful as once thought.

Obtain an axillary or rectal temperature from patients receiving oxygen by mask. The mask interferes with placing the thermometer in the mouth. Removing the mask may cause laboured breathing due to a drop in the patient's oxygen level. The effect of oxygen therapy on oral temperatures has been studied in patients receiving oxygen by catheter or cannula. The conclusion was that the effect was so small that it probably had no significance for most clinical purposes.

Avoid obtaining an axillary temperature when the patient is in a state of shock. Blood circulation to the axillary area is likely to be poor and, as a result, the axillary temperature will be inaccurate. Shock is further discussed in Chapter 21.

References

Campbell, K. (1983) Taking temperatures. *Nursing Times,* **79**(32), 63–5.

Close, J. (1987) Oral temperature measurement. *Nursing Times,* **83**(1), 36–9.

Davies, S.P., Kassab, J.Y., Thrush, A.J. and Smith, P.H.S. (1986) A comparison of mercury and digital clinical thermometers. *Journal of Advanced Nursing,* **5**(11), 535–43.

JNC (1985) The 1984 Report of the Joint National Committee on Detection, Evaluation and Treatment of High Blood Pressure. *Nurse Practitioner,* **10**(7), 9–10, 13–14, 19–20.

Stronge, J.L. and Newton, G. (1980) Electronic thermometers: a costly rise in efficiency? *Nursing Mirror,* **151**(8), 21–9.

Thompson, D.R. (1981) Recording patients blood pressure: a review. *Journal of Advanced Nursing,* **6**(4), 283–90.

Further reading

Boylan, A. and Brown, P. (1985) Student observations: More than "doing the obs" . . . the significance of pulse and blood pressure measurement. *Nursing Times,* **81**, 24–5.

Boylan, A. and Brown, P. (1985) Student observations: Respiration. *Nursing Times,* **81**, 35–8.

Boylan, A. and Brown, P. (1985) Student observations: The pulse and blood pressure. *Nursing Times,* **81**, 26–9.

Boylan, A. and Brown, P. (1985) Student observations: Temperature. *Nursing Times,* **81**, 36–40.

Hill, M.N. (1980) Hypertension: What can go wrong when you measure blood pressure. *American Journal of Nursing,* **80**, 942–5.

18
Administering medications

Learning objectives

When the content of this chapter has been mastered, the learner should be able to:

Define the terms appearing in the glossary.

Identify the components of a prescription sheet and types of prescription sheets.

Describe how medications, including narcotics, are supplied and safeguarded in hospitals.

Identify information about a patient that may affect medication administration.

Discuss guidelines the nurse would follow in the safe preparation and administration of medication.

List the practices that have been linked with contributing to medication errors.

Describe the recommended techniques for administering oral, topical and parenteral medications.

Demonstrate the recommended procedures for administering oral medications, medications through a nasogastric tube, topical medications, intramuscular injections, subcutaneous injections, intradermal injections and intravenous medications.

List strategies to help overcome noncompliance in the self-administration of medication.

Describe suggested measures for administering medications to patients in selected situations, as described in this chapter.

Summarize suggestions offered in this chapter for teaching patients about medications.

Glossary

Ampoule A glass container holding a single dose of a parenteral medication.

Bolus A single dose of a medication that is instilled into an intravenous line in a short amount of time.

Buccal A route used for administering drugs that involves placing the medication in the mouth against the mucous membranes on the inside of the cheek.

Diluent The liquid component of a solution.

Drug Any substance that chemically changes body function when administered to or taken in by an individual. Synonym for *medication*.

Enteric coated A covering on an oral drug that prevents it from becoming dissolved until the medication is within the small intestine.

Generic name A drug name that is usually descriptive of a drug's chemical structure and is not protected by a company's trademark. Synonym for *nonproprietary name.*

Individual supply A quantity of medication provided for a single patient that may last for 1 to 3 days.

Inner canthus The area of the eye near the nose.

Inunction A medication incorporated into a vehicle, such as an ointment, and rubbed into the skin.

Intradermal injection The administration of a solution just below the epidermis.

Intramuscular injection The administration of a solution into one muscle or muscle group of the body.

Medication Any substance that chemically changes body function when administered to or taken in by an individual. Synonym for *drug.*

Noncompliance The failure to follow instructions related to health care.

Nonproprietary name A drug name that is usually descriptive of a drug's chemical structure and is not protected by a company's trademark. Synonym for *generic name.*

Oral medications Drugs that are swallowed or instilled through a tube leading to the stomach.

Outer canthus The area of the eye near the temple.

Parenteral route All methods other than oral for administering medications; the term has come to refer more specifically just to administration by injection.

Prescription The information related to the administration of a drug.

Proprietary name The name of a drug used by the manufacturer for the product it sells. Synonym for *trade name.*

Reconstitution The process of adding a liquid to a powdered substance to form a solution.

Stock supply A large quantity of frequently prescribed drugs.

Subcutaneous injection The administration of a drug between the epidermis and the muscle.

Sublingual A route for administering drugs that involves placing the medication within the mouth under the tongue.

Teratogenic effects The production of abnormal structures in a developing foetus causing severe deformities.

Topical administration The application of medication to the skin or mucous membranes.

Trade name The name of a drug used by the manufacturer for the product it sells. Synonym for *proprietary name.*

Transdermal A word meaning through the skin.

Vial A glass container of parenteral medication with a self-sealing stopper.

Wheal A raised area within the skin.

Z-track technique An injection method used to administer irritating medications into the muscle in such a way that the drug cannot leak back into subcutaneous tissue.

Introduction

Among the nurse's most important responsibilities is the administration of medications. A *medication* is any substance that chemically changes body function when administered to or taken in by an individual. In this chapter the terms *medication* and *drug* will be used synonymously.

The emphasis of this chapter is the safe preparation and administration of medications. Information concerning specific drugs is more appropriately discussed in pharmacology texts.

The UKCC (1986) takes the view that first level practitioners should be responsible and accountable for their actions taken in the administration of medicines. This chapter will illustrate the practices associated with correct administration of medications. It must be stated that no student practice in association with the administration of medications should take place unless under the direct supervision of a first level practitioner (registered nurse).

Since the publication of guidelines from the UKCC, the Royal College of Nursing (1987) has also published a policy and practice statement on drug administration. This chapter has taken into account both of these advisory papers.

Checking the prescription sheet

The doctor is the only person authorized to determine the patient's drug therapy. The *prescription* includes the necessary information related to the administration of a drug. The nurse is the person within a hospital who is responsible for checking and carrying out the prescription.

Safe practice is to follow only a written prescription to help avoid misunderstandings and errors. The prescription is written on a special form provided by the hospital. A prescription is complete when it contains all of the following seven parts:

1. The name of the patient
2. The date and time the prescription is written
3. The name of the medication
4. The dosage to be administered
5. The route for administering the medication
6. The frequency of administering the medication
7. The signature of the person who has written the prescription

The nurse must determine that the prescription is valid by checking that all the seven essential parts are included.

Identifying the name of the patient. The name of the patient is ordinarily imprinted on each page of his record. His full name, including first name, middle initial and last name, is used. If there is any chance for confusion, a second name is used instead of a middle initial. If the patient's name is not imprinted on each page of the record, the full name should be written clearly on each page. If there is a patient with the same or a similar name a warning label must be placed on the prescription sheet of both patients.

Noting the date and time of the prescription sheet. The doctor writing the sheet indicates the date and time it is written. This information is important and is needed when discontinuation dates and times are calculated. Dating and timing an order also help to prevent oversights and errors. The information is typically written as follows: 11/1/91 10:15 A.M.

Specifying the name of the medication. Each drug has both a trade, or proprietary, name and a generic, or nonproprietary, name. The *trade* or *proprietary name* is the name used by the manufacturer for the drug it sells. The drug's *generic* or *nonproprietary name* is a name that is usually descriptive of the drug's chemical structure and is not protected by a company's trademark. For example, Valium is a proprietary name. It is the manufacturer's brand name for diazepam, which is its generic name. It is common practice that generic names are used when prescribing medication within the hospital.

Indicating the dosage of the medication. The amount of a drug represents its dosage. The amount may be written in whole numbers, decimals, fractions or symbols, followed by the measure to be used. Drug measurements are indicated using terms or abbreviations in the metric system, which is listed in Table 18-1.

Designating the route of administration. The prescription designates by what manner, or route, the drug is to be administered. Table 18-2 lists and describes common routes of administration. The

Table 18-1. Terms used when designating dosage measurements

Metric Term	Abbreviation
Gram	G or Gm (lower case letter may be used)
Milligram	mg
Microgram	mcg
Litre	L or l
Millilitre	ml

prescription should indicate specifically which route should be used, whether oral, a specific injection route or some other manner of administration. Some medications may be given by various routes. Meperidine hydrochloride is an example. The prescription should be questioned if the route is not specified, in order to clarify any doubt about which to use.

Prescribing the frequency of administration. The frequency with which a medication is to be given is most commonly written in standard abbreviations, which are listed and defined in Table 18-3.

Signing the prescription sheet. The person authorized to write a prescription most often is the doctor, but it may also be a dentist, or a doctor's assistant. The legally authorized person's signature must appear at the end of the prescription sheet.

Questioning a prescription sheet. The nurse is expected to question any prescription sheet that does not contain all seven parts of the prescription. The nurse should also clarify any aspect of the seven parts of the prescription sheet that may seem unclear or inaccurate. For example, if the writing is not legible, if the dosage or frequency is significantly different from the usual administration, if the appropriateness of giving a particular medication to a patient is questionable and so forth, the nurse should communicate with the person who has written the prescription. Errors are serious. A prescription sheet should *never* be implemented if the nurse has a question about it until after the nurse has consulted the doctor.

Implementing the prescription

The nurse is held accountable for accurately interpreting the prescription so that it is implemented correctly.

Table 18-2. Routes for administering medications

Term Used to Describe Route	How Drug is Administered
Oral administration Given by mouth	Having the patient swallow the drug
Inhalation Given via the respiratory tract	Having the patient inhale the drug
Parenteral Given by injection	Injecting the drug into:
Subcutaneous or hypodermic injection	Subcutaneous tissue
Intramuscular injection	Muscle tissue
Intracutaneous or intradermal injection	Corium (*i.e.,* upper layers of the skin)
Intravenous injection	A vein
Topical administration Given by placing on the skin or mucous membrane	
Transdermal administration	Placing a unit-dose of the drug on the skin; the drug is absorbed through the skin over a 24-hour period
Vaginal administration	Inserting the drug into the vagina
Rectal administration	Inserting the drug into the rectum
Sublingual administration	Placing the drug under the tongue; the drug is not to be swallowed or chewed
Buccal administration	Placing the drug between the cheek and gum; the drug is not to be swallowed or chewed
Inunction	Rubbing the drug into the skin
Instillation	Placing the drug into direct contact with mucous membranes
Irrigation	Flushing the mucous membranes with a drug in solution

Drugs may also be injected into the arteries, heart tissues, spinal cord, joints and peritoneal cavity. The drugs are ordinarily administered by the doctor when using these routes.

Drugs that are ordered to be given on a routine basis may be scheduled according to a predetermined time-table set for drug administration within the particular hospital. A drug that is ordered to be given four times a day may be scheduled in a variety of patterns. For example, it may be scheduled to be given at:

8 A.M., 12 noon, 4 P.M. and 8 P.M., or
10 A.M., 2 P.M., 6 P.M. and 10 P.M., or
6 A.M., 12 noon, 6 P.M. and 12 midnight

Any of these schedules will still provide the administration of the drug according to the prescribed frequency of four times a day as indicated on the prescription sheet. The nurse should be familiar with the policies concerning the routine times for administering medications within each hospital.

Discontinuing a prescription

The nurse must be aware of the limitations in the length of time that a prescription is valid. The administration of some drugs must be discontinued at a specified time. For instance, there may be restrictions on the length of time that a narcotic, antibiotic or anticoagulant may be administered. The date and time of the original prescription will be important in determining when the drug administration must be discontinued. The date and time for the last admin-

Table 18-3. Common abbreviations used when prescribing medications

Abbreviation	Meaning
$\overline{aa}$	of each
a.c. (ante cibum)	before meals
ad lib	freely
Aq	water
b.i.d. or b.d.	twice each day
BNF	British National Formulary
BP	British Pharmacopoeia
BPC	British Pharmaceutical Codex
c̄	with
h	hour
h.s.	at bedtime
IM	intramuscular
IV	intravenous
o.d. (omni die)	every day
OD	right eye
o.m. (omni mane)	every morning
o.n. (omni nocte)	every evening
OS	left eye
OU	both eyes
p.c. (post cibum)	after meals
PO (per os)	by mouth
prn (pro re nata)	according to necessity
q3h, q4h and so on	every three hours, every four hours and so on
q.d.	every day
q.h.	every hour
q.i.d.s. or q.d.s.	four times each day
q.o.d.	every other day
q.s.	a sufficient amount
rep. (repetateur)	let it be repeated
RX	take
s̄	without
s.c.	subcutaneous
S.O.S.	if necessary
ss	one half
stat	at once
subq	subcutaneous
t.i.d. or t.d.s.	three times each day
tinct	tincture

istration of a drug should be identified on the medication record. The drug may be renewed when a new prescription sheet is written.

It is usual to discontinue drugs the patient has been taking before surgery. After surgery, the doctor writes new prescriptions that should be followed. This practice is common also when patients are transferred to another hospital. Upon a patient's admission to a hospital, drugs that he had been taking at home are not continued unless the doctor so orders. Hospital policies vary about allowing the patient to keep drugs at his bedside and take them as he would at home. The nurse will observe the policies of each particular hospital.

Supplying medications

Prescriptions are filled and the drugs are dispensed to the nursing unit by a pharmacist in the hospital. Drugs may be supplied to the nursing unit in several ways. It may either be in the form of a stock supply or a personal individual supply. In most hospitals the pharmacist will come to the wards on a daily basis and check prescription sheets and order the appropriate drugs to be sent to the ward.

Safeguarding medications

Medications can be dangerous if they are not administered in the manner in which they are prescribed. Therefore, various safeguarding mechanisms are utilized for protecting the supply from improper or illegal use.

Storing medications

In each hospital, there is at least one area where drugs are kept in readiness for dispensing to patients. Drugs may be kept in one central area or they may be kept in separate locations for more efficient administration to individual patients.

There is currently a move towards self-administration of medication, to promote patient involvement in care. Where this is not possible, the responsibility would lie with the primary nurse, or the relatives or other carers if the patient is at home.

Legislation associated with drug administration

Drugs intended for use within the UK must conform to the standards specified by the British Phar-

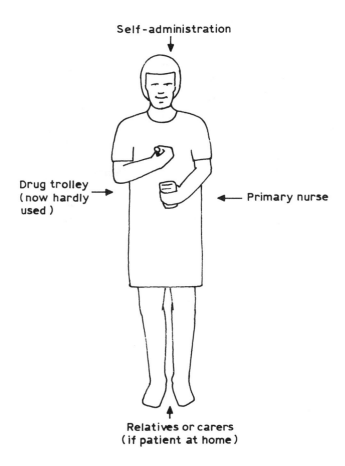

Self-administration

Drug trolley
(now hardly
used)

Primary nurse

Relatives or carers
(if patient at home)

Figure 18-1 Drug administration.

macopoeia (BP) or the British Pharmaceutical Codex (BPC).

There are three statutes which relate to administration of:

1. Opioids
2. Poisons
3. Medicines

The Misuse of Drugs Act 1971. This Act lists and classifies certain drugs to be controlled. It prohibits the use of these drugs except for controlled medical, dental and veterinary use. The Act divides the drugs into five schedules. In Table 18-4 Pritchard and David (1988) have summarized the requirements of the Act in relation to nurses working in a hospital with a pharmacy department.

The Poisons Act 1972. This Act deals with four aspects of poison control:

1. The establishment of a Poisons Board.

2. The listing of controlled poisons.
3. The control of the sale of listed poisons.
4. The system of inspection to enforce the provisions of the Act.

There are some substances that are poisons which are used for medicines; they come under the juristiction of the Medicines Act 1968.

The Medicines Act 1968. This Act controls all medicines. It covers all of the following:

1. The administrative system.
2. The licensing system.
3. The sale and supply to the public.
4. The retail pharmacies.
5. Packing and labelling.
6. The promotion of medicines.
7. The British Pharmacopoeia.

Calculating dosages

It is the nurse's responsibility to administer the quantity of a drug that equals the prescribed dosage. When medications are supplied in the same dosage and system of measurement as that prescribed by the doctor, no calculation is required. Special formulas and mathematical computations must be used when the dosages are dissimilar.

Determining the quantity to administer

When dosages are supplied in a different amount but the same system and unit of measurement as that written on the prescription sheet, the nurse must compute how much of the supplied drug to give. The following formula may be used:

$$\frac{\text{Dose Desired}}{\text{Dose on Hand}} \times \text{Quantity on Hand}$$

$$= \text{Quantity to Administer}$$

Example: 80 mg of a drug is prescribed. It is supplied in tablets containing 40 mg per tablet. How many tablets should be administered?

Answer: $\dfrac{80\,\text{mg}}{40\,\text{mg}} \times 1\text{ tablet} = 2\text{ tablets}$

This formula can also be used to compute liquid dosages as well. It can be used to compute any problem as long as the system and the unit of measurement of the two dosages are the same.

Table 18-4. Summary of the legal requirements for the handling of controlled drugs as they apply to nurses in hospitals with a pharmacy

	Schedule 1	Schedule 2	Schedule 3	Schedule 4	Schedule 5
Drugs in schedule	Cannabis + derivatives but excluding nabilone LSD	Most opioids in common use including: alfentanil amphetamines cocaine diamorphine methadone morphine papaveretum fentanyl phenoperidine pethidine codeine dihydrocodeine pentazocine	Minor stimulants. Barbiturates (but excluding: hexobarbitone thiopentone methohexitone). Diethylpropion	Benzodiazepines	Some preparations containing very low strengths of: cocaine codeine morphine pholcodine and some other opiods
Ordering	Possession and supply permitted only by special licence from the Secretary of State issued (to a doctor only) for scientific or research purposes	A requisition must be signed in duplicate by the nurse in charge. The requisition must be endorsed to indicate that the drugs have been supplied. Copies should be kept for 2 years	As Schedule 2	No requirement[1]	No requirement[1]
Storage[5]	As Schedule 2	Must be kept in a suitable locked cupboard to which access is restricted	Diethylpropion: as Schedule 2. All other drugs: no requirement	No requirement[1]	No requirement[1]
Record keeping	As Schedule 2	Controlled Drugs[3] Register must be used	No requirement	No requirement[1]	No requirement[1]
Prescriptions	As Schedule 2	See below for detail of requirement[4]	As Schedule 2 except for phenobarbitone[2]	No requirement[1]	No requirement[1]
Administration to patients	As Schedule 2. Under special licence only	A doctor or dentist or anyone acting on their instructions may administer these drugs to	As Schedule 2	No requirement[1]	No requirement[1]

Continued

Table 18-4. *Continued*

	Schedule 1	Schedule 2	Schedule 3	Schedule 4	Schedule 5
		anyone for whom they have been prescribed			

1 "No requirement" indicates that the Misuse of Drugs Act imposes no legal requirements additional to those imposed by the Medicines Act 1968.

2 All references to phenobarbitone should be taken to include all preparations of phenobarbitone and phenobarbitone sodium. Because of its use as an anti-epileptic, phenobarbitone is exempt from the handwriting requirements only of the full prescription requirements (see 4 below).

3 *Record keeping.*
There is no legal requirement for the nurse in charge or acting in charge of a ward or department to keep a record of Schedule 1 or 2 Controlled Drugs obtained or supplied. However the Aitken Report (Central Health Services Councils, 1958) recommended that this should be done and in practice a Controlled Drug Register is invariably kept according to the following guidelines:
  (a) Each page should be clearly headed to indicate the drug and preparation to which it refers. Records for different classes of drug should be kept on separate pages.
  (b) Entries should be made as soon as possible after the relevant transaction has occurred and always within 24 hours.
  (c) No cancellations or obliteration of an entry should be made. Corrections should be made by means of a note in the margin or at the foot of the page and this should be signed, dated and cross-referenced to the relevant entry.
  (d) All entries should be indelible.
  (e) The Register should be used for Controlled Drugs only and for no other purposes.
  (f) A completed register should be kept for 2 years from the date of the last entry.

4 *Prescription requirements.*
  (a) The prescription *must* state:
    (i) The name and address of the patient.
    (ii) The drug, the dose, the form of preparation (e.g. tablet).
    (iii) The total quantity of drug, or the total number of dosage units to be supplied. This quantity must be stated in *words* and *figures*.
        All the above must be indelibly written in the prescriber's own handwriting and he/she must sign the prescription.
    (iv) The date of the prescription.
    (v) If the prescription is to be dispensed in instalments, the number of instalments and the intervals between them. It is illegal to write or dispense a prescription which does not comply with these requirements.
  (b) The full handwriting requirements and statement of quantity to be supplied do not apply to prescriptions for hospital inpatients if the Controlled Drugs concerned are administered from ward or department stocks. They do, however, apply to prescriptions for drugs "to take home" or for outpatients.

5 *Storage and safe custody.*
  (a) All Controlled Drugs should be stored in a suitably secure (usually metal) cupboard which is kept locked and to which access is restricted. This cupboard (which may be within a second outer cupboard) should be used only for the storage of Controlled Drugs.
  (b) The Aitken Report recommends that all Controlled Drug record entries be checked by two nurses. In conjunction with the pharmacy a procedure should be developed to ensure regular checking of records and reconciliation of receipts and issues.
  (c) A programme for regular stock checking should be established and adhered to.

6 *Destruction.*
Unwanted or unused Controlled Drugs in Schedule 2 must not be destroyed on the ward but should be returned to the pharmacy.

Reproduced with permission from Pritchard and David, Royal Marsden Manual of Clinical Nursing Procedures, 3rd Edition; published by Blackwell Scientific, 1992.

Converting metric equivalents

The metric system is used for prescribing and supplying medications. At times a medication is supplied in a metric unit of measure that is different from the one prescribed. For example, the doctor may prescribe 0.5 g of a drug. The drug may be supplied with a label that reads 500 mg. The nurse may follow one of the following two methods for converting one or the other of these measurements to the equivalent of the other.

1. To convert a metric unit into the next larger unit, move a decimal point three places to the left of the number. The resulting number will be smaller than the original.

Example: 500 mg = •• g

Answer: 500 mg = 0.500 g or 0.5 g

2. To convert a metric unit into the next smaller unit, move a decimal point three places to the

right of the number. The resulting number will be larger than the original.

Example: 0.5 g = ●● mg

Answer: 0.5 g = 500 mg

Once the measurements are in equivalent units of measure, the nurse will be able to determine the quantity of medication to give. In this case, once the nurse has determined that the dose supplied and the dose ordered are equal, no further mathematical calculation is necessary. If the amounts were dissimilar, the formula used to calculate the quantity to administer would be used.

Nursing assessment

There is certain information the nurse should know about each patient before administering any medications. This information can be reviewed in the nursing assessment obtained at the time of the patient's admission. The collected data provide a base of information related to drug therapy. The following information concerning medications should be noted:

- Nonprescription medications the patient uses, the reason, frequency and length of time he has been using them.
- Prescription medications the patient has been taking, the reason, frequency, and length of time he has been using them.

Figure 18-2 A nurse carefully checks the prescription before administering any medication. (Courtesy Royal Marsden Hospital)

- The patient's pattern for following the directions for medication use.
- Any allergies the patient has to medications.
- The patient's habits of daily living that may influence drug therapy, such as alcohol and caffeine consumption.

The nurse should understand the patient's diagnosis, medical plan of care and the expected results of drug therapy. Understanding the unique characteristics of the patient will be helpful when comparing his drug therapy with that described in reference manuals. Pharmacology texts and resources on medications provide descriptions of the medication's usual dosage range, indications for use, possible undesired effects, contraindications, symptoms of toxicity and common routes of administration. These will be helpful when observing and evaluating the desirable and undesirable effects of the drug's action.

Following basic guidelines for administering medications

In April 1986 the UKCC published an advisory paper on the administration of medicines. It advises that a first level practitioner should be seen to be competent to administer drugs on her own. If two persons are involved, as seems to be common practice in most hospitals, then the senior is the one responsible.

The learner nurse must develop the competencies associated with drug administration but only under direct supervision of a first level practitioner.

Certain guidelines apply specifically to the preparation and administration of medications given orally and those given by injection. They are described later in this chapter. The following are basic actions the nurse performs whenever preparing and administering any medication, regardless of the route to be used.

Before preparing medications

Prior to preparing the drugs that will be administered to a patient, the nurse should do the following:

- Check the patient's prescription prior to preparing the drugs.
- Question any part of a drug order that appears inappropriate before proceeding.
- Be alert to any unusual changes, such as

new additions or deletions, of entries on the prescription.

- Question any unusual abbreviations that have been used. Errors have occurred when the person writing the prescription has used unacceptable abbreviations. This practice can cause misinterpretations when administering the medication.
- Check the prescription carefully with the drug that has been supplied, as the nurse in Figure 18-2 is doing.
- Organize the nursing care so that medications are given as near to the scheduled routine as possible. It is common policy to give the drug no earlier or later than 30 minutes from the time specified. A medication given outside this range of time is considered a drug error. This policy does not apply to drugs ordered to be given at once. Also, a preoperative medication should be given as close as possible to the exact specified time because surgery is planned accordingly. This also holds true when patients are given drugs before certain diagnostic procedures.

While preparing medications for administration

Safety is of the utmost importance in the preparation and administration of medications. The following guidelines are recommended when a nurse prepares medications for administration:

- Prepare medications while using a good light, without interruptions or distractions.
- Check the label of the drug container *three* times to ensure safety and accuracy:
  1. When reaching for the medication.
  2. Immediately prior to pouring the medication.
  3. When returning the container to its storage place.
- Do not use medications from containers on which the label is difficult to read or has come off. Guessing at the contents of a medication container is unsafe, even when one feels absolutely certain about what is inside. Return the container to the pharmacy.
- Do not return medications to a container or transfer medications from one container to another. This prevents mismatching drugs within labelled containers.
- Check expiry dates on medications, especially those that are in solution. Do not use a medi-

cation that has sediment at the bottom of the container unless the medication is to be shaken well before using. Do not use one that appears cloudy or has changed colour. The potency and potential usefulness may have changed.

- Protect needles for injecting drugs according to hospital policy to prevent contamination.
- Use an individual medicine dropper for each liquid medication dispensed in this manner. Medication that remains within a dropper may contaminate other liquid medications when a dropper is reused.

While administering medications

Recommended guidelines when administering medications to patients include the following:

- Do not give medications that have been prepared by another person. If an error was made in preparation, the person administering the medication is responsible.
- Allow enough time to assist patients who will require help with taking medications.
- Identify the patient by checking the patient's identification bracelet, as illustrated in Figure 18-3. Also ask the patient to state his name when he is able. Be very careful when the identity of a patient is not known, when a language barrier or impediment exists or when the patient is con-

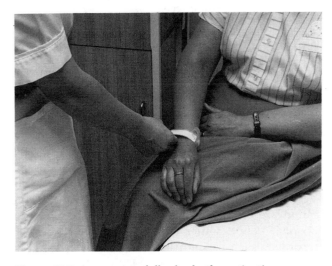

Figure 18-3 A nurse carefully checks the patient's name on the identification bracelet and also asks the patient her name before administering any medication. (Courtesy Royal Marsden Hospital)

fused. He may respond to a name whether the name is his or not.

- Remain with the patient as he takes the medication. If there are several medications, offer each separately to the patient.
- Do not leave medications at the bedside for the patient to take at a later time. The patient may forget to take the medication or someone else may take it.
- Omit giving a drug if the patient has symptoms suggesting an undesirable reaction to a previous administration of the drug. Report the observation immediately.
- Do not give a drug if the patient states that he is allergic to it. An allergic reaction can be serious and can even threaten the patient's life.
- Do not give a medication without further checking if the patient indicates that the drug appears different from what he has been receiving. A mistake may have been made when supplying the medication or when preparing the medication. Withholding it while checking further may avoid an error.
- Report immediately when a patient refuses a drug so that necessary adjustments in the patient's care can be made.

After administering medications

- Leave the patient in a comfortable position after medications have been administered.
- Check the patient in 30 minutes for desired and undesired drug effects.

Recording medication administration

The patient's prescription sheet is a legal document. Medications are recorded as soon as possible after they are administered. This helps other members of the nursing and health care team know that the patient has received the prescribed medication. The date, time, name of the drug, dosage and route by which it was given are recorded on the sheet. The site used for an injection is recorded. The initials and signature of the nurse who administered the medication are entered in a specified area according to hospital policy. Other patient information may be recorded, such as the patient's pulse rate or blood pressure, when this is indicated.

Occasionally a notation and explanation concerning drug administration should be entered on the chart. Record any medication that has been withheld and the reason for omitting the administration. An example is when drugs are withheld when a patient is fasting in preparation for a diagnostic test. Enter the administration of a drug that may be given irregularly, as needed by the patient, and explain the reason for its use.

Reporting medication errors

An error in medication administration occurs whenever stated procedures are not followed (McNeilly, 1987). Medications that are inadvertently omitted are also considered errors.

If a medication error occurs, the patient's condition is checked and the error is reported to the doctor and the supervising nurse immediately. Hospitals have a special form for reporting medication errors, called an incident sheet or accident sheet. In this report, a full explanation of the situation is provided. The report serves as a method for preventing future errors by examining the practices that contributed to the error. The incident sheet is not a part of the patient's permanent record nor should any reference be made in the chart to the fact that an incident sheet has been compiled.

Analysis of past medication errors indicates that some of the following actions are often the basis for mistakes in administering drugs:

- The nurse does not clarify an unclear prescription sheet.
- The nurse inaccurately reads labels on medication containers.
- The nurse incorrectly calculates the quantity of the drug that is administered.
- The nurse carelessly switches medications prepared for one patient with those for another.
- The nurse does not identify patients by checking their identification and asking the patient to say his name (Cobb, 1986).

Administering oral medications

Oral medications are those drugs administered by mouth or through a tube leading to the stomach. They are intended for absorption in the gastrointestinal tract. The oral route is the most frequently used route for medication administration. Oral medications are either solid or liquid in form.

Solid preparations of oral medications include tablets, capsules and pills. Some tablets are scored for easy breaking if part of the tablet is needed. Certain tablets are covered with a substance that does not dissolve until the medication reaches the small intestine. These tablets are *enteric coated*. If the coating is destroyed, the medication is released in the stomach, where it is irritating to the gastric mucosa. Enteric coated tablets should never be crushed or chewed.

Liquid preparations of oral drugs include elixirs, spirits, suspensions and syrups. The dosage of liquid medications is measured in calibrated cups. There are also extractors that can be used for measuring liquid medications. These devices resemble syringes and fit tightly into the neck of a bottle. The medication is withdrawn with the extractor and then the appropriate amount of the drug is placed in a cup or glass.

Principles of Care 18-1 describes the actions that may be followed for administering medications by the oral route.

Administering oral medications through a nasogastric tube

Medications should not be administered through a nasogastric tube if the tube is connected to suction.

However, when the tube is being used as a route for providing nourishment, oral medications may be administered through the nasogastric tube.

Liquid medications can be administered through the tube easily. Solid medications require additional preparation in order not to obstruct the lumen of the tube. They must be crushed and combined with a liquid. However, they should not be added to the formula being administered for a continuous feeding. If the patient is unable to take all of the formula, there is no way to estimate accurately how much of the medication the patient has received. A continuous feeding can be interrupted and resumed after administration of the medication. Remember that enteric coated tablets and similar drugs designed for sustained release should not be crushed.

To administer medications through a nasogastric tube, the suggested actions in Principles of Care 18-2 may be followed.

Administering topical medications

The application of medication to the skin or mucous membranes is referred to as the *topical administration*

Principles of Care 18-1. Administering oral medications

Nursing Action	Rationale
Check the prescription sheet.	Making sure that the information and directions are correct helps to avoid errors.
Observe medical asepsis by washing hands before preparing medications.	Handwashing removes organisms that can be transferred to drug administration articles and subsequently to patients.
Read the label of the medication container when removing the container from the shelf or drawer.	Many drugs appear similar. Reading the label verifies the contents of the container.
Check the label a second time before placing the drug into a dispensing cup.	Repetition ensures that the label has not been misread.
Pour capsules and tablets into the cap of the drug container. Then pour the proper amount into a medication cup.	Touching oral medications must be avoided so that organisms are not spread from the nurse's hands, which are never completely free of organisms.
Place all solid medications in the same cup with the exception of those that require special assessment of the patient prior to administration.	Some medications should not be administered until it has been determined that the drug will not harm the patient. Separation helps to avoid administration until the assessment is made.
Read the label on the drug container a third time before returning it to its place of storage.	Attention and concentration on the label for a third time provide the opportunity for a final safety check on the contents of the container.

Continued

Principles of Care 18-1. *Continued*

Nursing Action	Rationale
Place the bottle cap upside down on a working surface when preparing to pour a liquid medication.	Keeping the inner surface clean prevents contamination of the bottle cap and the contents of the container.
Use an appropriate measuring device when pouring liquids and read the amount at the bottom of the meniscus, as illustrated in Figure 18-4.	Accuracy is possible when an appropriate calibrated cup is used and the level of the drug is assessed at eye level.

Figure 18-4 For a liquid medication, the nurse places a thumbnail at the marking on the dispensing container at the level indicated for the proper dosage. Holding the calibrated cup at eye level ensures that the amount will be read at the most accurate point of the meniscus.

Nursing Action	Rationale
Pour liquids from the side of a bottle opposite the label to prevent liquids from running onto the label.	A liquid that drips onto the label may lead to errors if the information becomes illegible.
Place each liquid medication in a separate container.	Mixing liquids may produce a chemical change and certainly makes the taste unpleasant.
Help the patient into a sitting position.	Swallowing is easier and safer when the patient is in a sitting position.
Identify the patient by checking the wristband and by asking the patient his name.	Using two separate methods of identification helps to ensure that the medication will be given to the patient for whom it was ordered.
Offer water before giving solid medication in the amount desired by the patient.	Liquids moisten the mucous membranes and help prevent oral drugs from sticking to the mouth or oesophagus.
Discourage liquids after the patient has swallowed cough medications.	Liquids dilute and wash cough medications from the area where they may have a local effect.
Help the patient to take the medication in amounts that he feels safe in swallowing.	A patient may prefer to swallow one medication at a time. This is probably the safest approach.
Provide the patient with a drinking straw and encourage a generous intake of liquid, if permitted, to facilitate swallowing.	A straw may help the patient acquire a higher volume of water in the mouth without displacing the medication from its position for swallowing.
Have the patient suck on ice chips before taking a drug with an objectionable taste. Follow with warm or hot water.	Ice numbs the taste buds. Warm or hot water removes the aftertaste more quickly than does cold water.

Continued

Principles of Care 18-1. *Continued*

Nursing Action	Rationale
Use other liquids or foods, such as fruit juices, to disguise the unpleasant taste of a drug, but use them carefully.	A vehicle can lessen or overcome an unpleasant taste. However, the patient may come to dislike the vehicle due to its association with an unpleasant experience.
Offer oily medications after they have been refrigerated.	Cold oil is less aromatic and hence less objectionable than it is when administered at room temperature.
Remain with the patient until the medication is swallowed.	The nurse may need to provide assistance if the patient chokes. The nurse is responsible for documenting that the drug was taken by the patient. It is possible that a patient could discard a drug, misplace it or accumulate many in order to harm himself.
Help the patient into a position of comfort and safety before leaving.	The position for swallowing medications need only be temporary.
Record the volume of fluid taken with the medication if the patient's intake and output are being recorded.	All liquid that is ingested or instilled is considered part of the fluid intake. Incomplete records are inadequate for accurate assessment.
Dispose or return medication administration equipment to its proper location.	Other nursing team members may need medication trays and other equipment to complete their patient care responsibilities.
Record the administration of the medication on the prescription sheet as soon as possible.	Records must be kept current to avoid omission or possible duplication of a medication administration.
Check the patient in 30 minutes for desired and undesired drug effects.	Pertinent assessments help to identify the patient's response to the action of a medication.

of medication. Drugs administered topically may be placed externally or internally. Topically applied drugs may have a local or systemic effect; however, most are given in order to achieve a direct effect on the tissue to which they are applied.

Using an inunction

A medication incorporated into a vehicle, such as oil, lotion, cream, ointment or powder, and rubbed into the skin is an *inunction*. This word is derived from a term that referred to the religious practice of anointing. It may be acceptable for patients to self-administer some of these medications. The nurse's role then becomes one of teaching the patient the proper technique and supervising the application. An inunction is given as follows:

- Cleanse the area of application and the hands with soap or detergent and water before applying the oil, lotion, cream or ointment. This frees the skin of debris and body oil, both of which retard absorption.
- Shake the contents of mixtures that may have become separated.
- Apply most inunctions with the fingers and hands or using a cotton ball or gauze square.
- Wear gloves if the patient has a contagious skin condition or there are breaks in the skin of fingers or hands.
- Warm the inunction if it will be applied to a sensitive area such as the face or back. This may be done by holding the container or the inunction itself in the hands or submerging a tightly closed container in warm water.
- Apply local heat to the area as ordered. This increases blood circulation, which helps absorption.
- Keep powders away from the nose and mouth. If they are to be applied near the face, do so as the patient exhales.

Principles of Care 18-2. *Administering medications through a nasogastric tube*

Nursing Action	Rationale
Prepare prescribed solid medications by crushing and mixing with about 30 ml of warm water.	Tablets or the contents of capsules must be in a solution to move through the nasogastric tube. Warm water is more likely to help dissolve solid drugs than cold water.
Take the prepared medication, 30 to 50 ml of water, a clean towel, and a syringe barrel or funnel to the patient's bedside.	Having equipment and supplies in readiness saves time and energy.
Check the location of the tube following the techniques described in Chapter 10.	The nurse must verify that the end of the tube is in the stomach and not in the airway.
Help the patient into a Fowler's position. Drape the patient with a towel.	Having the patient in a sitting position uses gravity to move the medication through the tube. The towel protects the patient from becoming wet or soiled.
Attach the syringe barrel or funnel to the nasogastric tube and, while the tube is still clamped, pour the medication into the funnel or syringe.	Less air is introduced into the stomach when the entire solution is poured while the tube remains clamped.
Open the clamp on the tube and allow the medication to flow into the stomach by gravity.	Gravity avoids the use of pressure that may cause discomfort or injure the mucosa of the stomach.
Add 30 to 50 ml of water before the syringe barrel or funnel is completely empty.	Water introduced after most of the medication is given helps clear the tubing of medication so that the patient receives the entire dosage, and it keeps the lumen from becoming obstructed.
Clamp the tube while water still remains in it.	Maintaining fluid in the tubing prevents air from entering the stomach when subsequent fluid is instilled.
Remove the syringe or funnel and have the patient remain in a sitting position for about 30 minutes, or have him lie on his right side with the head of the bed slightly elevated.	These positions help the stomach to empty and prevent regurgitation and possible aspiration.
Place the patient on his left side if the medication is to remain in the stomach for a local effect.	Antacids are one type of drug that produce a desired effect when in the stomach. Lying on the left side delays movement of the stomach contents into the duodenum of the small intestine.
Record the amount of water used to administer the medication if the patient's fluid volume is being assessed.	Accurate assessment depends upon accurate recording.
Record the administration of the medication as for other medications. Indicate that the drug was given through the nasogastric tube.	The record should reflect the modifications that were utilized while oral medications were administered.

Using the transdermal route

The prefix trans- means across or through. The word *transdermal* means through the skin. A drug intended for application by this route enters the bloodstream after being absorbed through the skin's hair follicles and sweat glands. The most common medication given transdermally is nitroglycerine. This drug is used primarily to control angina pectoris, which is the chest pain associated with an insufficient amount of blood flow to the heart muscle. Scopolamine, used

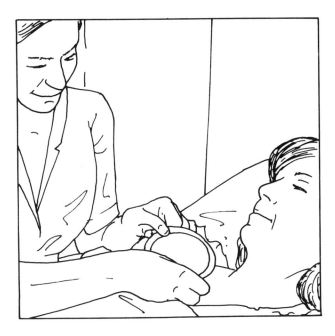

Figure 18-5 The nurse applies a self-adhering disc containing nitroglycerine on the patient's anterior chest wall. The medication is absorbed transdermally.

to relieve motion sickness, has also been prepared for transdermal application. It is generally applied in the form of a patch behind the ear. It is predicted that still other medications will soon be administered in this manner.

Applying nitroglycerine to the skin. Nitroglycerine for transdermal application is presently dispensed in two ways: in an ointment that is placed·on application paper, which is then secured to the skin, and in a round, adhesive disc containing a unit dose of the drug. Figure 18-5 illustrates a nurse applying a medicated disc to a patient's chest wall. The medication is absorbed slowly and one application is intended for each 24 hour period. It has been shown that nitroglycerine starts taking effect about 30 minutes after it has been applied to the skin and lasts for about 30 minutes after it is removed.

The following discussion describes directions for applying nitroglycerine ointment. Although each manufacturer prepares the ointment slightly differently, the following can serve as general guidelines:

- Remove any previous application from the patient's skin.
- Squeeze a ribbon of ointment from the tube onto

the manufacturer's application paper. The dosage is prescribed in centimetres or inches. The typical dosage is a 2.5 to 5 cm (1 to 2 inches) ribbon of ointment. Directions for increasing or decreasing the length of the ribbon may be provided when the drug is first prescribed. This is done in order to adjust the dosage to the most appropriate amount for each individual.

- Place the application paper containing the ribbon of ointment on a clean, nonhairy surface of the skin. The chest wall and the upper arm are usual sites.
- Cover the application paper with a square piece of plastic, such as the type for kitchen use, and secure the plastic with tape on four sides. A plastic bag with the bottom cut open may be applied over the application paper on the upper arm. The plastic cover retains heat and moisture in the arm, thereby improving the absorption of the medication. The patient may bathe or shower while wearing a properly applied ointment patch.
- Check the patient and his vital signs approximately 30 minutes after the application to determine the response of the patient.
- Rotate the sites on which the ointment is placed each day to prevent skin irritation. Some hospitals require the application on the skin to be dated and initialled. This validates that the application is current.
- Do not touch the ointment. The medication can be absorbed through any skin surface. If it becomes necessary to manipulate the ribbon of ointment, use a tongue blade.
- Do not rub or massage the ointment into the skin.
- Store the ointment in a cool place.

Administering eye medications

Eye medications may be applied topically either in the form of an ointment or as eye drops. The eye is a delicate organ. It is highly susceptible to infection and injury. Direct application of a solution or ointment into the eye is not recommended for fear of injuring the cornea. Instead, drops and ointments are instilled into the lower conjunctival sac. Although the eye is never free of microorganisms, the solutions, ointments and equipment used to administer eye medications should be sterile. Principles of Care 18-3 describes the techniques for administering eye medications.

Principles of Care 18-3. *Instilling eye medications*

Nursing Action	Rationale
Warm eye drops and ointments to room temperature. Roll the container between the hands for a minute or two if the medication storage area is unusually cool.	Instilling cold medication into the eye is startling and uncomfortable.
Wash the hands just before administering the eye medication.	Handwashing controls the spread of organisms into the patient's eye.
Position the patient supine or sitting with his head tilted back and slightly to the side into which the medication will be instilled.	Positioning in this manner allows optimal placement of the medication without excessive loss down the cheek or into the duct leading to the internal surface of the nose.
Clean the lids and lashes prior to instilling medication. Use one cotton ball for each wipe.	The area around the eye should be as clean as possible to avoid introducing organisms or debris into the eye.
Move the cotton ball from the area of the eye near the nose, called the *inner canthus*, outward to the area near the temple, the *outer canthus*.	Wiping in this direction will remove secretions, residual medication from previous instillations, and organisms away from the nasal duct.
Read the label on the medication at least three times.	Ointments and containers of eye drops look similar. The nurse must read each label carefully to avoid instilling the wrong medication.
Instruct the patient to look toward the ceiling.	When the patient does not look directly at the applicator, the blink reflex is less likely to occur.
Place the thumb or two fingers of the nondominant hand below the margin of the eyelashes under the lower lid and exert pressure downward over the bony prominence of the cheek, as the nurse in Figure 18-6 is doing.	This manoeuvre pulls the lower lid downward and creates a pouch in the conjunctiva. This small area is a convenient pocket into which the medication may be placed.
Move the medication container from below the line of vision or from the side of the eye.	Keeping the moving object out of the patient's direct vision will help to prevent the patient from becoming startled and moving away.

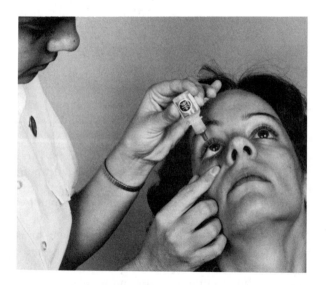

Figure 18-6 The patient tilts her head back and looks upward in preparation for receiving eyedrops. She also tilts her head slightly toward the eye receiving drops to help prevent medication entering the duct at the inner canthus. Pressure applied downward high on the cheek exposes the lower conjunctival sac.

Continued

Principles of Care 18-3. *Continued*

Nursing Action	Rationale
Hold the tip of the container steady above the conjunctival sac without actually touching the eye itself.	The tip of the medication container may injure the cornea or other structures if it is forced into the eye. Touching the eye contaminates the tip of the container.
Deposit the prescribed number of drops into the centre of the conjunctival sac or squeeze a ribbon of ointment from the inner canthus to the outer canthus.	Placing the drug in this manner facilitates its distribution throughout the eye when the nurse's hand is released from the patient's face.
Instruct the patient to close his eyelids gently and move the eye after the medication has been instilled.	Gently closing the eye prevents the patient from blinking eye drops out onto the cheek. Moving the eye within the orbit delivers the drug over the surface of the eye.
Apply gentle pressure over the opening to the nasolacrimal duct.	Nasal occlusion prevents systemic absorption of medication through the mucous membrane of the nose.
Provide the patient with a clean tissue to catch any medication or tears that may escape from the eye and roll down the face.	A clean tissue may be used to absorb liquids. The medication may irritate the patient's skin and the sensation of a substance running down the cheek is unpleasant.
Instruct the patient to avoid rubbing the eyes after medication has been administered.	Pressure may cause additional irritation of the eye.

Instilling ear medications

Topical medications may be instilled into the outer, or external, ear. The outer ear is separated from the other structures of the ear by the eardrum, or tympanic membrane. Normally this barrier is intact and clean technique is used when administering medications into the ear canal. When the eardrum has been opened, by disease, injury or surgery, sterile technique is used since organisms have a direct passage into the deeper tissue. The techniques for administering ear medications are described and illustrated in Principles of Care 18-4.

Administering medications into the nose

Topical medications may be dropped or sprayed within the nose. The nose is not a sterile cavity. However, because it connects with the sinuses, techniques of medical asepsis should be used. Nose drops that contain medication in normal saline solution are recommended rather than oily solutions that may be aspirated into the lungs and cause inflammation of the tissues.

Principles of Care 18-5 describes the suggested actions for instilling nasal medications.

Administering medications within the mouth

Some medications are intended to become absorbed through the blood vessels within the mouth rather than be delivered to the gastrointestinal tract. A *sublingual* administration involves placing a drug under the tongue. A *buccal* administration involves placing a drug against the mucous membranes of the cheek. The patient should be instructed to allow the medication to dissolve. Eating, chewing and smoking are contraindicated as the medication is being dissolved and absorbed.

Applying medications to the throat

The most frequently used method for applying topical medication to the throat is with the use of lozenges. These hard discs dissolve slowly when they are sucked, distributing the medication over the surface of the throat. Chewing or swallowing the

Principles of Care 18-4. Instilling medications into the ear

Nursing Action	Rationale
Warm the medication to room temperature.	Cold or hot medication instilled within the ear can cause discomfort, dizziness and nausea in some patients.
Clean the outer ear with cotton balls and normal saline, if that appears necessary.	The ear canal may contain dried secretions or drainage that may interfere with the absorption of the drug.
Fill the applicator with sufficient medication.	Most ear medications are instilled using a medication dropper.
Position the patient on his side with the ear into which the instillation is to be made uppermost.	This prevents loss of any medication from the effect of gravity.
Straighten the ear canal, as illustrated in Figure 18-7. Gently pull the ear upward and backward for an adult or downward and backward for a child.	Straightening the ear canal helps the medication to reach the lowest area of the ear canal and become distributed over all the surfaces in the outer ear.

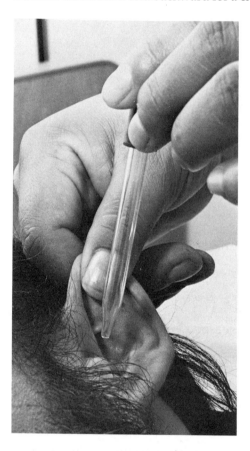

Figure 18-7 To instill eardrops in this adult patient, the nurse pulls the ear upward and backward and drops the solution along the side of the ear canal.

Hold the dropper with the tip above the ear canal.	The tip of the dropper should not touch the ear; this may cause the patient to pull away. Touching the tip to the skin contaminates the dropper.

Continued

Principles of Care 18-4. Continued

Nursing Action	Rationale
Allow the prescribed number of drops to fall on the side of the ear canal.	When drops fall directly on the eardrum they may cause an unpleasant sensation.
Encourage the patient to remain in this position for 5 minutes.	Maintaining the position allows time for medication to flow into the lowest area of the ear canal, avoiding the possibility of excessive loss from the ear.
Massage the cartilage below the opening to the ear canal.	Massage promotes the movement and distribution of the drug.
Insert cotton *loosely* within the ear canal if it is likely that the medication will drain out after the patient assumes an upright position.	The cotton wick will trap the medication within the ear canal and prevent its loss after the instillation.
Never pack cotton tightly within the ear canal.	Tightly packed cotton may interfere with the outward movement of normal secretions and could create undue pressure in the ear canal.
Wait 15 minutes between instillations if drops are to be placed in both ears.	Sufficient time must be allowed to prevent immediate loss of medication from its site of instillation.

Principles of Care 18-5. Administering nasal medications

Nursing Action	Rationale
Have the patient clear his nasal passages with a tissue.	Clearing nasal passages removes debris that may interfere with the instillation, distribution or absorption of medication.
Help the patient into a sitting position with his head tilted back if the drug is intended for the pharynx.	This position will facilitate the flow of the drug downward along the nasal passages leading to the pharynx and the opening to the eustachian tube of the ear.
Have the patient lie down with his head tilted slightly backward or to the side if the drug is intended to become distributed to the sinuses on one side of the face.	Gravity and positioning can facilitate movement of the medication toward the sinuses rather than downward toward the pharynx.
Use a rolled towel or pillow beneath the patient's neck to facilitate support and positioning.	Positioning devices may help to ensure or increase hyperextension of the neck or abduction of the head.
Remove the cover or applicator from the container of medication without touching any unclean objects in the area.	The contents of the container will become contaminated if the surfaces of the applicator or the inner cap touch areas where organisms are present.
Hold the dropper over one nostril while pressing against the tip of the nose, as the nurse in Figure 18-8 is doing.	The medication can be instilled properly after providing for the best visualization of the nasal passage.
Instruct the patient to breathe through his mouth as the proper number of drops are instilled.	Breathing through the nose may deliver a large amount of the medication into the respiratory passages, where it may cause coughing or aspiration into the lungs.

Continued

Principles of Care 18-5. Continued

Nursing Action	Rationale

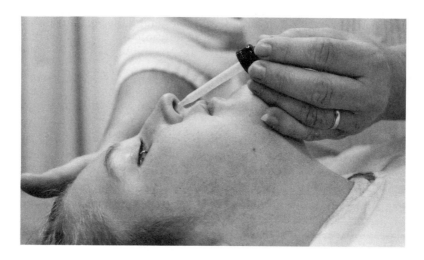

Figure 18-8 The nurse is about to instill medicated drops into the patient's nose. The patient's head is resting over a pillow. While straightening the nasal passage the nurse may assess the condition of the mucosa.

Nursing Action	Rationale
Help the patient to self-administer a nasal spray, if that is possible.	It is difficult to coordinate the spraying with simultaneous inhalation when two people are involved.
Place the tip of a nasal atomizer just inside the nostril.	Proper administration of the medication depends upon confining the spray within the nasal passage.
Compress the opposite nostril and instruct the patient to inhale as the container is squeezed.	Inhalation will distribute the drug within one nasal passage. No more force than that required to bring the spray into contact with the mucous membrane should be used.
Instruct the patient to remain in position for approximately 5 minutes.	Changing position may alter the movement and distribution of the medication from its intended location.

lozenge renders it largely ineffective. The patient should not take fluids during or soon after using a lozenge. The fluids will dilute and flush the drug away and decrease its local effect.

Throat irrigants, sprays and paints are very rarely used. The hospital's procedures should be observed on those occasions when they may be prescribed.

Inserting vaginal medications

Medicated vaginal creams are ordinarily applied by using a narrow tubular applicator with an attached plunger. Suppositories that melt when exposed to body heat are also prepared for vaginal insertion. Practices of medical asepsis are used because the vagina is not sterile. The techniques in Principles of

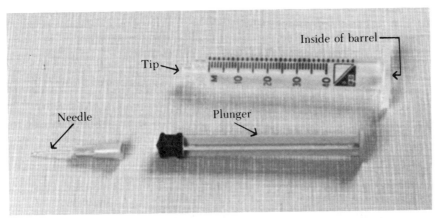

Figure 18-9 The parts of a needle and syringe have been disassembled and labelled in this illustration. The arrows indicate the areas of the equipment that must be kept free of organisms during the time of preparation and administration of parenteral drugs.

Care 18-6 may be followed when inserting medications within the vagina.

Inserting rectal medications

Rectal medications are used primarily for their local action. Occasionally, a medication may be given rectally for its systemic effect. Medications for rectal administration are most often in the form of a suppository, cream or solution. The technique for inserting a rectal suppository and instilling solutions within the rectum may be reviewed in Chapter 12. Rectal creams are generally inserted using a pre-lubricated applicator tip attached to a tube of medication. The applicator tip is designed so that it cannot be inserted any further than safely indicated. Principles of medical asepsis should be followed when removing the applicator and storing the medication.

Administering parenteral medications

The term *parenteral* refers to all routes of administration other than oral. However, the term is used most commonly to indicate injection routes. It is used in that manner in this text.

Drugs that are administered by injection must be prepared and administered following principles of surgical asepsis described in Chapter 20. Using sterile technique minimizes the danger of injecting organisms into body tissues.

Selecting equipment for parenteral administration

Drugs that are administered parenterally must be prepared using various types of syringes and

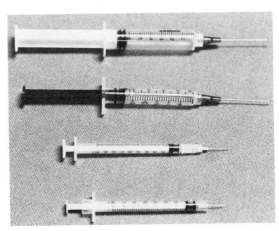

Figure 18-10 This collection of syringes shows variations in the types used for the administration of parenteral medications. Note that the syringes have the potential for holding and measuring different volumes of medication. This variety of needle lengths and gauges shows possible combinations that may be selected according to the characteristics of the medication, the size of the patient, or the site that will be used.

needles. Figure 18-9 illustrates a typical example of the equipment. Note the marked areas that must be kept free of contamination. The same areas are to remain sterile for any size or type of syringe and needle.

Syringes come in various sizes and calibrations depending upon the volume and type of drug that will be administered. Figure 18-10 shows some typical syringes used to administer drugs parenterally. Syringes for medication administration generally hold amounts ranging from 1 to 5 ml. Some

Principles of Care 18-6. Administering vaginal medications

Nursing Action	Rationale
Ask the patient whether she needs to void prior to inserting medications within the vagina.	A full bladder may cause discomfort during insertion, or the patient may wish to get up too soon after the drug has been administered.
Provide privacy by closing the curtains surrounding the patient's bed.	The patient should be protected from being viewed by others during any procedure involving exposure of the genital area.
Cover the patient with a cotton bath blanket and then pull the top linen toward the bottom of the bed.	Bed linen that remains tucked around the patient interferes with inspection and access to the genital area.
Place the patient in a dorsal recumbent position with the knees flexed and slightly spread upon the bed.	This position helps when locating the vagina for proper insertion of the medication.
Remove any perineal pad that the patient may have currently in place. Use gloves or touch only the outside surface of the pad.	Patients who require vaginal medications may use a perineal pad to absorb drainage or dissolved medication. The pad should be considered contaminated with organisms.
Discard the contaminated pad into a waterproof container for disposal or pull the glove inside out over the pad and dispose of both at the same time.	Contaminated articles must be contained within a barrier that controls the spread of organisms to others.
Perform proper handwashing.	The hands should be washed after handling any soiled or contaminated articles.
Fill the applicator with cream or insert the vaginal suppository into its dispenser.	Applicators help to insert the medication deep within the vaginal canal.
Lubricate the applicator or tip of the suppository with a water-soluble lubricant.	Lubrication reduces friction as the applicator is inserted into the vagina.
Apply gloves and spread the labia in order to identify the opening to the vagina.	The opening to the vagina is best visualized when the labia are retracted.
Insert the applicator tip gently downward and backward following the contour of the vaginal wall.	The vagina is a curved cavity that may be injured unless the insertion is performed correctly.
Depress the plunger of the applicator when it has been inserted approximately 7.5 to 10 cm (3 to 4 inches).	The medication is more effectively distributed and safely inserted at this distance.
Remove the applicator while keeping the plunger depressed and allow the labia to fall into place.	Preventing the parts of the applicator from moving during withdrawal prevents discomfort for the patient.
Pull the glove inside out over the applicator until it can be properly cleaned within the utility room.	The same applicator is used for repeated administrations of the medications and should be cleaned thoroughly before being stored for future use.
Apply a clean perineal pad.	A clean perineal pad absorbs vaginal drainage and prevents soiling of underclothing or bed linen.
Instruct the patient to remain lying down for at least 5 to 10 minutes, or longer if possible.	Maintaining this position allows time for the medication to become distributed at the deepest area of the vagina near the cervix.

Continued

Principles of Care 18-6. Continued

Nursing Action	Rationale
Clean the applicator with water and soap or detergent. Dry it thoroughly, wrap and replace it with the container of medication.	The applicator should be kept clean and ready for use at the next administration of the drug.
Perform proper handwashing before carrying out any other activities.	Handwashing is an effective technique of medical asepsis that controls the spread of organisms.

Table 18-4. Common sizes of syringes and needles

Type of Injection	Size of Syringe	Size of Needle
Subcutaneous	2, 2.5 or 3 ml calibrated in 0.1 ml	23-, 25- or 26-gauge
Intramuscular	5 ml calibrated in 0.2 ml	20-, 21-, 22- or 23-gauge
Intradermal	1 ml calibrated in 0.1 ml or 0.01 ml and/or in minims	25-, 26- or 27-gauge
Insulin, which is given subcutaneously	1 ml calibrated in units	25-, 26- or 27-gauge

syringes holding the equivalent of 1 ml may be calibrated in units for insulin administration or in minims for administering very small volumes beneath the skin.

Needles are available in various lengths and gauges. The size of the needle depends upon the tissue that will be entered during the injection of the drug (Lenz, 1983). Needle lengths vary from 2.5 to 15 cm. The needle gauge is identified in numbers that refer to the width of the needle. The common sizes of needle gauges used for parenteral administration of drugs range from 18 to 27 gauge. The smaller the number of the gauge, the larger the lumen of the needle. An 18-gauge needle is larger than a 27-gauge needle. A needle with a large lumen is needed when the solution to be injected is thick or oily. Table 18-4 identifies common sizes of syringes and needles used for various types of injections.

The nurse must use good judgement in selecting the appropriate syringe and needle based upon several criteria that affect the administration of the medication. The following should be considered:

- The *route* of administration; a longer needle is required to reach deeper layers of tissue.
- The *viscosity*, or thickness, of the solution; some medications are more viscous than others and

require a larger lumen through which to inject the drug.
- The *quantity* to be administered; the larger the volume of medication to be injected, the greater the holding capacity must be within the syringe.
- The *body size* of the patient; in an obese person a longer needle may be required to reach various layers of tissue than in a thin or paediatric patient.
- The *type of medication*; some drugs should only be measured or administered using specific equipment. For example, insulin is most accurately prepared using a syringe calibrated in units. Drugs that are irritating to subcutaneous tissue should be administered using a long needle to ensure proper placement of the medication deep within the muscle.

Reconstituting a powdered parenteral medication

Some drugs intended for parenteral administration are supplied as powders. The powdered drug must be combined with a liquid or *diluent* before it can be injected. The process of adding a diluent to a powdered substance is called *reconstitution*.

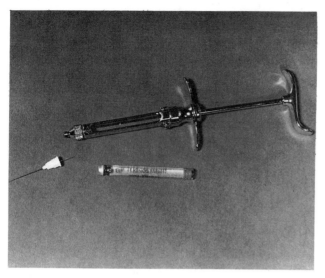

Figure 18-11 This syringe accepts prefilled cartridges. The needle has a point at both ends. The cartridge is labelled with the name of the drug, the dosage and route of administration. Once the cartridge is inserted into the barrel of the syringe, the shorter point punctures the rubber bung and the drug is ready for administration. (Courtesy Royal Marsden Hospital)

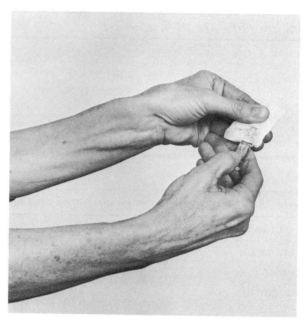

Figure 18-12 The nurse's fingers are protected with a moist pledget when the stem of the glass ampoule is snapped.

The label on the drug container will provide the nurse with the following information:

- The type of diluent to add to the powder; common diluents are sterile water for injection and sterile normal saline.
- The amount of diluent to add.
- The dosage of the medication per liquid volume when reconstituted.
- The directions for storing the reconstituted medication.

If the reconstituted drug will be used for more than one administration of the medication, the nurse must indicate certain information on the drug label. The date, initials of the nurse who added the liquid to the powdered drug and amount of drug per volume of solution should be indicated.

Placing medication in a syringe

Medications for injection may be supplied in one of three ways: prefilled cartridges, glass ampoules or rubber-capped vials containing single or multiple dosages of a drug. A prefilled cartridge is shown in Figure 18-11. An *ampoule* is a glass container holding a single dose of a parenteral medication. An ampoule is opened by scoring and snapping the neck of the glass container. The fingers should be protected from

being cut by using gauze or a similar substance, such as a premoistened pledget. A *vial* is a glass container of parenteral medication with a self-sealing stopper. Medication is removed from a vial by piercing the rubber stopper with a needle following appropriate cleansing techniques.

Removing medication from an ampoule. When a syringe is filled with a drug supplied in an ampoule, the following techniques may be utilized:

- Assemble the needle with the syringe.
- Distribute any medication trapped in the top of the ampoule into the bottom by tapping the upper area of the container.
- Score the neck of the ampoule with a file.
- Protect the thumb and fingers with a gauze square or premoistened pledget, as shown in Figure 18-12.
- Snap the neck of the ampoule away from the body when breaking the top free from the ampoule.
- Insert the needle into the ampoule, being careful not to touch the outside surface or the rim.
- Stabilize the ampoule, holding it securely within the hand or inverting the ampoule in the non-dominant hand, as illustrated in Figure 18-13.
- Withdraw the solution into the syringe by

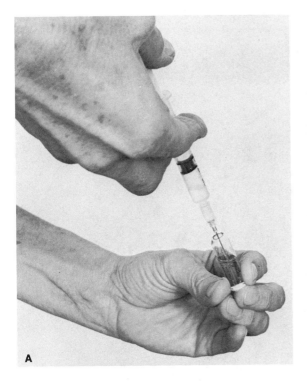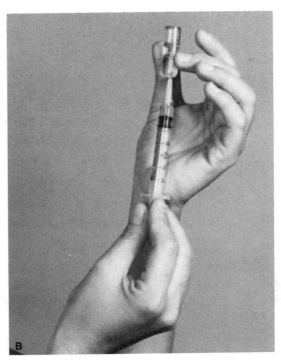

Figure 18-13 *Left*: When the stem of a glass ampoule is removed, the drug is drawn up into the syringe easily because air displaces the fluid. *Right*: The ampoule may be inverted when medication is withdrawn. When medication is removed in this manner, the trick is to keep the needle in the solution at all times, even as the ampoule is inverted.

pulling back the plunger. Keep the tip of the needle within the solution.

- Remove the syringe and tap the barrel to move any bubbles of air towards the end of the syringe.
- Cover the needle with its protective sheath.
- Expel the air bubbles and any excess medication.
- Discard the ampoule and any remaining medication in a container that will not injure someone who will be disposing of nonburnable refuse.
- Do not keep medications contained within an opened ampoule since there is no way of ensuring the continued sterility of the drug.

Removing medication from a vial. When a syringe is to be filled with a drug supplied in a vial, the following techniques may be utilized:

- Remove the metal cover from the vial.
- Clean the exposed rubber cap with a swab premoistened with an antiseptic solution.
- Attach the needle to the syringe and fill the syringe with the same volume of air as the medication that will be withdrawn, as the nurse in Figure 18-14 is doing.

- Insert the needle through the rubber stopper while holding the syringe and the vial at a slightly oblique angle. Piercing the rubber stopper in this manner helps to prevent instillation of a core of rubber into the vial when the air is instilled.
- Invert the vial without touching the needle and allow the medication to enter the syringe, as illustrated in Figure 18-15.
- Remove the needle when the desired volume of medication has entered the barrel of the syringe.
- Cover the needle with its protective sheath and replace with a new needle.
- Expel any air or excess medication from the syringe, as shown in Figure 18-16.

When the syringe has been filled with the correct dosage of medication from an ampoule or vial, a small amount of air, approximately 0.2 cc, may be pulled into the syringe. Providing an air bubble ensures that the entire dosage of medication will be administered during the time of injection. If the medication that is withdrawn can cause irritation of

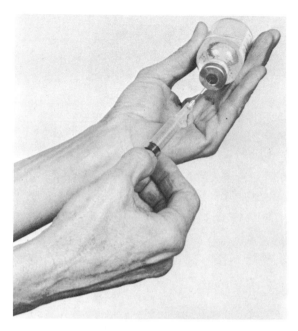

Figure 18-14 This nurse adds air to the contents of the vial. This increases pressure within the vial, making withdrawal of the solution easy. If air is not instilled, a partial vacuum is created in the vial as fluid is withdrawn. This makes it difficult to withdraw solution. If too much air is instilled, the pressure within the vial will propel solution into the syringe, making control and accurate filling difficult to achieve.

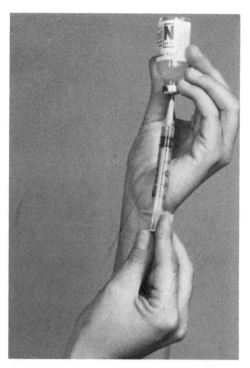

Figure 18-15 This nurse holds the inverted vial at eye level as medication is removed from it. Holding the vial in this manner assures accuracy in filling the syringe with the desired volume of medication.

tissue, the needle should be removed and replaced with another sterile needle before it is inserted into the patient.

It is possible to mix two medications together in one syringe but this must only be carried out if the drugs concerned are compatible.

Cleansing the skin at the site of injection

The skin is cleansed with an antiseptic solution prior to being pierced with the needle. Using a moistened cotton ball or pledget, move in a circular pattern beginning at the point of injection outward for a distance of about 2.5 to 6 cm (1 to 2.5 inches). This technique carries debris and microorganisms away from the site of injection (McConnell, 1982). Use firm pressure and friction when cleansing to help remove surface contaminants.

Reducing the discomfort of an injection

Following certain practices can lessen the potential for discomfort. Several techniques can greatly reduce

the pain associated with an injection. The nurse may wish to utilize some of the methods described as follows (McConnell, 1982; Newton and Newton, 1979; Kruszewski et al., 1979; Field, 1981):

- Select the smallest gauge that is appropriate for the route of administration and type of medication.
- Avoid inserting a needle that is coated with irritating medication; some drugs are more prone to causing discomfort than others. The best technique is to change the needle. However, the needle can be wiped using a sterile gauze pledget. Care must be taken to avoid contaminating the needle if this method is used.
- Select a site that is presently free of irritation.
- Develop a system for rotating the injection sites when the patient is receiving frequent administration of drugs by the parenteral route.
- Numb the skin if the patient has shown an unusual sensitivity during previous insertions of a needle. Apply cold compresses or an ice cube over the area to be injected; gently tap the site of

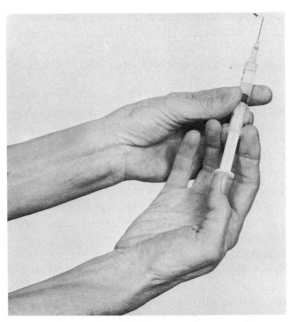

Figure 18-16 The medication has been placed within the syringe, which is held vertically—that is, the needle points upwards. Air and excess medication are then removed by pressing the plunger for the necessary distance.

injection with the fingers several times; or spray an anaesthetic, such as ethyl chloride, over the area to be injected. With the doctor's approval, a small amount of local anaesthetic, such as procaine hydrochloride, may be added to a medication injected intramuscularly.
- Position the patient prone with the feet pointing inward when an injection will be placed into the muscle in the buttock.
- Assist the patient to relax using deep breathing or other distraction techniques. Avoid having the patient watch the area where the needle will be placed. The mind can anticipate the entry of the needle and the imagery can intensify the discomfort.
- Insert the needle without hesitation.
- Instill the solution slowly, especially when the amount is sizable.
- Divide volumes in excess of 2.5 to 5 ml into two syringes and inject them in separate sites.
- Remove the needle rapidly to decrease the amount of medication that may spread into the surrounding tissue.
- Instill the medication by performing the Z-track or zig-zag technique discussed later in this chapter.

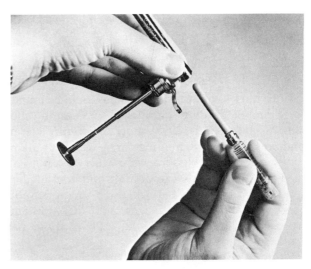

Figure 18-17 A nurse safely disposes of both syringe and needle in a sharps bin. (Courtesy Royal Marsden Hospital)

- Place pressure against the site of injection with a gauze pledget as the needle is withdrawn. This technique prevents pulling skin with the needle, which is an uncomfortable sensation.
- Massage the site after giving the injection unless contraindicated for the particular type of medication.

Disposing of contaminated needles and syringes
Reusable equipment is handled according to hospital policy. Care must be taken to avoid needle punctures and the possible transmission of pathogens spread by blood or serum. To prevent self-injury, needles may remain uncapped after their use. Disposable needles may be separated from the syringe using a special device, as shown in Figure 18-17. The needles fall directly into the puncture-resistant sharps bin and the syringes are discarded in the same container.

Administering an intramuscular injection

An *intramuscular injection* is the administration of a solution containing medication into one muscle or a muscle group of the body. Since very few nerve endings are in deep muscles, irritating medications are commonly given intramuscularly. Except for medications injected directly into the bloodstream, absorption from an intramuscular injection occurs more rapidly than from other routes.

Selecting sites for intramuscular injections

Various muscles may be used as sites for injection of a parenteral medication. In order to select an injection site, the nurse must know how to identify certain landmarks to avoid injuring large nerves, striking bones, or entering blood vessels. Muscles commonly used for the intramuscular administration of medications are located in the buttock, thigh and upper arm. There are unique advantages and disadvantages associated with the muscles in each of these particular injection sites.

Using the dorsogluteal site. This is a common site for injecting medications into the gluteus maximus muscle in the buttock. This muscle can receive a relatively large volume of drug with minimal post-injection discomfort associated with walking. If the site is not identified correctly, damage to the sciatic nerve with subsequent paralysis of the leg can result. Palpation of anatomical landmarks aids in the identification of the dorsogluteal site. This site should be avoided when the patient is under 3 years of age since the muscle is not developed enough at this age.

Using the ventrogluteal site. The ventrogluteal site utilizes the gluteus medius and gluteus minimus muscles in the hip area. This site has several advantages over the dorsogluteal site. There are no large nerves or blood vessels in the injection area. It is generally less fatty and cleaner because faecal contamination is rare at this site. The ventrogluteal site is safe for use in children.

Using the vastus lateralis muscle. This thick muscle is located in the lateral thigh. Large nerves and blood vessels are generally absent in this area. The vastus lateralis site is particularly desirable for infants and small children and other thin or debilitated individuals whose gluteal muscles are poorly developed.

Using the rectus femoris muscle. This muscle is located on the anterior aspect of the thigh. The muscle is quite visible in infants and is the preferred injection site for this age group.

Using the deltoid muscle. The deltoid muscle is located in the lateral aspect of the upper arm. It is not often used because it is a small muscle in comparison with the others. The deltoid muscle is not capable of absorbing large amounts of solution. Damage to the radial nerve and artery is a risk when this site is used.

Intramuscular injections into the deltoid muscle should be limited to 1 ml of solution. The deltoid muscle should be used only for adults. It is not developed enough in infants and children to absorb medication adequately.

Principles of Care 18-7 describes the techniques for locating and safely injecting medications intramuscularly into the various described sites.

Injecting an intramuscular medication

Principles of Care 18-8 describes and illustrates how to inject medication into an intramuscular site. The suggested actions assume that the nurse observes the basic guidelines for preparing and administering medications.

Using the Z-track technique. The *Z-track technique*, sometimes called the *zigzag technique*, is an injection method used to administer medications that are irritating to subcutaneous tissues. It acquired its name because of the manipulation of the tissue that appears somewhat like the letter Z. When this method is used, the medication is sealed within the muscle so that it cannot leak back through other layers of tissue following the path of the needle.

Before administering a medication using this technique, the nurse should select a needle that is a minimum of 6 cm long so that there is no danger of injecting into subcutaneous tissue. The original needle used to fill the syringe must be changed. This prevents distribution of any irritating medication covering the needle into subcutaneous tissue along the path of injection.

Principles of Care 18-9 describes and illustrates the procedure for administering a medication using the Z-track technique. It is assumed that the nurse observes the basic guidelines for preparing and administering medications when following the suggested actions for utilizing the Z-track technique for intramuscular injection.

Administering a subcutaneous injection

A *subcutaneous injection* involves the administration of a medication into the tissue that lies between the epidermis and the muscle. This involves a much wider area into which injected medication may be administered. The medication is absorbed fairly rapidly and begins acting within half an hour of being administered. The equipment selected for use requires some modification from that used for intra-

Principles of Care 18-7. Locating sites for intramuscular injections

Nursing Action	Rationale

The Rectus Femoris Site

Nursing Action	Rationale
Position the patient in a supine or sitting position.	The rectus femoris muscle is one of the large muscles that makes up the quadriceps group of muscles on the anterior aspect of the thigh.
Divide the thigh into thirds using the hands or the mind's eye, as shown in Figure 18-18.	The upper and lower thirds are not suitable for injecting medications.

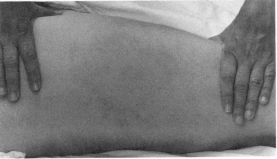

Figure 18-18 The hands are being used here to divide the thigh into thirds when determining the area for injecting a drug into the rectus femoris muscle.

Nursing Action	Rationale
Inject the medication into the middle third of the thigh, as the patient in Figure 18-19 is doing.	This site may be used as an alternative when rotating sites or when other sites show signs of irritation. It is often a convenient site for teaching patients how to self-administer injectable medication.

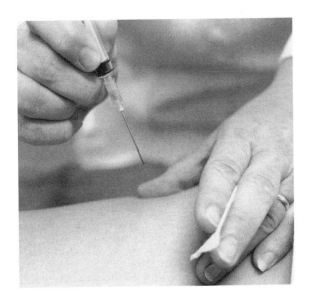

Figure 18-19 The patient is giving herself an intramuscular injection, using the rectus femoris muscle on the front of the thigh. Because this patient's muscle is relatively small, it is being bunched to elevate the muscle to avoid striking the femur. This injection site is associated with post-injection discomfort.

Continued

Principles of Care 18-7. *Continued*

Nursing Action	Rationale
The Ventrogluteal Site	
Place the patient on his side with the upper knee bent and the leg placed slightly ahead of the lower leg. The patient can also be in a supine or prone position.	A side-lying position is best for exposing and palpating the anatomic landmarks prior to injecting a medication into this muscle group.
Palpate the greater trochanter at the head of the femur, the anterior superior iliac spine and the iliac crest.	A triangular area between these structures provides the proper location for an injection.
Place the palm of the hand on the greater trochanter and the index finger on the anterior superior iliac spine.	The line between these two forms one boundary of the triangle.
Move the middle finger away from the index finger as far as possible along the iliac crest, as the nurse is doing in Figure 18-20.	The line between the palm and the middle finger forms another boundary of the triangle. The iliac crest is the base of the triangle.
The Dorsogluteal Site	
Inject into the centre of the triangle formed by the index, middle finger and iliac crest.	This area does not contain any major nerves or blood vessels.

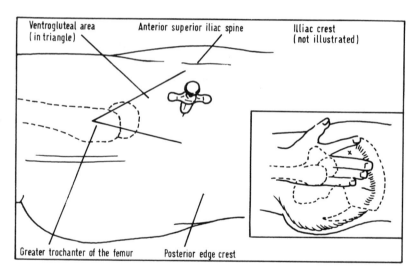

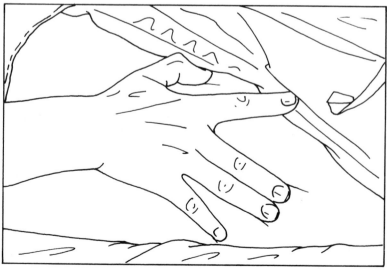

Figure 18-20 Although the side-lying position is the best to use, the sketch and photo here have the patient in the supine position. *Top*: The needle shows the position for injecting into the ventrogluteal area. Notice how the nurse's palm is placed on the greater trochanter and the finger is on the anterior superior iliac spine. The middle finger is spread posteriorly as far as possible along the iliac crest. The injection is made in the middle of the triangle formed by the nurse's fingers and the iliac crest. *Bottom*: The ventrogluteal area is identified on a patient.

Continued

Principles of Care 18-7. *Continued*

Nursing Action	Rationale

The Dorsogluteal Site

Position the patient on his abdomen with the buttock well exposed.

Use either of the following methods to identify safe areas for injecting medication into this site:

- Palpate the posterior iliac spine and the greater trochanter. Draw an imaginary diagonal line between the two landmarks.

  Insert the needle superior and lateral to the midpoint of this line.

The anatomy of the patient must be properly assessed in order to identify this site accurately.

When medication is injected into the dorsogluteal site, the sciatic nerve, trochanters of the femur and large blood vessels must be avoided.

These methods utilize the location of anatomical landmarks to determine the safe area for injection.

Structures that may become injured can be avoided by inserting the needle into the upper outer areas of these anatomical landmarks.

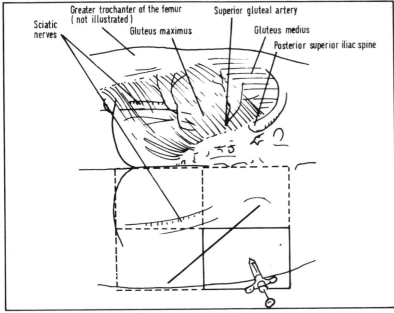

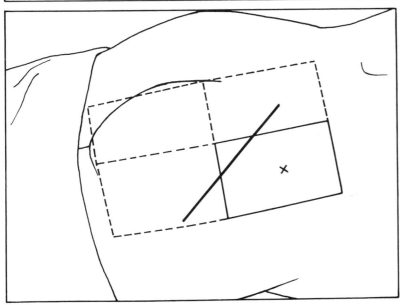

Figure 18-21 *Top*: The needle is in the proper place for an intramuscular injection into the dorsogluteal site. Notice how this site avoids entrance into any area near the sciatic nerve and the superior gluteal artery. The heavy dark diagonal line represents the imaginary line between the superior iliac spine and the greater trochanter. The lighter rectangular quadrants show the imaginary lines created when the buttock is divided into sectors, using the ridge of the superior iliac spine and the cleft in the buttock. The upper, outer corner of the quadrant identified with a solid line can be safely used for injections. *Bottom*: The imaginary lines indicating the dorsogluteal site are superimposed on the exposed buttock. The area identified with an *x* identifies the area for safe needle insertion.

Continued

Principles of Care 18-7. Continued

Nursing Action   **Rationale**

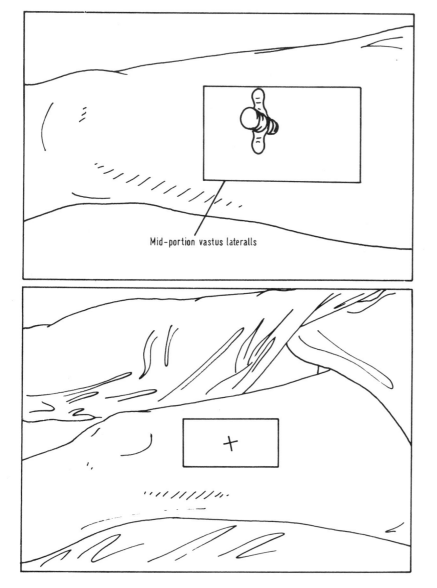

Mid-portion vastus lateralis

Figure 18-22 *Top*: The needle is in position for injecting into the centre of the vastus lateralis muscle. *Bottom*: The same area is identified on a patient. The imaginary mid-rectangle can be located by positioning a hand's breadth from all four perimeters of the thigh.

Continued

Principles of Care 18-7. Continued

Nursing Action	Rationale
The Dorsogluteal Site	
• Divide the buttock into four imaginary quadrants by drawing an imaginary vertical line through the bony ridge of the posterior superior biliac spine and an imaginary horizontal line from the upper cleft in the fold of the buttock.	The imaginary lines and various anatomical landmarks are identified in Figure 18-21.
Inject the medication in the upper outer area of the quadrant that lies superior and lateral to where the lines intersect.	
The Vastus Lateralis Site	
Have the patient lie supine or sit in a chair with the thigh well exposed.	The vastus lateralis is located on the lateral anterior aspect of the thigh.
Instruct the patient to point the toes inward.	Internally rotating the hip helps to position the leg for better exposure of the lateral aspect of the leg.
Divide the thigh into thirds to identify an imaginary rectangle.	The injection should be made into the middle rectangle of this thick muscle.
Use the breadth of the hand as a convenient measure to divide the thigh both vertically and horizontally in the following manner:	The hand can be used to section off the perimeter of the imaginary rectangle.
• Place one hand's breadth below the greater trochanter at the top of the thigh, and a hand's breadth from the knee.	This defines the superior and inferior sides of the middle rectangle.
• Place one hand's breadth along the middle of the inner side of the thigh and one hand's breadth on the outer side of the thigh.	This defines the medial and lateral sides of the middle rectangle.
• Inject into the centre of the imaginary midrectangle, as illustrated in Figure 18-22.	This area is safe for use in both adults and children.
Using the Deltoid Site	
Have the patient lie down, stand or sit with the upper arm and shoulder well exposed.	This site is easily located in virtually all positions.
Palpate the lower edge of the acromion process and draw an imaginary horizontal line.	This forms the upper boundary of the deltoid site.
Imagine another horizontal line at the lower boundary of the axilla.	This forms the lower boundary of the deltoid site.
Inject within the centre of the imaginary lines, as shown in Figure 18-23.	The deltoid muscle is much smaller than the other sites used for injections.

Continued

Principles of Care 18-7. *Continued*

Nursing Action	Rationale

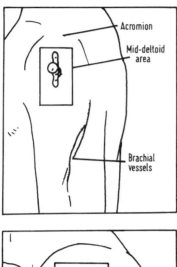

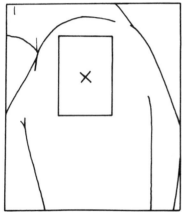

Figure 18-23 *Top*: The needle has been inserted in the deltoid muscle. The area for injection is bounded by the lower edge of the acromion process on the top to a point on the arm opposite the axilla on the bottom. The side boundaries are perpendicular to the lines described above about one-third and two-thirds of the way around the side of the arm, as indicated by the enclosed rectangle. *Bottom*: The deltoid site is identified on the arm of a patient.

muscular injections since the tissue is not as deep. Usually a smaller volume of medication is injected when using the subcutaneous route.

Selecting subcutaneous injection sites

The sites for giving a subcutaneous injection include the upper arm, thigh, abdomen and back. Figure 18–36 illustrates the appropriate locations of these areas.

When a patient, such as the insulin-dependent diabetic, must receive repeated subcutaneous injections, it is important to rotate the sites of injection. Rotation avoids repeated use of the same site, which can contribute to discomfort and possible tissue damage. In such cases, it is recommended that a

sketch of the body be used. Each time an injection is given, the nurse indicates on the sketch exactly where the medication was injected. The site is dated so that the next time an injection is given another site may be used. It is best to rotate areas of the body at the time of each injection rather than rotate among adjacent areas at the same site. The patient may also use a sketch so that he can keep an accurate account of the rotation sites he is using when self-administering the medication.

Assembling equipment for a subcutaneous injection

The subcutaneous route is used to administer insulin, heparin, certain narcotics and some immunizations.

Principles of Care 18-8. Injecting medication intramuscularly

Nursing Action	Rationale
Evaluate the possible injection sites that may be used.	Sites that are irritated or bruised should be excluded as should any site where the anatomical landmarks cannot be easily palpated.
Select an appropriate site for the injection. The dorsogluteal site, shown in Figure 18-24, will be the example used in this procedure.	Following selective criteria in choosing a site decreases patient discomfort and possible damage to body tissues.

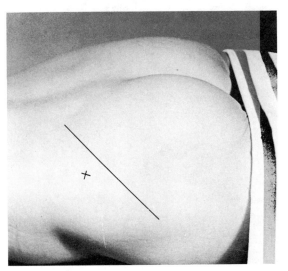

Figure 18-24 The buttock is well exposed to palpate and locate anatomical landmarks for determining the safe area for injecting the medication. In this case, the dorsogluteal site is identified.

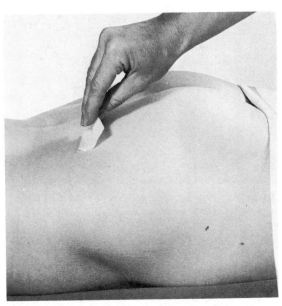

Figure 18-25 An injection site is being prepared by thorough cleansing with a swab containing an antiseptic of the hospital's choice.

Using friction, cleanse the site of entry using a swab that has been premoistened with an antiseptic. Use a circular motion outward for 2.5–6 cm (1 to 2.5 inches), as illustrated in Figure 18-25. Allow the skin to dry.	Cleansing the area of injection reduces the danger of forcing organisms into tissues. Introducing antiseptic into tissues with the needle causes tissue irritation. Allowing the skin to dry gives more time to inhibit the presence of organisms.
Remove the sheath protecting the needle.	Keeping the needle protected until just prior to the injection ensures its sterility.
Using the thumb and first two fingers, press the tissue down firmly, as illustrated in Figure 18-26.	Compression of the tissue helps to ensure that the needle will enter the muscle and not the subcutaneous layer of tissue.
Holding the syringe like a dart, insert the needle at a 90-degree angle quickly into the skin, as shown in Figure 18-27.	This angle facilitates needle insertion within muscle tissue. Hesitation during insertion can increase discomfort.
Continue to insert the needle firmly and steadily for almost its full length, as illustrated in Figure 18-28.	Sufficient penetration of the needle places it into the muscle.

Continued

Principles of Care 18-8. *Continued*

Nursing Action	Rationale

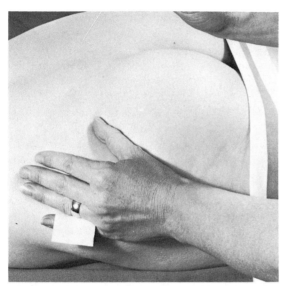

Figure 18-26 The thumb and fingers spread the skin at the injection site. The nurse is careful not to contaminate the site of entry.

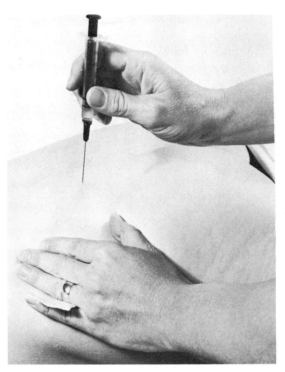

Figure 18-27 The nurse holds the syringe like a dart and introduces the needle quickly.

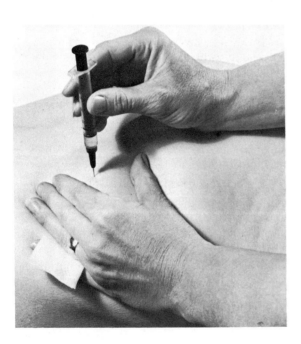

Figure 18-28 After entering the skin, the needle is introduced for almost its full length.

Continued

Principles of Care 18-8. *Continued*

Nursing Action	Rationale

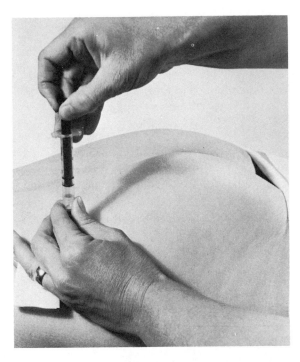

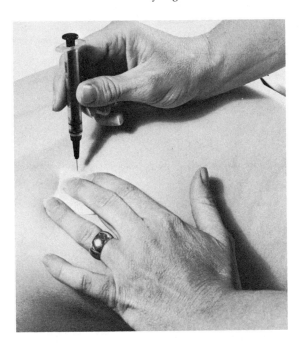

Figure 18-29 While steadying the syringe, the nurse pulls back gently on the plunger to see if blood can be brought back into the barrel of the syringe.

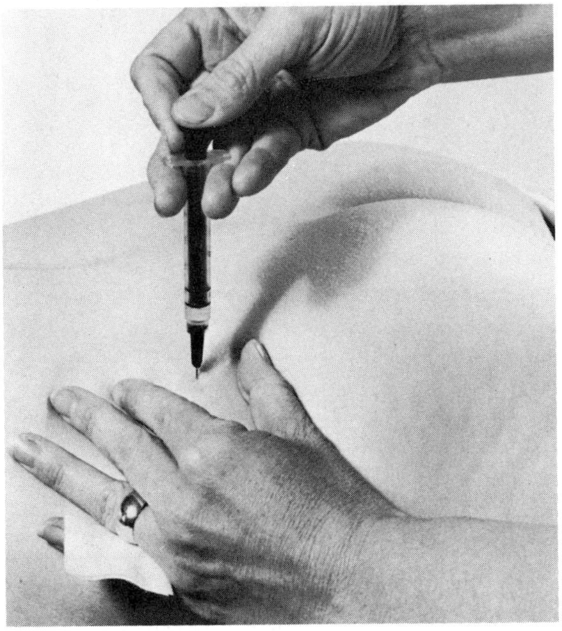

Figure 18-30 The nurse pushes the plunger its entire length. This forces the solution and the air bubble through the needle and into the muscle.

Figure 18-31 After the solution has been injected, pressure on the swab is applied against the injection site.

Continued

Principles of Care 18-8. Continued

Nursing Action	Rationale
Pull back gently on the plunger and observe the barrel of the syringe, as the nurse in Figure 18-29 is doing.	Aspiration is a method for assessing if a blood vessel has been entered. Drugs injected intramuscularly are intended for slower absorption and may be dangerous if placed in the bloodstream, since they would be absorbed immediately.
Inject the medication slowly if no blood appears in the barrel of the syringe by pushing the plunger into the barrel, as the nurse in Figure 18-30 is demonstrating.	Slow injection allows the solution to disperse into the surrounding tissue without creating excessive pressure.
Withdraw the needle quickly while applying pressure against the skin surrounding the site, as shown in Figure 18-31.	Quickly withdrawing the needle while applying pressure on the injection site reduces discomfort and the risk of medication leaking into subcutaneous tissue.
Massage the injection site with the premoistened swab, as the nurse in Figure 18-32 is doing, unless this action is contraindicated with the administration of that particular medication.	Massaging the site helps distribute the medication and hastens absorption by increasing the blood supply to the area.

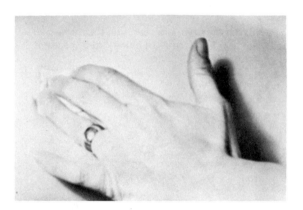

Figure 18-32 After the needle is removed, the injection site is massaged.

Equipment used for subcutaneous injection may depend on the type of medication that has been prescribed. Insulin is prepared in an insulin syringe that is calibrated in units. Heparin may be prepared in a tuberculin syringe or it may be supplied in a prefilled cartridge in some hospitals. Most of these medication dosages are within a volume of 1 ml.

A shorter needle, usually 1.5 cm, may be selected since the tissue into which the medication will be injected is not as deep as muscular tissue. A 25-gauge needle is most often used since the medications administered by the subcutaneous route are generally not viscous.

Modifying injection techniques

Some modifications in the injection technique are recommended when the nurse administers a subcutaneous injection. The goal is to inject into subcutaneous tissue. However, depending upon the patient's body size and layer of body fat, the angle of needle insertion or length of the needle, or both, may require some adjustments.

Principles of Care 18-9. Utilizing the z-track technique

Nursing Action	Rationale
Replace the needle used for filling the syringe with another sterile needle that is at least 6 cm long.	The needle must be free of irritating medication and long enough to be introduced deeply within the muscle.
Select the intramuscular site where the medication will be injected.	A large, thick muscle should be used when irritating drugs must be injected.
Cleanse the skin over a wider area, approximately 6.5 to 8.5 cm (3 to 4 inches).	A wider area of the skin must be manipulated, so the area that is cleansed should be of a comparable amount.
Grasp the muscle and pull it laterally about 2.5 cm (1 inch), until it is taut, as the person in Figure 18-33 is doing. Continue to hold the tissue in this position.	This provides a straight path in the tissue during the time of the needle insertion, but a diagonal path when the needle is withdrawn and the tissue is released.

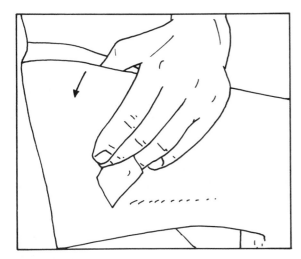

Figure 18-33 The patient has grasped the rectus femoris muscle in the left hand and has moved it laterally about 2.5 cm (1 in), as the arrow indicates.

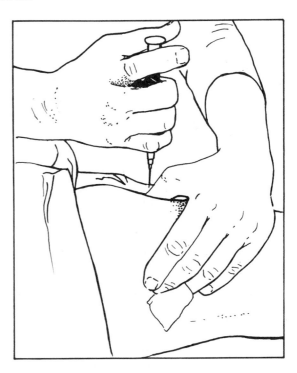

Figure 18-34 Notice that the patient steadies the syringe with the last three fingers while manoeuvring the plunger to check the location of the tip of the needle.

Insert the needle at a 90-degree angle using a dartlike motion.	This directs the needle tip well within the muscle.
Use the last three fingers of the hand holding the syringe to steady the barrel. Use the thumb and index finger on the same hand to aspirate, as shown in Figure 18-34.	The nondominant hand must not be released from its hold on the tissue.

Continued

Principles of Care 18-9. Continued

Nursing Action	Rationale
Aspirate by pulling back on the plunger. Inject the medication with slow even pressure if no blood appears in the barrel of the syringe during aspiration, as shown in Figure 18-35.	Medications intended for intramuscular injection should not be administered into the bloodstream. Slow instillation allows time for the medication to become evenly distributed within the muscle.

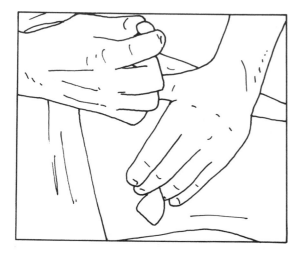

Figure 18-35 The patient continues to hold the muscle to the side and when no blood appears, pushes the plunger in to inject the medication.

Nursing Action	Rationale
Wait about 10 seconds with the needle still in place.	Pausing allows the medication to be distributed widely from the needle site.
Withdraw the needle and immediately release the skin.	The injection track will now become a diagonal path sealing the original route of entry with layers of released tissue.
Apply pressure but *do not* massage the site unless the manufacturer indicates that this is appropriate.	Massaging the site may cause some of the trapped medication to leak from the pocket where it has been deposited and irritate surrounding tissue.

Authorities suggest that for a larger patient the nurse use a 90-degree angle for needle insertion; a 45-degree angle may be used when the patient is thin. Figure 18-37 illustrates needles being introduced at different angles on patients who are of different weights.

A shorter needle, for example 1.5 cm, must be inserted at a 90-degree angle in order to reach subcutaneous tissue on an individual of average weight. A longer needle may be inserted at a 45-degree angle for a patient of average size.

Opinion also differs about whether the nurse should grasp the patient's tissues between the thumb and fingers or whether the skin should be stretched taut at the site of injection. The basis for the decision depends on the length of the needle and also on the body size of the patient. For a dehydrated or very thin patient and for most children and infants, grasping the tissue is preferred to stretching the skin. The nurse injecting patients in Figure 18-37 did not grasp the sites of injection. Just by changing the angle at which the needle was injected into the two adult patients of different weights, one can readily reach the subcutaneous tissue with the needle.

Preparing insulin

Insulin is a natural hormone that may not be produced by certain individuals with diabetes mellitus in

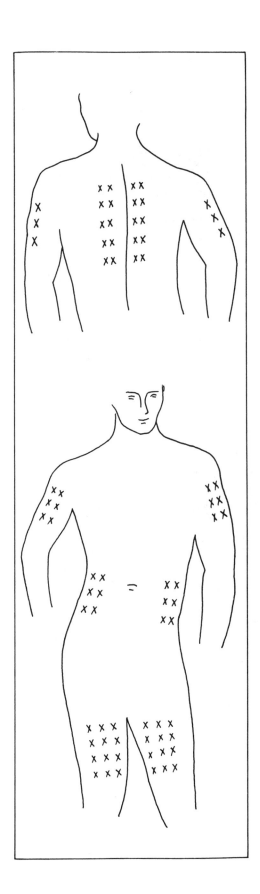

sufficient amounts to meet the body's needs. Insulin must be injected since it is destroyed by digestive enzymes if given by the oral route. It is administered using the subcutaneous route. Nurses must often teach newly diagnosed diabetics how to prepare insulin as well as the technique for administering a subcutaneous injection.

Insulin is supplied in a dosage strength called a unit. The equivalent now commonly used for measuring insulin is referred to as U-100. This means that when insulin is prepared by pharmaceutical companies, the standard strength is 100 units of insulin per 1 ml. This standardization has helped to prevent dosage errors. Insulin is supplied in multiple-dose vials.

Insulin preparations vary in their onset and duration of action. The nurse must take care when reading insulin labels since many containers of insulin look similar to one another. Some preparations of insulin separate on standing and must be remixed before a syringe is filled with them.

It is common practice for one nurse to check the insulin preparation of another nurse because errors in the dosage or type of insulin can have life-threatening consequences. When teaching a patient to administer insulin, it is advantageous also to instruct a family member.

Injecting medication subcutaneously

Principles of Care 18-10 describes how to administer a medication subcutaneously. It is assumed that the nurse observes the guidelines for preparing and administering a medication in addition to the suggested actions in the procedure.

Administering an intradermal injection

An *intradermal injection* involves the administration of a substance within the layers of the skin. Such an injection is placed just below the epidermis. Intradermal injections are commonly used for diagnostic purposes. Examples include the tuberculin test and allergy testing to determine a patient's sensitivity to various substances.

A common site for an intradermal injection is the inner aspect of the forearm, although other areas are also satisfactory, such as the back and upper chest.

Figure 18-36 These are sites on the body where subcutaneous injections can be given.

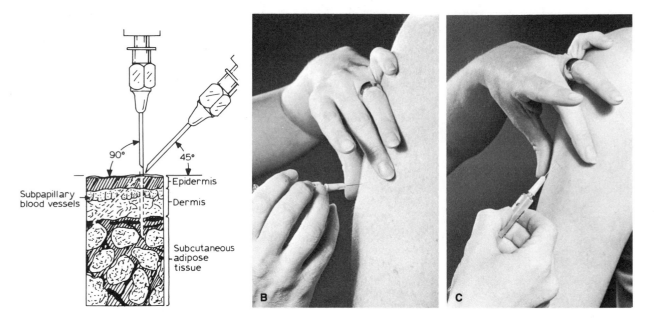

Figure 18-37 *Left*: The sketch illustrates that a shorter needle at a 90° angle and a longer needle at a 45° angle will be located in subcutaneous tissue. *Centre*: The nurse is using a 1.5 cm needle, inserted at a 90° angle, to inject a patient weighing 190 pounds. *Right*: It is inserted at about a 45° angle when injecting a patient weighing 120 pounds.

Small amounts of solution are administered, usually not more than 0.5 ml. A tuberculin syringe is used for measuring the dosage. A 25- to 27-gauge needle 1.5 cm in length is used when administering an intradermal injection.

The needle is inserted at a 10 to 15-degree angle for proper placement of medication. A small raised area or *wheal*, like the one shown in Figure 18-38, should appear at the injection site as the medication is instilled.

Principles of Care 18-11 describes and illustrates how to administer an intradermal injection. It is assumed that the nurse observes the basic guidelines for preparing and administering a medication in addition to utilizing the suggested actions in the Principles of Care.

Administering intravenous medication

Medications administered intravenously have an immediate effect. The intravenous route is the most dangerous route of administration. The medication is delivered directly into the bloodstream. It cannot be recalled nor can its actions be slowed. For these reasons usually only selectively qualified nurses are permitted to administer intravenous medications.

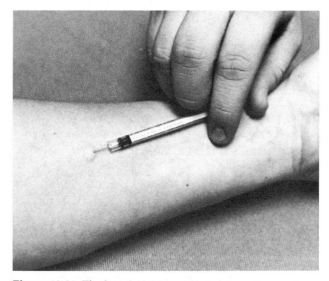

Figure 18-38 The bevel of this needle has been inserted between the layers of skin at about a 10° angle. A wheal forms as the solution is instilled. It appears to be similar in size and appearance to the bite of a mosquito.

Even those who are responsible for intravenous medication administration must exercise extreme caution in preparing and instilling them. Patients receiving intravenous therapy must be observed

Principles of Care 18-10. Injecting medication subcutaneously

Nursing Action	Rationale
Select an appropriate site for the injection. Refer to a site rotation guide if one is available.	The selection of a site should include consideration of how often a site has been used. Avoid using any site that appears to be bruised or swollen and tender.
Using friction, clean the skin thoroughly with a pledget moistened with an antiseptic. Allow the skin to dry.	Cleansing reduces surface contaminants. Drying prevents introducing antiseptic that may irritate the tissue. As the skin dries, the antiseptic continues to be active.
Hold the skin taut over the injection site or grasp the area surrounding the injection size and hold it in a cushion manner. The choice depends on the size of the patient and the length of the needle.	Holding the tissue taut helps the nurse to be sure that the subcutaneous tissue is being entered in most well-nourished, hydrated persons. Grasping the tissue facilitates entering subcutaneous tissue when the patient is thin, dehydrated or small.
Insert the needle to almost its full length at an angle of 45 to 90 degrees depending on the body size and length of the needle.	Subcutaneous tissue is abundant in well-nourished persons. It is usually sparse in thin, dehydrated or small persons.
When the needle is in place, release the grasp if the tissue has been bunched.	Injecting the solution into relaxed tissue allows the drug to enter with less discomfort.
Pull back gently on the plunger of the syringe to determine the location of the needle.	Placement is checked to assess if the needle has been inserted into a blood vessel.
Do not aspirate if heparin is being administered.	Aspiration increases the potential for causing a pocket of blood to form at the injection site. Heparin is not dangerous if absorbed into the bloodstream.
Inject the solution slowly.	Slow injection allows the solution to disperse into the surrounding tissue.
Withdraw the needle quickly while applying pressure against the injection site.	Rapid withdrawal of the needle while pressure is applied on the injection site reduces discomfort.
Massage the area where the injection was made unless contraindicated by the type of drug that has been administered.	Massaging the area of injection may help spread the medication in subcutaneous tissues and hastens absorption. Massage would be contraindicated when heparin has been injected since it will cause excessive bruising of the tissue.

for any signs of distress. The cannula site must be checked for signs of infection, whilst the cannula itself must be checked as to its patency. On insertion of the cannula, record in the nursing records to ensure replacement on the correct day.

Intravenous administration is the route chosen in an emergency when immediate action is required. However, there are many clinical situations in which drugs are administered intravenously. A number of antibiotics can be administered to a patient via the intravenous route. When there is already access to the bloodstream in place, intravenous administration of medications replaces the discomfort experienced from repeated intramuscular injections. Intravenous medications can be administered continuously using a syringe driver such as a sage pump or IVAC, or intermittently.

Overcoming noncompliance

Noncompliance is the failure to follow instructions related to health care. One of the areas with the highest rate of noncompliance involves self-administration of medications. Despite nurses teaching patients about

Principles of Care 18-11. Injecting a solution intradermally

Nursing Action	Rationale
Select an area on the inner aspect of the forearm, about a hand's breadth above the patient's wrist.	The forearm is a convenient and easy location for introducing an agent intradermally.
Cleanse the skin with a swab moistened with an antiseptic using a circular motion outward from the site of entry.	Debris and organisms are removed from the centre outward toward the periphery.
Cleanse the area with acetone if the skin is oily. Allow the area to dry.	Acetone is a defatting agent and is effective for removing oils from the skin. Allowing time for the antiseptic to dry also allows time for it to continue working.
Hold the patient's arm and stretch the skin taut with the thumb.	Taut skin provides an easier entrance into the intradermal area.
Place the syringe almost flat against the patient's skin, and insert the needle, bevel side up, at a 10 to 15-degree angle, as the nurse in Figure 18-39 is doing.	The intradermal area is only a short distance beneath the skin.

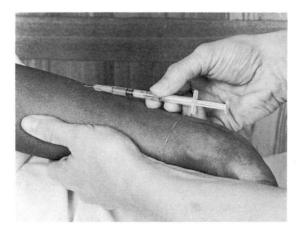

Figure 18-39 The nurse holds the needle almost parallel to the skin on the forearm when administering an intradermal injection.

Insert the needle about 0.5 cm and slowly inject the solution while watching for a small wheal to appear.	The bevel must be completely under the skin so that the solution does not leak out on the surface of the skin. If the needle is inserted too deeply, the wheal will not be seen.
Withdraw the needle quickly at the same angle at which it was inserted.	Withdrawing the needle in this manner minimizes tissue damage and discomfort for the patient.
Do not massage the area after removing the needle.	Massaging the area where an intradermal injection is given may interfere with test results.
Observe the patient's condition frequently within the first half hour after instilling an allergy test substance.	Severe allergic reactions may occur in the early period following the injection of substances to which the patient may be allergic.
Observe the area for signs of a local reaction at ordered intervals, usually in 24 hours and again in 48 hours.	The response to the injected substance must be assessed to determine future treatment. It may take 1 to 2 days for a definitive response to appear.

Table 18-5. Suggestions for overcoming noncompliance

Reason for noncompliance	Ways to help overcome noncompliance
Having an attitude of seeing no value in bothering with taking medications	This attitude is most often noted among patients with chronic diseases. The following measures are suggested to help overcome it: reviewing the patient's medications and the role they play in controlling or overcoming an illness; including the patient in a plan of care in relation to taking his medications; having a written contract with the patient indicating that he will take his medications as prescribed; and seeking help from family members who can give the patient support without threats of consequences for not taking medications.
Forgetting whether medications were taken	Overcoming this reason for noncompliance usually depends on developing a system of reminders with the patient. The following measures are suggested: having instructions for taking medications in writing, being sure that the patient has a clock and calendar handy for his use; keeping a diary, checklist or record that requires the patient to make a notation each time he takes a medication rather than depending on memory; using a colour coding system as a reminder to take medications; marking medication containers with reminders, such as placing an AM on the bottom of a container and a PM on the top of it and having the patient flip the container so that the next time the medication due is on the top; rotating places where medications are placed after taking each dose; and using an alarm, such as on a wristwatch, that is set to ring when a medication is due and reset immediately to ring when the next dose is due.
Being confused about when and how often to take medications	This common reason for noncompliance occurs especially frequently when the patient is expected to follow a complex drug programme. In addition to developing a system of reminders with the patient, as described above, it is helpful to consult the patient's doctor to see whether a simpler but equally effective programme of drug therapy can be developed.
Feeling better, no better, or worse after taking medications	The important teaching point when these causes lead to noncompliance is to be sure to explain the importance of continuing with medications for as long as prescribed, how long it may be necessary to take them before their effect is noted, and what symptoms to expect while taking medications.
Being discontented with the side-effects associated with medications and the way they interfere with activities of daily living	When this cause results in noncompliance, consultation with a doctor may help by finding substitute medications that produce fewer side-effects or by changing a dosage, if permissible. Other suggested measures are as follows: help the patient in learning how to adjust to and cope with side-effects; and be sure the patient understands the importance of drug therapy for treating his illness.
Having a variety of personal reasons, such as the cost of medications, pride, a need to be free of drug therapy, and pressure from others who use other types of medications or speak of the dangers of the prescribed medications	Helping to overcome various personal reasons for overcoming noncompliance requires individualized attention and care. Very often the nurse can seek help from others, such as from social service personnel when the patient cannot afford prescribed medications. It is important when helping a patient to overcome personal reasons for noncompliance that the nurse give the patient ample opportunity to describe his feelings and attitudes about drug therapy and that the nurse *listen* to what the patient is saying.

self-administration of medications, including injections, studies have shown that a remarkable number of patients do not follow directions. Common reasons and suggested ways of helping to overcome the nonuse, misuse and abuse of medications are described in Table 18-5. The creative nurse may find still other ways to help overcome noncompliance.

Suggested measures when administering medications in selected situations

When the patient is pregnant or lactating

Caution pregnant women that medications should be avoided because of *teratogenic effects* on the foetus. This means that some drugs can produce abnormal structures in the developing infant causing severe deformities. The foetus is particularly susceptible to the effects of chemicals during the first 3 months of a pregnancy when the organs are developing rapidly.

Encourage a pregnant woman to discuss the effects of certain self-prescribed and prescription medications with her doctor.

Explain that medications are excreted through breast milk in the lactating mother. Although many drugs appear to produce no harmful effects, certain drugs have been identified as harmful to the infant. The mother who breast-feeds an infant would be wise to discuss with the paediatrician the types of medications that may be taken safely.

When the patient is an infant or child

Be sure to check dosages carefully when administering medications to infants and children. Youngsters respond faster and more noticeably to drugs than adults.

Use a liquid preparation of a medication whenever possible for a child under 5 years of age. Children have difficulty swallowing solid forms of medications.

Use a syringe, without the needle, or a dropper to administer medications to infants and small children. Place the syringe in the side of the mouth and instill the medication in small amounts. Allow the child to swallow before administering additional medication. A liquid dispenser is illustrated in Figure 18-40.

Stimulate swallowing by gentle downward stroking motions over the larynx.

Crush or mix medications with soft foods, such as strained fruits or potatoes. Place the medication in the minimum amount of food needed.

Avoid mixing medications with milk formula or any essential item in the child's diet. The child may refuse foods he associates with medication.

Tell a child that an injection will hurt but that he can cry if he wishes. Telling a child a lie destroys confidence in the nurse.

Proceed in giving an injection without delay. Allowing a child to stall for time will not decrease his discomfort and may heighten his anxiety.

Place a sticking plaster over the injection site and praise the child for his endurance of the discomfort.

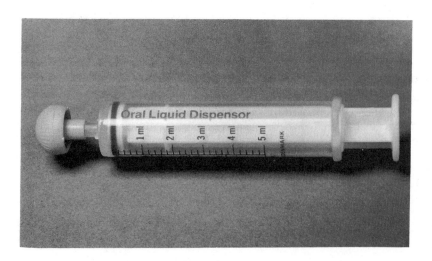

Figure 18-40 An oral liquid dispenser, calibrated for accurate measurement. The dispenser is placed beyond the sensitive taste buds on the tongue so that the youngster is less likely to resist taking the medication because of its taste.

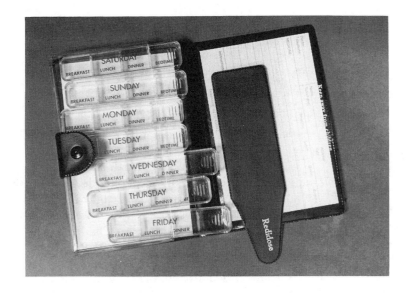

Figure 18-41 This is one type of pill organizer that many patients find helpful. The manufacturer points out that the organizer is easy to use and fill. (Courtesy Royal Marsden Hospital/The Redidose Company, Shoreham by Sea, West Sussex)

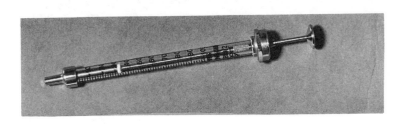

Figure 18-42 A re-usable hypodermic syringe for insulin injection for use by the blind and visually impaired. (Courtesy Royal Marsden Hospital/Rand Rocket Ltd, Consett, Co. Durham)

When the patient has a physical handicap

Help visually impaired or blind persons organize and identify containers so that medications are taken accurately. There are pill organizers on the market with individual compartments for tablets and capsules. One is illustrated in Figure 18-41. Other techniques include identifying bottles in some way such as with rubber bands or a cotton ball taped to the bottle, using a characteristic cap, and placing each medication container in a special place and always returning it to the same place.

Suggest that the visually impaired or blind person obtain a preset syringe as shown in Figure 18-42, for administering insulin.

Write instructions for self-administration for the hearing impaired individual. Provide directions to a family member or friend also.

Have the patient request that the pharmacist give him a medication container cap that is not child-proof if he has difficulty removing these types of caps. This advice is not recommended if there are children in the home. In such instances, a family member must help the patient to open the container.

When the patient is elderly

Take into consideration the elderly person's medical history when planning his care. Many elderly patients see several doctors who each prescribe medications. Patients may be taking nonprescription medications as well. The combination of drugs, with their potential side-effects, may lead to serious complications.

Monitor the elderly person's medication carefully while taking into account the effects of ageing. As a result of ageing, the risk of adverse side effects and toxicity to drugs increases. Decreased gastrointestinal motility and ability to absorb drugs tend to reduce the drug action because the drugs are not being taken into the bloodstream well.

Use a pill organizer, as described earlier in this section, when the elderly patient needs help in remembering to take medications as prescribed. Expect that a safe dosage for medications prescribed for the elderly will generally be lower than that for younger adults.

Teaching suggestions for the administration of medications

Suggestions for teaching patients when giving medications have been described in this chapter. They are summarized below:

It is recommended that in addition to observing a demonstration, the patient or family member should practise in the presence of the nurse until skill for safe administration is achieved.

The patient should be taught the name of the drug, what it is for, how much to take, how long and how often he is to take the medication, what the desired and undesired effects are and what alterations he must make in daily living, such as a dietary modification.

The nurse should teach the patient to notify his doctor promptly if undesirable symptoms occur. He should also be taught not to discontinue or make any changes in his medication schedule without consulting his doctor.

When a patient is to take liquid medications and

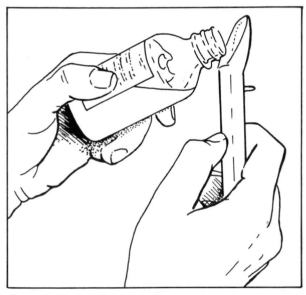

Figure 18-43 This dosing spoon has a hollow stem that is calibrated so that the prescribed amount of liquid medication can be measured accurately. When the spoon is tipped, the liquid fills the bowl of the spoon for easy administration.

the dosage is stated in teaspoons or tablespoons, he may be advised to purchase a dispenser to measure dosages accurately. The dispenser may be a special syringe, a dosing spoon like the one illustrated in Figure 18-43, or a calibrated medicine cup. It has been found that the sizes of household teaspoons and tablespoons vary considerably, with the result that the patient may not take prescribed dosages accurately when using them.

Disposable equipment is recommended whenever possible so that sterilizing and caring for needles and syringes are not necessary. The patient will need to be taught how to dispose of this equipment carefully to prevent its use by others.

It is recommended that patients taking medications over a long period of time be encouraged to carry a card or wear a bracelet that indicates special medical information. This practice helps in an emergency because health personnel are aware of what the patient is taking and can plan care accordingly. The same advice applies to individuals with allergies to medications or other substances.

Occasional treatment of minor problems with over-the-counter drugs is a common practice. However, repetitious or long-term self-administration of these drugs can be dangerous. It is recommended that the following advice is given and discussed with patients.

Don't be casual about taking drugs.
Don't take drugs you don't need.
Don't overbuy and keep drugs for long periods of time.
Don't combine drugs carelessly.
Do be cautious when using a drug for the first time.
Do dispose of old prescription drugs and outdated medications.
Don't continue taking drugs if symptoms persist.
Don't take prescription drugs not prescribed specifically for you.
Do read and follow directions for use.
Do seek professional advice before combining drugs.
Do seek professional advice when symptoms persist or return.
Do get medical check-ups regularly.

The nurse should plan to teach family members

when the patient is an infant or child or when the patient is elderly and cannot assume responsibility for taking his own medications. Parents should be taught of the dangers that are present when children are able to take medications that are not stored safely.

Problems with noncompliance often can be overcome when the patient helps prepare a plan for self-administration and when he is taught adequately about his medications and the reasons for taking them.

References

Central Health Services Councils (1958) *Report of the Joint Sub-Committee on the Control of Dangerous Drugs and Poisons in Hospitals* (Chairman J.K. Aitken). HMSO, London.

Cobb, M.D. (1986) Evaluating medication errors. *Journal of Nursing Administration*, **16**(4), 41–4.

Field, P.A. (1981) A phenomenological look at giving an injection. *Journal of Advanced Nursing*, **6**(4), 291–6.

Kruszewski, A.Z., Lang, S.H. and Johnson, J.E. (1979) Effect of positioning on discomfort from intramuscular injections in the dorsogluteal site. *Nursing Research*, **28**(2), 103–5.

Lenz, C.L. (1983) Make your needle selection right to the point. *Nursing (US)*, **13**(2), 50–1.

McConnell, E.A. (1982) The subtle art of really good injections. *Research Nurse*, **45**(2), 25–34.

McNeilly, J.L. (1987) Medication errors: a quality assurance tool. *Nursing Management*, **18**(12), 53–8.

Newton, D.W. and Newton, M. (1979) Route site and technique, three key decisions in giving parenteral injections. *Nursing (US)*, **9**(7), 18–25.

Pritchard, A.P. and David, J.A. (eds) (1988) *The Royal Marsden Hospital Manual of Clinical Nursing Procedures*, 2nd edn, Harper and Row, London.

Royal College of Nursing—Department of Nursing Policy and Practice (1987) *Drug Administration—A Nursing Responsibility*, Royal College of Nursing, London.

UKCC (1986) *Administration of Medicines—A framework to assist individual professional judgement and development of local policies and guidelines*, UK Central Council for Nursing, Midwifery and Health Visiting, London.

Further reading

Birsell, G. and Uretsky, S. (1984) How do I administer medication by NG? *American Journal of Nursing*, **84**, 1259–60, 1284.

Chaplin, G., Shull, H. and Welk, P. (1985) How safe is the air-bubble technique for IM injections? *Nursing*, **85**(15), 559.

Shepherd, M.J. and Swearingen, P.L. (1984) Z-track injections. *American Journal of Nursing*, **84**, 746–7.

19

The needs of the individual undergoing examinations and special tests

Learning objectives

When the content of this chapter has been mastered, the learner should be able to:

Define terms appearing in the glossary.

Describe the types of responsibilities a nurse assumes when assisting with patient examinations.

List common types of instruments, equipment and supplies that are used during a physical examination.

Describe suggested nursing actions when assisting with an examination.

Interpret the word endings that pertain to tests and examinations.

Describe common examination procedures and give some indications for their use.

List suggested measures for assisting with examinations in selected situations, as described in this chapter.

Summarize suggestions for instruction of patients offered in this chapter.

Glossary

Allergy An unfavourable reaction of the body to a substance to which the body is sensitive.

Angiography X-ray examination of blood vessels.

Biopsy The removal of a small specimen of tissue from the body for microscopic examination.

Bronchoscopy An examination that uses a bronchoscope to inspect the trachea and bronchi.

Cannula A hollow tube through which air or fluids may flow.

Cholecystography X-ray examination of the gall bladder and its ducts.

Computerized axial tomography An examination that uses narrow x-ray beams to view horizontal sections of a body part from various angles. Abbreviated CAT or CT.

Contrast medium A substance that makes hollow structures of the body more dense and, therefore, more distinct on an x-ray.

Cystoscopy An examination that uses a cystoscope to inspect the bladder and urethra.

Dorsal recumbent position The position in which a patient is on his back with his legs separated, the soles of his feet flat on the bed, and his knees bent.

Draping Covering a body part in such a manner that

it does not interfere with access to an area being examined.

Echography An examination that produces images of structures through the use of ultrasound. Synonym for *ultrasonography*.

Electrocardiography An examination that produces an image of the electrical impulses produced by the contracting heart muscle. Abbreviated EKG or ECG.

Electrode A wire that connects the body, usually through contact with the skin, to a machine that records electrical impulses.

Electroencephalography An examination that records electrical impulses in the brain. Abbreviated EEG.

Electromyography An examination that records the electrical impulses produced by contracting skeletal muscle. Abbreviated EMG.

Endoscope An instrument used to view an internal part of the body.

Endoscopy An examination of a body part with an endoscope.

Erect position The normal standing position.

Fluoroscopy The study of body organs in motion with a fluoroscope. A fluoroscope uses roentgen rays to perform the examination.

Gastric analysis An examination of stomach secretions.

Genupectoral position The position in which a patient rests on his knees and chest. Synonym for *knee-chest position*.

Graft Living tissue that is relocated and substitutes for diseased tissue.

Head mirror A mirror worn on an examiner's head to direct light into an area.

Horizontal recumbent position The position in which a patient lies flat on his back with his legs together.

Intravenous pyelography X-ray examination of the urinary tract following the introduction of a dye into a vein. Abbreviated IVP.

Invasive procedure An examination, test, or treatment in which the skin or parts of the body are entered.

Knee-chest position The position in which a patient rests on his knees and chest. Synonym for *genupectoral position*.

Lithotomy position A position that is similar to the dorsal recumbent position except that the feet are supported in stirrups.

Lumbar puncture A procedure for collecting cerebrospinal fluid by inserting a needle beneath the arachnoid layer of the meninges between the third and fourth or fourth and fifth lumbar vertebrae. Synonym for *spinal tap*.

Mammography X-ray examination of breast tissue.

Myelography X-ray examination of the spinal canal following the introduction of a dye into the subarachnoid space.

Ophthalmoscope An instrument used for examining the inside of the eye.

Pap test An examination of secretions from the female genital tract to determine whether cancer cells are present. Pap is from Papanicolaou, the name of the doctor who devised the test.

Paracentesis The withdrawal of fluid from the abdominal cavity.

Proctoscopy An examination that uses a proctoscope to inspect the rectum.

Radiation Energy that cannot be seen or felt.

Radionuclide A substance with an altered atomic structure that releases one or more types of radiation. Replaces the term radioisotope.

Radiopharmaceutical A radionuclide that has been prepared for administration to humans.

Retrograde pyelography X-ray examination of the ureters and kidneys following the introduction of dye directly into the ureters.

Roentgen rays Electromagnetic energy that passes through structures, producing an image on special film. Synonym for *x-rays*.

Roentgenogram The actual film image produced through roentgenography. Synonym for an *x-ray*.

Roentgenography A general term for all procedures that use x-rays to produce images of body structures.

Sigmoidoscopy An examination that uses a sigmoidoscope to inspect the lower colon.

Sims position, right or left The position in which a patient lies on one or the other side of the body with the upper knee more bent than the other.

Specimen A sample of tissue, body fluid, secretions or excretions.

Speculum An instrument used for opening a cavity so that it can be examined.

Spinal tap A procedure for collecting cerebrospinal fluid by inserting a needle beneath the arachnoid layer of the meninges between the third and fourth or fourth and fifth lumbar vertebrae. Synonym for *lumbar puncture*.

Stirrups Foot supports used when the patient is in the lithotomy position.

Suture Material used to stitch an incision closed.

Thoracentesis The withdrawal of fluid from the pleural cavity.

Tilt table A device that elevates or lowers the patient's body as he lies on it.

Tonometer An instrument used to measure pressure within the eye.

Transducer An instrument that picks up echoing sound waves.

Trocar An instrument used to pierce the skin and underlying tissue.

Tuning fork An instrument used to examine the patient's ability to hear or feel sensations.

Ultrasonography An examination that produces images of structures through the use of ultrasound. Synonym for *echography*.

Ultrasound Very high frequency, inaudible sound waves.

X-ray The actual film image produced through roentgenography. Synonym for *roentgenogram*.

X-rays Electromagnetic energy that passes through structures producing an image on special film. Synonym for *roentgen rays*.

Introduction

Many health personnel carry out examinations and special tests that are performed to obtain information about the patient. These are done to study how a patient's body is functioning and to locate disease processes. The nurse is often required to provide assistance by teaching and preparing the patient, supporting the patient physically and emotionally during an examination, assisting other health practitioners during an examination or test and caring for the patient and equipment afterwards. This chapter gives a general overview of the nursing responsibilities when the nurse is not the primary examiner.

Descriptions of many common diagnostic tests are also discussed. Most of the tests described are not done routinely. They are performed only when the patient has a suspected health problem. However, a few, such as electrocardiography, may be used during routine, preventive examinations on well people who are at potential risk for a certain disease condition.

An understanding of what is done during common procedures is important for the nurse to know. That information, and the reasons for which tests are usually performed, are necessary knowledge.

The nurse is responsible for carrying out test re-quirements. Policy and procedure manuals prepared by each hospital are available to the nurse. They describe the protocols that apply to individual tests. The usual preparation and aftercare of patients can be found in clinical or laboratory texts, which include nursing implications. Excellent examples are listed in this chapter's further reading list. These types of references are a valuable investment as a personal resource.

Nursing responsibilities when special procedures are performed

The responsibilities of the nurse who assists with examinations and tests fall into several broad categories.

Understanding the patient, his illness, and his plan of care

Certain information is basic to understanding the measures that are being used to restore an individual's health. Answers to questions such as the following will help a nurse apply general knowledge to the specifics of the individual:

- What is the patient's diagnosis?
- What is the probable cause of the patient's illness?
- How is the patient's illness interfering with normal body functions?
- How is the patient feeling physically and emotionally?
- How well is the patient responding to his present treatment?
- How does the examination or test to be carried out fit into the plan for care?
- What does the patient know about his illness, tests and treatment?
- What teaching possibilities exist?

Understanding the procedure

To appropriately assist with an examination or test, the nurse must understand the nature of the procedure. Answers to questions such as the following will help provide the necessary information.

- What is the procedure and how is it defined?
- What are the purposes, or indications, for which the procedure is commonly used?
- What part of the body will be entered?
- Does the procedure require clean or sterile equipment?

- How shall the patient be positioned so that the procedure may be carried out efficiently and safely and with comfort for the patient?
- Will a specimen be obtained?
- What signs and symptoms will the patient be expected to experience?
- What measures can be used to prevent complications?
- What signs and symptoms indicate that the patient is not responding well to the procedure?
- What actions may be necessary if the patient develops complications?
- Where is emergency equipment kept?

Instructing the patient

Ordinarily, the doctor is responsible for explaining any *invasive procedure*, that is, one in which the skin or parts of the body are entered. These types of tests or examinations are often associated with potential health risks. The patient's signature on a special consent form is usually required. Informed consent was discussed in Chapter 7. The doctor must provide information to the patient on which he can decide to allow or refuse a procedure. It is recommended that each hospital's policies be observed concerning a consent, but examples of procedures requiring one include thoracentesis, paracentesis and computerized axial tomography. These are all discussed later in the chapter.

Though the nurse does not hold the primary responsibility for providing information about tests and examinations, it often happens that the nurse must re-explain or repeat explanations. An anxious patient may not grasp all the information the first time it is explained. There may be questions that come after the doctor has left. The nurse should be sure that the patient understands the information. A thorough explanation will not eliminate all the stress a patient experiences, but it will reduce it. Stress can contribute to discomfort during an examination and may alter certain results.

No exact rules can be stated as to the best way to provide explanations to a patient. In general, the nurse is guided by the patient's questions, the requirements for the examination, the patient's condition, and each individual set of circumstances. Following the suggestions for teaching the patient and for providing emotional support, as discussed in Chapter 4, should lay a solid foundation for meeting the patient's needs.

Carrying out test requirements

Many examinations and tests require special preparation of the patient in order to obtain accurate results. For example, some tests or examinations require that food or fluids be withheld, that the diet be modified, or that laxatives be administered before a test. The requirements for certain tests are usually located in a reference manual on each ward. The nurse should refer to these written instructions each time a patient is undergoing a test rather than rely on memory. Special test preparations vary among hospitals. Nurses should follow the common practices of each place.

After reviewing the special requirements, the nurse must provide directions to the patient, nursing staff and other hospital departments affected by the test. All must cooperate so that the test can be carried out properly. If the nurse discovers that the preparations have not been carried out, it should be reported promptly. It may be necessary to cancel and reschedule the procedure in such instances.

Preparing equipment and supplies

The doctor may wish to examine the patient from time to time. The nurse should have equipment and supplies ready for an examination. Items likely to be used are checked first to see that they are clean and in good working order. Most hospitals have a tray or trolley for equipment ordinarily used during an examination. Although there are differences among hospitals, items usually kept in readiness for a physical examination are described in Table 19-1. Additional instruments may be used for a more extensive examination.

When special diagnostic examinations and tests are performed on the ward, the nurse is usually responsible for obtaining certain supplies and preparing test equipment prior to the procedure. The equipment and supplies will depend on the procedure and will vary among hospitals. Some hospitals have prepackaged trays with most, if not all of the necessary items in readiness; other hospitals may require that the nurse gather all of the items. While assembling and preparing materials, the nurse must maintain the cleanliness or sterility of the equipment. Practices that help to control microorganisms are discussed in Chapter 20.

Nurses giving patients daily care are not responsible for the equipment and supplies when an examination or test is carried out in another location, such as the x-ray department, the operating room or a

Table 19-1. Common equipment and supplies required to examine a patient

Item	Description
Ophthalmoscope	An ophthalmoscope is an instrument used for examining the interior of the eye.
Otoscope	An otoscope is an instrument used for observing the eardrum and external ear canal.
Speculum	A speculum is an instrument used for opening a cavity so that it may be more easily examined. Nose and vaginal specula are those most commonly used.
Tonometer	A tonometer is an instrument used to measure the pressure within the eyeball. A mild anaesthetic solution applied directly to the surface of the eye is used before placing a tonometer onto the eye's surface.
Head mirror	A head mirror is an instrument worn on the examiner's head to direct light into an area, such as into the throat.

The following items may also be used:

Sphygmomanometer	Stethoscope
Torch	Tongue depressors
Tape measure	Tuning forks
Skin pencil	Tissues and waste container
Sterile or clean gloves	Lubricant
Paper towels	Waste container for soiled instruments
Percussion hammer	Patient's gown
Material for draping	Lightweight blanket
Disposable pad	Pins, cotton, test tubes for hot and cold water, and various materials having different odours are included if a neurological examination is to be done.
Containers and slides for specimens, as indicated	

cardiac laboratory. Nor are nurses responsible for equipment or supplies when a special technician performs the procedure.

Preparing the working area

If the procedure is to be performed at the patient's bedside, the nurse will want to clear the area of unnecessary articles and provide privacy. Many wards contain an examination room that is clean, well-lighted, and stocked with frequently used equipment. If the patient is transported to such an area, the nurse will wish to explain that the reason is for the patient's comfort and convenience.

Any equipment and supplies that are needed should be arranged for easy access by the examiner. The functioning of instruments that require electric power, batteries or lights should be checked prior to their use. This provides time to replace any non-functioning equipment or parts before the examination has begun.

Cleanliness or sterility of equipment should be

maintained. The examination table should be covered with clean material, such as sheets or paper dispensed from a roll.

Preparing the patient

Before an examination is performed, the nurse should check the patient's identity bracelet to establish that the right patient is being examined, and check one more time that the consent form is signed, if it is required. Double-checking that test requirements have been fulfilled further prevents delays.

Just prior to the procedure, the nurse should provide the patient with the opportunity to care for his personal hygiene. Being clean promotes the patient's self-esteem and self-confidence in an unfamiliar situation.

In addition to the patient's hygiene measures, the nurse should observe the skin or site that will be examined. It may be necessary to cleanse it more thoroughly than just simple washing. The area may even require shaving; this applies particularly to procedures that require entry through the skin. The skin always contains microbes, some of which can cause disease if transferred to other tissues that the skin ordinarily protects. Antiseptics may also be used to reduce the numbers of organisms prior to entry through the skin.

The patient should be encouraged to use the bathroom or bedpan before the examination. While maintaining the privacy for elimination, the patient should be provided with a gown or other examination garments. These allow easy access to the various body areas, protect the patient from exposure and avoid soiling personal clothing. Extra covers should be available if chilling occurs.

Positioning and draping a patient

The nurse is responsible for helping a patient to assume various positions and for draping a patient properly while he is examined. *Draping* is a term that refers to covering a body part in such a manner that it does not interfere with access to the area being examined. Draping avoids exposing the patient unnecessarily. Only those parts of the body being examined are exposed. Some hospitals use disposable paper drapes. A bath blanket, drawsheet or a bed sheet may also be used.

When the nurse places the patient in certain positions, it facilitates the examination of specific body parts. With practice, and knowing which area will be examined, the nurse can develop competence in positioning patients in an appropriate manner for any test or examination. Table 19-2 provides the names of common positions, describes the position and identifies areas of the body that are usually examined in each position.

Assisting with an examination

During an examination the nurse has responsibilities both to the patient and to the examiner. The doctor, or technician, may need help with handling equipment, directing lighting and caring for specimens.

Specimens are samples of tissue, body fluids, secretions, or excretions. They may be sent to the laboratory following an examination. Each hospital has its own policies concerning items such as the type of container for the specimen, how the specimen is to be preserved, how the specimen is to be labelled, etc. The nurse will wish to follow these policies so that test results of the specimen are not inaccurate or delayed. Laboratory test results become a part of the patient's record. Figure 19-1 illustrates several examples of laboratory reports on specimens. The care of specimens, such as urine, stool and sputum, that the nurse collects are discussed later in this text.

The examiner may exchange certain pieces of equipment with the nurse. The nurse may also be required to hold drugs and injectable anaesthetics. The nurse must check these labels carefully as described in Chapter 18. In addition, the container should be held in such a manner that the examiner can also read the label. These practices help to avoid errors and misunderstandings.

In relation to patient responsibilities, the nurse should always be aware of the patient's reactions during the examination. For example, the patient may be cold, perspiring, in pain, and so on. The nurse may need to provide comfort measures and emotional support for the patient. Holding the patient's hand and offering words of encouragement may help the patient to withstand temporary discomfort. Assessments made by the nurse of the patient's physical condition may alert the doctor to shorten or modify the examination in some manner.

Principles of Care 19-1 is a summary of the nurse's responsibilities when assisting the patient during an examination. For information about the responsibilities for preparing the patient and the aftercare associated with specific examinations, clinical texts that discuss the medical or surgical care of patients should be consulted.

Recording and reporting data

The hospital policies indicate what information to record and where it is recorded. Usually, the following items are included: the type of examination, the time the examination was done, the name of the examiner, a description of what took place including any observations related to the patient's general condition. The person who performed the examination usually summarizes the findings on a different form than that used by the nurse.

If specimens were obtained, the nurse should describe the characteristics and note if they were sent for laboratory testing. The nature and amount of any drainage may also be described. Or, the nurse may wish to use general descriptive words that explain what was observed.

In addition to the written account of the examination, the nurse should report significant information to other nursing team members. This may include that the examination has been completed, the patient's reactions during and immediately after the pro-

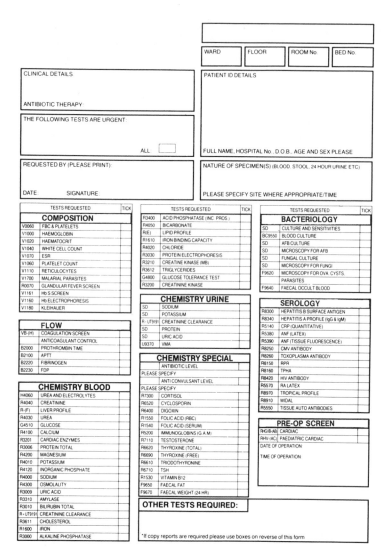

WARD	FLOOR	ROOM No.	BED No.

CLINICAL DETAILS:

ANTIBIOTIC THERAPY:

THE FOLLOWING TESTS ARE URGENT:

ALL:

REQUESTED BY (PLEASE PRINT):

DATE: SIGNATURE:

PATIENT ID DETAILS

FULL NAME, HOSPITAL No., D.O.B., AGE AND SEX PLEASE

NATURE OF SPECIMEN(S) (BLOOD, STOOL, 24 HOUR URINE ETC):

PLEASE SPECIFY SITE WHERE APPROPRIATE/TIME

	TESTS REQUESTED	TICK
	COMPOSITION	
V0060	FBC & PLATELETS	
V1000	HAEMOGLOBIN	
V1020	HAEMATOCRIT	
V1040	WHITE CELL COUNT	
V1070	ESR	
V1060	PLATELET COUNT	
V1110	RETICULOCYTES	
V1700	MALARIAL PARASITES	
R0070	GLANDULAR FEVER SCREEN	
V1161	Hb S SCREEN	
V1160	Hb ELECTROPHORESIS	
V1180	KLEIHAUER	

	FLOW	
VB-(H)	COAGULATION SCREEN	
	ANTICOAGULANT CONTROL	
B2000	PROTHROMBIN TIME	
B2100	APTT	
B2220	FIBRINOGEN	
B2230	FDP	

	CHEMISTRY BLOOD	
H4060	UREA AND ELECTROLYTES	
R4040	CREATININE	
R-(F)	LIVER PROFILE	
R4030	UREA	
G4510	GLUCOSE	
R4100	CALCIUM	
R3201	CARDIAC ENZYMES	
R3006	PROTEIN TOTAL	
R4200	MAGNESIUM	
R4010	POTASSIUM	
R4120	INORGANIC PHOSPHATE	
R4000	SODIUM	
R4300	OSMOLALITY	
R3009	URIC ACID	
R3310	AMYLASE	
R3010	BILIRUBIN TOTAL	
R-UT919	CREATININE CLEARANCE	
R3611	CHOLESTEROL	
R1600	IRON	
R3000	ALKALINE PHOSPHATASE	

	TESTS REQUESTED	TICK
R3400	ACID PHOSPHATASE (INC. PROS.)	
R4050	BICARBONATE	
R(E)	LIPID PROFILE	
R1610	IRON BINDING CAPACITY	
R4020	CHLORIDE	
R3030	PROTEIN ELECTROPHORESIS	
R3210	CREATINE KINASE (MB)	
R3612	TRIGLYCERIDES	
G4800	GLUCOSE TOLERANCE TEST	
R3200	CREATININE KINASE	

	CHEMISTRY URINE	
SD	SODIUM	
SD	POTASSIUM	
R-UT919	CREATININE CLEARANCE	
SD	PROTEIN	
SD	URIC ACID	
U9370	VMA	

	CHEMISTRY SPECIAL	
	ANTIBIOTIC LEVEL	
PLEASE SPECIFY		
	ANTI CONVULSANT LEVEL	
PLEASE SPECIFY		
R7300	CORTISOL	
R6520	CYCLOSPORIN	
R6400	DIGOXIN	
R1550	FOLIC ACID (RBC)	
R1540	FOLIC ACID (SERUM)	
R5200	IMMUNOGLOBINS (G.A.M)	
R7110	TESTOSTERONE	
R6620	THYROXINE (TOTAL)	
R6690	THYROXINE (FREE)	
R6610	TRIODOTHYRONINE	
R6710	TSH	
R1530	VITAMIN B12	
F9650	FAECAL FAT	
F9670	FAECAL WEIGHT (24 HR)	

OTHER TESTS REQUIRED:

*If copy reports are required please use boxes on reverse of this form

	TESTS REQUESTED	TICK
	BACTERIOLOGY	
SD	CULTURE AND SENSITIVITIES	
BC9550	BLOOD CULTURE	
SD	AFB CULTURE	
SD	MICROSCOPY FOR AFB	
SD	FUNGAL CULTURE	
SD	MICROSCOPY FOR FUNGI	
F9620	MICROSCOPY FOR OVA. CYSTS.	
	PARASITES	
F9640	FAECAL OCCULT BLOOD	

	SEROLOGY	
R8300	HEPATITIS B SURFACE ANTIGEN	
R8340	HEPATITIS A PROFILE (IgG & IgM)	
R5140	CRP (QUANTITATIVE)	
R5380	ANF (LATEX)	
R5390	ANF (TISSUE FLUORESCENCE)	
R8250	CMV ANTIBODY	
R8260	TOXOPLASMA ANTIBODY	
R8150	RPR	
R8160	TPHA	
R8420	HIV ANTIBODY	
R5570	RA LATEX	
R8970	TROPICAL PROFILE	
R8910	WIDAL	
R5550	TISSUE AUTO ANTIBODIES	

	PRE-OP SCREEN	
RHGVB(AB)	CARDIAC	
RHV-(AC)	PAEDIATRIC CARDIAC	
DATE OF OPERATION		
TIME OF OPERATION		

Figure 19-1 This is an example of a form used for laboratory reports. Each specimen has its own colour-coded section on which laboratory findings are entered. Copies are made easily, and one is sent to the nursing unit, where it is attached to the patient's record.

cedure, and any delayed reactions. When all the nursing team is kept aware of current events and changes in the patient's condition, the plan of care can be revised and kept up-to-date.

Caring for equipment and supplies

Local policy indicates the responsibilities of the assisting nurse in relation to caring for used equipment and supplies. Everything that was used must be returned or replaced. Soiled, nondisposable equipment should be delivered to an area for cleaning, disinfection or sterilization. Supplies for discard are placed in the proper receptacle to prevent the spread of disease-causing organisms. In some hospitals, part or all of these responsibilities may be delegated to non-nursing personnel.

Advancements in examinations and tests

Technology now allows examination of internal areas of the body without major surgery. There are machines that can record electrical impulses, the deflection of sound waves and the energy released from the circulation of radioactive substances. New tests on blood and other body fluids are constantly being developed. All these advances in testing and examinations have improved the ability to detect disease processes early. The remaining part of this chapter provides information about specific examinations and tests. The outcomes and values and the significance of abnormal results can be found in texts that discuss laboratory tests.

Table 19-2. Common positions for examinations and tests

Description	Indications for Use

Erect Position

The *erect position* is a normal standing position. The arms are held in a relaxed position at the sides of the body. The feet are 6 to 8 inches apart. The face should look straight ahead. The patient should wear a gown that opens in the back. Slippers may be worn.

This position is used to examine body contours, posture, balance, muscles and extremities. When the patient walks, gait and muscle coordination can be observed.

Sitting Position

The buttocks are firmly on the edge of the bed or at the foot of the examination table. The thighs are well supported. The knees should be bent and the feet should be positioned flat against the floor or a foot rest. A gown or paper vest may be used to cover the upper body; a bath blanket or paper sheet covers the waist and legs. This position is shown in Figure 19-2.

This position allows auscultation of the anterior, lateral and posterior areas of the lungs. It facilitates inspection and palpation of the thyroid, breasts and axillary areas. The reflexes in the elbows, wrists, knees and ankles are easily examined in this position. Having the patient sitting helps prevent back strain for the examiner while assessing the head and its related structures, such as the eyes, ears, nose and throat.

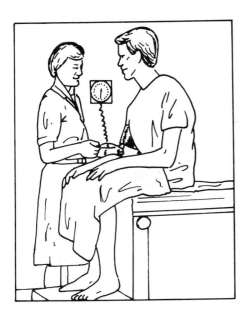

Figure 19-2 The nurse has instructed the patient to take this sitting position prior to his physical examination. The nurse has provided him with an examination gown and a drape. While waiting for the examiner, the nurse obtains the patient's vital signs.

Horizontal Recumbent Position

The *horizontal recumbent position* is one in which the patient lies flat on his back. The head is supported with a small pillow. The legs are together with the knees bent slightly to help relax the muscles in the abdomen. The patient is covered with a sheet and wears a gown. Areas of the sheet may be folded back when a body part is examined.

This position may be used to examine the anterior parts of the body if the patient is too weak or uncomfortable in a sitting position. It is most commonly used to examine the heart, chest and abdomen.

Dorsal Recumbent Position

The *dorsal recumbent position* is one in which a patient is on his back lying close to the edge, or centre, of the

The dorsal recumbent position is used most often to examine the rectum and vagina.

Continued

Table 19-2. *Continued*

Description	Indications for Use

Dorsal Recumbent Position *Continued*

bed or examination table. One pillow may be placed under the head. The legs are separated and the knees bent. The feet are flat against the surface on which the patient is lying. Figure 19-3 illustrates a dorsal recumbent position. A bath blanket is used to drape the patient. It is folded in such a way that the legs are covered, but a corner may be raised to expose the area between the legs as shown in Figure 19-4. A disposable pad may be placed under the patient's buttocks to avoid soiling bed linen.

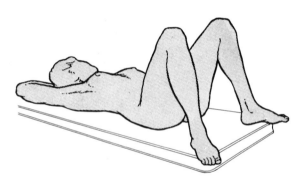

Figure 19-3 The dorsal recumbent position.

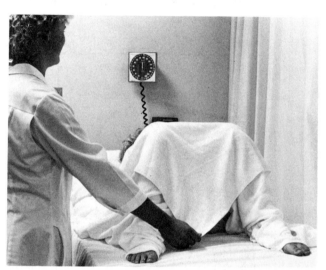

Figure 19-4 A bath blanket is used to drape a patient in a dorsal recumbent position. A corner of the rectangular drape is positioned at the head and between the feet, allowing the legs to be wrapped. When a procedure is about to be performed, the area covering the genitals is raised and placed over the abdomen.

Lithotomy Position

The *lithotomy position* is similar to the dorsal recumbent position except that the feet are supported in stirrups. *Stirrups* are foot supports. In this position the patient's buttocks are brought to the edge of the end of the table. The draping is the same as for the dorsal recumbent position. An illustration of the lithotomy position can be seen in Figure 19-5.

The lithotomy position is used to examine the vagina with a speculum. It is also used when the internal female reproductive organs are palpated. Specimens from the cervix or vagina may be obtained in this position. It is also a position in which the rectum may be examined. Males or females undergoing inspection of the bladder with a cystoscope may be placed in a lithotomy position.

Table 19-2. *Continued*

Description	Indications for Use

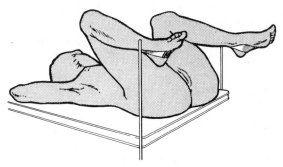

Figure 19-5 The lithotomy position.

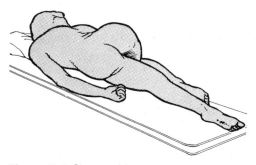

Figure 19-6 Sims position.

Sims Position

Sims position is a side-lying position. In the left Sims position, the patient lies on his left side and rests his left arm behind his body. The right arm is forward with the elbow bent, and the arm rests on a pillow placed under the patient's head. The patient's body is slightly forward. The right knee is sharply bent; the left one is slightly bent. A left Sims position is shown in Figure 19-6. A right Sims position is the reverse of left Sims. A disposable pad may be used under the buttocks. A bath blanket or paper sheet may be lifted at the hip to expose the area being examined.

The Sims position is used to examine the external anus or examine the rectum internally with a lubricated, gloved finger. It is often a position used for certain nursing procedures such as administering an enema or inserting a rectal tube. These are discussed in Chapter 12. This position may be used in lieu of the lithotomy position when examining the vagina of a woman who has difficulty bending the knees or hips, as may be the case with arthritis.

Knee-Chest or Genupectoral Position

The *knee-chest or genupectoral* position is one in which the patient rests on his knees and chest as illustrated in Figure 19-7. The head is turned to one side and may rest on a small pillow. A pillow may also be placed under the chest for added comfort. The arms are above the head, or they may be bent at the elbows and rest alongside the patient's head. The drape is placed so that the patient's back, buttocks and thighs are covered. Only the area to be examined is exposed. It is a very difficult position for most patients, especially the elderly. Therefore, the nurse should not assist the patient into this position until the examiner is ready to begin. There are now examination tables with sectional parts that may facilitate maintaining this position without much patient effort.

This position is used when the internal condition of the bowel is examined with various endoscopes.

Figure 19-7 The knee-chest or genupectoral position.

Principles of Care 19-1. Assisting with an examination

Nursing Action	Rationale
Check to see that any required consent form has been signed and dated by the patient and a witness to the signature.	Lawsuits are possible when examinations, tests, and treatments are performed without the patient's informed consent.
Determine that all test requirements have been accomplished.	Incomplete or inadequate preparation for a test may result in its cancellation and need for rescheduling.
Inform the patient that the examination will occur shortly.	The patient may use the opportunity to complete personal hygiene, use the toilet or bedpan, and change to a clean examination gown.
Inquire if the patient has any questions about the examination.	Providing information can reduce anxiety.
Inspect the examination room. Determine if it is clean and contains the supplies and equipment that will be needed.	Ensuring the readiness of the work area and examination equipment prevents delays and inconvenience for the patient and the examiner.
Check the function of instruments. Arrange items that are likely to be used for the examination.	Nonfunctioning equipment can cause frustration and prolong the examination time as replacements are located.
Note that there is a supply of clean gowns, drapes and protective pads.	It is just as important to have supplies available for the patient's use as they are for the doctor's use.
Complete any last minute test requirements, such as cleansing or shaving the examination site.	Some measures are performed just prior to the examination.
Assist the patient in whatever manner is needed.	The patient may need help with completing his hygiene, tying the gown or donning a robe and slippers.
If the patient's room is used for the examination, clear articles from the working area.	Clutter can result in disorganization and possible breakage of examination equipment and contamination.
Provide privacy around the bed or transport the patient to a private examination room.	The nurse must protect the patient from being observed and overheard during the examination.
Help the patient onto the examination table.	An examination table is generally higher than an average bed. The patient may need a step stool or a steady hand.
Assist the patient into a position that will facilitate the examination.	Various positions, previously discussed, allow the examiner access to the body part that will be examined.
Drape the patient and provide extra covers if he is chilled.	Examination gowns are lightweight. Though they cover the patient and allow access to the body, they do not provide much warmth.
Talk with the patient. Provide explanations for the actions that will take place.	Good communication techniques can help put the patient at ease.
Do not leave the patient alone.	Falls from an examination table can cause serious injury.
Introduce the patient to the doctor if they are unfamiliar with one another.	By extending social courtesy, the nurse can reduce the anxiety that comes from unfamiliarity.

Continued

Principles of Care 19-1. *Continued*

Nursing Action	Rationale
Remain throughout the examination. This is especially important if the doctor and the patient are different sexes.	Having a third person present protects the examiner from accusations concerning the manner of sometimes intimate examinations.
Adjust the lighting to the specifications of the examiner.	Examinations requiring inspection are more accurately performed with adequate lighting.
Provide the examiner with instruments, supplies and equipment as they are needed.	The doctor may be using sterile gloves and require the help of the nurse to keep them free of organisms.
Be prepared to receive and label specimens that may be obtained.	Improperly contained specimens and lost or mislabelled forms can delay necessary and vital information about the patient's state of health.
Talk with and support the patient throughout the examination.	Attention and encouragement from the nurse may help the patient endure the experience.
After the procedure is completed, help the patient to a position of comfort.	Some examination positions are difficult to assume and maintain.
Clean the patient of any substances that caused soiling. Assist the patient with a clean gown.	The patient's comfort and hygiene should be restored.
Return the patient to his bed, making sure that the signal is available if he requires further assistance.	The patient may wish to request medication, water, his meal tray, or other comfort and care measures.
Check the patient for signs and symptoms related to the procedure at frequent intervals.	The nurse is accountable for the safety of the patient. Regular, frequent observations may detect desirable and undesirable outcomes.
Record information concerning the examination performed and the condition of the patient.	A record is kept, documenting the care of the patient while in the hospital.
Report significant information about the examination to others responsible for the patient's care.	Sharing information provides current data that contribute to changes in the patient's plan for care.
Restore the examination room to order. Return equipment to its proper location.	Facilities and equipment should always be in readiness for the next use.

Interpreting terms that describe tests

By combining a root word, which refers to a part of the body, with a word ending that has a common meaning, the nurse can interpret the definition of medical terms. Words ending in "ography" are used with many names of tests. This suffix indicates a procedure in which an image is produced. For example, the word *cholecystography* combines the root word referring to the gall bladder, "cholecyst", with the ending "ography", to mean a procedure in which an image of the gall bladder is produced.

The actual image, or results of the test, is described by using a root word followed by the suffix "ogram".

The term *cholecystogram* refers to the image of the gall bladder, which may be held in the hand and examined. The word *electrocardiogram* refers to the visual image or paper strip showing waves produced during electrocardiography.

Words ending with "oscopy" describe examinations in which body structures are visualized by the eye helped with the aid of an instrument. For example, a sigmoidoscopy is an examination in which the sigmoid area of the colon is viewed by a doctor. Some instruments enhance the ability to see structures. They are described using the word ending "scope". Most people are familiar with words like microscope and telescope. A sigmoidoscope is an instrument used to look at the sigmoid section of the colon. The terms otoscope and ophthalmoscope have already been used and defined in this text.

When a procedure involves puncturing a body cavity, the ending "centesis" is attached to a word. A thoracentesis is a puncture of the pleural cavity, which lies in the thorax. Procedures involving this type of action usually are done to collect body fluids, which are examined microscopically by laboratory personnel. Sometimes the word *puncture* or *tap* is used in the name of these same types of procedures. For example, it is common that a nurse may assist with a bone marrow puncture or a spinal tap.

Learning root words for body structures, many of which come from Latin words, is a basic task for nurses. With this foundation and an understanding of the meanings of word endings, the nurse can interpret many technical terms. Only those referring to tests and examinations have been discussed here.

Examinations that use x-rays

Roentgenography is a general term referring to all procedures that use roentgen rays to produce images of body structures. *Roentgen rays* are also known as *x-rays*. They produce electromagnetic energy that passes through body structures leaving an image on special film. X-rays cannot be seen or felt. The actual film image that is produced is called a *roentgenogram*, but it is commonly known as an *x-ray*. *Fluoroscopy* is a technique that combines roentgen rays and a fluoroscope to visualize internal body structures in motion. It is performed at the same time that an x-ray is obtained.

When no other substance is used but the x-rays, it is called a plain film x-ray. X-ray examinations using plain film may be performed on almost any part of the body. For example, the chest, abdomen, teeth, sinuses and bones may be studied. A plain film x-ray may be taken any time because there is no special preparation that is required before the procedure. No special care or observations are necessary following a plain film x-ray.

At times, details in the body cannot be visualized sufficiently through plain film x-ray examinations. Therefore, a contrast medium may be used. A *contrast medium* is a substance that fills a body organ or cavity and makes it appear more dense. This serves to make the shape of the structure more distinct when viewed on x-ray film. X-rays in which a contrast medium is used require special preparation of the patient.

Scheduling these x-rays requires allowing time during which the patient is prepared. The nurse is responsible for the special preparation and aftercare of the patient following tests in which a contrast medium is used.

Some patients have adverse allergic reactions to certain contrast media (plural for medium). An *allergy* is an unfavourable reaction of the body to a substance to which the body is sensitive. The reactions may be mild, causing signs and symptoms, such as nausea and vomiting, a skin rash or itching. Others may have severe reactions that cause a collapse of heart and blood vessel functioning, kidney failure, coma and death. All patients should be asked if they have any allergies. When there is a history of a reaction, this should be clearly indicated on the patient's record and the examiner notified. Even if there is no history of allergies, the patient should be observed for allergic reactions to contrast media. A patient is least likely to be allergic to barium, one type of contrast medium. Allergic reactions to other contrast media substances, particularly those that contain dyes such as iodine, are relatively common.

There is a tendency now to be cautious about the number of x-rays that are taken. The energy that is used for imaging can cause cell changes when there is excessive or accumulated exposure.

Chest x-rays

Description. A chest x-ray is a plain film x-ray that provides an image of the structures within the chest. Back, front and side views are most commonly obtained. This is described as posterior and anterior and lateral views of the chest.

Common indications. Chest x-rays show the condition of the lungs, the ribs, the upper spine and the size of the heart. They are useful, for example, in diagnosing pneumonia, broken ribs and lung tumours.

Kidneys, ureters, and bladder, or abdominal plain film

Description. A plain film of the kidneys, ureters and urinary bladder provides images of these three structures and also other soft tissues of the abdomen.

Common indications. Used to help diagnose abnormalities in structures within the abdomen. Conditions such as enlarged kidneys, distended or narrowed areas of the ureters, an unusually shaped bladder, or obstructions in the intestinal tract can be detected.

Upper gastrointestinal x-ray

Description. An upper gastrointestinal x-ray, sometimes called an upper GI, uses barium as a contrast medium to study the oesophagus, stomach and duodenum. Despite flavourings that are added to the barium, most people find them distasteful. The structures in the upper gastrointestinal tract may be studied in motion with fluoroscopy as the barium is swallowed. X-ray images are also obtained. The patient may return to the x-ray department later to have further x-rays taken of the movement of the barium into the small intestine.

It is important that the patient be instructed that the characteristics of his stool will be assessed. The stool will appear white due to the presence of barium. If the barium is slow to be passed, it can thicken and obstruct the passage of normal stool. Laxatives are given prior to the examination to prevent this from occurring.

Common indications. An upper GI x-ray is done commonly to help diagnose ulcers, tumours or narrowing of the structures in the upper digestive system.

Lower gastrointestinal x-ray or barium enema

Description. A lower gastrointestinal x-ray may also be called a lower GI or a barium enema. This x-ray utilizes both air and barium, instilled as an enema, to enhance images of the lower intestine of the digestive tract. Most patients find this examination tiring and embarrassing. Helping to reassure and support them is important.

To promote the emptying of barium from the lower bowel, laxatives are generally prescribed. Observation of the pattern and characteristics of the patient's bowel elimination is an important nursing responsibility associated with this test.

Common indications. A lower GI is used to examine the position, contour, filling and movement of barium within the colon. It is most often used to help diagnose growths within the bowel, obstructions and other changes in the interior surface of the large intestine.

Cholecystography

Description. *Cholecystography* is an x-ray examination of the gallbladder and its ducts. A dye that serves as a contrast medium is given orally or, on occasion, the dye is introduced into a vein at the time of the examination. The x-ray image is called a cholecystogram.

Patients undergoing cholecystography, and other tests of structures that lie behind the intestine, are required to receive laxatives and enemas in order that stool or gas should not obscure the image that is being examined. It is not uncommon that this x-ray must be repeated. Usually this is necessary when the bowel was not sufficiently cleansed or when there was insufficient concentration of the dye. The patient should always be offered an explanation so that he does not become alarmed and worried.

Common indications. Cholecystography is most often used to determine the presence of stones and obstructions in the gallbladder or its system of ducts.

Intravenous pyelography (IVP)

Description. *Intravenous pyelography*, abbreviated IVP, is an x-ray examination to study the urinary tract. A contrast medium that contains a dye is introduced into a vein during this procedure. The image that is produced is called an intravenous pyelogram.

The patient should be forewarned that the dye is likely to cause him to feel warm and to have a salty taste in his mouth. He may also experience nausea. These symptoms are not forms of an allergic reaction, but rather a common effect when the concentrated dye is instilled directly into the circulatory system.

Common indications. An IVP is commonly used to help diagnose conditions that cause abnormal functioning of the urinary tract. It may help identify malformations, tumours, stones, cysts, and obstructions in the kidneys and ureters.

Retrograde pyelography

Description. *Retrograde pyelography* is an x-ray examination of the urinary tract, similar to an IVP, except that the dye is introduced through small catheters. The catheters are threaded directly into the ureters guided by the view through an instrument called a cystoscope. The procedure using a cystoscope is discussed later in the chapter. The name *retrograde* is used because the dye is instilled in a direction opposite to the normal flow of urine.

Common indications. This test is performed for the same reasons as an IVP. It is generally done when an IVP has not given sufficient results for diagnostic purposes. The IVP is more commonly performed because retrograde pyelography requires that the procedure be carried out in an operating room. A general or local anaesthetic may be used.

Angiography

Description. *Angiography* is an x-ray examination of blood vessels. The blood vessels that supply the heart are those that are frequently examined. A contrast dye is used; it is introduced through a catheter that is inserted into a blood vessel.

Common indications. An angiography is done to determine the location, extent and degree to which blood vessels have narrowed. Narrowing interferes with the amount of blood that can reach cells delivering oxygen and other chemicals. Surgery may be done following an angiography. During surgery a graft is performed. A *graft* is living tissue that is relocated and substitutes for diseased tissue. In one type of surgery, a vein from the leg is removed and reattached so that it provides a bypass for blood around the narrowed blood vessel. The examination helps the surgeon know exactly where the graft must be placed before any incision is made. This test may be performed after surgery to evaluate the improvement that was achieved.

Myelography

Description. *Myelography* is an x-ray examination that uses contrast material to study the spinal canal. Water-soluble or oil-based contrast media may be used. It is instilled during a lumbar puncture that is described later in this chapter. The x-ray image that is obtained is called a myelogram.

The patient should be taught that a tilt table is used during the examination. A *tilt table* is a device that elevates or lowers the patient's body. This helps to move the contrast medium to various levels within the spinal canal.

Common indications. Myelography is commonly used to detect spinal tumours, ruptured discs and bony changes in the vertebrae.

Computerized axial tomography (CAT or CT)

Description. *Computerized axial tomography*, abbreviated CAT or CT, is a type of x-ray examination that views horizontal sections of the body from various angles. CAT involves the use of narrow x-ray beams, much more sensitive than ordinary x-rays. A contrast dye may be used in some instances. A computer makes mathematically calculated observations as the test is in progress. The CAT machine

rotates about the motionless patient obtaining various views. Because a large area of the body is examined in layers, the name of this test may also be combined with the word *scan*, as in CAT scan.

As a result of the high technology associated with the manufacturing and operation of this equipment, many small hospitals cannot afford to purchase one. Patients may be referred to larger hospitals for this specialized test.

Common indications. Any part of the body may be examined by CAT. The most common uses include examinations of the head, chest, lungs, abdomen, spine, heart and blood vessel system, and liver and gall bladder. A CAT scan is useful in providing an image from which the size of normal and abnormal tissue can be evaluated.

Examinations of electrical impulses

When nerves send messages to other nerves or structures in the body, electrical impulses are produced. Machines have been developed that can record these electrical impulses. Analysing the image of the electrical impulses can help identify normal and abnormal conditions. The electrical impulses produced by the heart, brain and skeletal muscles are commonly examined. Wires, called *electrodes*, attached to the skin with suction and the help of a clear gel pick up the electrical impulses and transmit them to the machine. The machine converts the electrical energy into a visual image. The patient should be taught that although electrodes are connecting him to a machine, he will not receive any electrical shocks. Except for an awareness of the presence of electrodes, the patient usually does not experience any other sensations during the test.

Most of these tests can be performed without any prior preparation. Some special preparation may be ordered before an examination of the electrical impulses from the brain. This is usually to eliminate conditions or circumstances that may cause the test results to be misinterpreted.

Electrocardiography (ECG)

Description. *Electrocardiography* is an examination that records electrical impulses produced by the contracting heart muscle. It is abbreviated ECG. The recorded image of the electrical impulses, called an electrocardiogram, is illustrated in Figure 19-8.

Common indications. ECG is used to assess the pattern of impulses associated with the contraction of

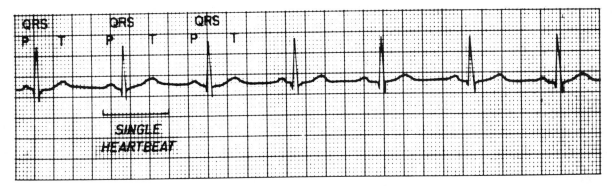

Figure 19-8 This is an example of an electrocardiogram. It illustrates normal heart functioning.

the heart muscle. The electrocardiogram can be interpreted to determine the heart rate, the rhythm, and evidence of heart damage, especially associated with a heart attack. This test may be performed on seemingly healthy people to determine an individual's potential risk for increasing his level of activity and exercise. Stress ECG was discussed in Chapter 11.

Electroencephalography (EEG)

Description. *Electroencephalography* is an examination that records an image of the electrical activity in the brain. It is abbreviated EEG. The recorded image is an electroencephalogram. The patient's usual amount of sleep is restricted before a scheduled examination. It is helpful to record the electrical impulses while the patient is awake and asleep. Natural sleep during the test is preferred to administering a drug to induce sleep.

The hair should be shampooed before the examination. This helps ensure that the electrodes, when applied to the head, remain in place. Natural oils on the scalp and hair may cause them to become loose. The hair will need to be rewashed following the test to remove the gel that was used to attach the electrodes.

Common indications. EEG is used to help diagnose epilepsy, tumours, bleeding into the brain tissues, and various other diseases of the brain. The test is also used to determine if an unresponsive, comatose patient is brain dead.

Electromyography (EMG)

Description. *Electromyography* is an examination that records the electrical impulses produced by contracting skeletal muscle. It is abbreviated EMG. The

record made of the electrical impulses is called an electromyogram.

There may be discomfort during this examination. Electrodes are inserted through the skin, which may cause slight pain. Uncomfortable sensations may also be felt when electrical stimulation is applied to muscles. This must be done to evaluate the ability of the muscle to respond. If the electrode makes contact with a nerve, an even greater amount of discomfort will occur. The patient should be told to indicate when he feels pain so the examiner may make adjustments.

Common indications. EMG is used to help identify and diagnose conditions that result in abnormal sensations, weakness or paralysis. These may be due to nerve diseases or injuries. This technology is also being used in other ways. The electrical impulses from nerves are being harnessed to stimulate artificial limbs to operate.

Examinations that detect radiation

Radiation is energy that cannot be seen or felt. The sun gives off radiation as well as heat and light. Types of radiation are identified as alpha, beta and gamma. Gamma radiation is the most powerful of these. It can pass through objects and body tissue.

The atomic structure of some chemical elements, such as iodine, can be altered in such a way that it gives off radiation. It is then referred to as a *radionuclide*. This is a more current term replacing the longused term *radioisotope*. Radionuclides prepared in forms that allow them to be administered to humans are called *radiopharmaceuticals*.

After a radionuclide is given, it will be circulated throughout the body. Certain organs absorb only certain types of radionuclides. The organ that is targeted by the radionuclide emits radiation. A radionuclide is usually distributed fairly uniformly in normal tissues. It will be distributed unevenly, or be absent, in diseased tissues. A machine scans the organ and converts the energy into light. This makes it possible to produce an image in shades of black and white according to the amount of energy being released. Organs that are often studied for disease with radionuclides include the thyroid gland, liver, bones and brain.

Tests using radionuclides are contraindicated for pregnant women or nursing mothers. The energy that is released can be harmful to the rapidly growing cells of an infant or foetus.

Thyroid scan

Description. A thyroid scan is a type of examination in which a radionuclide is used. Radioactive iodine, identified as ^{131}I, is administered to the patient. It can be given either orally or injected into a vein. After allowing time for the thyroid to absorb the iodine, a scanner passes over the area of the patient's thyroid gland. The patient experiences no discomfort from the iodine or the machine.

Common indications. A thyroid scan is done to evaluate the size, shape and functioning of the thyroid gland. A normal thyroid gland absorbs the radioactive form of iodine evenly. The test is usually performed to diagnose a gland that is functioning excessively or insufficiently. These conditions will show alterations in the rate of absorption. Tumours may result in an uneven absorption within the gland, and the shape or position of the gland may be abnormal.

Examinations that use sound waves

Ultrasonography is an examination that produces images of structures as they reflect or bounce back sound waves. This is similar to a bat or dolphin's echo location system. A synonym is *echography*. The sound produces waves of vibrations. They are of very high frequency, which neither can be felt, nor can be heard by the human ear. For this reason they are called *ultrasound*. The various densities of body tissues reflect sound in different ways and thereby produce an image that the examiner can study. Structures surrounded by fluid are the most readily examined by ultrasound.

A machine converts the deflected sound waves into a visual image. It can be viewed similarly to television. A recorded image is also obtained. It is called an ultrasonogram, sonogram or echogram.

Ultrasonography is used to study the position, form and functioning of various organs of the body. Ultrasonography can also be used to examine moving structures, such as the heart or a foetus.

Obstetric sonogram (B scan)

Description. The examination of a pregnant, or possibly pregnant, uterus using ultrasound is often called a B scan. This term refers to one of several methods for recording the echoing sound waves.

The pregnant uterus is especially appropriate to be studied in this manner since the foetus is surrounded by fluid. A full bladder further enhances the transmission of sound waves. Fluid helps make the image of the structure within the fluid more distinct.

A gel is applied to the abdomen. The examiner moves a *transducer*, an instrument that picks up the echoing sound waves, over the abdomen while observing the image on a screen. The mother can also view her unborn child. Movement, if there is any, such as a beating heart or moving arms and legs, can also be observed. The sex of a foetus can sometimes be determined by the outline of its anatomy in the late stages of a pregnancy. A permanent image is made as a record of the findings of the test.

Common indications. This test is often used to confirm that a pregnancy exists earlier than other laboratory tests that are available. It can also be used to determine the approximate age and growth of a developing foetus. Complications during pregnancy, such as an ill-located or attached placenta or some defects in the developing baby, can be identified.

Examinations using endoscopes

An *endoscope* is an instrument that can be inserted into a body area for direct observation and inspection of internal body structures and tissues. The endoscope has an illuminated mirror-lens system attached to a tube, which is sometimes flexible. *Endoscopy* is an examination of a body part with an endoscope. There are attachments for endoscopes that allow the examiner to obtain a biopsy. A *biopsy* is the removal of a small amount of tissue from the body for microscopic examination.

Bronchoscopy

Description. A *bronchoscopy* is the direct inspection of the trachea and bronchi with a bronchoscope. It is generally carried out in an outpatient surgical department or in an operating room. The throat of the patient is anaesthetized to prevent coughing and gagging as the scope is inserted. Food and fluids must be restricted until the patient can swallow and cough again. The nurse is held accountable for the safety of the patient who may have difficulty breathing due to swelling or aspirating secretions.

Common indications. Bronchoscopy is used most commonly to help in the diagnosis of tumours, to remove foreign objects, to remove thick respiratory secretions and to obtain specimens from the respiratory tract.

Proctoscopy and sigmoidoscopy

Description. A *proctoscopy* and a *sigmoidoscopy* are examinations that allow direct observation and inspection of the rectum and sigmoid colon with a proctoscope or sigmoidoscope. The patient will be placed in a knee-chest or Sims position. There is no pain. The patient may experience some discomfort when the instrument is inserted its full distance, and he may experience a strong urge to defaecate.

Common indications. A proctoscopy and a sigmoidoscopy are done most commonly to help in the diagnosis of inflammatory conditions of the bowel and to identify tumours in the rectum and sigmoid colon.

Cystoscopy

Description. A *cystoscopy* is an examination that permits direct viewing of the urinary urethra, bladder and openings to the ureters with a cystoscope. The patient will be placed in a lithotomy position for this examination. It is generally performed in an operating room, but the patient is usually awake. He is given a local anaesthetic. General anaesthetics may be given in certain circumstances.

Common indications. A cystoscopy is used to study the functioning and internal condition of urinary tract structures, to remove stones, to identify where a catheter should be threaded for retrograde pyelography and to view and treat bladder tumours.

Examinations of body fluids

Most examinations that require the collection of body fluids are carried out at the patient's bedside. The nurse acts as an assistant to the doctor when these examinations are performed. Prepackaged trays that contain most, if not all, of the necessary equipment are generally available. If they are not, the nurse should assemble supplies according to a prepared list.

Collection of blood is usually done by a laboratory technician. The nurse often coordinates the test requirements and patient preparation with laboratory personnel. Occasionally, the nurse may need to help restrain or position the patient so that a specimen may be collected.

Four representative examples of procedures that are performed to collect body fluids will be discussed. While assisting with these examinations, the nurse should be observing and supporting the patient. If any unusual signs or symptoms are assessed, the nurse should inform the doctor in a manner that will not alarm the patient.

Gastric analysis

Description. A *gastric analysis* is a procedure in which stomach secretions are obtained for examination. The secretions are removed through a nasogastric tube to obtain the specimen. Principles of Care 10-3, which describes suggested actions for inserting a nasogastric tube, may be reviewed. Some forms of this test include the administration of drugs known to stimulate the production of gastric acid to evaluate the stomach's response.

Common indications. This test is generally performed to analyse the amount of gastric acid present in the stomach. Abnormally high levels are associated with ulcers. This test may be repeated to evaluate the response of ulcer patients to forms of treatment. Abnormally low levels are also significant.

Lumbar puncture

Description. A *lumbar puncture* or *spinal tap* is a procedure that involves the insertion of a needle beneath the arachnoid layer of the meninges in the space between the third and fourth or fourth and fifth lumbar vertebrae. Cerebrospinal fluid is located in this space. It is collected and specimens are sent to the laboratory for microscopic examination. The spinal cord is not located in the area of entry, so it cannot be injured. A local anaesthetic is administered so that only sensations of pressure are experienced.

The patient is assisted to curl up in a ball, as shown in Figure 14-10 while lying on his side in bed, or he is helped to assume a sitting position. This widens the space between the bony vertebrae so that the needle can be inserted easily. The nurse may need to help the patient maintain this position during the procedure.

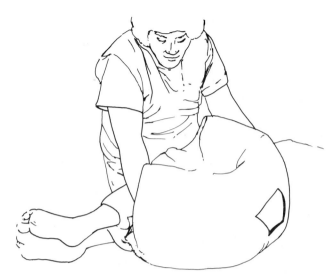

Figure 19-9 The patient is in position for a lumbar puncture. Note that his back is sharply arched as the nurse holds him at his knees and shoulders. The sterile drape has been secured in place with adhesive strips. Helping the patient relax by taking slow deep breaths makes assuming and holding the position easier for him. A small pillow is allowed under the head. Be sure the knees are not forced into the abdomen, which would affect spinal pressure.

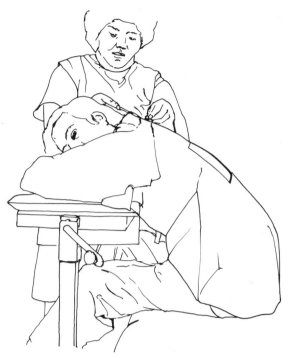

Figure 19-10 The patient rests over his bedside table in readiness for a thoracentesis. The nurse is securing the sterile drape with adhesive strips so that it cannot slip out of place over the working area. Some patients can rest over the back of a straight chair for a thoracentesis.

Common indications. This test may be performed for various reasons. It may be used to diagnose conditions that cause the intracranial pressure to be elevated, which may occur with a brain or spinal cord tumour. A lumbar puncture may be used to lower the intracranial pressure by withdrawing some of the volume of fluid. Specimens of cerebrospinal fluid may be collected and sent to the laboratory to diagnose infections, like meningitis, and other diseases. A lumbar puncture may be performed in order to instill contrast medium when myelography is carried out. Finally, some infections and tumours may be treated by instilling drugs directly into the spinal fluid after a similar amount of fluid has been withdrawn.

Thoracentesis

Description. A *thoracentesis* is a procedure during which the pleural cavity is entered and fluid is withdrawn. Normally fluid does not accumulate in the thorax. The patient is assisted into a sitting position, as shown in Figure 19-10. If the patient cannot sit, the nurse may have him lie on his unaffected side.

Common indications. This test is performed to remove fluid or sometimes air from the pleural cavity.

The fluid that is collected can be examined in the laboratory to determine if organisms are causing an infection. They may also be examined to help diagnose the presence of cancer. Removing accumulated fluid from the pleural cavity can be performed to ease a patient's laboured respirations. This provides more room for the lungs to fill with air.

Paracentesis

Description. A *paracentesis* is a procedure that involves puncturing the skin and subsequently the abdominal cavity so that body fluid may be withdrawn. The patient is placed in a position shown in Figure 19-11. A local anaesthetic is administered prior to using a piercing instrument called a *trocar*. A hollow sheath called a *cannula* surrounds the trocar. Once the trocar has been advanced to the depth desired, it is removed. Fluid drains through the cannula and tubing and eventually into a drainage container. Large volumes of fluid can be expected.

It is important to have the patient urinate before the procedure. A full bladder could be accidentally punctured. The nurse may also obtain some evaluative assessments such as the patient's weight and the measurement of the abdomen. By repeating these assessments after the procedure, the nurse can collect objective information about the effects of the procedure on the patient.

Common indications. This procedure is most commonly done to relieve pressure and dyspnoea caused by the accumulation of excessive amounts of fluid. When this is done, the patient's ability to breathe may be improved because there will be more room for lung expansion. The patient, having had the weight from a large volume of fluid removed, should also be more comfortable. A sample of the fluid may be sent to the laboratory for further microscopic examination.

Suggestions for assisting with examinations in selected situations

When the patient is an infant or child

Tests and examinations performed on adults may also be performed on children. Test preparations and procedures may be adjusted in keeping with the child's body size or ability to cooperate.

Expect that the number of enemas or amount of laxatives are likely to be reduced when this is required prior to a test.

The use of laxatives or enemas should always be questioned if a child has abdominal pain or diarrhoea.

The amount of time during which food and fluids are restricted before an examination may vary, depending on the doctor's wishes.

Expect that the external jugular veins and femoral arteries are most likely to be used to obtain blood samples from an infant.

Expect that a sedative may be prescribed if a child has difficulty lying quietly during an examination.

Lead shielding, which protects the thyroid and genitals, should be provided for children and adolescents undergoing dental x-rays.

Stroke and touch an infant or young child after a painful procedure. The warmth and touch offer reassurance and often console the youngster.

When the patient is elderly

Expect that the elderly patient, especially one who is debilitated from illness, may not be able

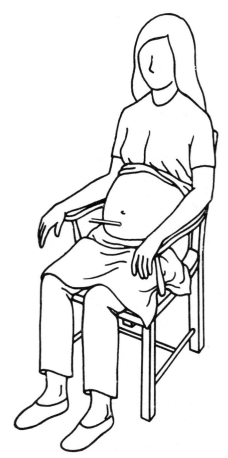

Figure 19-11 This illustrates the positioning for an abdominal paracentesis. Drainage occurs by gravity.

to tolerate having food and fluids withheld for long periods of time before certain examinations, such as an IVP.

Laxatives and enemas may exhaust certain elderly patients. When there is a question, be sure to consult the doctor. Be available to assist elderly patients with a bedpan or ambulating to the bathroom.

Elderly patients are often on daily medications for chronic conditions. The doctor should be consulted about withholding medications when an elderly patient must remain fasting for a test or examination.

When the patient is pregnant or breast feeding

Assume that any female who is sexually active and not using any form of birth control could be pregnant. X-rays should be delayed until the patient is questioned about the possibility of being pregnant.

Provide a lead apron to cover the chest and abdomen of any woman in reproductive years for whom x-rays are necessary.

Expect that examinations using x-rays or radionuclides will not be used for women who are pregnant or breast feeding.

Radiation may affect the cells of the rapidly growing foetus or infant.

Consult with a doctor about omitting enemas and laxatives to prepare women in the advanced stages of pregnancy for tests and examinations.

Medications that are administered with tests or examinations may need to be withheld for the woman who is pregnant or breast feeding. Medications enter the bloodstream and breast milk of the woman and subsequently are distributed to the foetus or infant.

Teaching suggestions about tests and examinations

Descriptions of what a patient may expect during a test or examination should be provided to all patients to prevent or relieve anxiety.

The patient should be instructed about test requirements or preparations associated with an examination. If the patient is going to be responsible for his own preparation, such as when a test is performed as an out-patient, the test instructions should be written. The patient should be given a phone number of a contact person if there are any questions.

Suggestions for the instruction of patients were given several times when describing specific examinations.

Women should be taught the importance of scheduling examinations that include Papanicolaou's test, commonly called a *Pap test*. The test can be helpful in detecting cancer of the cervix during its early, still curable stages. It has been usual to recommend that regular Pap testing start at about 35 to 40 years of age. Some doctors perform this test at younger ages on women who take oral contraceptives. Some authorities state that after two negative Pap tests, done at one-year intervals, a woman who is not at risk for cancer need have a Pap test only every three years.

Mammography, an examination of the breast tissue using x-rays, should be done as a baseline at about the age of 40. Mammographic examinations should be continued throughout the lifetime of an ageing woman. This test can identify a cancerous lesion at least two years earlier than it can be felt. Women should consult with a doctor about the frequency of these examinations. This often depends on risk factors obtained from a woman's health history.

Men should understand the importance of an examination of the prostate gland. This is usually performed at the time of a physical examination. This gland undergoes changes, and may develop cancer, as men age. When the doctor feels the outline of the prostate gland using a lubricated gloved finger inserted into the rectum, its size and texture may be assessed.

Further reading

Anon. (1984) Lumbar puncture, *Consultant*, **24**, 217.

Beare, P.G., Rahr, V.A. and Ronshausen, C.A. (1985) *Nursing Implications of Diagnostic Tests*, 2nd edn, J.B. Lippincott, Philadelphia.

Beck, M.L. (1981) Diagnostic tests: Guiding your patient . . . one step at a time . . . through colonoscopy. *Nursing 81*, **11**, 28–31.

Brown, S.R. (1984) An anxiety reduction technique during lumbar punctures in infants and toddlers. *Journal of the Associaton of Pediatric Oncology Nurses*, **1**, 24–5.

Bubb, D. (1981) RN's instant refreshers: Teaching patients about ultrasound and CAT brain scans. *RN Magazine*, **44**, 64–5.

Bubb, D. (1982) RN's instant refreshers: Neurodiagnostic studies: Pre- and post-procedure care. *RN Magazine*, **45**, 64–5.

Cameron, T.J. (1981) Fiberoptic bronchoscopy. *American Journal of Nursing*, **81**, 1462–4.

Fischbach, F.T. (1984) *A Manual of Laboratory Diagnostic Tests*, 2nd ed., J.B. Lippincott, Philadelphia.

Gelmann, G.R. (1985) The predictive value of diagnostic procedures. *Nurse Practitioner*, **10**, 25, 28–30, 32.

Haughey, C.W. (1981) Understanding ultrasonography. *Nursing 81*, **11**, 100–4.

Haughey, C.W. (1981) What to say . . . and do . . . when your patient asks about CT scans. *Nursing 81*, **11**, 72–7.

Kenyon, S. (1985) Midwifery: Obstetric scanning, *part 3*. *Nursing Mirror*, **160**, 52–5.

Stiklorius, C. (1982) RN's instant refreshers: GI studies. *RN Magazine*, **45**, 64–5.

Stiklorius, C. (1982) RN's instant refreshers: When patient preparation is the key to success. *RN Magazine*, **45**, 64–5.

Sugarbaker, P.H. (1984) Endoscopy in cancer diagnosis and management. *Hospital Practice*, **19**, 11–122.

Via Monte, M.Jr. (1985) New images of imaging. *Emergency Medicine*, **17**, 22–6, 28–30, 32.

Part 4

Nursing Skills

Related to Health

Restoration

20

The need for infection control

Learning objectives

When the content of this chapter has been mastered, the learner should be able to:

Define the terms appearing in the glossary.

Discuss the conditions that must usually be present to support the growth of microorganisms.

List examples of natural body defences that protect individuals from acquiring infections.

List factors that increase the potential risk for acquiring infections.

Describe the cycle that explains how microorganisms are spread.

Demonstrate proper handwashing; identify the actions that would be different when performing a surgical scrub.

Discuss practices that should be followed when cleaning supplies and equipment.

Identify the difference between disinfection and sterilization.

Identify four methods for destroying microorganisms with heat and four methods for destroying microorganisms with chemicals.

List principles that should be applied when carrying out aseptic technique.

Demonstrate how to don and remove sterile gloves.

List the routes by which microorganisms are most often transmitted. Give examples of each route.

List two general approaches for preventing microbes from spreading.

Describe two categories of isolation.

Describe the general principles of isolation techniques.

Discuss the psychological needs of a patient who requires infection control practices.

Identify factors related to controlling infectious diseases in young children and patients in intensive care areas.

Summarize the suggestions for instruction of patients that are offered in this chapter.

Glossary

Aerobic microorganism A microbe that requires free oxygen in order to exist.

Airborne transmission A route by which pathogens are transferred from an infected person to another on air currents containing suspended dust particles or residue of evaporated droplets.

Anaerobic microorganism A microbe that depends on an environment without oxygen for its survival.

Antibiotics A classification of drugs that have an anti-infective action. Synonym for *antimicrobial agent*.

Antimicrobial agent A chemical that kills or suppresses the growth of microorganisms. Synonym for *anti-infective agent*.

Antiseptic A chemical used to prevent, or inhibit the growth of microorganisms, which is safe to use on skin or living tissue.

Asepsis The absence of infection.

Aseptic technique Practices that render and keep objects and areas free of all microorganisms.

Bacteriocide A chemical that kills microorganisms, but not necessarily spores. Synonym for *disinfectant* and *germicide*.

Barrier nursing Practices that prevent the transmission of pathogens from host to another. Synonym for *isolation techniques*.

Blood/body fluid precautions Infection control practices used to prevent the transmission of pathogens present in the blood or serum of an infected person.

Category isolation Several groups of infection control practices designed to limit the transmission of a variety of pathogens spread by a common route.

Clean technique Practices that help reduce the number and spread of microorganisms.

Contagious disease A disease that can easily spread to others. Synonym for *communicable disease*.

Contaminate To make something unclean or unsterile.

Direct contact The route of transmission in which microorganisms are transferred when one is with or touching an infected person.

Disinfectant A chemical that kills microorganisms but not necessarily spores. Synonym for *bacteriocide* and *germicide*.

Disinfection A process by which pathogens, but not necessarily their spores, are destroyed.

Droplet transmission A route of transmission spread by particles of moisture released from the nose or mouth of an infected person.

Germicide A chemical that kills microorganisms but not necessary spores. Synonym for *bacteriocide* and *disinfectant*.

Host A person or animal on which or in which microorganisms live.

Indirect contact A route of transmission in which pathogens on contaminated objects are carried to a susceptible host.

Infectious disease A disease that can be easily spread to others. Synonym for *contagious disease*.

Infectious period The time when pathogens exit from an infected host.

Isolation techniques Practices that prevent the transmission of pathogens from one host to another.

Microorganism A tiny living animal or plant, also called a microbe or organism, which can only be seen with a microscope.

Nonpathogen A harmless microorganism.

Nosocomial infection An infection acquired in hospital.

Pathogen A microorganism that can cause an infection or a contagious disease.

Portal of entry The part of the body where organisms enter.

Protective isolation Infection control practices used to prevent a highly susceptible person from acquiring an infection.

Reservoir A place on which or in which microorganisms grow and reproduce.

Sepsis A state of infection.

Source isolation Practices to prevent the transmission of pathogens from an infectious person.

Spore A state in which a microbe can survive extreme living conditions until more favourable ones exist.

Sterile field A work area that is free of all microorganisms.

Sterilization A process by which all microorganisms, including spores, are destroyed.

Susceptible host An animal or person who has the potential for acquiring an infection.

Terminal cleaning Final cleaning of a patient's contaminated equipment and supplies after he is discharged from hospital.

Transmission barrier A garment or technique that blocks the transfer of pathogens from one person, place, or object to another.

Vaccine A substance given to susceptible individuals to promote the body's natural defence against a specific contagious disease.

Vector An insect or animal that spreads pathogens.

Vehicle of transmission The means by which organisms are carried about.

Introduction

Microorganisms, or what most people call germs, are everywhere though they cannot be seen without a microscope. They cover objects; they are in air and water and on the surfaces of food. They are found on and within the body. Many are harmless; they are called *nonpathogenic*. Those that cause infections or contagious diseases are called *pathogens*. The organism *Escherichia coli*, for example, is normally found in the intestinal tract where it does not cause disease. However, if it spreads to another part of the body, such as the urinary bladder, it is considered a pathogen because it may cause infection there. A *host* is a person or an animal on which or in which microorganisms live.

Some germs cause illnesses that are referred to as infections or infectious diseases. The human body has natural defences that reduce the risk of acquiring infections. Still, all humans are affected from time to time. Sick persons are even more likely to acquire an infection because of weakened defences.

A high priority in health care is to prevent disease, which includes infections, among individuals who are healthy and ill. Nurses do this by protecting an individual's natural body defences and by safeguarding individuals who are at higher risk from pathogens. Health personnel do not wait until an infection develops; steps are taken to keep it from happening. The challenge to health personnel has been to carry out methods that prevent microorganisms from living, growing and spreading. Techniques that are used to control organisms will be discussed in this chapter.

Characteristics of microorganisms

A *microorganism* is a tiny living animal or plant. The word microorganism is often shortened to microbe or organism. Microorganisms include bacteria, viruses, fungi, yeasts, moulds, rickettsia and protozoa. Most nurses study the specific characteristics of each of these in a course in microbiology.

All microorganisms are living substances and share some common characteristics in order to grow and survive. Certain conditions must be present, just as for humans, to support life.

- *Warmth*. Microorganisms can survive at a wide range of temperatures. The normal temperature of the human body supports and promotes the growth of microorganisms.
- *Air*. Most microorganisms require free oxygen to exist. These are called *aerobic microorganisms*. Those that survive without free oxygen are called *anaerobic microorganisms*. Some anaerobes are very dangerous because they grow rapidly in

deep wounds where free oxygen is scarce, such as in nail punctures. The microorganism that causes tetanus (lockjaw) is of this kind.
- *Water and nourishment*. Microbes do not generally survive well in dry areas or places where nutrients are lacking. They depend on other sources, such as a human or animal, for water and food. Blood and the contents within cells can provide a continuous supply of the ingredients needed for the growth of organisms.
- *Chemical environment*. An environment that is neither too acid nor alkaline is preferred by most microorganisms. Blood is relatively neutral and microbes often seek this as a medium to support their existence.

Some microbes are able to survive adverse conditions by forming spores. A *spore* is a state in which a microbe changes its structure, usually by forming a thick outer cellular wall, which permits it to survive extremes of heat, cold, dryness or lack of food. Spores can then develop into active microorganisms when conditions are more favourable for their growth.

Natural body defences

The human body is equipped with various ways to protect itself. These methods are what allow the body to resist being overcome by microorganisms and to defend itself once they have become established in a part of the body. Table 20-1 is a summary of natural body defences and the manner in which they provide protection.

Factors that weaken natural body defences

At times changes occur that weaken a person's normal defences against microorganisms. An individual then becomes a *susceptible host*, one who is at risk of acquiring an infection. The following factors can result in reduced resistance to the entry of disease-causing organisms.

Poor nutrition. The body depends on nutrients to grow, maintain, and repair healthy cells. Without proper nutrition, cells become weakened. Nutritional substances needed to produce body secretions and chemicals, examples of the body's natural defences, can also be depleted.

Table 20-1. Natural body defences

Natural Defence	Effect on Microorganisms
Intact skin and mucous membranes	Unbroken surfaces of the body and body openings act as barriers, preventing the entry of organisms into the body.
Body hair	Hair that is present on or within areas of the body, such as the nose, trap and hold particles that contain microorganisms.
Body secretions, such as saliva, mucus, sebum, tears, perspiration, gastric enzymes and urine	Body secretions contain chemical substances that weaken or destroy microbes.
Reflexes, such as sneezing, coughing, blinking, tearing and vomiting	Reflex reactions occur spontaneously to expel microorganisms that enter a particular area of the body.
Physiological responses, such as the inflammatory response and the immune response	The body is capable of producing additional specialized cells and chemicals that are responsible for inhibiting the growth and spread of microorganisms.
Temperature regulation	By raising the body temperature above the normal range, many organisms can be destroyed or weakened by the heat.
Cell repair and replacement	Manufacturing new cells that repair and replace those that are diseased, injured, or destroyed protects the body from further invasion of microorganisms.

Poor personal hygiene. The body traps microorganisms on the skin and hair, under nails, and in areas such as the mouth. Daily or more frequent hygiene removes microbes from those areas. Accumulation of trapped organisms provides the opportunity for their growth and multiplication.

Broken skin or mucous membranes. Once the body's natural barriers have been broken, infectious microorganisms can invade more susceptible areas of the body. When cuts, incisions or burns occur, individuals are at an increased risk for infection.

Age. Premature and newborn infants are at risk for infections because many of the natural defences are not fully developed. The elderly are similarly at high risk because their defensive mechanisms are not always functioning at an optimum level.

Illness. When a disease disrupts normal functioning, the entire body is affected. Any reserves that would be ordinarily available to resist infection may be used up or reduced.

Certain medical treatments. Some useful forms of therapy, such as various drugs, may be prescribed for one illness yet reduce the body's ability to defend itself against infection. For instance, steroids, a type of hormone used to treat severe forms of arthritis, cancer, or transplant patients, may reduce the number of specialized cells that attack microorganisms.

The infectious process cycle

Microorganisms move from place to place in a cycle. This is illustrated in Figure 20-1. If the cycle is broken anywhere, the organisms cannot grow, spread and cause disease. Methods for controlling microorganisms are based on interrupting the cycle and thus preventing their spread. The focus of this chapter will be those practices that alter the *reservoir*, the place on which or in which organisms grow and reproduce, and practices that affect the vehicle of transmission. The *vehicle of transmission* is the means by which organisms are carried about.

Hospital patients are particularly prone to infection. Many are exposed to invasive procedures, such as catheterization, cannulation and surgery, which compromise their natural defences. Staff and equipment can act as vehicles of transmission carrying microorganisms between patients.

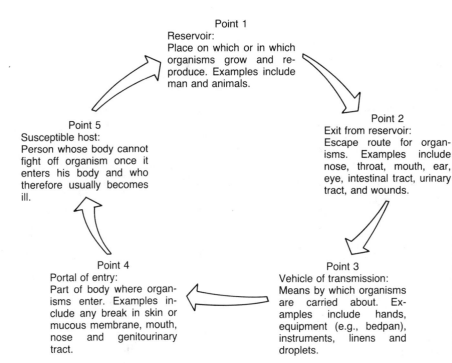

Point 1
Reservoir:
Place on which or in which organisms grow and reproduce. Examples include man and animals.

Point 2
Exit from reservoir:
Escape route for organisms. Examples include nose, throat, mouth, ear, eye, intestinal tract, urinary tract, and wounds.

Point 3
Vehicle of transmission:
Means by which organisms are carried about. Examples include hands, equipment (e.g., bedpan), instruments, linens and droplets.

Point 4
Portal of entry:
Part of body where organisms enter. Examples include any break in skin or mucous membrane, mouth, nose and genitourinary tract.

Point 5
Susceptible host:
Person whose body cannot fight off organism once it enters his body and who therefore usually becomes ill.

Figure 20-1 This sketch illustrates the infectious process cycle. Infections and infectious diseases are spread by starting from the reservoir, point 1 on the diagram, and moving through the full circle of points to a susceptible host, point 5 on the diagram. Microorganisms can be controlled by using methods that interfere at any point within the cycle.

Preventing the transmission of infection

Preventing the transmission of infection depends on a number of simple precautions upon which good nursing practice should be based. There are many times when such infection control practices are carried out in the course of daily living. Examples of practices that reduce the spread of microorganisms are given in Table 20-2.

Handwashing

Handwashing is the most important method of preventing the transmission of microorganisms. It is the single most effective way to prevent *nosocomial infections*, which are infections acquired after being admitted to a hospital. Despite being warned about the importance of washing hands, carelessness still continues.

The importance of handwashing cannot be overemphasized. Washing the hands with soap and water removes the microorganisms acquired from touching patients, body fluid and objects. However, to remove all these organisms, all parts of the hands must be washed. Drying the hands thoroughly also removes microorganisms and prevents the skin becoming damaged.

Handwashing is a conscientious activity that shows a healthy respect for the potential hazards involved in spreading microorganisms, and it is assumed throughout the text that it is always performed before and after giving care.

Principles of Care 20-1 describes the recommended actions for reducing the presence of organisms from the hands.

The handwashing procedure used prior to the activities in operating theatre and labour ward is called a surgical scrub. Principles of Care 20-2 describes the differences in the handwashing technique that should be followed when performing a surgical scrub.

Antimicrobial agents

An *antimicrobial agent* is a chemical that kills or suppresses the growth or reproduction of microorganisms. Antimicrobial agents are used in the prevention and treatment of many kinds of infection.

Soaps and detergents can be considered antimicrobial agents. They are used for cleansing. By removing dirt, body oils, and debris, such as blood and secretions, from skin or objects, the nurse also removes microbes that are present. Cleansing must be combined with some other sterilization method to completely remove all microorganisms and their

Table 20-2. Common infection control practices

Examples of Practices in Everyday Living	Examples of Practices When Giving Care	Examples of Practices in Personal Grooming
Cover the nose and mouth when coughing and sneezing. A cough or a sneeze forces large numbers of organisms from the mouth, nose and throat into the environment, where they may be inhaled by others.	Wash hands before and after giving nursing care and after handling equipment and supplies used for care. A discussion of handwashing is found in the next section of this chapter.	Keep your hair cut short or tied back if long. Some persons have questioned whether organisms grow on hair shafts, but most believe that hair allowed to hang on the health worker's uniform could serve as a vehicle for carrying organisms about. In addition, many patients find it offensive to have persons around them with long, loosely arranged hair, especially when food is being handled.
Wash hands before handling food to prevent the spread of organisms from your hands to the food.	Always handle body fluids as though they contain pathogens and discard promptly. Bandages, dressings, tissues and cotton balls are commonly used to absorb body fluid. They can easily spread organisms if not discarded properly into leakproof waste-bags.	
Use individual personal care items, such as towels, tooth-brushes, combs, hair brushes, razors and so on. This helps to prevent the spread of organisms from one person to another.	Discard disposable equipment according to hospital policy. All equipment used for patient care is considered contaminated after use.	Wear only plain band rings on duty. Rings with stones or grooves are not recommended, primarily because they are difficult to keep clean. Organisms can easily lodge in corners and crevices and be carried from person to person. It is also possible that some stones and grooves could scratch the patient.
Wash hands after using the toilet to prevent the spread of organisms found in excretions.	Flush away content of bedpans and urinals promptly, unless they are being saved for a specimen. It is considered safe to flush contents into the sewage system. Sewage treatment destroys pathogens.	
Environmental Health Officers inspect public eating places for protection from persons carrying diseases and from poor practices of hygiene.	Use equipment and supplies for one patient only. If they are to be reused by another patient, clean them thoroughly and then disinfect or sterilize them in the manner described later in this chapter to prevent spreading organisms among patients.	Keep fingernails short and well groomed. The surfaces under the nails, ragged nails and hangnails are likely to harbour organisms that are difficult to remove but easy to transmit to others.
Control pests, such as rats and mosquitoes, that may spread diseases.		
Immunize against infectious disease.		
	Cover breaks in the skin with sterile dressings. Breaks in the skin are a good portal of entry for many organisms.	Do not wear nail polish. Chipped polish offers areas that may harbour organisms that can be easily spread to others.
	Keep soiled equipment and supplies, especially linens, away from your uniform so that you do not carry organisms from patient to patient and to yourself.	
	Consider the floor heavily contaminated. Discard any item if	

Continued

Table 20-2. Continued

Examples of Practices in Everyday Living	Examples of Practices When Given Care	Examples of Practices in Personal Grooming
	it falls to the floor, or clean, disinfect or sterilize it as necessary.	
	Do not allow the accumulation of dust. Institute regular cleaning to remove dust.	
	Do not shake linens. This creates draughts that will carry contaminated dust and lint from place to place.	
	Clean the least soiled areas first and the most soiled areas last. This prevents having cleaner areas soiled even more by material from dirtier areas.	
	Handle contaminated needles and sharp instruments with extreme care. Discard promptly into a designated bin for sharps.	

Principles of Care 20-1. Handwashing

Nursing Action	Rationale
Turn on the water, using elbow taps where fitted.	Organisms accumulate on water taps. Touching them after the hands are clean leads to recontamination and the possibility of spreading microbes to oneself or others.
Regulate the temperature of the water so that it is comfortably warm.	Warm water makes better soap suds than cold. It also decreases the surface tension of body oils, which trap dirt and microorganisms. Hot water may dry and chap skin by removing oils from the skin.
Control the flow of water so that it does not splash from the sink.	Water splashed from the contaminated sink may spread organisms onto a uniform.
Wet the hands and soap them well (Figure 20-2). Liquid soap is preferred; apply about a teaspoon.	The soap dish can act as a reservoir for microorganisms.
With firm rubbing and circular motions, wash the palms and backs of the hands, each finger, the area between the fingers, and the knuckles as illustrated in Figure 20-3.	Friction caused by firm rubbing and circular motions helps to loosen dirt and organisms. Dirt and organisms lodge between fingers and in skin crevices of knuckles, as well as on the palms and backs of the hands.

Continued

Principles of Care 20-1. *Continued*

Nursing Action	Rationale

Figure 20-3 The nurse scrubs well while continuing to hold the bar of soap in her hand.

Figure 20-2 The nurse has regulated the temperature of the water and is wetting her hands.

Figure 20-4 A thorough handwashing includes washing the wrists. It also includes washing up the forearms to a distance at which contamination is considered present.

Wash the wrists and forearms. Wash up the forearms at least as high as contamination is likely to be present. Use firm rubbing and circular motions as illustrated in Figure 20-4.

Organisms may be present on the wrists and forearms as well as on the hands. The hands are considered to be more contaminated than other areas. Cleaning least contaminated areas (wrists and forearms) after the hands are clean prevents spreading organisms from the hands to the forearms and wrists.

Continued

Principles of Care 20-1. Continued

Nursing Action	Rationale
Wash the hands for at least 15 to 30 seconds before and after giving care if exposure to contamination is minimal. Use a 1- to 2-minute wash if exposure to contamination has been extensive.	The amount of contamination on the hands determines the amount of time for washing the hands. For the safest precaution, it is best to overdo rather than underdo the washing.
Repeat the wetting, relathering, and washing procedure if the hands have been heavily contaminated.	When hands are heavily contaminated, second and third washings may be necessary to assure that all dirt and organisms have been removed.
Rinse the forearms, wrists and hands, in that order, under running water.	Running water rinses dirt and organisms loosened with soap, water and friction into the sink.
Using as many paper towels as necessary, pat the forearms, wrists and hands, respectively, to dry them well.	Drying the skin well prevents chapping. Drying more contaminated areas last prevents spreading remaining microbes to cleaner areas.
Apply handcream to the forearms, wrists and hands.	Handcream helps keep the skin soft and easier to clean. It helps prevent chapping. Chapped skin is difficult to keep clean because dirt and microbes may lodge in roughened areas.

Principles of Care 20-2. *Performing a surgical scrub*

Nursing Action	Rationale
Turn on and regulate the water, using elbow, knee or foot controls.	Controls that do not require hand regulation reduce the possibility for recontamination.
Let the water flow over the skin while keeping the hands higher than the elbows.	In a surgical scrub, practices are used to keep the hands as free of microorganisms as possible. Wetting, scrubbing, rinsing and draining should always be in a direction away from the hands.
Apply cleansing solution. Work up a lather and scrub the hands, using friction and circular motions as described for general handwashing.	An initial washing will remove a great deal of surface debris.
Rinse in a direction from the fingertips to the elbows.	Sources of microorganisms flow away from the area that is to remain cleanest.
Relather the hands. Using a soft sterile nail brush, scrub the nails of each hand.	Microorganisms can be trapped under the nails. Nail brushes can harbour organisms, so they must be discarded or sterilized after each use.
Discard the brush and rinse in a direction from the fingers to the elbows.	Water should flow away from the cleanest area, the hands.
While keeping the hands higher than the elbows, dry each hand with a sterile towel. Use a different towel for each hand. Move the towel from the hand toward the elbow when drying.	A second towel maintains the same degree of cleanliness for both hands.
Without touching any clothing being worn or letting the hands fall below the level of the waist, apply a sterile gown and gloves.	Unsterile clothing is a source of organisms that could recontaminate freshly scrubbed hands.

spores from an object. Skin can never be completely free of microorganisms.

Antiseptics are chemical antimicrobial agents used to reduce the growth of microorganisms on living tissues. A synonym for an antiseptic is *bacteriostatic agent*. The category of anti-infective agents only prevents or inhibits the growth and reproduction of microorganisms. Bacteriostatic agents do not completely destroy all microbes; therefore, their use is not a form of sterilization. Examples of common antiseptics include iodine and hydrogen peroxide.

A *bactericide* is a substance that can destroy or kill microorganisms, but not necessarily spores. A *disinfectant* is a bactericidal substance. A synonym for bactericide and disinfectant is *germicide*. These antimicrobials are not intended for use on people. They are quite strong and would damage living tissue if used for the amount of time and strength necessary to destroy organisms. Though they render an object free of all active microbes, but not necessarily inactive spores, their use is not a form of sterilization. Examples of disinfectants include phenol, hypochlorite and formaldehyde.

Antibiotics, such as penicillin, are examples of drugs that are antimicrobial agents. Antibiotics have been lifesaving for many patients. However, they are only useful in reducing or destroying the growth of bacteria, one type of microorganism. Even so, not all bacteria are affected by all antibiotics. The doctor must selectively match the type of bacteria with the appropriate antibiotic. Earlier indiscriminate use of antibiotics has been associated with adaptive changes among some bacteria. Now bacteria have changed in ways that allow them to resist the once effective action of many antibiotics.

Disposal of waste materials

Most hospitals now use disposable equipment, which is used only once, or for only one patient, and then discarded. The use of central supply units and disposable equipment has helped reduce the spread of microorganisms in hospitals and the work required of nurses. However, the large volume of waste generated in hospitals creates major disposal problems. A certain amount of this waste is contaminated with body fluids and may therefore contain pathogens. A national colour-coding policy for hospital waste indicates that yellow bags must be used for contaminated or clinical waste. This enables segregation of clinical waste to ensure it is disposed of by incineration (Health and Safety Commission, 1982).

Sharp, disposable instruments, such as needles, present particular problem. Bloodborne viruses, such as HIV and hepatitis B virus, can be transmitted through injury by a contaminated needle or sharp instrument. Sharp instruments must therefore be discarded directly into the special rigid bins provided with the minimum of handling. Needles should not be resheathed as this increases the risk of injury (Expert Advisory Group on AIDS, 1990).

Cleaning and decontamination of supplies and equipment

Although the use of disposable equipment has reduced the amount of cleaning required, nurses may still be responsible for cleaning some equipment and work areas. Equipment should be decontaminated according to the risk posed to the patient.

High-risk equipment is that which penetrates the skin, enters sterile body areas or has contact with damaged mucous membranes. These items must be sterilized; e.g. surgical instruments, intrauterine devices.

Medium-risk equipment is used in contact with intact mucous membranes. These items should also be sterilized, but disinfection is adequate; e.g. vaginal speculum used for examination only, proctoscopes.

Low-risk equipment is used only on intact skin and should be washed or disinfected after use; e.g. commodes, beds (BMA, 1989).

Table 20-3 summarizes methods of suppressing the growth of microorganisms.

Cleaning. In general, items that have been in contact with a patient should be cleaned before use by another patient. About 80% of microorganisms can be removed by thorough washing with detergent and hot water. This method is usually adequate for the environment (floors, furniture) and must also form the first step in preparing equipment for disinfection or sterilization.

The following guidelines describe a safe and effective method of using detergent and water to clean supplies and equipment:

- Wear disposable gloves if items are contaminated or if the skin is broken.
- Disassemble and rinse reusable equipment as soon as possible after use, especially when time does not permit a thorough cleaning immediately. This prevents parts from becoming locked together.

Table 20-3. Methods for suppressing growth of organisms

Method	Examples	Explanation
Heat	Boiling Steam under pressure Hot air oven Pasteurization	Temperatures that exceed those at which microbes can survive will destroy organisms. Most of these techniques require special equipment that measures heat and pressure. The heat must be constantly maintained for a specific period of time.
Cleaning	Handwashing Detergent	Removing dirt, body oil, blood and other secretions that contain microbes, water and nutrients can reduce the ability of microorganisms to grow.
Chemicals	Antiseptics Disinfectants Antibiotics Ethylene oxide gas	Chemicals work in a variety of ways to create a harmful environment that interferes with the ability of organisms to live, grow and multiply.

- Rinse items *first* under cool, running water. Hot water causes many substances to *coagulate* (that is, to thicken or congeal), making them difficult to remove.
- Use hot water and detergent for cleaning purposes. Hot water and detergent break up dirt and body secretions into tiny particles that can be more easily rinsed off with water.
- A sponge or cloth may be used to create friction that helps loosen dirt and organisms from the surfaces of objects.
- Use a brush with stiff bristles to loosen dirt as necessary. A brush is a necessity for cleaning small grooves and joints in instruments.
- Force soapy water through the hollow channels of instruments to loosen dirt.
- Rinse items well under running water after cleaning with detergent and water. This will rinse loosened dirt and organisms into the sink.
- Dry equipment well to prevent rusting.
- Treat gloves, brushes, sponges, cleaning cloths, and water used for cleaning as reservoirs for microorganisms. Clean or discard them accordingly.
- Avoid splashing or spilling water on yourself or on the floor or other equipment during the entire procedure.
- Consider hands heavily contaminated after cleaning equipment. Even when wearing gloves during cleaning, the nurse should perform handwashing as described earlier in this chapter.

For most purposes, thorough laundering of linen is sufficiently safe for cleaning.

Certain items cannot be washed without being ruined, for example instruments used for taking blood pressure.

Terminal cleaning

When the patient is discharged, all contaminated supplies and equipment are cleansed a final time to prepare them for reuse by another patient. This is called *terminal cleaning*. Policies differ from hospital to hospital about who is responsible for cleaning the patient's room, supplies and equipment after he is discharged. After the cleaning has been completed, the bed is made ready to receive another patient, as described in Chapter 16.

Disinfection and sterilization

Disinfection is a process by which pathogens, but not necessarily bacterial spores, are destroyed; sterilization destroys all microorganisms and bacterial spores. Physical methods of sterilization or disinfection, such as heat, are the most reliable. Chemical *disinfectants* are compounds which can destroy microorganisms. *Antiseptics* are nontoxic disinfectants which can be applied to skin or living tissues.

The greater the number of organisms, the longer it will take to destroy all of them. When organisms are protected under layers of grease, oil, blood and pus, removing microorganisms becomes more difficult; therefore, any method of disinfection or sterilization becomes potentially less effective and unreliable. Scrupulous cleaning is therefore essential to ensure as many organisms as possible are removed before disinfection or sterilization takes place.

Microorganisms are not destroyed instantly, therefore all methods of disinfection or sterilization must be sustained for a period of time.

Methods of sterilization

Steam under pressure. Moist heat under pressure provides the most dependable method of destroying all forms of microorganism and bacterial spores. The autoclave is the most common type of pressure steam sterilizer. The pressure makes it possible to achieve much higher temperatures than the boiling point of water. The usual cycle is a temperature of 121°C for 15 minutes. Autoclaves sterilize by transferring the latent heat of condensation to the microorganisms on the surface of the instruments. It is therefore essential that all the surfaces of the instruments are exposed to the steam. To ensure that instruments are sterile at the point of use, paper wrappings are often used. Sterilization of wrapped or hollow equipment requires a special "porous-load" autoclave in which the steam can penetrate the packs and dry them at the end of the cycle. Autoclaving is the method of choice for sterilizing metal instruments but it is unsuitable for items which would be damaged by the high temperatures, for example, most plastics and fibre-optic endoscopes.

Dry heat. The transfer of heat by steam is far more efficient than air, therefore the dry heat method of sterilization, such as a hot air oven, requires much higher temperatures and a longer time than an autoclave. Instruments can be sterilized in a hot air oven at a temperature of 160°C for 60 minutes, but like steam under pressure, this method is not suitable for heat-sensitive equipment.

Ethylene oxide gas. Items sterilized in this way are exposed to the gas in a chamber. It is a useful method for heat-sensitive items and can also be used to penetrate hollow or wrapped items. The gas is toxic and irritant so following exposure items must be aired for about a week. Ethylene oxide is often used by manufacturers to sterilize plastic single-use items, but is not widely used in hospitals.

Methods of disinfection

Hot water. Disinfection by heat is most efficient in water because water conducts heat well to all parts of an immersed object. Boiling will disinfect items but cannot sterilize, as some bacterial spores can withstand boiling. Items should be placed in the water and held at 100°C for 15 minutes to ensure bacteria and viruses are destroyed. Hot water at temperatures between 65°C and 80°C is also commonly used in combination with cleaning, as a highly effective method of disinfecting low-risk equipment, for example, bedpan washers, laundry and dish-washing machines.

Glutaraldehyde. This chemical disinfectant is effective against a wide range of microorganisms. It will destroy bacterial spores if items are immersed in the solution for three hours. It is more commonly used for shorter immersion periods where it will only disinfect. Glutaraldehyde is irritant to skin, eyes and mucosa. It must therefore be handled very carefully and items thoroughly rinsed after immersion.

Alcohol can rapidly destroy microorganisms but it only works well on clean surfaces. A 70% solution is often used in hand disinfection preparations and impregnated wipes.

Chlorhexidine. Chlorhexidine destroys most bacteria but not spores or viruses. It is easily inactivated by organic matter or soap and is therefore not usually used for chemical disinfection of equipment. It can be used as an antiseptic for skin and mucous membranes.

Principles of asepsis

Asepsis means the absence of infection. Asepsis is based on the underlying principle that equipment and areas that are free of microorganisms must be protected from contamination. *Aseptic technique* refers to the methods used to prevent the transfer of microorganisms; it is used whenever invasive procedures are performed, e.g. surgery, insertion of catheters, dressing wounds, administering injections, and so on. These procedures increase the possibility of introducing organisms into the body, causing infection and disease, because the natural body defences are breached. Table 20-4 lists principles that promote surgical asepsis.

There are many occasions on which the nurse will need to apply principles of asepsis. The following are some common practices that are often components of various nursing skills, which are discussed later in this text.

Creating a sterile field

A *sterile field* is a work area that is free of microorganisms. The inner surface of a wrapper that holds sterilized equipment is often used as a sterile field much like a tablecloth would be used. It acts as a sterile surface for resting pieces of sterile equipment or supplies that may be used for patient care. The nurse must open the sterile package in such a way as to keep the inside of the wrapper and its

Table 20-4. Aseptic technique

Principle	Explanation
An item that has only been disinfected is not considered sterile.	Disinfection does not destroy spores. Spores may become active and cause infections.
A sterile object becomes contaminated when touched by an unsterile object.	Even clean objects contain microorganisms. Sterile objects may only touch other sterile objects.
The inside of a wrapper and its contents are sterile. They should never be touched with the bare hand; sterile gloves or sterile instruments should be used if the contents must be rearranged.	Touch only the outer wrapper or inside surface of the wrapper. The inside is sterile; the outside is contaminated.
A sterile object or area may become contaminated by microorganisms in air currents, dust, lint and moisture.	Microbes are everywhere, not just on physical objects. Sterile areas must be protected from exposure to other sources of microorganisms.
Talking, coughing, sneezing or reading over a sterile area must be avoided.	Microorganisms are present in the moisture from respiratory secretions. These droplets can fall onto sterile areas, causing contamination.
The back should never be turned on a sterile area.	Since vision is obscured while turning away, it is possible that contaminated areas of the body or clothing may touch sterile objects.
A sterile area should never be left unattended.	Leaving sterile areas and equipment provides a situation in which undetected contamination may occur.
Cover a sterile field and equipment with a sterile drape if the equipment will not be used immediately.	Covering sterile areas with another sterile object maintains its sterility, but only for a short period of time.
Do not use equipment and supplies if there is any doubt about their sterility.	Because organisms cannot be seen, it is far better to err on the side of safety than to take a chance and have the patient acquire an infection.
Avoid the use of sterile equipment that has been partially opened, has an expired use date or has an unchanged sterilizer tape.	Evidence such as this indicates that the current sterility of the equipment is suspect.
Any wet areas on a sterile field should be considered contaminated.	Moisture on sterile cloth or a paper liner can act as a wick, pulling microorganisms from the contaminated surface underneath to the sterile field.

contents sterile. This may be done by performing the following steps, which are also illustrated in Figure 20-5.

- Position the wrapped package so that the outermost triangular edge can be moved away from the nurse when the sealed tape is broken or removed as shown in the photograph on the left in Figure 20-5.
- The sides of the wrapper may be unfolded by touching the areas that will become the underneath surface of the sterile field when it is opened as the nurse is doing in the centre photograph of Figure 20-5.
- The final triangular fold can be pulled in the direction of the body. Opening the package in this manner avoids the possibility of touching a sterile field with the nurse's uniform and avoids having to reach across a sterile field.

Adding sterile items to the sterile field

There are times when sterile procedures will require supplies or equipment that may not be totally con-

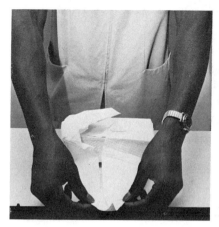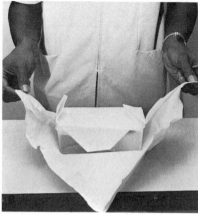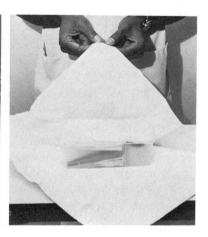

Figure 20-5 *Left*: The nurse opens a sterile set or tray by folding the topmost part of the covering wrapper *away* from him. This leaves sterile equipment and supplies well covered so that they cannot be contaminated by the nurse reaching across the set or tray to open the wrapper. *Centre*: Next, the nurse opens the second layer of the wrapper to the sides of the set or tray. This still leaves sterile equipment and supplies covered with the last layer of the wrapper. *Right*: As the last step, the nurse opens the final layer of the wrapper *towards* himself. The wrapper now becomes the sterile field for the equipment and supplies within the set or on the tray. Note that at no time did the nurse reach across an uncovered sterile field or sterile equipment and supplies.

tained in one wrapped package. Some supplies, such as gauze dressings, come packaged separately. These packages usually have two loose flaps that extend above the sealed edges that enclose the contents. By separating the flaps, the sterile contents can be dropped onto the sterile field without any contamination occurring. Using individually wrapped sterile items for a single use has reduced the spread of microorganisms from supplies and equipment.

Donning and removing sterile gloves

To *don* means to put on an article of wear. For certain procedures the nurse dons sterile gloves. When applied correctly, sterile gloves may be safely used to handle sterile equipment and supplies without contaminating these objects. They may be used to prevent transferring microbes, which are always present on the hands, to patients. Sterile gloves are included in some packages of supplies. They may also be packaged separately in glove wrappers. Principles of Care 20-3 describes how to don sterile gloves and remove them.

Nonsterile gloves may be used as a barrier that protects the nurse from contact with contaminated material. In this case, the gloves do not require any special technique for their application. However, nonsterile gloves should be removed following the techniques described in Principles of Care 20-3.

Teaching suggestions for asepsis

The nurse may have many opportunities to teach patients practices and facts about asepsis.

It is important to teach patients common practices of asepsis that relate to everyday living. Many patients recognize the importance of common practices such as covering the nose and mouth when sneezing and coughing, and washing the hands after using the toilet and before handling food, but some do not. By observing patients, the nurse may identify areas where instruction would be helpful in controlling the spread of microorganisms. Teaching can then be directed toward areas where it is most appropriately needed.

The patient who gives himself care at home needs guidance in the proper way to handle sterile equipment and supplies and in how to sterilize reusable items. Teaching how to clean items properly is important also. Using boiling water at home is generally satisfactory. However, for the greatest safety, using disposable equipment should be recommended whenever practical.

The nurse acts as a model by observing sound practices of asepsis when giving care. This is a form of teaching also. Patients are generally quick to notice when questionable practices are

Principles of Care 20-3. Donning and removing sterile gloves

Nursing Action	Rationale
Thoroughly wash the hands, following the techniques described.	The hands can never be sterile, but the number of microorganisms can be reduced by conscientious handwashing.
Dry the hands well and dust with powder if necessary.	Wet hands interfere with glove application. Powder helps the gloves glide over the skin. Some gloves come prepowdered.
Select a package of gloves of the appropriate size and place the wrapped gloves on a work area.	Gloves that are too small will be difficult to don and may be easily contaminated. Gloves that are too large may be cumbersome to use.
Open the wrapper containing the gloves without touching the inner surface.	The inside of the wrapper and certain areas of the gloves must remain untouched or they will become contaminated.
Expose and identify the right and left gloves. They should appear similar to diagram A in Figure 20-6.	Gloves that are mismatched or are in reverse positions may prove awkward to apply and become contaminated.
Make sure that the cuff of the each glove is folded down as represented by the shaded areas throughout the diagrams that are used as illustrations.	The side of the cuff that will eventually face the skin surface of the gloved hands is the only part that can be touched by bare hands as the gloves are applied.

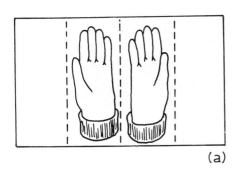

(a)

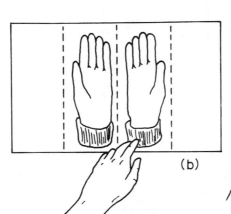

(b)

(c)

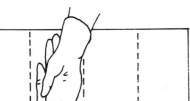

(d)

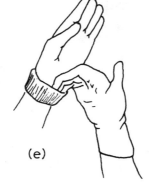

(e)

Figure 20-6 This illustrates the correct way of putting on sterile gloves. The shaded portion of the gloves may be touched by a bare hand but not by any part of a gloved hand.

Continued

Principles of Care 20-3. Continued

Nursing Action	Rationale
Using the thumb and fingers of the nondominant hand, pick up the glove that will cover the dominant hand. Touch only the folded edge of the cuff, as shown in diagram B of Figure 20-6.	The outer surface of the glove must remain untouched to remain sterile.
Pull and stretch the glove while inserting the dominant hand. Do not allow any of the outside surface of the glove to touch the skin of either hand, the uniform or other unsterile areas.	The sterile surface of gloves becomes contaminated when it comes in contact with skin or any other unsterile items.
Touching only the edge of the glove, as shown in diagram C of Figure 20-6, unfold the cuff.	The unfolded edge now exposes the maximum sterile surface of the gloves.

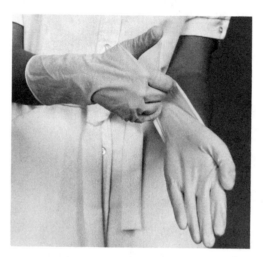

A

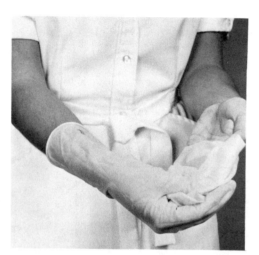

B

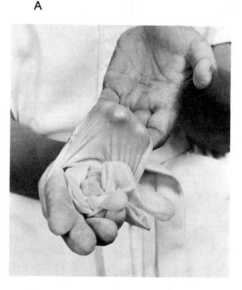

C

Figure 20-7 *A:* The nurse grasps the first glove to be removed without touching her skin or the inside (clean surface) of the contaminated gloves. *B:* The nurse pulls off the first glove, holding it inside out with the other gloved hand. *C:* Next, the second glove is removed while touching only the inside (clean surface) of the glove. The nurse pulls the second glove off by turning it inside out also. Both gloves now enclose the contaminated areas; the clean surfaces are on the outside. The gloves are ready to be discarded.

Continued

Principles of Care 20-3. *Continued*

Nursing Action	Rationale
Insert the gloved hand beneath the folded cuff of the remaining glove, as shown in diagram D of Figure 20-6.	As long as sterile areas touch other sterile areas, no contamination occurs.
Using the gloved hand to pull and stretch, insert the hand, as illustrated in diagram E of Figure 20-6. Care must be taken that the gloved thumb, fingers and hand do not touch the skin of the ungloved hand.	Sterile objects become contaminated with organisms when contact is made with unsterile areas.
Touching only the sterile surfaces of the gloves, pull and stretch them until they fit smoothly and firmly over all the fingers and surfaces of the hands.	Sometimes wrinkles or air pockets form as gloves are being applied. These conditions can be corrected once the gloves have been applied to both hands.
Maintain gloved hands above the level of the waist.	Lowering or dropping the hands to the sides creates the potential for contamination.
To remove the gloves, grasp and stretch the area covering the wrist, as shown in photograph A of Figure 20-7.	Following their use, the gloves are considered more contaminated than the bare hands. They should be removed so that additional organisms are not transferred to the hands.
Pull the glove, turning it inside out as illustrated in photograph B of Figure 20-7.	Microorganisms from the patient are now enclosed within the inverted glove.
Reach under the cuff of the remaining glove. While touching only its inner surface, stretch it so that it too may be turned inside out as the nurse is doing in photograph C of Figure 20-7.	Neither ungloved hand should contact the contaminated surface of the gloves. This technique controls the spread of microorganisms to the nurse.
Discard the gloves into a lined, covered waste bin for soiled equipment.	Asepsis includes proper disposal, to control the spread of microbes. Disposable gloves and other equipment are generally incinerated to destroy microbes with heat.
Perform thorough handwashing before proceeding with further nursing responsibilities.	Even though the hands were gloved, handwashing is an aseptic practice that reduces the potential for spreading microorganisms if undetected contamination occurred.

used. The nurse who has not been attentive to personal grooming quickly loses credibility.

Infectious disease

Infectious diseases include *contagious diseases* which are transmitted by contact. These diseases are caused by pathogens. Practices called *isolation techniques* or barrier nursing are used to prevent the transmission of these infectious pathogens from one host to another.

Understanding the infectious process cycle, previously illustrated in Figure 20-1, is a foundation for the principles of infection control. Isolation techniques confine the reservoir of pathogens, block the vehicle or route of their transmission, interfere with the portal of entry and protect susceptible hosts. The nurse should be familiar with the terms and practices of asepsis before proceeding with the study of the skills associated with preventing the spread of infectious diseases.

Progress towards the control of infectious disease

At one time, contagious diseases were the leading cause of death. Today, many of these diseases in the

UK have been controlled or eliminated. Examples of two such diseases are poliomyelitis and smallpox.

There are several reasons for this accomplishment. One of the main factors has been the production and use of vaccines. *Vaccines* are substances given to individuals to promote the body's defences against contagious diseases. Vaccines are given to infants, children and susceptible individuals according to a routine schedule or immediate need.

The discovery and use of various types of drugs, such as antibiotics, have helped prevent the spread of diseases. While many people still become ill with contagious diseases, drugs often help bring the infection under control more rapidly. Their use reduces the *infectious period*, the time when pathogens exit from their reservoir. The drugs make it possible to shorten the time during which infection control techniques are necessary.

Despite these advances, contagious diseases have not disappeared. Some predict that they will increase in the future. This prediction is made on the basis that our society contains growing numbers of susceptible individuals. Among these are premature infants who would not have previously survived, an increase in the population of ageing individuals who may gradually lose immunity, more and more recipients of transplanted organs who must take drugs that suppress the body's natural defences, and a rising incidence of people with AIDS (Acquired Immune Deficiency Syndrome) who also cannot resist pathogens.

Other facts that explain the continued occurrence and spread of contagious diseases include the following:

- Some individuals are indifferent to the seriousness of infectious diseases and neglect acquiring vaccinations for themselves and their children.
- Vaccinations are refused by some on the basis of religious beliefs.
- Some organisms have developed methods to resist antibiotic drugs and remain a potential threat to health.
- More young children are being cared for in preschool and day-care centres. One ill child can easily infect others.
- Immigrants enter this country already sick or susceptible to contagious diseases.

Therefore, despite past accomplishments, nurses can expect a continued challenge to use nursing skills that prevent the spread of contagious diseases.

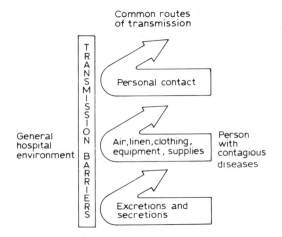

Figure 20-8 Following isolation guidelines, transmission barriers can be used to prevent pathogens from being transferred from the infected person to the general hospital environment.

Isolation techniques

Microorganisms are transmitted by various routes. It is important to be aware of these routes because they form the bases for several kinds of techniques developed to control the spread of infectious diseases. The routes of transmission are described in Table 20-5.

Isolation techniques are used for two reasons. Firstly, to protect patients and staff from the pathogens released from a person with an infectious disease, often called source isolation. Secondly, to protect a highly susceptible individual from microorganisms in the environment and from other people. These methods are illustrated in Figures 20-8 and 20-9.

Facilities available for nursing infectious patients in the UK vary. Some hospitals have separate rooms on ordinary wards, whilst others may have special isolation wards. Isolation policies may also vary among hospitals; often categories of isolation are used where infectious diseases spread by a common route are grouped under one isolation category. Cards with instructions relevant to the category of isolation are used to notify other staff and visitors that isolation precautions are necessary. An example of an isolation card is illustrated in Figure 20-10.

General principles of isolation techniques

The practices used in isolation of infectious individuals aim to block the transmission of the pathogen

Table 20-5. Routes of transmission

Route	Explanation
Contact Route—the transmission of communicable pathogens by touching the microorganisms	
Direct contact	A nurse or others may acquire an infectious disease by being with or touching an infected person.
Indirect contact	Pathogens that remain on the surfaces of objects can spread diseases when they are touched and then enter a susceptible host. Common objects include bed linens, instruments, soiled tissues and dressings.
Droplet spread	Moist material released when an infected person sneezes, coughs, talks or laughs is considered contact spread because of the close association necessary between the infected person and the susceptible host. Droplets do not travel very far.
Vehicle Route—the transmission of communicable pathogens through various media	
Contaminated food, water, blood	When pathogens or their spores remain within food, water and blood they can be transferred through a portal of entry in the susceptible host.
Airborne	As air currents are created by walking, changing linen, sweeping, dusting, fans, open windows and so forth, pathogens suspended on dust particles or droplets can be transferred into a portal of entry.
Vectorborne	Insects and animals may carry pathogens from an infected person or contaminated water or food to a portal of entry in a susceptible host. Mosquitoes, flies, ticks and rats are examples of vectors.

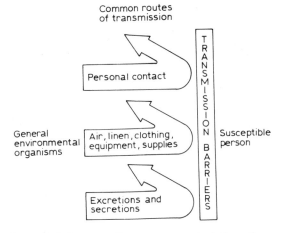

Figure 20-9 In protective, or reverse, isolation, the susceptible person is protected from microorganisms. Transmission barriers are used to keep pathogens away from the patient with weakened defences.

and should be based on principles of microbiology and asepsis. As illustrated in Table 20-6 the precautions may be varied according to the route by which the microorganism is transmitted or the category of isolation.

Use of a single room

If an infection is spread by the airborne route then a single room with the door kept shut will be necessary. In other cases a separate room may not be essential. For example, as an enteric infection, such as salmonella, is transmitted by hands and fomites after contact with faeces, a single room will not contribute to preventing the spread of this infection. A separate room may be desirable if the patient has profuse diarrhoea or, in the case of bloodborne infection, uncontrolled bleeding.

Where an outbreak of infection occurs, individuals with the same infection can be nursed together in one ward instead of many single rooms.

Exclusion from normal social contact can be a distressing experience which can have serious psychological effects. The period of enforced isolation due to infectious disease should therefore always be kept to a minimum.

Handwashing

Microorganisms acquired on the hands from the patient or his environment are usually easily removed by thorough handwashing with soap (see Principles of Care 20-1). Hands must always be washed after the

```
┌─────────────────────────────────────────────────────┐
│                                                       │
│                  STANDARD ISOLATION                   │
│                                                       │
│   Visitors report to Nurses' station before entering  │
│                     the room                          │
│                                                       │
│   APRON:   must be worn when attending patient        │
│   GLOVES:  must be worn for contact with infectious   │
│            material                                   │
│   MASKS:   not necessary                              │
│   WASTE:   discard into yellow bag                    │
│                                                       │
│      HANDS MUST BE WASHED ON LEAVING THE ROOM         │
│                                                       │
└─────────────────────────────────────────────────────┘
```

Figure 20-10 Instructions describing the precautions that must be practised for isolation are printed on a card and displayed on the door of the isolation room. This card is an example of a single category of source isolation.

Table 20-6. Examples of categories of source isolation

Category of Isolation	Disease	Aim	Specification
Strict	Lassa fever, anthrax	To prevent contact and aerosol spread. Usually nursed in special isolation units.	Single room necessary, door must be kept closed. Apron, mask and gloves must be worn to enter the room.
Respiratory*	Tuberculosis, meningococcal meningitis	To prevent spread from respiratory secretions and aerosols.	Single room necessary, door must be closed. Gloves must be worn for contact with respiratory secretions. A mask may be necessary for close contact. People susceptible to the disease must be excluded. Hands must be washed before leaving the room.
Enteric*	Salmonella, cholera	To prevent spread by contact with excreta.	Single room not essential. Apron and gloves must be worn for contact with excreta. Masks are not necessary. Hands must be washed before leaving the room.
Wound and skin*	Multi-resistant bacteria, impetigo	To prevent spread from wounds or skin lesions.	Single room not always necessary. Apron and gloves must be worn for contact with infectious material. Masks are not necessary. Hands must be washed before leaving.
Protective	Leukaemias, organ transplant	To prevent spread from people or the environment to highly susceptible individuals.	Single room necessary. Protective clothing may be necessary for direct contact with the patient. People with infections, e.g. respiratory, must be excluded. Hands must be washed before entering the room.

*These categories can be combined to form a single category of Standard Isolation.

protective clothing has been removed and before leaving the room.

Protective clothing

Aprons. Transmission of microorganisms on staff clothing is theoretically possible but unlikely to occur.

Plastic disposable aprons provide the most practical form of protection. Microorganisms can pass through a fabric gown, especially when it becomes wet. Plastic aprons are impermeable and therefore fully protect the clothing. The apron should be discarded before leaving the room. If cotton gowns are used, care should be taken to ensure that the inside and outside of the gown is clearly marked so that it cannot be worn inside out.

Masks. These are rarely indicated whilst caring for infectious patients. Masks which are damp do not filter microorganisms effectively, and hands are easily contaminated when adjusting or removing the mask. It is more reliable to exclude individuals who may be susceptible to the disease; for example, a nurse who has not had chickenpox should not care for a patient who has the infection.

Gloves. These should be used to protect the hands from becoming grossly contaminated. They should be worn for contact with infectious material, such as faeces from a patient with salmonella.

Linen

Linen from infected patients should not be handled by laundry staff before it is washed. Infected linen is distinguished by placing it into red bags on the ward, instead of the usual white laundry bag. All linen is safely disinfected during the wash cycle where it will reach a temperature of at least 65°C for 10 minutes.

Equipment

Nondisposable equipment such as washbowls and commodes should remain in the room until the isolation precautions are discontinued, when they can be decontaminated. Crockery and cutlery is an unlikely vehicle of microorganism transmission. Washing of crockery and cutlery in hot water and detergent, preferably in a dishwasher, ensures adequate decontamination between uses. Disposable crockery is not necessary.

Waste material

Potentially contaminated waste should be placed into yellow refuse bags. These bags will then be incinerated. Provided care is taken to ensure that the bag is effectively sealed there is no reason to enclose the waste in a second bag. Urine and faeces can be discarded in the usual manner into a toilet, bedpan washer or bedpan macerator.

Protective isolation

Protective isolation is used to prevent an immuno-suppressed and highly susceptible person from acquiring an infection. These individuals have weakened defences and may become seriously ill with an infection which most people would easily overcome. They include patients undergoing organ transplantation, and patients with leukaemia or with extensive burns.

Research has shown that these patients most commonly become infected by microorganisms carried on and within them (Nauseef and Maki, 1981). However, protective isolation is used to ensure that microorganisms carried by other patients in the ward are not transferred to these highly susceptible patients. Conscientious asepsis, such as hand-washing, has been shown to be the most important method of preventing this transmission. It is considered unnecessary to wear sterile gowns or gloves. Equipment such as bedpans, commodes and crockery should be clean but sterilization is unnecessary. Most importantly, hands should always be washed before attending to the patient, and staff or visitors who themselves have an infection, such as a cough or a cold, must be excluded.

Psychological implications of infectious disease control

Regardless of the isolation technique that is used, one need for patient care remains a priority: attention to the psychological effects of isolation.

Understanding the patient's feelings

Experienced nurses have found that patients requiring infection control measures often feel feared by others. They, themselves, are generally frightened of the disease, since special precautions are required for their care. They feel "unclean" because everyone must wash their hands so frequently and be careful of handling contaminated articles. They feel alone and neglected because they cannot leave the room; visitors sometimes leave, finding that the patient is in isolation. Particular effort needs to be made to demonstrate that the microorganisms, not the isolated patient, are unwanted.

When the patient resents the isolation precautions, the nurse needs to show acceptance of the patient as a person and allow him time for expressing his feelings. The nurse understands the holistic concept that emotions can influence the patient's recovery.

Providing human contact

Loneliness is often a problem for the patient in isolation because the patient is usually deprived of the usual contact with others. Studies have shown that the extensive separation of persons from others can be very traumatic. The goal, therefore, is to minimize this situation as much as is safely possible. While precautions are being used, it is important to plan frequent contact with the patient, not only when giving nursing care. Visitors should be encouraged to come whenever and as often as the hospital's policies and the patient's condition permit. The nurse should emphasize that as long as the precautions are followed, they are not likely to acquire the disease.

Providing sensory stimuli

Being isolated from others and prevented from participating in activities outside the isolation room can easily lead to sensory deprivation and depression. The nurse must use preventive measures to help the patient experience a variety of sensory stimulation. Suggestions for providing sensory stimulation were discussed in Chapter 16.

Suggested measures for controlling infectious diseases in selected situations

When the patient is an infant or child

Infants and children represent a group of individuals that are often at high risk for acquiring contagious disease. Young children often play in close contact with one another for long periods of time. Their use of handwashing is often infrequent and inadequate. They share eating utensils and food. They may not cover their mouth while coughing and sneezing. For these reasons, as well as others, they acquire contagious diseases at a higher frequency than other age groups. Prevention and care for them is often a special challenge.

Newborns who have a contagious disease require special care. Some hospitals separate a sick infant from healthy infants in a nursery. However, if there is adequate personnel, opportunity for thorough handwashing, and sufficient space between newborns, a private room for the infant may not be necessary.

Until the source of an infection in a nursery is identified, groups of infants born within the same 24- to 48-hour period may be kept in a single nursery. Personnel assigned to care for these infants should remain constant. The room is then cleaned thoroughly when all the infants have been discharged.

Children with the same contagious disease may be placed in a room together. Nurses must observe closely, since young patients cannot always be relied on to remain within the isolated area.

When the patient is in an intensive care unit

Patients in intensive care units are at higher risk for acquiring an infection than most others within the hospital because they require more invasive equipment while in a weakened condition. Furthermore, these patients are grouped closely together. In an emergency, personnel may be required to move quickly and frequently from patient to patient without time for handwashing.

The optimum precaution would be to place the intensive care patient with a contagious disease in a private room. When this is not possible, the isolation area may be marked off by cubicle curtains. Instructional cards are posted nearby. Conscientious handwashing continues to be one of the most critical precautions for limiting infectious diseases.

Teaching suggestions for infectious disease control

The following are teaching suggestions that may be carried out while providing care for the patient in isolation.

The patient and his family need to have an accurate understanding of the disease and of how to carry out the required precautions.

Family members may need much help in understanding why the patient may be depressed and how to cope with it.

Nursing staff should review the practices involved in isolation technique frequently. Patients are quick to observe differences in the practices of personnel. This can cause confusion and even mistrust in the quality of care.

References

BMA (1989) *A Code of Practice for Sterilisation of Instruments and Control of Cross-infection*, British Medical Association, London.

Expert Advisory Group on AIDS (1990) *Guidance for Clinical Health Care Workers: Protection Against Infection with HIV and Hepatitis Viruses*, Recommendations of the Expert Advisory Group on AIDS. HMSO, London.

Health and Safety Commission (1982) *The Safe Disposal of Clinical Waste*, Health and Safety Commission, Health Services Advisory Committee. HMSO, London.

Nauseef, W.M. and Maki, D.G. (1981) A study of the value of simple protective isolation in patients with granulocytopenia. *New England Journal of Medicine*, **304**, 448–53.

Further reading

Ayliffe, G.A.J., Coates, D. and Hoffman, P.N. (1984) *Chemical Disinfection in Hospitals*, Public Health Laboratory Service.

Bagshawe, K.D., Blowers, R. and Lidwell, O.M. (1978) Hospital topics: isolating patients in hospital to control infection—sources and routes of infection. *British Medical Journal*, **2**, 26 August, 609–12.

Bagshawe, K.D., Blowers, R. and Lidwell, O.M. (1978) Hospital topics: isolating patients in hospital to control infection—who should be isolated and where? *British Medical Journal*, **2**, 2 September, 684–6.

Gidley, C. (1987) Now, wash your hands. *Nursing Times*, **83**(29), 40–2.

Gould, D. (1987) *Infection and Patient Care—a Guide for Nurses*, Heinemann Nursing, London.

Report of the ICNA working party on ward protective clothing, January 1984, Infection Control Nurses Association.

21

The needs of the individual undergoing surgery

Learning objectives

When the content of this chapter has been mastered, the learner should be able to:

Define the terms appearing in the glossary.

List the benefits that occur when patients are well taught and prepared for surgery.

Design a plan of care for the preparation of a patient who is to have surgery, including psychological care.

Demonstrate teaching deep breathing, coughing and leg exercises.

Measure and correctly apply antiembolism stockings.

Discuss methods for preoperatively preparing the surgical site.

Describe the actions that are generally included in the immediate preparation of a patient for surgery.

Describe the postoperative care after receiving a patient from the postanaesthetic recovery room.

List possible postoperative discomforts and complications, indicate typical signs and symptoms, and describe nursing measures to prevent and to help overcome them.

Discuss several ways in which the nurse can help the family of a surgical patient and the benefits of such efforts.

Summarize suggestions offered in this chapter for teaching the surgical patient and his family.

Glossary

Anaesthesia The loss of sensation.

Anticoagulant A medication that inhibits or delays blood clotting.

Day surgery Surgery performed on patients who enter and leave hospital on the same day.

Dehiscence The separation of layers of a wound.

Depilatory cream A substance used to remove hair.

Evisceration The separation of a wound with exposure of body organs.

General anaesthesia The use of an anaesthetic agent that eliminates all sensation as well as consciousness.

Hiccups Intermittent spasms of the diaphragm. Synonym for *singultus*.

Holding area An area where patients are received and wait immediately prior to surgery.

Micro-abrasion Scraping away of skin not usually visible with ordinary vision.

Nebulizer A device that converts a liquid into a fine mist.

Operating theatre The area in which a surgical procedure is performed.

Parotitis An inflammation of the parotid glands. When the condition occurs postoperatively, it is frequently called surgical mumps.

Pneumonitis An inflammation of the lungs.

Postanaesthetic recovery room The area in which a patient is closely observed after surgery until his condition is stable.

Receiving room The area in which a patient waits immediately prior to surgery.

Regional anaesthesia Loss of sensation in an area of the body without affecting consciousness.

Shock The reaction of the body to inadequate circulation. Hypovolaemic shock occurs with the loss of blood volume.

Singultus Intermittent spasms of the diaphragm. Synonym for *hiccups*.

Surgery Procedures that involve entering tissue and removing or reconstructing structures that are diseased, injured or malformed.

Trendelenburg position The position of the patient in bed with the head lower than the feet.

Introduction

Some illnesses or conditions can be treated through surgery. *Surgery* is defined as the treatment of disease, injury or deformity by manual or instrumental procedure (Miller and Keane, 1986). This chapter discusses basic care of the surgical patient. It includes care that, in general, applies to all surgical patients, regardless of diagnosis or type of surgery. Clinical textbooks more appropriately discuss specific disorders that require particular kinds of surgery.

Types of surgery

Surgical procedures are classified according to the urgency with which they must be carried out, as described in Table 21-1. Nursing care of the patient is frequently influenced by the type of surgery a patient is having. For example, providing psychological support, physical care, and teaching is affected by the time the nurse has available with the patient prior to surgery. Emergency surgery requires split-second coordination and attention to priorities, whilst elective

Table 21-1. Classification of surgical operations

Class	Description	Example
Elective	Surgery is not necessary for the patient's survival but is expected to improve the quality of the patient's life.	Removal of a superficial cyst.
Essential	Surgery is necessary to remove or to prevent a threat to the patient's life.	Removal of the uterus.
Emergency	Surgery is required immediately for survival.	Surgery to relieve an intestinal obstruction.

surgery allows a more relaxed pace with time to attend to details. Regardless of the type of surgery, the nurse must be competent in performing the skills required for preoperative and postoperative care for all patients undergoing surgery.

Location for surgery

Traditionally, surgery has been performed in special departments within hospitals. The operating department generally includes a *holding* or *waiting area* where the patient is received and waits immediately prior to surgery, one or more *operating theatres* where surgery is performed and a *postanaesthetic recovery room* where the patient is closely observed after surgery until his condition is stable.

Until recently, most surgical patients were admitted to the hospital one or two days prior to surgery. Now there is a trend to perform more and more *day surgery*. This type of surgery is performed usually within specialized *day units* where patients arrive early in the morning of the day of surgery and leave the same day. The provision of this type of surgery is useful for those minor procedures which require general anaesthesia of 30 minutes duration or less (Royal College of Surgeons, 1985). This service is generally reserved for those patients who are in an optimum state of health and whose outcome is expected to remain uneventful. Some advantages and disadvantages of day surgery are listed in Table 21-2.

Table 21-2. Advantages and disadvantages of day surgery

Advantages	Disadvantages
Large numbers of patients treated.	Regarded by some health professionals as a "second class" service.
Interferes less with individual's daily routine.	Patients present for surgery straight off the street (good preoperative selection is essential).
Fewer nurses required.	Requires intensive preoperative teaching in a short amount of time.
Good recruitment of nursing staff (no nights or weekends).	Doubts about the ideal anaesthetic technique.
Psychological benefits for children (no hospitalization).	Minor sequelae will occur after surgery and anaesthesia.
Reduced surgical waiting lists.	Medico-legal considerations in terms of patient recovery and driving.
Reduced cross-infection rates.	Possible increase in workload of community services.
Economic benefits (dependent on a reduction in inpatient beds).	

Reproduced with permission from Ogg, T.W., Aspects of Day Surgery and Anaesthesia, Anaesthesia Rounds, 18, 1985.

Types of anaesthesia

The term *anaesthesia* implies *without sensation*. The choice of the type of anaesthesia used for surgery is based on several factors:

- The location and extent of the surgical procedure.
- The potential for experiencing pain or other discomfort with the procedure.
- The patient's current state of health.
- The level of the patient's anxiety.
- The personal feelings of the patient about certain types of anaesthesia.

Following consideration of these factors, the patient may receive general or regional anaesthesia. *General anaesthesia* eliminates all sensation and produces loss of consciousness, reflex responses and skeletal muscle tone. This relaxation of muscle facilitates the surgery. It can be administered by the inhalation of gases or by injection of chemicals into the circulatory system. Regional anaesthesia temporarily blocks the sensory receptors in the surgical area. The patient remains conscious throughout the surgical procedure but may be drowsy due to preoperative sedation.

Regional anaesthesia can be produced by the following methods:

- Local infiltration by injection of anaesthetic agent into the surgical area.
- Instillation of an anaesthetic agent into the spinal canal, thereby producing loss of feeling into a large area of the body.
- Topical application of an anaesthetic agent to the surface of the mucous membranes, thereby eliminating discomfort for a relatively short period of time.

Identifying surgical risk factors

Each patient who will undergo surgery should be evaluated for potential risks. The nurse shares the responsibility for assessing factors that pose a hazard for the patient undergoing surgery. Experience has shown that common factors increase the possibility that complications will occur. The number and type of risk factors influence the preoperative preparation, the type of anaesthetic and postoperative care of surgical patients. Some risk factors may be so great that surgery may be postponed to improve a patient's state of health.

Some risk factors and complications that may result are listed in Table 21-3. Old age, obesity and chronic diseases, such as diabetes mellitus, are common

Table 21-3. Surgical risk factors

Condition	Complication	Explanation
Old age	Delayed healing	The elderly patient may have decreased body functions that prolong cell growth and repair. Inactivity may lead to many complications.
Dehydration	Reduced circulation, reduced urine output, blood clots	When the water volume of blood is low, cells may not receive adequate chemicals or oxygen. Blood that is thick is more apt to clot.
Inadequate nutrition	Poor healing, skin breakdown	Without appropriate nutrients, cell maintenance, growth and repair cannot take place.
Cigarette smoking or use of other tobacco products	Pneumonia, atelectasis, poor circulation, blood clots	Smoking causes an increase in mucous production that can plug air passages or leads to an inflammation in the lungs. Nicotine constricts blood vessels, slowing the movement of blood.
Obesity	Poor healing, hypostatic pneumonia	Fatty tissue has a reduced blood supply. This interferes with the delivery of oxygen, nutrients and other chemicals needed for tissue repair. An overweight person generally moves less and breathes less deeply.
Certain drugs, like anticoagulants, aspirin, oral contraceptives, steroids	Bleeding, clotting, slowed healing, reduced response against infection	Anticoagulants, including aspirin, can interfere with clotting. Oral contraceptives increase the tendency to clot. Steroids alter the ability to heal and fight infection due to their anti-inflammatory action.
Substance abuse or dependence, such as alcohol	Withdrawal symptoms, altered reaction to anaesthetic agents	Self-administration or reduction in the usual amount of an addicting substance may cause dangerous symptoms.
Psychological fear	Emotional stress, tensed muscles, elevated blood pressure, rapid heart rate	Stimulation of the sympathetic nervous system accelerates many body functions. Tense muscles and an overly excited state of consciousness may interfere with achieving the desired state of anaesthesia.

surgical risk factors that are discussed in more detail at the end of the chapter. In addition to the conditions listed, the nurse should report any abnormal vital signs and laboratory test results that may affect the outcome of surgery. Specific complications associated with surgery are discussed later in this chapter.

Informing the patient

A patient is usually told about the need for surgery by his own doctor. This often happens in the outpatient department before the patient is admitted to the hospital. In some instances, the patient may have been admitted to the hospital for diagnostic studies and then learn that surgery is advised. The doctor must inform the patient of the risks and benefits of surgery, the likely outcome if surgery is not performed and alternative methods of treatment other than surgery. These are components of informed consent that were discussed previously in Chapter 7. Obtaining written consent will be discussed again later in this chapter.

Providing psychological support

Keeping in mind holistic concepts, the nurse understands that a patient's emotional state can affect his physical condition. Because fear and stress create potential risk factors for the surgical patient, the nurse has an important responsibility for providing psychological support for the patient.

The need for psychological support will vary greatly among patients. For example, the patient's age, diagnosis, cultural and educational background, family responsibilities, sex and occupation are typical factors that affect the need and approaches for psychological support.

By putting oneself in the patient's position, a nurse can begin to help patients cope with forthcoming surgery. Answering certain questions such as the following can provide a beginning:

How would I feel if I were about to have the type of surgery this patient is to have?
What would frighten me most about the surgical experience?
Who would I most like to be with me?
What would I like the nurse to do to help me through this experience?

Psychological stress associated with surgery is usually based on a fear of the unknown. Therefore, another way to provide emotional support is by anticipating common concerns of the patient. Then, by providing information and instructions, the patient's stress level may be reduced. Experience has shown that the following questions are most frequently asked by patients about to have surgery:

- What is the surgical procedure and why is it being done?
- Will I lose control of my body functions while I am unconscious?
- How long will I be in the operating and recovery rooms?
- When may I see my family after surgery?
- Will I have pain when I wake up?
- Will I know where I am?
- Will I be sick from the anaesthesia?

- Will I have tubes in me when I wake up?
- Will I need a blood transfusion?
- What can I eat and drink after surgery?
- What kind of incision will I have? How long will it take to heal?
- Will I be disfigured? Can I lead a normal life?
- How long will it take before I can return home, go to work, or go to school?

This list of questions is by no means complete, some patients may ask still other questions. On the other hand, not every patient will be interested in answers to every question listed. However, these questions may help to guide the nurse in being alert to areas in which the patient may have concerns.

Psychological support not only involves providing information. It includes observing and taking the time to listen to the patient and others who are concerned about the patient. It is usually of no help simply to say that everything will be all right and that there is no cause for worry. The helpful nurse will be available to provide an opportunity for individuals to talk about their problems and express feelings. In this manner, the nurse can often determine whether the patient wishes to see some other support person, such as his minister, priest or rabbi, before surgery. Steps can be taken to arrange a visit if this has not already been done.

Emotional care continues during the postoperative period in a manner similar to that in preoperative care. The nurse should be alert to feelings and worries that patients may not be able to express specifically. For example, the patient may ask, "How am I doing?" when he really means, "Do you think I'll make it?" The nurse may need to interpret the patient's underlying question and explain what is happening to the extent to which individuals are interested or able to understand.

Caring for the patient before surgery

Research has shown that the better patients are taught and prepared for surgery, the fewer postoperative problems or complications that occur. When compared with patients who have had little or no preparation during their preoperative care, studies have noted the following results about patients who are well prepared for surgery:

- Well-prepared patients understand more about the surgery they are to have.

- They feel more in control of the actions and consequences affecting their care.
- They experience less postoperative pain and anxiety.
- They are better motivated for self-care.
- They require less time in the hospital.
- Their recuperative period is shortened (Hayward, 1975; Boore, 1978; Wilson Barnett, 1976, 1979, 1988; Wilson Barnett & Garrigy, 1978).

These findings most certainly indicate the advantages for preparing patients for their surgical experiences.

Most often, teaching is done on an individual basis but nurses have also learned that it is very helpful to include close family members in preoperative teaching. This is especially important when a patient may be unable to understand all the nurse's teaching or when the patient will be going home the same day of surgery. Most relatives are eager to be informed, cooperative and helpful.

The discussion that follows includes information that could be included in the preparation of patients undergoing surgery. Any preoperative teaching should be documented on the patient's chart as it is carried out. This provides a record of what teaching has been done and what still needs to be completed. The skills discussed in Principles of Care 21-1 to 21-3 are primarily the responsibility of the physiotherapist. However, it is necessary for the nurse to understand and help teach the patient these various procedures in the pre- and postoperative situation.

Promoting activity and exercise

Inactivity poses a hazard for the surgical patient. Postoperative patients tend to want to move about as little as possible. They are often fearful of pain and of opening an incision. If patients are allowed to function in this manner, postoperative complications are very likely to develop.

The nurse should explain to the preoperative patient that postoperatively he will be helped to move and turn, to change his position frequently and to walk soon after surgery. Most surgical patients are helped out of bed the same day of their operation. Skills for promoting movement and mobility, described in Chapter 16, can be applied when caring for the surgical patient.

Preventing respiratory complications

Many factors increase the risk of respiratory complications even for the patient who is reasonably healthy and active before surgery. As mentioned previously, inactivity interferes with adequate ventilation. Refraining from food and water tends to thicken respiratory secretions. Inhaled anaesthetics are combined with oxygen, which has a drying effect on mucous membranes. The nurse has an opportunity preoperatively to teach the patient measures that will counteract these effects in order to prevent or restore respiratory function.

Performing deep-breathing exercises. Normally, individuals yawn, sigh or take deep breaths automatically every 5 to 10 minutes to keep the small air passageways of the lungs open. Those who receive general anaesthesia are dependent on the person administering the anaesthetic to provide occasional deep breaths. The reduction of automatic deep-breathing, inactivity during surgery, and a tendency to breathe less deeply after surgery to avoid pain combine to predispose the surgical patient to respiratory complications. Less than optimal ventilation may be accompanied by the collection of thickened secretions within the respiratory tract. Deep-breathing and, in some cases, coughing are important measures to prevent the possibility of hypostatic pneumonia and atelectasis.

Deep-breathing exercises consist of helping a patient to use diaphragmatic and pursed-lip breathing. This helps open small air passageways and to inflate the lungs fully with air. Principles of Care 21-1 describes and illustrates the actions that the nurse can teach the patient in order to improve ventilation.

Raising secretions. Cilia, hairlike structures that line the respiratory tract, move secretions to the upper airways. Coughing is an automatic method for clearing airways of secretions. Deep breathing alone may provide enough stimulus to produce a natural cough. Encouraging patients to drink adequate amounts of fluid will help keep the secretions thinned so they are more easily raised.

It is generally agreed that, unless moist secretions can be heard in the lungs, forced coughing should not be routinely performed postoperatively. The forced exhalation created by coughing tends to collapse small airways and alveoli, doing more harm than good. Patients undergoing some types of surgery, such as that on the eye or brain, or those having had a hernia repaired, should not cough unless specifically ordered to do so. Coughing is dangerous for these patients because it increases pressure in the operative area. However, these surgical patients may perform deep-breathing exercises.

Principles of Care 21-1. *Teaching deep-breathing exercises*

Nursing Action	Rationale
Place the patient in a sitting position, if that is possible.	A sitting position lowers the abdominal organs away from the diaphragm so that the lungs have the maximum amount of room for expansion. A sitting position may not be allowed following all surgical procedures.
Place a pillow between the lower back and the bed or have the patient sit 2 to 4 inches from the back of a chair.	Having the back away from the bed or chair further allows room for full expansion of the lungs.
Flex the knees if the patient has an abdominal incision.	Flexion creates less tension on abdominal muscles and therefore less discomfort when the chest expands.
Help the patient relax.	Tense muscles interfere with full lung expansion.
Explain that the pattern for deep breathing should be repeated three or four times with a few seconds rest between each inspiration.	To compensate for the period of inactivity during surgery and restricted ventilation afterwards, deep breathing must be performed several times when it is actively practiced.
Emphasize that the breathing should be done *slowly*.	Rapid breathing causes hyperventilation. It does not allow enough time to exhale carbon dioxide, which can lead to dizziness, lightheadedness, weakness, tingling around the mouth and fingertips, and even fainting.
Have the patient place his hands on his abdomen, as the nurse is demonstrating in Figure 21-1.	Practising with the patient helps reinforce the correct movements for diaphragmatic breathing.

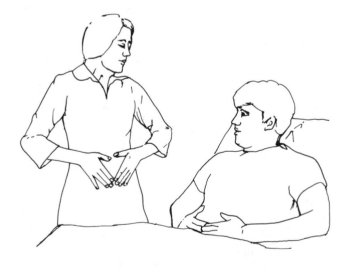

Figure 21-1 The nurse teaches the patient to make his abdomen larger as he takes a deep breath through his mouth. He holds his breath to the count of three before exhaling.

Instruct the patient to take a deep breath while counting to about five or seven, with a second for each count, making the abdomen swell to become larger.	This type of breathing moves the diaphragm downward, increasing the area of the thorax and elevates the lower ribs to allow the greatest amount of room for the lungs to expand.

Continued

Principles of Care 21-1. Continued

Nursing Action	Rationale
Follow local policy for explaining the process for inhalation. In some hospitals, the patient is instructed to inhale through his mouth, or nose, or both.	Inhaling through the nose prevents gulping and swallowing air, which can lead to discomfort if the stomach and intestines fill with air.
Have the patient hold his breath to the count of three to four after inhaling deeply.	Retaining a high volume of air opens and fills air passages throughout the lungs and helps prevent bronchioles and alveoli from narrowing or collapsing.
Instruct the patient to exhale slowly through pursed lips to the count of 12 to 15 or, if he cannot exhale for that long, for as long as it took him to inhale.	Exhaling slowly through pursed lips increases the air pressure within the alveoli greater than during quiet expiration, opens air passageways and helps to maximize the exhalation of carbon dioxide.
Have the patient compress his abdomen toward the spine while exhaling or bend slightly forward.	Rather than passively releasing air, this movement increases intra-abdominal pressure, which moves the diaphragm upward to empty the lungs of a higher volume of expired air.
Practise the deep-breathing exercise several times until the patient can perform it correctly.	Patients should be competent at performing this before surgery. Pain and anxiety after surgery limit the patient's attention and may interfere with the ability to learn.
Explain that postoperatively he should plan to breathe deeply every 1 to 2 hours while he is awake. These exercises should continue for the first 2 to 3 postoperative days, or possibly longer if he has respiratory problems.	To achieve the goal of preventing respiratory complications, this exercise must be performed at frequent intervals until the patient breathes well and normal breath sounds are heard throughout the lungs.

For those patients who have noisy respirations or wet lung sounds, coughing should be performed to help raise and expectorate the accumulated secretions. Principles of Care 21-2 describes the technique for teaching a patient how to cough properly.

Avoiding thrombi and emboli

Inactivity and gravity cause blood to pool and settle in lower areas of the body. Blood tends to become thickened due to the restriction of fluid and food prior to surgery. The surgical patient should avoid positions that tend to keep blood trapped in the lower extremities. Such things as sitting for a prolonged period of time should not be allowed. Placing pillows directly beneath the knees can interfere with blood flow, leading to the formation of clots. Measures can be used during the postoperative period to prevent circulatory complications. The nurse can explain their use preoperatively.

Performing foot and leg exercises. The temporarily inactive surgical patient can perform foot and leg exercises to promote circulation and help prevent the formation of blood clots. Alternate contraction and relaxation of muscles create a pulselike effect on vein walls that helps move blood toward the heart. Recommended techniques for leg and foot exercises are described in Principles of Care 21-3.

Wearing antiembolism stockings. To help prevent thrombi formation, antiembolism stockings are often ordered for patients with limited activity. The stockings are manufactured by several companies. They come in thigh length or knee length in various sizes. Some stockings fit either leg; others are designed for right or left. Their elastic woven fibre acts to support the walls and valves of veins much as a girdle supports abdominal muscles. The support of the vein wall prevents it from stretching and distending with blood. As blood is pumped from the lower areas of the legs upward, the stockings help the valves close. Closed valves prevent blood that has been moved forward toward the heart from falling back into the lower legs and feet due to the effect of gravity.

Principles of Care 21-2. Teaching a patient to cough

Nursing Action	Rationale
Position the patient in a sitting position, unless contraindicated, with the patient leaning slightly forward. A side-lying position may be used by those who may not sit.	A sitting position lowers abdominal organs away from the diaphragm so that the lungs have the maximum amount of room for expansion. A sitting position may not be allowed for all surgical patients. Leaning forward increases intrathoracic pressure, promoting raising of secretions.

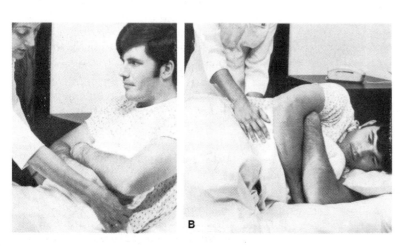
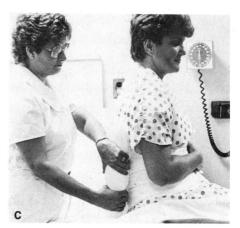

Figure 21-2 *Left*: A rolled towel with the patient's arms across it can be used as a splint over a wound when the patient coughs. *Centre*: The patient can bring up his knees while lying on his side and put pressure on a pillow against an incision for support when coughing. *Right*: This nurse has wrapped a bath blanket around the patient's chest and abdomen. When the blanket is rolled to support the incision snugly, the patient is encouraged to cough.

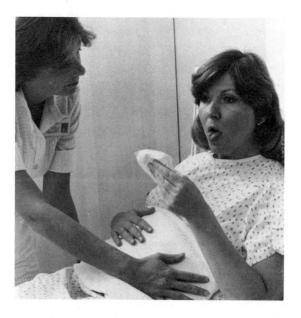

Figure 21-3 The patient is producing a hacking cough, tongue extended, to practise the method for raising secretions from the respiratory tract.

Continued

Principles of Care 21-2. Continued

Nursing Action	Rationale
Splint the abdomen if that is where the operative site will be. This can be done with applied hand pressure, with a folded towel or pillow, or with a bath blanket about the middle of the body, as shown in Figure 21-2.	Applying pressure supports the area of an abdominal incision. The patient will feel less discomfort with a splinted incision and will probably produce a more effective cough.
Have the patient inhale deeply and then have him give two or three hacking coughs as he exhales. The mouth should be open with the tongue out for best results, as illustrated in Figure 21-3.	Hard coughing should be avoided because it may injure the tissues in the respiratory tract.
Follow the coughing effort with a deep breath and then with another cough if secretions are still present.	Deep breathing following coughing helps inflate collapsed lung tissues.
Explain and expect that the patient should be able to expectorate raised secretions into a tissue.	The pressure created by coughing should move secretions to a higher area, where they can be expelled.
Have the patient dispose of the tissue in a waste container.	Secretions may contain pathogens that could be spread if touched by others.
Listen postoperatively for the presence of secretions after the patient coughs.	Normal breath sounds should sound like air moving in and out of passageways. When secretions accumulate, the nurse may not hear any sounds in an area or they will sound like wheezes, crackles or gurgles as the patient breathes in and out.

In addition to inactive and bedridden patients, people with vein disorders or circulatory disturbances, those who spend a great deal of time on their feet, and pregnant women often find elastic stockings helpful to prevent oedema and improve circulation in the legs. Principles of Care 21-4 describes and illustrates the actions for applying and using anti-embolism stockings.

Obtaining written consent

The importance of having a consent form signed preoperatively was discussed in Chapter 7. It is a nursing responsibility to check that one has been obtained before proceeding with preparing a patient for surgery. It is not the nursing responsibility to explain the procedure or obtain written consent. A consent form for a surgical procedure is illustrated in Figure 21-8.

Preparing the surgical site

Hair and skin harbour organisms. For this reason, the skin at and around the site of the surgery is specially prepared preoperatively. The skin cannot be sterilized, but measures can be taken to reduce the chances of introducing organisms into the operative site.

Cleansing the skin. An area of skin much larger than the immediate area around the incision is ordinarily prepared before surgery. This precaution further reduces the chances of infection. When the exact area to be prepared has not been specified, Figure 21-9 may be used as a guide.

Some hospitals permit the patient to participate in preparing his skin by showering or scrubbing with a specified type of soap for a certain period of time. Usually the nurse is required to scrub the surgical site (Date, 1984).

Shaving the hair. Recent studies have shown controversy about the traditional approach used to prepare the surgical site, which includes shaving hair from the skin (Bond, 1980; Pettersson, 1986; Winfield, 1986). Though intended to remove microorganisms attached to the hair, it has been found that the razor causes micro-abrasions. A *micro-abrasion* is a microscopic scraping away of skin. The skin is ordinarily a barrier against pathogens but when abraded, it

Principles of Care 21-3. *Teaching leg and foot exercises*

Nursing Action	Rationale
Position the patient on his back with the head of the bed slightly elevated.	Leg exercises require that the patient flex the knee and toe, which is most easily performed in a supine position. Raising the head helps the patient observe foot movements and relaxes the abdominal muscles.
Instruct the patient, as the nurse is doing in Figure 21-4, to alternately dorsiflex and plantarflex his feet followed by moving each foot in clockwise and then counterclockwise circles.	Movement of the feet helps to move blood, pooled there by inactivity and gravity, out of the most distant areas of the legs.

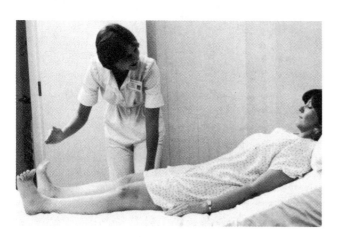

Figure 21-4 The patient is being taught to exercise the feet by performing alternate dorsiflexion and plantarflexion followed by moving the toes in circles. This begins to circulate blood that has pooled in the lowest areas of the legs back to the heart.

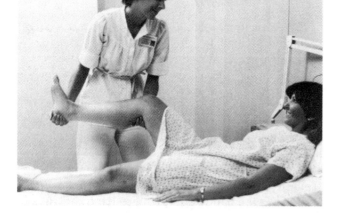

Figure 21-5 The patient is taught to bend her knee. The nurse provides assistance if the patient cannot independently perform the exercise.

Request that the patient bend one knee and then the other, sliding each as far up the mattress as possible and then back again. Or, the nurse can assist the patient with this movement, as shown in Figure 21-5.	Actively using the muscles of the thigh to flex and extend the knee creates a pumping action that moves blood back to the heart.

Continued

Principles of Care 21-3. *Continued*

Nursing Action	Rationale
Have the patient straighten and then raise each leg alternately as high off the bed as comfort will allow and return it to the bed, as illustrated in Figure 21-6.	Elevation assists gravity to move blood in the direction of the heart.

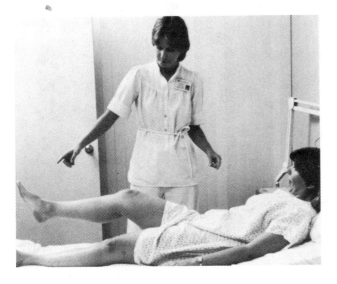

Figure 21-6 The patient extends her knee as she allows her leg to drop slowly back onto the bed. Each leg is exercised in this manner.

Inform the patient that foot and leg exercises should be performed five times each and repeated when awake every 2 hours postoperatively until resuming ambulation and normal activity.	Until a reasonable level of activity is resumed, foot and leg exercises must be performed as a substitute for ambulation.

Principles of Care 21-4. *Using antiembolism stockings*

Nursing Action	Rationale
Measure the patient's leg from the flat of the heel to the bend of the knee, and the calf circumference. For thigh-high stockings, measure the length to midthigh; in addition to the calf measurement, also measure thigh circumference.	Determining a patient's size is important for achieving the purpose of the stockings. Improperly fitting stockings are uncomfortable and will do little good and may even do harm.
Plan to apply stockings in the morning before the patient is out of bed or after elevating the feet for at least 15 minutes.	Before the feet are lowered, there is a minimal amount of pooled blood in the lower legs and feet. Elevation helps gravity move blood toward the heart.
Clean and dry the feet. Apply talcum powder if desired.	Hygiene provides an opportunity for assessment. Powder helps reduce friction when the stockings are applied.
Take care not to massage the legs during hygiene.	Massaging may break a clot loose, if it is present, and cause it to circulate in the body.

Continued

Principles of Care 21-4. *Continued*

Nursing Action	Rationale
Apply the stocking using either of two methods. Turn the stocking inside out and insert the toes. Or, gather the stocking down from the top, insert the foot and thread the leg through the stocking. Both methods are shown in Figure 21-7.	Though elastic, these stockings do not have a wide range of stretch. Applying the stockings in graduated amounts helps ease their application and prevents forming uncomfortable wrinkles.

 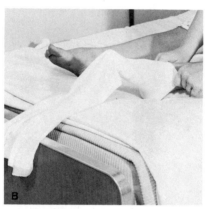 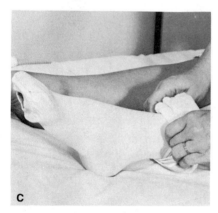

Figure 21-7 *Left*: This type of anti-embolism stocking is turned inside out to the foot. *Centre*: The inverted stocking is then put on the foot and properly positioned over the heel. *Right*: This stocking has been gathered and is pulled the length of the leg. The opening, which should cover the toes, is somewhat larger to allow for extra room and comfort.

Check the position of the patient's heel in the stocking.	An improperly positioned heel area may interfere with wearing slippers and walking or cause discomfort to the skin.
Stretch the toe area of the stockings and mould the toes and forefoot into good alignment if the stockings do not have a toe opening.	Pressure and poor alignment of the toes should be relieved so that circulation, the condition of the skin, or movement are not restricted.
Smooth the stocking of wrinkles.	Folds and wrinkles can cut off circulation and cause enough pressure to break down skin.
Remove the stockings and assess the patient's comfort, colour, temperature and signs of swelling, at least twice a day or on each shift.	Damage to skin and problems with circulation can develop quickly. Frequent observation aids detection and correction of problems early.
Wash soiled stockings at least every three days or more often if necessary.	Laundering clothing is an example of personal hygiene.
Dry the stockings on a flat surface.	Drying on a flat surface prevents altering the shape and size of stockings due to stretching.
Immediately replace soiled stockings with a clean pair.	Removing stockings for an extended period of time defeats their purpose.

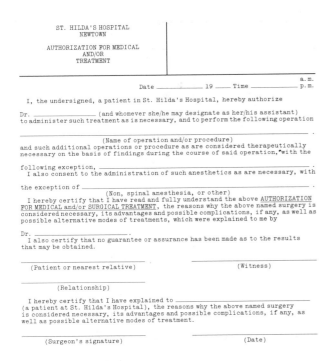

Figure 21-8 Form granting consent for surgery.

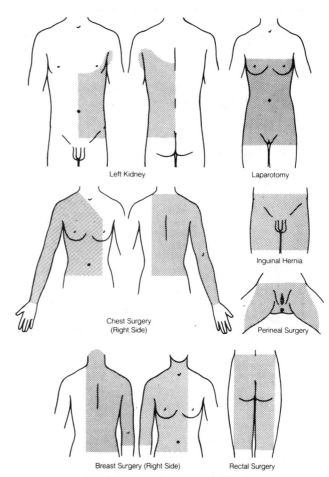

Figure 21-9 This illustrates the areas of skin that are ordinarily scrubbed and shaved preoperatively for various types of surgery. Follow the doctor's order or local policy, which may differ regarding preparation of the surgical site.

allows an entry site for microorganisms. These same studies show that the time interval between shaving and the time of the operative procedure affects the extent of organism growth; the longer the time between the two, the more numerous the microorganisms. Many surgeons now request that a depilatory cream be used. A *depilatory cream* is a substance that is applied to the skin and removes hair. Some surgeons wait to shave the skin until the patient is in the operating room. Others rely only on scrubbing the skin as preparation of the site prior to surgery.

If the skin preparation includes shaving, the same wide areas that are cleansed are also shaved. The actions described in Principles of Care 21-5 may be used when the nurse is responsible for shaving the operative area.

Carrying out the preoperative routine

Most hospitals follow similar routines for the basic physical preparation of the preoperative patient. Principles of Care 21-6 provides a sequence of care that is most commonly performed before a patient's surgery. Not all the actions will be required for all patients. Any omission of a commonly practised preoperative routine, such as missing lab results, no preoperative prescriptions or no documentation of

having given a cleansing enema, should be questioned. There could have been an oversight on the part of the nurse, attending doctor, or other hospital personnel. Appropriate steps may be taken to rectify the situation to avoid delaying the surgery.

Judgement is required in emergency situations. The preoperative preparation of the patient is adapted to meet the patient's needs in the best possible manner while still conserving time.

Completing a preoperative checklist. Most hospitals have a checklist to guide the nurse's actions while preparing the preoperative patient for surgery. The checklist is a summary of priority actions that must be completed before an operation can begin. Having all the information on one sheet of paper eliminates the

Principles of Care 21-5. *Shaving the operative area*

Nursing Action	Rationale
Assemble equipment. Some hospitals have a prepared kit that contains the needed items, such as razor, soap, basin and gauze squares. Water may be added at the patient's bedside.	Having equipment ready saves time.
Expose the area to be shaved and drape the patient, as shown in Figure 21-10.	The nurse considers the comfort and modesty of the patient.

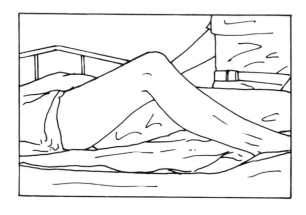

Figure 21-10 The operative site is the knee, but the entire leg will be prepared. Notice that the nurse has draped the patient, exposed the leg for shaving and protected the bed linen under the leg.

Figure 21-11 The nurse works up a good lather over one area of the leg, which is about to be shaved.

Apply soap solution to small areas of the skin and work up a lather, as illustrated in Figure 21-11.	Soap breaks up normal fatty substances on the skin and loosens dirt so that water can penetrate and soften the hair.

Continued

Principles of Care 21-5. Continued

Nursing Action	Rationale
Hold the razor at about a 30-degree angle to the skin.	This angle keeps nicking and cutting the skin to a minimum.
Shave in the direction of the hair growth with one hand while stretching the skin with the other hand. Use long, gentle strokes, as illustrated in Figure 21-12.	Shaving in the direction of the hair growth removes the hair as close as possible to the surface of the skin. Stretching the skin eliminates pits and wrinkles so that the nurse can see the area and achieve a close shave.

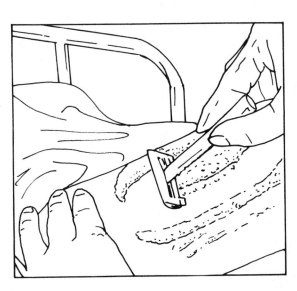

Figure 21-12 Notice that the nurse holds the patient's skin taut with one hand while shaving with the other.

Figure 21-13 After completing the shave, the nurse stoops so that her eyes are at the level of the patient's leg. She then inspects the leg carefully to be sure that all hair has been removed.

Check to see where hair has been removed by stooping so that the eyes are at the level of the shaven area, as the nurse in Figure 21-13 is doing.	Looking closely at the area helps the nurse see whether all the hair has been removed.
Rinse the skin well and dry the area with gauze.	Rinsing removes any residue of soap, skin and hair. Drying the skin promotes comfort for the patient.

time involved in searching through other areas of the patient's chart to determine that they have been carried out. Before the patient is received into the operating department, the nurse responsible for his care and a nurse/technician who works in the operating room review the checklist. If any areas of the checklist are incomplete, the patient remains in the reception area until clarification takes place. An example of a preoperative checklist is illustrated in Figure 21-15.

Principles of Care 21-6. Preparing the patient for surgery

Nursing Action	Rationale
Day/Evening Before Surgery	
Determine that a physical examination, laboratory tests and special examinations have been ordered and completed.	Knowledge of the patient's condition is important to help prevent complications, correct abnormalities and reduce surgical risks.
Assess the health status of the patient.	Being aware of each individual's problems is the basis for the preparation and planning of each patient's care.
Make sure the doctor has obtained a signed consent for surgery.	Legal implications are serious when surgery is performed without proper consent.
Assess temperature, pulse, respiration and blood pressure on admission and again periodically before surgery. Report abnormal measurements promptly.	Abnormal measurements may indicate conditions that increase the surgical risks. Surgery may need to be postponed or cancelled if they are not within normal ranges.
Provide a light evening meal and then nothing by mouth after midnight.	A nonactive and empty gastrointestinal tract prevents aspiration of undigested food if vomiting occurs. It reduces postoperative nausea and abdominal distention.
Carry out the doctor's orders for special measures to promote bowel elimination.	While anaesthetized, the patient may have an involuntary bowel movement when the colon has not been emptied preoperatively. An empty bowel reduces postoperative abdominal distention and constipation associated with diminished eating, inactivity and the use of pain medication.
Attend to the patient's need for personal hygiene, such as bathing and mouth care.	The patient usually feels more relaxed and comfortable when personal hygiene needs are met. Cleanliness helps prevent infections. Special antiseptic soaps may be used.
Cleanse or shave the surgical site according to the policy of the hospital.	Having the operative area free of hair and scrupulously clean reduces chances of introducing organisms into the operative field.
Administer prescribed bedtime medication.	Medication, usually a sedative, is given to assure a good night's rest before surgery and to relieve fears and anxiety.
Day of Surgery	
Provide for mouth care and a partial or complete bath as time permits.	Early scheduling of surgery may shorten the time available for complete bathing in the morning.
Care for valuables, such as jewellery, a watch or money, the day of surgery. If the patient objects to removing a ring, it can be secured in place with adhesive tape or with a strip of gauze, as shown in Figure 21-14.	Lost or damaged valuables may result in serious legal problems. Observe hospital policy on how to label and store these items.
Remove prostheses, such as artificial limbs and eyes. Follow hospital policy regarding the removal of	Prostheses may be lost or accidentally damaged during surgery. Dental appliances may become

Continued

Principles of Care 21-6. Continued

Nursing Action	Rationale

Day of Surgery

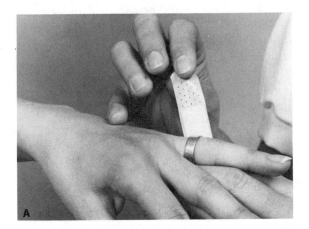 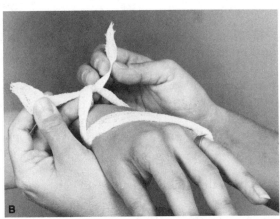

Figure 21-14 *Left*: A plastic bandage strip can be used to secure a ring in place when a patient does not wish to remove it before going to surgery. The gauze section of the strip is placed over a stone in the ring, if present. *Right*: Another way to secure a ring is to use bandaging gauze to tie the ring in place.

Nursing Action	Rationale
dentures and bridgework. Store prostheses properly and safely according to hospital policy.	dislodged or chipped, and cause choking during surgery.
Remove glasses, contact lenses, wigs, false eyelashes and cosmetics such as lipstick, nail polish and rouge.	Glasses and other items may become lost or damaged. Contact lenses may damage the eyes. Cosmetics interfere with the assessment of skin, lips and nailbeds.
Assist the patient to dress in surgical apparel, such as a hospital gown and hair covering. Antiembolism stockings are applied preoperatively in some hospitals.	Hospital garments are used for convenience and to prevent soiling or damage to personal garments. Caps prevent the transmission of organisms on loose strands of hair. Stockings reduce the formation of thrombi due to inactivity during surgery.
Remove hairpins, clips and combs. If the patient does not object, braid long hair. Rubber bands may be used to secure hair in place.	Sharp hair devices may accidentally injure the scalp. Braiding long hair reduces the possibility that loose strands will fall out.
Provide an opportunity for bowel and bladder eliminaton shortly before surgery.	Incontinence is less likely to occur during anaesthesia if the bowel and bladder are empty. A full bladder or bowel may interfere with the surgeon's view or exploration.
Verify that the patient is wearing an identification bracelet.	Misidentification of surgical patients can lead to serious physical injury and legal problems.
Check the patient's history of allergies and administer preoperative medications at the time specified in the doctor's orders if there are no contraindications.	A sedative, usually a narcotic, is given to help the patient into a relaxed state. A drug to dry mouth secretions may also be given to minimize the danger of aspiration. Some patients may be allergic to the

Continued

Principles of Care 21-6. Continued

Nursing Action	Rationale
Day of Surgery	

drugs; the medication should be withheld and the doctor notified if that is the case.

Explain to the patient that he will feel drowsy and thirsty depending on the medications that have been administered.

Informing the patient about the action of drugs will reduce the anxiety and fear of the unexpected.

Raise cotsides, draw curtains around the bed area, attach the buzzer cord and inform the patient to remain in bed.

It is unsafe for the patient to walk around after receiving preoperative medications, since they may cause the patient to feel dizzy and fall.

Complete all charting and the preoperative checklist.

Personnel in the operating and recovery rooms will need the patient's complete record for reference and to provide continuity of care.

Assist with transferring the patient from the bed onto a trolley.

A medicated patient may not be able to assist with moving onto a trolley.

Direct the family or friends to the surgical waiting area.

The surgeon or personnel from the operating or recovery rooms may come to this area to personally communicate with the family.

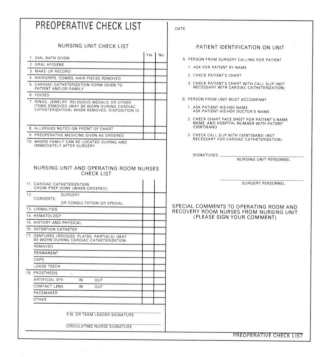

Figure 21-15 An example of a pre-operative checklist.

Resuming care after surgery

Most hospitals have postanaesthetic recovery rooms where patients remain until they are conscious and their condition stabilizes. Nurses working in post-anaesthetic recovery rooms have special training in the immediate care of the postoperative patient. Their role is not discussed here.

Preparing a patient's bed

While the patient is in the operating and recovery room, the nurse prepares an unoccupied bed, as described in Chapter 16. The top linen is folded to the side or bottom of the bed until the patient is transferred from the trolley. Absorbent pads may be placed over the drawsheet to protect bottom linens from soilage. Equipment and supplies that are likely to be needed are in readiness. They will include items such as blood pressure equipment, extra tissue wipes, a vomit bowl and a pole for hanging intravenous fluid bottles, suction and oxygen equipment.

Receiving the patient

When the patient returns from the recovery room, the nurse should be prepared to continue making frequent and appropriate assessments of his condition. Principles of Care 21-7 describes the actions

Principles of Care 21-7. *Caring for the postoperative patient*

Nursing Action	Rationale
Verify the identify of the patient by checking his wristband.	Misidentification of the patient can lead to serious errors. An identification bracelet is more reliable than verbal response.
Loosen or transfer intravenous fluid bottles, equipment used for oxygen, drainage tubes and containers to the hospital bed.	Stretching or pulling tubing may cause discomfort or dislocation unless there is sufficient slack to allow for the distance during transfer.
Assist with moving the patient from the stretcher to the bed.	A patient who is drowsy, in pain, or who has not fully regained feeling in his legs will not be able to provide much help during transfer.
Place the patient on his side when possible, or if he must be on his back, turn his head to one side. Keep the patient who has had spinal anaesthesia flat for as long as ordered, usually 8 to 12 hours, although some suggest a much shorter time.	A side-lying position or turning the head to one side prevents secretions from draining into air passageways. A flat position for a patient who has had spinal anaesthesia helps prevent headaches.
Cover the patient with extra blankets if he seems to be chilled.	Operating and recovery rooms are usually air-conditioned. Blood loss and a lowered room temperature can lower the patient's body temperature.
Fasten the buzzer cord within the patient's reach.	The patient should not attempt to get out of bed. The buzzer cord provide a means for ensuring the safety of the patient.
Obtain a full report from the person in charge of transporting the patient.	To provide continuity of care, the nurse who assumes responsibility for the patient should be aware of anything unusual that may have occurred in the operating or recovery room.
Measure and record the patient's pulse, respirations and blood pressure. A typical routine is to check them every 15 minutes for 1 or 2 hours, every half hour for the next 2 hours and then every 4 hours if stable. Frequent checking, as often as every 5 to 10 minutes, is indicated if the patient's condition is not stable.	A change in measurements may be one of the earliest indications that a complication is occurring.
Temperature should be measured less frequently.	A patient's temperature is easy to measure by touch except in cases where hypothermia has been carried out intraoperatively; then temperature should be measured in the axillary site until the patient is conscious.
Note the colour of the patient's skin especially around the mouth and nailbeds.	Blood loss and poor ventilation can be detected by pale or cyanotic colour in these areas.
Allow an oral airway to remain in place if one is present. If an endotracheal tube is in place, special management by a qualified nurse is required.	An airway keeps upper air passages open. The patient will expel an oral airway when reflexes in his throat return to normal. An endotracheal tube is inserted more deeply and requires special assessment skills and care.
Check the patient's dressings. Report if there is a large amount or bright red bleeding. Feel under the	Dressings absorb blood. An unusual amount of bright red blood may indicate that haemorrhage is occurring.

Continued

Principles of Care 21-7. *Continued*

Nursing Action	Rationale
patient's body and along the side; also check the bottom linen.	Gravity may influence the direction of drainage so that instead of saturating the dressings, the blood flows down the side or under the patient.
Check the patient's postoperative orders for instructions about specific settings for oxygen, suction and so on.	The nurse is responsible for carrying out any orders that affect the patient's immediate care.
Observe the site of an IV. Count the rate at which intravenous fluid is infusing.	Intravenous fluid is used to supplement oral fluids and nourishment. The infusion and rate must provide appropriate amounts.
Assess the patient's level of consciousness. Help the patient become oriented by telling him that his surgery is over and that he is back in his bed.	General anaesthesia alters consciousness. The patient may still be sleepy but easily aroused. Though he may not communicate, he may understand what he hears.
Instruct the patient to take several deep breaths and move his feet and legs as soon as he is able to cooperate.	Preoperative instructions should be implemented as soon as possible to avoid respiratory and circulatory complications.
Provide mouth care using specially prepared swabs, or wet a wash cloth or gauze to moisten the patient's lips and tongue.	The patient recovering from anaesthesia may be disturbed by thirst, yet not be alert enough to swallow safely.
Administer pain-relieving medication as soon as the patient's condition safely permits.	Pain-relieving medication can cause drowsiness, decrease respirations and lower other measurements. This may tend to interfere with the accurate assessment of the patient's recovery from anaesthesia.
Assess the patient's bladder for distention. Offer the use of a urinal when the patient feels the need to urinate. Measure the amount voided. Notify the doctor if more than 8 hours have passed since the patient last micturated.	An accurate record of the patient's fluid balance must be kept after surgery. Additional measures may be needed if the patient is not able to void.
Communicate with the patient's relatives about his condition and the plans for nursing care.	The family are naturally concerned. Without explanations, they may misjudge the patient's condition or the priorities for care.

that are commonly carried out during the immediate postoperative period on the ward.

Planning postoperative care

The patient's postoperative care is guided by written nursing and medical orders. Many hospitals follow previously adopted care plans. The plan for care is designed to include measures for preventing postoperative complications and discomforts and treating them when they occur. The following are general types of measures included in postoperative orders:

- The frequency with which measurement of temperature, pulse, respiration and blood pressure are to be checked once they have stabilized.

- The type, amount and rate at which intravenous fluid therapy is to be administered.
- The concentration and method for administering oxygen.
- Medications to be given following surgery. Ordinarily, orders include drugs to control pain and sleeplessness.
- The type of food and fluids that the patient may have. Typically, the patient has ice chips and sips of water to determine if nausea or vomiting are likely to occur. If the patient tolerates this well, clear fluids, and finally a soft diet may be ordered. Food and fluids are restricted if the patient has gastric or intestinal suctioning.
- The recording of fluid intake and output.

- Care for the wound.
- The frequency and positions in which the patient is to be turned.
- The time when walking should be started.
- Laboratory examinations to be done immediately or on the day following surgery.

Detecting postoperative complications

The nurse must be alert for changes in the patient's condition that indicate that complications may be occurring. Some signs and symptoms indicate a life-threatening situation, while others may only be minor discomforts. Table 21-4 is a list of common problems that may occur during the postoperative period and their implications for nursing care.

Assisting the family of a surgical patient

Keep in mind that relatives, too, are fearful and worried about the patient. To ease their anxiety, they should be taught and given information about what to expect when the patient returns from surgery.

The nurse should be sure to explain the hospital's visiting policy to family members. The family support system is an important part of every patient's care. Both the patient and his family benefit when a nurse takes this into account and wisely uses the family's support for the patient.

Suggested measures when giving preoperative and postoperative care in selected situations

When the patient is an infant or child

Remember that a properly signed consent form is as important for an infant or child as for an adult. Parents or guardians must sign consent forms for minors.

Carefully check the child preoperatively for signs of a skin rash, fever and an upper respiratory infection. Children are more likely than adults to have an upper respiratory infection or a communicable disease. The onset is often rapid. Unless an emergency exists, surgery needs to be postponed if an infection is present.

Take into account that an infant or child receives most of his emotional support from his parents. Therefore, the parents should be taught about the surgical experience, as described in this chapter, so that they can anticipate what will happen and be in a position to support their children through the experience. Parents are being allowed to accompany their child in some hospitals during the induction of anaesthesia and also as the child awakens in the recovery room (Day, 1987).

During the preoperative period, work at developing a friendly and trusting relationship with a youngster having surgery. The child will then be ready to trust the nurse who provides postoperative care.

Just as for an adult, teach a youngster about the surgical experience, equipment likely to be used, the experience of pain and so on, at a level the child understands. Some hospitals include tours in advance of outpatient surgery. With such teaching, the child will enjoy benefits similar to those of an adult who has been properly taught preoperatively.

Assure a child that he will not be left alone. Encourage him to talk about his fears as much as he is able. Tell him it is all right to cry, answer his questions and correct the misconceptions most children have of surgery.

Allow the child to take his own stuffed animal, doll or familiar blanket with him to the operating room as a form of emotional support. Communication among personnel will generally provide for its safe-keeping during surgery and replacement with the child in the recovery room.

Use visual aids to explain a surgical procedure, to the extent to which a child can understand them. Drawings, x-ray films and pictures are helpful (Doroshow and London, 1988). Use of a doll as a substitute for a patient has been successful for role-playing with many youngsters (Smallwood, 1988).

Modify methods for encouraging deep breathing. Balloons, party horns or pinwheel toys may be used.

When the patient has diabetes mellitus

Preoperatively, help work toward good control of a patient's diabetes. Surgical risks are lessened when the patient's disease is under control.

Be prepared to make adjustments in the patient's insulin dosage. A longer acting dose may be prescribed the night before, or a somewhat smaller dose than usual may be ordered in the morning by injection or by intravenous drip. Postoperatively, insulin dosages are generally

Table 21-4. Common postoperative problems

Discomfort/Complication	Implications for Nursing
Cardiovascular Problems	

Haemorrhage and Shock

Shock is the body's reaction to inadequate circulation. Clinical texts describe various types of shock. Hypovolaemic shock is discussed here and occurs postoperatively when blood volume is lost due to haemorrhage. It constitutes an emergency situation.

- Observe for signs and symptoms of haemorrhage and shock, which include excessive blood on dressings; a rapid, thready pulse; a drop in blood pressure; pale or cyanotic and cold, clammy skin; rapid and deep respirations; rapid and shallow respirations as shock becomes more severe; low body temperature; restlessness and anxiety; and finally listlessness and unconsciousness. The patient will die if remedial action is not taken.
- Check pulse, respirations and blood pressure frequently and report adverse changes promptly.
- Check dressings frequently for signs of excessive bleeding. Be sure to check under the patient for bloody drainage.
- Be prepared to place the patient in shock in the *Trendelenburg position*, in which the head is lower than the feet, as illustrated in Figure 21-16. This positioning encourages blood to flow from the extremities to vital body organs. The position is *not* used for patients who have had spinal anaesthesia or brain surgery.

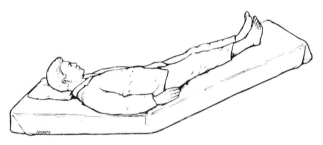

Figure 21-16 This illustrates the Trendelenburg position. The lower extremities are elevated to an angle of about 20°, the knees are straight, the trunk is horizontal, and the head is slightly elevated. (Brunner and Suddarth, 1984)

- Place an extra covering on the patient for warmth. Do *not* overheat the patient. This would cause blood to be diverted from vital organs to the body's superficial surfaces.
- Be prepared to administer prescribed emergency drugs, intravenous infusions, a blood transfusion or blood components, and oxygen therapy.
- Put manual pressure on a bleeding area, if possible, to try to stop the bleeding. The patient may need to be returned to the operating room if bleeding does not stop.

Thrombophlebitis

Thrombophlebitis occurs as a result of various factors, singly or in combination: injury to veins, dehydration and slowed circulation after surgery. Thrombophlebitis usually develops between 7 and 10 days after surgery.

- Observe for signs of thrombophlebitis, which include pain or cramping in the calf, painful swelling of the leg. Body temperature may be elevated.
- Use measures to help prevent thrombophlebitis, which include keeping the patient well hydrated, using leg and foot exercises and using early ambulation as prescribed.

Continued

Table 21-4. Continued

Discomfort/Complication	Implications for Nursing
Cardiovascular Problems	
	• Avoid anything that may decrease circulation to the legs, such as sharply flexing the knees or hips.
	• Avoid massaging the legs and use antiembolism stockings, as prescribed.
	• Sit the patient carefully and prevent the legs from hanging down over the edge of the bed. Support the feet on a chair or on the floor.
	• When thrombophlebitis develops, be prepared to restrict the patient's activity, elevate the affected leg in straight alignment if elevation is prescribed and administer a prescribed *anticoagulant*, which is a drug that inhibits or delays blood clotting.
	• Expect that hot, moist packs may be ordered to be placed on the affected leg.
Respiratory Problems	
Atelectasis Atelectasis is the most common postoperative respiratory complication. It is often accompanied by *pneumonitis*, which is an inflammation of the lungs. Atelectasis is caused by a mucous plug that closes off small respiratory passages.	• Observe for signs and symptoms of atelectasis, which include dyspnoea, cyanosis, pain in the chest and decreased breath sounds and chest movement on the affected side. Fever is often present. • Use measures to encourage respiratory functioning, especially deep-breathing exercises, coughing when secretions are present, and early ambulation. • Oxygen therapy may be necessary when atelectasis is present.
Pulmonary embolism A pulmonary embolism is most often caused by a blood clot that has dislodged from its original site. It is often preceded by deep-vein thrombophlebitis.	• Observe for signs and symptoms of pulmonary embolism, which include coughing, bloody sputum, a sharp pain in the chest, cyanosis, extreme anxiety, dyspnoea, and a rapid and irregular pulse rate. • Use preventive measures such as early ambulation, exercise and activity, antiembolism stockings and encouragement of a liberal fluid intake. • Be prepared to administer prescribed oxygen therapy, analgesics, bedrest and anticoagulants when a pulmonary embolism has occurred.
Hiccups *Hiccups* are intermittent spasms of the diaphragm. A synonym is *singultus*.	• If possible, remove the cause of hiccups, such as gastric or abdominal distention and irritation from drainage tubes in the upper gastrointestinal tract. • When the cause cannot be eliminated, the following measures often relieve hiccups: Have the patient rebreathe in and out of a paper bag. Have the patient hold his breath while taking large swallows of water. • Be prepared to administer a prescribed medication, such as chlorpromazine hydrochloride (Thorazine), if hiccups persist.

Continued

Table 21-4. Continued

Discomfort/Complication	Implications for Nursing
Respiratory Problems	

Respiratory infections
Respiratory infections include bronchitis, lobar pneumonia, bronchopneumonia and pleurisy.

- Observe for signs and symptoms of various respiratory infections; these include fever, expectorations of purulent sputum, cough, elevated pulse and respiratory rates, flushed skin, dyspnoea and pain with inspirations. An elevated temperature within 24 hours after surgery suggests a respiratory tract infection.
- Use preventive measures to improve respiratory functioning; these include deep-breathing exercises, leg and foot exercises, coughing to raise sputum, incentive spirometry, early ambulation and activity as prescribed.
- Encourage fluid intake and use analgesics as indicated when an infection is present.
- Be prepared to administer prescribed antibiotics and oxygen therapy when an infection is present.

Blocked respiratory passages

- Observe for signs and symptoms of blocked respiratory passages; these include cyanosis, noisy and difficult respiration, or lack of respirations.
- Use suction as indicated to remove secretions and debris that may be blocking air passages.
- Open the patient's mouth by pressing down on the chin and up at the angle of the jaw under the ear; pull the tongue out with gauze if the tongue has fallen back into the throat.
- Be prepared to use an airway to facilitate breathing.
- Expect that an endotracheal tube or a tracheostomy may be needed when other measures fail to open respiratory passages.

Gastrointestinal Problems

Nausea and vomiting
Nausea and vomiting occur in many postoperative patients. They often result from an accumulation of stomach contents before peristalsis returns and from manipulation of organs during surgery.

- Offer fluids and food only as ordered. Intravenous infusions are ordinarily used during the postoperative period, while the patient takes nothing by mouth.
- Use measures described in Chapter 10 to help prevent and relieve nausea and vomiting and to care for the patient suffering with nausea and vomiting.
- Support and splint the surgical wound when the patient retches and vomits.

Thirst
Thirst is the result of preoperative medications used to decrease secretions, fluid loss during surgery and preoperative fluid intake restrictions.

- Provide mouth care as described in Chapter 9.
- Moisten the lips and tongue with a clean wet washcloth or gauze square.
- Offer ice chips or sips of fluid, if permitted. Hot tea with lemon juice is often helpful.
- Use measures described in Chapter 23 for the care of patients with limited fluid intake.

Continued

Table 21-4. *Continued*

Discomfort/Complication	Implications for Nursing
Gastrointestinal Problems	
Parotitis *Parotitis* is inflammation of the parotid glands. It is often called surgical mumps when it occurs after surgery. Poor oral hygiene predisposes a patient to parotitis.	• Observe for signs and symptoms of parotitis; these include pain, swelling and redness in the area of the parotid glands. • Use measures described in Chapter 9 to assure good oral hygiene.
Abdominal distention Abdominal distention generally results from inactivity of the gastrointestinal tract due to medications, anaesthesia, handling of internal organs during surgery, the patient's inactivity and changes in fluid and food intake.	• Observe for signs and symptoms of abdominal distention; these include a swollen abdomen and abdominal pain. • Keep the patient nil by mouth postoperatively until bowel sounds are heard upon auscultation. • Use measures described in Chapter 12 for the prevention and relief of abdominal distention. • Encourage exercise and activity to the extent permitted to help prevent and relieve distention.
Constipation Constipation may be due to reduced fluid and food intake, and inactivity. Postoperative constipation is also often a problem when the patient has a history of constipation.	• Observe the patient for signs and symptoms of constipation, as described in Chapter 12. • Begin postoperative exercise and activity as soon as permitted after surgery. • Use measures described in Chapter 12 to relieve and prevent constipation.
Urinary Tract Problems	
Retention, retention with overflow and urinary tract infections These complications occur most often among patients having surgery on the anus, vagina or lower abdomen. Infections are common when the patient must be catheterized or has an indwelling catheter.	• Observe for signs and symptoms of retention, retention with overflow and infection in the urinary tract, as described in Chapter 12. • Use measures described in Chapter 12 to help prevent and relieve retention, retention with overflow and urinary tract infections. • Use measures described in Chapter 12 when catheterizing a patient and when caring for a patient with an indwelling catheter.
Pain and Sleeplessness	
Pain is almost always present at the site of surgery, but it may also cover a larger body area. Sleeplessness is common postoperatively, especially when pain is present.	• Observe the patient for signs and symptoms of pain and sleeplessness, as described in Chapter 14. • Administer prescribed medications to relieve pain and sleeplessness, as indicated. • Use measures described in Chapter 14 to promote comfort, rest and sleep.

Continued

Table 21-4. *Continued*

Discomfort/Complication	Implications for Nursing
Problems Related to the Skin and Mucous Membranes	
Dehiscence *Dehiscence* means that layers of the wound separate. Dehiscence may involve only top layers or it may include all layers of the wound. It usually occurs about 1 week after surgery. *Evisceration* is present when internal organs are exposed and escape from the wound.	• Observe for signs and symptoms of dehiscence, which include a separation of the wound. When evisceration occurs, the patient is likely to say that "something gave way" and is likely to be very anxious. • Handle evisceration as an emergency and be prepared to return the patient to the operating room. • When evisceration occurs, cover exposed organs with sterile gauze moistened with warm sterile normal saline. Do *not* try to replace organs. • Use measures described in Chapter 22 to care for the wound and to help prevent dehiscence. When the patient coughs, be sure the wound is well supported.
Wound infection A wound infection may be localized or it may affect the patient systemically.	• Observe for signs and symptoms of a wound infection; these include fever, rapid pulse and respiratory rates, general malaise, discomfort, swelling in the area and redness. An elevated temperature occurring after 72 hours postoperatively suggests a wound infection. • Use measures described in Chapter 22 to care for the surgical wound.
Decubitus ulcers and symptoms of poor personal hygiene.	• Observe measures to promote personal hygiene described in Chapter 9 and to prevent and care for decubitus ulcers as described in Chapter 22.
Musculoskeletal Problems	
General muscle weakness and contractures are likely to occur if efforts to prevent them are not taken.	• Observe for signs and symptoms of musculoskeletal weakness, as described in Chapter 16. • Use measures described in Chapter 16 to prevent musculoskeletal problems by using exercise and activity for the patient to the extent permitted.
Nutritional Problems	
Fluid imbalances and malnutrition may result when efforts to prevent them are not taken.	• Observe for signs and symptoms of fluid imbalances and malnutrition, as described in Chapters 23 and 10, respectively. • Expect that intravenous therapy, certain medications and a nourishing diet as soon as the patient can tolerate it will be used to help prevent fluid imbalances and malnutrition.

Continued

Table 21-4. *Continued*

Discomfort/Complication	Implications for Nursing
Hypothermia	
Hypothermia decreases the availability of oxygen for cells due to slowed circulation. It can also cause a slow or irregular heart beat. A body temperature below 35.6°C is typical of hypothermia.	• Observe for signs of hypothermia; these include a low body temperature, shivering and skin that is cold to touch. • Apply blankets to the patient to prevent and correct hypothermia. • Expose the patient as little as possible when assessing him postoperatively. • Consider pain as a possible cause of hypothermia and use measures to overcome it. • Be prepared to administer warm, humidified oxygen when hypothermia is present.
Disturbances in Psychological Status	
Disorientation is likely to occur as a result of sensory alterations and the use of analgesics. Emotional distress may occur owing to alterations in body image.	• When caring for the patient postoperatively, observe for signs of disorientation. Also observe for signs of emotional distress in the patient's behaviour and communication patterns. • Use measures described in Chapter 16 to prevent and overcome sensory alterations. • Be prepared to listen to the patient so that he can express his concerns freely. • Use measures described in Chapter 3 to develop and maintain a helping nurse-patient relationship.

regulated according to periodic urine and blood testing for glucose levels.

Expect that it may be likely that wound healing will be delayed in patients with diabetes. Wound dehiscence is also more likely, especially if the patient is obese.

When the patient is obese

Expect that the prevention and care of an obese postoperative patient is likely to be more difficult than for a patient who is of average weight. Much of this is due to the inactivity associated with an overweight condition.

Be especially careful to use nursing measures meticulously to promote respiratory functioning. The obese person tends not to move about and takes shallow breaths. Therefore, special efforts are required to help prevent respiratory complications.

Observe the patient carefully for wound dehiscence and poor wound healing because of the reduced blood supply to fatty tissue. Delay in wound closure increases the risk for postoperative wound infections.

When the patient is elderly

Expect that many elderly persons suffer from poor nutrition. Most elderly persons require a diet high in protein before and after surgery.

Anticipate that elderly patients suffering with chronic diseases are more likely to experience postoperative complications. Chronic diseases especially likely to predispose a patient to postoperative complications include anaemia, diabetes mellitus, and various respiratory and cardiovascular diseases.

Administer medications with caution, since most elderly persons do not metabolize or excrete medications as well as do younger adults. Therefore preoperative and postoperative medications are ordinarily prescribed in smaller than average doses. Use noninvasive measures described in Chapter 14 to help control pain and sleeplessness. This practice reduces the dangers of adverse medication reactions.

Monitor the temperature, pulse, respirations and blood pressure, urinary output and laboratory findings carefully when the surgical patient is elderly. With advancing age, the patient is more susceptible to shock and other postoperative complications.

Anticipate the need to help elderly persons become oriented postoperatively. They often are more likely to be disoriented in a strange environment and after anaesthesia or the use of other drugs that affect a state of alertness.

Expect slower wound healing in most elderly persons due to less than adequate nutrition and poorer circulation to tissue.

Take into account that the elderly have diminished physical reserves. This explains why their organ functions slowly return to normal after surgical intervention. Therefore, meticulous preoperative and postoperative care are especially important to help prevent postoperative complications (Kupferer et al., 1988).

Teaching suggestions related to a surgical experience

Many teaching suggestions for the care of the surgical patient preoperatively and postoperatively were given in this chapter. Although teaching must be geared to meet each patient's needs, the following additional teaching suggestions are appropriate in most situations:

Many patients will not have used a bedpan or urinal before hospitalization for surgery. It is helpful to show the patient a bedpan or urinal and demonstrate its use preoperatively. Understanding this alternative method for elimination may be helpful in reducing or eliminating postoperative urine retention or constipation.

Patients are generally fearful of tubes. They accept them better and are more cooperative when they are taught why they are used and are prepared for those that are likely to be in place when they awaken after surgery. Commonly used tubes include urinary catheters, intravenous lines and drainage tubes at the site of the incision. Patients should also be prepared if it is likely

that oxygen therapy and suctioning equipment will be used postoperatively.

Checking temperature, pulse, respirations, blood pressure and dressings may seem routine to a nurse. However, many patients are disturbed and fear their condition is poor when a nurse is present to check frequently. If the patient understands why he will be checked frequently, it relieves unnecessary postoperative anxiety.

The fear of pain and sleeplessness often contributes to anxiety. Therefore, the patient should be taught that measures will be used to keep him as comfortable as possible and to promote rest and sleep. Explaining that he will be consulted postoperatively about pain and sleeplessness and measures to relieve them is especially reassuring for most patients.

The purposes of not being allowed to eat or drink for a period of time postoperatively should be explained. Most patients are interested in knowing how nutritional and fluid needs are met when they are not eating and drinking normally.

Explanations and the purposes for measures provided before and after surgery should always be offered before carrying them out.

Teaching postoperatively should also include instructions on whatever the patient needs to learn about self-care for when he goes home.

Family members of patients who experience surgery are very often of critical importance. As this chapter pointed out, it is important that they, too, are taught so that they are able to support the patient in the best way possible.

References

Bond, S. (1980) Shave it or save it? *Nursing Times*, **76**(9), 362–3.

Boore, J. (1978) *A Prescription for Recovery*, Royal College of Nursing Research Publications, London.

Brunner, L.S. and Suddarth, D.S.(1984) *Textbook of Medical-Surgical Nursing*, 5th edn, J.B. Lippincott, Philadelphia, p. 406.

Date, J. (1984) Sterile pursuit. *Nursing Mirror*, **23**(19), 14.

Day, A. (1987) Can Mummy come too? *Nursing Times*, **83**(51), 51–2.

Doroshow, M.L. and London, D.L. (1988) Surgery and children—a colorful way to introduce children to surgery. *AORN Journal*, **47**(3), 696–700.

Hayward, J. (1975) *Information—a Prescription against Pain*, Royal College of Nursing Research Publications, London.

Kupferer, S.S., Uebele, J.A. and Levin, D.F. (1988) Geriatric ambulatory surgery patients—assessing cognitive functions. *AORN Journal*, **47**(3), 752–66.

Miller, B.F. and Keane, C.R. (1986) *Encyclopaedia and Dictionary of Medicine, Nursing and Allied Health*, 3rd edn, W.B. Saunders, Philadelphia.

Ogg, T.W. (1985) Aspects of day surgery and anaesthesia. *Anaesthesia Rounds*, No. 18.

Pettersson, E. (1986) A cut above the rest? *The Journal of Infection Control Nursing*, **68**(5 March), 70.

Royal College of Surgeons Commission on the Provision of Surgical Services (1985) *Guidelines for Day Case Surgery*, Royal College of Surgeons of England, London.

Smallwood, S.B. (1988) Preparing children for surgery through play. *AORN Journal*, **47**(1), 177–85.

Wilson Barnett, J. (1976) Patients' emotional reactions to hospitalization: an exploratory study. *Journal of Advanced Nursing*, **1**, 351–8.

Wilson Barnett, J. (1979) *Stress in Hospital*, Churchill Livingstone, Edinburgh.

Wilson Barnett, J. (1988) Patient teaching or patient counselling? *Journal of Advanced Nursing*, **13**, 215–22.

Wilson Barnett, J. and Garrigy, A. (1978) Factors influencing patients' emotional reactions to hospitalization. *Journal of Advanced Nursing*, **3**, 221–9.

Winfield, W. (1986) Too close a shave? *Journal of Infection Control Nursing*, **68**(5 March), 67–8.

22

Wound healing— the needs of the individual

Learning objectives

When the content of this chapter has been mastered, the learner should be able to:

Define the terms appearing in the glossary.

Discuss how the body reacts to injury and how healing occurs.

List and describe types of open and closed wounds.

Describe factors that predispose a patient to the development of a pressure sore. Describe susceptible patients, common locations and how a pressure sore is best prevented and treated.

List reasons for leaving a wound undressed and purposes of a dressing.

Demonstrate how to change a dressing on a clean, open wound and how to secure it.

Describe how to care for a drain, pack a wound and remove sutures and staples.

Demonstrate how to irrigate a wound and the vagina.

List purposes of bandages and binders and recommended actions when applying them.

Demonstrate the application of a roller bandage using each of six basic turns.

Discuss factors that guide the nurse when using applications of heat and cold and list common purposes for using such applications.

Demonstrate the application of cold or hot compresses.

List suggested measures for promoting tissue healing in selected situations, as described in this chapter.

Summarize suggestions for the instruction of patients offered in this chapter.

Glossary

Abscess A collection of pus or a foreign body surrounded by tissue.

Bandage Material applied in a manner to cover a part of the body.

Binder A type of bandage designed to cover or support a large body part, such as the abdomen or chest.

Circular turn A technique for wrapping a roller bandage in which one turn completely overlaps another.

Closed wound Injured tissue without a break in skin or mucous membrane.

Compress Local application of moisture to the skin or a wound.

Debridement A method of cleaning a wound of debris.

Douche A vaginal irrigation.

Dressing A protective covering placed over a wound.

Figure-of-eight turn A technique for wrapping a roller bandage by overlapping turns that ascend and descend in the manner of the number 8.

First intention A type of wound healing in which the edges are directly next to one another. Synonym for *primary intention*.

Granulation tissue An area of repaired cells that appears pinkish red from an increased blood supply.

Hyperthermia A high body temperature.

Hypothermia A low body temperature.

Inflammation The naturally occurring, defensive response of the body to injury.

Insulator A substance that is a poor conductor.

Irrigation A procedure that involves instilling solution into an area of the body.

Malaise Loss of energy.

Many tailed binder A binder with many tails.

Open wound Injured tissue in which there is a break in the skin or mucous membrane.

Recurrent turn A technique of wrapping with a roller bandage in which an area is covered by carrying the bandage back and forth over a rounded surface.

Regeneration A process in which destroyed cells are replaced with identical cells.

Resolution A type of healing process in which damaged cells are able to recover.

Scar formation A process in which destroyed cells are replaced by connective tissue.

Second intention A type of wound healing in which widely separated edges must heal inward toward the centre.

Shearing force Damaging effect to skin that occurs when compressed layers of tissue move upon each other.

Spica turn An adaptation of the figure-of-eight turning technique in which all turns overlap and cross each other, forming a sharp angle.

Spiral-reverse turn A wrapping technique in which a roller bandage is wrapped in a spiral turn in which reverses are made halfway through each turn.

Spiral turn A technique for wrapping with a roller bandage in which one turn partly overlaps the previous one.

Staples Wide metal clips used to hold a wound together.

Straight binder A rectangular piece of material that is long enough to encircle the body.

Sutures Threads of various materials used to encircle a wound to join the edges of tissue together.

T-binder A binder shaped like the letter T.

Third intention A type of wound healing in which temporarily separated wound edges are eventually brought together at a later time.

Trauma A general term for injury.

Wound A condition that results from an injury to the skin or other soft tissues of the body.

Introduction

Everyone acquires a wound at one time or another. A *wound* is a form of damage to the skin and soft tissues of the body. It occurs as a result of *trauma*, a general term referring to an injury. Some examples of trauma include physical injury, such as cuts, blows or even poor circulation to tissue, strong chemicals and excessive heat or cold.

The body has remarkable ability to recover when tissue is injured. This chapter will discuss several methods through which the body repairs wounds. It will also describe nursing actions that can be taken to prevent certain wounds from occurring and actions that support the healing processes of the body when a wound does occur.

The nurse should observe the policies of the hospital where care is given. Hospital policy is also followed when nursing care described in this chapter is recorded.

Types of wounds

In general, there are two types of wounds, open and closed. An *open wound* means there is a break in the skin or mucous membrane. Such a wound may be caused by an accident, or it may be an intentional wound, such as that made by a surgeon when cutting tissue while performing an operation. A *closed wound* has no break in skin or mucous membrane. Table 22-1 provides a list and descriptions of various types of open and closed wounds.

The body's reaction to injury

Regardless of the type of wound, the body immediately reacts to the injury. First, the body produces an inflammation and later implements one of several mechanisms for tissue healing.

Table 22-1. Types of wounds

Open Wounds	Description
Incision	A clean separation of skin and tissue with smooth, even edges
Laceration	A separation of skin and tissue in which the edges are torn and irregular
Abrasion	A wound in which the surface layers of skin are scraped away
Avulsion	Stripping away of large areas of skin and underlying tissue, leaving cartilage and bone exposed
Ulceration	A shallow area in which skin or mucous membrane is missing
Puncture	An opening of skin, underlying tissue, or mucous membrane caused by a narrow, sharp, pointed object
Closed Wounds	**Description**
Contusion	Injury to soft tissue underlying the skin from the force caused by contact with a hard object; sometimes called a bruise

The inflammatory response

An *inflammation* is a naturally occurring defensive response of the body to injury. Its purpose is to limit tissue damage, remove injured cells and debris, and prepare the wound for permanent repair. Several activities occur during an inflammation before the wound can actually heal. The sequence of these activities gives the characteristic local signs and symptoms associated with an inflammation: swelling, pain, decreased function, redness and warmth. Systemic signs and symptoms also occur; they include *malaise*, a general loss of energy and a slightly elevated temperature.

The sequence of events that are associated with the inflammatory response include the following:

- The injured cells release chemical substances that set the inflammation in motion. These chemicals alter cell membranes and allow fluid from within the cells to pour out into the surrounding tissue. This causes swelling and congestion, limiting movement or function. In turn, this acts to prevent any injuring substance from travelling to other parts of the body as well as prevent further injury. Another chemical, released at the same time, causes the sensation of pain to be transmitted along nerve cells. Finally, chemicals cause blood vessels to dilate, producing the redness and warmth associated with inflamed tissue.
- White blood cells, called neutrophils and monocytes, are drawn to the injured area and begin to engulf dead cells and debris. Neutrophils, the body's largest number of white cells, appear first. They encircle the injured area and begin to consume small particles. Monocytes, which migrate somewhat later, are able to remove larger sized debris in the area of injury. Any substances that escape these cells travel to the lymph system and are destroyed there.
- Once the area has been cleaned, cells called fibroblasts and a substance called collagen fill the injured area. These two act as building blocks and "glue" to temporarily repair the area that was damaged. They are the components in a scab.
- The body begins to send new projections of capillaries into the area to supply replacement cells with oxygen and nutrients. This produces pinkish red tissue, called *granulation tissue*, that is gradually replaced later by skin and scar tissue. The supply of blood through these capillaries will eventually diminish and the area will appear similar in colour to the surrounding tissue.

Healing mechanisms—reconstruction and maturation

Wound healing involves the body's efforts to restore the structure and function of cells in the injured area. This is done either by the recovery of injured cells, a process called *resolution*; by replacement of damaged cells with identical new ones, called *regeneration*, or by the production of a nonfunctioning substitute for the destroyed cells, a process called *scar formation*. Cells that can no longer be duplicated when injured are replaced with scar tissue. A scar consists of connective tissue that is strong but does not have the elasticity or capacity to function like the cell it replaces. The aim is to minimize the amount of scar tissue and thereby preserve the appearance and the function of the injured tissue. The type of healing and the time required for permanent repair depends on the extent of injury and the type of tissue involved.

There are three mechanisms by which wounds heal. They are called healing by first intention, second intention and third intention. Each is illustrated in Figure 22-1. The distance between the edges of a wound determines the area of scar tissue.

First intention healing. *First intention* healing, also called *primary intention*, occurs when wound edges are directly next to one another. There is only a narrow space that must be filled with replacement tissue. Only a small scar results. Closing a wound with sutures, or material that produces a similar effect, such as butterfly strips, steri-strips or staples, facilitates healing by first intention.

Second intention healing. Healing by *second intention* involves replacing damaged cells between wound edges that are relatively far apart. This occurs when the edges of the wound cannot be stretched to achieve closure. In some cases the rate of second intention healing is slowed by the presence of drainage from an infection, a blood clot or debris that fills the space between the wound edges. Granulation tissue extends from the edges of the wound toward the centre. This tissue is easily dislodged. Therefore, the nurse must take care to avoid reinjuring the healing wound.

Third intention healing. *Third intention* healing involves a wound with widely separated edges that are later brought together with some type of closure material. The wound is usually one that is fairly deep and likely to contain accumulating fluid. In some cases, the surgeon may intentionally place a drain or pack gauze into the wound to provide for drainage. This keeps the edges of the wound temporarily apart. Once the drain or gauze is removed, the edges of the wound can be closed and the healing completed. The amount of scar tissue that develops with third intention healing is similar to the end result of second intention healing.

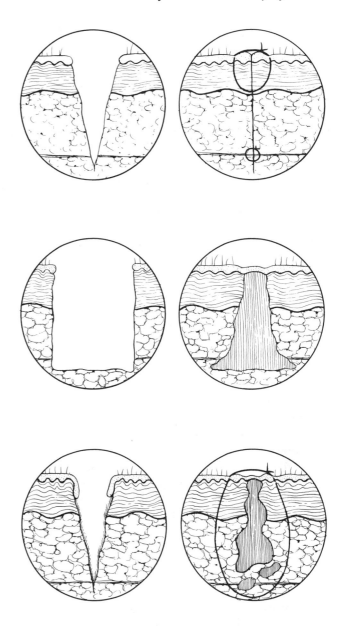

Figure 22-1 *Top*: Smoothly separated wound edges are held together with suture facilitating first intention healing. This is the optimum method of healing because it requires the least amount of time with minimal scar formation. *Centre*: Second intention healing requires that the body produce meterial to fill the area between separated wound edges. Healing takes place slowly from the wound margin towards the centre. *Bottom*: Third intention healing shows delayed closure, early formation of granulation tissue around the margin of the edges, and then the use of suture to join the wound edges together.

Factors affecting healing

If the injury is overwhelming and the body is unable to cope with it, even with assistance, death occurs. When this is not the case, several factors, mentioned below, affect the outcome of healing.

The extent of injury. The more tissue that is damaged, the greater the demand on the body's reparative processes. It will take longer for healing to take place as the limited supplies of the body must be replenished to meet the continued demands. The ability to close an open wound greatly affects the rate of healing and prevention of complications. It may be necessary to use skin grafts to close a wound when the skin covering a large area has been destroyed.

The blood supply to the area. An adequate blood supply is necessary for healing. Healing is delayed when oxygen, nutrients and specialized cells cannot be delivered to the injured area. The tissue of an obese person heals more slowly; individuals with poor circulation, such as the elderly, take longer to heal. The nurse must assess the injured area frequently to determine that oedema, tight bandaging or positioning do not interfere with an adequate blood supply.

The type of injured tissue. Skin and mucous membranes close and heal fairly quickly, sometimes in a day's time. Deeper structures take longer to repair. Surgeons account for this by using different types of suture material for joining various layers of tissue. Sutures that hold muscle layers together are designed to dissolve at a slow rate. Some damaged cells, such as heart muscle and nerve tissue, never regenerate. Healing is prolonged and less than satisfactory as the dead cells are removed and replaced by scar tissue.

The presence of debris. Drainage, dead or damaged tissue cells, embedded fragments of bone, metal, glass or other substances can act as foreign bodies and interfere with good tissue healing. Cleaning an area of this sort of material is referred to as *debridement*. The doctor performs debridement. The nurse is usually responsible for the initial cleansing of a wound and wound irrigation.

The presence of infection. Because the patient's primary protective barrier is weakened when skin and mucous membranes are opened, the need for preventing microorganisms from entering the body becomes especially important. Careful handwashing before caring for the wound probably is the single most effective method of preventing infections.

Although it is not possible to sterilize the skin, practices of surgical asepsis are used when caring for an open wound. Precautions are also taken for persons with closed wounds because of the lowered resistance of the damaged tissue to infection.

When an infection is present, a collection of white blood cells and dead pathogens collects within a wound. This material is called pus. Until the body absorbs it, or it drains from the wound, healing will be delayed. An *abscess* occurs when the body walls off a collection of pus and healing occurs around it. Treatment of an abscess varies, but healing will not completely take place until it is removed. In some cases a surgical procedure to open and drain the abscess may be performed. Local application of heat and immobilization of the part may also be used.

The health of the patient. The promotion of good health helps the body deal with trauma. Adequate rest, relief from emotional tensions, a nourishing diet and adequate fluid intake are particularly important for persons undergoing a response to injury. As mentioned in Chapter 21, individuals with chronic diseases, such as diabetes mellitus, and those with conditions or medications affecting the immune system or blood cell production will have a reduced capacity for healing.

Promoting skin integrity

Intact skin is a barrier against microorganisms. It also helps to retain fluids and proteins within cells and tissues. A pressure sore is an area where skin tissue has been injured; there may be eventual destruction of underlying tissue as well. The terms pressure sore, decubitus ulcer and pressure ulcer are used interchangeably. Nurses are wiser to channel their energies into promoting skin integrity than to be faced with the need for aggressively treating a pressure sore.

Understanding the causes of pressure sores

The primary cause of a pressure sore is prolonged, unrelieved pressure. The body's cells can tolerate pressure, but only for brief periods of time. Therefore, the duration of the pressure is more important than the amount of pressure in the formation of a pressure sore. The mechanism for destruction is as follows: the body weight compresses the tissue and blood vessels against the hard surface of a bed, chair, bedpan and so on. As a result, the cells in the skin

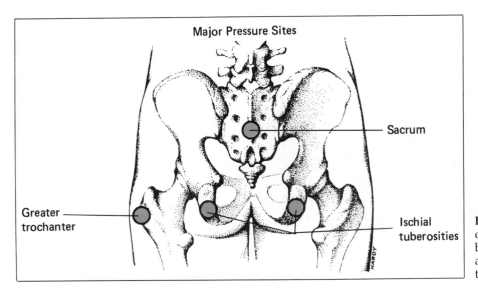

Major Pressure Sites

Greater trochanter

Sacrum

Ischial tuberosities

Figure 22-2 Sites at which about 75% of all pressure sores occur. Other bony prominences include the areas at the heels, the elbows, the ankles, the knees, and the back of the head.

and underlying areas lack oxygen and nourishment; cells die under these conditions.

Friction to the skin and shearing forces also contribute to altering the integrity of skin. Friction causes abrasions to the skin. *Shearing force* is the damaging effect that occurs when compressed layers of tissue move upon each other. This tends to tear and separate the attachment between the epidermal and dermal layers of the skin. For example, a patient who is partially sitting up in bed will experience shearing forces when his skin sticks to the sheet and tissues underlying the skin move downward with his body. This may also occur in the patient who sits in a chair but slides down while his skin sticks to his clothing and the back of the chair.

Wrinkles in linen and various types of debris in a bed or on a chair, such as crumbs, hairpins and buttons, irritate and damage skin so that a pressure sore is likely to develop. Other contributing factors include faecal and urinary incontinence, inadequate nutrition low in calories and protein, and poor hydration.

Pressure sores most often develop on areas of the body where there is too much pressure on bony prominences. Figure 22-2 illustrates common areas where pressure sores tend to develop. They also frequently occur over the heels, the ankles, elbows and even over the ears.

Recognizing the signs of a pressure sore

The earliest sign of excessive pressure is a pale appearance to the skin over a bony area of the body.

The pallor is due to poor blood circulation in the area. This is followed by reddened skin as the body oversupplies the area with blood to improve the effect caused by diminished circulation. Unless the circulation is improved promptly, the area will become dark and cyanotic. As cells die, the skin breaks down, forming an open ulcer.

Pressure sores may be classified according to stages, depending on the assessed characteristics of the skin. Table 22-2 lists the stages of pressure sores, illustrates each stage and describes the characteristics of each classification.

Identifying individuals at risk for developing pressure sores

Any patient, regardless of diagnosis, who is not moving about normally is at risk of developing a pressure sore. Other candidates are patients who are eating poorly, have a low haemoglobin, have lost a great deal of weight or are very thin. Consider the potential risk for others who are unable to control urination and bowel movements, have draining wounds, are feverish and perspire freely or have illnesses that make it difficult for the body to nourish cells and get rid of waste products from cells. Totally or partially paralysed patients and those who are in casts and require immobilization need careful watching. The bedridden patient is especially susceptible, but patients in chairs and wheelchairs also develop decubitus ulcers. Table 22-3 provides an assessment guide for predicting individuals who are at risk for developing pressure sores. Using this

Table 22-2. Classification of pressure sores

Classification	Appearance	Description
Stage I	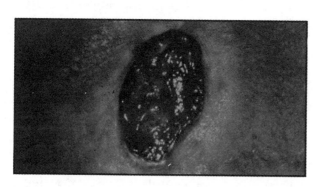	Blanching hyperaemia—momentary light finger pressure onto the site of erythema, following a prolonged period of pressure on the skin, causes the skin to blanch, indicating that the skin's microcirculation is intact. **Figure 22-3** First stage pressure sore.
Stage II	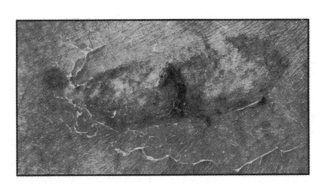	Non-blanching hyperaemia—the erythema remains when light finger pressure is applied, indicating some microcirculatory disruption. Superficial damage, including epidermal ulceration, may be present. **Figure 22-4** Second stage pressure sore.
Stage III	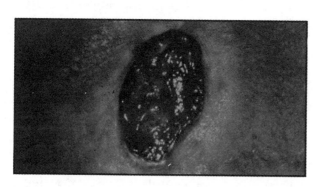	Ulceration progresses through the dermis to the interface with the subcutaneous tissue. **Figure 22-5** Third stage pressure sore.

Continued

Table 22-2. *Continued*

Classification	Appearance	Description
Stages IV and V	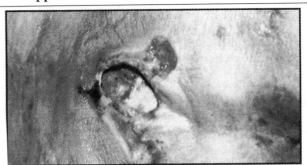	The ulcer extends into the subcutaneous fat. Underlying muscle is swollen and inflamed. The ulcer tends to spread laterally, temporarily impeded from downward progress by deep fascia. Infective necrosis can now penetrate down to the deep fascia, where upon destruction of the muscle occurs rapidly. **Figure 22-6** Fourth stage pressure sore.

After Morison, M.J. (1992) *A Colour Guide to the Nursing Management of Wounds*, Wolfe Publishing, London, p. 73 and Torrance, C. (1983) *Pressure Sores: Aetiology, Treatment and Prevention*, Croom Helm, Beckenham.

Table 22-3. *The Norton scale for risk assessment*

Physical condition		Mental state		Activity		Mobility		Incontinence	
Good	4	Alert	4	Ambulant	4	Full	4	None	4
Fair	3	Apathetic	3	Walks with help	3	Slightly limited	3	Occasional	3
Poor	2	Confused	2	Chairbound	2	Very limited	2	Usually urinary	2
Very bad	1	Stuporous	1	Bedridden	1	Immobile	1	Double	1

Adapted from Norton *et al.*, An Investigation of Geriatric Nursing Problems in Hospital; published by Churchill Livingstone, 1975.

guide, the nurse may develop nursing orders using measures designed to prevent the occurrence of pressure sores in susceptible individuals.

Preventing skin breakdown

There are many interventions nurses can use to help prevent pressure sore formation. Some recommended techniques are provided in Principles of Care 22-1.

Treating pressure sores

Preventive measures described in Principles of Care 22-1 should continue if a pressure sore develops.

However, additional actions must be taken to restore the skin's integrity. The approaches that are appropriate are different, depending on whether the pressure sore is a closed wound, as in Stages I and II, or has extended to an open wound, as in Stages III, IV and V.

One of the principal differences involves whether to keep the area of the pressure sore moist or dry. During the prevention and treatment of a closed pressure sore, the focus is on keeping the area dry. When the surface of the skin is broken, the nurse must maintain a moist environment. Moisture promotes the movement of epidermal cells to the surface

Principles of Care 22-1. Preventing pressure sores

Nursing Action	Rationale
Change the patient's position *often*, as frequently as every hour or two, for a patient at risk for bedsores.	Changing the patient's position helps relieve pressure and restore circulation.
Use the supine position as infrequently as possible.	Lying on the back causes pressure to many vulnerable areas on the body.
Tilt the body obliquely at a 30-degree angle. Use pillows to support the body in this position.	An oblique position is the ideal position for avoiding pressure over bony prominences on the posterior and lateral sides of the body.
Keep the skin dry and clean.	Dampness and uncleanliness predispose the patient to skin breakdown.
Use skin cleansers that do not destroy the natural acid condition of the skin.	Bathing with alkaline soaps destroys the ability of the skin to retard the growth of bacteria and fungi.
Rinse off soap, detergent or skin cleansers well using water.	Residues left on the skin can be irritating and predispose the patient to skin breakdown.
Avoid using waterproof materials on the patient's bed.	Waterproof materials tend to cause the patient to perspire and to prevent evaporation of water. They also retain urine next to the skin of incontinent patients. Moisture on the skin predisposes the patient to skin breakdown.
A sheepskin is no longer being advocated for preventing pressure sores.	Synthetic sheepskins tend to become stiff and hard after washing. The hide backing on natural sheepskins will not allow urine to drain away from an incontinent patient.
Avoid massaging reddened areas.	Once a pressure sore is forming, massage may cause separation of skin layers. Massage of healthy tissue promotes circulation to the area.

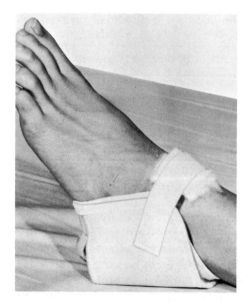

Figure 22-7 This device protects the heel from friction when moving across the bed linen and mattress. Other pressure-relieving measures are recommended in addition to the use of this type of product. (Courtesy J.T. Posey Co., Arcadia, CA)

Continued

Principles of Care 22-1. Continued

Nursing Action	Rationale

Protect areas especially prone to friction, shearing forces, and pressure, such as the heels and elbows. Figure 22-7 shows a heel protector.

Special protective devices reduce friction and provide a cushioning effect to body areas subject to skin breakdown when turning, moving and positioning the patient.

Use a bridging technique like the one illustrated in Figure 22-8 to protect the tissue over bony areas.

Relieving counter-pressure from a hard surface can improve the circulation of blood to an area prone to skin breakdown.

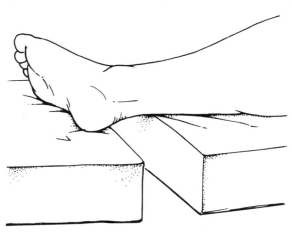

Figure 22-8 This illustrates a way to create a bridging effect by supporting the leg and foot. This positioning technique prevents pressure on the ankle and bottom of the heel.

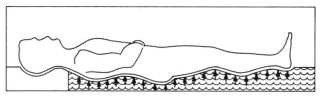

Figure 22-9 The water mattress allows for even distribution of the patient's weight, thereby reducing areas of pressure. It can be used for the prevention of decubitus ulcers and as an aid in healing them.

Avoid using a mattress that is so hard that it causes pressure on parts of the body. A water mattress, as illustrated in Figure 22-9, shows how pressure is distributed on the mattress. Other types of pressure-relieving mattresses, such as an alternating air pressure mattress or convoluted foam pads, are also available.

The even distribution of the patient's weight, at the same time as the counter-pressure from the mattress is reduced, helps improve circulation and prevent injury to skin.

Use only one sheet and avoid tightly tucked linen covering a pressure-relieving mattress.

Re-creating a rigid surface defeats the purpose of the mattress.

Use smaller pressure-relieving pads, like the one shown in Figure 22-10, for those times when the patient is sitting in a chair.

Sitting increases the weight and pressure on bony areas in the buttocks greater than that when lying down. A portable small pad relieves pressure during inactive time spent out of bed.

Change a patient's sitting position frequently. Try not to raise the head of the bed more than 30 degrees.

Pressure and shearing forces increase in proportion to the head elevation of the patient.

Use talcum powder if the patient's skin sticks to the bed, chair or bedpan.

Friction and shearing force have a damaging effect on skin. Talcum powder absorbs moisture and reduces trauma to skin.

Continued

Principles of Care 22-1. Continued

Nursing Action	Rationale

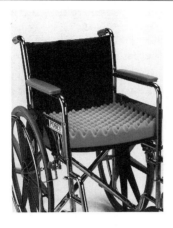

Figure 22-10 This example of a flotation pad illustrates how weight can be distributed to relieve pressure areas. This type is especially handy for patients who are allowed to sit in a chair or wheelchair. (Courtesy J.T. Posey Co., Arcadia, CA)

Nursing Action	Rationale
Lift or use a turning sheet rather than slide the patient when he is moved.	Reducing friction can promote and maintain skin integrity.
Avoid using doughnuts and air-inflated rings, or use them only with the greatest of care and for very short periods of time.	Rings may relieve pressure over an area but they restrict circulation where the body part rests on the ring, causing more problems than they solve.
Keep bed linens and clothing dry, clean and free of wrinkles.	Wrinkles, soilage and moisture irritate the skin and predispose the patient to skin breakdown.
Do everything possible to help keep the patient in the best possible physical condition. This includes seeing that he eats a nutritious diet, takes plenty of fluids, has sufficient rest and gets as much exercise as possible.	Healthy, well-nourished, hydrated patients are less prone to injury and deterioration.

of the wound, causing it to seal over and heal. A dry, crusted area retards this process. Many health care personnel are now using occlusive dressings, such as Op-Site, Tegaderm and Duoderm over open pressure sores. These prevent tissue fluid from draining away from the area of skin breakdown. The manufacturers' directions should be followed regarding application and removal of these dressings.

Other measures, including the use of enzyme ointments, debridement techniques and direct application of oxygen, are being used to promote healing of late stage pressure sores. They have been reported to be effective for at least some patients. The selection of methods depends on local policy. Nursing orders should clearly direct the schedule and techniques that should be followed. By far the best

approach is to prevent the formation of pressure sores with good nursing care in the first place.

Caring for a wound

The tissues of open and closed wounds are more susceptible to further injury than is healthy, intact tissue. Prevention of additional injury and the promotion of healing are two principal goals of wound care.

The undressed wound

Closed wounds are left undressed. Certain open wounds are left undressed if the wound has sealed itself and can be protected from injury and irritation.

This is true even of wounds that have been surgically created and sutured.

There are common reasons for leaving some wounds undressed:

- Friction and irritation of the dressing may injure skin tissues.
- A dark, warm, moist area under the dressing is the type of environment that promotes the growth of microorganisms.
- A dressing may interfere with good circulation to the part, causing a delay in healing.

The dressed wound

A protective covering over a wound is called a *dressing*. Common purposes of a dressing include the following:

- To help keep a wound clean and restrict entry of organisms
- To absorb drainage
- To control oedema and bleeding when applied with pressure
- To protect the healing area from additional injury
- To help hold antiseptic medication next to the wound
- To protect an area that may be sensitive to environmental temperature changes
- To cover an area of disfigurement

Preparing a patient for a dressing change

It helps improve a patient's outlook and his self-esteem when he is included in planning for dressing changes. Mutual cooperation makes the patient a partner in his care. The patient and the nurse should discuss where, when and how the dressing will be changed. If changing a dressing is likely to be a painful experience, the nurse should give the patient a prescribed medication about 15 to 30 minutes before a dressing change to reduce discomfort.

Dressings may be changed in a treatment room or in an operating room in some hospitals. In other hospitals, dressings are changed while the patient is in bed. Commercially prepared, sterilized and individually packaged supplies selected according to the patient's needs are used.

It is best to avoid changing a dressing immediately before or after a meal because of the effect it may have on the patient's appetite or digestion. A considerate nurse will schedule a dressing change other than during visiting hours. The patient will feel more in control of the events surrounding his care if the nurse considers his wishes about when his dressing may be changed as long as the choice does not create a potential hazard to his care.

The patient should receive explanations about the steps that will be followed when changing his dressing. In some instances, patients do not wish to look while their wounds are dressed. This is particularly true for patients whose wounds involve changes in their appearance or body functions, such as when an extremity has been amputated or a breast has been removed. The nurse can make positive statements, such as "There's less drainage today", as a verbal progress report. Patience and empathy will have a more positive effect on the nurse-patient relationship than coercion or shaming.

Organizing equipment and supplies for a dressing change

The following equipment and supplies are suggested for a dressing change on a clean open wound:

- A sterile cloth or paper on which to set up a working field. This can be the wrapper that covers a sterile dressing kit or an instrument set.
- Forceps or a clean glove to handle soiled dressing materials.
- Sterile forceps and a pair of sterile gloves with which to apply sterile dressing materials.
- A sterile cup in which to place antiseptic solution of the hospital's choice or commercially prepared sterile antiseptic swabs.
- A special solvent if a spray-on adhesive preparation was used to secure the previous dressing.
- Sterile normal saline and a sterile cup in which to place it if the dressing tends to stick to the wound.
- A waterproof bag to receive soiled dressings and wet cleansing materials.
- Dressings of various sizes and amounts depending on the size and condition of the wound.
- Tape for securing the dressing. Many patients are allergic to adhesive tape. Micropore tape, or paper tape, is less damaging to skin when it is removed. Also, few individuals seem to experience skin reactions with its use.

Principles of Care 22-2 describes how to use this equipment and supplies when changing a dressing on a clean open wound. Practices of surgical asepsis are required to prevent introduction of organisms into the wound.

Principles of Care 22-2. Changing a dressing

Nursing Action	Rationale
Provide privacy.	The patient has a right to expect that others will not be able to see the procedure.
Position the patient so that he is comfortable and so that the working height promotes the nurse's good posture and body mechanics.	Comfort for the patient and convenience for the nurse make contamination of the area while working less likely.
Expose the area of the wound but cover the areas that do not require attention.	Unnecessary exposure can cause chilling and embarrassment.
Remove materials securing the dressing. If materials other than tape have been used to secure the dressing, loosen and place them away from the wound.	The soiled dressing must be removed and properly disposed in order to prepare the wound for cleansing and redressing.
Loosen the end of an adhesive strip and gently pull it with quick, short, strokes toward the wound. Pull the tape while holding it as nearly parallel to the skin as possible, as illustrated in Figure 22-11. When hair is present, pull the tape in the direction of hair growth, if possible.	Pulling adhesive tape toward the wound prevents separating wound edges in the process of repair. Short, quick strokes and pulling in the direction of hair growth help prevent discomfort for the patient.

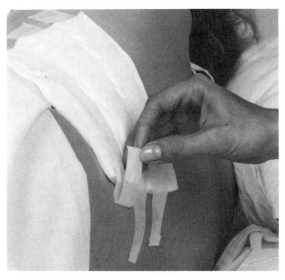

Figure 22-11 The nurse removes adhesive that is securing the patient's dressing. Notice that it is being pulled toward the wound and that the tape is held as nearly parallel as possible to the patient's skin.

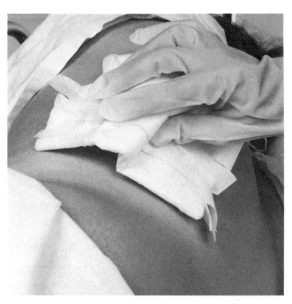

Figure 22-12 The nurse's hand is protected from contact with organisms that may be present on the soiled dressing by a glove that acts as a transmission barrier. Forceps may be used in place of a glove. The distance between the hand and the tip of the forceps prevents contact with a source of organisms.

Lift off the dressing while touching only the outside area. If the dressing is soiled, use a forceps or gloved hand, as illustrated in Figure 22-12.	Microorganisms can be transferred by contact with the drainage on soiled dressings.

Continued

Principles of Care 22-2. *Continued*

Nursing Action	Rationale

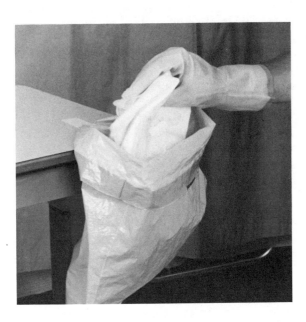

Figure 22-13 The soiled dressing and contaminated disposable equipment and supplies are placed in a waterproof container for burning. In this case, a waxed bag has been attached to the overbed table.

Discard the soiled dressings in a waterproof bag, as illustrated in Figure 22-13, for later disposal, preferably by burning. Be careful not to touch the dressing materials to the outside of the bag.

Confining organisms within a waterproof bag acts as a transmission barrier controlling the spread of organisms to others. Burning destroys organisms.

Place used forceps on a paper towel away from the work area. If a disposable glove or forceps is used to remove the soiled dressing, it may also be placed in the waterproof container with the soiled dressing.

Equipment used to handle soiled dressings are contaminated and should not be placed near sterile materials to possibly contaminate them. The material from which disposable items are made will melt and be destroyed when burned.

If a dressing sticks to a wound, moisten it with sterile water or normal saline, unless contraindicated. Remove the dressing only when it is completely free.

Granulation tissue is easily dislodged by gauze that contains dried secretions. Moistening the dressing will liquefy the dried secretions, thereby reducing trauma and bleeding in the healing wound.

Wash hands before continuing to care for the wound.

Handwashing is one of the most important medical aseptic techniques to reduce the spread of pathogens that may have been transferred to the nurse.

Set up the sterile field on the overbed table or a similar stable, convenient work area.

Using good judgement regarding the location of the sterile field will help prevent contamination of the equipment later.

Add all the equipment and supplies for the dressing change, including the antiseptic solution, to the sterile field.

Poor organization wastes time. Having all necessary materials ready prevents having to seek assistance. Leaving to obtain the items would risk contaminating the sterile field.

Continued

Principles of Care 22-2. *Continued*

Nursing Action	Rationale
Don sterile gloves.	To prevent contaminating items that will be placed in contact with an open wound, sterile gloves must be worn.
Gather the edges of a small gauze square containing no cotton filler with sterile forceps, as the nurse in Figure 22-14 has done.	Gathering permits absorption of a greater volume of antiseptic without dripping. Fibres from cotton-lined gauze squares tend to remain in the wound.

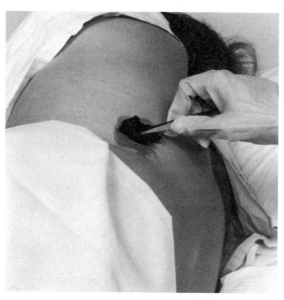

Figure 22-14 The wound is cleaned with a gathered gauze square moistened with povidone-iodine (Betadine).

Nursing Action	Rationale
Using one gauze square or swab for each stroke, cleanse the wound and skin around it, following one of the three methods illustrated in Figure 22-15.	Moving away from the wound and using one swab for each stroke prevents bringing organisms present on the skin into the wound.
Dispose of the gauze squares or swabs used for cleansing with the other soiled material in the waterproof container. Take care not to touch the sterile forceps or glove to any contaminated or unsterile areas.	Placing a wet gauze or swab on a cloth or paper sterile field will pull organisms from the underneath surface, thereby contaminating that area.
Allow the antiseptic to dry well.	Dressings may become moist and pull organisms into the wound if excessive antiseptic remains on the skin. Tape may not securely hold the dressing in place if the skin is wet.
Look at the wound carefully. Assess the healing process and look for signs of infection, such as unusual drainage, puffiness, and tenderness.	The nurse is responsible for assessing the wound and recording the findings that are observed on the patient's record.
Cover the wound with sterile gauze dressings, as illustrated in Figure 22-16. Position the dressing with sterile forceps or gloved hands. The outermost surface of the last dressing may be considered clean rather than sterile.	Touching surfaces with one's hands that will be in close contact with the open wound can transfer pathogens that may lead to a wound infection.

Continued

Principles of Care 22-2. Continued

Nursing Action	Rationale

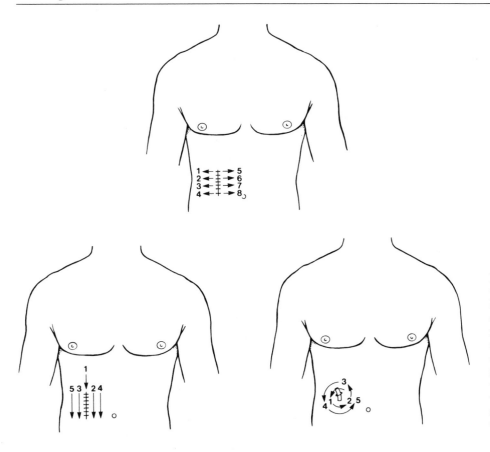

Figure 22-15 The nurse follows a principle of medical asepsis when cleaning a wound; that is, the order and direction of strokes are made from the cleaner area to the one that is likely to contain more organisms. This principle can be maintained by following any of the numbered patterns shown in the illustration. Any round area should always be cleansed using the circular technique.

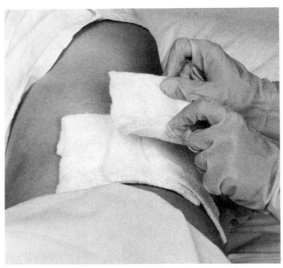

Figure 22-16 The nurse has removed soiled gloves and donned a sterile pair. Layers of gauze squares and pads are placed over the wound to absorb the drainage while keeping the outer dressing dry. Excess dressing material should be avoided, since it may cause discomfort.

Continued

Principles of Care 22-2. Continued

Nursing Action	Rationale
Consider the effect of gravity on the drainage from wounds. Use extra amounts of dressing materials on the lower sides of draining wounds.	Material from a wound will drain downward due to gravity. Applying extra material at the lower end and sides will help absorb drainage when the patient walks or lies in bed.
Secure the dressing with tape. Fold a portion of the end of the tape back over on itself.	Tape helps prevent the dressing from coming loose or changing position. Fashioning a tab promotes ease of tape removal and may reduce discomfort the next time the dressing is changed.
See the text for suggestions for other methods of securing dressings.	Some patients may be sensitive to tape or their wounds may require some additional reinforcement.
Dispose of the contaminated, soiled material. Care for used instruments according to hospital policy.	Careless handling of equipment and supplies spreads organisms to others.
Record the care and appearance of the wound.	Careful documentation is important in validating the care provided and the progress of the patient's condition.

Performing an irrigation

Wounds and other cavities of the body sometimes require an irrigation. An *irrigation* is a procedure that involves instilling solution into an area of the body. Irrigations are generally performed to cleanse and remove drainage and debris. All irrigations will require a solution, an instillation device and a basin to receive soiled irrigation solution as it drains away from the area.

Various types of solutions may be used from plain tap water, normal saline or other medicated solutions. The nurse should follow the doctor's order or the hospital policy regarding the choice of irrigating solution. Warming the solution may produce some comfort for the patient and stimulate increased blood flow that will aid in healing. Solutions that contain an antiseptic or other medication may achieve some additional intended action, such as preventing or inhibiting the growth of organisms.

The instillation device will often depend on the volume of solution that must be instilled. A syringe, a bulb syringe or even a commercial wound-irrigating device may be used. Any irrigation that is performed in a body area that contains intact skin or mucous membranes will need to follow principles of sterile technique. However, when an irrigation is required for an incision or other open wound, surgical asepsis should be followed. The drainage basin must be sterile, although it will receive solution contaminated with organisms and debris from the irrigated area.

A wound irrigation is usually carried out at the time that the dressing is changed. Principles of Care 22-3 describes the suggested actions for performing irrigations. Special modifications are also mentioned for modifying the procedure for irrigating the vagina; a vaginal irrigation is called a *douche*. Irrigation of wounds or body cavities must only be undertaken by nurses who are directly supervised by a qualified nurse.

Caring for a wound with a drain

Drains are hollow tubes through which liquid secretions from a wound are removed. At one time most drains were inserted directly into the wound. This has been found to delay healing and provide an entry site for pathogens. Now surgeons insert drains so that they exit from a separate location beside the wound. Some drains are sutured in place while others may be prevented from slipping beneath the skin by placing a safety pin or clip on the end extending from the wound.

Closed drains are being used more often in place of open drains. A closed drain is connected to a drainage receptacle, such as the one in Figure 22-17. A vacuum or suction machine causes a pulling action to remove drainage. The end of an open drain re-

Principles of Care 22-3. *Performing an irrigation*

Nursing Action	Rationale
Assemble all equipment.	Organization saves time and prevents frustration.
Inspect the equipment, especially reusable or plastic devices, such as douche nozzles, for damage.	Faulty or broken reusable equipment can cause injury. A douche nozzle, unlike other irrigating devices, actually comes in contact with the patient's tissue.
Provide privacy.	The nurse should protect the patient from the view of others.
Explain the procedure to the patient and provide time for comfort measures such as using the bathroom.	The patient who receives a vaginal irrigation should void, since a full bladder may cause discomfort and interfere with filling the vagina with solution.
Warm the irrigating solution.	A warmed solution is more soothing.

For a wound irrigation:

Warm 100 to 200 ml of irrigation solution, for example, to 32.2°C to 35°C.	A higher temperature may cause tissue injury; a colder one may cause chilling.

For the vagina:

Prepare 1000 to 1500 ml of irrigation solution to a temperature of 40.5°C to 43.3°C.	The vagina tolerates relatively high temperatures. Cooler temperatures are uncomfortable.
Inspect the area to be irrigated. Cleanse and remove any gross debris from the area, using clean or sterile technique, as indicated.	Removing superficial debris from the genital area prevents dislodgement into the area being irrigated.
Position the patient in such a manner that the irrigation solution can be directed into the wound or body cavity without excessive overflow into other structures of the body.	The patient may experience chilling and discomfort if other areas of his body, clothing and bed linen become wet. Drainage may contain pathogens that should not be transferred to other areas.

For an abdominal wound:

Place the patient in a supine or dorsal recumbent position.	The solution will flow into the wound and drain out into a basin at the patient's side by gravity.

For the vagina:

Place the patient in a dorsal recumbent position so that the hips are higher than the opening to the vagina.	Gravity will cause the solution to flow into all portions of the vagina. With elevated hips the solution will fill and distend the vaginal walls so that all areas are reached.
Drape the patient and protect the area beneath the irrigation area with absorbent material.	The patient should be protected from unnecessary exposure. Absorbent material may prevent the need to change bed linen.
Place the basin for receiving the draining solution below yet near the area being irrigated.	Gravity causes liquids to flow from a higher to a lower level.
Place a bedpan beneath the patient.	When the head of the patient is elevated, the solution will drain into the bedpan.

Continued

Principles of Care 22-3. Continued

Nursing Action	Rationale
Empty air from tubing that is attached to an irrigating device by letting some solution be washed into the drainage basin.	Air occupies space and may decrease the amount of solution that can be instilled. It may also cause unpleasant sensations.
Allow some of the solution to flow onto tissue near the area to be irrigated.	The patient should be consulted about the comfort of the warmed solution. The area to be irrigated may be even more sensitive than adjacent tissue.
Position the container of solution at a distance that will not cause the fluid to flow too quickly. For a vaginal irrigation, the container may be placed above the hips about 45 to 60 cm (18 to 24 in). If syringes are used, exert gentle pressure.	The higher the container of fluid from the area of instillation, the faster and more forceful the flow. Undue force may cause additional injury.
Direct the flow of the solution toward the body cavity or wound opening in such a manner that structures will not be injured.	The flow of water mechanically breaks up debris and moves it out of the area.

For an abdominal wound:

Nursing Action	Rationale
Without touching the wound itself, let generous amounts fill the open wound without a great deal of pressure.	The solution will be instilled so that debris will move out of the wound by gravity rather than be deposited or forced into tissue pockets.

For the ragina:

Nursing Action	Rationale
While wearing gloves, separate the labia. Allow some solution to flow over and cleanse the outer area. Introduce the nozzle of the irrigating device downward and backward and gently rotate it within the vagina during the instillation. Have the patient contract the perineal muscles, as though attempting to stop urination, and then relax them, four or five times during the irrigation.	Moistening the area promotes the ease of insertion while following the normal anatomic contour of the vagina, avoiding injury to the mucous membranes. Rotation helps direct the solution to all vaginal surfaces. Contracting and relaxing muscles helps to distribute the solution.
Dry any skin areas that may have become wet with solution or drainage.	Wet skin is uncomfortable.
Position the patient over the drainage basin while providing time for draining to occur.	The larger the volume of solution and the area into which it was instilled, the longer the time for draining.
Complete any comfort measures, such as applying a clean dressing, absorbent pad, hospital gown, or bed linen.	The patient should be left feeling clean and refreshed.
Remove soiled equipment and care for it according to hospital policy.	Special cleansing or disinfection may be necessary to avoid spreading microorganisms.
Assess the condition of the irrigated tissue and the results of the irrigation. Record the observations on the patient's record.	The nurse's recorded observations are a tool for evaluating the effectiveness of measures ordered on the nursing care plan.

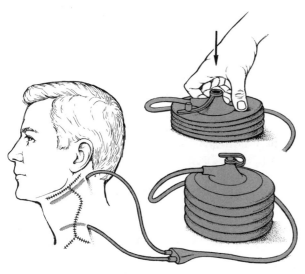

Figure 22-17 A closed drain may be used to remove fluid from a wound. The fluid travels through the catheters into a collector. This device facilitates wound drainage by creating a vacuum suction when it is flattened and sealed.

mains free. It relies on gravity to remove secretions that are then deposited into an absorbent dressing. Open drains are made from various materials. Some are flat flexible rubber tubes, called a Penrose drain; some are silicone or plastic with one or more openings at the base for removing drainage.

When caring for a drain, the nurse should do the following:

- Assess the characteristics and amount of drainage. Drains can become kinked or plugged. If this happens, an abscess may develop within the wound or drainage may ooze from the insertion site.
- Cleanse the area around a drain using separate equipment and gloves than that used for cleansing the wound. This avoids transferring organisms that may be present in one area but not in another.
- Clean the skin around the drain, using the circular method described earlier. It may be helpful and may provide more comfort to the patient if the drain is elevated with several thicknesses of gauze squares while care is being provided. This avoids pulling on the drain from its point of attachment.
- Shorten a drain by using forceps and a *gentle* twisting motion to pull the drain out for the prescribed distance. Cut off the excess length with sterile scissors. Place a sterile safety pin or clip near the exposed end of the drain. Periodic shortening of a drain promotes healing from the base of a wound to the surface.
- Remove a drain using the same techniques for shortening. The patient may be premedicated to reduce any potential discomfort. Refer to the discussion later in this chapter concerning removal of sutures, if the drain has been secured in this manner.

Packing a wound

A draining wound, especially when it is deep and has pockets, may be packed. Packing materials help to soak up drainage and remove large debris from a wound that may not move freely through a drain. Long strips of gauze impregnated with an antiseptic substance may be used. The strip may be cut when the desired amount has filled the wound. The nurse generally changes the packing at the same time that the dressing is changed. This requires assembling additional supplies. The wound should be packed using sterile forceps or gloved hands. The packing should be inserted gently and with care to prevent injury to the wound or displacement of any granulation tissue that may be present. Packing promotes second or third intention healing.

Securing a dressing

Securing a dressing often requires ingenuity and resourcefulness. Factors such as the size of the wound, its location, whether drainage is present, and the amount and nature of the drainage, the frequency with which the dressing needs changing, and the activities of the patient should be taken into account.

The following recommendations describe basic techniques for securing a dressing:

- Plan to use adhesive or paper tape for most dressings. These are available in various widths. The length is cut according to need. Elasticized tape permits more movement of a body part without pull on adjacent tissues.
- Consider shaving the area if tape must be applied over hairy areas. Shave with great care because shaving can cause micro-abrasions and an entry site for organisms.
- Remove adhesive remnants when applying new tape. The remains of adhesive may be removed

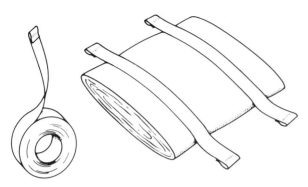

Figure 22-18 This illustrates how to fold back the ends of adhesive strips. The technique helps in the removal of tape so that the ends can be easily grasped. The edges had been turned back for easy removal of tape from the patient shown earlier in Figure 22-11.

with acetone, but it is very drying and irritating to the skin.

- Fold under each end of an adhesive strip creating a tab, as illustrated in Figure 22-18. This technique helps in grasping the tape and lifting it off when it is to be removed.

- Apply a protective coating on the skin before using tape when dressings must be changed frequently. This helps protect the skin from irritation. Some products, such as karaya paste or powder, or Skin Gel, used for protecting the skin around an ostomy, may also be used around some wounds.

- Moisten adhesive with a little alcohol if the adhesive does not stick well to the skin. Alcohol dissolves the oils present on skin surfaces.

- Do not cover the entire surface of the dressing with tape. To do so does not permit the escape of heat and moisture from the skin. This predisposes the patient to skin irritation and destruction.

- Observe the patient for sensitivity to adhesive. Investigate any complaint or discomfort associated with adhesive. Signs include redness, swelling and blister formation. Various kinds of nonallergic tapes, such as those made of silk or paper, are available for a sensitive patient.

- Secure a dressing so that it is snug enough to prevent the dressing from slipping about but not so tight that circulation is obstructed. Loose-fitting dressings cause friction as the patient moves, which produces irritation on the wound and skin. Also, try to secure a dressing so that it fits a body contour for the patient's comfort.

- Use protection judiciously when drainage is profuse. If waterproof material is used, it should not be applied so that the dressing is airtight. This traps secretions and heat, which tend to cause irritation and a breakdown of the skin around the wound. Also, these conditions favour the growth of organisms.

- Consider using a type of bandage or binder when adhesive is impractical. Bandages and binders are discussed later in the chapter.

Removing sutures and staples

Clean, open wounds are held together with temporary materials to promote healing by first intention. Some methods of wound closure include butterfly tapes, steri-strips, sutures and staples. Butterfly tapes and steri-strips are adhesive backed materials applied to the skin surface.

Sutures are threads of natural fibres, like silk wire, or synthetic substances, like nylon, that provide a union between open edges of a wound. Lay people refer to them as stitches. *Staples* are metal clips that also hold tissue together. Sutures and staples are inserted into the skin and underlying tissues. Staples have an advantage in that they are less likely to compress tissue if a wound swells. This is prevented because staples do not encircle the wound; they merely form a bridge that holds the two sides together.

All wound closure material is intended to remain in place until the wound surface has healed sufficiently to prevent reopening. The nurse will be directed by the doctor to remove the sutures or staples. Figure 22-19 illustrates the technique of suture removal. Staples are removed with a special instrument. The staple remover is placed in the middle of the metal staple. Squeezing on the staple remover bends the bridge area and lifts the embedded teeth of the staple from the skin. On individuals with slower healing, every other suture may be removed on one occasion followed by removal of the others a few days later. Sometimes steri-strips are placed over the incision line in between areas where sutures have been removed.

Using bandages and binders

A *bandage* is material applied in a manner to cover a body part. Usually, bandages are dispensed in rolls of various widths. A *binder* is a type of bandage. The term binder is generally used when the bandaging

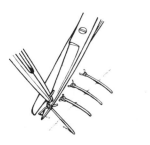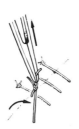

Figure 22-19 To remove sutures, begin by cleansing the incision line. Use a forceps to grasp and elevate the knot. Carefully insert the tip of the scissors just under the knot. If sutures seem to stick, moisten then with normal saline for a few minutes. If the patient is allowed to shower, schedule suture removal following personal hygiene. Cut the suture *below* the knot as close to the skin as possible. Pull the knot gently in one continuous movement to remove the suture.

covers or supports a large body area, such as the abdomen, chest or breasts. Some texts use the terms synonymously, although in the strictest sense they do not have the same meaning.

Purposes of bandages and binders

Bandages and binders serve a variety of purposes:

- They can be used to hold dressings in place, especially when adhesive cannot be used or when the dressing is large.

- They prevent tension on sutures when properly applied.
- They limit motion to promote healing.
- They are used to support a part of the body, protect an injured area and prevent further injury.
- They provide comfort and a sense of security for the patient.

Fabrics for bandages and binders

Manufacturers have prepared bandages and binders utilizing various fabrics to achieve certain desired results. Table 22-4 describes each type of material and indicates the purposes for their use.

Selecting a bandaging technique

Most fabrics used for covering a body part are roller bandages. A *bandage* is a continuous strip of material wound on itself to form a cylinder or roll. These rolls are prepared in various widths and lengths. When applying a bandage, it is wrapped around a body part. The outer surface of the bandage is placed next to the patient's skin. When the bandage is begun, the end is held in place with one hand while the other hand passes the roll around the part. Once the bandage is anchored, the remainder of the roll is passed from hand to hand, with care being taken to exert equal tension with each turn. Unequal tension may interfere with proper circulation to the part. The

---

Table 22-4. Comparison of fabrics used for bandages and binders

Fabric	Description	Uses
Gauze	Light, porous, soft, prepared in a roll or tube	Readily fits a body part. Promotes a cool feeling because it allows circulation of air.
Muslin, flannel, synthetic fabrics	Tightly woven, strong, firm	Useful when support and comfort are desired. Feels more like a garment of clothing. Helps keep an area warm. Well suited for home use, since they may be washed and reused.
Elasticized materials	Strong, stretchable, moulds well to body contours; some are self-adhering, i.e., sticks to itself	Provides firm support and immobilization. Can exert pressure to control bleeding and swelling.
Stockinet, Tubinet, Tubigrip, Netalast	Tubular, stretchable material in various widths or diameters	Encircles a body part, making it convenient for covering the head, chest or length of an extremity. Applies a uniform amount of pressure. Remains in place better than a wrapped bandage. Simple and quick to use.

Table 22-5. *Basic wrapping techniques for roller bandages*

Circular turn (Figure 22-20): Hold the free end of the bandage with one hand and return to the exact point of starting without pulling so tightly as to create a tourniquet effect.

Purpose: To anchor and secure a bandage when it is started and ended.

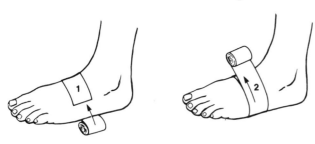

Figure 22-20 A circular turn is wrapped firmly but not tightly around the end of the foot. Note that bandaging is started at the side of the foot so that the end will not cause pressure over a bony area on the upper foot or create discomfort on the bottom of the foot when the patient walks.

Spiral turn (Figure 22-21): Partly overlap the previous turn. The overlapping varies from half to three quarters of the width of the bandage, depending on the purpose of the bandage.

Purpose: To wrap a part that is cylindrical in shape, such as the fingers, arms, legs, chest and abdomen.

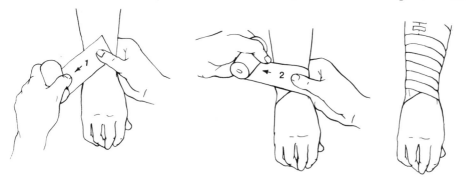

Figure 22-21 A roller bandage is applied using a spiral turn. Note that instead of an initial circular turn, the bandage was started obliquely to anchor it around the wrist.

Spiral-reverse turn (Figure 22-22): This is wrapped similarly to a spiral, the difference being that each layer is reversed halfway through the turn.

Purpose: To bandage a cone-shaped body part, such as the thigh or leg.

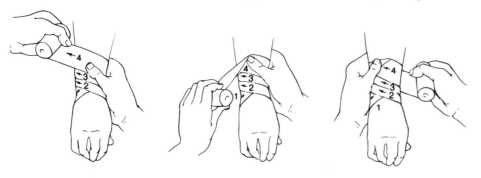

Figure 22-22 This is the procedure for making the spiral reverse turn with a roller bandage.

Figure-of-eight turn (Figure 22-23): This turn consists of oblique overlapping turns that ascend and descend alternately. Each turn crosses the one preceding it so that it resembles the number 8.

Continued

Table 22-5. *Continued*

Purpose: To bandage around joints such as the knee, elbow, ankle and wrist. This turn provides for a snug bandage, which in some cases is useful for immobilization.

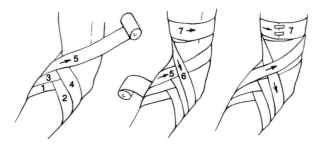

Figure 22-23 This illustrates the figure-of-eight turn.

Spica turn (Figure 22-24): The spica turn is an adaptation of the figure-of-eight turn. The turn consists of ascending and descending turns with all turns overlapping and crossing each other to form a sharp angle.

Purpose: To bandage the thumb, breast, shoulder, groin, or hip.

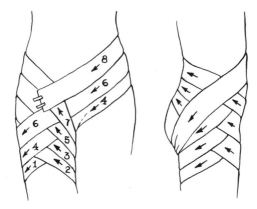

Figure 22-24 The numbers and arrows indicate the technique for wrapping a roller bandage in a spica.

Recurrent turn (Figure 22-25): In the recurrent turn, the roll is passed back and forth over the tip of the body part from one side to the other after the free end has been anchored. It is important to be sure that the tension on each turn is equal. Unnecessary and uneven overlapping of turns should be avoided. All skin should be covered to prevent swelling of exposed tissue. To hold the recurrent turns in place, the bandaging may be completed by using a figure-of-eight turn.

Purpose: To bandage rounded surfaces, such as the head or the stump of an amputated limb.

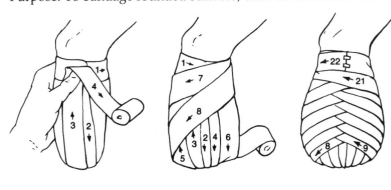

Figure 22-25 This illustrates the sequence for wrapping a roller bandage around a stump. A circular turn is followed by several recurrent turns. A circular turn should not be used to anchor a bandage on a stump if circulation will be compromised. The patient or an assistant can hold the recurrent turns securely. The bandaging can then be completed, using a figure-of-eight technique covering the length of the stump and the previous recurrent turns.

terminal end of the bandage may be secured with adhesive. This should be done in such a way that pressure is not exerted on the patient's skin or over the wound.

There are six basic turns used when applying bandages. The choice of turning technique depends on the shape of the body part. Some wrapping techniques may be used separately or in combination, depending on the purpose and the part being bandaged. Table 22-5 describes each turn, lists its purpose and provides illustrations for its application.

Applying bandages and binders

The nurse should follow some basic guidelines when applying bandages and binders. Principles of Care 22-4 describes suggested actions that can provide principles to follow when covering a body part.

Removing a bandage

If a bandage is not going to be reused, it is best to remove it by freeing the bandage material with bandage scissors. Cutting should be done on the side opposite the injury or wound, from one end to the other, so that the bandage can be opened for its entire length. If the material is to be reused, it may be unwrapped and rewound by rolling the loosened end and passing it as a ball from one hand to the other while unwinding.

Applying commonly used binders

Some commonly used binders include the T-binder, four-tailed binder, scultetus binder and straight binder. A triangular binder known as a sling, is discussed further in Chapter 16. The following is information concerning the application of binders that are frequently used in the care of patients.

Using a T-binder. A *T-binder* looks like the letter T and is used for securing dressings on the perineum and in the groin. A single T-binder has a tail attached at right angles to a belt. The belt is placed around the waist and tied. The single tail is passed between the legs and tied to the belt. A T-binder is illustrated in Figure 22-26.

Using a many tailed binder. Each tail is about 5 cm (2 in) wide, attached to the sides of a rectangular piece of flannel or muslin. Among other purposes, it may be used to support the wound of an obese patient to prevent dehiscence. When a many tailed binder is applied to the abdomen, the patient lies on his back and on the centre of the binder. The nurse should be sure the area of the binder under the

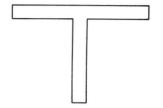

Figure 22-26 A single T-binder.

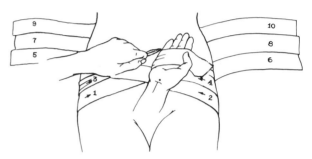

Figure 22-27 This illustrates the procedure for applying a many-tailed binder. Occasionally, the tails may be applied in the opposite direction—that is, they are wrapped from top to bottom—when the patient has had a caesarean section or a vaginal delivery. This method of application promotes uterine drainage from the vaginal canal.

patient is free of wrinkles. The lower end of the binder is placed well down on the hips but not so low that it will interfere with the use of a bedpan or walking. The tails are brought out to either side to wrap around the lower part of the abdomen first. A tail from each side is brought up and placed obliquely over the abdomen until all tails are in place. The last tails are fastened with adhesive. Figure 22-27 illustrates the application of a many tailed binder to the abdomen.

Using a straight binder. A *straight binder* is a rectangular piece of material, usually about 15 to 20 cm (6 to 8 in) wide and long enough to more than circle the body. This straight piece of fabric can be applied to the abdomen or chest. Sometimes a binder is applied to the breasts of a newly delivered mother to suppress the formation of milk. A breast binder is often equipped with shoulder straps so that it will not slip down on the trunk. When straight binders are used, they must be adjusted to fit the contours of the body. This is usually done by making small tucks in the binder. The tucks can be secured with safety pins.

Principles of Care 22-4. *Applying bandages and binders*

Nursing Action	Rationale
Observe principles of medical asepsis when applying bandages and binders.	Bandages and binders should be clean and dry. Handwashing controls the transfer of organisms.
Select a bandage or binder material according to the effect desired.	Some bandages or binders are meant only to hold a dressing in place, while others are intended to exert pressure, immobilize and so on.
Avoid an unnecessarily thick or extensive bandage.	Heavy and extensive bandaging makes the area uncomfortably warm and cumbersome for the patient.
Choose the size of bandage or binder appropriate for covering the body part.	Covering the chest or thigh will require larger sized materials than that for a forearm or finger.
Support the part to be bandaged in normal anatomic alignment. Joints should be slightly flexed rather than extended or hyperextended.	Improper alignment contributes to healing in a position of deformity.
Use absorbent material to separate any two skin surfaces that touch one another, such as between fingers and toes, in the axillary area, under the breasts, in the folds of the groin or abdomen.	Padding absorbs moisture and reduces skin irritation or breakdown. It also promotes separate healing for surfaces that may each contain an open wound.
Pad bony prominences over which bandages and binders are placed. Hollows in the body contour may be filled with padding.	Padding cushions and distributes pressure equally over all skin surfaces. It promotes comfort and prevents skin breakdown.
Determine the appropriate technique for encircling a body part if a rolled bandage is being used.	Various turning techniques are used depending on the body part that is bandaged.
Begin at the lowest point of the body part and bandage in a direction toward the heart. The heel should not be left exposed when the foot or leg is bandaged.	Bandaging toward the heart helps prevent venous congestion and interference with circulation. Swelling is likely to be accentuated in the unbandaged area due to uneven compression on tissue and blood vessels.
Leave a small portion of an extremity, such as the fingertips or toes, exposed.	Exposing fingertips and toes on a bandaged extremity helps a nurse observe for signs of swelling and changes in circulation.
Apply a bandage or binder with sufficient pressure, using neither too little nor too much. Avoid applying a binder on the chest too snugly.	Sufficient pressure provides for adequate support and immobilization, and ensures that the bandage will stay in place. Too much pressure may interfere with circulation or respiration, and cause discomfort.
Unwind a bandage gradually and only as it is required.	This provides better control of the roll to keep equal tension throughout the area being covered.
Apply a bandage over a wet dressing or draining wound less tightly than usual.	If a wet dressing, saturated with secretions, dries, it is likely to shrink, causing more pressure than when it was originally applied.
Test the circulation in a bandaged extremity by applying pressure on the nailbeds. Compare with an unbandaged extremity if possible.	In normal circumstances, the area will blanch first and then return to its original colour quickly when pressure on the nailbed is released. If the bandage is too tight, the blood may be trapped or it may not be able to leave and return very quickly.

Continued

Principles of Care 22-4. Continued

Nursing Action	Rationale
Report any of the following signs promptly: coldness, numbness of the part, swelling, bluish or very red colouring, throbbing, tingling or pain.	Prolonged poor circulation to an area can result in death of cells or slowed healing. Corrective action should be taken if signs of impaired circulation are present.
Place adhesive used to secure the bandage or binder well away from a wound or tender and inflamed area, to prevent unnecessary pressure on a part of the body.	Pressure from adhesive is uncomfortable, may interfere with circulation, and may cause injury to skin and nerve tissues.

Understanding the use of heat and cold

Before applying heat or cold to the body, the nurse will wish to be familiar with certain facts to give safe care.

The immediate effect of cold applications. The immediate effect of cold applications is that blood vessels in the area constrict; that is, they become smaller. The opposite occurs when heat is applied. The reverse effect occurs with prolonged use of heat or cold. For example, eventual blood vessel constriction will occur with prolonged use of heat. Therefore, applications should not be left in place for long periods of time. The recommended durations for various heat and cold applications are provided when they are described later in this chapter.

Nerve receptors for heat and cold in the skin adapt to temperature. An important characteristic of heat and cold receptors is that they adjust readily if the stimulus is not extreme. For example, if the arm is placed in warm water, the sensation of warmth soon diminishes because of the adaptability of the heat receptors. The same phenomenon occurs if cool water is used. This is important to remember. Once the receptors adapt, the patient may become unaware of temperature extremes until tissue damage occurs. The patient usually is not familiar with this adaptability process and may request that the heat or cold be increased beyond the point of safety.

The temperatures that the skin can tolerate vary among persons and on different parts of the body. Some can tolerate very warm and cold applications more safely than others; young children, elderly, diabetic patients and individuals with circulatory diseases have a low tolerance for safety. Certain areas of the skin are also more tolerant of temperature than are others. Those parts of the body where the skin is thinner, for example the inner forearm, chest and abdomen, generally are more sensitive to temperature than exposed areas where the skin is often thicker. Therefore, it is important to apply warm and cold applications well within the generally known safe limits of temperature. In addition, the skin should be observed so that persons who are more sensitive to temperature will not suffer tissue damage, even though applications have been applied within recommended temperature ranges.

Heat and cold are transferred directly from one substance to another by conduction. A poor conductor is called an *insulator*. Water is a relatively good conductor of heat while air is a poorer conductor. Therefore, the skin will tolerate greater extremes of temperature if the heat or cold is dry rather than moist. For example, a moist hot compress should be applied at a lower temperature than a cloth-covered hot water bottle to prevent burning the skin. The air between the bag and the dry cloth that covers the hot water bottle acts as an insulator.

The body tolerates greater extremes in temperature when the duration of exposure is short. When duration is lengthy, the temperature range that the body can tolerate safely is narrower. The area involved is also important. In general, the larger the area to which heat or cold is applied, the less tolerant is the skin to the extreme in temperature.

The condition of the patient is an important factor to consider when heat and cold are being applied to the body. Special care is indicated for patients who are debilitated or unconscious. Patients who have disturbances in circulation are more sensitive to heat and cold. Broken skin areas are also more subject to tissue damage and less tolerant of heat and cold.

Common uses of cold applications

There are times when the decision concerning whether it is best to use hot or cold application requires judgement. Generally, using a cold application immediately following an injury is best to control swelling and pain. Later, the use of heat promotes comfort and improved circulation, which speeds healing.

Cold is most commonly used for the following clinical reasons:

- To limit the accumulation of fluid in body tissues (oedema). If oedema is already present, the application of cold acts to retard its relief because circulating blood in the area is at a minimum and excess fluid will not be reabsorbed efficiently.
- To control bleeding by constricting blood vessels.
- To relieve pain, such as at the site of a sprain.
- To produce an anaesthetic effect. Cold may be used for this purpose for certain surgical procedures and for the relief of discomfort at the site of an injection.
- To reduce body temperature and the body's metabolic rate.

Common uses of heat applications

Heat is most commonly used for the following clinical reasons:

- To promote circulation to an injured area and thereby hasten healing.
- To aid in removing debris from an infected or dirty wound.
- To relieve muscle spasms.
- To relieve pain by promoting muscle relaxation. Some individuals have learned that they have good relief from pain when they use warm applications. Others use cold applications. Still others may find that alternating between hot and cold applications works best for them. The reason for the difference is not clearly understood.
- To help overcome feelings of chilliness.
- To help raise body temperature when applied over a large area of the body.

Table 22-6. Temperature ranges for applications of heat and cold

Level of Heat	Temperature Range
Very hot	40.5°C to 46.1°C
Hot	36.6°C to 40.5°C
Warm and neutral	33.8°C to 36.6°C

Level of Cold	Temperature Range
Tepid	26.6°C to 33.8°C
Cool	18.3°C to 26.6°C
Cold	10°C to 18.3°C
Very cold	Below 10°C

Ensuring safe temperatures for applications of hot and cold

No one optimum temperature can be stated for hot or cold applications. The selection of temperature depends on factors such as the duration of the application, the method of the application, the condition of the patient and the condition and sensitivity of the skin. For short periods of time and for small areas, the maximum safe limits for hot or cold temperatures can be tolerated without discomfort or tissue damage. For longer periods, it is considered dangerous to expose skin to extreme temperatures except in rare life-threatening situations. These situations require constant monitoring. Table 22–6 provides the temperature ranges for various levels of hot or cold water.

Other special considerations should guide the safe temperature for applications of heat or cold. Very hot and cold temperatures should be avoided in an area of skin disease. They should also be avoided when patients have circulatory or heart disorders because of the danger of causing damage to tissues already in a state of distress.

Selecting a method for applying cold

There are several ways that cold temperatures can be applied to the skin. Some of the more common methods are discussed below.

Using an ice bag. Rubber or plastic ice bags are frequently used for applying cold to an area. Ice collars are smaller than most ice bags and are used for the neck and other small areas.

An ice bag should be prepared as follows:

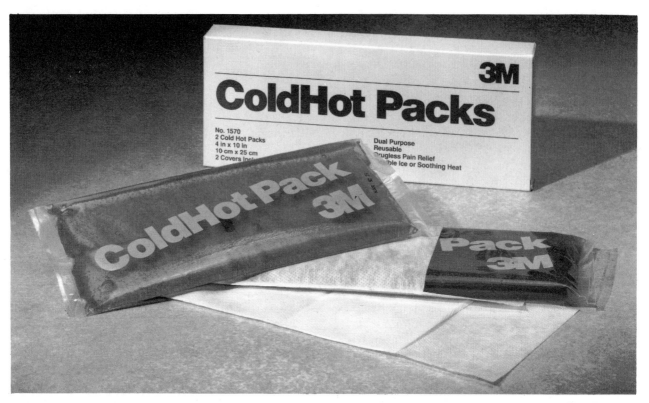

Figure 22-28. A prefilled and re-usable hot and cold gel pack. A gel pack can be stored in a freezer without its sleeve for cold applications. The gel remains malleable even when below freezing. It can be dropped in hot water or heated in a microwave for hot applications. (Courtesy 3M Health Care Limited, Loughborough, England.)

- Fill an ice bag half to two-thirds full with ice chips or small cubes. This makes it easy to mould the bag to fit body contours. Also, small pieces of ice reduce the amount of air, which acts as an insulator in the bag.
- Pour water over the cubes or chips to eliminate sharp edges and then remove the water from the bag.
- Twist the top of the bag and cap it. This technique removes excess air from the bag.
- Check for leaks in the bag and at the cap to prevent the patient from becoming wet should there be a flaw in the bag.
- Cover the ice bag and place it on the patient. The cover provides for comfort for the patient and absorbs moisture that condenses on the outside of the bag. Many bags are made with a soft outer covering, making another covering unnecessary.
- Allow the ice bag to remain in place no more than half to one hour and then remove it for approximately one hour. In this way, the tissues are able to react to the desired immediate effects

of the cold. Signs of excessive cold include mottled skin and numbness in the area being treated.
- Try using a rubber or plastic glove when a small area is involved. The ice is placed in the glove, excess air is removed, and the glove is tied shut securely. This type of ice bag has been found useful for patients who have had mouth or dental surgery.
- Wrap an ice cube in gauze with one side of the cube exposed to massage an area. Use a small circular motion when massaging. This technique is useful for applying cold to a small area for a short period of time when an ice bag is unsuitable for a small area.
- Place ice chips in a zip-lock plastic bag when a plastic bag is not available.

Commercially prepared cold packs are available. They retain a constant degree of cold for several hours. Figure 22-28 illustrates and describes one pack that can be used for either cold or hot applications.

Principles of Care 22-5. Applying a compress

Nursing Action	Rationale
Assemble equipment following appropriate principles of medical or surgical asepsis.	Medical asepsis is used most often, but sterile technique is practised when there is an open wound.
Place an appropriate amount of solution over absorbent material, such as gauze or even a clean washcloth.	The texture and the thickness of the material used depend on the area to which the compress is applied.
Warm or cool the solution to the desired temperature within those considered in a safe range to achieve the desired purpose of the application.	Consider the duration of the application, the condition of the patient, the condition and sensitivity of the skin, and the area to be covered.
Explain and plan the procedure with the patient.	A patient can cooperate and feel more in control of his care when he can understand and is permitted to participate.
Place the patient in a position of comfort.	An uncomfortable position can lead to muscle strain if maintained for the duration of the compress.
Protect the bed linen with absorbent material.	Covering the linen and ensuring absorption will reduce the need to change all the bed linen.
Wring the compress material of excess liquid. Sterile forceps or gloves may be used for sterile compresses.	The compress should be moist but not dripping. Cold or hot saturated compresses can injure tissue, since water is a relatively good conductor.
Shake the compress once or twice quickly.	Incorporating air into the layers of compress material acts to trap air, keeping the compress at a rather constant temperature.
Allow some of the liquid to drop onto thinner skin near the area of the intended compress.	Thinner skin is generally more sensitive than other areas. If the temperature feels comfortable in this area, it will be easily tolerated in other areas.
Place the compress gently on the affected area.	Pressure or rapid change in surface temperature may cause discomfort.
Lift the compress after a few seconds to inspect the patient's skin.	Assessing the effect of the compress on the skin helps prevent subsequent injury.
Place a dry covering over the moist compress and enclose both in waterproof material. Some nurses prefer placing the dry cover on the outside and the waterproof material next to the wet compress.	The dry covering and waterproof cover will act as insulators and prevent rapid temperature change and moisture loss from the compress.
Mould and secure the coverings to fit the contours of the body surface.	Air is a poor conductor of heat or cold. When openings allow air movement, rapid changes in the original temperature decrease the effectiveness of the compress.
Remoisten the compress material frequently enough to maintain the temperature. Usually the patient can indicate when this should be done.	The temperature should be maintained within a fairly constant range within the duration of the compress.
Use warming or cooling devices, such as an ice bag or hot water bottle, over the compress material, if available.	Heat or cold may be conducted from one source to another and promote a constant temperature.

Continued

Principles of Care 22-5. *Continued*

Nursing Action	Rationale
Continue applying the compress for approximately 15 to 20 minutes four or five times a day.	Prolonged applications of hot or cold may cause the reverse effect to tissue.
Provide comfort measures during and following treatment.	The patient may need to be warmed or cooled due to the effect of the compress, draughts and exposure of the compress area.
Remove the compress and dispose of the wet material according to hospital policy. If compress material contains body secretions, bag them in a waterproof container and dispose of them properly.	Unsoiled wet compress material can be placed in a lined receptacle. Soiled compresses must be wrapped separately in a waterproof container for burning to avoid spreading organisms.
Dry the patient as necessary after completing the procedure.	Restoring the comfort of the patient is a considerate act.
Assess the effect of the compress on the skin as well as the patient's evaluation.	Changes in the plan of care are based on the responses of the patient to treatment measures.
Chart significant observations and any other pertinent information according to hospital policy.	The patient's chart is a written record of the patient's care and progress.

Using cold compresses. *Compresses* are local applications of moisture. They may be either hot or cold depending on their desired purpose. They are applied similarly with the exception of the temperature of the solution. Principles of Care 22-5 describes the suggested actions for applying compresses.

Selecting a method for applying heat

Various methods may be used for applying heat. The applications of heat must be treated just as cautiously as the applications of cold. When heat is applied, the patient may require certain monitoring. If a large area of the body is involved with the application of heat, it is best to determine the patient's temperature before and after the heat is removed to determine any influence on body temperature. If the condition of the patient is poor or if he appears to be reacting unfavourably, monitoring all the vital signs is recommended.

Using electrical heating pads. The electric heating pad is a popular means for applying dry heat locally. It is easy to use, provides constant and even heat, and is relatively safe when used on low settings. Careless handling may result in injury to the patient or the nurse as well as damage to the pad.

Because of possible injury, many hospitals have a policy that prohibits the use of heating pads. If the patient insists on using a heating pad, the hospital may require him to sign a release to free the hospital of responsibility.

Because heating pads are commonly used in the home and in some hospitals, the nurse should be familiar with their proper use. The heating element of an electric pad consists of a web or wires that converts electric current into heat. Crushing or creasing the wires may impair proper functioning, and portions of the pad will overheat. Burns or a fire may result. Pins should be avoided for securing the pad because there is danger of electric shock if a pin touches the wires. Pads with waterproof coverings are preferred, but they should not be operated in a wet or moist condition because of the danger of short circuiting the heating element and consequently causing electric shock.

Heating pads for home use have a selector switch for controlling the heat within easy reach of the patient. After the heat has been applied and a certain amount of adaptation of nerve endings in the skin has taken place, the patient often increases the heat. Many persons have been burned in this manner. Hospitals that use heating pads usually have preset pads, which cannot be reset to temperatures that may burn the patient.

Heating pads should be covered with flannel or similar material. This helps make the heat more comfortable for the patient and protects the skin. The pad can be used repeatedly when the cover is washed after each patient's use. However, it is important not to cover the pad too heavily because heavy covering over an electric pad prevents adequate heat dissipation. The patient should not lie on a heating pad because heat will accumulate and may cause burns.

Suggested measures to promote tissue healing in selected situations

When the patient is an infant or child

Plan to promote general well-being when a youngster sustains trauma, especially if it involves a large area. Infants and children tolerate injury less well than do adults. Be sure the patient receives proper nourishment, sufficient fluid intake, rest and sleep, and emotional support to promote healing.

Take into account that infants and children tolerate applications of heat and cold less well than do adults. Be *sure* that the temperatures of applications are within normal safe ranges. Check the youngster's skin and the general physical reaction to heat and cold applications frequently. Heating pads are not recommended for infants and children because of the danger of burning. Hot water bottles and ice bags should never be placed directly on the skin without proper protection of the bag and skin.

In an emergency, recommend that a parent use a bag of frozen vegetables, such as peas, as a method of applying cold. It moulds easily to body contours and will not drip as much as melting ice cubes when becoming warm.

When the patient is unconscious

Be especially careful when applying hot and cold applications to an unconscious patient. His circulation is usually poor and he is unable to report symptoms of discomfort and tissue injury.

When the patient is elderly

Plan to give the best possible nursing care to promote general well-being when tissue trauma is present. Elderly persons tolerate injury and heal wounds less well than do younger adults. Physical reserves wane with the years. Be sure the patient receives proper nourishment, sufficient fluid intake, rest and sleep, and emotional support to promote healing.

As individuals age, they lose body fat underlying the skin. This, combined with a tendency to have drier skin, and inactivity predispose the elderly to decubitus ulcers.

Check bedridden elderly persons frequently for early signs of skin breakdown. They ordinarily have a decreased sense of pressure on the skin, as well as of pain, heat, and cold. Plan preventive measures described earlier in this chapter for anyone at high risk for developing pressure sores.

Be especially careful to apply heat and cold applications with care to prevent tissue damage. Be sure the temperatures of heat and cold are within the normal safe range and inspect the patient's general response to therapy frequently.

Teaching suggestions for promoting tissue healing

Suggestions for teaching patients who have had tissues injured are summarized below:

Patients with tissue injuries are often not hospitalized when the injury is relatively small; if hospitalized, they may be discharged before wounds are healed. Therefore, they or family members need to be taught how to care for the wound and signs indicating complications, such as profuse or foul-smelling drainage, puffiness and tenderness in the area of the wound.

Teaching patients about the normal characteristics of the body's reaction to injury and how to care for an open wound helps them to overcome commonly held fears about the strength of wound healing and wound closure techniques.

Patients being taught how to give themselves a douche at home should be instructed to lie in the bath. Administering a douche while sitting on a toilet will not result in a thorough cleansing since the solution will not come in contact with all the tissue within the vagina. This occurs because there are no muscles to retain the solution; therefore, solution will flow out by gravity before reaching the upper levels of the vaginal canal.

23

Fluid balance— the needs of the individual

Learning objectives

When the content of this chapter has been mastered, the learner should be able to:

Define terms appearing in the glossary.

List the chief functions and sources of body water and ways in which the body normally loses water.

Discuss assessment techniques for detecting fluid imbalances.

Describe how to determine fluid intake and fluid output and the usual practices involved in recording measured amounts.

Describe measures to promote fluid balance, especially ways to increase and limit oral fluid intake.

List the primary functions of each of the following electrolytes and list several food sources that supply the body with each of them: sodium, potassium, chloride, phosphate, calcium, magnesium and bicarbonate.

List signs and symptoms that may suggest electrolyte imbalance.

Discuss measures that help prevent or correct electrolyte imbalance.

List reasons for administering fluids intravenously.

Describe the difference between a crystalloid solution and a colloid solution.

List examples of commercially prepared isotonic, hypotonic and hypertonic solutions.

Discuss assessments that may be useful for determining a patient's response to fluid therapy.

Identify the equipment that the nurse should prepare when a patient will receive intravenous fluids.

Calculate the infusion rates using common drop factors.

Describe the actions involved in providing the following aspects of patient care: caring for the venepuncture site, changing solution containers, and discontinuing an infusion.

Describe possible complications of intravenous infusion and the appropriate nursing response for each.

List and describe various types of transfusion reactions; identify the nurse's actions when responding to a possible reaction.

List possible substitutes for blood and components of blood that may be infused separately.

List suggested measures that help promote fluid

imbalance in selected situations, as described in this chapter.

List suggested measures for administering intravenous fluids in selected situations as described in this chapter.

Glossary

Acid A substance containing hydrogen ions that can be liberated or released.

Acidosis A condition in which the pH of blood falls below 7.35.

Active transport A process requiring energy and sometimes a carrier substance to move dissolved substances through a semipermeable membrane from an area of low concentration to one that is more highly concentrated.

Air embolism A rare, but potentially deadly, complication that occurs when a large volume of air enters a vein.

Alkali A substance that can accept or bind with hydrogen ions. Synonym for *base*.

Alkalosis A condition in which the pH of blood measures more than 7.45.

Angiocath A flexible catheter threaded over a needle into a vein.

Anion An electrolyte with a negative electrical charge.

Base A substance that can accept or bind with hydrogen ions. Synonym for *alkali*.

Bevel The tapered tip of a needle.

Blood transfusion The intravenous infusion of whole blood.

Body fluid The mixture of body water and dissolved chemicals.

Carrier substance A constituent in body fluid that helps transport a dissolved chemical compound through a semipermeable membrane.

Cation An electrolyte with a positive electrical charge.

Circulatory overload A complication caused by administering too much intravenous fluid for the patient's system to circulate and eliminate.

Colloid solution A mixture of water and molecules of protein that remain suspended in the solution and do not become dissolved.

Crossmatching A laboratory test that determines whether blood specimens of the donor and recipient are compatible.

Crystalloid solution A mixture of water and uniformly dissolved crystals, such as salt and sugar.

Dehydration A condition that results from a low volume of body water.

Dialysis A procedure that removes water and toxic chemicals from the body when the kidneys are not functioning adequately.

Diffusion A process in which dissolved substances move passively through a semipermeable membrane from an area of higher concentration to an area of lower concentration.

Donor The person giving blood.

Drop factor The number of drops of solution that equal one millilitre, determined by the manufacturer of a particular brand of IV equipment.

Electrolytes Chemical compounds that dissolve and separate into individual molecules, each carrying either a positive or negative electrical charge.

Extracellular fluid All body water except that contained within cells.

Fluid balance The state in which water remains in normal amounts and percentages within various locations within the body.

Fluid intake All sources of fluid consumed or instilled into the body.

Fluid output All fluid eliminated from the body, including drainage from tubes, catheters and wounds.

Haemoconcentration A condition in which the fluid content of blood is decreased.

Haemodilution A condition in which the fluid content of blood is increased.

Hypercalcaemia An excess of calcium in the blood.

Hyperkalaemia An excess of potassium in the blood.

Hypermagnesaemia An excess of magnesium in the blood.

Hyperphosphataemia An excess of phosphate in the blood.

Hypertonic solution A mixture of water and crystals in higher concentration than found in intravascular fluid.

Hypervolaemia An excess of water in the circulating blood.

Hypocalcaemia An insufficient amount of calcium in the blood.

Hypokalaemia An insufficient amount of potassium in the blood.

Hypomagnesaemia An insufficient amount of magnesium in the blood.

Hypophosphataemia An insufficient amount of phosphate in the blood.

Hypotonic solution A mixture of water and crystals in lower concentration than found in intravascular fluid.

Hypovolaemia Below average amount of water in the circulating blood.

Infiltration The escape of an infusing solution into tissues.

Insensible water loss Water that is lost in a form that is not seen or felt.

Interstitial fluid Water surrounding the outside of cells; a subcategory of extracellular fluid.

Intracath A flexible catheter threaded through a needle into a vein.

Intracellular fluid Water located within the inside of cells.

Intravascular fluid Water within blood known as plasma or serum; a subcategory of extracellular fluid.

Intravenous fluids Those solutions instilled within a patient's vein.

Isotonic solution A mixture of water and crystals in equal concentration to that found in intravascular fluid.

Millimole The unit for measuring electrolytes. Abbreviated mmol.

Nonelectrolytes Chemical compounds that remain bound together when dissolved in a solution and cannot conduct electricity.

Oedema An excess of water in the interstitial space within body tissues.

Osmosis The movement of water through a semipermeable membrane from an area of lower concentration of dissolved substances to one where there is higher concentration.

pH The expression of hydrogen ion concentration in a fluid.

Plasma The fluid component of blood and lymph.

Recipient The person receiving blood.

Semipermeable membrane A layer of tissue that selectively allows certain substances to move in and out.

Serum Plasma from which the clotting factors have been removed.

Skin turgor The fullness of the skin in relation to underlying tissue.

Typing The laboratory test that identifies the proteins on red blood cells.

Venepuncture The act of entering a vein.

Introduction

Water is one of the chief necessities of life. All the water in the body contains chemical substances. For this reason it is common to use the term *body fluid* when referring to the mixture of water and dissolved chemicals. The body normally has a remarkable ability to discard or conserve body fluid to maintain an environment in which cells continue to thrive. This chapter summarizes the process involved in fluid and chemical balance and discusses common imbalances that are likely to occur.

It is part of the nurse's responsibility to assess a patient's state of fluid and chemical balance. This chapter describes some of the skills that are useful for gathering that data accurately. When alterations occur, the nurse may be required to implement measures discussed in this chapter for restoring balance.

Understanding fluid balance

Fluid balance is the state in which water remains in normal amounts and percentages within various locations within the body. Healthy persons maintain fluid balance automatically. They take in a wide variety of fluids and foods in various quantities and dispose of wastes and excesses as a result of complicated chemical mechanisms. One of the most basic measures for maintaining fluid and chemical balance is consuming an adequate fluid intake and eating a nourishing diet.

Body fluid proportions

The human body is made up of approximately 45% to 75% water. The amount of water varies according to an individual's age, sex and body fat composition. Table 23-1 shows a comparison of percentages based on the variables of age and sex.

Water content within the body decreases in proportion to increases in body fat. There may be wide differences in body composition among both sexes and age groups. Women tend biologically to have greater amounts of body fat. It could be said that, in general, women have less body water than men. This is reflected in the figures listed in Table 23-1.

The main functions of body water

Because the body is almost primarily a fluid structure, water plays a major role in dissolving and transporting substances. The main functions of water include:

- Transporting dissolved nutrients, oxygen, vitamins, hormones, enzymes and blood cells within the body. These are called nonelectrolytes. They are more descriptively defined later in this chapter.

Table 23-1. Average water percentages according to age and sex

Location of Body Water	In Infants	In Adult Males	In Adult Females	In the Elderly
In the blood (intravascular)	4%	4%	5%	5%
In tissues surrounding body cells (interstitial)	25%	11%	10%	15%
Within body cells (intracellular)	48%	45%	35%	25%
Total body water	77%	60%	50%	45%

- Transporting substances called electrolytes, such as sodium, chloride, bicarbonate and so on. These are also discussed later in more detail, since an imbalance of water often results in an imbalance of one or more electrolytes.
- Removing and transporting the wastes from metabolism, such as carbon dioxide, so that they may be eliminated from the body.
- Helping to regulate body temperature. Evaporation aids cooling; water promotes warmth by conducting heat produced by cell metabolism.
- Aiding digestion and elimination.
- Contributing the major component to the body's secretions.

From the length of this list, it is obvious that water is vital to life. Life can be sustained without food for many days; however, an individual will die much sooner when deprived of water.

The chief sources of water

The total amount of water that most adults consume is between 2000 and 3000 ml per day. A range between 1500 and 3500 ml would not be considered abnormal. Most of that amount is obtained by consuming liquid beverages and drinking water. The second largest source is from eating food, all of which contains liquid. Certain foods, such as fresh fruit, contain large quantities of water; some foods, such as cereal and dried fruits, contain little. Water is also an internal by-product from the metabolism of food. Table 23-2 lists the average amounts of water that a normal adult acquires from each of these three sources per day.

Methods of eliminating water

The same amount of fluid that is consumed every day is also similar to the amount that is eliminated. Most of the water is lost through the kidneys. Some moisture is lost in stool and in obvious perspiration from

Table 23-2. Average adult daily sources of water

Source of Water	Amount of Water (ml)
Ingested water	1200–1500
Ingested food	700–1000
Metabolic oxidation	200–400

areas where the skin contains abundant sweat glands. A certain amount of water is lost in a form that cannot usually be seen or felt. This is called *insensible water loss*. It occurs from the lungs during expiration and through the skin. The amount of water loss varies among people and under various circumstances. Variations can be associated with changing factors such as environmental temperature and humidity, body temperature and activity. A comparison of the variations in water loss under certain conditions is listed in Table 23-3.

Fluid distribution

Though body fluid is literally located throughout all the structures of the body, it is common to speak about fluid as being located in specific compartments. It should be kept in mind that these areas are not separate and distinct from one another. Water moves constantly in and about all these locations. Changes in the distribution of fluid in one area will automatically set in motion fluctuations in other areas.

Generally, body fluid is located inside and outside cells. The fluid within cells is called *intracellular fluid*. It represents the highest volume of water in the body. All the remaining fluid is called *extracellular fluid*. This category is further subdivided into *intravascular fluid*, fluid within the blood-vessel (vascular) system also known as *plasma* or *serum*, and fluid between cells,

Table 23-3. Average adult water losses per day

Exit Route	Normal Loss	With Elevated Body Temperature	Following Active Exercise
Urine	1200–1700	1200	500
Faeces	100–250	200	200
Perspiration	100–150	1400	5000
Insensible losses			
Skin	350–400	350	350
Lungs	350–400	250	650
Total	2100–2900	3400	6700

called *interstitial fluid*. Figure 23-1 illustrates the locations and percentages of fluids in the body. The proportions of fluid in each area tend to remain at a fixed amount when an individual is healthy.

When the ratio of water to dissolved substances in any body fluid location changes, water will relocate. This process restores proper proportions to maintain homeostasis. The movement and relocation of water is governed by the principle of *osmosis*. That is, water moves from an area where there is a lower concentration of dissolved substances to one where there is greater concentration. The process of osmosis is illustrated in Figure 23-2.

To redistribute itself, water moves through a *semipermeable membrane*. Cell walls and capillary walls are examples of semipermeable membranes in the body. A semipermeable membrane can be compared to openings like windows in a building. The windows keep birds out but let light and air in. Semipermeable membranes in the body allow substances, like water, to move in or out.

Fluid regulation

There are numerous, complex mechanisms that automatically adjust the volume of fluid within the body to maintain a constant state of balance. They include the stimulation of thirst and the activation of hormones that influence kidney filtration and reabsorption. A text that discusses physiology is an excellent resource for reviewing these biological controls.

However, certain circumstances can threaten the body's ability to regulate fluid amounts and distribution. When fluid losses are severely reduced or excessive, or intake is similarly affected, the body may not be able to adjust automatically to sustain the

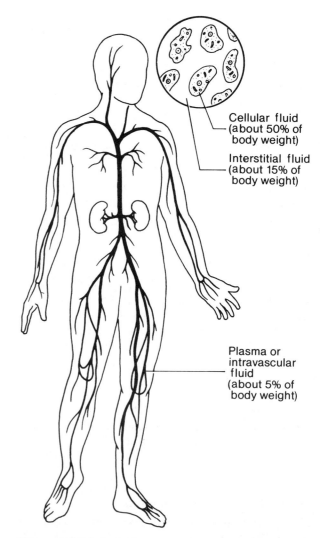

Cellular fluid (about 50% of body weight)

Interstitial fluid (about 15% of body weight)

Plasma or intravascular fluid (about 5% of body weight)

Figure 23-1 Normal placement of fluids in the body and distributed amounts based on the percentages of body weight.

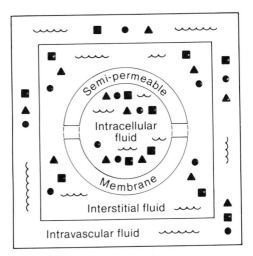 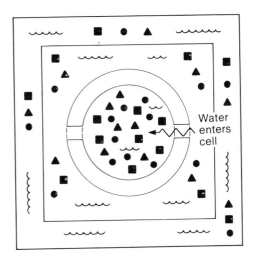

Figure 23-2 *Left*: This simplified drawing depicts a state of fluid balance in all locations of body water. Note that there is an equal ratio of dissolved substances, depicted as geometric figures, in each of the fluid areas, indicated by a wave. *Right*: When a fluid area becomes concentrated with dissolved substances, as shown within the cell of this drawing, water will move by osmosis from a less concentrated area to dilute and restore the proper proportions of water to dissolved substances. The size of the cell, in this case, will increase as more water enters through its semipermeable membrane.

health of an individual. The nurse must be able to recognize when additional support measures may be necessary to restore fluid balance.

Assessing fluid balance

The nurse should become familiar with the patient's state of health, the history of his present illness and the medical plan of care. Because balance is maintained normally when the intake of food and beverages is in proper proportion to output, anything that upsets these functions should act as a warning to the nurse. These are a few typical questions for which the nurse will wish to seek answers:

Has the patient's normal food and fluid intake changed? If so, for how long has it differed from usual?
Have there been restrictions on what the patient could eat or drink?
Has there been any abnormal loss of body fluids? If so, how long has the loss been occurring?

Any situation in which the patient has lost or retained excessive fluids warns of imbalance. Examples include extreme perspiration, vomiting or diarrhoea, wound or body drainage and blood loss. With fever, patients lose more fluid than when their body temperature is normal, as Table 23-3 indicates. Inade-

quate fluid intake can result from nausea, a poorly balanced diet, an inappropriate self-restriction of fluid to control urinary incontinence, or the unavailability of food or fluids. Fluid retention is associated with kidney failure, heart failure and some liver diseases. Imbalances also can result from the indiscriminate use of diuretic drugs, salt and tap water enemas. In fact, it is the rare illness or indisposition that does not threaten fluid or chemical balance.

One of the simplest methods for objectively assessing fluid balance is to compare the amount of a patient's fluid intake with fluid output. Other data that help the nurse determine the patient's fluid status will eventually be discussed.

Measuring and recording fluid intake and output

When an individual is healthy, the amount of fluid that is taken in should approximate the same amount that is lost. To determine that a balanced ratio exists, the nurse may collect data by measuring and recording various amounts of fluids.

Determining fluid intake. *Fluid intake* is determined by measuring all sources of fluid consumed or instilled into the body. The nurse must be constantly aware of the sources of water even though they may not be in the form of food or beverages. Fluid intake includes all the liquids a patient drinks and some

Table 23-4. Volume equivalents for common containers

Container	Volume
Teaspoon	5 ml
Tablespoon	15 ml
Drinking glass	240 ml
Coffee cup	210 ml
Water pitcher	900 ml
Paper cup	180 ml
Soup bowl	200 ml
Cereal bowl	120 ml

	INTAKE			OUTPUT		
	Oral	IV	Other	Urine	NG	BM/Other
7–3						
3–11						
11–7						
TOTAL						

Figure 23-3 This hospital's form shows an example of the area where the total from the bedside record of fluid intake and output are recorded on the patient's permanent record.

foods, nourishment instilled during a tube or parenteral feeding, intravenous fluid administration, and irrigation solutions instilled into tubes or catheters. When there is any question about the type of fluid that should be measured, the nurse should consult with a supervising nurse or refer to hospital policy.

Each hospital may develop a list that may be used as a guide for measuring the liquids that a patient consumes from his dietary tray. An example of the amounts of liquid that common food and beverage containers hold is listed in Table 23-4. Keep in mind that these amounts may vary, depending on the sizes of containers that each hospital uses. When the amount of a liquid is not known, a calibrated jug should be used to measure the volume. The nurse should avoid estimating an approximate amount. Too often the estimate is inaccurate.

Recording fluid intake. Hospital policies should be followed concerning the frequency and times of day when the amount of liquid intake is recorded. A good practice to follow is to record the amount of a patient's intake either immediately after it has been consumed or at frequent intervals during the day. Trying to recall the type and amount of fluids after several hours is likely to result in errors.

The nurse uses a form supplied by the hospital for recording intake. Most hospitals have a bedside form for recording amounts throughout the day. The bedside form, known as a fluid balance chart, usually has large spaces where the time, type of fluid and amount can be recorded. The hospital may also require that totals from the fluid balance chart be recorded each shift in a specific area on the patient's permanent

record. At the end of each 8-hour and 24-hour period, the nurse totals the amount, records it and prepares a new form for the next day. Figure 23-3 is an example of a hospital form used for a summary recording. A form used for bedside recording and other information about the oral intake or fluids can be reviewed in Chapter 10.

Determining fluid output. Patients whose intake is measured and recorded ordinarily need to have fluid output measured and recorded. *Fluid output* is the sum of all the liquid eliminated from the body. Fluid output is determined by measuring urine, emesis, drainage from tubes and the fluid drained following an irrigation. In some cases, to ensure accurate assessment of fluid loss, the nurse may be required to measure liquid stool or weigh wet linens, nappies or dressings saturated with blood or other secretions. The weight of wet items is compared to the weight of a similar dry item. An estimate of output is based on the knowledge that one pint (475 ml) of water weighs about 1 pound (0.47 kg).

Urine is the chief source of fluid output. For accurate measurement of urine, the nurse should do the following:

- For the patient who uses the bathroom for voiding, a container is placed inside the toilet bowl underneath the toilet seat. The container is calibrated in millilitres to make measurement of the urine convenient.
- For the patient confined to bed, a bedpan or urinal may be used. Pour the voided urine into an appropriate measuring device provided by the hospital. Place the calibrated container on a flat surface for an accurate reading.
- If the patient has a catheter, the drainage container is calibrated for easy measurement. It should be measured at least at the end of every

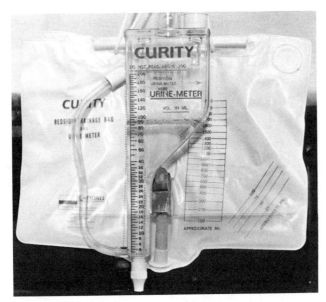

Figure 23-4 This gravity drainage container collects small amounts of urine in a separate collector. At periodic intervals, the nurse can measure and record the amount. The urine can then be added to the total being collected within the larger drainage receptacle.

shift. If urine output must be assessed more frequently, Figure 23-4 shows a urine collection device that allows smaller volumes to be kept separate from the total amount until they have been measured.

- The contents of a leg bag can be emptied and measured using a jug with markings that indicate graduated amounts.
- Be sure to instruct patients who are up and about when their urinary output is to be measured. They will then be less likely to urinate directly into the toilet. Some patients can be taught how to measure their urinary output. This is a good idea when the patient can be depended upon for accuracy. It helps the patient develop independence and involves him with his care.
- Teach the patient or a member of his family how to measure urinary output in home situations. Any calibrated container may be used for measuring. It is aesthetically preferable to use one that can be discarded when it is no longer necessary to measure output.

Recording fluid output. The nurse should follow the same practices and hospital policies for recording fluid output as described for recording fluid intake. Figure 23-3 also illustrates an example of one form commonly used at the patient's bedside for the periodic recording of measured amounts of fluid output.

Analysing other measurable data

Information taken for other purposes may help in analysing if a patient has a fluid imbalance. The nurse may wish to evaluate the cluster of measurable data listed in Table 23-5 if there are indications that the patient may have a problem with fluid deficit or fluid excess.

Physical assessments related to fluid balance

No single sign or symptom in itself necessarily indicates fluid imbalance. Each must be reviewed in re-

Table 23-5. Measurable data that may indicate fluid imbalance

Type of Data	Fluid Deficit	Fluid Excess
Body weight	Recent weight loss	Recent weight gain
Blood pressure	Hypotensive	Hypertensive
Body temperature	Elevated	Normal
Pulse	Rapid, weak, thready	Full, bounding
Respirations	Rapid, shallow	Moist, laboured
Specific gravity of urine	Elevated	Low
Red blood cell count	Elevated	Low
Haematocrit	Elevated	Low
Haemoglobin	Elevated	Low

lation to the patient's state of health. It is also especially important to compare findings with the person's usual characteristics. The following is a review of data gathered during a physical assessment of various systems of the body that may be associated with a fluid imbalance.

The integumentary system. The nurse may observe various signs and symptoms typical of fluid imbalances when examining the skin and mucous membranes.

- The skin may appear warm, flushed, and dry when the patient is experiencing fluid deficit. It may appear cool, pale, and moist in fluid excess.
- The lips chap and a whitish coating may be present on the lips and tongue when the patient experiences a low volume of fluid. The mucous membranes may feel dry and sticky. With adequate or excess fluid, tissues will appear moist.
- The eyes appear sunken as subcutaneous tissues around them lose fluids; they may appear small with fluid excess as the surrounding tissues swell with water.
- The turgor of the skin may change with alterations in fluid volume. *Skin turgor* is the fullness of the skin in relation to the underlying tissue. With low levels of body fluid, skin can be lifted almost separately from the tissue underneath. With excessive levels of body fluid, it will be difficult to grasp the skin between the forefinger and thumb. A normally hydrated person's skin should return to its original position immediately after being grasped.
- An individual with fluid excess may exhibit oedema. *Oedema* is an excess of fluid in the interstitial space within body tissues. It causes swelling and makes the skin appear tight. Oedema is often seen around the eyes and in the parts of the body that tend to collect fluid due to gravity, such as the fingers, ankles and feet. The patient may indicate that rings or shoes no longer fit. The impression of the weave in stockings may remain on the skin even after they have been removed for some time. The person who lies in bed may exhibit oedema in the lower part of the back and buttocks. One way to assess the presence of oedema is to press a finger gently into an area of the body. If the impression remains after pressure has been released, the condition is called pitting oedema. It is illustrated in Figure 23-5.

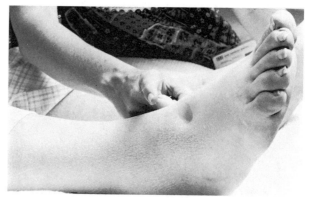

Figure 23-5 The nurse has applied pressure on this patient's foot for a few seconds. The imprint in the oedematous tissue demonstrates pitting oedema.

The gastrointestinal and urinary systems. These two systems are commonly affected by the patient's intake of food and fluids. Some common signs and symptoms typical of fluid imbalances include the following:

- Thirst is a common symptom when fluid intake has been low.
- Consumption of salty foods can affect the intake and retention of fluids.
- The patient with a fluid deficit may expel drier stool or experience constipation. An individual with kidney failure who retains fluid may have frequent, moist bowel movements.
- The urine is light in colour and almost odourless when fluid levels are high. It is dark and has a strong odour when fluid levels are low. The nurse may wish to measure the specific gravity of urine, as discussed in Chapter 12.

The circulatory and respiratory systems. These systems are also often affected as a unit when the patient is experiencing fluid imbalances. This occurs because the heart circulates blood, which has a major fluid component, through the lungs. The following are typical of fluid imbalances:

- The lung sounds may seem wet when fluid levels are high. The patient may find it easier to breathe when sitting up rather than lying down when there is an excess of body fluid.
- The patient may experience fatigue and chest pain if the volume of blood is inadequate to supply oxygen to the heart muscle.

- The neck veins may distend from the skin when the patient is in a sitting position. This usually indicates fluid excess. When the patient has a low fluid volume, it may be difficult to distend any peripheral veins when obtaining a specimen of blood or inserting a needle for an intravenous infusion.

The nervous system. An individual's level of consciousness often becomes affected when there are dangerous changes in the person's fluid status. The following are typical:

- Normal personality characteristics may change. The active, outgoing person may become withdrawn and quiet, or vice versa as the brain struggles to adjust to the changes in body fluid distribution.
- The person with low fluid volume is likely to seem weak, sleepy and disoriented as the fluid imbalance worsens.
- A patient with fluid excess may appear tense and worried. Insomnia may be present.
- Eventually convulsions, coma and death may occur with either type of fluid imbalance.

Describing common fluid imbalances

Fluid imbalance is a general term describing any of several conditions in which the body's water is not in the proper volume or location within the body. One of the locations in which fluid levels are likely to become imbalanced is the blood, or the area of intravascular fluid. When describing an imbalance in this area, certain prefixes and the suffix *aemia*, referring to blood, are used in combination. When fluid is excessive in this location, the term *hypervolaemia* is used to describe it. This term means that there is a high volume, or amount, of water present in the blood. *Hypovolaemia* is a term that indicates a below average amount of water in blood. Other terms used to describe imbalances in the chemicals within intravascular fluid follow a similar pattern and are listed later in the chapter.

When an individual eventually experiences fluid deficits in all the areas where fluid is distributed, he is in a state of *dehydration*. The body no longer has the ability to restore fluid balance by redistributing fluid from one area to another. There simply is an insufficient supply to meet the need. An example of an individual suffering from dehydration can be seen in Figure 23-6.

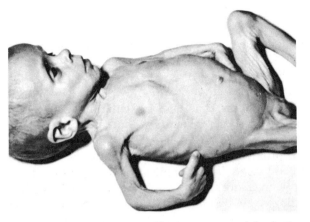

Figure 23-6 This youngster illustrates severe dehydration. Note the sunken eyes and poor skin turgor.

Last, fluid imbalance can occur when fluid becomes trapped in interstitial areas. It often occurs when there is a loss of proteins from the plasma of blood. This can occur suddenly when a person is burned, experiences a crushing injury or has a severe allergic reaction. It can occur slowly with some types of kidney and liver diseases. The total volume of body fluid essentially remains the same. However, the percentages of fluid within various compartments are changed. The percentage of water located within the interstitial space is greater than it should be, and the percentage of water in the intravascular area is lower than its normal amount. The body cannot relocate the water until the level of plasma proteins is restored to normal.

Correcting fluid imbalances

Certain principles help in planning actions when correcting fluid imbalances becomes a necessary part of a patient's care.

- Fluid deficits need to be corrected by replacing fluids and controlling their loss.
- Fluid excesses can be reduced by limiting fluid intake and increasing fluid loss.
- The degree and type of fluid imbalance and the body's ability to cope with them determine the type and intensity of therapy needed.

The nurse and the doctor usually work together when planning measures to correct fluid imbalances. Whenever possible, it is desirable to have the patient participate in correcting the fluid imbalance to whatever extent he can.

Several approaches are commonly used to help correct fluid imbalances. To reduce fluid deficits, oral liquid intake may be increased by providing additional servings of food and beverages during the day. Tube feedings may be used both for the benefit of fluid replacement and nourishment. Intravenous infusions are often used to increase fluid volume when there is an urgent need to do so. Infusions and transfusions are discussed later in this chapter.

To promote fluid loss, diuretic drugs may be prescribed by the doctor. Some individuals with kidney failure may need temporary or permanent dialysis treatments. *Dialysis* is a procedure that removes water and toxic chemicals from the body when the kidneys are not functioning adequately.

The nurse's contribution to promoting the restoration of fluid balance includes developing and implementing a plan for increasing or limiting the intake of oral fluids.

Encouraging oral fluid intake

The nurse may independently order and implement measures that replace fluid loss by increasing the patient's oral fluid intake. This action has been referred to in the past as pushing fluids. Because that term conveys a negative image of the nurse-patient relationship, more nurses are using the term *encouraging fluids*.

The specified amount the patient should take is indicated in a nursing order. An amount equal to or somewhat above the average daily requirement, for example 3000 ml, may be an acceptable oral fluid intake goal per day. It may be helpful to specify the goal for each shift, planning that a greater portion of the total amount will be consumed during the day rather than during the evening and night.

The techniques in Principles of Care 23-1 may be used when increasing the daily intake of oral fluids.

Restricting oral fluid intake

Though diuretic drugs may achieve dramatic results in promoting fluid loss, restricting oral fluid intake can also have a positive effect. The patient will still need to consume some liquid. Many patients can temporarily reduce their oral fluid intake to between 1000 to 1500 ml in 24 hours. In some cases, the patient's oral intake is restricted to the same volume as the urine that is excreted. Occasionally, the doctor will determine the amount of fluid restriction. When the nurse must limit the intake of oral liquids, the

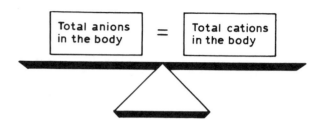

Figure 23-7 The total anions in the body are equal to the total cations in the body when they are described in millimoles per litre.

actions in Principles of Care 23-2 may be useful in the nursing care plan.

Understanding electrolyte balance

All body fluid contains chemicals called nonelectrolytes and electrolytes. *Nonelectrolytes* are chemical compounds that remain bound together when dissolved in a solution and, therefore, cannot conduct electricity. Glucose is an example of a nonelectrolyte. *Electrolytes* are chemical compounds that dissolve and separate into individual molecules, each carrying either a positive or negative electrical charge. For example, the chemical compound of salt is sodium chloride. These two molecules separate when dissolved. The sodium molecule carries a positive electrical charge while the chloride molecule carries a negative charge. In general, these separated molecules are called ions. More specifically, a *cation* is an ion with a positive electrical charge. An *anion* is an ion with a negative electrical charge.

The total cations in the body normally equal the total anions. They balance each other, as illustrated in Figure 23-7. Electrolytes are measured in *millimoles*, abbreviated mmol, per litre. Table 23-6 is a list of various electrolytes and the amounts that are normally found in the plasma, or serum, of blood.

Electrolyte distribution

Electrolytes are distributed in different proportions in extracellular and intracellular tissue. Their proportions remain relatively constant due to the movement and relocation of various ions through the processes of diffusion and active transport. Diffusion is the process in which ions move from an area of greater concentration to an area of lesser concentration through a semipermeable membrane. This

Principles of Care 23-1. Increasing oral fluid intake

Nursing Action	Rationale
Explain the reasons for increasing consumption of oral fluids to the patient.	Obtaining and encouraging the patient's participation will ensure better achievement of the goal.
Develop a list of beverages that the patient generally enjoys drinking.	Increasing fluid intake when not feeling well is not always a pleasant or easy task.
Plan a schedule for the amount that will be consumed over a 24-hour period.	The patient should understand that the fluids can be replaced gradually.
Divide the total allotment of fluids so that the patient will drink greater amounts during the early hours of the day and less in the evening.	Larger amounts of fluid are easier to take after a night of sleep when there has been little or no fluid intake. Taking fluids in the evening tends to disturb sleep because the patient may need to void.
Set an hourly goal with the patient and provide some means of measuring the progress toward the goal. Indicate on a graph or picture when the patient moves closer to reaching the goal.	It helps to see evidence of the progress made toward reaching a goal. The nurse can use creativity in designing a graph or picture that illustrates the current efforts toward the goal.
Keep fluids handy at the bedside at all times and in containers the patient can handle.	Lack of accessibility can be one reason for not reaching a goal.
Offer a variety of fluids to avoid monotony and lack of interest. Change the serving glass or container frequently.	Drinking the same thing, even though it may be something the person likes, can become unpleasant after a while.
Provide small amounts of a favourite liquid frequently. Serve the refreshment in small containers.	The patient is likely to feel defeated if the nurse brings a large volume of fluid to drink at any one time.
Serve fluids at the proper temperature.	It is unappetizing to sip drinks normally served cold when they are warm, and vice versa.
Include jelly, ice lollies and ice cream as alternatives to liquid beverages.	These items are considered fluids and can be substituted for beverages consumed from a glass.
Keep an accurate record of fluid intake and output.	Records will help in evaluating the effectiveness of the plan.

happens very passively with no release of energy. However, when it is necessary that molecules move in the opposite direction, it requires active transport. *Active transport* is a process requiring energy to move molecules through a semipermeable membrane from an area of low concentration to one that is higher. Movement of molecules may also require a carrier substance. A *carrier substance* facilitates the transfer of an electrolyte or nonelectrolyte through a semipermeable membrane. For example, insulin is the carrier substance that is needed to transfer glucose, a non-electrolyte, through a cell's membrane.

Major electrolytes and their chief functions

Body fluid is a mixture of electrolytes and other chemical substances. Those ions that are found in the

Table 23-6. Normal serum electrolyte levels

Serum Electrolyte	Normal Level (mmol/l)
Sodium (Na)	140
Potassium (K)	5
Chloride (Cl)	105
Phosphate (HPO_4^{-2})	1.1
Calcium (Ca)	2.5
Magnesium (Mg)	1
Bicarbonate (HCO_3)	25–29 (adult)
	20–25 (child)

Principles of Care 23-2. Limiting oral fluid intake

Nursing Action	Rationale
Explain the purpose for restricting the intake of oral liquids.	Understanding promotes cooperation.
Indicate the total amount the patient may consume in one day, using measurements the patient will understand.	Patients are often unfamiliar with terms such as millilitres or litres. Using terms like two pints or four drinking glasses to explain the equivalent of 1000 ml may help the patient understand the extent of his limitation.
Schedule the distribution of the fluid intake throughout the 24-hour period.	It is unwise to let the patient consume the total amount early in the day and then totally restrict his intake later.
Ration the fluid so that the patient will have the opportunity to drink fluids other than at meal times.	Food contains liquid, and the patient's thirst may be relieved temporarily just from the water in food.
Keep fluids out of sight as much as possible.	Seeing something that is forbidden is frustrating. The patient may be tempted to drink it.
Use small containers for serving liquids.	Serving small amounts of fluid in large containers reminds him of what he cannot have.
Avoid serving foods and fluids that tend to increase thirst.	Sweet drinks and foods and dry or salty foods increase thirst.
Serve liquids at their proper temperture.	When the patient can only drink a small amount, liquids should be served so that the patient will experience the maximum pleasure with their consumption.
Offer ice chips, but calculate it as part of the total amount of fluid that the patient is allowed.	Ice appears to be greater than its actual volume. Melted ice is about one half the volume of the frozen state. It melts slowly and the patient may extend the time during which the liquid is consumed.
Use water in a plastic squeeze bottle with a spray top or an atomizer to moisten the patient's mouth.	This technique helps decrease thirst while using little fluid.
Help the patient maintain good oral hygiene.	Oral hygiene helps lubricate the lips and mucous membranes of the mouth. This relieves thirst and prevents drying and chapping of the lips.
Permit the patient to rinse his mouth with water as long as he is not tempted to swallow the water.	Keeping the mouth moist will reduce thirst.
Maintain an accurate record of the patient's fluid intake and output.	An accurate record helps in evaluating the effectiveness of the plan.
Evaluate the urinary output.	To excrete adequate amounts of toxic wastes, the patient should eliminate at least 500 ml of urine per 24 hours. Fluid restriction may need to be adjusted if the urine output is lower than this amount.

greatest proportions in the body are called major electrolytes. There are other electrolytes, no less important, but in lesser amounts. They are called minor electrolytes. Zinc, selenium and chromium are examples.

The following is a description of the major electrolytes and a brief summary of their function and food sources.

Sodium. Sodium is a cation. It is the most abundant

cation in extracellular fluid. It has important functions in the body, such as helping to maintain the correct volume of body fluid, acid-base balance, and normal nervous and muscle cell activity. Sodium is found in many foods and especially in bacon, ham, processed luncheon meats, sausages, mustard, cheese and other dairy products, and table salt.

Potassium. Potassium is a cation. It is the most abundant cation in intracellular fluid. It functions in the body to help maintain proper cell activity and transmit electrical impulses, especially through the heart. Gastrointestinal secretions contain large quantities of potassium. Most fresh fruits and vegetables are rich in potassium. Especially rich food sources include bananas, peaches, figs, dates, oranges, prunes, apricots, potatoes and tomatoes.

Chloride. Chloride is the chief extracellular anion. It is essential for the production of hydrochloric acid in gastric juices and plays a role in acid-base balance. Chloride is found in foods that are also high in sodium.

Phosphate. Phosphate is the major anion in intracellular fluid. It is important for maintaining acid-base balance, plays a role in nerve and muscle activity, and carbohydrate metabolism. It is necessary for proper cell division and for the transmission of hereditary traits. Phosphorus, from which the electrolyte phosphate derives, is found in most foods, but especially in beef, pork, and dried beans and peas.

Calcium. Calcium, the most abundant mineral in the body, forms the framework for bones and teeth. In its electrolyte form, calcium is a cation and is important for the transmission of nerve impulses, blood clotting and muscle contraction. Calcium is found in milk, cheese and dried beans, and, to a lesser extent, in meats and vegetables.

Magnesium. Magnesium is a cation. It is especially important for the promotion of enzyme activity. Because it is widespread and found in almost all foods, deficiencies are seldom found in persons who are eating normally.

Bicarbonate. The bicarbonate molecule is an anion that is essential for acid-base balance. Acid-base balance and its related imbalances will be discussed later in this chapter. Bicarbonate can come from food and drug sources, but it is also formed within the body.

Electrolyte imbalances. It is possible that an individual could suffer an excess or deficiency of any one or a combination of electrolytes. The type of electrolyte depends on the nature of the fluid loss or gain, and the individual's diet. For instance, the individual with severe diarrhoea may experience a potassium deficit, since gastrointestinal secretions are high in potassium; electrolyte levels of calcium, for example, may remain normal. Table 23-7 is a list of terms that are used when describing specific imbalances of the serum levels of certain specific electrolytes.

Table 23-7. Terms describing electrolyte imbalances

Imbalance	Definition
Hypernatraemia	An excess of sodium in the blood
Hyponatraemia	A deficit of sodium in the blood
Hyperkalaemia	An excess of potassium in the blood
Hypokalaemia	A deficit of potassium in the blood
Hyperchloraemia	An excess of chloride in the blood
Hypochloraemia	A deficit of chloride in the blood
Hyperphosphataemia	An excess of phosphate in the blood
Hypophosphataemia	A deficit of phosphate in the blood
Hypercalcaemia	An excess of calcium in the blood
Hypocalcaemia	A deficit of calcium in the blood
Hypermagnesaemia	An excess of magnesium in the blood
Hypomagnesaemia	A deficit of magnesium in the blood

Detecting electrolyte imbalances

The source of electrolytes is the food and beverages that are consumed daily. Therefore, any change in the intake of nourishment and water will probably affect the amount and balance of electrolytes. Because these electrolytes become dissolved in body fluid, any condition that affects fluid loss or retention is also going to affect the balance of electrolytes. It is unlikely that a person would experience an imbalance of one kind without also experiencing an imbalance of the other.

There are certain related signs and symptoms that may accompany abnormal levels of electrolytes. However, because each electrolyte has diverse and unique functions, it is difficult to detect an imbalance based only on physical assessment alone. The most conclusive assessment technique involves an analysis of blood in which the serum levels of electrolytes are measured.

Despite the fact that physical assessments cannot be totally relied on to detect imbalances of electrolytes, some of the following should suggest that the nurse collect more data:

- Any chronic or acute loss or retention of fluid
- The recent or prolonged administration of medications, such as diuretics, that are likely to cause a change in fluid volumes or electrolyte levels
- Loss of muscle strength, twitching muscles or leg cramps
- ECG changes, specifically changes in the normal appearance or timing of a wave and wave complexes
- Bradycardia, a tachycardia and other abnormalities of pulse rate and rhythm
- Numbness or tingling in the fingers, toes or lips
- Confusion, disorientation, depression, seizures or changes in levels of consciousness

Preventing and correcting electrolyte imbalances

Severe electrolyte deficits may require infusions of specific electrolytes or electrolyte solutions. Other invasive procedures, such as dialysis or the administration of certain drugs that promote electrolyte excretion, may be used when there are electrolyte excesses. Severe electrolyte imbalances can lead to death if they are not restored to balance quickly.

The following is a list of measures that may prevent or help promote normal levels of electrolytes:

- Help the patient maintain proper nutrient and fluid intake.
- Carefully assess any patient who receives medications that predispose to fluid or electrolyte imbalances.
- Provide additional dietary sources of certain electrolytes that are likely to be depleted. For example, the patient who routinely takes certain diuretics may be served orange juice or a banana daily to replace the potassium that may be lost in urine. A patient with diarrhoea, vomiting or excessive perspiration may benefit from drinking gastrolyte, a beverage that contains a mixture of replacement electrolytes.
- Diligently perform skills that prevent or close areas of the body that may drain fluids, for instance, pressure sores and burns.
- Maintain accurate recordings of fluid intake and output, as well as body weight. Notify the doctor early when there are significant changes in these figures.
- Communicate with laboratory personnel when the results of laboratory tests are urgently needed.
- Inform the doctor when laboratory tests indicate abnormal results.
- Implement prescription or intravenous infusion administration as soon as possible when the patient is experiencing altered levels in fluid or electrolytes.

Understanding acid-base balance

All body fluids are either acidic, base or neutral. An *acid* is defined as a substance containing hydrogen ions that can be liberated or released. An *alkali* or *base* is a substance that can accept or bind with hydrogen ions. A combination of these two tends to balance each other, resulting in a condition that is neither acidic or base, but neutral.

The nature of the fluid can be determined by measuring its *p*H. The term *p*H is an expression of hydrogen ion concentration. The range of *p*H is based on a numerical scale from 1 to 14; 7 is considered neutral. A *p*H in the range of 1 to 7 is acid; the lowest number represents the highest acidic level. A *p*H above 7 up to 14 is considered base; the highest number represents the highest base level. The *p*H of pure water is 7; gastric secretions have a *p*H of about 1.0 to 1.3; secretions from the pancreas have a *p*H of about 10.

Table 23-8. *Types of acid-base imbalances*

Type	Description	Nursing Observation
Respiratory acidosis	Respiratory acidosis results from a respiratory phenomenon. The primary cause is a deficiency in respiratory ventilation, resulting in hypoventilation. Pneumonia, emphysema and respiratory obstructions are common causes.	Dyspnoea Disorientation Coma Plasma pH below 7.35
Respiratory alkalosis	Respiratory alkalosis results from increased respiratory ventilation. The primary cause is hyperventilation associated with extreme emotions, anxiety, an elevated temperature or salicylate intoxication.	Deep, rapid breathing Eventually convulsions Plasma pH above 7.45
Metabolic acidosis	Metabolic acidosis results from an accumulation of acid components or a decrease in alkaline components in the blood. Common causes include a decreased food intake, infections, diabetic acidosis, renal failure and diarrhoea.	Hyperventilation Weakness Disorientation Coma Plasma pH below 7.35
Metabolic alkalosis	Metabolic alkalosis results from an excess of alkaline components or a decrease in acid components in the blood. Common causes include excessive ingestion of alkalis, fluid loss from gastric suction and therapy to increase urinary excretion.	Disorientation Stupor Deep, rapid breathing Plasma pH above 7.45

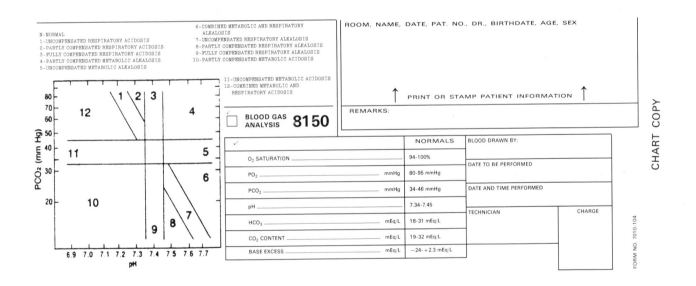

Figure 23-8 Arterial blood gas analysis form.

The normal pH of blood is slightly alkaline, measuring a pH in the range of 7.35 to 7.45. The pH of blood is primarily maintained by a fixed ratio between carbonic acid molecules and bicarbonate molecules. Normal acid-base balance is maintained primarily by the body's ability to retain or eliminate hydrogen ions, by carbon dioxide excretion from the lungs and by the ability of the kidneys to excrete or reabsorb substances that influence acid-base balance.

The ratio of carbonic acid molecules and bicarbonate

molecules must remain constant or the narrow range of balance will be disrupted. Death will occur rapidly when an acid-base imbalance occurs. When the levels of blood *p*H change, the terms acidosis and alkalosis are used to identify the altered state. *Acidosis* is the condition in which the *p*H of blood falls below 7.35. *Alkalosis* is the condition in which the *p*H of blood measures more than 7.45. Types of acidosis and alkalosis are described further in Table 23-8.

Identifying acid-base imbalance

Besides various abnormal yet nonspecific signs and symptoms, an arterial blood gas analysis provides the best data for establishing that an acid-base imbalance exists. Among other data, this test measures the blood *p*H; the level of dissolved carbon dioxide in the blood, abbreviated PCO_2; the level of dissolved oxygen in the blood, abbreviated PO_2; and the amount of bicarbonate, abbreviated HCO_3. The normal ranges for these substances are indicated on the sample form in Figure 23-8.

Preventing and correcting acid-base imbalance

Most acid-base imbalances must be treated aggresively as soon as they are detected. Balance can be promoted by treating the metabolic or respiratory cause creating the imbalance. Some cases of acidosis may be treated by administering sodium bicarbonate intravenously. Respiratory acidosis and alkalosis can be treated by methods that restore normal respirations.

The nurse can help prevent acid-base imbalances by:

- Providing a patient with adequate fluids and nutrients.
- Implementing skills that reduce the loss of fluids and electrolytes.
- Ensuring adequate ventilation.
- Instructing patients on the proper dosage and self-administration of medications that predispose to alterations in acids, bases and other electrolytes.

Administering intravenous fluids

As already mentioned, one of the measures that can be taken to prevent or promote normal levels of electrolytes is intravenous infusion administration.

Intravenous fluids are those solutions instilled within a patient's vein. They may include solutions of water and chemicals normally found within the body, dissolved medications, or blood, blood extracts and blood substitutes. The term IVs is commonly used when referring to solutions instilled into a vein.

Policies and practices vary concerning who may administer and regulate intravenous fluids. This chapter has been prepared to help those nurses who will be responsible for these skills. Nevertheless, the information within this chapter is recommended reading for nurses who may be assigned to care for patients receiving parenteral fluids. All nurses may not necessarily start intravenous infusions, but may still be responsible for monitoring the infusion, for observing the patient and for discontinuing the therapy.

Purposes for administering intravenous fluids

There are several reasons for which a patient may receive fluids intravenously, among which are the following:

- To restore fluid balance quickly when a patient experiences a significant fluid loss
- To prevent fluid imbalance for a patient who is currently or potentially likely to experience a loss of body fluid
- To maintain fluid balance when the patient temporarily is unable to eat and drink
- To replace specific electrolytes or other chemicals, such as water-soluble vitamins
- To provide some measure of nutrition
- To administer medications, such as anaesthetics, antibiotics and so on
- To establish access to the vascular system in case emergency medications may need to be administered quickly
- To replace blood cells or specific components of blood

Criteria for selecting an intravenous solution

Intravenous solutions are selected and prescribed by the doctor. They are considered to be a form of medication. The specific type of solution, volume and rate of administration are part of the prescription. The nurse must exercise extreme caution that the correct solution is infused. This is a priority of concern, since any substance that is instilled directly into the circulatory system produces a rapid effect due to its almost instant distribution throughout the body. Chapter 18 discusses specific actions for ensuring accurate administration of medications.

The type of intravenous fluid is selected on the basis of the intended purpose of the infusion and the effect a particular fluid will have on the distribution of water and dissolved substances within the body. In other words, water will be distributed according to the principle of osmosis and dissolved substances will become distributed by diffusion and active transport. These physiological processes have been discussed earlier in this chapter.

Types of intravenous solutions

Intravenous fluids fall into two basic categories. They are either a crystalloid or a colloid solution. A *crystalloid solution* is a mixture of water and uniformly dissolved crystals, such as salt and sugar. A *colloid solution* is a mixture of water and molecules of protein that remain suspended in the solution and do not actually become dissolved. Whole blood, packed cells, plasma and plasma proteins, such as albumin, are examples of colloid solutions. The substances in a colloid solution remain in the intravascular space because the molecules are too large to move through a semipermeable membrane.

Crystalloid solutions are further subdivided into isotonic, hypotonic and hypertonic solutions on the basis of the amount of dissolved crystals present in the solution. An *isotonic solution* contains an equal amount of dissolved crystals, as normally found in plasma. The distribution of water and chemicals will remain relatively unchanged when an isotonic solution is infused.

A *hypotonic solution* contains fewer dissolved crystals than normally found in plasma. It represents a dilute solution in comparison to the fluid within and around cells. Therefore, when infused intravenously, the water in the solution will enter through the semipermeable membrane of blood cells. The blood cells will become larger as they fill with water. This can temporarily increase blood pressure as it expands the circulating volume. Water may also pass through capillary walls and become distributed within other body cells and the interstitial spaces. This acts to equalize the ratio of water to dissolved substances throughout the body. It is, therefore, an effective mechanism for rehydration of individuals experiencing fluid deficits.

A *hypertonic solution* has a higher amount of dissolved crystals than present in plasma. It will draw water into the intravascular compartment from the more dilute areas of water within the cells and interstitial spaces. This can help to relieve oedema as cells and tissues shrink and dehydrate from fluid loss. It can be expected that urine output will increase as a regulatory mechanism compensating for the added fluid volume present in the blood.

Table 23-9 provides a list of intravenous solutions that are either isotonic, hypotonic or hypertonic. These commercially available solutions are commonly used in clinical situations in which fluid balance must be maintained or restored. The pharmaceutical companies that prepare intravenous solutions have excellent literature explaining the nature of and common indications for the solutions they prepare.

Assessing the patient requiring fluid therapy

The nurse should gather a base of data that can be useful for evaluating the effect and results of fluid therapy. Focus assessments should be made throughout the period of fluid replacement and continue until the patient's fluid balance is no longer an actual or potential clinical problem.

The following are observations that can help with comparative assessments:

- The patient's vital signs, including temperature, pulse, respiration and blood pressure, should be taken prior to and at periodic intervals during fluid infusion. The variations in these physiological signs may reflect early, subtle responses of the patient to changes in fluid volume.
- The body weight should be recorded. It may be compared with the patient's admission weight or weights that have been recorded on previous days. The conditions for recording weight should be as similar as possible. In other words: same time of day, same scale and same type of clothing.
- A record of intake and output should be collected and continued throughout the period of fluid therapy. If no prior record is available, the nurse may assess the colour, odour and specific gravity of urine.
- The nurse may selectively note physical assess-

Table 23-9. Classification of intravenous solutions

Solution	Components	Special Comments
Isotonic Solutions		
0.9% Saline, also called Normal Saline	0.9 g of sodium chloride per 100 ml of water	Contains amounts of sodium and chloride in physiologically equal amounts to that found in plasma.
5% Dextrose and Water	5 g of dextrose (glucose/sugar) in each 100 ml of water	Isotonic when infused but the glucose is metabolized quickly, leaving a solution of dilute water.
Ringer's Solution or Lactated Ringer's	Water and a mixture of sodium, chloride, calcium, potassium, bicarbonate, and in some cases, lactate	Replaces electrolytes in amounts similarly found in plasma. The lactate, when present, helps maintain acid-base balance.
Hypotonic Solutions		
0.45% Sodium Chloride, or also called Half-Strength Saline	0.45 g of sodium chloride in each 100 ml of water	A smaller ratio of sodium and chloride than found in plasma causing it to be less concentrated in comparison.
5% Dextrose in 0.45% Saline	5 g of dextrose and 0.45% sodium chloride per 100 ml of water	The sugar provides a quick source of energy, leaving a hypotonic salt solution.
Hypertonic Solutions		
10% Dextrose in Water	10 g of dextrose per 100 ml of water	Twice the concentration of glucose than present in plasma.
3% Saline	3 g of sodium chloride per 100 ml of water	The high concentration of salt in the plasma will dehydrate cells and tissue.

ments, such as the condition of skin and mucous membranes, filling of veins and level of consciousness.

- Laboratory test results may reflect haemoconcentration or haemodilution. *Haemoconcentration* is a condition in which the fluid content of the blood is decreased; *haemodilution* is a condition in which the fluid content of the blood is increased. Cell counts and levels of serum electrolytes may appear abnormal, but this may only be a paper deficit or excess rather than an actual clinical state. In other words, when a specimen of blood is analysed, the levels and numbers of substances within the blood sample may appear low or high in relation to the proportion of fluid that is present. Correcting the fluid imbalance often restores the reported levels of other substances found in the blood to normal ranges.

Preparing the infusion solution and equipment

Wards generally stock commonly used intravenous solutions and equipment within utility rooms. Blood and blood products are stored, undergo extensive safety checks and then are released by the laboratory or blood bank.

Preparing the solution and equipment must be done while following the principles of medical and surgical asepsis. The nurse should practise good handwashing technique and be prepared to use skills that prevent the contamination of any openings or connection areas on equipment that could introduce organisms into the patient's circulatory system.

Preparing the intravenous solution

Solutions for intravenous infusions are dispensed in bottles or in collapsible plastic bags. The variety of solutions on the market is almost without limit. Manufacturers of fluids may use different names for identical, interchangeable solutions. If a nurse has questions about the particular solution that is ordered and the name of a stocked solution, the supervising nurse, doctor in charge of the patient or the hospital pharmacist generally is glad to interpret.

Solutions come in various volumes. They are usually in amounts of 1000 ml, 500 ml, 250 ml, 100 ml and 50 ml. The volume that the doctor orders depends on

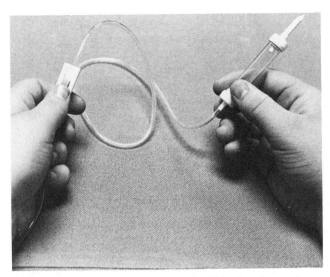

Figure 23-9 IV tubing showing spike, drip chamber and regulator clamp.

the length of time over which the fluid therapy will be required.

It is common that if a patient requires continuous intravenous therapy, an average of three 1000-ml containers of solution may be needed per day. The doctor should specify the amount and sequence in which the solutions should be infused if they are different. Smaller volumes of intravenous solutions, such as 250 ml of normal saline, are used prior to and after administering blood. The amount of saline solution used may vary according to the hospital policy. Whatever the type or amount of solution, the nurse should always know which is currently being infused and which solution is to follow.

Solutions containing a medication that must instill in an hour or less may be diluted in 50 or 100-ml solutions. The hospital pharmacist generally prepares the medication with the solution. Certain substances may be incompatible with various solutions. Having pharmacy personnel prepare additives in solutions decreases the likelihood of administering undesirable combinations. Any substance added to solutions should be clearly labelled on the bottle or bag. In addition, most pharmacies are now equipped with a laminar airflow hood. Mixing medications and solutions under this air-filtering device reduces the danger of contamination.

Some solutions that contain medications are prepared in advance and refrigerated to slow their decomposition. If this is the case, the nurse will want to remove the solution from the refrigerator and let it warm to room temperature prior to the scheduled

infusion. This can prevent the patient from feeling chilled or experiencing a change in body temperature.

Attaching intravenous tubing

Tubing is used to transport the fluid from the solution container to the needle or catheter within the patient's vein. Tubing comes in a variety of lengths with possibilities for additional extensions or connections. The top of the tubing contains a spike that is used to perforate the seal on the solution container. Just below the spike lies the drip chamber. The drip chamber is partially filled by squeezing and releasing the empty reservoir. Tubing and related equipment is illustrated in Figure 23-9.

In addition to gravity, the infusion can be controlled with a regulator clamp that is usually attached to the tubing. The nurse may use this device to adjust the rate of flow manually by opening or partially occluding the lumen of the tubing.

The nurse must use judgement in selecting the type of tubing designed to infuse a crystalloid or colloid solution. It is important to match the type of tubing that will best infuse each type of solution at an appropriate rate. The relationship between drip size and calculation of rates will be discussed later.

Using filters. Filters are used when there is a possibility that substances in the solution may form a precipitate. Filters can be attached to or come manufactured within tubing. They are designed to restrict any undissolved particles from entering the patient's vein. Hospital policy indicates whether and when a filter is to be used. Many experienced health personnel now tend to recommend the use of filters whenever administering an intravenous infusion. These people have found that filters help reduce infections as well as expel air bubbles through their vents.

Hanging the infusion equipment. Once the solution and tubing have been connected, they may be hung from a portable standard or one attached to the patient's bed. Normally, the pressure in the patient's vein is higher than atmospheric pressure. The solution is placed on a standard at a level approximately 45 to 60 cm (18 to 24 in) above the level of the vein. At this height, gravity is sufficient to overcome the pressure within the vein and allow the solution to infuse. The height of the solution will affect the rate of flow. The higher the solution, the faster it will infuse. As the bottle is lowered, the flow will become slower.

Some hospitals use a pump or controller on a portable standard when administering intravenous

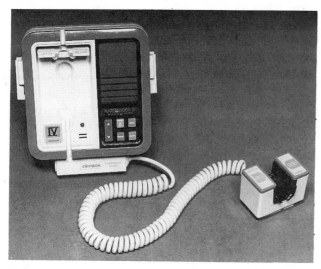

Figure 23-10 This is a volumetric infusion controller which automatically delivers a preset amount of solution. An alarm system alerts the nurse to various problems that may interfere with the delivery of solution (e.g. an empty container, a closed clamp, or kinked tubing). (Courtesy Royal Marsden Hospital)

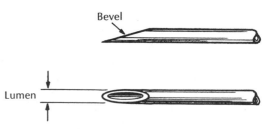

Figure 23-11 The bevel of a needle is its slanting edge, and its lumen is the space within the tubular needle shaft. The size of the lumen is indicated by the gauge size of the needle. A smaller number indicates a larger opening, and vice versa.

fluids. This equipment, shown in Figure 23-10, automatically delivers fluid at a preset rate. It also sounds an alarm to indicate the presence of an empty solution container or an obstruction in the intravenous tubing line. The device also has the ability to detect and warn the nurse that there is air rather than fluid in the tubing. Controllers and pumps are especially helpful when the volume of a solution the patient is to receive is critical, such as when a medication must be administered through an infusion line at a very slow rate.

Selecting a venepuncture device

Venepuncture is a term that refers to the act of entering a vein. Since the circulatory system is a continuous loop, there is no other means of access other than puncturing. Hollow needles are inserted through the skin and into a vein when fluids are administered intravenously.

Because venepuncture is an invasive procedure and the skin is no longer an intact barrier against pathogens principles of asepsis are very important. Most hospitals use disposable needles dispensed in sterile packages. This eliminates possible sources of contamination from reusable equipment.

Whenever possible, the needle size should be smaller than the vein to reduce tissue damage and discomfort when it is introduced. The lower the size of gauge, the larger is the lumen of the needle. For

most intravenous infusions for adults, a 20, 21, or 22 gauge, flexible needle is used. A size 18 or 19 gauge needle should be selected when colloid solutions are infused because a smaller needle may become plugged with the suspended proteins.

The venepuncture needle ideally should be short with a sharp bevel to facilitate puncturing and reduce tissue damage. A *bevel* is the tapered tip of the needle. Figure 23-11 illustrates the bevel and lumen of a needle. Most needles used for entering a vein are 2.5 to 4 cm (1 to 1.5 in) long. Butterfly needles are also called winged-tip or scalp vein needles. They are short, thin-walled needles with plastic tabs. Many prefer to use this type of venepuncture device because of the ease of handling and stabilizing them. The needle may be found in an infusion set or selected separately.

An intravenous catheter may be inserted under certain circumstances, once the needle punctures the vein. Intravenous catheters may also be called intracaths or angiocaths; angio is a prefix that refers to vein. An *intracath* is a venepuncture device that is a flexible tube located on the inside of a needle. Once the needle is in place, the catheter is threaded through the needle and into the vein. The needle is subsequently removed. An *angiocath* is a narrow, flexible tube that is positioned around the outside of an inflexible needle. The tip of the needle extends from the end of the catheter. The needle tip acts only to puncture the vein. The catheter is threaded over the needle tip and into the vein. The needle is then removed from the vein. An angiocath is illustrated in Figure 23-12.

Because catheters are flexible, they are less likely to become displaced; however, they may become kinked. This type of venepuncture device may be used when:

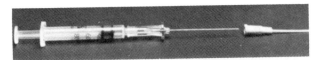

Figure 23-12 This catheter threads over the needle. After the needle and catheter have been introduced into the vein, the needle and syringe are carefully withdrawn, leaving only the catheter in place in the vein. The tubing from the intravenous solution is then connected to the catheter.

- An infusion is to run for an extended period of time.
- The veins are unusually difficult to locate and enter.
- The patient is young or active, or unable to exercise some degree of protection of the infusion site.
- The solution or medication is likely to cause discomfort or damage to tissue if it does not remain within the vein.

Assembling miscellaneous equipment

The nurse may gather additional equipment, some of which may be optional, when an infusion of intravenous fluids will be started. The following items are usually necessary: a tourniquet, a antiseptic swab to cleanse the area at the site of the injection; a dry, sterile swab or two; antiseptic spray, if hospital policy requires its use at the puncture site; a gauze square to cover the venepuncture site; and adhesive strips to secure the needle and dressing.

The nurse should use judgement and follow hospital policy when collecting other equipment. For instance, an armboard may be needed to anchor the arm and hand when a patient may not be relied upon to be cautious when moving about.

In the UK it is the responsibility of the doctor to perform venepuncture to administer an intravenous infusion. In some hospitals doctors are allowed to delegate this procedure to qualified nurses who have undergone specific training in this area. However it still remains the doctor's responsibility.

Calculating the infusion rate

The doctor prescribes the flow rate but it is the responsibility of the nurse to regulate and maintain the proper flow rate. The rate is calculated by the nurse on the basis of drops of solution per minute.

There is no standard equivalent of drops per millilitre among commercially manufactured IV equipment. The size of the opening into the drip chamber of the tubing, and subsequently the size of the drop

itself, varies among manufacturers. Most hospitals use the products of a single company. The nurse should become familiar with those used. The more common equivalents, called the *drop factor*, are: 15 drops equal 1 ml, 20 drops equal 1 ml and 60 drops equal 1 ml. Because blood is a colloidal solution, the drop size must be larger to permit the molecules of protein to flow through. Therefore, when blood is infused, tubing different from that used for infusing crystalloid solutions must be utilized. The drop factor when using a blood set is usually 10 drops equal 1 ml.

To determine how many millilitres of solution are to be given each hour, the nurse should use the following formula:

$$\frac{\text{Total number of ml to be given}}{\text{Hours in which the solution is to be infused}}$$

$$= \text{ml to be given per hour}$$

For example, a doctor orders 3000 ml of solution to be infused over a 24-hour period:

$$\frac{3000\,\text{ml}}{24\,\text{hr}} = 125 \text{ ml to be infused per hour}$$

The nurse then determines the number of drops to be infused per minute. This requires using the drop factor determined by the manufacturer of the IV tubing being used. The formula is as follows:

$$\frac{\text{Number of ml per hour} \times \text{drop factor}}{60 \text{ minutes}}$$

$$= \text{drops to infuse per minute}$$

For example, using the amounts in the order given in the first example in which 125 ml are to be infused every hour, assume that the intravenous equipment has a drop factor of 20 drops equal 1 ml.

$$\frac{125\,\text{ml} \times 20}{60} = 41.6 \text{ rounded to 42 drops per minute}$$

The nurse would then count the number of drops falling into the drip chamber of the tubing per minute. By adjusting the regulator clamp, the number of drops per minute can be increased or decreased until the infusion rate matches the calculated rate.

Monitoring the rate of infusion

Maintaining the proper rate of flow is important. Too slow a flow may not meet the patient's needs for fluid. Infusing fluid too rapidly may overtax the body's ability to adjust to the increase in the fluid volume, the electrolytes, or the medications that may have been added.

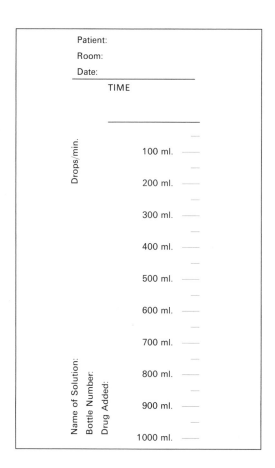

Patient:

Room:

Date:

TIME

Drops/min.

100 ml. —

200 ml. —

300 ml. —

400 ml. —

500 ml. —

600 ml. —

700 ml. —

Name of Solution:

Bottle Number:

Drug Added:

800 ml. —

900 ml. —

1000 ml. —

Figure 23-13 Sample marker for a solution container.

The nurse should make timely observations, at least every hour, to determine that the volume of intravenous solution is infusing according to schedule. The task may be simplified by marking the container at points indicating the amounts that should be infusing hour by hour. The nurse should be able to tell at a glance whether the solution is being infused at the proper hourly rate. An example of a marker that can be placed on the solution container is illustrated in Figure 23-13. Some nurses mark directly on a plastic bag of solution. However, it is probably better not to use a heavy felt-tipped pen because questions have been raised about the possibility of the ink penetrating the bag and entering the solution.

The rate of flow of an intravenous infusion may be altered by several factors. These factors are listed and explained in Table 23-10.

Readjusting the rate of flow

If an infusion is not progressing according to schedule, it may be necessary for the nurse to make adjustments in the rate. However, the volume should never be rapidly increased or decreased to adjust the rate of infusion in a short period of time. To compensate for a deficit or excess of infused volume, the rate should be adjusted over each remaining hour of administration. Even so, the increased or decreased rate should never exceed 25% of the original infusion rate. If the difference is over 25% then the doctor must be informed.

Table 23-10. Common factors affecting the rate of flow

Factor	Explanation
Changing distances between the height of the container and the insertion site	Distances may change as the patient ambulates, moves to a chair, stretcher or toilet, or alters the position of the hand in which the solution is infusing. As distances increase, the rate speeds, and as distances decrease, the rate will slow.
Occlusion of the tubing or lumen of the venepuncture device	Tubing can become compressed by the patient's weight or parts of the bed, thus slowing or stopping the rate of infusion. A blood clot, inflammation or swelling at the tip of the needle may similarly affect the infusion rate.
Faulty regulator clamp or tampering	A faulty regulator clamp may become loose, causing an increased volume to be infused in a short time. Some patients purposely or accidentally change the adjustment of the clamp, causing it to slow or infuse more rapidly.
Administration of cold fluid	Cold fluid may cause localized constriction of the blood vessels slowing the rate of infusion.
Changes in the patient's blood pressure	The fluid infuses once it overcomes the venous pressure within the vessel. Changes in arterial pressure are likely to affect venous pressure, since the vascular system is a continuous loop. The rate of flow will slow or speed according to the rise and fall of blood pressure.

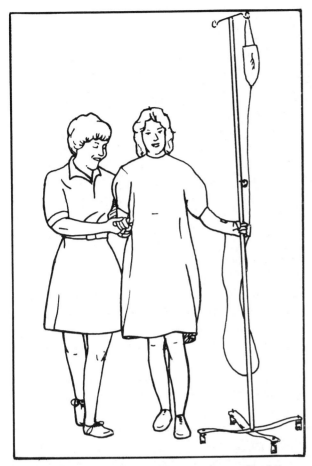

Figure 23-14 This patient is taking her first walk while receiving intravenous therapy. She is wearing rubber-soled shoes that reduce the risk of slipping and falling.

Providing patient care

The nurse must continue to provide the care that has been individually planned for each patient receiving an infusion of intravenous fluids. This includes personal hygiene needs as well as specific skills involving the maintenance of the infusion.

Some modifications may be utilized when providing routine care. Infusing solutions may be made portable by using a standard on wheels, as shown in Figure 23-14. This facilitates the patient's need for activity and exercise. Special gowns that facilitate insertion and removal of the arm used for an infusion are available in some hospitals. The sleeves of these gowns unsnap to the neckline, opening the entire length. Such gowns eliminate the need to slip a sleeve over the needle, tubing and solution container.

When these gowns are not available, the following technique may be used for removing a patient gown with a closed sleeve. The sleeve is slipped over the venepuncture device, tubing and solution container while the nurse holds the container temporarily. The reverse set of actions is used to replace the gown, beginning with slipping one sleeve of the gown over the solution container and then down over the tubing and needle and into place.

Caring for the venepuncture site

The venepuncture site represents a type of open wound. It is important to inspect and dress the wound at routine intervals specified by the hospital. Some notation about its condition should appear daily in the permanent record.

Hospital policy may indicate a particular antimicrobial spray that should be used. The principles of asepsis are no less important when changing this dressing than when changing the dressing over an incision. In fact, sterile technique is particularly important in this case, since the venepuncture site is a direct line to the bloodstream. Pathogens may be circulated easily to other parts of the body.

Changing solution containers

When the patient requires continuous or repeated infusions of solutions, it may become necessary to change solution containers as they become nearly empty. Also, a solution container that has been hanging up to 24 hours should be changed to reduce the potential for growing pathogens. If a venepuncture site must be changed, it may be convenient, in some cases, to change the solution container at the same time. This may not always be possible. Principles of Care 23-3 describes the actions that should be followed when only the solution container must be changed.

Changing infusion tubing

Most hospitals set infection control policies that indicate the length of time that tubing may continue to be used. Tubing is usually changed at least every 48 hours. This is best done when the solution and the site are changed. However, it may be necessary to change the tubing without changing the solution container or the venepuncture device.

Detecting complications

Regular assessments of the site of the infusion, the equipment that is delivering the infusion and the patient's overall responses during the fluid infusion

Principles of Care 23-3. Changing solution containers

Nursing Action	Rationale
Determine that the solution that is scheduled to replace the current infusion is available about one hour before it is needed.	The replacement solution should be available before the current solution has completely infused. Delay may facilitate clotting, and a new venepuncture may be required.
Be ready to switch containers when the infusion container is empty but the drip chamber still contains fluid.	If air enters the tubing, it will have to be removed using techniques described further in this procedure.
Tighten the regulator clamp on the infusion tubing to slow the rate of infusion.	The rate should be fast enough to keep the solution infusing, but slow enough to prevent partially emptying the tubing.
Lower the empty solution container, with its tubing, from the standard. Position the container on a slant or resting on its wide base with the neck facing upward.	Keeping the opening upward will prevent any solution within the container from leaking out the punctured opening.
Pull out the spike from the container, without touching the tip.	The tip will be inserted within the sterile replacement solution and lead to its contamination if touched.
Remove the seal from the replacement solution container.	The seal protects the solution from contamination; it should not be removed until just prior to puncturing with the spike.
Immediately insert the spike into the container of the fresh solution.	Prolonged exposure of the tip to the air increases the potential for contamination with pathogens.
Hang the solution container from the infusion standard.	The height of the container should be 45 to 60 cm (18 to 24 in) above the level of the vein.
Inspect for the presence of air bubbles in the tubing and proceed to displace them from the tubing.	Air bubbles probably are not dangerous in small amounts. However, they may cause the patient to become concerned for his safety.
Displace the air bubbles by using one of the following two methods: <ul><li>Move the regulator clamp below the air and tighten to stop the flow. Tap the bubbles as shown in Figure 23-15.</li><li>Milk the air in the direction of the drip chamber or the filter, or work the air upward by wrapping the tubing around a circular object as illustrated in Figure 23-16.</li></ul>	Air will rise or take the path of least resistance.
Loosen the regulator clamp and adjust the infusion rate to deliver the ordered volume over the prescribed amount of time.	The rate will need to be timed and readjusted once the position of the regulator clamp has been changed.
Attach a new monitoring strip to the solution container, identifying the hourly increments of the volume to be infused.	A monitoring strip aids observation of the schedule of the infusing solution.
Record the volume of infused solution on the intake portion of the fluid record.	An accurate record of fluid intake and fluid output should be maintained on all patients receiving intravenous fluids.

Continued

Principles of Care 23-3. Continued

Nursing Action	Rationale

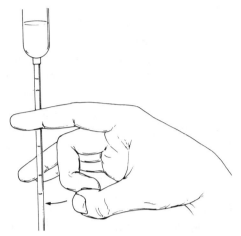

Figure 23-15 Beginning directly below the lowest level of air in the tubing, thump the tubing, proceeding upward until the air escapes from the tubing.

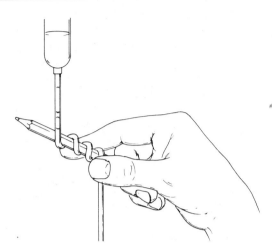

Figure 23-16 Beginning below the level of air in the tubing and twisting the tubing round a pen, pencil, scissors or other object will also displace air from the tubing.

Nursing Action	Rationale
Record the addition of new solution wherever it is designated by hospital policy.	Many hospitals require that a new volume of intravenous solution be recorded similarly to medications.

should be made frequently. The nurse should be on the alert and be prepared to take action if any signs of complications occur when a patient is receiving intravenous fluids.

- Immediately report signs and symptoms of respiratory problems such as dyspnoea, noisy breathing and coughing. Respiratory and cardiac problems are often caused by *circulatory overload*. This is a condition that is caused by administering too much solution too quickly in relation to a patient's ability to circulate the added volume or eliminate it through urination. The flow rate should be decreased, the patient should be placed in a Fowler's position, vital signs should be assessed, and the doctor should be notified for further orders. The complication is serious and the infusion may have to be stopped entirely.
- Check for *infiltration* of the solution, which is the escape of solution into tissues. A dislodged

needle or a needle that has penetrated the wall of the vein may cause fluid to pass into subcutaneous tissue. Typical signs include a slow flow rate or no flow of solution, swelling in the area of the venepuncture site, a burning sensation, local pallor of the skin and coldness. A penlight is often helpful to detect infiltration. The light will illuminate the skin differently in the area of infiltration.
- Check for phlebitis, which may occur when a solution is particularly irritating to the vein or the venepuncture device remains in the same site for a prolonged period of time. The area will appear red, warm, swollen and painful. The rate may slow due to localized oedema. Further use of the vein should be avoided. Notify the doctor of the observations.
- Infection at the site may occur and could spread to other parts of the body via pathogens within the blood stream. The site may appear red and

puffy. Purulent drainage may be present. The patient may have a rise in temperature and chills. Discontinue the infusion at its present site. Follow principles of asepsis when dressing the wound. Notify the doctor for further orders. A culture may be necessary to identify the type of pathogens that are present. Subsequent treatment and care will depend on measures required for controlling the spread of the microorganisms.

- An *air embolism* is a rare, but deadly, complication that occurs when a large volume of air enters the vein. If proper techniques are followed when tubing is attached, infusions usually do not permit lethal amounts of air to enter the patient. The minimum quantity of air that would be fatal to humans is not known, but animal experimentation indicates that it is much larger than the quantity that could be present in the entire length of infusion tubing. The average infusion tubing holds about 5 ml of air, an amount not ordinarily considered dangerous. Patients, however, are often frightened when they see air in the tubing, and every effort should be made to keep this from happening. If a patient experienced an air embolism, the nurse would probably detect a sudden and extreme drop in blood pressure, tachycardia, cyanosis and diminished level of consciousness. The nurse should position the patient on his left side and elevate

his feet above the level of the heart. Since air rises, the air will enter the right atrium where it will remain trapped at that level. This position is maintained until the air can be absorbed.

Discontinuing the infusion

When the amount of ordered solution has been infused and no more is scheduled to follow, the nurse discontinues the infusion as follows:

- Clamp the tubing and remove the tape that held the dressing and venepuncture device in place.
- Gently press a swab moistened with antiseptic solution over the site of entry.
- Remove the needle or catheter by pulling it out without hesitation, following the course of the vein. If the needle or catheter is removed by twisting, raising or lowering, it could damage the vein.
- Apply pressure to the injection site for 30 to 45 seconds while elevating the forearm, as illustrated in Figure 23-17. This technique helps stop bleeding from the injection site. Then apply a small, dry pressure dressing.
- Flex and extend the arm or hand several times to help the patient regain sensation and mobility in the area where the needle was located.
- Record the amount and type of fluid infused

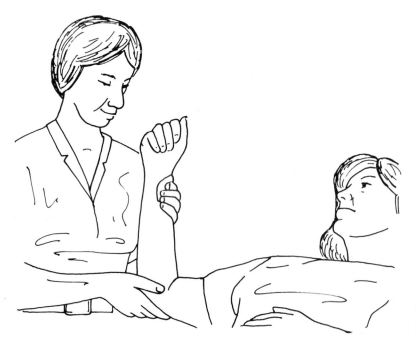

Figure 23-17 The nurse elevates the patient's forearm and places pressure at the injection site after removing the needle when discontinuing an intravenous infusion.

during the current shift on the bedside fluid intake record.

Administering a blood transfusion

A *blood transfusion* is the intravenous infusion of whole blood. Most often, blood is collected from one person, called the *donor*, and given to another, called the *recipient*. Donors are screened in order to ensure that the person giving the blood is healthy and will not be endangered by the loss of a fraction of his blood volume.

Donated blood is tested for serum hepatitis and AIDS antibodies to avoid the possibility of spreading these diseases from infected blood. Blood that tests positive is automatically not used. Nevertheless, the fear associated with acquiring these blood-transmitted diseases has caused many individuals in good health to have their own blood collected and stored. It is then administered at a later date if it is needed. This method has been found safe because there are no dangers related to passing organisms from one person to another or receiving mismatched blood. The disadvantage is that instances are relatively rare in which it can be predicted that a person will need a blood transfusion. Blood is generally collected and stored from 21 to 35 days.

Before blood can be given to a patient, it must be determined that the blood of the donor and that of the recipient are compatible. Incompatible red blood cells can react with one another, causing clumping within the vascular system and possible death to the recipient.

Blood is categorized into four major groups—A, B, AB and O—depending on the type of protein present on the surface of the red blood cells. In addition to the four groups, there are many other factors that differentiate one group of blood cells from another, Rh factor being one example. The laboratory test that identifies the proteins on red blood cells is called *typing*.

The blood type of the donor and the blood type of the recipient are tested, using a test called *crossmatching*, to determine the compatibility between the two blood specimens. Though the recipient is almost always given an identical blood type during a transfusion, there may be exceptions made in an emergency. Table 23-11 provides a list of blood types that are compatible.

Blood is collected and dispensed in 500-ml bottles or plastic containers. Each container is called a unit of

Table 23-11. Compatible blood types

Recipient's Blood Type	Donated Blood Type*
A	A and O
B	B and O
AB (Universal Recipient)	AB, A, B, and O
O (Universal Donor)	O

* A recipient with Rh positive blood may receive Rh positive or Rh negative blood although it is preferred to match this factor as well. (Rh negative means that the factor is absent from the surface of the blood cell). However, an Rh negative person should *never* receive Rh positive blood.

blood. An anticalcium agent is added to the blood to prevent clotting. Blood is a colloid solution; it is not unusual for individuals to be sensitive to the various protein molecules in blood and other blood products.

Policies may vary among hospitals about the administration of a blood transfusion. In some hospitals a written consent form must be signed by the patient before blood is administered.

Infusing blood extracts and blood substitutes

Some patients do not need all the components of whole blood. For example, one may need red blood cells but not the plasma and its contents. Packed red blood cells, which must be crossmatched, may be given to such a patient intravenously. In other situations, only plasma is required. Frozen or fresh serum is particularly useful in emergencies for immediate restoration of fluid volume. Serum presents no compatibility problem, and time need not be lost typing and crossmatching blood and seeking donors. Still other patients may require only blood platelets or just albumin, a single plasma protein. These can be collected separately from whole blood and administered intravenously.

Several substitute solutions for blood may be used in certain situations. Dextran is a synthetic plasma expander. It is used intravenously as an emergency measure until whole blood becomes available. A relatively new product is a synthetic blood substitute with the trade name Fluosol-DA. It contains substances that carry oxygen, but no red blood cells, and has been used effectively for patients needing components of whole blood. It is also acceptable to persons who, for religious reasons, refuse blood transfusions. The product holds promise for selected use.

Monitoring the patient undergoing blood transfusion

The patient must be monitored every 30 minutes for any signs or symptoms of a reaction to the blood. The following are signs or symptoms that may indicate a reaction:

- Hypotension, tachycardia, dyspnoea, restlessness, constriction in the chest, back pain, flushing, are a few manifestations of an incompatibility reaction.
- A febrile reaction may be characterized by a sudden onset of fever with shaking chills during or following the infusion, with headache, tachycardia and generalized muscle aches.
- Fever, chills, gastrointestinal symptoms and a drop in blood pressure may be associated with the infusion of blood contaminated with pathogens.
- Mild allergic reactions may be manifested by large hives, itching and discomfort, but usually no drastic changes in vital signs.
- Moderate chilling during the reaction with little or no significant change in body temperature may just be a temporary reaction to the cold blood. However, the nurse should substantiate that conclusion with other assessments.
- Hypertension, dyspnoea, moist breath sounds, distended neck veins and a bounding pulse may indicate circulatory overload.
- Tingling in the fingers, low blood pressure, cramps and finally convulsions may be associated with an effect caused by the chemical added to prevent blood clotting of the stored blood.

Take the following steps if the patient has any signs or symptoms of a reaction to the blood:

- Stop the transfusion *immediately. Do not remove the needle from the vein.*
- Place the patient in a Fowler's position, unless ordered to the contrary.
- Report all observations immediately and follow any orders the doctor prescribes.
- Monitor the vital signs frequently and continue to make careful observations of the patient's condition.
- Save the blood and tubing.

Follow an uneventful infusion of blood with an administration of a small volume of the normal saline solution.

Record the volume of blood and saline that was infused on the patient's bedside fluid intake form.

Record all assessments, care, and the patient's response in the permanent record.

Suggested measures to promote fluid and chemical balance in selected situations

When the patient is an infant or child

Take into consideration that infants and children have a greater proportion of body water and that their mechanisms to maintain fluid balance are less well-developed than are those of adults. As a result, fluid and chemical imbalances often develop rapidly and become severe quickly. The premature infant and the newborn are especially quick to develop fluid imbalances.

Think of infants and young children as "smaller vessels with a larger spout" when compared with adults. This means that youngsters lose water more quickly because of a comparatively large skin surface in terms of body weight than adults.

Take into consideration that normal serum electrolyte concentrations are not strikingly different among infants, children, and adults, except that bicarbonate levels are lower in youngsters. Children and infants tend to develop imbalances relatively quickly and easily.

Expect the signs and symptoms of fluid imbalances in general are similar in children and adults, except that behavioural changes include irritability and increased crying.

Provide children with cool drinks or ice lollies on hot days when they become so involved in play that they do not take time for fluid intake.

When the patient is an adolescent or young adult

Discourage fad or crash dieting that severely restricts the intake of food or fluids.

Explain the dangers of using starvation, self-administered laxatives or self-induced vomiting to control weight gain.

Encourage exercise-conscious individuals to select alternative forms of active exercise when temperatures and humidity levels are extremely high.

Advise an individual who exercises during hot, humid weather to drink extra water, orange juice or other beverages to replace fluids and electrolytes lost through perspiration.

When the patient is elderly

Take into account that the elderly gradually lose physical reserves and, hence, mechanisms of the body that maintain fluid balance become fragile with increasing years. As a result, fluid imbalances develop relatively quickly, can become severe rapidly and respond slowly to treatment.

Expect that the concentration of electrolytes remains essentially the same as persons grow older, except that the plasma concentration of sodium is somewhat higher in the elderly.

Explain to an elderly patient the importance of identifying all medications, both prescription and nonprescription drugs, that are taken. For example, many nonprescription drugs taken by the elderly for the relief of constipation and antacids contain magnesium. Overuse of these can lead to hypermagnesaemia. Excessive self-administration of sodium bicarbonate can alter acid-base balance. Cough medicines containing ammonium chloride can affect kidney regulation of acid-base and electrolyte balance.

Teaching suggestions for promoting fluid and chemical balance

Chapter 10 discussed nursing measures and described the importance of patient teaching about ways to promote proper nutrition. This chapter has explained the benefits of proper nutrition and fluid intake as they relate to fluid and chemical balance.

To the extent that a patient can understand it, information in this chapter should be shared with patients so that they know why it is so important to eat a well-balanced diet and have an adequate fluid intake. Similarly, information in this chapter will help the nurse teach patients the importance of observing special diets, or using recommended food supplements, and of increasing or limiting fluids, as ordered. Teaching has been found to be more effective and patients to follow ordered therapy better when they understand why their therapy is important and how it will help promote health and well-being.

Suggested measures when administering intravenous fluids in selected situations

When the patient is an infant or child

Try to arrange to start an intravenous infusion in a treatment room rather than at a child's bedside. A child is comforted when he can think of his own room as being safe from painful procedures.

Explain the procedure for administering intravenous fluids and let the child act out the procedure on a doll. This helps decrease fear and lets the child displace and express his own feelings in a non-threatening way.

Select equipment of an appropriate size for infants and children when starting an intravenous infusion. Select a small needle, such as a 27-gauge, or a butterfly needle. Catheters are often used because of their flexibility.

For an infant, a small armboard can be made with two tongue blades wrapped in gauze and secured with tape when a small-sized board is unavailable.

Select veins for administering an intravenous infusion in the same manner as for an adult. A scalp vein is often used for an infant, although

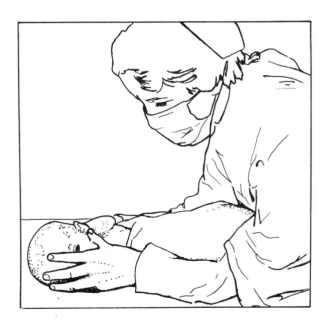

Figure 23-18 This is one method of holding an infant when a scalp vein is to be entered. The hands are cupped over the occiput and the face, while holding and rotating the head 90°. The forearms are used to immobilize the infant's trunk.

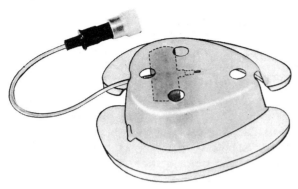

Figure 23-19 This transparent protective shield can be placed over a needle in a vein to help keep it in place. It is especially helpful when a scalp vein on a child has been entered for an intravenous infusion. (Courtesy J.T. Posey Co., Arcadia, CA)

some nurses prefer peripheral veins. The technique for holding an infant when a scalp vein is used is illustrated in Figure 23-18.

Anchor a needle or catheter well for intravenous therapy. When a scalp vein is used for an infant, a protective shield can be placed over the needle. One is illustrated in Figure 23-19.

Monitor intravenous therapy used for infants and children carefully. In terms of the flow rate and amounts of added medications and electrolytes, the margin of error is small in young-sters. A controller helps considerably to maintain an appropriate flow rate and is often used for infants and children receiving intravenous therapy.

Look for reactions to solutions of intravenous medications, intravenous fluids and blood transfusions as for an adult when caring for an infant or child. Crying and restlessness are frequently present in the child too young to describe when he feels ill.

When the patient is elderly

Expect that veins in the elderly are often hardened (sclerotic) and also fragile. Small-gauge needles, such as a 27-gauge needle, should be used for intravenous therapy and inserted, secured and removed with care. Because the elderly person's veins are easily injured, every effort should be taken to preserve those that are available.

Inspect an IV site when leaking occurs. As individuals age, skin turgor around the venepuncture device is likely to be less than that found in younger patients.

Monitor intravenous therapy closely. The elderly are very susceptible to water and electrolyte imbalances, but measures to restore balance must be used with caution to avoid imbalances of the opposite nature.

Part 5

Nursing Skills

Associated with the Dying Patient

24

Caring for terminally ill and grieving individuals

Learning objectives

When the content of this chapter has been mastered, the learner should be able to:

Identify and describe the stages of dying, as described by Dr. Elisabeth Kübler-Ross.

Describe the options for care that are generally available to patients with a terminal illness.

Describe nursing measures that may be useful when meeting the emotional needs of dying patients.

List common fears shared by many dying individuals.

Discuss approaches for meeting the dying patient's spiritual needs.

Identifying unique physical problems of dying patients and nursing interventions that may be useful.

List various signs associated with aproaching death.

Describe approaches when informing and supporting a family member when death is near.

Describe the nursing responsibilities associated with care of the body and patient's belongings.

Discuss typical grief reactions and methods that help others to resolve the loss of a loved one.

Describe the nursing measures that may facilitate grieving a perinatal death.

List suggested measures for the care of the terminally ill patient in selected situations as described in this chapter.

Summarize suggestions for patient and family teaching as offered in this chapter.

Glossary

Active euthanasia The deliberate ending of the life of an individual who is suffering from an incurable condition.

Anticipatory grief The grief that begins when learning that a death will occur.

Avoidance A technique used to separate oneself from situations that are threatening or unpleasant.

Brain death A term meaning that there is no evidence of brain functioning in an individual who is being kept alive with life support machines.

Denial A psychological technique in which an individual does not believe certain information to be true.

Euthanasia A term meaning an easy death.

Grief The physical and emotional feelings related to separation and loss.

Grief work Activities that lead to resolving a loss. Synonym for *mourning*.

Hope The ability to cling to the possibility of a positive outcome in spite of overwhelming odds.

Hospice An organization dedicated to providing care and services for dying patients and their families.

Last offices Care of the body after death.

Mourning Activities that lead to resolving a loss. Synonym for *grief work*.

Passive euthanasia Using techniques that relieve pain but that do not delay natural death from occurring.

Pathological grief Actions that indicate an individual is not accepting the reality of a death.

Perinatal death The death of an infant that occurs prior to, during or shortly after birth.

Shroud A garment for enclosing a dead body.

Symbolic language Communication that involves terms or statements that carry a double meaning.

Terminal illness One from which recovery is beyond reasonable expectation.

Tolerance A condition in which a person requires more of a drug to achieve a similar effect once obtained with a lower dosage.

Table 24-1. Selected causes of death in England and Wales, 1991

Cause of death	ICD code	Total number of deaths, all ages
Ischaemic heart disease and myocardial infarction	410–414	150,090
Malignant neoplasms (cancer)	140–208	143,610
Cerebrovascular disease	430–438	68,669
Respiratory disease	460–519	63,273
Accidents and adverse effects	E800–E949	11,066
Suicide	E950–E959	3,893
Injury–undetermined whether accidentally or purposefully inflicted	E980–E989	2,054
Congenital anomalies	740–759	1,643
Homicide	E960–E969	269
Complications of pregnancy, childbirth and the puerperium	630–676	45

Source: Office of Population Censuses and Surveys, Deaths by Cause: 1991 registrations, Series DH2 92/2; published by OPCS, 1992. Crown Copyright.

Introduction

Scientific technology, improved nutrition and advancements in health care have all added increased years to life expectancy. It continues to lengthen year by year. Yet death is a certainty. The only unknowns are when, where and how death will occur. Nurses and other health personnel are probably involved more than any other group with individuals who are experiencing impending death.

Death may be sudden and unexpected for some; but it may be somewhat predictable for individuals with a terminal illness. A *terminal illness* is one from which recovery is beyond reasonable expectation. The condition that contributes to death may be a disease or it may be the result of injury. Table 24-1 shows the current leading causes of death in England and Wales.

When a patient is dying, the nurse is faced with dual responsibilities. The dying patient requires holistic care in perhaps the fullest meaning of the term. At the same time, those individuals who have developed a significant relationship with the dying patient, which may include family, friends and even health care staff, will need support. All will be dealing with grief. *Grief* encompasses the physical and emotional feelings related to separation and loss.

This chapter will deal with many aspects of the dying and grieving experience. The unique emotional, spiritual and physical problems of the terminally ill will be discussed. Approaches that are helpful in dealing with anticipatory grief will also be described. *Anticipatory grief* is the grief that begins when learning that a death will occur.

Examining attitudes and responses to dying

It is difficult to deal with any problem that does not seem to be a reality. Death seems to be one of those unrealistic events. It is not unreasonable to understand the futility that individuals feel when dealing with the certainty of approaching death.

People have been left vulnerable as a result of many social changes. Most individuals have been sheltered from death by institutions that provide care for the terminally ill or that relieve the family's involvement by arranging the funeral.

Life-sustaining advancements occur now with such frequency as to make death seem as though it could be postponed almost indefinitely. Transplant procedures provide dying individuals with not only a new healthy organ but also a second chance at life. Intensive care techniques literally snatch many a person from almost guaranteed death. The examples go on and on.

As a result of the lack of experience with death, most individuals react somewhat instinctively when personally involved with impending death. Some common reactions among patients, family members, and health care professionals include:

Denial: denial is a psychological technique in which an individual does not believe certain information to be true. This approach is difficult to sustain as accumulating evidence tests its logic.

Avoidance: avoidance is a technique used to separate oneself from situations that are threatening or unpleasant. Health care personnel are more often inclined to use this approach since the dying person represents a personal defeat.

Hope: hope is the ability to cling to the possibility of a positive outcome against overwhelming odds. This human quality helps individuals to endure a hardship while believing that it will ultimately be resolved.

Most individuals prefer to ignore thoughts of death as much as possible. They prefer to think and deal with death only when it becomes absolutely necessary to do so. However, this approach does not always provide the best resources for dealing with death and dying. More and more individuals are studying death and dying and encouraging others to do so.

Preparing to provide terminal care

Each nurse will more than likely become involved with the care of a terminally ill patient. Personal values and attitudes are closely associated with the quality of care that a nurse provides. Since the subject of death is not one that most nurses have thought about, it is best to take the opportunity to explore various aspects of death and dying before being faced with the actual experience. This intellectual approach may help to resolve future conflicts before becoming emotionally involved.

Exploring feelings about death

Since nurses are a product of their culture, it is not difficult to understand that they would share similar values. In our culture, youth, health and productivity are valued in contrast to ageing, illness or retirement. Most individuals are strongly dedicated towards life

and the future. We live in a death-denying society. For these reasons, nurses may experience difficulty when caring for individuals who are chronically ill, elderly or approaching death.

One's personal feelings about death and dying are particularly important to understand before providing terminal care. The nurse who neglects to do so is in a questionable position to be able to meet the needs of terminally ill patients and their families. The easy way is to avoid involvement and remain detached. Sadly enough, as a result, the dying person and the family are often emotionally abandoned. They are often left to face a very frightening situation alone while the nurse performs care like an unfeeling robot.

Discussing ideas with others is one of the most effective ways of developing insight concerning personally held attitudes about death and dying. This can be done in a formal conference with other health or nursing personnel; it can be done informally through discussions with friends, family, counsellor or clergyman.

The answers to the following questions often help a nurse to clarify feelings about personal death and dying:

- What is my concept of death?
- Who or what has contributed to my feelings about death?
- What kinds of goals or experiences are especially important to me before I die?
- Would I want to know that my condition is terminal?
- If I could control the events that lead to my death, what would I want them to be?
- Whom would I want to have present during my terminal illness?
- Where would I prefer to die?
- What fears do I have about death?

Developing a support system

The nurse is often looked to as the source of strength that others find they need during a period of crisis. However, there may be times when the nurse may feel the need to vent frustration and receive support rather than always give it. Most often nurses find their co-workers extremely empathetic and comforting. The nurse must never feel that the burden of care depends on only one person. Other health team members include the doctor, pharmacist, psychologist, social worker, dietician, clergyman and others. All are allies who may provide help that complements and supplements the nursing care of the terminally ill patient and his family. When nurses feel a sense of support, they are better able, in turn, to support others.

A support system among peers begins by developing an environment in which nurses working together know that they can turn to each other. It includes being able to share daily work problems, sadness and humour—and, possibly most of all, being able to share themselves and their personal feelings. Such nonverbal communication techniques as using touch in the form of a pat on the back or a hug are often helpful. Weeping, laughing and also being silent together can be comforting and supportive. Peer support works best when nurses not only reach out for support they need but also recognize when their peers need help and can readily say, "How can I help you?"

Examining euthanasia

When caring for a terminally ill patient, a nurse must often deal with ethical and legal issues about ending life or prolonging it by artificial means. *Euthanasia* literally means an easy death. The term has also been applied to mean mercy killing. The use of euthanasia is generally considered when death is inevitable and life-saving measures are of questionable benefit. *Passive euthanasia* refers to using techniques that relieve pain but that do not delay natural death from occurring. *Active euthanasia* is the deliberate ending of the life of an individual who is suffering from an incurable condition; this form of euthanasia is illegal.

Despite a hopeless situation, the patient and the family remain the focus of attention. They are the ones who should control decisions affecting medical care. They often need time to work through their feelings. At one time the medical emphasis was on extending the quantity of life no matter what the cost. Today, there is a greater concern about providing quality and dignity to the dying patient's life. Each set of circumstances is unique. What may be reasonable or ordinary care for one individual may be unreasonable or extraordinary to another. The important factor is that communication occurs.

Decisions are often made about whether to implement resuscitative procedures for a terminally ill patient. It is good practice to involve the patient and family in the decision, but the doctor has the ultimate say. His decision is taken when a patient has a chronic incurable illness for which there is no further treatment and no justification for prolonging life. The order must be written in the patient's notes. A verbal or telephone order is not sufficient.

Table 24-2. Criteria for acceptable organ donation according to age of the donor

Organ	Age Range
Kidney	2 years to 70 years
Liver	Up to 55 years
Heart	Up to 40 years
Pancreas	2 years to 50 years
Corneas	Acceptable at any age
Lung	Up to 40 years

Reproduced with permission from Keogh, A.H., Transplantation and Organ Donation, Nursing, 16, p. 591, 1987.

Requesting organ donations

Body organs and tissues, such as the kidneys, heart, liver, pancreas, corneas, the lungs and skin, may be needed for transplants. Organs cannot be bought or sold. Donations remain the one and only method by which organs are available for transplants. They must be voluntarily given. Prior to death, patients may grant such permission. However, if the patient has not granted permission or signed a donor card, permission must be obtained from the next of kin. Verbal consent is adequate and need not be confirmed in writing. Figure 24-1 is an example of an organ donation card.

Approaching the next of kin is a very sensitive area and should be done by someone with experience, whether it is the doctor in charge of the patient, the nurse, the GP, a religious leader or the transplant coordinator. They should be sensitive, compassionate and articulate. Care must be taken that no one feels that another patient is being given preferential treatment at the expense of the donor. It is not uncommon for those approached as potential donors to feel victimized and extremely distraught. Care must be taken that these individuals are not coerced into agreeing to organ donations or made to feel guilty for refusing.

Table 24-2 provides age criteria when considering the use of various organs.

Informing the dying patient

Arguments can be made for both concealing and revealing the truth about a terminal condition. However, there is growing evidence that most individuals wish to be informed when their condition is terminal. One poll in the USA showed that up to 90% of adults surveyed said they would want to know when their

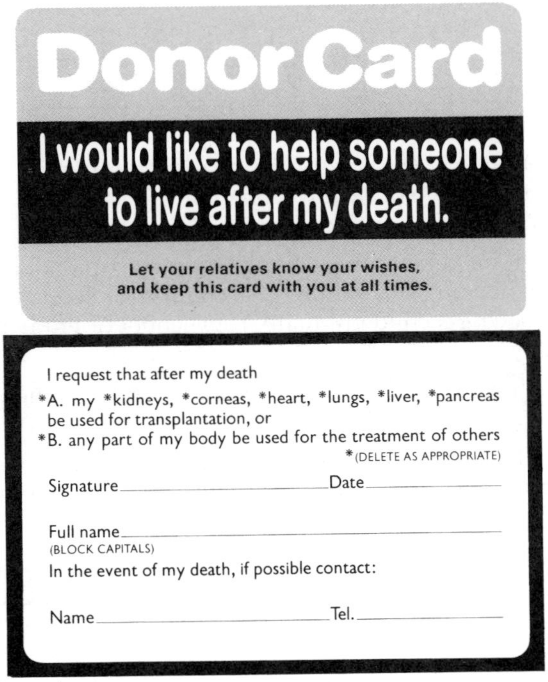

Figure 24-1 An organ donor card. (Courtesy Dept of Health/HMSO)

illness is most probably terminal. In general, health practitioners support the position that patients should be told. This is usually the responsibility of the attending doctor. When patients are informed, it is also important that they understand that no one is giving up on the treatment of the condition nor the quality of care they receive.

From many observations, it has been seen that most patients realize even without being told that they are suffering from an incurable illness. The nonverbal communication of the patient's family and the health personnel often speak louder than words. Patients often feel even more isolated, lonely and rejected when the truth is withheld, especially when they are told falsehoods.

In some situations, the decision may be not to tell the patient about his illness. At times, this is valid. Some people indicate that they simply do not want to know. When this is the case, the person's wishes should be respected. In other situations, when the patient's mental condition is such that he cannot comprehend, trying to help him understand may serve no good purpose.

Informed patients usually react negatively to the news at first. Despite this, studies have shown that there are several advantages when the truth is revealed. These include:

- Maintaining all relationships with the patient on the basis of honesty rather than sustaining the false pretence that recovery will occur.
- Providing the patient with the opportunity to complete unfinished business. That is, to put his legal and personal affairs in order and accomplish any remaining tasks or goals.
- Permitting the use of still unidentifiable inner resources that have been demonstrated to prolong life. This has often been called the "will to live".
- Promoting more meaningful communication between the patient, family and health care personnel.
- Resolving grief earlier and more effectively. Grief is resolved better when individuals feel free to say and do things with the dying patient that they would later regret not having done.

Identifying patterns of emotional reactions

Although every person provided with the knowledge of impending death responds in his own distinctive way, studies have shown that there is a common pattern. Dr. Elisabeth Kübler-Ross, a recognized authority on the subject, has described stages that a dying person experiences. These stages are listed and described in Table 24-3.

Not all persons go through the stages in the precise order in the table. Also, a person may skip one stage or fall back a stage. Stages may overlap. The length of any stage may range from a few hours to months. Nevertheless, knowing about these stages is valuable when trying to understand and help patients and their families cope with dying.

Kübler-Ross and others have offered suggestions on how to help patients through stages of dying, as follows:

- Accept whatever manner in which the patient responds.
- Provide a nonjudgemental atmosphere in which the patient can express his feelings freely.
- Be ready to *listen*, especially at night when patients tend to awaken and want to talk.
- Work to understand the patient's feelings. His feelings, not the nurse's, should take precedence.
- Provide the patient with a broad opening for communication, such as, "Do you want to talk about it?" By not defining "it", the nurse allows

Table 24-3. Stages of dying, according to Kübler-Ross

Stage	Typical Emotional Response	Typical Comment
First stage	Denial	"No, not me." The patient may think there has been a mistake.
Second stage	Anger	"Why me?" The patient's hostility may be directed toward family members, friends, or health workers.
Third stage	Bargaining	"Yes, me, but . . ." The bargain may be a promise to God, if the patient is a religious person, in exchange for more time; or a person may say he will do anything in exchange for such experiences as seeing a child graduate from school or enjoying his next birthday.
Fourth stage	Depression	"Yes, me." The patient feels sadness and often cries, as though he is mourning his own death.
Fifth stage	Acceptance	"I am ready." The comment is characterized by a positive feeling and a readiness for death. This stage is usually peaceful and tranquil.

From Kübler-Ross, on Death and Dying; published by McMillan, 1969.

the patient to choose the topic that he wishes to discuss.

Supporting options for care

Any competent adult has the right to request aggressive treatment or refuse therapy and all variations in between. Depending upon the choice that is made, the patient may require continuous hospitalization, extended care in another hospital, home or hospice care.

Coordinating home care

In most early cases, the terminally ill patient remains at home and the family assumes responsibility for his care. The patient may travel to and from the hospital for periodic outpatient treatment and evaluation.

In the latter stages the majority of the health care of any patient at home is the responsibility of the primary health care team, i.e. the GP, the district nurse, the social worker, etc. At present health authorities have no uniform policy for the provision of specialist nursing support for terminally ill patients and their families in the community. Arrangements differ from area to area.

Some authorities fund their own continuing care teams, while others now run joint schemes with the Macmillan Nursing Services to provide specialist advice, support and encouragement for terminally ill patients and their relatives at home.

However, true continuity of care must include a realistic assessment of the relatives' ability to cope at home:

- The family and the patient should prefer home care to other options.
- The family and the patient should be aware of the patient's diagnosis and prognosis.
- There should be support systems available, such as professional personnel to call for consultation and to help with care as necessary.
- Special equipment needed for the patient should be available.
- There should be one person ready and able to assume primary responsibility for the patient's care.

It has been shown that, in general, terminally ill patients cared for at home, compared with patients receiving care in a hospital, enjoy greater emotional comfort and dignity and their families adjust better to their dying and death. When the terminally ill patient is surrounded by his family members and is in a familiar environment, he usually feels more secure. He often can enjoy following his own routines, have food that he likes, and can continue to function to some degree in his family role. Family members have more opportunity to communicate and demonstrate their love and affection without feeling intimidated by the presence of others. Guilt feelings may be lessened by having family members care for the person. Children can participate more extensively in the last days and can be helped to understand death with less fear. Because the process of dying generally is a gradual one, family members can have the opportunity to work through some of the beginning phases of grieving that are often more difficult when the patient is in a hospital.

However, the nurse must realize that in some instances the care needed by dying patients is too complex or demanding for family members. Families may have neither the physical nor the emotional strength to deal with the terminally ill person in the home. Care must be taken that the family is not made to feel guilty about not having the ill person at home.

The role of the hospice in the care of the terminally ill

Dame Cicely Saunders is given credit for developing special care facilities for the terminally ill called a *hospice*. She defined a hospice as a way station where terminally ill persons can live out their final days with dignity and meaningfulness in a caring environment. The concept is an application of the shelter provided for weary travellers going from one destination to another. On a more allegorical level, the dying are on a journey to another destination as well.

Hospice care emphasizes helping the patient *live* until he dies, with his family with him, and helping the family return to normal living after the patient's death. Hospice personnel consider their patient to be a terminally ill person *and* his family. The care they offer emphasizes preserving a bond between the patient and his family and helping them to be prepared so that death can more readily be accepted as a normal part of life.

In the UK the hospice may be a separate facility, it may be a special unit in a hospital, either inpatient or day care unit, or it may be a service provided in the home.

The care is provided by a multidisciplinary team of which the nurse is a key member. They are specially trained and committed to assist dying individuals and their families. They focus all their attention entirely on the needs of the terminally ill patient. The aim is to maximize the life that is left to the patient by keeping his symptoms under control and allowing him to maintain his independence and dignity until death.

Every effort is made by the hospice personnel to carry out any of the patient's last wishes. Families are encouraged to visit and assist in the care of the dying person as much as possible in order to keep the family unit intact.

Responding to emotional needs

The patient who is dying requires emotional support perhaps more than at any other time during his life. It is also a time when others find support most difficult to give. The patient's helpless feelings cause him naturally to depend upon others to provide him with a sense of being safe, secure, loved and worthwhile. The nurse can help the patient and his family by sustaining realistic hope, understanding common fears, facilitating communication and helping the family accept reality.

Sustaining realistic hope

Hope may not always be realistic and is likely to change with circumstances surrounding the illness. Yet hope always involves a positive rather than negative outlook. Realistic hope involves a wish for something that is more than likely possible.

The patient, the family and health care personnel will all manifest some degree of hope. However, the hope expressed by these various people may not be altogether realistic nor in agreement with one another. For example, as the patient begins to face impending death, he may hope for a quick end to his suffering. The family may still be hoping for a miraculous cure. Realistic hope should be supported. A comment such as the following may help in situations when the nurse recognizes unrealistic hope: ''We will continue to do everything we can and we hope you are right about your expectations.'' Such a comment neither shatters hope nor supports unrealistic hope.

Errors in judgement about recovery sometimes are made. Some may recall, from personal experiences or publicized reports, people whose illnesses were considered terminal but who survived and lived for many years. Also, during the course of an illness medical progress may bring forth a means of saving a life. Many diabetics, for example, faced certain premature death until insulin was discovered. Hence, there is good reason to remain hopeful while caring for terminally ill patients.

Understanding common fears

Fears are as varied as attitudes toward death. Both may change from time to time as a terminal illness progresses. Most fear death because it represents a force over which there is no control. However, it is understandable that many choose to fight it. Some look forward to death as a relief from earthly suffering and sorrow. Still others feel so depressed and desperate that they have suicidal tendencies. Generally, by relieving an individual's fears concerning death, the nurse can facilitate moving to the stage of acceptance in which the patient can die in peace and dignity.

Some common fears associated with the process of dying include:

Abandonment. Any threatening and unknown experience produces fear. It can be reduced when it is shared with another. Many dying patients feel isolated and alone. Encouraging the family to be present and involved relieves the feeling of separation from others. Touch can be used to communicate closeness to a patient.

Extreme pain. Discomfort that cannot be relieved is both physically and emotionally exhausting. Measures for controlling pain are discussed later in this chapter.

Loss of control. This fear may be related to the inability to control bodily functions, such as faecal or urinary elimination, diminished intellectual capacity, or the inability to maintain a previously held role within the family unit.

Dependence. Most adults resent having to depend on others for measures that once were performed independently.

Body alterations. Some terminal illnesses must be treated by the surgical removal of body structures. Drug therapy too may cause hair loss or other changes in the patient's overall appearance. The patient may feel that he will repulse others.

Loss of dignity. The use of highly technical equipment sometimes is associated with the intensive care of machines rather than intensive caring for the patient. Dying patients fear being treated as an object rather than as a person.

Facilitating communication

Sometimes a patient verbalizes statements that mask his true feelings. Or, he may talk in symbolic language. *Symbolic language* is a means of communication using terms or statements that carry a double meaning. The comments may be made to determine if others can tolerate talking about a certain subject. They may also be used as a substitute for revealing thoughts that are too frightening to discuss. Children may draw symbolic pictures that convey a

message since their ability to verbalize is not as finely developed.

Open communication between the nurse, the patient, and the family can help individuals to cope and deal with the reality of the issues concerning death. The nurse may need to interpret what a patient may be trying to say abstractly. Nonverbal communication often conveys messages more clearly than verbal communication. In summary, the nurse may wish to:

- Listen to what is being said. It is possible that the patient is sending a mixed message. There may be important clues about feelings or ideas that he is too frightened to express openly.
- Paraphrase, or restate, what may be the message.
- Provide time for the patient to perceive, confirm or deny the interpretations.
- Pace, but do not press the patient to communicate. Too slow a response may be equated with disinterest. Firing questions may be associated with insensitivity.
- Be honest rather than clinical in communicating with a patient. When a relationship is based on trust, shortcomings are easily tolerated.

Accepting reality

Eventually it becomes apparent that death will not be delayed much longer. The patient and family often find comfort in knowing that the patient's wishes have been followed, that the dying patient's discomfort is eased, and that there has been an opportunity to express how meaningful and appreciated the dying person has been.

Sometimes it must be explained to the family that patients may prolong dying while awaiting a sign that others are prepared to accept the loss. This has been described as "waiting for permission" to die. Death often occurs peacefully and shortly after a significant family member indicates that it is okay to "let go". Letting go can be a devastating experience. Many are afraid that it will be interpreted as giving up or demonstrating that they no longer care. By having this phenomenon, which has been identified in various studies on the dying experience, explained to them family members may feel less guilty.

Meeting spiritual needs

Attitudes toward death are influenced by various cultural factors, religion being one of them. Some patients, especially those with strong religious beliefs, may be ready to enter another life to which they look forward with joy. They believe that their death will be followed by great reward and peace for having lived a good and faithful life. Others may believe that death may involve some form of punishment; and perhaps others may believe that when life ends so does all form of existence.

Many terminally ill patients find great comfort in the support they receive from their religious faiths. It is important to help in obtaining the services of a clergyman as each situation indicates. However, it must be remembered that a religious faith is not an insurance policy guaranteeing security from the sorrow, fear and loneliness of dying. The clergyman's visit does not replace the kind words and the gentle touch of the nurse. Rather, the minister, rabbi or priest should be considered as one of the team assisting the patient to face terminal illness.

Nondenominational chapels are available in some hospitals. They may be used by the patient, when he is able, or by his family members.

Attending to physical needs

Unless death occurs suddenly, the nurse has an important responsibility in helping to meet the patient's physical needs at the same time as other needs of the terminally ill patient are being met. The physical care generally includes actions that prevent debilitation and provide comfort.

Providing nourishment

The patient who is terminally ill usually has little interest in nourishment. The physical effort of eating or drinking may simply be too great for him. Or, nausea and vomiting may interfere with adequate food consumption. Poor nutrition leads to exhaustion, infection, and other complications such as the development of pressure sores. When the patient is unable to take fluids and food by mouth, intravenous therapy, total parenteral nutrition or tube feedings may be used for maintaining nutrition and fluid intake.

When death is pending, normal activities of the gastrointestinal tract decrease. Offering the patient large quantities of food may only predispose him to distention and added discomfort.

If the swallowing reflex is present, offering sips of water at frequent intervals is helpful. As swallowing becomes difficult, aspiration may occur when fluids are given. The patient may suck on gauze soaked in water or on ice chips wrapped in gauze without difficulty because sucking is one of the last reflexes to disappear as death approaches.

Withholding food and fluids is now being considered when there is a request to withdraw life support systems from hopelessly ill or irreversibly comatose patients. This action would be considered a form of passive euthanasia.

Maintaining elimination

Some patients may be incontinent of urine and faeces. Others may need to be observed for retention of urine and for constipation, all of which are uncomfortable. Cleansing enemas may be ordered. It should be remembered that, if the patient is taking little nourishment, there may be only small amounts of faecal material in the intestine.

When urine and faecal incontinence becomes a problem, catheterization is indicated. Care of the skin becomes particularly important to prevent odours and skin breakdown. Incontinence sheets are easier to change than all the bed linen.

Administering hygiene

The dignity of a patient is largely influenced by the image that he feels he projects to others. It is especially important to keep the dying patient clean, well groomed and free of unpleasant odours.

If the patient is taking food and fluids without difficulty, oral hygiene is similar to that offered other patients. As death approaches, the mouth usually needs additional care. Mucus that cannot be swallowed or expectorated may need to be removed. The mouth can be wiped out with gauze, or suctioning may be necessary. Positioning the patient on his side helps in keeping the mouth and the throat free of accumulated mucus.

The mucous membranes should be kept free of dried secretions. Lubricating the mouth is helpful as well as comfortable for the patient.

Sometimes, secretions from the eyes accumulate. The eyes may be wiped clean with tissues or cotton balls moistened in normal saline. If the eyes are dry, it is usually because they tend to stay open. A lubricant in the conjunctival sac may be indicated to prevent friction and discomfort.

As death approaches, the patient's temperature usually is elevated, but as his circulatory system fails, the skin usually feels cold to the touch and the patient often perspires profusely. Sponging him and keeping him dry often promote relaxation and quiet sleep as well as cleanliness. A complete bath may be tiring and cause extreme discomfort.

Open lesions may be a source of offensive odours as dead tissue and bacterial growth accumulate within the wound. Charcoal pads can be used to eliminate the odour. They act by absorbing the contaminating microorganisms, hence improving the quality of life of the patient. Masking the odour with room deodorizers is not usually an adequate solution.

It is important to keep the bed linens and bed clothing dry by bathing the patient and changing linens as necessary. Using light bed clothing and supporting it so that it does not rest on the patient's body usually give additional comfort. The patient often is restless and may be observed to pick at his bed linen. This may be because he feels too warm.

The dying patient's hair should be kept clean and groomed. Dry shampoos may be used. A male patient who has preferred to be clean shaven should have that practice continued throughout his remaining life.

Positioning the patient

Good nursing care provides for proper positioning of the patient and includes frequent changes in position even though the patient may appear to be unconscious. Poor positioning without adequate support is fatiguing as well as uncomfortable.

When dyspnoea is present, the patient will be more comfortable when supported in the semi-sitting position. Noisy breathing frequently is relieved when the patient is placed on his side. This position helps to keep the tongue from obstructing the respiratory passageway.

Controlling the patient's pain

There are many factors affecting a patient's pain threshold, which are important when assessing the individual's pain, as illustrated in Table 24-4. Pain may remain intractable if mental and social factors are ignored.

Relief of pain should be assessed in relation to comfort achieved:

- during the night
- in the daytime at rest
- on movement

The goal is to keep a patient free from pain yet not dull his consciousness or ability to communicate. Table 24-5 gives examples of the types of analgesia used to control pain of varying intensities. It is usual

Table 24-4. Factors affecting pain threshold

Threshold Lowered	Threshold Raised
Discomfort	Relief of symptoms
Insomnia	Sleep
Fatigue	Rest
Anxiety	Sympathy
Fear	Understanding
Anger	Companionship
Sadness	Diversional activity
Depression	Reduction in anxiety
Boredom	Elevation of mood
Introversion	
Mental isolation	Analgesics
Social abandonment	Anxiolytics
	Antidepressives

From Twycross, R. and Lack, S.A., Therapeutics in Terminal Cancer; published by Churchill Livingstone, 1984.

Table 24-5. Classification of pain intensity

Pain Intensity	Relieved by
Mild	Paracetamol, aspirin
Moderate	Dihydrocodeine, coproxamol
Severe	Morphine, diamorphine

to commence with a lower dosage and continue to increase until the pain is under control.

It is expected that a stage may be reached when tolerance develops. *Tolerance* is a condition in which the body requires more of a drug to achieve an effect once obtained with a lower dosage.

When pain is intense, relief is more difficult to obtain with irregular administration of drugs. Therefore, it is better to try to control pain when it is minimal rather than wait until it is excruciating. Peaks and valleys of pain can be reduced by administering pain-relieving drugs on a routine schedule throughout the 24 hour period rather than just when it becomes absolutely necessary to do so.

Many patients are now being provided with syringe drivers as a method of drug administration. This is a portable battery operated pump which allows small amounts of fluid to be administered subcutaneously or intravenously over a 12 or 24 hour period. The need for regular injections is removed and drug levels are maintained in the blood stream, hence allowing for better pain control.

Morphine is the most common drug given in this way when the patient is unable to tolerate oral medication for reasons such as nausea, vomiting or dysphagia. Antiemetics and tranquillizers can also be added. The syringe driver can be used at home by the patient under the supervision of the GP or the home care nurse. If the pump is used subcutaneously the site should be checked daily for signs of inflammation and the needle resited when indicated.

Some nurses are concerned that the patient will become addicted to the pain medication which is generally a narcotic, such as morphine. This development is expected to occur. Since death is near, the possibility of addiction should not stand in the way of pain control.

Unfortunately, though tolerance develops to the pain-relieving quality of the drug, tolerance to other drug actions do not appear as quickly. Therefore, respirations may become slower and constipation is more likely with regular use of these drugs.

Sometimes pain is intensified by fear and anxiety. Other medications may be given for very anxious or depressed patients. Supplemental techniques, such as imagery, biofeedback and relaxation, may be useful in potentiating the effect of the drug. Persons working with the terminally ill have noted that patients experiencing a warm supportive relationship require less pain-relieving drug therapy.

Protecting from harm

The terminally ill patient may be very restless at times. The use of siderails on the bed is indicated. The patient's relatives may offer to remain with him so that he does not injure himself. However, family members should not be left with the complete burden of the patient's safety. The patient should be checked frequently because his welfare is still the nurse's responsibility. Well-meaning but unprepared, fatigued and stressed family members sometimes misjudge the patient's need for safety precautions. The guilt, if some unexpected occurrence results in injury, is an unfair price for family members to pay.

Modifying the environment

It is economical of nursing time to place the hospitalized terminally ill patient in a room close to the nursing station. This arrangement is convenient for giving nursing care and for observing him at frequent intervals.

Having familiar objects in view can help to make the patient feel more comfortable and secure. The family may be encouraged to make his room meaningful to him. Pictures, books and other significant objects can be very important. Whether the patient is at home or in a hospital, it is desirable to have the environment reflect his preferences. Once the environment is pleasing to the patient, it can remain thus unless he chooses to make alterations. In this way, the patient is being given some degree of control over his environment when he has lost control of most other aspects of daily living. The home environment is generally not difficult to maintain according to the patient's wishes.

It is not necessary that the patient remain in his room at all times. If his condition permits, trips outside are a pleasant change.

Normal lighting should be used in the patient's room. Terminally ill patients often complain of loneliness and various fears precipitated by poor vision, all of which are exaggerated by darkening the room. The room should be well-ventilated and the patient protected from draughts.

When conversing at the patient's bedside, it is preferable to speak in a normal tone of voice. Whispering may be annoying to the patient and may make him feel that secrets are being kept from him. It generally is believed that the sense of hearing is the last sense to leave the body. Many patients retain this sense almost to the moment of death. Therefore, care should be exercised concerning topics of conversation. Even when the patient appears to be unconscious, he may hear what is being said in his presence. It generally is comforting to the patient for others to say things that he may like to hear. Even when he cannot respond, it is kind and thoughtful to speak to him. It also remains important for the nurse to explain to the patient what care will be given so that the patient does not misunderstand the actions or become fearful.

Involving family members in the patient's care

It is helpful to remember that family members are in the process of having to make tremendous adjustments during the patient's terminal illness. There are instances when the nurse must focus more on the needs of the relatives than the patient.

Family members often appreciate helping with the patient's care. They feel helpless and welcome the opportunity to assist the patient. Their cooperation helps to maintain a family bond. Allowing relatives to help with the patient's care serves other purposes. Family members often find that helping with care improves their ability to cope with the situation. It also helps to begin and promote the grieving process, which is discussed later in this chapter.

However, the nurse needs to check on the patient frequently to determine his condition as well as the relatives' ability to cope with the situation. The nurse should explain that the family can call for nursing assistance at any time. Family members also need to know that when members leave or are too tired to give care a nurse will intervene. The nurse should be sensitive to the amount of care and involvement the family can assume. Expecting relatives to accept undue responsibility for the patient's care is an unkindness.

Recognizing the signs of approaching death

Most persons die gradually over a period of hours or days. Human cells cease to live when there is a lack of sufficient oxygen. The capacity of tissues varies as to the length of time they can live with insufficient oxygen. During the process of dying, there are signs that usually indicate clearly that death is imminent.

Motion and sensation are gradually lost. This usually begins in the extremities, particularly the feet and legs. The normal activities of the gastrointestinal tract begin to decrease, and reflexes gradually disappear. The jaw and facial muscles relax and the patient's expression, which may have appeared anxious, becomes peaceful. The eyes may remain partly open.

Although the patient's temperature usually is elevated he feels cold and clammy. This begins with his extremities and the tip of the nose. It reflects the beginning of circulatory collapse.

Respirations may be noisy and the "death rattle" may be heard. These occurrences are due to an accumulation of mucus in the respiratory tract when the patient is no longer able to raise and expectorate sputum. Cheyne-Stokes respirations occur commonly.

Circulation fails and the blood pressure falls. The patient's skin becomes cyanotic, grey, or pale. The pulse becomes irregular, weak, and rapid.

Pain, if it has been present, subsides. As the patient's level of consciousness changes, the brain may no longer perceive pain.

The patient's mental condition usually deteriorates. Such terms as being mentally "fuzzy" or "clouded", confused and disoriented are often used to describe mental deterioration. Eventually, complete unconsciousness and coma ordinarily occur, but some patients may remain conscious until death. The amount of mental alertness varies among patients, which is important to remember when giving care.

Summoning the family

Even though signs of approaching death are appearing, the nurse should realize that no one can predict the amount of time before death actually occurs. However, it is important to make the family aware that the end is near at hand. It is the responsibility of the sister or the most senior nurse to inform them. The following suggestions for communicating this information to the family may be used.

- Give your name and title, and indicate from where the call is being made.
- Determine the identity of the person who has answered the phone.
- Explain that you are calling because the patient's condition has worsened.
- Speak in a calm and controlled voice. The next of kin should feel that health personnel are in command of the serious nature of the patient's condition.
- Use short sentences to provide small bits of information. It is difficult to follow lengthy or technical explanations with any kind of understanding when under stress.
- Pause to allow the receiver of the call time to comprehend.
- Inform the family member of the care that is being provided at the moment. It should not appear as if the patient or his care is being abandoned.
- Urge the individual to come at once to the hospital.
- Document the time and the individual to whom the information was communicated.

The doctor should be responsible for informing a patient's nearest relative if a death has occurred. This information is usually delayed until after the family member arrives in order to avoid precipitating any desperate acts, such as suicide, or contributing to a traffic accident.

Helping arriving relatives

Relatives of the dying patient should be met by the nurse who informed them by telephone. When everyone has the benefit of continuity in the communication, there is less confusion. If it is not possible for the nurse to meet with the family, some other designated support person should be available. The family should not be left alone; however, they may appreciate being shown to a room or area that provides privacy.

There may be a variety of emotional reactions expressed at this time. It is important that the individuals not feel inhibited because they are in the presence of strangers. It is not unusual for family members to weep and sob uncontrollably. However, the genuineness of their grief should not be misinterpreted if there is not a great display of emotions. In this culture, men are encouraged to control their emotions. If the family has had a period of time to anticipate the patient's death, much of the emotion may already be spent.

Expect a rather severe emotional reaction if the dying person has been a victim of a sudden and unexpected accident. These family members have not had the opportunity to prepare for the loss. They are especially in need of emotional support that includes allowing them to express their grief and listening to them as they vent their feelings.

Confirming death

The patient must be pronounced dead by a doctor. Generally the nurse can determine that a patient is dead when there is no evidence of pulse, respirations or blood pressure. The pupils will become dilated and fail to respond to light. These were at one time the traditional signs of death.

In the case of extensive use of artificial means for maintaining life support, other criteria have been adopted in order to redefine death. New assessments are now used to declare individuals "brain dead". *Brain dead* means that despite the fact that the heart is beating and ventilation is occurring mechanically, the brain is no longer functioning. Brain wave activity is determined by electroencephalography. Recordings are taken over a period of 24 hours to validate the conclusion before any life-support measures are discontinued.

Obtaining permission for a post mortem

A post mortem is an examination of the organs and tissues of a human body following death. A coroner has the right to order that a post mortem be performed if the death involved a crime, was of a suspicious nature or occurred without any medical consultation prior to the death. Otherwise, a post mortem cannot be performed without the written consent of the next of kin.

It is generally the doctor's responsibility to obtain permission for a post mortem. It involves the same delicate communication as when requesting organs for transplant. When permission is being sought, the nurse often can assist by helping to explain the reasons for a post mortem. This requires tact and compassion. Many relatives will find comfort when they are told that a post mortem may help to further the development of medical science as well as to establish proof of the exact cause of death.

Issuing a death certificate

A death certificate is required by law for each person who has died. In the first instance, the doctor confirms the death and signs the medical certificate. This is then taken to the registrar in the borough in which the person has died, where two forms are issued. One is the certificate which is given to the funeral director for disposal of the body and the other is used in any dealings with the Department of Health. Information on the medical certificate is used to compile statistics which become important in identifying trends, needs and problems in the field of health and medicine.

Nursing responsibilities following the patient's death

The nurse is still involved with both the patient and the family even after death occurs. Sometimes, relatives are not present at the bedside at the time of death. It is customary for the relatives to view the body when they arrive. It is kind to ask relatives if they wish to be alone during viewing. Often they do, but the nurse should accompany them if that is their wish. Other special approaches will be discussed later concerning the death of an infant.

It is also very important for nurses to know something of the cultural and religious background of the patients they care for. Neuberger (1987) provides a very important contribution to this area. She gives an informative account of the beliefs and customs of different religions, with practical advice and suggestions for care.

Nurses are often confused about the effect that showing their own emotions will have on the family. The current feeling is that it is only human for nurses to become involved and attached to patients and their families. Many families are touched that the nurse has also shared their loss. Therefore, nurses should not fight to control expressing how they feel. Words of comfort are hard to come by. Speaking sincerely is always a good guide. Many times, just listening and allowing persons the time to reminisce or express their emotions is the best course of action.

The survivors of a sudden death should especially be encouraged to view the body. Seeing and touching the body confirms the reality of death. The nurse can clean and cover mutilated areas; however, most families tend to ignore the evidence of trauma and relate to the dead individual as if the injuries were not there. Sedating survivors is not recommended because it delays the normal grieving process.

Accounting for valuables

Each hospital has policies about the care of valuables when patients are admitted to the institution. Those valuables that the patient has chosen to keep with him—a ring, a wristwatch, money and so on—require careful handling after death. Occasionally, the patient's family may take the valuables home when death becomes imminent. If valuables are still with the patient at the time of death, they should be identified, accounted for and sent to the appropriate department for safekeeping until the family claims them. If it is impossible to remove jewellery, such as a wedding ring, the fact that it remains on the body should be noted. As a further safeguard, the article should be secured with adhesive so that it cannot slip off and be lost. The nurse owes it to the patient's family as well as to the hospital to use every precaution to prevent loss and misplacement of valuables.

Performing last offices

After the doctor has pronounced the patient dead, the nurse is responsible for performing last offices. This means caring for the body after death. The body is cleaned and identified appropriately before it is taken to the mortuary. The nurse will be guided by local procedures as they vary among hospitals. The actions in Principles of Care 24-1 may be used as a guideline. It is important also that the nurse is sensitive to different religious beliefs when carrying out last offices. In the case of Christians and nonbelievers, the body is laid out in the normal way. With other religions, procedures vary.

Islam. Muslims have strict washing rituals which are usually performed by close relatives. Disposable gloves should be worn by the nurse who is assigned to straighten the body and remove drainage tubes, etc.

Judaism. In the case of Orthodox Jews, a strict ritual also applies. The nurse may straighten the body, close the eyes, remove drainage tubes, etc. The nurse may or may not be required to wear disposable gloves when carrying out the above.

With progressive Jews, the body can be laid out in the normal way. It is advisable to check with the relatives or rabbi before proceeding.

Hinduism. There is usually no restriction among Hindus concerning the touching of the body by non-Hindus in the performance of last offices. Some relatives may request the body to be dressed in special clothing.

Understanding the grieving process

Grieving is a painful yet normal experience that facilitates the resolution of a death. Some compare this to emotional healing. The activities that lead to resolving the loss are called *grief work* or *mourning*.

Each culture has its rituals associated with death, burial and mourning. These traditions help to facilitate grieving. They provide a means for attending to those who have been touched by death and who deserve special compassion and understanding. Unfortunately, many cultural traditions have been abbreviated or abandoned in recent years. This has led to ineffective grieving and, for some, a pathological state. It is important for nurses to understand the physical and emotional effects of grieving that are experienced by surviving individuals. Further, nurses should share with others the methods that will facilitate the grief process.

Identifying common grief reactions

The normal grieving process may extend on the average from 6 months to 2 years. When anticipatory grieving has occurred, the mourning period may be less lengthy. Regardless of its length, individuals tend to all experience similar reactions. These grief

Principles of Care 24-1. Giving last offices

Nursing Action	Rationale
Screen the deceased off from the rest of the ward.	The other patients may be upset by witnessing the activities surrounding the death. The family will appreciate privacy with the body.
Notify the nursing administration office and the hospital switchboard.	Calls concerning the dead patient's condition should be screened. Supervisors may adjust staffing patterns when the nurse is involved with last offices.
Assemble equipment for cleaning, wrapping and identifying the body.	The body is prepared in a clean condition before it is transferred to the mortuary.
Determine that the family and clergyman have spent all the time they want with the body.	Many individuals request that certain religious services be performed before the body is removed from the room.
Place the body supine with the arms extended at the side or folded over the abdomen.	A normal anatomical position prevents discoloration of the skin from pooling blood in the areas visible in a coffin.
Remove hairpins or clips.	Hard objects about the face can scratch the tissue and detract from its appearance when the body is viewed at the undertakers.
Close the eyelids by applying gentle pressure in the lowered position.	The eyes may not be easily closed if the time between death and preparation of the body is prolonged.
Replace or retain dentures within the mouth. If the dentures are not in the patient's mouth, label and send them with the body.	Dentures maintain the natural contour of the face. They may be difficult to insert several hours after the body has been transferred.
Use a small towel under the chin to close an open mouth.	If the mouth is allowed to remain open, it may be difficult to close later.
Apply gloves and remove soiled dressings or other infected sources of pathogens.	Live pathogens may continue to be present in drainage from areas of the body even though the patient is dead.
Leave all equipment in place and attached if a coroner suspects that the patient is a victim of a crime.	The equipment may become part of the evidence that establishes that a crime was committed.
If a patient died of natural causes, remove venepuncture devices, indwelling catheter, monitor leads and so on.	Only the body should be delivered to the undertaker for burial care.
Dispose of all contaminated and soiled articles in appropriate containers.	A container acts as a transmission barrier to control the spread of organisms.
Remove gloves and discard them with contaminated articles.	The gloves are considered a source of pathogens if they have handled heavily soiled or contaminated drainage.
Wash the hands thoroughly.	Even though gloves were worn, the hands should be washed in order to ensure cleanliness.
Cleanse any obviously soiled areas of the body, such as faeces that may have been expelled.	The body is completely washed by the undertaker and so a complete bath is not required before transferring the body.

Continued

Principles of Care 24-1. Continued

Nursing Action	Rationale
Leave the hospital identification bracelet intact.	The importance of proper and complete identification of the body cannot be overstressed. Mistakes cause embarrassment and additional sorrow. Padding avoids damaging visible tissue if the identification is applied too tightly. The hospital bracelet ensures proper identification if the tag is lost.
Remove or make an inventory of the valuables still attached to the body.	All personal valuables must be accounted for.
Wrap the body with a *shroud*, a garment for enclosing a dead body.	The shroud covers the patient and preserves the dignity and respect due the body from any unauthorized onlookers.
Attach an identification tag to the shroud.	This prevents having to unwrap the body in order to make proper identification.
Notify the hospital porters that the body is ready for removal from the ward.	The porters will transfer the body to the mortuary for collection by the undertaker.
Lock removed articles in a safe and note their placement on the permanent record.	Valuable belongings of the patient must be safeguarded for proper return to the family.
Complete the patient's permanent record indicating in what manner the body was removed.	The permanent record should reflect where and to whom the body was transferred.
If the patient was HIV+ the body is treated with extreme care as with other infectious diseases such as hepatitis. Protective clothing must be worn by the nurse when dealing with the body and contaminated materials must be disposed of according to local procedures. The body is wrapped in a sheet with a HIV+ sticker on top and then put in a cadaver bag. This bag will be labelled with a "danger of infection" sticker. The undertaker should be alerted prior to accepting the body.	This is to protect all staff who come in contact with the deceased from contaminated body fluids. The undertakers also need to take precautionary measures.

reactions have been studied by noted authorities, such as C.M. Parkes of the UK and G.L. Engel of the USA. In separate studies most have found that grieving involves both physical and emotional reactions. These results support the concept that the mind and the body are truly interrelated. Parkes (1972) states that: "On the whole, grief resembles a physical injury more closely than any other type of illness, the 'wound' gradually heals; at least, it usually does. But occasionally complications set in, healing is delayed, or a further injury reopens a healing wound. In such cases abnomal forms arise, which may even be complicated by the onset of other types of illness. Sometimes it seems that the outcome may be fatal."

Common physical reactions. Grieving individuals may experience various physical symptoms, such as anorexia, tightness in the chest and throat, difficulty breathing, lack of strength and sleep pattern disturbances. Some claim to see, hear or feel the continued presence of the deceased. It is not understood yet if these should be considered paranormal experiences or if they are simply the result of wishful thinking.

Despite an inability to connect these physical manifestations to any identifiable pathology, studies have shown that the incidence of death is higher among individuals who have lost a spouse in the previous 6 months to a year. It may really be possible to die of a "broken heart".

Table 24-7. Stages of grief, according to Engel

Stage	Description
Shock and Disbelief	Shock and disbelief are characterized by a refusal or inability to accept the fact that a loved one is about to die or has died. They are a form of denial.
Developing Awareness	This stage is characterized by physical and emotional responses. The grieving person may feel sick or experience pain; he may feel emptiness or show anger and cry.
Restitution	The stage of restitution is characterized as a period during which the loss is recognized. It is time in which one accepts the reality of the death.
Idealization	During the idealization stage, the grieving individual often exaggerates the good qualities of the person. Eventually the deceased is viewed in a more realistic perspective.

Adapted from Engel, G.L., Grief and Grieving, American Journal of Nursing, 64, 1964.

Common emotional reactions. There are several emotional phases through which grieving individuals pass. They have been identified by various individual researchers. Table 24-7 shows phases of grief described by Engel.

Comforting grieving individuals

Each individual grieves differently depending upon the significance of the dead person, the amount of anticipatory grieving, the mode of death and their own network of support. The nurse can perform some of the techniques in Principles of Care 24-2 when facilitating the grief process. The suggested actions may also be useful to others who may be influential in helping grieving individuals to resolve their loss.

Identifying pathological grief

Pathological grief involves actions that indicate an individual is not accepting a death. These activities tend to be categorized as bizarre or morbid behaviour. Examples include: retaining all of the deceased's possessions as if in readiness for use, refusing to leave the house to attend the funeral or any other activity, attempting to make contact with the deceased through various forms of spiritualism, and, in rare instances, keeping a dead body within a residence for an extended period after death.

Grieving in special circumstances

Grief is a process that is generally experienced somewhat commonly among all individuals. However, when the loss involves a suicide or the death of a child, there are unique problems for the survivors.

Grieving a suicide. Survivors of a suicide are not only saddened by the loss but they suffer extreme guilt for not anticipating the despair felt by another individual. The guilt may be further reinforced if a vindictive note was left.

Many may also be angry at being publicly embarrassed, yet feel uneasy about expressing it. Instead of using communication with support persons to resolve the death, the survivor may avoid any discussion of the death with others. It has also been found that many fear that they may also end their own life some time in the future. A professional grief counsellor may be extremely helpful when individuals are tormented by these feelings.

Grieving a perinatal death. A *perinatal death* is the death of an infant that occurs prior to, during, or shortly after birth. This type of death requires special techniques that facilitate grief since the parents literally have no past memories to share about the child. The nurse and those associated with the grieving couple must guard against giving the impression that the baby and his unique identity never existed.

Researchers have found that ignoring the death is extremely traumatic even though it is done in the spirit of attempting to shelter and protect the parents. Some suggestions that nurses can use when there is a perinatal death include the following:

- Remove any trappings that may interfere with expressing sincere feelings about the baby's death. Such things as wearing a lab coat or

Principles of Care 24-2. Facilitating the process of grieving

Nursing Action	Rationale
Express words that convey sympathy with an individual's loss. Speak from the heart.	Communication, even if it is not the most articulate, is better than ignoring an individual who is experiencing pain.
Demonstrate feelings and emotions. Do not hold back tears and sadness if they are sincerely felt.	Showing emotional involvement indicates to the family that the deceased person was meaningful and adds dignity to the deceased's memory.
Use spontaneous touching, such as a handshake, an arm on the hand, or embrace, as a comforting gesture.	Grieving individuals miss being touched. Touching may be done in ways that are not sexually suggestive.
Answer any questions the individuals may have had about the treatment and the response of the patient.	Family and friends are often troubled by the fantasy that an individual was in extreme pain or had an awareness of dying.
Expect that the same questions may be asked several times by grieving family and friends.	It is difficult to comprehend information when in a distraught frame of mind. Many facts or the sequence of events may seem distorted and in need of clarification.
Mention names of nurses and doctors that were with the patient at the time of death.	Families need assurance that their loved one was not alone at the time of death. Later the family may want to talk personally with those who were present.
Encourage the family members to view, touch and talk to the dead body.	Seeing and touching the dead individual provides reality to the death.
Discourage the self-administered use of alcohol or drugs.	Abused substances can suppress grief and contribute an unreal quality to the circumstances surrounding the death and memorial service.
Listen as the grieving individual discusses the death and the significance of the loss.	Repetition helps to reinforce the order of events and personal meaning of the loss.
Encourage individuals to talk about the deceased even though grieving individuals may cry.	Suppressing talk of the deceased implies that the event never occurred or that the death is easily forgotten.
Tolerate expressions of anger and guilt.	Normal grieving involves verbalizing helpless feelings and regrets concerning the deceased.
Help the mourner to list areas where assistance is needed, such as in making funeral arrangements, and so on.	Listing specifics helps others to understand where their efforts are most appropriately needed.
Caution the survivor to make life changes slowly, such as taking an expensive trip or moving in with another relative.	Some may act impetuously and eventually regret making various financial or social decisions.
Suggest that others invite the survivor out for social activities both in mixed or solitary company.	The survivor should be made to feel valued as an individual and not be ignored because he is no longer coupled in a former relationship.
Send cards, make phone calls or spend time on significant anniversary dates and holidays.	The grieving individual is likely to feel more depressed on the date of a wedding anniversary or birthday.

stethoscope, or sitting behind a desk, create distance and physical barriers that are non-verbally inconsistent with expressing empathy.

- Speak aloud the most important words. Say "death", "dead", "baby", "your son", or "your daughter". Avoiding the use of certain words may communicate to the bereaved person that you are uncomfortable.
- Listen. The parents need to talk about their loss and express a variety of intense feelings. Be willing to allow them to do so without judgement and without trying to minimize their loss.
- Refer to the baby by its name or the pronoun referring to its gender. This reinforces that the baby was a unique individual.
- Offer the parents the opportunity to see and hold the infant. Many parents are unaware that this is even possible. They tend to fantasize, often unrealistically, for the rest of their lives about how the baby looked.
- Prepare the couple who wish to see the baby for its appearance. They may expect to see something quite different. Explaining that the baby may be disoloured, stiff, macerated, or that there are certain defects, helps to lessen any shock that would otherwise ultimately occur.
- Wrap the baby in a warm blanket, not a towel or pathology drape. The message that is conveyed is that this infant was a person and is therefore deserving of being treated with dignity and respect.
- Carry the body of the baby as if it was alive. The nurse sets an example that the baby is lovable and can be touched and held as closely as any other infant may be.
- Offer to unwrap the infant or encourage the parents to hold the baby and do so. This relieves any future doubts about the severity of any disfigurement. Most parents somehow see past defects, if there are any, and find comfort in discussing the baby's resemblance to other live children or relatives.
- Point out the aspects of the baby that are normal. This helps the parents to keep the presence of any defects in perspective.
- Allow the family time to be alone with the infant if they feel they do not require the nurse's presence. Parents may feel inhibited from communicating or examining the baby thoroughly when in the presence of the nurse.
- Encourage young siblings to describe or draw a picture of the dead brother or sister. This provides the child with information to work on later. It also helps others know what impressions seem important to them.
- Avoid bombarding the bereaved parents into making decisions. People who are in shock have great difficulty making decisions. They tend to be overly passive and may later deeply regret a decision they felt pressured into. Allow them ample time for consideration. It is seldom absolutely necessary to hurry the family. Many decisions and procedures can wait.
- Encourage delaying any memorial service until the mother can be discharged to participate. Funerals and memorials facilitate grieving.
- Help the family to seek the help of a supportive person who can make telephone calls for the family. "Telling the story" again and again can be very draining.
- Discourage disposing of all the furniture, layette, and gifts at home before the mother's discharge from the hospital. This may be done to shield the mother from going home to a houseful of sad reminders. However, emptying the house tends to communicate a message that it is better to act as if the baby was never expected.
- Avoid sex-role stereotyping. You may find that you are inviting the father to be strong, and denying the impact of his loss, while you are more understanding of the mother's expressions of her feelings.
- Expect that family members will find different ways of experiencing and expressing their grief. People grieve at varying paces, too. It is not unusual for bereaved parents to be affected for years following the loss. One parent may feel things very intensely, while the other may "shut down" for a time. These roles may switch occasionally.
- Encourage communication about the death between father and mother even though it causes painful feelings to surface. Silence about such an emotional incident is often misinterpreted as lack of concern or value for the lost child.
- Avoid suggesting that the death of a child is a predictor of future emotional problems or divorce. If, after becoming familiar with the aspects of normal grief, there is concern that the family needs outside help, suggest that option and offer to help them find the appropriate resource.

- Share the intense feelings that you are experiencing personally as a result of assisting the grieving family. Helpers need to have their own sources of support.

(Portions adapted from *Grief Notes*© 1986 with permission of Stephen and Naomi Shelton, East Lansing, Michigan)

If the family prefers not to see the body of the dead infant, other alternatives for realizing the loss may be made available. These help to provide the parents with some tangible token that represents the existence of the infant. Some examples include taking photographs, providing a lock of hair, and supplying footprints and handprints of the infant. These could also be given to parents who view the baby. If the photographs are refused, they may be kept with the permanent record. The parents should be informed that they may have them at any time in the future.

Recognizing signs of grief resolution

Mourning is not finished immediately after a funeral. It may take longer for some than for others. However, one sign that grief is becoming resolved is when an individual is able to talk about the dead person without becoming emotionally overwhelmed. Another sign is that the grieving individual describes the deceased's good and bad qualities. It is common in the early stages of grief to idealize a dead individual to a point near perfection. A more realistic concept of a person's memory indicates that there has been some progress toward adjustment.

Suggested measures when the patient is terminally ill or grieving in selected situations

When the patient is an infant or child

Be familiar with how children understand death. The following guidelines are offered.

Infants and toddlers. Infants and toddlers generally have not enough life experience to have formulated a concept of death.

Three- to 5-year-old children. Children between these ages usually consider death similarly to the loss of an object. They may be curious about death but often view it as reversible. Fear is usually associated with separation from parents rather than fear of death.

School-age children. School-age children generally see death as a permanent situation.

Ten- to twelve-year-old children and adolescents. Children in this age range view death very much as adults do. Teenagers in particular often consider death an injustice because they yearn to continue with life and are saddened about leaving loved ones.

- Be prepared to observe that most children become aware of the fact that they are terminally ill. Therefore, in general, authorities recommend that children be told about their prognosis in language they can understand. Just as with adults, being told the truth appears to help prevent feelings of fear, of being deserted and alone, and of suffering with guilt when they believe that death is a punishment.
- Expect that when the primary caretaker, usually the mother, has trouble accepting the reality of her child's impending death, the child may turn to a mother substitute, generally the nurse, for help and the emotional support he needs.
- Understand that the death of a child represents an event that is out of sequence with the normal pattern of life and will therefore be more difficult to accept.
- Expect that parents often suffer serious guilt feelings when a child dies. They almost always believe they neglected to do something and they may become hostile towards health personnel as their psychological pain reaches high levels. These feelings may be part of anticipatory grief and they eventually change, especially when psychological support is present. Allowing parents to participate in the care of a terminally ill child to the extent that they wish has been found helpful in promoting the resolution of grief.

When the patient is elderly

- Do not expect that an elderly patient will have a peaceful and accepting attitude toward death. Just as no two lives are the same, death also is an individualized experience.
- Include the elderly person in as many aspects of his care as possible so that he has a feeling of dignity and of having at least some control over his destiny.
- Recognize that the elderly may not always consider nursing measures as helpful, especially if they wish to die. More so than with younger

adults, their dignity is often destroyed when they feel that technology and machines are taking over the ownership of their body.

Teaching suggestions involving terminally ill and grieving individuals

Unusual equipment or drugs may be used in the treatment of some illnesses. The patient and the family need to have frequent explanations for whatever is done and why. This demonstrates respect for the patient and the family. It helps to relieve fears and feelings of guilt that are common during the time a loved one is dying.

Demonstrate measures that the family members are capable of carrying out for the dying patient. Most relatives have at least some fear because they think they may harm the patient, even though they may wish to help. Careful explanations are important so that family members understand how to carry out safe and considerate care.

Teaching also includes keeping the family informed about the patient's condition.

Explain that it is healthy to talk with children and other family members about death and personal wishes for terminal care. Open communication prepares individuals to deal with death as a realistic part of life.

Inform patients of organizations who may provide assistance with organ or body donation.

Encourage individuals to use all of life's opportunities to say and do meaningful things with one another so that there are few regrets or guilt when death is imminent.

Refer individuals to support groups within the community or to printed resources, such as the further reading list below, that may help them to understand and deal with their own personal grief experience.

References

Engel, G.L. (1964) Grief and grieving, *American Journal of Nursing*, **64**, 93–8.

Keogh, A.H. (1987) Transplantation and organ donation *Nursing*, **16**, 591.

Neuberger, J. (1987) *Caring for Dying People of Different Faiths*, The Lisa Sainsbury Foundation Series, London.

OPCS (1992) *Office of Population Censuses and Surveys Monitor*, DH2 92/2.

Twycross, R. and Lack, S.A. (1984) *Theraputics in Terminal Cancer*, Churchill Livingstone, Edinburgh, 11–12.

Parkes, C.H. (1972) *Bereavement—Studies of Grief in Adult Life*, Penguin, Harmondsworth, 25.

Further reading

Edwards, A.C. (1983) *The Nursing Care of the Dying Patient*, Beaconsfield Publishers, UK.

Hinton, J. (1967) *Dying*, Penguin, Harmondsworth.

Kübler Ross, E. (1969) *On Death and Dying*, Macmillan, New York.

Kübler Ross, E. (1975) *Death: The Final Stages of Growth*, A Spectrum Book, Prentice-Hall, London.

Lugton, J. (1987) *Communicating with Dying People and Their Relatives*, The Lisa Sainsbury Foundation Series, London.

Editorial (1988) Coping with death and loss. *Nursing*, **32**.

Saunders, C. (1978) *The Management of Terminal Disease*, Edward Arnold, London.

Saunders, C., Summers, D. and Teller, N. (1981) *Hospice: The Living Idea*, Edward Arnold, London.

Stedford, A. (1984) *Facing Death. Patients, Families and Professionals*, William Heinemann Medical Books, London.

Worden, J.W. (1984) *Grief Counselling and Grief Therapy*. Tavistock Publications, London.

Index